Y0-BDP-832

Coding for Data
and
Computer Communications

Coding for Data
and
Computer Communications

David Salomon
California State University, emeritus
Northridge, CA, USA

 Springer

Professor David Salomon (emeritus)
Computer Science Dept
California State University
Northridge, CA 91330-8281
USA

Email: david.salomon@csun.edu

Library of Congress Cataloging-in-Publication Data

Salomon, D. (David), 1938-
   Coding for Data and Computer Communications/ David Salomon
   p.cm.
   Includes bibliographical references and index.

ISBN: 0-387-21245-0   / e-ISBN: 0-387-23804-2 Printed on acid-free paper.
ISBN-13: 978-0387-21245-6

TK5102.94.S35 2005
005.8—dc22

                                                2005042510

Printed in the United States of America.

9 8 7 6 5 4 3 2 1   SPIN 10986165 (HC) / 11345305 (eBK)

springeronline.com

Dedicated to the memories of Claude Shannon, Richard Hamming,
David Huffman, and the many other pioneers in this field.

Preface

On the evening of 23 June 1995, the well-known painter Franz Hutting (not his real name) sent a digitized copy of his latest masterpiece *Barricade* from his studio in New York to his friend Percival Bartlebooth in Paris. In itself, this data transmission was not different from the millions of other, similar transmissions taking place all over the globe all the time. A close examination of the individual steps of this process, however, reveals how certain mathematical disciplines have become indispensable in our everyday lives and how they affect our behavior, our assumptions, and our outlook on the world around us.

Consider the following. The original painting was placed in a scanner and converted into many millions of small dots, termed *pixels*, that were recorded magnetically on a computer disk. Each dot was converted to a 24-bit number that specifies the color at a certain point in the painting. It was these bits that were later sent thousands of kilometers around the world, to be recorded on another magnetic disk in Paris and eventually printed. Many computer programs, mathematical algorithms, international protocols, and individual pieces of hardware were employed in the execution of this data transfer. This book examines only three crucial factors that contributed to the success of this process, as well as to those of the many other data transmissions taking place all over the globe all the time.

The first factor is time. It takes time to transfer even a single bit over any communications channel, and it takes much longer to transfer millions of bits. Time, as we all know, is money, so decreasing the number of bits being transferred saves money—always an important consideration. This factor, reducing the size of a data file, is popularly referred to as *data compression*, while its formal name is *source coding* (coding done at the source of the data, before it is stored or transmitted).

The second factor is reliability. We often experience noisy cell phone conversations because of electrical interference. In general, any type of data sent over any kind of communications channel may get corrupted as a result of channel noise. When the bits of a data file are sent over a telephone line, a dedicated communications line, or a satellite connection, errors may creep in and corrupt bits. Looking at the freshly printed picture in his Paris apartment, Bartlebooth may not have noticed several small dots with wrong colors (especially since *Barricade* is an example of modern art and depicts what the artist sees in his mind's eye, not what the rest of us may see). An image, therefore, is an example of data where absolute reliability may not be an important consideration. Other types of data, such as an executable computer program, a legal document, or genetic information, may not be so forgiving. Change one bit in the executable code of a program, and the program will not run, or worse, it may run and do the wrong thing. Reliability is therefore important and is achieved by means of error-control codes. The formal name of this mathematical discipline is *channel coding* because these codes are employed when information is transmitted on a communications channel.

The third factor that affects the storage and transmission of data is security. Mr. Hutting did not want his painting to be intercepted and copied on its way to his friend. He therefore protected it by encrypting the data file with a modern, strong encryption algorithm that depends on a long, randomly selected key. Anyone who doesn't possess the key and wants access to the data may have to resort to a long, tedious process of either trying to break the code (deduce the key by logic combined with trial and error) or trying every possible key. Encryption is especially important for diplomatic communications, messages that deal with money, or data sent by members of secret organizations. A close relative of data encryption is the field of data hiding (steganography). A data file A (a payload) that consists of bits may be hidden in a larger data file B (a cover) by taking advantage of "holes" in B that are the result of redundancies in the way data is represented in B.

These three factors are the topics of this book. Not every data file requires all three. A small piece of data can be stored and transmitted without any compression. A routine text message can suffer the corruption of a few characters and still be readable and recognizable. A noncritical business or personal email may not cause any damage if it falls into the wrong hands, so it does not have to be encrypted. Still, source coding, channel coding, and encryption are examples of three modern mathematical fields that affect our lives even though most of us are not aware of their existence.

Cryptography has its origin in the ancient world. Julius Caesar used simple cryptography to hide the meaning of his messages (see [Salomon 03]). Source and channel codes, however, are modern concepts that have their origins in information theory. This important discipline was created in 1948 by Claude Shannon at Bell Labs. We normally consider information a qualitative concept. We may or may not understand, like, or benefit from a piece of information, but we don't normally assign it a number (a size, a price, or a weight). Shannon, however, was able to precisely and quantitatively define and measure information. An unexpected result of information theory is the *channel coding theorem*, proved by Shannon, which says that there exist codes that make it possible to transmit information through a noisy channel with any desired reliability, as long as the transmission rate (the number of bits transmitted per second) does not exceed a limit called the channel capacity. When the transmission rate exceeds the channel capacity, it is impossible to achieve reliable transmission. Two points should be mentioned in connection with this theorem: (1) the theorem guarantees the existence of such codes, but does not show how to design them; and (2) the codes in question do not prevent errors during transmission, but instead detect errors and correct them automatically.

Shannon's channel coding theorem became the starting point for researchers looking for powerful error-control codes. Work done since the 1950s has resulted in the sophisticated error-correcting codes used today in many areas where data has to be stored or transmitted reliably.

Shannon was also responsible for the use of the term redundancy in connection with source and channel coding. Part II of this book shows that source coding (compression) is achieved by removing redundancy from data, while channel coding (in Part I) is based on adding redundancy to the data. Thus, data compression and data reliability are opposite concepts. Compressing data makes it less reliable, whereas increasing data reliability inevitably leads to increasing its size.

Shannon was also the originator of the two important cryptographic concepts of confusion and diffusion (Section 11.1). He was also active in the search for better cryptographic methods.

This book is an attempt to bring the three disciplines of data compression, error-control codes, and cryptography and data hiding to the attention of the general public. As a result, it is mostly nonmathematical and does not attempt to be complete. It is naturally divided into three parts, each of which discusses the most important approaches, methods, and techniques that are currently employed in one of these fields to make the storage and transmission of data fast, secure, and reliable.

The book has been written mostly as a professional text for those interested in the basic problems and methods of data coding. It can, however, also serve as a textbook in a course dealing with aspects of data coding. Some features that enhance this aspect of the book are the many exercises sprinkled throughout the text, the proposed projects for self-study (Appendix D), and the Glossary.

The book's Web site, with an errata list and BibTEX information is part of the author's Web site, located at `http://www.ecs.csun.edu/~dsalomon/`. Domain name `www.DavidSalomon.name` has been registered and is used as a mirror. The author's email address is `dsalomon@csun.edu`, but ⟨*anyname*⟩`@DavidSalomon.name` is an alternative address.

> Kindness is a brief preface to ten volumes of exaction.
> —Ambrose Bierce

Contents

As for editorial content, that's the stuff you separate the ads with.

—Lord Thomson of Fleet

Part I:
Channel Coding

Errors are all around us. We hate them, but we make them all the time, we expect them, and we try to learn to live with them. We say "to err is human," but it is not only humans who err. Tools, instruments, and machines of all kinds misbehave, bite back, and break down from time to time. One area where errors are particularly critical is data processing and communications. One bad bit in a computer program can completely corrupt the program. Similarly, the smallest error in a data file can change the meaning of the data in a crucial way. Fortunately, it is possible to detect, and often also to correct, errors in data.

This particular area of coding theory is commonly referred to as *channel coding* because these codes are used mostly when information is transmitted in a communications channel. They are also used when data is stored, especially when it is stored in a device prone to reading errors, such as a CD or a DVD. Channel codes are also sometimes referred to as error-control codes because they consist of two types, error-detecting and error-correcting codes.

The key to error-control codes is added redundancy. Any method that results in reliable data also increases the size of the data. Perhaps the simplest example is doubling the data. When two copies of a file are stored or transmitted, then compared, most errors can easily be detected. When three copies are employed in this way, most errors can also be corrected. Such methods (Section 1.3) are very inefficient, though, and many error-control algorithms use parity bits (Section 1.5). Modern error-control methods are based on sophisticated mathematical concepts such as polynomials and finite fields.

Chapter 1 introduces the main concepts of reliable codes, such as redundancy, parity, Hamming distance, Hamming codes, periodic codes, and Reed–Solomon codes. The text avoids the use of advanced mathematics, which makes it easy to read and understand, at the cost of not delving into more sophisticated methods.

Chapter 2 is devoted to error detection in the various decimal numbers used to identify and protect important documents such as checks, credit cards, airline tickets, and books. These methods are based on the concept of a check digit, which is computed, appended to the number, and later used to validate it.

> In Russia we only had two TV channels. Channel One was propaganda. Channel Two consisted of a KGB officer telling you: Turn back at once to Channel One.
>
> —Yakov Smirnoff

1
Error-Control Codes

1.1 Information Theory and Algebraic Coding

Information theory is the mathematical field dealing with the transfer of information from one location to another and with the storage of information for later retrieval and use. Both tasks can be regarded as passing information or data through a channel from a source to a receiver. Consequently, information theory deals with the following three aspects:

- Reliability—detection and removal of errors caused by noise in the channel (channel coding or error-control coding).
- Efficiency—efficient encoding of the information (source coding or data compression).
- Security—protection against eavesdropping, intrusion, or tampering with the data (cryptography).

Figure 1.1 shows the stages that a piece of digital data may go through when it is created, transmitted, received, and used at the receiving end.

The information source produces the original data to be transmitted. If this is in analog form, such as sound, electrical signal, or a paper document, it has to be digitized before it proceeds to the next step. The digitized data is first encrypted, if necessary, to hide its meaning from prying eyes. The source encoder translates the encrypted data into an efficient form by compressing it. The channel encoder adds an error-control (i.e., detection or correction) code to the encrypted, compressed data to provide robustness before it is sent through the noisy channel. The modulator (normally a modem) translates the digital data into a form that can be sent on the channel (usually an

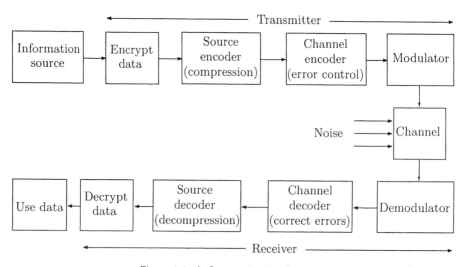

Figure 1.1: A Communication System.

electromagnetic wave). The channel itself may be a wire, a microwave beam, a satellite link, or any other type of hardware that can transmit signals. After demodulation (by another modem), channel decoding (error check and correction), source decoding (decompression), and decryption, the received data finally arrives at the receiving end, where it can be used confidently. The encryptor, source encoder, channel encoder, and modulator are sometimes called the *transmitter*.

We denote by p the probability that a 1 bit will change to a 0 during transmission. The probability that a 1 will remain uncorrupted is, of course, $1 - p$. If the probability that a 0 bit will be degraded during transmission and recognized as 1 is the same p, the channel is called *binary symmetric*. In such a channel, errors occur randomly. In cases where errors occur in large groups (bursts), the channel is a *burst-error channel.*

1.2 Error Control Codes

Every time information is transmitted, on any channel, it may get corrupted by noise. In fact, even when information is stored in a storage device, errors may suddenly occur, because no piece of hardware is absolutely reliable. This also applies to noncomputer information. Printed information may fade with time and may deteriorate from high use. Speech sent through the air may deteriorate due to noise, wind, and variations in temperature. Speech, in fact, is a good starting point for understanding the principles of error-detecting and error-correcting codes. Imagine a noisy cocktail party where everybody talks simultaneously, on top of blaring music. We know that even in such a situation it is possible to carry on a conversation, except that more attention than usual is needed.

What makes our language so robust, so immune to errors? There are two properties: *redundancy* and *context*.

■ Our language is redundant because only a very small fraction of all possible words are valid. A huge number of words can be constructed with the 26 letters of the Latin alphabet. Just the number of 7-letter words, for example, is $26^7 \approx 8.031$ billion. Yet only about 50,000 words are commonly used, and even the Oxford English Dictionary lists "only" about 640,000 words. When we hear a garbled word, our brain searches through many similar words for the "closest" valid word. Computers are very good at such searches, which is why redundancy is the basis of error-detecting and error-correcting codes.

⋄ **Exercise 1.1:** The string "blibe" is not an English word. Suggest some words close to this string by swapping, deleting, or changing up to two letters.

■ Our brain works by associations. This is why we humans excel at using the context of a message to repair errors in the message. In receiving a sentence with a garbled word or a word that doesn't belong, such as "pass the thustard please," we first use our memory to find words that are associated with "thustard," and then we use our accumulated life experience to select, among many possible candidates, the word that best fits in the present context. If we are driving on the highway, we pass the bastard in front of us; if we are at dinner, we pass the mustard (or custard). Another example is the (highly corrupted) written sentence "a∗l n∗tu∗al l∗∗gua∗es a∗e red∗ ∗ ∗ant", which we can easily complete. Computers don't have much life experience and are notoriously bad at such tasks, which is why context is not used in computer codes. In extreme cases, where much of the sentence is bad, even we may not be able to correct it, and we have to ask for a retransmission: "Say it again, Sam."

The idea of using redundancy to add reliability to information is due to Claude Shannon, the founder of information theory. It is not an obvious idea, since we are conditioned against it. Most of the time, we try to reduce redundancy in computer information, in order to save space. In fact, all the data-compression methods do just that.

We discuss two approaches to reliable codes. The first one is to duplicate the code, an approach that leads to the idea of *voting codes*; the second approach uses *check bits* and is based on the concept of *Hamming distance*.

Both approaches result in increasing the size of the data. An error-control code may start with k-bit data symbols and convert each to an n-bit codeword. We use the notation (n, k) for such a code and denote the difference $n - k$ by m. This is the number of extra bits added to achieve reliability.

> Mistakes are almost always of a sacred nature. Never try to correct them. On the contrary: rationalize them, understand them thoroughly. After that, it will be possible for you to sublimate them.
>
> —Salvador Dali

1.3 Voting Codes

Perhaps the first idea that comes to mind, when thinking about redundancy, is to duplicate every bit of the message. Thus, if the data 1101 has to be transmitted, the bits 11|11|00|11 can be sent instead. A little thinking shows that this results in error detection, but not in error correction. If the receiver receives a pair of different bits, it cannot tell which bit is correct. This is an example of a *receiver failure*. The next natural idea is that sending each bit in triplicate can lead to reliable (although not absolute) error correction. We can transmit 111|111|000|111 and tell the receiver to compare the three bits of each triplet. If all three are identical, the receiver assumes that they are correct. Moreover, if only two are identical and the third one is different, the receiver assumes that the two identical bits are correct. This is the principle of *voting codes*. To fully understand this approach, we enumerate all the possible cases as follows:

1. All three copies are identical. There are two subcases.
   1.1. All three copies are correct.
   1.2. All three are bad in the same way.
2. Two copies are identical and the third one is different. Again, there are two subcases.
   2.1. The two identical copies are correct.
   2.2. The two identical copies became corrupted in the same way. The third copy may or may not be correct.
3. All three copies are different.

> What I tell you three times is true.
>
> —Lewis Carroll, *The Hunting of the Snark*

Using the principle of voting codes, the decoder makes the correct decision in cases 1.1 and 2.1. In case 3, the decoder detects an error but cannot correct it. In cases 1.2 and 2.2, the decoder makes a wrong decision, so we conclude that voting codes are not absolutely reliable. However, if the probability of cases 1.2 and 2.2 is small enough, then voting codes can be used in the many applications where high but not absolute reliability is required. We next realize that the probability of case 1.2 is smaller than that of case 2.2, so we have to estimate only the probability of the latter case.

If we duplicate each bit an odd number of times, the receiver may sometimes make the wrong decision, but it can *always* make a decision. If each bit is duplicated an even number of times, the receiver will fail (i.e., will not be able to make any decision) in cases where half the copies are 0s and the other half are 1s.

In practice, errors may occur in bursts, so it is preferable to separate the copies of each bit and send them interleaved. Thus, it is better to send 1101...1101...1101... instead of 111|111|000|111. The receiver has first to identify the three bits of each triplet, then compare them.

A voting code where each bit is duplicated n times is an $(n, 1)$ voting code. It is intuitively clear that the reliability of the voting code depends on n and on the quality of the transmission channel. The latter can be estimated by measuring the probability p that any individual bit will be corrupted during transmission. This measurement can be made by transmitting large quantities of known data through the channel and counting the number of bad bits received. Such an experiment should be carried out with many millions of bits and over long time periods in order to account for differences in channel reliability due to day or night, summer or winter, intense heat, high humidity, sunspot activity, lightning, and so on. Actual values of p for typical channels used today are in the range 10^{-7} to 10^{-9}, meaning that, on average, one bit in 10 million to one bit in a billion bits transmitted gets corrupted.

Once p is known, we compute the probability that j bits out of the n identical bits transmitted will go bad. Given any j bits of the n bits, the probability of those j bits going bad is $p^j(1-p)^{n-j}$, because we have to take into account the probability that the remaining $n-j$ bits did not go bad. However, it is possible to select j bits out of n bits in several ways, and this also has to be taken into account in computing the probability. The number of ways to select j objects out of any n objects without selecting the same object more than once is denoted by ${}^nC_j$ and is

$$ {}^nC_j = \binom{n}{j} = \frac{n!}{j!(n-j)!}. $$

⋄ **Exercise 1.2:** When asked to derive this probability, many people mistakenly pick p^j, not realizing that the fact that the remaining $n-j$ bits did not go bad affects the probability. Suggest a way to demonstrate the effect of $(1-p)^{n-j}$ on the probability.

We therefore conclude that the probability of any group of j bits out of the n bits going bad is $P_j = {}^nC_j p^j (1-p)^{n-j}$. Based on this equation, we can analyze the behavior of voting codes by computing three basic probabilities: (1) the probability p_c that the receiver will make the correct decision (i.e., will find and correct an error), (2) the probability p_e that the receiver will make the wrong decision (i.e., will "detect" and correct a nonexistent error), and (3) the probability p_f that the receiver will fail (i.e., will not be able to make any decision). We start with the simple case $n = 3$, where each bit is transmitted three times.

When $n = 3$, the receiver will make a correct decision when either all three bits are correct (case 1.1) or one bit goes bad (case 2.1). Thus, p_c is the sum $P_0 + P_1$ which equals $\left[{}^3C_0 p^0 (1-p)^{3-0}\right] + \left[{}^3C_1 p^1 (1-p)^{3-1}\right] = (1-p)^3 + 3p(1-p)^2$. Similarly, the receiver will make the wrong decision when either two of the three bits go bad (case 2.2) or all three have been corrupted (cases 1.2 or 3). The probability p_e is therefore the sum $P_2 + P_3$, which equals $\left[{}^3C_2 p^2 (1-p)^{3-2}\right] + \left[{}^3C_3 p^3 (1-p)^{3-3}\right] = 3p^2(1-p) + 3p^3$. Since n is odd, the receiver will always be able to make a decision, implying that $p_f = 0$. Any code where $p_f = 0$ is a *complete decoding* code. Notice that the sum $p_c + p_e + p_f$ is 1.

Example: We compute p_c and p_e for the $(3,1)$ voting code for $p = 0.01$ and for $p = 0.001$. The former yields $(1 - 0.01)^3 + 3 \times 0.01(1 - 0.01)^2 = 0.999702$ and $p_c = 3 \times 0.01^2(1 - 0.01) + 3 \times 0.01^3 = 0.000298$. The latter yields $(1 - 0.001)^3 + 3 \times 0.001(1 - 0.001)^2 = 0.999997$ and $p_c = 3 \times 0.001^2(1 - 0.001) + 3 \times 0.001^3 = 0.000003$. This evaluation shows that the simple $(3,1)$ voting code features excellent behavior even for large bit failure rates.

The $(3,1)$ voting code can correct up to one bad bit. Similarly, the $(5,1)$ voting code can correct up to two bad bits. In general, the $(n,1)$ voting code can correct

$\lfloor(n-1)/2\rfloor$ bits (in future, the "$\lfloor$" and "$\rfloor$" symbols will be omitted). Such a code is simple to generate and to decode, and it provides high reliability, but at a price: an $(n, 1)$ code is very long and can be used only in applications where the length of the code (and consequently, the storage space or transmission time) is acceptable. It is easy to compute the probabilities of correct and incorrect decisions made by the general $(n, 1)$ voting code. The code will make a correct decision if the number of bad bits is 0, 1, 2,...,$(n-1)/2$. The probability p_c is therefore

$$p_c = P_0 + P_1 + P_2 + \cdots + P_{(n-1)/2} = \sum_{j=0}^{(n-1)/2} {}^nC_j p_j (1-p)^{n-j}.$$

Similarly, the $(n, 1)$ voting code makes the wrong decision when the number of bad bits is greater than $(n+1)/2$. Thus, the value of p_e is

$$p_e = P_{(n+1)/2} + P_{(n+3)/2} + P_{(n+5)/2} + \cdots + P_n = \sum_{(n+1)/2}^{n} {}^nC_j p_j (1-p)^{n-j}.$$

Notice that $p_f = 0$ for an odd n because the only case where the receiver cannot make a decision is when half the n bits are bad, and this can happen only with an even n. Table 1.2 lists the values of p_e for five odd values of n and for $p = 0.01$. Values of the redundancy (or the *code rate*) R are also included. This measure is the ratio k/n, i.e., the number of data bits in the $(n, 1)$ code (i.e., 1) divided by the total number n of bits.

n	p_e	R
3	3.0×10^{-4}	0.33
5	9.9×10^{-6}	0.20
7	3.4×10^{-7}	0.14
9	1.2×10^{-8}	0.11
11	4.4×10^{-10}	0.09

Table 1.2: Probabilities of Wrong Decisions for Voting Codes.

$\diamond$ **Exercise 1.3:** Compute p_e for the $(7, 1)$ voting code, assuming a bit failure rate of $p = 0.01$.

Example: We calculate the probability p_f of failure for the $(6, 1)$ voting code, assuming that $p = 0.01$. We know that failure occurs when three out of the six identical copies have been corrupted and now have the opposite value. The probability of that occurring is $p_f = P_3 = {}^6C_3 p^3 (1-p)^3 = 1.94 \times 10^{-5}$. Thus, on average, the decoder will not be able to make a decision in one error out of every $1/(1.94 \times 10^{-5}) \approx 51,546$ bits.

> Life has a self-correcting mechanism—things that we once thought were terrible have a way of becoming stepping stones for new discoveries.
>
> —Raymond Soh

1.4 Check Bits

In practice, voting codes are normally too long and are rarely used. A better approach to error detection and correction is to add *check bits* to the original *information bits* of each word of the message. In general, k check bits are appended to the original m information bits to produce a *codeword* of $n = m + k$ bits. Such a code is referred to as an (n, m) code. The codeword is then transmitted to the receiver. Only certain combinations of the information bits and check bits are valid, in analogy with a natural language. The receiver knows what the valid codewords are. If a nonvalid codeword is received, the receiver considers it an error. Section 1.9 shows that by adding more check bits, the receiver can also *correct* certain errors, not just detect them. The principle of error correction is that, on receiving a bad codeword, the receiver selects the valid codeword that is the "closest" to it.

Example: A set of $2^7 = 128$ symbols needs to be coded. This implies $m = 7$. If we select $k = 4$, we end up with 128 valid codewords, each 11 bits long. This is an $(11, 7)$ code. The valid codewords are selected from a total of $2^{11} = 2048$ possible codewords, so there remain $2048 - 128 = 1920$ nonvalid codewords. The big difference between the number of valid (128) and nonvalid (1920) codewords implies that, if a codeword gets corrupted, chances are that it will change to a nonvalid one.

It may, of course, happen that a valid codeword gets modified, during transmission, to another valid codeword. Thus, our codes are not absolutely reliable, but they can be made more reliable by adding check bits and by selecting the valid codewords carefully. One of the basic theorems of information theory says (page viii) that codes can be made as reliable as desired by adding check bits, as long as n (the size of a codeword) does not exceed the channel's capacity.

⋄ **Exercise 1.4:** (Easy.) Why not add more and more check bits to make our codes extremely reliable?

It is important to understand the meaning of the word *error* in data storage and transmission. When an n-bit codeword is sent and received, the receiver always receives n bits, but some of them may be bad. A bad bit does not disappear, nor does it change into something other than a bit. A bad bit simply changes its value, either from 0 to 1 or from 1 to 0. This makes it relatively easy to correct the bit. The code should tell the receiver which bits are bad, and the receiver can then easily correct the bits by inverting them.

In practice, bits may be sent on a wire as voltages. A binary 0 may, e.g., be represented by any voltage in the range 3–25 volts. A binary 1 may similarly be represented by the voltage range of −25v to −3v. Such voltages tend to drop over long lines and have to be amplified periodically. In the telephone network there is an amplifier (a *repeater*) every 20 miles or so. It looks at every bit received, decides if it is a 0 or a 1 by measuring the voltage, and sends it to the next repeater as a clean, fresh pulse. If the voltage has deteriorated enough in passage, the repeater may make a wrong decision when sensing it, which introduces an error into the transmission. At present, typical transmission lines have error rates of about one in a billion but, under extreme conditions—such as in a lightning storm, or when the electric power suddenly fluctuates—the error rate may suddenly increase, creating a burst of errors.

> The sooner you make your first five thousand mistakes the sooner you will be able to correct them.
>
> —Kimon Nicolaides

1.5 Parity Bits

A parity bit can be added to a group of m information bits to complete the total number of 1 bits to an odd number. Thus the (odd) parity of the group 10110 is 0, since the original group plus the parity bit has an odd number (3) of 1s. It is also possible to use even parity, and the only difference between odd and even parity is that in the latter case, a group of all zeros is valid, whereas with odd parity, any group of bits with a parity bit added cannot be all zeros.

Parity bits can be used to design simple, but not very efficient, error-correcting codes. To correct 1-bit errors, the message can be regrouped in a *rectangle* of dimensions $(r - 1) \times (s - 1)$. A parity bit is added to each row of $s - 1$ bits, and to each column of $r - 1$ bits. The total size of the message (Table 1.3, where parities are even) is now $s \times r$. Notice the single zero at the bottom-right corner of the rectangle (typeset in italics). This is the parity of the 7 parity bits in the bottom row and rightmost column. It helps verify the parity bits themselves.

```
0 1 0 0  1
1 0 1 0  0
0 1 1 1  1
0 0 0 0  0
1 1 0 1  1

0 1 0 0  0
```

Table 1.3: Row and
Column Parities.

```
0 1 0 0 1
1 0 1 0
0 1 0
0 0
1
```

Table 1.4: Diagonal
Parities.

If only one bit becomes bad, a check of all $s - 1 + r - 1$ parity bits will identify it, since only one of the $s - 1$ row parities and only one of the $r - 1$ column parities will be bad. A single-bit error can therefore be corrected by row and column parity bits. When two bits become bad, the error is detected but cannot be corrected. If the data bit at row 3 column 2 is bad, then parity bits R2 and C3 (the second in the row and the third in the column of parity bits) will immediately identify the error. However, if the two bits at positions $(3, 2)$ and $(2, 4)$ go bad, then the four parity bits R2, R4, C3, and C2 will indicate errors. These error indications, however, are ambiguous because they may refer either to data bits $(3, 2)$ and $(2, 4)$ or to $(3, 4)$ and $(2, 2)$. Similarly, if data bits $(3, 2)$ and $(3, 4)$ are bad, only parity bits R2 and R4 will be bad. Parity bit

C3 will be unchanged because of the two errors in row 3. We therefore conclude that the use of simple parity leads to codes that can detect 2-bit errors and can correct only 1-bit errors.

The overhead of a code is defined as the number of parity bits divided by the number of information bits. The overhead of the rectangular code is therefore

$$\frac{(s - 1 + r - 1)}{(s - 1)(r - 1)} \approx \frac{s + r}{s \times r - (s + r)}.$$

A similar, slightly more efficient code is a triangular configuration, where the information bits are arranged in a triangle, with the parity bits placed on the diagonal (Table 1.4). Each parity bit is the parity of all the bits in its row and column. If the top row contains r information bits, the entire triangle has $r(r + 1)/2$ information bits and $r + 1$ parity bits. The overhead is thus

$$\frac{r + 1}{r(r + 1)/2} = \frac{2}{r}.$$

It is also possible to arrange the information bits in several two-dimensional planes to obtain a three-dimensional box, three of whose six outer surfaces consist of parity bits.

It is not obvious how to generalize these methods to more than 1-bit error correction.

1.6 Hamming Distance

In the 1950s, Richard Hamming developed the concept of *distance* as a general way to use check bits for error detection and correction.

Example: To illustrate this concept, we start with a simple example involving just the four symbols A, B, C, and D. Only two information bits are required (we denote the number of information bits by m), but the codes of Table 1.5 add k check bits, for a total of 3–6 bits per symbol. The first of these codes, code$_1$, is simple. Its four codewords were selected from the 16 possible 4-bit numbers and are not the best possible ones. When the receiver receives one of them, say, 0111, it assumes that no error has occurred and the symbol received is D. When a nonvalid codeword is received, the receiver detects an error. Since code$_1$ is not the best code, not every error is detected. Even if we limit ourselves to single-bit errors, this code is not very good. There are 16 possible single-bit errors in our 4-bit codewords, and of those, the following four cannot be detected: a 0110 changed during transmission to 0111, a 0111 modified to 0110, a 1111 corrupted to 0111, and a 0111 changed to 1111. The error detection rate is therefore 12 out of 16, or 75%. In comparison, code$_2$ does a much better job. It can detect every single-bit error, because if only a single bit is changed in any of the codewords, the result is not any of the other codewords. We say that the four codewords of code$_2$ are sufficiently *distant* from each other. The concept of distance of codewords is simple and easy to define as follows:

1. Two codewords are a Hamming distance d apart if they differ in exactly d of their n bits.
2. A code has a Hamming distance of d if every pair of codewords in the code is at least a Hamming distance d apart.

Symbol	code$_1$	code$_2$	code$_3$	code$_4$	code$_5$
A	0000	0000	001	001001	01011
B	1111	1111	010	010010	10010
C	0110	0110	100	100100	01100
D	0111	1001	111	111111	10101
m:	2	2	1	4	3

Table 1.5: $(k = 2)$.

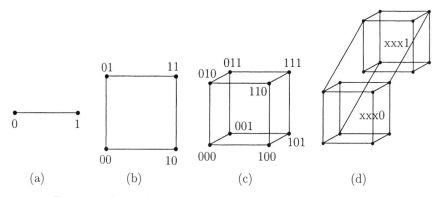

Figure 1.6: Cubes of Various Dimensions and Corner Numbering.

These definitions have a simple geometric interpretation (for the mathematical readers). Imagine a hypercube in n-dimensional space. Each of its 2^n corners can be numbered by an n-bit number (Figure 1.6) such that each of the n bits corresponds to one of the n dimensions. In such a cube, points that are directly connected (near neighbors) have a Hamming distance of 1, points with a common neighbor have a Hamming distance of 2, and so on. If a code with a Hamming distance of 2 is needed, only points that are not directly connected should be selected as valid codewords.

The reason code$_2$ can detect all single-bit errors is that it has a Hamming distance of 2. The distance between valid codewords is 2, so a 1-bit error always changes a valid codeword into a nonvalid one. When two bits go bad, a valid codeword is moved to another codeword at a distance of 2. If we want that other codeword to be nonvalid, the code must have at least a distance of 3.

In general, a code with a Hamming distance of $d + 1$ can detect all d-bit errors. In comparison, $code_3$ has a Hamming distance of 2 and can therefore detect all 1-bit errors even though it is short ($n = 3$). Similarly, $code_4$ has a Hamming distance of 4, sufficient to detect all 3-bit errors. It is now obvious that we can increase the reliability of our data, but this feature does not come free. As always, there is a tradeoff, or a price to pay, in the form of the overhead. Our codes are much longer than k bits per symbol because of the added check bits. A measure of the price is $n/k = \frac{m+k}{k} = 1 + m/k$, where the quantity m/k is the *overhead* of the code. In the case of $code_1$ the overhead is 2, and in the case of $code_3$ it is $3/2$.

Example: A code has a single check bit that is a parity bit (even or odd). Any single-bit error can easily be detected, since it creates a nonvalid codeword. Such a code therefore has a Hamming distance of 2. Notice that $code_3$ uses a single, odd, parity bit.

⋄ **Exercise 1.5:** Guess how $code_4$ was constructed.

> The mistakes made by Congress wouldn't be so bad if the next Congress didn't keep trying to correct them.
>
> —Cullen Hightower

1.7 Error-Correcting Codes

The principle of error-correcting codes is to separate the codes even farther by increasing the code's redundancy (i.e., adding more check bits). When an invalid codeword is received, the receiver corrects the error by selecting the valid codeword that is closest to the one received. An example is $code_5$, which has a Hamming distance of 3. When one bit is changed in any of its four codewords, that codeword is one bit distant from the original one but is still two bits distant from any of the other codewords. Thus, if there is only one error, the receiver can always correct it.

What code will correct 2-bit errors? When two bits go bad in a codeword A, the resulting codeword B is at a distance of 2 from A. Such an error can be corrected if the distance between B and all other codewords is greater than 2, i.e., at least 3. If this is true, then A is the codeword closest to B and the error is corrected by changing B to A. Thus, to correct 2-bit errors, a code with Hamming distance 5 or greater is needed.

In general, when d bits go bad in a codeword A, A turns into a codeword B at a distance d from A. (Notice that B should be invalid, which means that the code must have a Hamming distance of at least $d + 1$.) If the distance between B and any other valid codeword is at least $d + 1$, then B is closer to A than it is to any other valid codeword. This is why a code with a Hamming distance of $d + (d + 1) = 2d + 1$ (or greater) can correct all d-bit errors.

How are the codewords selected? The problem is to select a good set of 2^k codewords out of the 2^n possible ones. The simplest approach is to use brute force. It is easy to write a computer program that will examine all the possible sets of 2^k codewords and will select the first one that has the right distance. The problems with this approach are

(1) the time and storage required at the receiving end to verify and correct the codes received and (2) the amount of time it takes to examine all the possibilities.

Problem 1. The receiver must have a list of all the 2^n possible codewords. For each codeword, it must have a flag indicating whether the codeword is valid, and if not, which valid codeword is the closest to it. The list has to be searched for each codeword received in order to verify it.

Problem 2. In the case of four symbols, only four codewords need be selected. For $code_1$ and $code_2$, these four codewords had to be selected from among 16 possible numbers, which can be done in $\binom{16}{4} = 7280$ ways. It is possible to write a simple program that will systematically select sets of four codewords until it finds a set with the required distance. In the case of $code_4$, however, the four codewords had to be selected from a set of 64 numbers, which can be done in $\binom{64}{4} = 635{,}376$ ways. This is still feasible, but it illustrates the magnitude of the problem. In practical cases, where sets of hundreds of symbols are involved, the number of possibilities of selecting codewords is too large even for the fastest computers to handle in a reasonable time frame.

> Life is an error-making and an error-correcting process, and nature in marking man's papers will grade him for wisdom as measured both by survival and by the quality of life of those who survive.
>
> —Jonas Salk

1.8 Hamming Codes

Clearly, a clever algorithm is needed to select the best codewords and to verify them on the fly as they are being received. The transmitter should use the algorithm to generate the codewords right before they are sent, and the receiver should use it to check them when they are received. The approach discussed here is due to Richard Hamming [Hamming 86]. In Hamming's codes, the n bits of a codeword are indexed from 1 (least significant) to n (most significant). The check bits are those with indexes that are powers of 2. Thus, bits b_1, b_2, b_4, b_8, ... are check bits, and b_3, b_5, b_6, b_7, b_9, ... are information bits. The Hamming code is based on the fact that any integer can be expressed as a sum of powers of 2. Thus, for example $11 = 1 + 2 + 8 = 2^0 + 2^1 + 2^3$. The index of each information bit can therefore be written as the sum of the indexes of certain check bits. For example, b_7 can be written as b_{1+2+4}, which is why b_7 is used in determining check bits b_1, b_2, and b_4. The check bits are simply parity bits. The value of b_2, for example, is the parity (odd or even) of b_3, b_6, b_7, b_{10}, ... because each of the indexes 3, 6, 7, 10,... is expressed as a sum of powers of 2 that includes 2^1.

Example: We construct the Hamming code for the set of symbols A, B, C, D. Two information bits are needed to code the four symbols, so these must be b_3 and b_5. This implies that the parity bits are b_1, b_2, and b_4 (the next parity bit, b_8, is not needed because the indexes 3 and 5 can be expressed as sums that employ only 1, 2, and 4). We write $3 = 1 + 2$ and $5 = 1 + 4$, which defines the three parity bits as follows:

b_1 is the parity of bits b_3, b_5, b_2 is the parity of b_3, b_4 is the parity of b_5.

This is how code$_5$ of Table 1.5 was constructed. The codes of the four integers 00, 10, 01, and 11 are 01011, 10010, 01100, and 10101, respectively.

Example: Take the Hamming code of a set of 256 symbols. Eight information bits are required to code the 256 symbols, so these must be b_3, b_5, b_6, b_7, b_9, b_{10}, b_{11}, and b_{12}. The parity bits are, therefore, b_1, b_2, b_4, and b_8. The total size of a codeword is 12 bits. The four parity bits are defined by the relations $3 = 1 + 2$, $5 = 1 + 4$, $6 = 2 + 4$, $7 = 1 + 2 + 4$, $9 = 1 + 8$, $10 = 2 + 8$, $11 = 1 + 2 + 8$, and $12 = 4 + 8$.

This implies that b_1 is the parity of b_3, b_5, b_7, b_9, and b_{11}. The definitions of the other parity bits are as follows: b_2 is the parity of b_3, b_6, b_7, b_{10}, and b_{11}; b_4 is the parity of b_5, b_6, b_7, and b_{12}; b_8 is the parity of b_9, b_{10}, b_{11}, and b_{12}.

Thus, the 8-bit symbol 10111010 becomes the codeword 101**1**0101**0**010. When such a codeword is received, the receiver checks for errors by verifying the four parity bits. Assuming that b_7 has gone bad, the receiver will find that parity bits b_1, b_2, and b_4 are bad (because they are based on b_7) while b_8 is good. Adding the indexes $1 + 2 + 4$ of the bad parity bits will produce 7, the index of the corrupted bit. This method of decoding also works in cases where one of the parity bits gets changed. Assuming that b_4 has gone bad, verifying the parity bits will result in only b_4 being bad. Adding the indexes of the bad parity bits will again point to the culprit.

This method of decoding shows that only one error can be corrected, because adding the indexes of the bad parities produces a single number. The Hamming code is therefore a 1-bit error-correcting code, so its Hamming distance must be 3.

⋄ **Exercise 1.6:** What is the Hamming code for a set of 128 symbols?

⋄ **Exercise 1.7:** What Hamming codes use parity bit b_{16}?

The size of the Hamming code is easy to figure out because this is a simple code that corrects only 1-bit errors. Given a set of 2^m symbols, 2^m valid codewords are needed, each n bits long. The 2^m valid codewords should therefore be selected from a total of 2^n numbers. Each codeword consists of m information bits and k check bits, where the value of m is given, and we want to know the minimum value of k.

A single-bit error takes us to a codeword at distance 1 from the original. As a result, all codewords at distance 1 from the original codeword should be nonvalid. Each of the original 2^m codewords should therefore have the n codewords at distance 1 from it declared nonvalid. This means that the total number of codewords (valid plus nonvalid) is $2^m + n2^m = (1+n)2^m$. This number has to be selected from the 2^n available numbers, so we end up with the relation $(1 + n)2^m \leq 2^n$. Since $2^n = 2^{m+k}$, we get $1 + n \leq 2^k$ or $k \geq \log_2(1 + n)$. The following table illustrates the meaning of this relation for certain values of m.

n	:	4	7	12	21	38	71
k	:	2	3	4	5	6	7
$m = n - k$:		2	4	8	16	32	64
k/m	:	1	.75	.5	.31	.19	.11

This result has a geometric interpretation that provides another way of looking at the result and also of obtaining it. We imagine 2^m spheres of radius one, tightly packed in our n-dimensional cube. Each sphere is centered around one of the corners and encompasses all its immediate neighbors. The *volume* of a sphere is defined as the number of corners it includes, which is $1 + n$. The spheres are tightly packed but they don't overlap, so their total volume is $(1 + n)2^m$, and this should not exceed the total volume of the cube, which is 2^n.

The case of a 2-bit error-correcting code is similarly analyzed. Each valid codeword should define a set including itself, the n codewords at distance 1 from it, and the set of $\binom{n}{2}$ codewords at distance 2 from it, a total of $\binom{n}{0} + \binom{n}{1} + \binom{n}{2} = 1 + n + n(n-1)/2$. Those sets should be nonoverlapping, which implies the relation

$$\left(1 + n + n(n-1)/2\right)2^m \le 2^n \Rightarrow 1 + n + n(n-1)/2 \le 2^k \Rightarrow k \ge \log_2\left(1 + n + n(n-1)/2\right).$$

In the geometric interpretation we again imagine 2^m spheres of radius 2 each, each sphere centered around a corner and containing the corner, its n immediate neighbors, and its $\binom{n}{2}$ second-place neighbors (corners differing from the center corner by 2 bits).

> Mistakes are a fact of life. It is the response to the error that counts.
>
> —Nikki Giovanni

1.9 The SEC-DED Code

Even though we can estimate the length of a 2-bit error-correcting Hamming code, we don't know how to construct it! The best that can be done with Hamming codes is single-error correction (SEC) combined with double-error detection (DED). An example of such a SEC-DED code is code$_6$ of Table 1.5. It was created by simply adding a parity bit to code$_5$.

The receiver checks this code in two steps. In step 1, the single parity bit is checked. If it is bad, the receiver assumes that a 1-bit error occurred, and it uses the other parity bits, in step 2, to correct the error. It may, of course, happen that three, five, or any odd number of bits are bad, but the simple SEC-DED code cannot correct such errors.

If the single parity is good, then either there are no errors or two bits are bad. The receiver proceeds to step 2, where it uses the other parity bits to distinguish between these two cases. Again, there could be four, six, or any even number of bad bits, but this code cannot handle them.

The SEC-DED code has a Hamming distance of 4. In general, a code for c-bit error correction and d-bit error detection should have a distance of $c + d + 1$.

The following discussion provides better insight into the behavior of the Hamming code. For short codewords, the number of parity bits is large compared to the size of the codeword. When a 3-bit code, such as xyz, is converted to SEC-DED, it becomes the 7-bit codeword $xyb_4zb_2b_1p$, which more than doubles its size. Doubling the size of a code seems a high price to pay in order to gain only single-error correction and double-error detection. On the other hand, when a 500-bit code is converted to SEC-DED, only the 10 parity bits $b_{256}, b_{128}, b_{64}, b_{32}, b_{16}, b_8, b_4, b_2, b_1$, and p are added, resulting in a 510-bit codeword. The size of code is increased by 1.8% only. Such a small increase in size seems a low price to pay for even a small amount of increased reliability. With even larger codes, the benefits of SEC-DED can be obtained with even a smaller increase in the code size. There is clearly something wrong here, since we cannot expect to get the same benefits by paying less and less. There must be some tradeoff. Something must be lost when a long code is converted to SEC-DED.

What is lost is reliability. The SEC-DED code can detect 2-bit errors and correct 1-bit errors in the short, 7-bit codeword and also in the long, 510-bit codeword. However, there may be more errors in 510 bits than in 7 bits. The difference in the corrective power of SEC-DED is easier to understand if we divide the 500-bit code into 100 5-bit segments and convert each individually into a SEC-DED code by adding four parity bits. The result is a string of $100(5 + 4) = 900$ bits. Now assume that 50 bits become bad. In the case of a single, 510-bit long string, the SEC-DED code may be able to detect an error but will not be able to correct any bits. In the case of 100 9-bit strings, the 50 bad bits constitute 5.6% of the string size. This implies that many 9-bit strings will not suffer any damage, many will have just 1 or 2 bad bits (cases which the SEC-DED code can handle), and only a few will have more than 2 bad bits.

The conclusion is that the SEC-DED code provides limited reliability and should be applied only to reasonably short strings of data.

Richard Wesley Hamming (1915–1998)

Richard Hamming was born in 1915 in Chicago, Illinois. He was educated at the University of Chicago, the University of Nebraska, and the University of Illinois at Urbana-Champaign.

Hamming joined the Manhattan Project at Los Alamos in 1945, when the project was at its final stage. In 1946, after the war, Hamming joined the Bell Telephone Laboratories, where he was fortunate to work with both Claude Shannon and John Tukey. He stayed at Bell Labs until 1976, when he became a professor at the Naval Postgraduate School at Monterey, California. He stayed in Monterey until his death in 1998.

Hamming is best known for his pioneering work on error-detecting and error-correcting codes. His revolutionary paper on this topic was published in 1950 and started a new field within information theory. Hamming codes are of fundamental importance in coding theory and are used in many practical applications.

Work in codes is related to packing problems, and Hamming's work led to the solution of a packing problem for matrices over finite fields.

In 1956 Hamming helped develop the IBM 650, one of the early computers. As part of that project, he developed a programming language that has influenced the high-level computer languages of today.

Hamming also made important contributions to numerical analysis, integrating differential equations, and the Hamming spectral window.

Hamming has received important awards for his pioneering work. In 1968 he became a fellow of the IEEE and was awarded the Turing Prize by the ACM. In 1979 he was awarded the Emanuel R. Piore Award and in 1988 a medal, both by the IEEE.

1.10 Periodic Codes

No single error-control code provides absolute reliability in every situation. This is why, ideally, each application should have a special reliable code designed for it, based on what is known about possible data corruption. One common example of errors is a *burst*. Imagine a reliable cable through which data is constantly transmitted with high reliability. Suddenly a storm approaches and lightning strikes nearby. This may cause a burst of errors that will corrupt hundreds or thousands of bits in a small region of the data. Another example is a CD. Data is recorded on a CD (Section 1.11) in a continuous path that starts on the inside and spirals out. When the CD is cleaned carelessly, it may get scratched. If the cleaning is done in a circular motion, parallel to the spiral, even a small scratch may cover (and therefore corrupt) many consecutive bits (which is why a CD should be cleaned with radial motions, in a straight line from the inside toward the rim).

The SEC-DED, or any similar code, cannot deal with a burst of errors, which is why special codes must be designed for applications where such bursts may occur. One way to design such a code is to embed parity bits among the data bits, such that each parity bit is the parity of several, nonadjacent data bits. Such a code is called *periodic*.

As a simple example of a periodic code, imagine a string of bits divided into 5-bit segments. Each bit is identified by the segment number and by its number (1 through 5) within the segment. Each segment is followed by one parity bit. Thus, the data with the parity bits included becomes the string

$$b_{1,1}, b_{1,2}, b_{1,3}, b_{1,4}, b_{1,5}, p_1, b_{2,1}, b_{2,2}, b_{2,3}, b_{2,4}, b_{2,5}, p_2, \ldots, b_{i,1}, b_{i,2}, b_{i,3}, b_{i,4}, b_{i,5}, p_i, \ldots.$$

We now define each parity bit p_i as the (odd) parity of the five bits $b_{i,1}$, $b_{i-1,2}$, $b_{i-2,3}$, $b_{i-3,4}$, and $b_{i-4,5}$. Thus, each parity bit protects five bits in five different segments, with the result that any error affects five parity bits: one in its segment and four in the four segments that follow. If all the data bits of segment j become corrupted, the corruption will be reflected in the five parity bits p_j, p_{j+1}, p_{j+2}, p_{j+3}, and p_{j+4}. In general, errors will be detected if every two bursts are at least five segments apart.

This simple code cannot correct any errors, but the principle of periodic codes can be extended to allow for as much error correction as needed.

⬦ **Exercise 1.8:** If the index of the last data segment is n, then bit $b_{n,1}$ is protected by parity bit p_n, but the remainder of the segment does not participate in any parity bits. Suggest a way to remedy this situation.

1.11 Compact Disc Error Control

The compact disc (CD) was developed by Philips and Sony, starting in 1974. In June 1980 the two companies agreed on a common CD standard. In 1981 this standard was approved by the Digital Audio Disc committee, was ratified as standard IEC 908, and has been used since. The standard includes details of the signal format, disc material, and error-correcting code. Note the spelling "disc," as opposed to a magnetic "disk."

The immediate success of the audio CD motivated the development of the CD-ROM (for digital information) in 1985, the CD-V (for video), and the CD-I (interactive), both in 1987. For detailed sources for the history of the compact disc, see [Despan 04] and [Pohlman 92].

To understand the capacity requirements of the CD, let's consider the way sound is recorded digitally. A microphone converts sound (air vibrations) to an electrical signal (voltage) that varies with time according to the intensity and frequency of the sound. We can therefore consider sound to be a function $s(t)$ of the time t. The function goes up and down according to the intensity of the sound, so its frequency may change all the time. However, at each point in time, $s(t)$ has a value representing the intensity (amplitude) of the sound. The principle of digital recording is to examine $s(t)$ periodically and to record its value as a binary number. This process is called *sampling*, and each number is a sound sample.

Clearly, if we don't sample a sound often enough, we don't get enough information about it and therefore cannot reconstruct it (play it back) correctly from the sound samples. On the other hand, we don't want to sample too often. This is where the Nyquist theorem [Nyquist 28] comes to the rescue. It declares: If the sampling is done at a rate greater than twice the highest frequency of the sound, then the sound can always be fully reconstructed from the individual samples. This theorem applies to the sampling of any waves, and this sampling rate is called the Nyquist rate.

◇ **Exercise 1.9:** The Nyquist rate must be greater than twice the highest frequency of the wave being sampled. Show an example where sampling at exactly twice the rate is insufficient.

The human ear can normally hear sounds up to a frequency of about 20–22 kHz, which means that sound recording should use a sampling rate of more than 40–44 kHz. The CD standard specifies a rate of 44.1 kHz. An hour of music therefore requires $44,100 \times 3,600 = 158,760,000$ sound samples. To get high-quality sound, the CD standard specifies 16-bit samples, bringing the total number of bits to 2,540,160,000. Stereo sound requires two numbers per sound sample, resulting in 5,080,320,000 bits. This is equivalent to 635,040,000 bytes. Synchronization and modulation information, and parity bits for error correction (see below), increase this number significantly. Thus, one hour of music requires an impressive storage capacity.

(We say that stereo music requires two channels, while mono requires just one. The CD standard specifies three ways of recording sound: (1) stereo samples, recorded on the two channels; (2) mono samples recorded twice, on both channels; (3) mono samples on one channel with the other channel left empty. The standard does not allow for two different mono samples to be recorded on both channels.)

A CD-ROM contains digital information and is similar to a read-only memory (ROM). The fundamental unit of data on a CD-ROM is the sector. The amount of user data contained in a sector depends on the mode of the sector. A mode 1 sector (the most common) contains 2K = 2048 bytes of user data. Most PC, Macintosh, and UNIX CD-ROMs are mode 1. A mode 2 sector contains 2336 bytes of user data. Examples of mode 2 CD-ROMs are XA, Photo-CD, and CD-I. Older recordable CDs (CD-R) were labeled "74 min., 650 Mbytes." Such a CD had 336,075 sectors, which translates to 74 min., 43 sec. playing time. The capacity was $336{,}075 \times 2048 = 688{,}281{,}600$ bytes or 656.396484375 Mbytes (where mega is $2^{20} = 1{,}048{,}576$). However, it is possible to record more sectors on a CD, thereby increasing its capacity. This is somewhat risky, since the extra sectors approach the outer rim of the CD, where they can easily be scratched or get dirty.

Current CD-Rs are labeled as 700 Mbyte or 80 minutes. They have 359,849 sectors for a total capacity of $359{,}849 \times 2048 = 736{,}970{,}752$ bytes or 702.83 Mbytes.

In order to read 702.83 Mbytes in 80 minutes, a CD drive has to read 150 Kbytes per second. This speed is designated 1X and was typical for CD players made before 1993. Current CD drives (year 2004) can read CDs at speeds of up to 56X, where 700 Mbytes are read in just under 86 seconds!

The following table lists the capacities of a CD-ROM with 345,000 sectors in mode 1 and in mode 2.

	Mode 1 345000×2048	Mode 2 345000×2336
Bytes	706,560,000	805,920,000
Mbytes	673.828	768.585

Notice that *mega* is defined as $2^{20} = 1{,}048{,}576$, whereas a million equals 10^6. The playing time (at 75 sectors per second) is 76 min, 40 sec. in either mode.

1.12 CD Description

Physically, the CD is a disc, 1.2 millimeters thick, with a 120 mm diameter. The hole at the center is 15 mm in diameter. The distance between the inner and outer circumferences is therefore $(120 - 15)/2 = 52.5$ mm. Of this, only 35 mm is actually used, leaving a safety margin both inside and outside. The information is recorded on a metallic layer (typically aluminum, silver, or gold), that is 0.5μ to 1μ thick (where μ, or micron, is 10^{-6} meter). Above this layer there is a protective lacquer coating (10μ to 30μ thick), with the printed label. Below the metal layer is the disc substrate, normally made of transparent polycarbonate. It occupies almost the entire thickness of the disc. Since the protective layer on top is so thin, any scratches on the label can directly damage the metallic layer. Even pen marks can bleed through and cause permanent damage. On the other hand, scratches on the substrate are usually handled by the error correcting code (Section 1.14).

The digital information is recorded in pits arranged in a spiral track that runs from the inner circumference to the outer one. The pits are extremely small. Each is 0.5μ

wide and 0.11μ deep (Figure 1.7b). Pit lengths range from 0.833μ to 3.56μ. The track areas between pits are called *land*. The distance between successive laps of the track is 1.6μ. As a result, the track makes 22,188 revolutions in the 35 mm recording area. Its total length is about 3.5 miles. The information is recorded such that any edge of a pit corresponds to binary 1, and the area in the pits and in the lands (between pits) corresponds to consecutive zeros. To reduce fabrication problems, the pits should not be too short or too long, which means that the number of binary ones recorded should be carefully controlled (see below).

To read the disc, a laser beam is focused on the track through the disc substrate, and its reflection measured (Figure 1.7a). When the beam enters a pit, the reflection drops to almost zero, because of interference. When it leaves the pit, the reflection goes back to high intensity. Each change in the reflection is read as binary one. To read the zeros, the length of a pit, and the length of a land between pits, must be measured accurately.

The disc must therefore rotate at a constant linear velocity (CLV). This implies that, when the reading laser moves from the inner parts of the track to the outer ones, the rotational speed has to decrease (from 500 RPM to about 200 RPM). The track contains synchronization information used by the CD player to adjust the speed. The aim of the player is to read 4.3218 million bits per second, which translates to a CLV of 1.2–1.4 meter/sec.

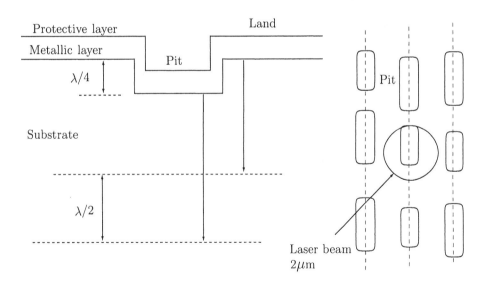

(a)   (b)

Figure 1.7: Pits and Lands on a CD.

The CD was made possible by two advances: a technological one (high precision manufacturing) and a scientific one (error-correcting codes). Here are some numbers illustrating the two points:

1. Remember the old LP vinyl records? Information is stored on such a record in a narrow spiral groove whose width is about the diameter of a human hair (about 0.05 mm). More than 30 laps of the CD track would fit in such a groove!

2. A CD is read at a rate of 4.3218 million bits per second. The reading is done by measuring the reflection of a laser beam from the track and is thus sensitive to surface scratches, to imperfections in the track, and to surface contamination because of fingerprints, dust particles, and so on. All these factors introduce errors in reading, but the digital nature of the recording allows for error correction.

(A note about cleaning: Clean a CD only if you must, since cleaning may create many invisible scratches and cause more harm than good. Use a soft, moistened cloth, and work radially, from the center to the rim. Cleaning with a circular motion might create a long scratch paralleling a track, thereby introducing a long burst of errors.)

1.13 CD Data Encoding

The CD data encoding process starts with a chunk of 24 data bytes (twelve 16-bit samples, or six 32-bit stereo samples), which is encoded with Reed–Solomon codes (Section 1.14). This results in a 32-byte frame that consists of scrambled data and parity bits. The encoding hardware generates another byte called the subcode (Section 1.13.1) and attaches it to the frame. The CD data overhead is therefore $8 + 1$ bytes for every 24 bytes, or 37.5%. It can be shown that even a burst of about 4000 bad data bits can be completely corrected by this code, which justifies the overhead.

Before writing a 33-byte frame on the CD, the recording hardware performs Eight-to-Fourteen Modulation (EFM). Each byte of the frame is used as a pointer to a table with 14-bit entries, and the table entry is written on the CD instead of the byte. The idea is to control the length of the pits by controlling the number of consecutive zeros. It is easier to fabricate the pits if they are not too short or too long. EFM modulation produces 14-bit numbers that have at least two zeros and at most ten zeros between successive ones. There are $2^{14} = 16{,}384$ 14-bit numbers, and 267 of them satisfy this condition. Of those, 256 were selected and placed in the table. (Two more are used to modulate the subcodes.) Table 1.8 lists the first ten of the 256 entries.

There is still the possibility of a 14-bit number ending with a binary 1, followed by another 14-bit number starting with a 1. To avoid that, three more *merging bits* are recorded on the track after each 14-bit number. Two of them are zeros, and the third one is selected to suppress the signal's low frequency component. This process results in about 3 billion pits being fabricated on the long CD track.

To summarize the encoding process, it starts with a group of 24 bytes (192 bits), which are encoded into $24+8+1 = 33$ bytes. These are translated into 33 14-bit numbers that are recorded, each with 3 merging bits, on the track. A synchronization pattern of 24 bits (plus 3 merging bits) is also recorded at the start of the track. Thus, the original

8-bit pointer	14-bit pattern
00000000	01001000100000
00000001	10000100000000
00000010	10010000100000
00000011	10001000100000
00000100	01000100000000
00000101	00000100010000
00000110	00100001000000
00000111	00100100000000
00001000	01001001000000
00001001	10000001000000
00001010	10010001000000

Table 1.8: 8-Bit Pointers and 14-Bit Patterns.

192 bits require $24 + 3 + 33 \times (14 + 3) = 588$ bits to be recorded, which corresponds to an overhead of $(588 - 192)/192 = 396/192 \approx 206\%$. To record 635,040,000 data bytes, we therefore need to record about 1,309,770,000 bytes (about 10.5 billion bits)! The following summarizes the format of a frame.

sync. 24	merg. bits 3	byte 0 14	merg. bits 3	byte 1 14	merg. bits 3	$\cdots$ $\cdots$	byte 32 14	merg. bits 3

The CD player has to read the information at the rate of 44,100 samples per second (corresponding to a 44.1 kHz sampling rate). Each (stereo) sample consists of two 16-bit numbers, so there are six samples per frame. This is why $44,100/6 = 7350$ frames have to be read each second, which translates to a bitrate of $7350 \times 588 = 4,321,800$ bits/sec.

1.13.1 The Subcode

Each frame contains an additional byte called the subcode. The eight bits of the subcode are labeled PQRSTUVW. In an audio CD, only the P and Q bits are used. When the CD is read, the subcode bytes from 98 consecutive frames are read and assembled into a *subcode frame*. Recall that the frames are read at a rate of 7350 per second. Since $7350/98 = 75$, this implies that 75 subcode frames are assembled each second by the CD player! A subcode frame has the two 14-bit sync patterns 00100000000001 and 00000000010010 (two of the 267 patterns not included in the EFM table). The frame is then considered eight 98-bit numbers. The 98 bits of P give the CD player information about the start and end of each song (each music track). The bits of Q contain more information, such as whether the CD is audio or ROM, and whether other digital recorders are legally permitted to copy the CD.

1.14 Reed–Solomon Codes

This section presents a simplified, geometric approach to the Reed–Solomon code used for error correction in CDs, DVDs and many other applications.

It is obvious that reading a CD-ROM must be error free, but error correction is also important in an audio CD, because one bad bit can cause a big difference in the note played. Consider the two 16-bit numbers 0000000000000000 and 1000000000000000. They differ by one bit only, yet when played as sound samples, the first corresponds to silence and the second produces a loud sound. The size of a typical dust particle is 40μm, enough to cover more than 20 laps of the track and cause several bursts of errors (Figure 1.9a). Without extensive error correction, the music may sound like one long scratch.

Any error correction method used in a CD must be very sophisticated, since the errors may come in bursts or may be individual. The use of parity bits makes it possible to correct individual errors but not a burst of consecutive errors. This is why *interleaving* is used, in addition to parity bits. The principle of interleaving is to rearrange the samples before recording them on the CD and to reconstruct them after they have been read. This way, a burst of errors during reading is translated to individual errors (Figure 1.9b), that can then be corrected by their parity bits.

The actual code used in CDs is called the Cross-Interleaved Reed–Solomon Code (CIRC). It was developed by Irving S. Reed and Gustave Solomon at Bell Labs in 1960 [Reed and Solomon 60] and is a powerful code. One version of this code can correct up to 4000 consecutive bit errors, which means that even a scratch that covers three millimeters of the track can be tolerated on a CD. The principle of CIRC is to construct a geometric pattern that is so familiar that it can be reconstructed even if large parts of it are missing. It's like being able to recognize the shape of a rectangular chunk of cheese after a mouse has nibbled away large parts of it.

Mathematician Gustave Solomon died on January 31 [1996] in Los Angeles. He was 65. Dr. Solomon was a co-inventor with Irving S. Reed of the Reed–Solomon codes, which have come into increasingly widespread use as a way of combating the inevitable errors that occur in the transmission and storage of information. He did early work concerning the algebraic theory of error-correcting codes, and, with H. F. Mattson, was co-author of the powerful tool for analyzing such codes known as the Mattson-Solomon polynomial. His other interests included composing popular songs and folksongs and teaching voice and movement.

—Dave Farber, farber@central.cis.upenn.edu

Suppose that the data consists of the two numbers 3.6 and 5.9. We consider them the y coordinates of two-dimensional points, and we assign them x coordinates of 1 and 2, respectively. We end up with the points $(1, 3.6)$ and $(2, 5.9)$ that we consider two points on a line. We now calculate four more points on this line, with x coordinates of 3, 4, 5, and 6. They are $(3, 8.2)$, $(4, 10.5)$, $(5, 12.8)$, and $(6, 15.1)$. Since the x coordinates are so regular, we only need to store the y coordinates of these points. We thus store (or write on the CD) the six numbers 3.6, 5.9, 8.2, 10.5, 12.8, and 15.1.

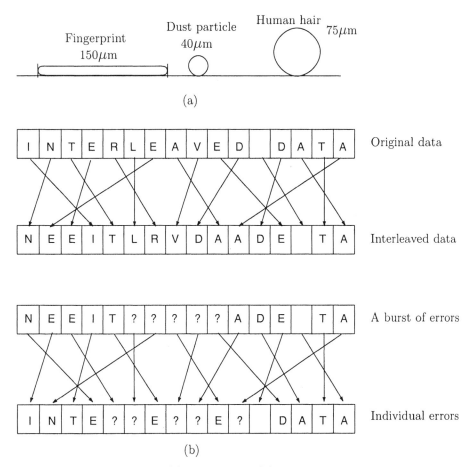

Figure 1.9: (a) Relative Sizes. (b) Interleaving Data.

Suppose that two of those six numbers have been damaged. When the new sequence of six numbers is checked for the straight line property, the remaining four numbers can be identified as being collinear and can still be used to reconstruct the line. Once the line is known, the two bad numbers can be corrected, since their x coordinates are known. Even three bad numbers out of those six can be corrected, since the remaining three numbers would still be enough to identify the original straight line. (Notice that there is a small but finite chance that any other set of three of the six numbers would be on a straight line, so this code may sometimes fail to correct two- or three-number errors.)

A more powerful code can be obtained by using a more complex geometric figure. A simple approach may start with three numbers a, b, and c, convert them to the points $(1, a)$, $(2, b)$, and $(3, c)$, and calculate the (unique) parabola that passes through these points. Four more points, with x coordinates of 4, 5, 6, and 7, can then be calculated on this parabola. Once the seven points are known, they provide a strong pattern. Even if three of the seven get corrupted, the remaining four can be used to reconstruct the parabola and correct the three bad ones. However, if four of the seven become bad, then no four numbers will be on a parabola (and any group of three will define a different parabola). Such a code can correct three errors in a group of seven numbers, but it requires high redundancy (seven numbers instead of four).

⋄ **Exercise 1.10:** Show how to compute the parabola that passes through three given points.

The mathematics of Reed–Solomon codes is based on polynomials. A polynomial $p(x)$ of degree n is the simple function

$$p(x) = a_0 + a_1 x + a_2 x^2 + \cdots + a_n x^n = \sum_{i=0}^{n} a_i x^i.$$

It depends on $n+1$ coefficients a_i that are normally real numbers but can be any other mathematical entities. A degree-1 polynomial has the form $a_0 + a_1 x$. When plotted, its curve is a straight line, so it can intercept the x axis at most once (except for the special, degenerate cases where the line is the x axis itself or runs parallel to it). A degree-2 polynomial has the form $a_0 + a_1 x + a_2 x^2$, which when plotted becomes a parabola; it intercepts the x axis at most twice (again, there are special cases). In general, the curve of a degree-n polynomial is wavy. It oscillates, goes up and down, and intercepts the x axis at most n times.

An (n, k) Reed–Solomon code, normally denoted by $\text{RS}(n, k)$, encodes a block of k data symbols a_0, a_1,...,a_{k-1} into a codeword of n symbols, where n is selected to be greater than k for increased redundancy. Specifically, $n = k + 2t$ for a certain t, and the code can correct errors in up to t symbols (i.e., its Hamming distance is $2t + 1$). Each symbol consists of s bits, where the maximum value of n is $2^s - 1$.

A common example is the $(255, 223)$ code with $s = 8$. Each symbol is an s-bit number (a byte), and 223 data bytes are combined with 32 extra bytes to produce a 255-byte codeword. Adding 32 bytes implies $t = 16$, so this code can correct errors in up to 16 bytes. One extreme case is where each byte has just one bad bit. In this case, the number of bits corrected is 16. Another extreme case is where each of the 16 bad bytes has been completely corrupted; every bit is bad. The decoder ends up correcting $16 \times 8 = 128$ bits in this case.

The codes may be shortened in cases where no convenient value of k is available. If for some reason it is inconvenient to use $k = 223$, it is possible to use another value such as $k = 168$. The encoder appends 55 zero bytes to a block of 168 data bytes, to end up with 223 bytes. An additional 32 bytes are then computed from the 223 bytes, and a codeword consisting of the original 168 data bytes and the extra 32 bytes is sent to the decoder, where the 55 zero bytes are implied.

We describe two intuitive approaches to generating the code. In both approaches the original k data symbols a_i are considered the coefficients of the degree-$(k - 1)$

polynomial

$$p(x) = a_0 + a_1x + a_2x^2 + \cdots + a_{k-1}x^{k-1}.$$

In the first approach, the polynomial is evaluated at n distinct, nonzero points x_i, and the n values $y_0 = p(x_0)$, $y_1 = p(x_1), \ldots, y_{n-1} = p(x_{n-1})$ become the codeword. The x_i values are built into both encoder and decoder. The decoder receives the codeword with the y_i's and combines each x_i with the corresponding y_i to end up with the n points (x_0, y_0) through (x_{n-1}, y_{n-1}). The points are used to reconstruct polynomial $p(x)$, whose coefficients a_i are the original data symbols. Without any errors, reconstruction is easy. The polynomial is of degree $k - 1$, so it can be determined by k points. With no errors, any k of the n points can be used, and any set of k points will determine polynomial $p(x)$.

In the presence of errors, decoding is more complex. The decoder generates the n points. It knows that the unknown, degree-$(k - 1)$ polynomial $p(x)$ passes through the points. Some of the points (at most t) may be bad. A set of k points is enough to determine a unique degree-$(k - 1)$ polynomial, but given more points, this polynomial may not pass through the extra points. The decoder starts by finding a subset of at least $k + t$ points through which a degree-$(k - 1)$ polynomial $q(x)$ passes. Such a subset is termed *consistent* and it always exists, because polynomial $p(x)$ that was computed by the encoder passes through all n points, and we assume that at most t points went bad. (If such a subset cannot be found, the decoder concludes that more than t errors have occurred.)

Finding such a subset and determining polynomial $q(x)$ is only the first step. Some of the points in the subset may be bad, so polynomial $q(x)$ determined by the subset may be different from $p(x)$. However, the subset consists of $k + t$ (or more) points, and of those, not more than t are bad. We therefore start with the case where there are no bad points in the subset. All the points in the subset are among the ones originally used by the encoder, so polynomial $q(x)$ determined by the subset is the one computed by the encoder. In such a case, every set of k points in our subset will determine the same polynomial $q(x)$, and this will be identical to $p(x)$. If the subset includes some bad points, then different sets of k points in the subset will determine different degree-$(k-1)$ polynomials.

In the second step, the decoder has to test every set of k points in the subset. If different sets determine different degree-$(k - 1)$ polynomials, then the subset contains some bad points, and another subset must be identified and tested. If no more subsets can be found, the decoder concludes that more than t points are bad and the error cannot be corrected.

This approach is impractical because of the many calculations required. The next approach, while also computationally infeasible, has the advantage of being simple in the common case where no errors are discovered. The idea is to generate a codeword where the first k symbols are simply the data symbols a_i, and these are followed by $2t$ parity check symbols. The parity symbols are of the form $p(x_i)$, where the x_i are distinct, nonzero values. Such a Reed–Solomon code is known as systematic, because in the common case where there are no errors, the decoder simply outputs the first k symbols of the codeword.

To check for errors, the decoder generates the system of $2t$ equations

$$a_0 + a_1 x_0 + \cdots + a_{k-1} x_0^{k-1} = y_0,$$
$$a_0 + a_1 x_1 + \cdots + a_{k-1} x_1^{k-1} = y_1,$$
$$\vdots$$
$$a_0 + a_1 x_{2t-1} + \cdots + a_{k-1} x_{2t-1}^{k-1} = y_{2t-1}.$$

As with the first approach, there must be at least one consistent subset of $k+t$ symbols, and any such subset has k correct symbols. Assume that a subset with k correct symbols has $k - l$ data symbols a_i and l polynomial values $p(x_i)$. Each polynomial value $p(x_i)$ contributes an equation, for a total of l equations. Each equation has k symbols a_i on the left side, but only l are unknown, so the system of l equations can be solved.

These two approaches are impractical not only because they are computationally intensive but also because they require the use of nonintegers. In the computer, nonintegers are normally represented (as floating-point numbers) with limited precision, which complicates the problem of reconstructing the parabola or any other geometric figure. The Reed–Solomon codes that are used in practice employ integers, which are stored in the computer (or written on a CD) in full precision. The problem is that operations on integers may result in very large integers, in negative integers, or in nonintegers, which is why these codes use arithmetic operations in finite fields. A finite field is a finite set of elements (integers or other symbols) with a special operation defined on the field elements that always results in a field element (the field is *closed* under this operation). Interested readers are invited to study the basics of finite fields in Appendix B. Once this topic is understood, the Reed–Solomon codes can be described more precisely. Here is a short summary.

An (n, k) Reed–Solomon code deals with elements of the finite field GF$(n + 1)$, which implies that $n + 1$ should be either a prime or a power of a prime. This code encodes a group of k field elements into a group of n field elements. A common example is the RS (255, 223) code that is based on the field GF(256). Each element of this field is a byte, and the code encodes a group of 223 field elements into 255 elements by adding 32 check field elements. It can be shown that an (n, k) RS code has a Hamming distance of $2t + 1$, where t is defined by $2t = n - k$. The code can therefore correct up to t errors. (The following is another interpretation of these numbers. Start with k data items, normally bits, and increase the data redundancy by adding $2t$ data items. The resulting code is $n = k + 2t$ long, and it can correct up to t errors.)

Given a finite field GF$(n + 1)$ and a string $a_0 a_1 \ldots a_{k-1}$ of k field elements to be encoded, the (n, k) RS code is computed in the following steps:

1. Select a primitive element g of the field. This is a generator of the multiplicative cyclic group of the nonzero elements of the field.
2. Treat the message as the polynomial $p(x) = a_0 + a_1 x + a_2 x^2 + \cdots + a_{k-1} x^{k-1}$.
3. Compute this polynomial at the n points $p(1), p(g), p(g^2), \ldots, p(g^{n-1})$.

The n field elements computed in step 3 are the RS code of the original string. This code can be stored or transmitted instead of the string. Because of the way g

is selected, the various powers g^i are nonzero and are all different. Returning to the geometric interpretation, these n elements are n points on the graph of the polynomial $p(x)$. This polynomial is of degree $k-1$, so k points are enough to determine it uniquely. The polynomial is computed at n points where $n > k$, so it is overcomputed by $2t = n-k$ points. Because of the way this particular polynomial is computed, it has the following useful property: Given any k of the n points, if we compute the degree-$(k-1)$ polynomial that passes through them, the result will be $p(x)$.

Decoding is complex and is beyond the scope of this book. It involves five main steps: (1) syndrome calculation, (2) Berlekamp algorithm, (3) Chien search, (4) Forney's algorithm, and (5) error correction. For one of several detailed references that describe this process, see [Berlekamp 68].

Another advantage of this code is its excellent behavior for burst errors. Its Hamming distance is $2t + 1$, so it can correct up to t errors, but if the locations of the errors are known, all of them (up to $2t$ errors) can be corrected. This process is easy to visualize when we consider the geometric interpretation. If we know the bad points, we can reconstruct the polynomial from k points, then correct up to $2t$ bad points by "pulling" them into the polynomial.

1.15 Generating Polynomials

There are many approaches to the problem of developing error-control codes for more than 1-bit error correction. These are, however, more complicated than Hamming's method and require a background in group theory and Galois fields (Appendix B). One such approach, using the concept of a *generating polynomial*, is briefly sketched here.

We consider the case $k = 4$. Sixteen codewords are needed that can be used to code any set of 16 symbols. We already know that three parity bits are needed for 1-bit correction, thereby bringing the total size of the code to $n = 7$. Here is an example of such a code:

```
0000000 0001011 0010110 0011101   0100111 0101100 0110001 0111010
1000101 1001110 1010011 1011000   1100010 1101001 1110100 1111111
```

Note that it has the following properties:

■   The sum (modulo 2) of any two codewords equals another codeword. This implies that the sum of any number of codewords is a codeword. Thus, the 16 codewords above form a *group* under this operation.
(Addition and subtraction modulo-2 is done by $0 + 0 = 1 + 1 = 0$, $0 + 1 = 1 + 0 = 1$, $0 - 1 = 1$. The definition of a group should be reviewed in any text on algebra.)

■   Any circular shift of a codeword is another codeword. Thus, this code is *cyclic*.

■   The Hamming distance is 3, as required for 1-bit correction.

Interesting properties! The sixteen codewords were selected from the 128 possible ones by means of a *generator polynomial*. The idea is to look at each codeword as a polynomial, where the bits are the coefficients. Here are some 7-bit codewords associated with polynomials of degree 6.

$$
\begin{array}{ccccccccccccccccc}
1 & 0 & 0 & 1 & & 1 & & 1 & & 1, & 0 & 1 & & 1 & 0 & 0 & 1 & 0, & 0 & 1 & 0 & 0 & & 1 & & 1 & & 1. \\
x^6 & & & +x^3 & & +x^2 & & +x & & +1 & & x^5 & & +x^4 & & & +x & & & x^5 & & & & +x^2 & & +x & & +1
\end{array}
$$

The 16 codewords in the above table were selected by finding the degree-6 polynomials that are evenly divisible (modulo 2) by the generating polynomial $x^3 + x + 1$. For example, the third codeword 0100111 in the table corresponds to the polynomial $x^5 + x^2 + x + 1$, which is divisible by $x^3 + x + 1$, because $x^5 + x^2 + x + 1 = (x^3 + x + 1)(x^2 + 1)$.

To understand how such polynomials can be calculated, let's consider similar operations on numbers. Suppose that we want to know the largest multiple of 7 that is less than or equal to 30. We divide 30 by 7, obtaining a remainder of 2, and then subtract the 2 from the 30, getting 28. Polynomials are divided in a similar way. Let's start with the four information bits 0010 and calculate the remaining three parity bits. We write 0010ppp, which gives us the polynomial x^4. We divide x^4 by the generating polynomial, obtaining a remainder of $x^2 + x$. Subtracting that remainder from x^4 gives us something that will be evenly divisible by the generating polynomial. The result of the subtraction is $x^4 + x^2 + x$, so the complete codeword is 0010110.

Any generating polynomial can get us the first two properties. To get the third property (the necessary Hamming distance), the right generating polynomial should be used, and it can be selected by examining its roots (see [Lin and Costello 82]).

A common example of a generating polynomial is $\mathrm{CRC}(x) = x^{16} + x^{12} + x^5 + 1$. When dividing a large polynomial by $\mathrm{CRC}(x)$, the result is a polynomial of degree 15, which corresponds to a 16-bit codeword. There are standard polynomials used to calculate the CRC (cyclic redundancy codes) at the end of blocks of transmitted data.

Other generating polynomials are $\mathrm{CRC}_{12}(x) = x^{12} + x^3 + x + 1$ and $\mathrm{CRC}_{16}(x) = x^{16} + x^{15} + x^2 + 1$. They generate the common CRC-12 and CRC-16 codes, which have lengths of 12 and 16 bits, respectively.

Example: The generating polynomial $1 + x^2 + x^4 + x^5 + x^6 + x^{10} + x^{11}$ generates the code listed in Figure 1.10. This is a $(23, 12)$ *Golay code*. Each 23-bit code has 12 data bits and 11 check bits. Its Hamming distance is 7, so it can correct three errors.

```
10000000000011111111110
01000000000000001111111
00100000000001110001111
00010000000010110110011
00001000000011011010101
00000100000011101101001
00000010000001111100101
00000001000001010111001
00000000100001101010011
00000000010010011001011
00000000001010100011101
00000000000111000100111
```

Figure 1.10: The $(23, 12)$ Golay Code.

1.15.1 Golay codes

In 1949, Marcel Golay discovered a way to construct the $(23, 7)$ and $(23, 12)$ binary codes and the $(11, 5)$ and $(11, 6)$ ternary codes [Golay 49]. In 1954, Golay discovered a geometric construction [Golay 54] of the $(23, 12)$ code. This construction is described here and can also be found in [Goettingen 04].

We start with five straight lines in the plane, no two of which are parallel and no three of which are concurrent. The lines are labeled A through E and each of their intersections is labeled with a pair of these letters. Figure 1.11 shows an example with 10 intersections. We construct a 10×5 matrix (Figure 1.12a) whose rows and columns correspond to the 10 intersections and the five line segments, respectively. In each column, the matrix elements are set to 0 if there is an intersection with the line labeling the column; otherwise, the elements are set to 1. For example, the first column corresponds to line A, which intersects lines B, C, D, and E. Thus, the first four elements of this column are set to 0 and the other six elements are set to 1. The five matrix columns are labeled 2 through 6.

The next step is to construct six more columns and append them to the original matrix as columns 7 through 12. We start with the string $ABEDC$ and select the five permutations of this string that are cyclic, that differ from $ABEDC$ by an even number of interchanges of symbols, and that are not equivalent to $ABEDC$. For example, permutation $ACDEB$ is equivalent to $ABEDC$ because a left circular shift of $ACDEB$ produces $CDEBA$ which is the reverse of $ABEDC$. The six permutations are $ABEDC$, $ABEDC$, $ABCED$, $ABDCE$, $ACEBD$, and $ADCBE$, and they are employed to produce the 10×11 matrix of Figure 1.12b. Column 1 is now added as a single 0 followed by nine 1s, to extend our matrix to 10 rows and 12 columns. Finally, the matrix is transposed (so it has 12 rows and 10 columns) and the 12×12 identity matrix is prepended on the left, to end up with the 12×23 matrix of Figure 1.10.

1.16 Codes and Geometry

In addition to generating polynomials, other methods have been developed to generate sets of numbers with a given Hamming distance. One such method, based on *projective planes*, is described here. This is an elegant method, but its practical use is limited because other, more advanced methods are more efficient. A projective plane is a geometric structure that consists of points and lines (where a line is defined by a set of points and does not have to be straight) and satisfies the following:

- Every two points lie on exactly one line.
- Every two lines intersect at exactly one point.
- There are four points such that no three of them are collinear.

Figure 1.14 shows two examples of such planes. The graph of Figure 1.14a has four points and six lines. There are exactly two points on each line and three lines intersect at each point. A set of six 4-bit codes with Hamming distance 2 can be constructed in the following way. We prepare a matrix whose rows and columns correspond to the lines and points, respectively, of the graph, and whose elements are bits. A matrix element

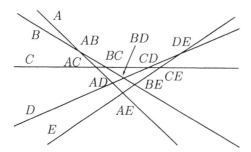

Figure 1.11: Five Intersecting Lines.

$$
\begin{array}{c}
\begin{array}{ccccc}
A & B & C & D & E \\
2 & 3 & 4 & 5 & 6
\end{array} \\
\begin{array}{l}
AB\ 1 \\ AC\ 2 \\ AD\ 3 \\ AE\ 4 \\ BC\ 5 \\ BD\ 6 \\ BE\ 7 \\ CD\ 8 \\ CE\ 9 \\ DE\ 10
\end{array}
\left(
\begin{array}{ccccc}
0 & 0 & 1 & 1 & 1 \\
0 & 1 & 0 & 1 & 1 \\
0 & 1 & 1 & 0 & 1 \\
0 & 1 & 1 & 1 & 0 \\
1 & 0 & 0 & 1 & 1 \\
1 & 0 & 1 & 0 & 1 \\
1 & 0 & 1 & 1 & 0 \\
1 & 1 & 0 & 0 & 1 \\
1 & 1 & 0 & 1 & 0 \\
1 & 1 & 1 & 0 & 0
\end{array}
\right)
\end{array}
\qquad
\begin{array}{c}
\begin{array}{cccccccccccc}
2 & 3 & 4 & 5 & 6 & 7 & 8 & 9 & 10 & 11 & 12
\end{array} \\
\begin{array}{l}
AB\ 1 \\ AC\ 2 \\ AD\ 3 \\ AE\ 4 \\ BC\ 5 \\ BD\ 6 \\ BE\ 7 \\ CD\ 8 \\ CE\ 9 \\ DE\ 10
\end{array}
\left(
\begin{array}{ccccccccccc}
0 & 0 & 1 & 1 & 1 & 0 & 0 & 0 & 1 & 1 & 1 \\
0 & 1 & 0 & 1 & 1 & 0 & 1 & 1 & 0 & 0 & 1 \\
0 & 1 & 1 & 0 & 1 & 1 & 0 & 1 & 0 & 1 & 1 \\
0 & 1 & 1 & 1 & 0 & 1 & 1 & 0 & 1 & 0 & 0 \\
1 & 0 & 0 & 1 & 1 & 1 & 0 & 1 & 1 & 0 & 0 \\
1 & 0 & 1 & 0 & 1 & 1 & 1 & 0 & 0 & 0 & 1 \\
1 & 0 & 1 & 1 & 0 & 0 & 1 & 1 & 0 & 1 & 0 \\
1 & 1 & 0 & 0 & 1 & 0 & 1 & 0 & 1 & 1 & 0 \\
1 & 1 & 0 & 1 & 0 & 1 & 0 & 0 & 0 & 1 & 1 \\
1 & 1 & 1 & 0 & 0 & 0 & 0 & 1 & 1 & 0 & 1
\end{array}
\right)
\end{array}
$$

(a)   (b)

Figure 1.12: Two Stages in Constructing Golay Code.

(i, j) is 1 if point j is located on line i and is 0 otherwise. Thus, the top row of the matrix corresponds to line L_1 that is defined by points P_1 and P_3. The row is therefore 1010. The entire matrix is shown in Table 1.15 together with its one's complement and the two 4-bit numbers 0000 and 1111. The result is a set of 14 4-bit codes with a Hamming distance of 2.

⋄ **Exercise 1.11:** The graph of Figure 1.14b has seven points and seven lines. Each line has three points and three lines intersect at each point. Write the seven 7-bit codes constructed by this graph and extend it to a set of 14 7-bit codes with Hamming distance of 3.

Figure 1.13 shows two larger projective planes and the codes generated by them, but the downside of this approach is that there is no explicit algorithm to generate any desirable projective plane, and it is even unknown which projective planes exist.

For references on this interesting and elegant approach, see [Hill 86], [Rosen 00] and [AMS 04]. Many diagrams of projective planes can be found in [Polster 98].

The author is indebted to Prof. Joseph Malkevitch for information on this method.

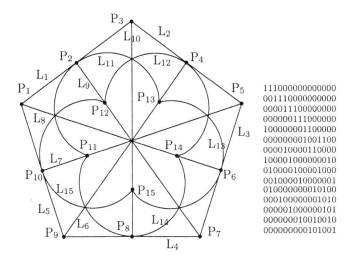

```
111000000000000
001110000000000
000011100000000
000000111000000
100000001100000
000000001001100
000010000110000
100001000000010
010000100001000
001000010000001
010000000010100
000100000001010
000001000000101
000000010010010
000000000101001
```

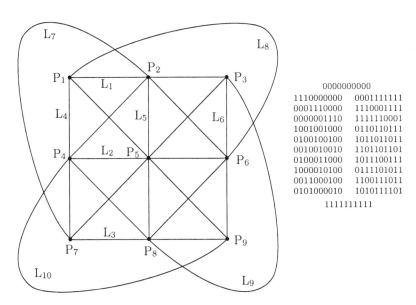

```
        0000000000
1110000000    0001111111
0001110000    1110001111
0000001110    1111110001
1001001000    0110110111
0100100100    1011011011
0010010010    1101101101
0100011000    1011100111
1000010100    0111101011
0011000100    1100111011
0101000010    1010111101

        1111111111
```

Figure 1.13: Two Projective Planes and Corresponding Codes.

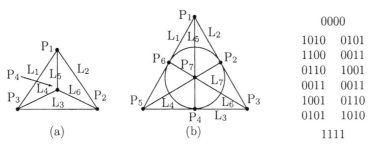

Figure 1.14: Two Projective Planes.   Table 1.15: Codes.

From the errors of others, a wise man corrects his own.

—Publilius Syrus

2
Check Digits for Error Detection

Computers process large amounts of data, and error correction is essential in many computer applications. There are, however, many common, important applications where only small quantities of data (such as a short identification number) are involved and where only error-detection capability is needed. Once an error has been detected, it can be manually checked and corrected. A typical example is a credit card. Any credit card has an identification number that is protected by a check digit. A typical credit card has a 16-digit number, where the rightmost digit is the check digit that is computed as a simple function of the other digits. When a consumer tries to use a credit card, the entire 16-digit number is transmitted to the card issuer and the check digit is verified. This process has two important advantages: (1) if the card is read incorrectly, either by a machine or by a human, at the point of sale, the verification process will almost always detect an error; and (2) not every 16-digit number is a valid credit card number, which adds redundancy to those numbers and makes it (at least in principle) harder for a casual forger to forge such a card.

The methods discussed in this chapter deal with decimal data. The serial numbers and identification numbers found on credit cards, airline tickets, checks, and other documents are decimal. The error-control methods of Chapter 1 are for binary numbers and are based on finite (Galois) fields (Appendix B). Such fields exist only for prime numbers or for powers of primes. The integer 2 is a prime, but 10 is neither a prime nor a power of a prime, so the finite field GF(10) does not exist. Thus, new methods are required for making decimal data reliable, and these methods are the topic of this chapter.

This chapter starts with several common applications of this type, such as ISBN, various types of barcodes, and the unique identification numbers found on airline tickets, money orders, and checks. These applications are based on a single *check digit*, an extra digit appended to the number, that provides redundancy and can detect many common errors. The chapter continues with a few sophisticated methods (Sections 2.9 and 2.10) that employ more than one check digit and can detect more errors and even correct a few. The last method, due to Verhoeff (Section 2.11), is based on symmetry groups and can detect virtually all common errors.

For recommended references for this chapter, see [Gallian 89], [Gallian 91], [Kirtland 00], [Palmer 95], and [Vinzant 99].

Before we can define check digits and examine their properties, we first have to find out what kinds of errors are likely to occur in a given application and then design the check digit to detect as many errors as possible. A common example is a traveler calling ahead to make a hotel reservation with a credit card. The credit card number has to be read into the telephone, heard by the hotel clerk, and entered into a computer by writing or keying it. This process is obviously error-prone, which is why the credit card issuer wants to be reasonably certain that the card number that it is about to approve is valid.

According to Hamming ([Hamming 86], p. 27) the two most common errors humans make, when keying numbers, dialing them, or reading and saying them, are transposing adjacent digits and changing a triplet of the form *aab* to *abb*. In 1969, the Dutch mathematician Jacobus Verhoeff published the results of a study [Verhoeff 69] of errors commonly made by humans in handling decimal numbers. Table 2.1 lists the types of errors that have been identified by him, and their frequencies.

Type of error	*Example*	Frequency
Single errors	$a \to b$	60–95%
Adjacent transpositions	$ab \to ba$	10–20%
Twin errors	$aa \to bb$	0.5–1.5%
Jump transpositions	$acb \to bca$	0.5–1.5%
Jump twin errors	$aca \to bcb$	< 1%
Phonetic errors*	$50 \to 15$	0.5–1.5%
Omitting or adding a digit		10–20%

* "phonetic" because in many languages 15 and 50, as well as other pairs, have similar pronunciations.

Table 2.1: Types of Common Errors and Their Frequencies

The omission or addition of a digit is easily detected without a check digit, so the table implies that the main task of a check digit is to detect a single corrupted digit and a transposition of two adjacent digits. All the other errors are rare.

Check digits normally use the concept of modulo. The mathematical function $a \bmod b$ (read: a modulo b) is simply the remainder of the integer division a/b, so it is an integer in the interval $[0, b-1]$. Given a number A that consists of the decimal digits $d_1 d_2 \ldots$, the simplest way to compute a check digit C for A is to solve the equation

$$(C + d_1 + d_2 + \cdots) \bmod n = 0, \qquad (2.1),$$

but the value of n should be chosen carefully. Notice that this equation can be solved by first computing the sum $T = (d_1 + d_2 + \cdots) \bmod n$ and then subtracting $C = n - T$.

Example: Assume a 3-digit integer $A = d_1 d_2 d_3$, where each digit is between 0 and 4. A good choice for n is the prime number 5. Given $A = 421$, it is easy to compute $T = (4 + 2 + 1) \bmod 5 = 2$ and $C = 5 - 2 = 3$. The check digit is appended to A, and the 4-digit number $421|3$ is read over the telephone, written, stored in a computer, or transmitted over a communication line. At the receiving end, the number is checked. If no digits got corrupted, the check $(4 + 2 + 1 + 3) \bmod 5$ will yield 0. If the number became, for example, $431|3$, then the check $(4 + \mathbf{3} + 1 + 3) \bmod 5$ will yield 1 (the difference between the bad digit and its original value). This simple check digit can therefore detect single-digit errors, but cannot correct them because the position of the error is unknown.

◇ **Exercise 2.1:** Develop a similar check digit for 2-digit decimal numbers.

A little thinking shows that this simple check digit cannot detect any transpositions of digits, which is why most of the methods described in this chapter use a check digit computed by means of certain weights w_i as

$$(C + w_1 \cdot d_1 + w_2 \cdot d_2 + \cdots) \bmod n = 0, \tag{2.2}$$

or equivalently $T = (w_1 \cdot d_i + w_2 \cdot d_2 + \cdots) \bmod n$ and $C = n - T$. Given $A = 421$, we can select the weights 2, 3, and 4 and compute the check digit by $T = (24 + 32 + 41) \bmod 5 = 3$ and $C = 5 - 3 = 2$. If two adjacent digits of A are swapped due to an error, to end up with $A' = 241$, a check would yield $(2 + 2 \cdot 2 + 3 \cdot 4 + 4 \cdot 1) \bmod 5 = 2$, thereby detecting an error.

The reason why the check digit defined by Equation (2.2) provides good reliability is that the weights w_i are relatively prime to 5 (i.e., 5 does not divide any of them evenly). Section 2.1 illustrates a practical application of Equation (2.2) for 9-digit identification numbers.

Section 2.10 shows how two check digits, defined by Equations (2.1) and (2.2), can correct, not just detect, single-digit errors.

2.1 ISBN

ISBN (International Standard Book Number) is an identifying number assigned to virtually every book published. (A reprint of a book has the same ISBN, but a new edition receives its own ISBN.) It serves to uniquely identify the book. An ISBN has four parts: a language/country code, a publisher code, a book number assigned by the publisher, and a check digit, for a total of 10 digits. For example, ISBN 0-387-95045-1 has language/country code 0, publisher code 387, book number 95045, and check digit 1. Table 2.2 lists some language/country codes. It's clear that widely used languages are assigned a short language/country code, thereby allowing for a long publisher code, while other countries and languages have been assigned long language/country codes, so their publisher codes must be short. When the number space of a language/country code is exhausted, another code is assigned to the language/country. Thus, Table 2.2 shows that India has country codes 81 and 93. For codes not included in the table, see [ISBN 04].

(The modern ISBN has evolved from the old Standard Book Number [SBN] used in the past in some English-speaking countries. An SBN is converted to an ISBN by appending a zero on the left.)

0	English (UK, US, Australia, NZ, Canada)	99917	Brunei Dar-es-salam
1	English (South Africa, Zimbabwe)	99918	Faroe Islands
2	French (France, Belgium, Canada, Switzerland)	99919	Benin
3	German (Germany, Austria, Switzerland)	99920	Andorra (see also 99913)
4	Japan	99921	Qatar
5	USSR	99922	Guatemala (see also 99939)
6	-	99923	El Salvador
7	China	99924	Nicaragua
80	Czechoslovakia	99925	Paraguay
81	India (see also 93)	99926	Honduras
82	Norway	99927	Albania
83	Poland	99928	Georgia (see also 5 and 99940)
84	Spain	99929	Mongolia
85	Brazil	99930	Armenia (see also 5 and 99941)
86	Yugoslavia	99931	Seychelles
87	Denmark	99932	Malta (see also 99909)
88	Italian (Italy, Switzerland)	99933	Nepal
89	South Korea	99934	Dominican Republic
90	Dutch/Flemish	99935	Haiti
91	Sweden	99936	Bhutan
92	International (Unesco and EEC)	99937	Macau
93	India (see also 81)	99938	Srpska (Serbia, see also 86)
950	Argentina	99939	Guatemala (see also 99922)
951	Finland	99940	Georgia (see also 5 and 99928)
952	Finland	99941	Armenia (see also 5 and 99930)

Table 2.2: Various ISBN Country/Language Codes.

⋄ **Exercise 2.2:** Find the ISBN of a book published in Malta.

The check digit is computed by multiplying the leftmost ISBN digit by 10, the next digit by 9, and so on, up to the ninth digit from the left, which is multiplied by 2. The products are then added, and the check digit is determined as the smallest integer that when added to this weighted sum will make it a multiple of 11. The check digit is therefore in the interval $[0, 10]$. If it happens to be 10, it is replaced by the Roman numeral X in order to make it a single symbol.

If we denote the nine leftmost ISBN digits by d_1 through d_9 (from left to right), then the ISBN I is computed by first calculating the weighted sum

$$T = (10d_1 + 9d_2 + 8d_3 + 7d_4 + 6d_5 + 5d_6 + 4d_7 + 3d_8 + 2d_9) \bmod 11 \qquad (2.3)$$

(notice that T is in the interval $[0, 10]$ because of the use of the modulo) and then subtracting $I = 11 - T$. For example, given the nine digits 038795045, the two steps produce

$$T = (10 \cdot 0 + 9 \cdot 3 + 8 \cdot 8 + 7 \cdot 7 + 6 \cdot 9 + 5 \cdot 5 + 4 \cdot 0 + 3 \cdot 4 + 2 \cdot 5) \bmod 11 = 241 \bmod 11 = 10$$

and $I = 11 - 10 = 1$, yielding ISBN 0-387-95045-1.

ISBNs are assigned, printed, scanned, and handled by both machines and humans, so errors can creep in. It is important to detect errors, but there is no need to automatically correct them by means of a sophisticated error-correcting code. When the check digit indicates an error in an ISBN, a human can easily identify the error and correct it manually. Obviously, a single check digit cannot detect every error, but it is easy to show that the ISBN check digits can detect all the most common errors.

The most common errors in an ISBN are a corrupted digit and two consecutive digits being transposed. It's easy to show that all these errors will be detected by the ISBN check digit.

To understand why single-digit errors are always detected, we try to find cases where such an error will go unnoticed. An error in digit d_i will not be detected unless it affects the value of T. Since T is computed modulo 11, this will happen if the corrupted digit changes the sum $10d_1 + 9d_2 + \cdots + 2d_9$ by 11 or by a multiple of 11. However, since 11 is prime and since the weights that multiply the nine digits are relatively prime to 11, this cannot happen. A change in d_1, for example, will change T by a small multiple of 10 (up to $9 \cdot 10$), and such a multiple is never a multiple of 11. Similarly, a change in d_2 will change T by a small multiple of 9 (up to $9 \cdot 9$), which is never a multiple of 11, and so on.

Now examine two consecutive digits, such as d_4 and d_5. Their contribution to T is the sum $7d_4 + 6d_5$, but when transposed they contribute $7d_5 + 6d_4$. In order for T to remain unchanged, the difference of the two contributions should be a multiple of 11, but the difference is $d_4 - d_5$ (or, equivalently $d_5 - d_4$) and the difference of two digits is a digit in the interval $[-9, +9]$, so it never equals 11.

See Section 2.10 for an extension of this technique that can also correct, not just detect, single-digit errors.

◇ **Exercise 2.3:** The ISBN check digit provides strong error detection because its base, 11, is a prime and the weights are not factors of 11. Show an example of a weak check digit that is similar to that of the ISBN but has a composite base and one weight that is a factor of the base.

2.2 Barcodes

The rapid progress of science and its applications in the twentieth century has created several technologies that are commonly used, while being little understood by the general public. Barcodes are a typical example of such a technology. This section starts with a short history of barcodes, followed by a detailed description of several types of barcodes and their check digits.

The first practical application of barcodes was in the food industry. Large, modern food stores (the so-called supermarkets) stock thousands of items, many of which are perishable, and sell them at a very low markup. Thus, a supermarket has to be efficient. It has to keep track of its inventory, which shouldn't be too large or too small, and it has to quickly and accurately identify each item purchased by a customer and add it to the customer's bill. For decades, inventories had to be done manually by counting each item in the store, and pricing accuracy depended on the skills of employees at the checkout counters.

In 1948, the president of a chain of food stores was trying to interest a dean at Drexel University in Philadelphia in his problems. The dean was not responsive, but the conversation was overheard by a student, Bernard Silver, who shared it with his friend, Norman Joseph Woodland.

Woodland became fascinated by the problem and devoted much time to solving it. He applied two existing technologies: the Morse code and the soundtrack used in movies. The former, as everyone knows, uses dots and dashes. A movie soundtrack consists of gray stripes printed on a narrow strip along the edge of the film. The stripes have different widths and shades of gray. Light shines through the stripes as the film rolls, and any light passing the stripes is detected on the other side of the film and is converted to an electrical wave, which is fed into a speaker to create the sound.

As a first step, Woodland extended the dots and dashes into vertical, black, narrow and wide stripes printed on paper. Light shined on the stripes is absorbed by the black stripes and reflected by the white gaps between them. The reflected light is then detected and used to generate the characters encoded in the stripes. This system was later modified to concentric circles of stripes, which could be scanned in any direction.

A patent was filed by Woodland and Silver and was granted in 1949. The patent expired in 1969 without having been used much. The state of the art of computers and electronics in the 1950s was not advanced enough to allow the development of fast, accurate, and inexpensive barcode scanners. However, the invention of the integrated circuit in the mid-1950s and the development of small, powerful, and inexpensive lasers in the 1960s have finally made such a scanner a reality.

It was again Woodland, this time at IBM, who came up with the modern form of barcodes and with the idea of the universal product code (UPC). A new body, the Uniform Code Council (UCC), was established to design barcode standards and assign barcodes to manufacturers and to individual products. The next paragraph is a brief timeline of the UCC.

The ad hoc Uniform Grocery Product Code Council (UGPCC) convened for the first time in August 1970 and agreed to jointly pursue a uniform grocery product identification code. Over 100 manufacturers and 84 retailers had joined the UGPCC by December 1972. In April 1973 the UGPCC adopted the use of barcodes for product identification. In September 1974 the UGPCC became the Uniform Product Code Council (UPCC) and in November 1984 it changed its name to become the Uniform Code Council (UCC). Manufacturers can register with the UCC to obtain a manufacturer identifier code and then register each of their products. This way, each item in a retail store has its own unique identification number. When brought to a checkout counter and scanned, the item's number is input into a computer that adds it to the total bill and updates the store's inventory. For more information on this important organization, see [UCC 04].

The first supermarket product to be barcode scanned was a pack of chewing gum. This historic event took place at a Marsh supermarket in Troy, Ohio, on June 26, 1974. Today, we rarely pay any attention to barcodes because they are so prevalent. Boats stored by the United States Army are labeled by huge, two-foot long barcodes.

Researchers tag insects and other animals under study by mounting small barcodes on them. Automobile parts, business documents, logs in lumberyards, and patients in a hospital are other examples of items tagged by barcodes. Packages routed by Federal Express and other delivery services are tagged by barcodes to make it easy to track their progress.

Because of the usefulness of barcodes, there are many barcode standards, each suitable for certain applications. Important examples are UPC, ISBN, postal zip codes, and EAN (European article numbering).

Figure 2.3: Various Barcodes.

2.2.1 The UPC Code

The UPC barcode consists of a 1-digit product type, a 5-digit manufacturer code, a 5-digit product code, and a single check digit. Figure 2.3a shows UPC code 8-37281-00321-1. UPC barcodes can also include a 5-digit or a 2-digit price code, as illustrated by Figure 2.3b. Each digit is encoded in seven bits, where each bar stands for a bit (white for 0 and black for 1) and up to four adjacent bars can have the same color. (Alternatively, we can say that there are four different bar widths and a bar can represent between 1 and 4 bits.) The barcode of Figure 2.3a encodes the following bits:

```
||    0110111 0111101 0111011 0010011 0110111 0011001    ||    1110010 1110010 1000010 1101100 1100110 1100110    ||
↑                                                         ↑                                                       ↑
separator              left side                      separator              right side                   separator
```

Table 2.4 lists the 7-bit codes of the 10 decimal digits. Each digit has two codes for the left and right parts of the barcode. The codes have been chosen to satisfy the following properties:

1. Each of the left codes has an odd number of 1s, and each of the right codes has an even number of 1s. This makes it possible to figure out the codes regardless of the direction of scanning.
2. All the left codes start with a 0 and end with a 1, while the right codes employ the opposite convention. This helps the scanner to determine the start and end of a 7-bar code.

We denote the 11 code digits by d_1 through d_{11} (from left to right). The check digit C is computed by first calculating the temporary quantity

$$T = 3d_1 + d_2 + 3d_3 + d_4 + 3d_5 + d_6 + 3d_7 + d_8 + 3d_9 + d_{10} + 3d_{11} \bmod 10,$$

	Left	Right		Left	Right
0	0001101	1110010	5	0110001	1001110
1	0011001	1100110	6	0101111	1010000
2	0010011	1101100	7	0111011	1000100
3	0111101	1000010	8	0110111	1001000
4	0100011	1011100	9	0001011	1110100

Table 2.4: UPC Codes of the Digits.

and then subtracting $C = 10 - T$. Thus, UPC code 8-37281-00321 results in

$$T = 3{\cdot}8 + 3 + 3{\cdot}7 + 2 + 3{\cdot}8 + 1 + 3{\cdot}0 + 0 + 3{\cdot}3 + 2 + 3{\cdot}1 \bmod 10 = 89 \bmod 10 = 9,$$

implying $C = 10 - 9 = 1$.

To estimate the reliability of such a check digit, we again examine its performance when one digit becomes bad and when two adjacent digits are transposed. The temporary quantity T is computed modulo 10, so its values are in the interval $[0, 9]$. Thus, a corrupt code will not be detected by the check digit if the weighted sum of T changes its value by 10 or by a multiple of 10. Each of the 11 digits has a weight of either 3 or 1. Changing a digit therefore modifies the weighted sum by either a small multiple of 3 (up to $9{\cdot}3$) or a small multiple of 1, and such small multiples are never multiples of 10.

The consecutive digits d_3 and d_4 contribute $3d_3 + d_4$ to the weighted sum. Switching these digits changes this contribution to $3d_4 + d_3$, with the result that the weighted sum is modified by the difference $2d_4 - 2d_3 = 2(d_4 - d_3)$. The difference $(d_4 - d_3)$ of two digits is in the interval $[-9, +9]$, so double the difference is in the interval $[-18, +18]$, and it may equal ± 10 in several cases. Error detection by the single UPC check digit is therefore not as reliable as that offered by the ISBN.

$\diamond$ **Exercise 2.4:** The two weights used by the UPC check digit are 1 and 3. They are relatively prime to 10. What other digits are relatively prime to 10?

2.2.2 The EAN-13 Code

The EAN (European Article Numbering) barcodes were initiated by the International Article Numbering Association (whose name originally was the European Article Numbering Association). EAN barcodes were adopted by the UCC in the early 1970s. They are longer, more informative, and more reliable than the UPC barcodes. An especially popular version is EAN-13. From being used by a few European countries in the late 1970s, EAN-13 has spread to all of western Europe as well as the United States, Canada, Australia and Japan. The United States is currently planning to replace UPC with EAN-13 by 2005. Close to half a million EAN-13 manufacturer codes have already been issued to manufacturing companies in about 90 countries.

Instead of the separators used by UPC, EAN-13 has three sets of guard bars, the middle of which separates the code into two zones.

As its name implies, EAN-13 consists of 13 digits. The first two (or three) digits (the flag characters) are a country code. The following five (or four) digits are a manufacturer code, and the next five digits are a product code. The 13th character is a check digit. Figure 2.5a shows the barcodes for 83-72810-03215-4 (the ">" character on the right is a quiet zone indicator). As in the UPC, each digit is represented as a 7-bit number, using bars of four different widths.

Figure 2.5: (a) EAN-13 and (b) ISBN Barcodes.

The check digit is computed as in the UPC barcode, so it offers the same reliability. The digits are denoted by d_1 (leftmost) through d_{12} (rightmost). Each digit with an odd index is multiplied by 3, and each digit with an even index is assigned a weight of 1. The weighted sum (modulo 10) is then subtracted from 10 to produce the check digit. In our example of 83-72810-03215, the weighted sum is 106, so taken modulo 10 it is 6, for a check digit of 4.

Another peculiarity of EAN-13 is that the bars encode only the rightmost 12 digits. The leftmost digit (the first flag character) is encoded indirectly. This is done by assigning each digit three 7-bit codes, denoted by A, B, and C. Code A is given by column "left" of Table 2.4, code C is given by column "right" of the table, and code B is the reverse of C (each 7-bit code is reversed). The six digits in the right zone are always encoded with their C codes. Each of the six digits of the left zone is encoded with either its A or B codes, and the sequence of six A and B codes is used by the computer to determine the value of the leftmost digit. In our example, the sequence is ABABBA, and Table 2.6 shows that this implies a leftmost digit of 8. This convention reduces the number of bars needed but also decreases the reliability of EAN-13. Any error in reading one of the six leftmost digits may cause an error in determining the left flag.

0	AAAAAA	5	ABBAAB
1	AABABB	6	ABBBAA
2	AABBAB	7	ABABAB
3	AABBBA	8	ABABBA
4	ABAABB	9	ABBABA

Table 2.6: EAN-13 AB Codes.

2.2.3 ISBN Barcodes

A special application of the popular EAN-13 barcode is the labeling of books. Once an ISBN is assigned to a book, a special barcode in EAN-13 format is printed on the back of the book to facilitate easy scanning and checkout. We already know that an ISBN has 10 digits and an EAN-13 code consists of 13 digits. An ISBN is therefore converted to an EAN-13 barcode by adding three digits, and the digits 978 have been assigned for this purpose. In addition, the check digit is computed as for a regular EAN-13 barcode. Thus, ISBN 0-387-95045-1 becomes the EAN-13 code 978-0-387-95045-7 (Figure 2.5b), and ISBN 1-890137-40-5 becomes EAN code 978-1-890137-40-3.

⋄ **Exercise 2.5:** Compute the barcode for ISBN 1579550088.

2.3 Zip Barcodes

In the United States, 5-digit postal codes, referred to as *zip* (zoning improvement plan) codes, were first assigned in the early 1960s. In order to facilitate speedier mail delivery, the post office extended the zip codes in 1983 by adding 4 digits, and these codes are known as zip + 4. In 1991, the 11-digit delivery point barcode, where the nine digits are followed by the last two digits of the address, was introduced and tested. This type of barcode virtually eliminates the need for mail carriers to sort mail in order of delivery.

Figure 2.7: Business Reply Mail.

Business reply cards are very popular in the United States. Figure 2.7 is a typical, hypothetical example. Such cards are distributed by a company as part of its advertising effort by, for example, placing them in a magazine. Anyone can mail back the card without a postage stamp. Because of the large number of such cards, the post office requires the zip code to appear on the card in machine-readable form. This is done by using a special barcode format that consists of short and long black vertical bars, corresponding to binary 0 and 1, respectively. Two long bars are placed at the extreme ends of the barcode pattern to serve as guide lines. The digits of the zip code are placed between the guidelines, and each digit is encoded by two long bars and three short bars, as listed in Table 2.8.

0	‖ııı	5	ıIılı
1	ııı‖	6	ıIlıı
2	ıIıl	7	Iııl
3	ııllı	8	Iıılı
4	ılıl	9	Iılıı

Table 2.8: Postal (Zip) Barcodes.

Figure 2.9: Zip Code 92040-5616-35-9.

Error detection is provided by a single check digit that follows the zip digits. The check digit simply completes the sum of the zip code digits to the next multiple of 10. The nine digits of zip code 50037-2706 of Figure 2.7 add up to 30, so the check digit is 0. Figure 2.9 shows the 11-digit zip code 92040-5616-35, where the digits add up to 41, so the check digit is 9. It is clear that the check digit can detect certain errors, but the check digit, combined with the fact that each of the 10 digits is encoded by two long and three short bars, also provides for a certain amount of error-correcting capability. When a zip barcode is read by machine, a short bar may be read as a long bar or vice versa because of smudges, dirt, or scratches on the paper. We examine three typical cases of such errors.

1. If one bar is read incorrectly, then its 5-bit pattern no longer has exactly two long and three short bars, so it is easily identified as bad. Because of the way the check digit is computed, once it is known that a certain digit is bad, it can be corrected by the check digit. For example, the 12-digits of 50037-2706-0 add up to a multiple of 10, so if the machine reads 50037270?0 (i.e., it identifies one bad digit), it adds up the remaining 11 digits (24 in our example) and immediately concludes that the bad digit is 6, because 6 completes the sum to the nearest multiple of 10. Notice that the bad digit may be the check digit itself, in which case there is no need to correct anything, but the error-detection capability provided by the check digit has been lost.

2. Two bars in two different groups are misread. Two digits are identified as bad, so an error is detected, but the single check digit cannot correct this error.

3. Two bars in the same group are misread. Each digit is encoded by two 1s and three zeros. The number of ways to combine two 1s and three zeros is $\binom{5}{2} = \binom{5}{3} = 10$ (this is the number of ways to select two of five objects or three of five objects without repetitions). This lack of redundancy means that if two bars in a group of five are

misread, the group is read as another valid group and the barcode reader cannot identify the bad digit. In such a case, an error is detected but cannot be corrected.

◇ **Exercise 2.6:** Suggest ways to increase redundancy so that more than 10 groups of bars are possible.

2.4 Postal Money Orders

Money orders sold by the United States postal service have a 10-digit identification number. The sum modulo 9 of the 10 digits becomes a check digit (the 11th digit). Figure 2.10 shows an example where the ten digits 0517708425 add up to 39, which equals 3 modulo 9.

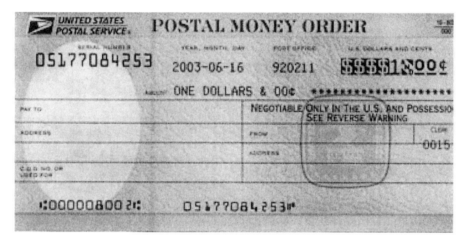

Figure 2.10: A US Postal Money Order.

It's easy to see why this scheme detects most single-digit errors. In order for an error to go undetected, the sum of the 10 digits should be modified by 9 or a multiple of 9. A change in one digit, however, changes the sum by less than 9, except when a 0 becomes 9 or vice versa. Notice that a change of the check digit itself between 0 and 9 will be detected.

A transposition of two adjacent digits does not affect the sum, so this type of error is not detected. However, if the check digit is one of the transposed digits, an error is normally detected, except in cases such as 1234567890|0, where the check digit happens to be identical to the tenth (rightmost) digit.

American Express traveler's checks use a similar scheme. The traveler's check has a 9-digit identification number, and a check digit C is computed by $T = d_1 + d_2 + \cdots + d_9 \bmod 9$ and $C = 9 - T$. Thus, the check digit for 123456789 is 9.

2.5 Airline Tickets

An airline ticket has a $(10+1)$-digit stock control number and a $(14+1)$-digit identification number. Each has a check digit that is computed as the modulo 7 of the 10- or 14-digit number. The ticket shown in Figure 2.11 has the 10-digit stock control number 5174917238. Dividing this number by 7 produces a remainder of 1, so this is its check digit. Similarly, the identification number is 0-114-1408967263, so its check digit 5 is the remainder of dividing the large integer 1141408967263 by 7. (The first digit, 0, is the coupon number. This number specifies the leg of the trip, except that a coupon number of 0 is printed on the traveler's receipt. The second part, 114, identifies the airline, and the third part is a unique identification. The 3-digit airline identification is sometimes not included in the check digit computation.)

```
FP CA53085101610081407 EXP0492 453450 FC 3JUL SAN AA
X/JFK 165.00  LY LHR   LY TLV 584.00  LY X/LAX
584.00  AA SAN 165.00  $1498.00 END
```

FARE	EQUIV. FARE PD		
TAX USD1498.00			ALLOW PCS WT UNCKD ✷✷✷✷✷✷✷✷✷✷
TAX US18.00		CPN	DOCUMENT NUMBER CK
TOTAL XU10.00	51749172381	0 114 1408967263 5	
USD1526.00	STOCK CONTROL NO. TX 889		

Figure 2.11: An Air Ticket.

Most other methods discussed in this chapter start by computing a weighted sum. This method can also be viewed as based on a weighted sum, because each digit in a number such as 5284 is multiplied by a power of 10.

This method is also used by Federal Express ground (but not air) and in other cases where tracking numbers are $14+1$ digits.

This interesting scheme has the disadvantage that it requires divisions of large integers. In addition, it does not detect all single-digit errors, because changing any digit may modify the number by 7 or by a multiple of 7. If a digit d_i is erroneously read as b_i, the number is modified by $(b_i - d_i)10^i$ and this product is a multiple of 7 whenever $b_i - d_i = \pm 7$, which occurs with a probability of 6.67%.

Similarly, most, but not all, transpositions of adjacent digits are detected by this scheme. When digits d_i and d_{i+1} are swapped, the number is modified by $(d_i \cdot 10^i + d_{i+1} \cdot 10^{i+1}) - (d_{i+1} \cdot 10^i + d_i \cdot 10^{i+1}) = 9 \cdot 10^i (d_{i+1} - d_i)$. The difference $(d_{i+1} - d_i)$ of two digits is in the interval $[-9, +9]$, which makes it easy to check all cases and verify that 9 times that difference is a multiple of 7 only when the difference itself equals ± 7.

Section 2.9 discusses an extension of this method to two or more check digits.

2.6 Banking

In the United States, each bank is assigned an 8-digit identification number, with a 9th check digit C computed as a weighted sum modulo 10:

$$C = 7 \cdot d_1 + 3 \cdot d_2 + 9 \cdot d_3 + 7 \cdot d_4 + 3 \cdot d_5 + 9 \cdot d_6 + 7 \cdot d_7 + 3 \cdot d_8 \bmod 10.$$

The check shown in Figure 2.12 has (hypothetical) bank identification number 12200450, so its check digit is

$$C = 7 \cdot 1 + 3 \cdot 2 + 9 \cdot 2 + 7 \cdot 0 + 3 \cdot 0 + 9 \cdot 4 + 7 \cdot 5 + 3 \cdot 0 \bmod 10 = 102 \bmod 10 = 2.$$

(The two other numbers printed at the bottom of the check are the account and check numbers. All three numbers are printed in the special MICR [magnetic ink character recognition] font to facilitate fast and reliable machine scanning and recognition of the digits.)

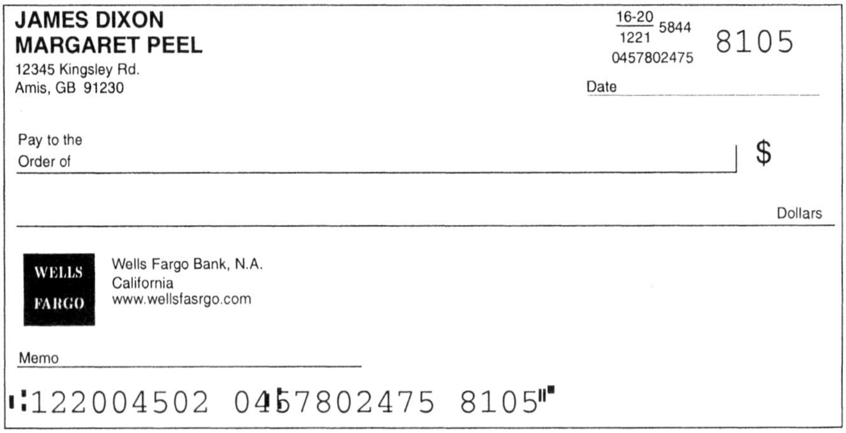

Figure 2.12: A Bank Check.

The particular choice of weights makes it possible for the check digit to detect all single-digit errors. When a digit d_i is read as another digit b_i, the weighted sum is modified by $w_i(b_i - d_i)$, where w_i is the weight for digit i. The difference $(b_i - d_i)$ is a nonzero integer in the interval $[-9, +9]$ and w_i is 7, 3, or 9. There are 18 nonzero integers in the interval $[-9, +9]$, so it is easy to check all 18×3 products of the form $w_i(b_i - d_i)$ and verify that none is a multiple of 10. Any change in a single digit modifies the weighted sum by an amount that is not a multiple of 10, so it modifies the check digit as well. It is also obvious that an error in the check digit itself will always be detected.

A similar analysis shows that most, but not all, transpositions of consecutive digits will be detected. When digits d_i and d_{i+1} are transposed, the weighted sum is modified by the difference $(w_i d_i + w_{i+1} d_{i+1}) - (w_i d_{i+1} + w_{i+1} d_i) = (d_i - d_{i+1})(w_i - w_{i+1})$. The difference $(w_i - w_{i+1})$ of two consecutive weights is one of the six integers $7 - 3 = 4$, $3 - 7 = -4$, $9 - 3 = 6$, $3 - 9 = -6$, $9 - 7 = 2$, and $7 - 9 = -2$. These integers are not relatively prime to 10, so multiplying any of them by even a small number may result in a multiple of 10 and therefore in an undetected error.

2.7 Credit Cards

Most credit cards have 16-digit numbers where the rightmost digit is a check digit C that is computed by first computing the special weighted sum modulo 10

$$T = 2\#d_1 + d_2 + 2\#d_3 + d_4 + \cdots + d_{14} + 2\#d_{15} \bmod 10$$

(where $2\#$ means multiply by 2, then add the digits of the product) and then subtracting $C = 10 - T$. This is also known as the IBM check (but see also Section 2.8 for a different algorithm bearing the same name).

Example: The weighted sum of the 15-digit number 123456789012345 is computed by

$$T = 2\#1 + 2 + 2\#3 + 4 + 2\#5 + 6 + 2\#7 + 8 + 2\#9 + 0 + 2\#1 + 2 + 2\#3 + 4 + 2\#5$$
$$= 2{+}2{+}6{+}4{+}(1{+}0){+}6{+}(1{+}4){+}8{+}(1{+}8){+}0{+}2{+}2{+}6{+}4{+}(1{+}0) \bmod 10 = 58 \bmod 10 = 8,$$

so $C = 10 - 8 = 2$.

A change in one digit from d_i to b_i modifies the weighted sum by either the difference $b_i - d_i$ or the product $2\#(b_i - d_i)$. The former is a nonzero integer whose absolute value is less than 10, so it cannot modify the weighted sum by a multiple of 10. The latter is a nonzero integer whose absolute value is one of 2, 4, 6, 8, $(1 + 0)$, $(1 + 2)$, $(1 + 4)$, $(1 + 6)$, or $(1 + 8)$, so it is also less than 10. A change in one digit is therefore always detected by the IBM check.

A transposition of two adjacent digits d_i and d_{i+1} modifies the sum by $(2\#d_i + d_{i+1}) - (2\#d_{i+1} + d_i)$. A careful review of all the possibilities reveals that the only swaps that leave the weighted sum unchanged are $9 \leftrightarrow 0$ or $0 \leftrightarrow 9$. These are two out of 90 possible digit pairs, so the reliability of the IBM check for adjacent transposition is $88/90 \approx 0.978$ or about 98%.

"You want 21 percent risk free? Pay off your credit cards."
—Andrew Tobias

"Modern man drives a mortgaged car over a bond-financed highway on credit-card gas."
—Earl Wilson

"Life was a lot simpler when what we honored was father and mother rather than all major credit cards."
—Robert Orben

2.8 The IBM Check Digit

The IBM check digit is a sophisticated error-detection scheme for an arbitrary number of data digits. It is based on the mathematical notion of permutations, so we start with a short introduction to this simple and useful concept (see also Chapter 8).

A permutation of n objects is simply a rearrangement of the objects. Thus, one permutation of the five symbols (a, b, c, d, e) is (b, c, d, e, a), which is denoted by

$$\begin{pmatrix} a\ b\ c\ d\ e \\ b\ c\ d\ e\ a \end{pmatrix}.$$

$\diamond$ **Exercise 2.7:**   There are $n!$ permutations of n objects. How can this property be proved?

Permutations can be combined or "multiplied" by combining the effect of two permutations. Thus, we can write

$$\begin{pmatrix} a\ b\ c\ d\ e \\ b\ c\ d\ e\ a \end{pmatrix} \begin{pmatrix} c\ b\ d\ e\ a \\ d\ a\ b\ e\ c \end{pmatrix} = \begin{pmatrix} a\ b\ c\ d\ e \\ a\ d\ b\ e\ c \end{pmatrix}.$$

The first permutation changes "b" to "c" and the second one changes "c" to "d," so the product changes "b" to "d."

Mathematicians use the *cyclic notation* to describe permutations. This notation is easy to understand by means of an example. The cyclic notation of the permutation

$$\begin{pmatrix} \texttt{abcdefghijklmnopqrstuvwxyz} \\ \texttt{QPALZMWOSKXEDCHRIFJVNTUGYB} \end{pmatrix}$$

is $(\texttt{aqisjkxgwunc})(\texttt{bprfmdlez})(\texttt{ho})(\texttt{tv})(\texttt{y})$. We start with the top-left symbol a. It corresponds to Q, q corresponds to I, i corresponds to S, and so on, up to c, which corresponds to A. This completes the first cycle. The second cycle starts with the first letter (in alphabetical order) not included in the first cycle. This is b, which corresponds to P, and so on, up to z, which corresponds to B, thereby completing the second cycle. The last cycle is (y), expressing the fact that y corresponds to Y in this particular permutation.

An *involutary permutation* is a permutation that is its own inverse. An involutary permutation is expressed in cyclic notation as a set of pairs. For example, the ROT13 permutation (Section 6.1), where the entire alphabet is rotated cyclically 13 positions, is expressed by

$$\begin{pmatrix} \texttt{abcdefghijklmnopqrstuvwxyz} \\ \texttt{NOPQRSTUVWXYZABCDEFGHIJKLM} \end{pmatrix}$$

or cyclically as $(\texttt{an})(\texttt{bo})(\texttt{cp})\ldots(\texttt{zm})$.

On the other hand, a permutation may have just one cycle. An example is the 26-letter alphabet where each letter is permuted to the one following it cyclically. The permutation is

$$\begin{pmatrix} \texttt{abcdefghijklmnopqrstuvwxyz} \\ \texttt{BCDEFGHIJKLMNOPQRSTUVWXYZA} \end{pmatrix}$$

and its cyclic notation is (abc ... z).

Permutations are also discussed in Chapter 8 and in Section 9.8.

The IBM check digit is based on the particular permutation

$$\sigma = (0)(1, 2, 4, 8, 7, 5)(3, 6)(9).$$

Given an $(n-1)$-digit decimal number $d_1 d_2 \ldots d_{n-1}$, its IBM check digit d_n is computed as follows:

- If n is even, d_n is assigned as the decimal digit that satisfies

$$\sigma(d_1) + d_2 + \sigma(d_3) + d_4 + \cdots + \sigma(d_{n-1}) + d_n \bmod 10 = 0.$$

- If n is odd, d_n is assigned as the decimal digit that satisfies

$$d_1 + \sigma(d_2) + d_3 + \sigma(d_4) + \cdots + \sigma(d_{n-1}) + d_n \bmod 10 = 0.$$

◇ **Exercise 2.8:** Write permutation σ explicitly.

This scheme is used by some libraries to identify their books. A typical example is the 5-digit number 12345. The check digit will be the 6th digit, so n is even, and d_6 is computed by means of

$$\sigma(1) + 2 + \sigma(3) + 4 + \sigma(5) \bmod 10 = 2 + 2 + 6 + 4 + 1 \bmod 10 = 5,$$

which yields $d_6 = 10 - 5 = 5$.

The IBM method detects all single-digit errors and virtually all adjacent digit transpositions. If d_i is corrupted to a different digit b_i, the value of the weighted sum is modified by either $b_i - d_i$ or $\sigma(b_i) - \sigma(d_i)$. The former difference is nonzero and can be at most 9. The latter difference is also nonzero because permutation σ maps two different digits $a \neq b$ to two different digits $x \neq y$. It is also less than 10, because it is a difference of two digits.

The IBM method detects virtually all transpositions of adjacent digits. Swapping d_i and d_{i+1} changes the weighted sum by either

$$[d_i + \sigma(d_{i+1})] - [d_{i+1} + \sigma(d_i)] = [d_i - d_{i+1}] + [\sigma(d_{i+1}) - \sigma(d_i)] \stackrel{\text{def}}{=} D_1 + D_2 \quad (2.4)$$

or

$$[\sigma(d_i) + d_{i+1}] - [\sigma(d_{i+1}) + d_i] = [d_{i+1} - d_i] + [\sigma(d_i) - \sigma(d_{i+1})] = -D_1 - D_2. \quad (2.5)$$

In either case, two differences D_1 and D_2 are added to the weighted sum. We examine two cases as follows:

1. $d_i \neq d_{i+1}$. In this case, each of the two differences D_1 and D_2 that are added to the weighted sum is nonzero, but because of the particular choice of permutation σ, their sum is never 0 or a multiple of 10. If, for example, $d_i d_{i+1} = 63$, then $d_i - d_{i+1} = 3$ and $\sigma(d_{i+1}) - \sigma(d_i) = 3$, so $D_1 + D_2 = 6$.

2. $d_i = d_{i+1}$. The only undetected errors are the two transpositions $0 \leftrightarrow 0$ and $9 \leftrightarrow 9$, because each of these digits is mapped to itself by σ. Every other digit is mapped to a different digit, so $D_1 = 0$, but $D_2 \neq 0$. There are 100 pairs of two decimal digits and transpositions of two of them are not detected. Thus, the reliability of the IBM check digit for this type of error is 98%.

The IBM check digit is almost as reliable as the ISBN scheme but is more general because it can handle an arbitrary number of data digits. It is also computationally simpler because the check digit is decimal and there is no need to worry about it being 11 (or X), as for an ISBN.

2.9 Two Or More Check Digits

Recall that the check digit for an airline ticket number N (Section 2.5) is computed as the remainder of dividing N by 7. Any integer N can be viewed as a weighted sum, where the weights are powers of 10, so this method computes the check digit as a weighted sum modulo 7. The number 7 is used for the modulo because it is the largest prime that is less than 10. This method can be extended to two or more check digits. The largest prime less than 100 is 97. Given a nonnegative integer N, we can therefore compute $C = N \bmod 97$, which yields a 2-digit integer C in the interval $[0, 96]$. This calculation is more computationally intensive than for a single-digit check, but results in a very powerful error-detecting capability.

This interesting scheme detects all single-digit errors because changing a digit cannot modify the number by 97 or by a multiple of 97. If a digit d_i of N is erroneously read as b_i, N is modified by the nonzero product $(b_i - d_i)10^i$ and this product cannot be a multiple of 97.

⋄ **Exercise 2.9:** Show why the simple claim above is correct.

Even more, this method detects every twin error! If a pair of identical adjacent digits $d_i d_i$ in N gets changed to an identical pair $b_i b_i$ of different digits, N is modified by

$$(d_i \cdot 10^i + d_i \cdot 10^{i+1}) - (b_i \cdot 10^i + b_i \cdot 10^{i+1}) = 10^i \cdot 11(d_i - b_i).$$

The product $11(d_i - b_i)$ can take the values 11, 22, 33,...,99, so multiplying it by 10^i cannot produce a multiple of 97.

(There may be cases of undetected twin errors if one digit of the twin is one of the check digits, but these cases are rare. The case where both check digits are identical and are replaced by identical digits is detected.)

What about a pair of consecutive digits $d_i d_{i+1}$ replaced by another pair $b_i b_{i+1}$ in N? Such an error modifies N by

$$(d_i \cdot 10^i + d_{i+1} \cdot 10^{i+1}) - (b_i \cdot 10^i + b_{i+1} \cdot 10^{i+1}) = 10^i[(d_i - b_i) + 10(d_{i+1} - b_{i+1})],$$

and this produces a multiple of 97 in several cases, the most obvious of which is $d_i - b_i = 7$ and $d_{i+1} - b_{i+1} = 9$.

Similarly, all transpositions of adjacent, nonidentical digits are detected by two check digits. When adjacent digits d_i and d_{i+1} in N are swapped, N is modified by $(d_i \cdot 10^i + d_{i+1} \cdot 10^{i+1}) - (d_{i+1} \cdot 10^i + d_i \cdot 10^{i+1}) = 9 \cdot 10^i (d_{i+1} - d_i)$. The difference $(d_{i+1} - d_i)$ of two different digits is nonzero and is in the interval $[-9, +9]$, which makes it easy to check all possible cases and verify that 9 times that difference is one of $9, 18, 27, \ldots, 81$. When any of these nine numbers is multiplied by a power of 10, can the result be a multiple of 97? Formally, the question is this: Does the equation $a \cdot 10^i = 97j$, where a is one of the nine numbers above, have any integer solutions i and j? It's easy to see why the answer is no. The prime factors of a are $9d$, where d is a single digit. The prime factors of 10^i are $2^i 5^i$. Thus, the left-hand side of the above equation does not have the prime 97 as one of its prime factors, so if this side is divided by 97, the result cannot be an integer.

A natural extension of this approach is to compute a 3-digit check for an integer N as the remainder of dividing N by 997, the smallest prime less than 1000. This requires more computations but results in extremely high reliability.

2.10 Hamming Check Digits

Section 2.1 shows how the simple ISBN check digit can detect all single-digit errors. It is possible to extend this technique to correct, not just detect, such errors by computing another check digit. We start with a 9-digit decimal number and denote the digits by d_1 through d_9 from left to right. Two check digits, a and b, are computed from the equations

$$b + 2d_1 + 3d_2 + 4d_3 + \cdots + 10d_9 \bmod 11 = 0 \tag{2.6}$$

$$a + b + d_1 + d_2 + d_3 + \cdots + d_9 \bmod 11 = 0. \tag{2.7}$$

Given the nine original digits, Equation (2.6) is first used to compute b, and then a is computed from Equation (2.7). Since the result is computed modulo 11, both a and b are in the interval $[0, 10]$. We can therefore consider them base-11 digits and use X to indicate a digit of 10.

When checking for a single-digit error, Equation (2.6) gives the position of the error (albeit indirectly), and Equation (2.7) gives the amount of the error. To see how a single-digit error is identified and corrected, we assume that digit d_i has been corrupted to a different digit b_i. Equation (2.7) becomes

$$a + b + d_1 + \cdots + b_i + \cdots + d_9 \bmod 11$$
$$= [a + b + d_1 + \cdots + d_i + \cdots + d_9] + (b_i - d_i) \bmod 11$$
$$= 0 + (b_i - d_i) \bmod 11 = b_i - d_i \stackrel{\text{def}}{=} \Delta.$$

(The difference Δ is a single base-11 digit, so $\Delta \bmod 11 = \Delta$.) This is how Equation (2.7) yields the amount Δ of the error. Once Δ is known, the position of the error can be deduced from Equation (2.6) which becomes

$$b + 2d_1 + \cdots + (i+1)b_i + \cdots + 10d_9 \bmod 11$$
$$= b + 2d_1 + \cdots + (i+1)d_i + \cdots + 10d_9 + (i+1)(b_i - d_i) \bmod 11$$
$$= 0 + (i+1)\Delta \bmod 11.$$

The weight $i+1$ is one of 2, 3,…,10, so it is relatively prime to 11, and the absolute value of Δ is in the interval $[1, 10]$. Since Δ is known from Equation (2.7), the value of $i+1$ can easily be computed. For example, if $i+1 = 2$, then the 10 values of $2\Delta \bmod 11$ are 2, 4, 6, 8, 10, 1, 3, 5, 7, and 9. In practice, Table 2.13 is computed once, and the software uses Δ from Equation (2.7) and $(i+1)\Delta \bmod 11$ from Equation (2.6) as row and column indexes, respectively, to the table to obtain the position $i+1$ of the error.

$(i+1)\Delta \bmod 11$

Δ	1	2	3	4	5	6	7	8	9	10
1	1	2	3	4	5	6	7	8	9	10
2	6	1	7	2	8	3	9	4	10	5
3	4	8	1	5	9	2	6	10	3	7
4	3	6	9	1	4	7	10	2	5	8
5	9	7	5	3	1	10	8	6	4	2
6	2	4	6	8	10	1	3	5	7	9
7	8	5	2	10	7	4	1	9	6	3
8	7	3	10	6	2	9	5	1	8	4
9	5	10	4	9	3	8	2	7	1	6
10	10	9	8	7	6	5	4	3	2	1

Table 2.13: Values of $i + 1$.

To illustrate this process, we use ISBN 0-387-95045. Equation (2.6) becomes

$$b + 2{\cdot}0 + 3{\cdot}3 + 4{\cdot}8 + 5{\cdot}7 + 6{\cdot}9 + 7{\cdot}5 + 8{\cdot}0 + 9{\cdot}4 + 10{\cdot}5 = b + 251.$$

The next multiple of 11 is 253, so b should be set to 2. Equation (2.7) becomes

$$a + 2 + 0 + 3 + 8 + 7 + 9 + 5 + 0 + 4 + 5 \bmod 11 = a + 43 \bmod 11,$$

so a must be set to 1.

Now assume that the digit 3 in the original number became corrupted to 9. When checking the number 12|098795045, the two equations yield

$$2 + 2{\cdot}0 + 3{\cdot}9 + 4{\cdot}8 + 5{\cdot}7 + 6{\cdot}9 + 7{\cdot}5 + 8{\cdot}0 + 9{\cdot}4 + 10{\cdot}5 \bmod 11 = 271 \bmod 11 = 7,$$
$$1 + 2 + 0 + 9 + 8 + 7 + 9 + 5 + 0 + 4 + 5 \bmod 11 = 50 \bmod 11 = 6.$$

The second equation yields $\Delta = 6$, and the first equation implies that $(i+1)\Delta \bmod 11 = 7$. Row 6, column 7, of Table 2.13 contains 3, so the error is corrected by subtracting (modulo 11) Δ from the digit whose weight is 3. This digit is 9, and subtracting 6 produces 3.

In a slightly different example, we assume that the 7 in 0-387-95045 has been modified to 1. The two equations yield $\Delta = 5$ and $(i+1)\Delta \bmod 11 = 3$. Row 5, column 3, of Table 2.13 contains 5, so Δ should be subtracted modulo 11 from the digit whose weight is 5. This digit is 1, and $1 - 5 \bmod 11 = -4 \bmod 11 = 7$ (because $7 + 4 = 11$).

This method resembles the original (binary) Hamming code and also corrects single errors in the two check digits. An important difference is that the current, decimal method will interpret many double-digit errors as certain single-digit errors. (Recall that the SEC-DED code of Section 1.9, which is the original Hamming method plus a parity bit, detects 2-bit errors.)

The method can be extended to more than nine data digits by increasing the number of check digits. It turns out that three check digits are enough to correct single-digit errors in up to 118 data digits. We denote the 121 digits by d_1 through d_{120}, where d_0, d_1, and d_{11} are the check digits. They are computed by means of the three equations

$$
\begin{aligned}
&[0d_0 + 1d_1 + 2d_2 + 3d_3 + \cdots + 10d_{10}+ \\
&0d_{11} + 1d_{12} + 2d_{13} + \cdots + 10d_{21}+ \\
&\cdots \text{eight more rows} \cdots + \\
&0d_{110} + 1d_{111} + 2d_{112} + \cdots + 10d_{120}] \bmod 11 = 0,
\end{aligned}
$$

$$
\begin{aligned}
&[0d_0 + 0d_1 + 0d_2 + 0d_3 + \cdots + 0d_{10}+ \\
&1d_{11} + 1d_{12} + 1d_{13} + \cdots + 1d_{21}+ \\
&\cdots \text{eight more rows} \cdots + \\
&10d_{110} + 10d_{111} + 10d_{112} + \cdots + 10d_{120}] \bmod 11 = 0,
\end{aligned}
$$

$$
[d_0 + d_1 + d_2 + \cdots + d_{119} + d_{120}] \bmod 11 = 0.
$$

The top two equations are first solved to compute d_1 and d_{11}, and then the third equation can easily be solved for d_0. If there are fewer than 118 data digits, the missing digits are treated in the above equations as zero.

When checking for a single-digit error, the third equation yields Δ and the first two equations produce the position p of the error as an integer in the interval $[0, 120]$. The first equation results in $p \bmod 11$, and the second equation results in $p \div 11$. These are the remainder and the quotient, respectively, of the integer division of p by 11. Once these numbers are known, p is computed as $p = (p \div 11) \times 11 + (p \bmod 11)$. As an example, if $p \div 11 = 5$ and $p \bmod 11 = 8$, then $p = 5 \times 11 + 8 = 63$.

Note again that this code may wrongly interpret two-digit errors as certain single-digit errors. Recall that the SEC-DED code of Section 1.9 can detect 2-bit errors and therefore does not try to correct such an error.

2.11 The Verhoeff Check Digit Method

The simplest check digit scheme, illustrated earlier in this chapter by the equation

$$(C + d_1 + d_2 + \cdots) \bmod n = 0,$$

can detect single-digit errors but not transposition errors, because addition is commutative. This suggests that a better method should use a noncommutative operation. A slightly more powerful check digit method illustrated earlier in this chapter is given by Equation (2.2):

$$(C + w_1 {\cdot} d_1 + w_2 {\cdot} d_2 + \cdots) \bmod n = 0. \tag{2.2}$$

This equation can detect transposition errors if n is a prime and the weights w_i are relatively prime to n. Of all the methods discussed here that use a single check digit, only the ISBN algorithm [Equation (2.3)] detects all single-digit errors and all transpositions of adjacent digits. However, the ISBN check digit has two drawbacks: it produces a base-11 check digit (which is why the symbol X is needed), and it is limited to nine data digits.

This section describes a check-digit algorithm that detects all single-digit and adjacent-digits transpositions, that uses just decimal digits, and that works with identification numbers of arbitrary lengths. The method was developed by the Dutch mathematician Jacobus Verhoeff in 1969 [Verhoeff 69] and has the added advantage that it also detects all the error types of Table 2.1 (except adding or omitting a digit) with almost 100% accuracy.

Given a set of n decimal data digits d_1 through d_n, Verhoeff's method computes their decimal check digit C by the weighted-sum equation

$$C * \sigma(d_1) * \sigma^2(d_2) * \cdots * \sigma^n(d_n) = 0. \tag{2.8}$$

Notice the similarity between this expression and the weighted sum of Equation (2.2). There are, however, two differences between these expressions, as follows:

1. The operation, denoted here by "$*$", is a special type of operation on integers. It is called multiplication in the finite dihedral group D_{10} and is given by Table 2.14a. Notice that it is noncommutative and is very different from standard addition or multiplication. The product $6 * 7$ is 0, while $7 * 6$ is 2. Also, the squares of the integers 5 through 9 are all zeros. The interested reader can find the necessary background material on groups and symmetry groups in Appendix A.

2. The notation σ is used for a *permutation*, and σ^i denotes the ith power of σ. Permutations are discussed in Section 2.8.

*	0	1	2	3	4	5	6	7	8	9
0	0	1	2	3	4	5	6	7	8	9
1	1	2	3	4	0	6	7	8	9	5
2	2	3	4	0	1	7	8	9	5	6
3	3	4	0	1	2	8	9	5	6	7
4	4	0	1	2	3	9	5	6	7	8
5	5	9	8	7	6	0	4	3	2	1
6	6	5	9	8	7	1	0	4	3	2
7	7	6	5	9	8	2	1	0	4	3
8	8	7	6	5	9	3	2	1	0	4
9	9	8	7	6	5	4	3	2	1	0

(a)

i	σ^i									
	0	1	2	3	4	5	6	7	8	9
1	0	4	3	2	1	6	7	8	9	5
2	0	1	2	3	4	7	8	9	5	6
3	0	1	2	3	4	9	5	6	7	8
4	0	1	2	3	4	8	9	5	6	7
5	0	1	2	3	4	7	8	9	5	6
6	0	1	2	3	4	9	5	6	7	8
7	0	1	2	3	4	8	9	5	6	7
8	0	4	3	2	1	6	7	8	9	5
9	0	1	2	3	4	7	8	9	5	6
10	0	1	2	3	4	9	5	6	7	8

(b)

Table 2.14: (a) The D_{10} Multiplication Table. (b) Ten Powers of σ.

Jacobus (Koos) Verhoeff, the Dutch mathematician responsible for the elegant system of designing a decimal check digit system based on the dihedral group of order 10, was born in 1927. He studied mathematics in Leiden and Amsterdam and wrote his doctoral dissertation in the area of coding theory. In fact, the publication in which his check digit system is included was a reworked version of his thesis. He had a very varied career. He worked at the mathematics research center in Amsterdam known as the Mathematical Center (now the Center for Mathematics and Computer Science) and taught at the Technological University in Delft. Later he worked in industry at Philips in Eindhoven. Finally, he became a full professor of Computer Science at Erasmus University in Rotterdam. He is now retired.

—from `http://www.ams.org/new-in-math/cover/verhoeff.html`

And now, back to the Verhoeff algorithm. We illustrate it for ten data digits, using the permutation $(0)(1,4)(2,3)(5,6,7,8,9)$ that has been identified and studied by Winters [Winters 90]. Written explicitly, the permutation and its first four powers are shown below. Its first 10 powers are listed in Table 2.14b. Notice that $\sigma^8 = \sigma$.

$$\begin{pmatrix} 0123456789 \\ 0432167895 \end{pmatrix} \begin{pmatrix} 0123456789 \\ 0123478956 \end{pmatrix} \begin{pmatrix} 0123456789 \\ 0123495678 \end{pmatrix} \begin{pmatrix} 0123456789 \\ 0123489567 \end{pmatrix} \begin{pmatrix} 0123456789 \\ 0123467895 \end{pmatrix}$$

Example: Compute the Verhoeff check digit for the 10-digit number 0387950451. Equation (2.8) becomes

$$C * \sigma(0) * \sigma^2(3) * \sigma^3(8) * \sigma^4(7) * \sigma^5(9) * \sigma^6(5) * \sigma^7(0) * \sigma^8(4) * \sigma^9(5) * \sigma^{10}(1)$$
$$= C * 0 * 3 * 7 * 5 * 6 * 9 * 0 * 1 * 7 * 1$$
$$= C * (0 * 3) * (7 * 5) * (6 * 9) * (0 * 1) * (7 * 1)$$
$$= C * 3 * 2 * 2 * 1 * 6 = C * 0 * 3 * 6 = C * 3 * 6 = C * 9 = 0,$$

which yields $C = 9$.

Verhoeff himself used the permutation $(1, 5, 7, 6, 2, 8, 3, 0, 9, 4)$, and it's possible that many other permutations yield excellent error-detection capability. Using his permutation, the equivalent of Table 2.14b can be computed by the following recursive function:

$$F(0, j) = j, \quad \text{for } 0 \leq j \leq 9,$$
$$F(1, j) = (1, 5, 7, 6, 2, 8, 3, 0, 9, 4), \quad \text{for } 0 \leq j \leq 9,$$
$$F(i, j) = F\big(i - 1, F(1, j)\big), \quad \text{for } 2 \leq i \leq 7,$$
$$F(8, j) = F(1, j), F(9, j) = F(2, j), \quad \text{for } 0 \leq j \leq 9.$$

Verhoeff's method is based on the noncommutativity of the D_{10} group operation and on the fact that the various powers of the permutation "mix" the individual digits in such a way that the weight σ^i for digit d_i depends on another digit in a somewhat random fashion. The method is powerful. It detects all single-digit errors, all adjacent digit transpositions, 95.555% of twin errors, 94.222% of jump transpositions and jump twin errors, and 95.3125% of all phonetic errors. Its main weakness is that it does not detect most jump twin errors involving digits with a difference of 5, such as $050 \leftrightarrow 505$, $161 \leftrightarrow 616$, $272 \leftrightarrow 727$, and $494 \leftrightarrow 949$ (although it does detect 383 read as 838).

> If there is known to be a check-digit calculation method for a credit institution, it is incumbent on the credit institution first involved (or the first collecting office) to check the accuracy of the account numbers of the recipients or payers. The basis for this procedure is the Cheque Agreement (Scheckabkommen), Part II, No 3, section 3 and the Credit Transfer Agreement (Überweisungsabkommen), No 2, section 3 applied by the German banking industry.
>
> —http://www.bundesbank.de/zv/zv_pruefziffer.en.php

Part II: Source Codes

Part I of this book introduces the concept of redundancy and shows how errors in digital data can be controlled by increasing redundancy in the data. Thus, all error-control methods (channel codes) end up increasing the size of the data. With this in mind, the reader may be surprised to learn that redundancy is also the basis for all the source code (data compression) methods that have become so prevalent. Computer programs for compressing data often have titles such as "zip," "implode," "stuffit," "diet," and "squeeze," but these terms are inappropriate and don't describe the actual process of compression. Data is not compressed by squeezing it but by reducing or completely eliminating any redundancies in its representation. Data with redundancy can be compressed; data without any redundancy cannot be compressed—period.

We are familiar with the term *information*. We use it all the time, we feel we intuitively understand it, but we consider it a qualitative concept. Information seems to be one of those entities that cannot be precisely defined, cannot be quantified, and cannot be dealt with rigorously. There is, however, a mathematical field called *information theory*, where information is treated quantitatively. Among its other achievements, information theory shows how to precisely define redundancy. In this introduction we try to understand redundancy intuitively by pointing out the redundancy in two common types of computer data and by trying to understand why redundant data is used in the first place.

The first type of data is text. Text is an important example of computer data. Many computer applications, such as word processing and software compilation, are nonnumeric; they deal with data whose basic components are characters of text. The computer can store and process only binary information (zeros and ones), so each character of text must be assigned a binary code. Present-day computers use the ASCII code (pronounced "ass-key," short for "American Standard Code for Information Interchange"), but many new computers and operating systems support the new Unicode

(Chapter 10). ASCII is a fixed-size code where each character is assigned an 8-bit code (the code itself occupies seven of the eight bits, and the eighth bit is parity, for simple error detection). A fixed-size code is a natural choice because it makes it easy for software applications to handle characters of text. On the other hand, a fixed-size code is inherently redundant.

In a file of random text, we expect each character to occur approximately the same number of times. Our text files, however, are rarely random. They have meaningful text, and we know from experience that in most texts certain letters tend to be more common than others. It is well known that "E," "T," and "A" are common in English text, while "Z" and "Q" are rare. This explains why the ASCII code is redundant and also suggests a way to eliminate the redundancy. ASCII is redundant because it assigns the same number of bits (eight) to each character, common or rare. The redundancy can be removed by assigning variable-size codes to the characters, with short codes assigned to the common characters and long codes assigned to the rare ones. This is precisely how Huffman coding (Section 3.5) operates.

Imagine two text files A and B with the same text, where A consists of ASCII codes and B has variable-size codes. We expect B to be smaller than A, and we say that A has been *compressed* to B. It is obvious that the amount of compression depends on the redundancy of the particular text and on the particular variable-size codes used in file B. Text where certain characters are very common while others are very rare has much redundancy and will compress well if the variable-size codes are properly assigned. In such a file, the codes of the common characters should be very short, while those of the rare characters can be long. The long codes do not degrade the compression because they occur rarely in B. Most of B consists of the short codes. Random text, on the other hand, does not benefit from replacing ASCII with variable-size codes, because the compression achieved by the short codes is canceled out by the expansion caused by the long codes. This is a special case of a general rule that says that random data cannot be compressed because it has no redundancy.

The second type of common computer data is images. A digital image is a rectangular array of colored dots, called *pixels*. Each pixel is represented in the computer by its color code. (In the remainder of this introduction, the term *pixel* is used for the pixel's color code.) In order to simplify the software applications that handle images, pixels have a fixed size. The size of a pixel depends on the number of colors in the image, and this number is normally a power of 2. If there are 2^k colors in an image, then each pixel is a k-bit number.

There are two types of redundancy in a digital image. The first type is similar to redundancy in text. In any particular image, certain colors may dominate, while others may be infrequent. This redundancy can be removed by assigning variable-size codes to the pixels (as is done with text) or by the use of a color lookup table (Section 14.1.1). The other type of redundancy is much more important and is the result of *pixel correlation*. As our eyes move along the image from pixel to pixel, we find that in most cases, adjacent pixels have similar colors. Imagine an image with blue sky, white clouds, brown mountains, and green trees. As long as we look at a mountain, adjacent pixels tend to be similar; all or almost all of them are shades of brown. Similarly, adjacent pixels in the sky are shades of blue. It is only on the horizon, where mountain meets sky, that adjacent pixels may have very different colors. The individual pixels are therefore not completely independent, and we say that neighboring pixels in an image tend to be *correlated*. This type of redundancy can be exploited in many ways, as described in Chapter 5.

Regardless of the method used to compress an image, the effectiveness of the compression depends on the amount of redundancy in the image. One extreme case is a uniform image. Such an image has maximum redundancy because adjacent pixels are identical. Obviously, such an image is not interesting and is rarely, if ever, used in practice. However, it will compress very well under any image compression method. The other extreme example is an image with uncorrelated pixels. The color of every pixel in such an image is very different from the colors of its near neighbors, so the image redundancy is zero. Such an image will not compress, regardless of the compression method used. However, such an image tends to look like a random jumble of dots and is therefore uninteresting. We rarely need to keep and manipulate such an image, so we rarely need to compress it.

The rest of this introduction covers important technical terms used in the field of data compression.

■   The *compressor* or *encoder* is the program that compresses the raw data in the input file and creates an output file with compressed (low-redundancy) data. The *decompressor* or *decoder* converts in the opposite direction. Notice that the term *encoding* is very general and has wide meaning, but since this part of the book discusses only data compression, we use the term *encoder* to mean data compressor. The term *codec* is sometimes used to describe both the encoder and decoder. Similarly, the term *companding* is short for "compressing/expanding."

■   A *nonadaptive* compression method is rigid and does not modify its operations, its parameters, or its tables in response to the particular data being compressed. Such a method is ideal for compressing a single type of data. Examples are the Group 3 and Group 4 methods for facsimile compression (Section 3.7). They are specifically designed for facsimile compression and do a poor job compressing any other type of data. In contrast, an *adaptive* method examines the raw data while compressing it and modifies its operations and/or its parameters accordingly. An example is the adaptive Huffman method of Section 3.6. Some compression methods are based on a two-pass algorithm, where the first pass reads the input file in order to collect statistics on the data to be compressed, and the second pass performs the actual compression using parameters or codes determined by the first pass. Such a method may be called *semiadaptive*. A data compression method can also be *locally adaptive*, meaning it adapts itself to local conditions in the input file and varies this adaptation as it moves from area to area in the input. An example is the move-to-front method [Salomon 2000].

■   *Lossy/lossless compression*. Certain compression methods are lossy. They achieve better compression by losing some information. When the compressed file is decompressed, the result is not identical to the original data. Such a method makes sense for the compression of images, movies, or sounds. If the loss of data is small, we may not be able to tell the difference. In contrast, text files, especially files containing computer programs, may become worthless if even one bit gets modified. Such files should be compressed only by a lossless compression method. (Two points should be mentioned regarding text files: (1) if a text file is the source code of a program, many blank spaces can normally be eliminated, since they are disregarded by the compiler anyway; and (2) when the output of a word processor is saved in a text file, the file may contain information about the different fonts and formatting used in the text. Such information may be discarded if the user wants to save just the text.)

■ *Symmetric compression* is the case where the compressor and decompressor use the same basic algorithm but work in "opposite" directions. Such a method is ideal for applications where the same number of files is compressed as is decompressed. In an asymmetric compression method, either the compressor or the decompressor may have to work significantly harder. Such methods have their applications and are not necessarily bad. A compression method where the compressor executes a slow, complex algorithm while the decompressor is simple is a natural choice for applications where files are compressed into an archive, but will be decompressed and used very often, such as mp3 audio files on a CD. The opposite case is useful in environments where files are updated all the time and backups are always made and compressed. There is only a small chance that a backup file will be used, so the decompressor isn't used very often.

■ *Compression performance.* Several measures are commonly used to express the performance of a compression method, as follows:

1. The *compression ratio* is defined as

$$\text{Compression ratio} = \frac{\text{size of the output file}}{\text{size of the input file}}.$$

A value of 0.6 means that the data occupies 60% of its original size after compression. Values greater than 1 indicate an output file bigger than the input file (negative compression or expansion). The compression ratio can also be referred to as *bpb* (bit per bit), since it equals the number of bits in the compressed file needed, on average, to compress one bit in the input file. In image compression, the similar term *bpp* stands for *bits per pixel*. In modern, efficient text compression methods, it makes sense to talk about *bpc* (bits per character), i.e., the number of bits it takes, on average, to compress one character in the input file.

Two more terms should be mentioned in connection with the compression ratio. The term *bitrate* (or *bit rate*) is a general term for bpb and bpc. Thus, the main goal of data compression is to represent any given data at low bit rates. In audio and video compression, the term *bitrate* refers to the number of bits generated by the encoder for each second of audio or video. The encoder may take more than a second to compress a second of video, but the decoder must decompress one second of video in one second of real time. The term *bit budget* refers to the functions of the individual bits in the compressed file. Imagine a compressed file where 90% of the bits are variable-size codes of certain symbols and the remaining 10% encode certain tables that are needed by the decompressor. The bit budget for the tables is 10% in this case.

2. The inverse of the compression ratio is the *compression factor*:

$$\text{Compression factor} = \frac{\text{size of the input file}}{\text{size of the output file}}.$$

In this case, values greater than 1 indicate compression, and values less than 1 imply expansion. This measure seems natural to many people, since the bigger the factor, the better the compression. This measure is distantly related to the sparseness ratio, a performance measure discussed on page 172.

3. The expression $100 \times (1 - \text{compression ratio})$ is also a reasonable measure of compression performance. A value of 60 means that the output file occupies 40% of its original size (or that the compression has resulted in savings of 60%).

4. In image compression, the quantity bpp (bits per pixel) is commonly used. It equals the number of bits needed, on average, to compress one pixel of the image. This quantity should always be compared with the bpp before compression.

■ The *probability model*. This concept is important in statistical data compression methods. Sometimes, a compression algorithm consists of two parts: a probability model and the compressor itself. Before the next data item (bit, byte, pixel, or anything else) can be compressed, the model is invoked and is asked to estimate the probability of the data item. The item and its probability are then sent to the compressor, which employs the estimated probability to compress the item. The better the probability estimation, the more compressed the item.

Here is an example of a simple model for a black and white image. Each pixel in such an image is a single bit. Assume that after reading 1000 pixels and compressing them, pixel 1001 is read. What is the probability that this pixel is black? The model can simply count the numbers of black and white pixels read so far. If 350 of the 1000 pixels were black, then the model can assign pixel 1001 a probability of $350/1000 = 0.35$ of being black. The probability and the pixel (which may, of course be either black or white) are then sent to the compressor. The point is that the decompressor can easily calculate the same probabilities before it decodes the 1001st pixel.

■ The term *alphabet* refers to the set of symbols in the data being compressed. An alphabet may consist of the two bits 0 and 1, of the 128 ASCII characters, of the 256 possible 8-bit bytes, or of any other symbols.

■ The performance of any compression method is limited. No method can compress all data files efficiently. The following simple argument illustrates the meaning of this statement quantitatively. The argument shows that most data files cannot be compressed, no matter what compression method is used. This seems strange at first because we compress our data files all the time. The point is that most files cannot be compressed because they are random or close to random and therefore have no redundancy. The (relatively) few files that can be compressed are the ones that we *want* to compress; they are the files we use all the time. They have redundancy, are nonrandom and are therefore useful and interesting. The argument consists of two simple parts, as follows:

1. Given two different files A and B that are compressed to files C and D, respectively, it is clear that C and D must be different. If they were identical, there would be no way to decompress them and get back file A or file B.

2. Compression must convert a large file L to a small file S, but there are many large files and only few small files, so not every file can be compressed. We denote the numbers of large and small files by M and F, respectively, and we show that for all files, regardless of their size, M is much greater than F.

Suppose that an n-bit large file L is given and we want to compress it into a small file S. The number M of large files is 2^n, and our task in this paragraph is to estimate the number F of small files S. Any compression method that can compress L to, say, 10 bits would be welcome. Even compressing it to 11 bits or 12 bits would be great. We therefore (somewhat arbitrarily) decide that compressing L to half its size or smaller should be considered good compression. There are 2^n n-bit files L, and they would have to be compressed into 2^n different files S of sizes less than or equal to $n/2$. However, the total number of S files is the sum

$$
\begin{aligned}
F &= (\# \text{ of files of size } 1) + (\# \text{ of files of size } 2) + \cdots + (\# \text{ of files of size } n/2) \\
&= 2^1 + 2^2 + \cdots + 2^{n/2} \\
&= 2 + 4 + \cdots + 2^{n/2} = 2^{1+n/2} - 2 \approx 2^{1+n/2},
\end{aligned}
$$

so only F of the 2^n original files have a chance of being compressed efficiently. The problem is that F is much smaller than 2^n. Here are two examples of the ratio between these two numbers.

For $n = 100$ (files with just 100 bits), the total number of files is 2^{100}, and the number F of files that can be compressed efficiently is 2^{51}. The ratio of these numbers is the ridiculously small fraction $2^{-49} \approx 1.78 \cdot 10^{-15}$.

For $n = 1000$ (files with just 1000 bits, about 125 bytes), $M = 2^{1000}$ and $F = 2^{501}$. The ratio F/M is the incredibly small fraction $2^{-499} \approx 9.82 \cdot 10^{-91}$.

Most files of interest are at least some thousands of bytes long. For such files, the percentage of files that can be efficiently compressed is so small that it cannot be computed with floating-point numbers even on a supercomputer (the result is stored in the computer as zero).

It is worth noting that this result does not depend on our arbitrary choice of $n/2$ as the limit of good compression. It's easy to show that even a higher limit such as $0.9n$ results in essentially the same small fractions of compressible files.

It is therefore clear that no compression method can hope to compress all files or even a significant percentage of them. In order to compress a data file, the compression algorithm has to examine the data, find redundancies in it, and try to remove them. Since the redundancies in data depend on the type of data (text, images, sound, etc.), any new compression method being developed should be designed for a specific type of data. There is no such thing as a universal, efficient data compression algorithm. Certain algorithms may perform well on several types of data, but they do not produce the best possible compression.

This sad conclusion, however, should not cause the reader to close the book with a sigh and turn to more promising pursuits. The interesting fact is that out of the 2^n

large files, the ones we actually *want* to compress are normally the ones that compress well. The ones that compress badly are random or close to random and are therefore uninteresting, unimportant, and not candidates for compression, transmission, or storage.

This part of the book consists of three chapters that deal with statistical compression methods, dictionary-based methods, and methods developed specifically for the compression of images.

> It is still an unending source of surprise for me how
> a few scribbles on a blackboard or on a piece of
> paper can change the course of human affairs.
>
> —Stanislaw Ulam

3
Statistical Methods

Statistical data compression methods exploit the statistical properties of the data being compressed to represent it with fewer bits. The term *statistical properties* normally means the probability (or equivalently, number of occurrences) of each symbol in the data. Thus, the simpler statistical methods assign variable-size codes to the individual symbols in the data and write the data with these codes on the output file.

The term *statistical properties* may have other, more complex meanings. A *digram* is a pair of consecutive symbols, and experience shows that in typical text, certain digrams are common while others are rare. In English texts, the digrams "ta," "he," and "ca," are common while "xa," "hz," and "qe," are rare. A sophisticated statistical compression method may therefore assign variable-size codes to the many digrams (or even trigrams), rather than to the individual symbols in the data.

Arithmetic coding (Section 3.8) is a sophisticated statistical method that uses symbol frequencies to replace the entire input file with a single number. The input file is read and the probability of each symbol is used to narrow a certain numeric interval. As the interval narrows, it takes longer numbers to specify it. When the entire input file has been read and processed in this way, the output is any number in the last (very narrow) interval. Each data file results in a different number (the number can be considered a fingerprint of the file) and compression is achieved because of the way the probability of a symbol is used to narrow the current interval.

> It is a statistical fact that the wicked work harder
> to reach hell than the righteous do to enter heaven.
> —Josh Billings

3.1 Basic Statistical Methods

A basic statistical compression method assigns variable-size codes to the individual symbols in the data and outputs these codes. Such a method has to perform the following tasks: (1) compute or estimate the probabilities of the individual symbols; (2) assign the best variable-size codes to the symbols; and (3) write those codes on the output file such that the decoder will be able to read them unambiguously. This section offers general ideas on these tasks, while the details appear in the remainder of the chapter.

1. There are three ways to compute or estimate the probabilities of individual symbols. An algorithm can use a fixed set of variable-size codes regardless of the symbol probabilities of any particular data file. The algorithm may read the input file twice (a two-pass job), where the first pass counts symbol occurrences and computes symbol probabilities and the second pass uses the probabilities to actually compress the data. Alternatively, an algorithm may adapt itself continuously to the statistical properties of the input file while the file is being compressed. These three approaches are discussed in detail in Section 3.4.

2. There is a simple algorithm, due to David Huffman, that assigns a set of the best codes to a set of symbols with known probabilities. This algorithm is described in Section 3.5.

3. It is possible to design variable-size codes that can be read unambiguously. Imagine the sequence of five codes 11100|01|1010|10. It's easy to write them on a file, but the decoder cannot tell where each code ends, because it does not know the sizes of the codes. Section 3.3 explains how to design a set of good variable-size codes.

3.2 Entropy

Information theory was created, in 1948, by Claude Shannon of Bell Labs. This theory took the scientific world by surprise because we normally consider information to be a qualitative concept. The only information-theoretical concept needed to understand data compression is *entropy*. The entropy of a symbol a with probability P is interpreted as the amount of information included in a and is defined as $-P \log_2 P$. For example, if the probability P_a of symbol a is 0.5, then its entropy is $-P_a \log_2 P_a = 0.5$.

Given an alphabet of symbols a_1 through a_n with probabilities P_1 through P_n, respectively, the sum $\sum_n -P_i \log_2 P_i$ is the entropy of the entire alphabet. Given any string of symbols from the alphabet, its entropy is similarly calculated.

Based on the entropy, information theory shows how to calculate the probability of any string from the alphabet and predict its best compression, i.e., the minimum number of bits needed, on average, to represent the string. This is demonstrated by a simple example. Given the five symbols ABCDE with probabilities 0.5, 0.2, 0.1, 0.1, and 0.1, respectively, the probability of the string AAAAABBCDE is $P = 0.5^5 \times 0.2^2 \times 0.1^3 = 1.25 \times 10^{-6}$. The base-2 logarithm of this probability is $\log_2 P = -19.6096$. Thus, the minimum number of bits needed, on average, to encode the string is $-\lceil \log_2 P \rceil$ or 20.

An encoder that achieves this compression is called an *entropy encoder*.

Example: We analyze the entropy of an alphabet consisting of the two symbols a_1 and a_2, with probabilities P_1 and P_2, respectively. Since $P_1 + P_2 = 1$, the entropy of the alphabet is $-P_1 \log_2 P_1 - (1 - P_1) \log_2(1 - P_1)$. Table 3.1 shows the values of the expression $-\log_2 P_1 - \log_2(1 - P_1)$ for certain values of the probabilities. When $P_1 = P_2$, at least one bit is required to encode each symbol, reflecting the fact that the entropy is at its maximum, the redundancy is zero, and the data cannot be compressed. However, when the probabilities are very different, the minimum number of bits required per symbol drops significantly. We may not be able to devise a compression method using 0.08 bits per symbol, but we know that when $P_1 = 99\%$, such compression is theoretically possible.

P_1	P_2	Entropy
99	1	0.08
90	10	0.47
80	20	0.72
70	30	0.88
60	40	0.97
50	50	1.00

Table 3.1: Probabilities and Entropies of Two Symbols.

3.3 Variable-Size Codes

The first rule of assigning variable-size codes is obvious: short codes should be assigned to the common symbols and long codes should be assigned to the rare symbols. There is, however, another aspect to variable-size codes: they have to be assigned such that they can be decoded unambiguously. A simple example will serve to make this point clear.

Consider the four symbols a_1, a_2, a_3, and a_4. If they appear in our data strings with equal probabilities ($= 0.25$ each), then we can simply assign them the four 2-bit codes 00, 01, 10, and 11. The probabilities are equal, so variable-size codes will not compress the data. For each symbol with a short code, there will be another symbol with a long code, and the average number of bits per symbol will be 2. The redundancy of a set of symbols with equal probabilities is zero, and a string of such symbols cannot be compressed by the use of variable-size codes (or by anything else).

Next, consider the case where the four symbols occur with different probabilities as shown in Table 3.2, where a_1 appears in the data (on average) about half the time, a_2 and a_3 have equal probabilities, and a_4 is rare. In this case, the data has redundancy and variable-size codes can compress it to less than 2 bits per symbol. In fact, information theory tells us that the smallest number of bits needed, on average, to represent each symbol is 1.57 (the entropy of this set of symbols).

Code 1 of Table 3.2 is designed such that the most common symbol, a_1, is assigned the shortest code. When long data strings are transmitted using Code 1, the average

Symbol	Prob.	Code 1	Code 2
a_1	.49	1	1
a_2	.25	01	01
a_3	.25	010	000
a_4	.01	001	001

Table 3.2: Variable-size Codes.

number of bits per symbol is $1 \times 0.49 + 2 \times 0.25 + 3 \times 0.25 + 3 \times 0.01 = 1.77$, very close to the theoretical minimum. An illuminating example is the 20-symbol string

$$a_1 a_3 a_2 a_1 a_3 a_3 a_4 a_2 a_1 a_1 a_2 a_2 a_1 a_1 a_3 a_1 a_1 a_2 a_3 a_1,$$

where the four symbols occur with (approximately) the right frequencies. Encoding this string with Code 1 results in the 37 bits

$$1|010|01|1|010|010|001|01|1|1|01|01|1|1|010|1|1|01|010|1$$

(without the vertical bars). Using 37 bits to encode 20 symbols yields an average size of 1.85 bits/symbol, not far from the calculated average size. (The reader should bear in mind that our examples are short. To get results close to the best that is theoretically possible, an input file with at least thousands of symbols is needed.)

However, when we try to *decode* the binary string above, it becomes obvious that Code 1 is bad. The first bit is 1, and since only a_1 is assigned this code, it (a_1) must be the first symbol. The next bit is 0, but the codes of a_2, a_3, and a_4 all start with a 0, so the decoder has to read the next bit. It is 1, but the codes of both a_2 and a_3 start with 01. The decoder does not know whether to decode the string as $1|010|01\ldots$, which is $a_1 a_3 a_2 \ldots$, or as $1|01|001\ldots$, which is $a_1 a_2 a_4 \ldots$. Code 1 is thus *ambiguous*. In contrast, Code 2, which has the same average size as Code 1, can be decoded unambiguously.

The property of Code 2 that makes it so much better than Code 1 is called the *prefix property*. This property requires that once a certain bit pattern has been assigned as the code of a symbol, no other codes should start with that pattern (the pattern cannot be the *prefix* of any other code). Thus, once the string "1" was assigned as the code of a_1, no other codes could start with 1 (i.e., they all had to start with 0). Once "01" was assigned as the code of a_2, no other codes could start with 01. This is why the codes of a_3 and a_4 had to start with 00. Naturally, they became 000 and 001.

Designing a set of variable-size codes is therefore done by observing two principles: (1) assign short codes to the more frequent symbols, and (2) obey the prefix property. Following these principles produces short, unambiguous codes but not necessarily the best (i.e., shortest) ones. In addition to these principles, an algorithm is needed that always produces a set of shortest codes (codes with minimum average size). The only input to such an algorithm is the frequencies (or the probabilities) of the symbols of the alphabet. Fortunately, there is a simple algorithm, due to David Huffman and named after him, that does just that. It is the subject of Section 3.5.

(It should be noted that not all statistical compression methods assign variable-size codes to the individual symbols of the alphabet. A notable exception is arithmetic coding, as described in Section 3.8.)

Prefix codes have applications in other areas, not just in data compression. Section 9.13 illustrates their use in cryptography.

3.3.1 The Unary Code

The *unary code* of the nonnegative integer n is defined as $n-1$ ones followed by a single zero (Table 3.3) or, alternatively, as $n-1$ zeros followed by a single one. The length of the unary code for the integer n is thus n bits. Stone Age people indicated the integer n by marking n adjacent vertical bars on a stone, so the unary code is sometimes called a *stone-age binary* and each of its $n-1$ ones (or $n-1$ zeros) is called a *stone-age bit*.

n	Code	Alt. Code
1	0	1
2	10	01
3	110	001
4	1110	0001
5	11110	00001

Table 3.3: Some Unary Codes.

⋄ **Exercise 3.1:** Discuss the use of the unary code as a variable-size code.

3.3.2 The Golomb Code

The Golomb code [Golomb 66] offers an alternative to the Huffman codes in certain cases. The JPEG-LS method [Salomon 04] is an example of how this code is employed.

Encoding. The Golomb code for nonnegative integers n depends on the choice of a parameter m. Thus, it is a parametrized prefix code, which makes it especially useful in cases where good values for the parameter can be computed or estimated. The first step in computing the Golomb code of the nonnegative integer n is to compute the three quantities q (quotient), r (remainder), and c by

$$q = \left\lfloor \frac{n}{m} \right\rfloor, \quad r = n - qm, \text{ and } c = \lceil \log_2 m \rceil,$$

following which the code is constructed in two parts: the first is the value of q, coded in unary (Section 3.3.1), and the second is the binary value of r, coded in a special way. The first $2^c - m$ values of r are coded, as unsigned integers, in $c - 1$ bits each, and the rest are coded in c bits each (ending with the biggest c-bit number, which consists of c 1s). The case where m is a power of 2 ($m = 2^c$) is special because it requires no $(c-1)$-bit codes. We know that $n = r + qm$, so once a Golomb code is decoded, the values of q and r can be used to easily reconstruct n.

Examples. Choosing $m = 3$ produces $c = 2$ and the three remainders 0, 1, and 2. We compute $2^2 - 3 = 1$, so the first remainder is coded in $c - 1 = 1$ bit to become 0, and the remaining two are coded in two bits each, ending with 11_2, to become 10 and 11. Selecting $m = 5$ results in $c = 3$ and produces the five remainders 0 through 4. The first three ($2^3 - 5 = 3$) are coded in $c - 1 = 2$ bits each, and the remaining two are each coded in three bits ending with 111_2—thus, 00, 01, 10, 110, and 111. The following simple rule shows how to encode the c-bit numbers such that the last of them will consist of c 1s. Denote the largest of the $(c-1)$-bit numbers by b and then construct the integer $b+1$ in $c-1$ bits and append a zero on the right. The result is the first of the c-bit numbers, and the remaining ones are obtained by incrementing.

Table 3.4 shows some examples of m, c, and $2^c - m$, as well as some Golomb codes for $m = 2$ through 13.

m	2	3	4	5	6	7	8	9	10	11	12	13	14	15	16
c	1	2	2	3	3	3	3	4	4	4	4	4	4	4	4
$2^c - m$	0	1	0	3	2	1	0	7	6	5	4	3	2	1	0

m/n	0	1	2	3	4	5	6	7	8	9	10	11	12
2	0|0	0|1	10|0	10|1	110|0	110|1	1110|0	1110|1	11110|0	11110|1	111110|0	111110|1	1111110|0
3	0|0	0|10	0|11	10|0	10|10	10|11	110|0	110|10	110|11	1110|0	1110|10	1110|11	11110|0
4	0|00	0|01	0|10	0|11	10|00	10|01	10|10	10|11	110|00	110|01	110|10	110|11	11110|00
5	0|00	0|01	0|10	0|110	0|111	10|00	10|01	10|10	10|110	10|111	110|00	110|01	110|10
6	0|00	0|01	0|100	0|101	0|110	0|111	10|00	10|01	10|100	10|101	10|110	10|111	110|00
7	0|00	0|010	0|011	0|100	0|101	0|110	0|111	10|00	10|010	10|011	10|100	10|101	10|110
8	0|000	0|001	0|010	0|011	0|100	0|101	0|110	0|111	10|000	10|001	10|010	10|011	10|100
9	0|000	0|001	0|010	0|011	0|100	0|101	0|110	0|1110	0|1111	10|000	10|001	10|010	10|011
10	0|000	0|001	0|010	0|011	0|100	0|101	0|1100	0|1101	0|1110	0|1111	10|000	10|001	10|010
11	0|000	0|001	0|010	0|011	0|100	0|1010	0|1011	0|1100	0|1101	0|1110	0|1111	10|000	10|001
12	0|000	0|001	0|010	0|011	0|1000	0|1001	0|1010	0|1011	0|1100	0|1101	0|1110	0|1111	10|000
13	0|000	0|001	0|010	0|0110	0|0111	0|1000	0|1001	0|1010	0|1011	0|1100	0|1101	0|1110	0|1111

Table 3.4: Some Golomb Codes for $m = 2$ through 13.

Decoding. The Golomb codes are designed in this special way to facilitate their decoding. We first demonstrate the decoding for the simple case $m = 16$ (m is a power of 2). To decode, start at the left end of the code and count the number A of 1s preceding the first 0. The length of the code is $A + c + 1$ bits (for $m = 16$, this is $A + 5$ bits). If we denote the rightmost five bits of the code by R, then the value of the code is $16A + R$. This simple decoding reflects the way the code was constructed. To encode n with $m = 16$, start by dividing it by 16 to get $n = 16A + R$ and then write A 1s followed by a single zero, followed by the 4-bit representation of R.

For m values that are not powers of 2, decoding is slightly more involved. Assuming again that a code begins with A 1s, start by removing them and the zero immediately following them. Denote the $c - 1$ bits that follow by R. If $R < 2^c - m$, then the total length of the code is $A + 1 + (c - 1)$ (the A 1s, the zero following them, and the $c - 1$ bits that follow), and its value is $m \times A + R$. If $R \geq 2^c - m$, then the total length of the code is $A + 1 + c$ and its value is $m \times A + R' - (2^c - m)$, where R' is the c-bit integer consisting of R and the bit that follows R.

An example is the code $0001xxx$, for $m = 14$. There are no leading 1s, so A is 0. After removing the leading zero, the $c - 1 = 3$ bits that follow are $R = 001$. Since $R < 2^c - m = 2$, we conclude that the length of the code is $0 + 1 + (4 - 1) = 4$ and its value is 001. Similarly, the code $00100xxx$ for the same $m = 14$ has $A = 0$ and $R = 010_2 = 2$. In this case, $R \geq 2^c - m = 2$, so the length of the code is $0 + 1 + c = 5$, the value of R' is $0100_2 = 4$, and the value of the code is $14 \times 0 + 4 - 2 = 2$.

The best value for m depends on p, and it can be shown that this value is the integer closest to $-1/\log_2 p$, or equivalently, the value that satisfies $p^m \approx 1/2$. It can also be shown that in the case of a sequence of run lengths, this integer is the median of the run lengths. Thus, for $p = 0.5$, m should be $-1/\log_2 0.5 = 1$. For $p = 0.7$, m should be 2, because $-1/\log_2 0.7 \approx 1.94$, and for $p = 36/37$, m should be 25, because $-1/\log_2(36/37) \approx 25.29$.

Given the right data, it is therefore easy to employ the Golomb codes to easily generate the best variable-size codes without going through the Huffman algorithm.

3.4 Decoding

Before we can describe any specific statistical compression methods, it is important to understand the way encoder and decoder (compressor and decompressor) communicate. Suppose that a data file (with text, images, or anything else) has been compressed by assigning variable-size (prefix) codes to the various symbols. In order to decompress the data, the decoder has to know the prefix code of every symbol. This problem can be approached in three ways:

1. A set of prefix codes is determined once and is used by all encoders and decoders. This approach is used in facsimile compression (Section 3.7). The designers of the fax compression standard have chosen a set of eight "representative" documents, analyzed their statistical properties, and used these as the basis for selecting the prefix codes shown in Table 3.18. In technical language, we say that the documents were used to "train" the algorithm. Training an algorithm is a simple approach to statistical compression, but its performance depends on how much the file being compressed resembles the training documents.

2. The encoder performs a two-pass job. In the first pass, it reads the data file to be compressed and collects the necessary statistics. In the second pass, the file is actually compressed. In between the passes, the compressor uses the information from pass 1 to compute a set of best prefix codes for the particular file. This approach results in excellent compression but is normally too slow to be practical. It also has the added inconvenience that the prefix codes have to be included in the compressed file for the decoder's use. This degrades the overall performance, but not by much. This approach to statistical compression is sometimes called *semiadaptive compression*.

3. Adaptive compression is used by both encoder and decoder. The encoder starts with no knowledge of the statistical properties of the data. The first part of the data is therefore poorly compressed, but while compressing it, the encoder collects more and more statistical information, improves the prefix codes that it uses, and thus improves its performance. The algorithm must be designed such that the decoder would be able to follow every step taken by the encoder, collect the same statistical information, and improve the prefix codes in the same way. An example of adaptive compression is shown in Section 3.6.

Buffy: It is statistically impossible for a 16-year-old girl to unplug her phone.

—Buffy the Vampire Slayer

3.5 Huffman Coding

Huffman coding is a simple algorithm for generating a set of variable-size codes with the minimum average size. It is a well-known, popular algorithm, and it serves as the basis for several common software applications used on personal and other computers to compress text and images. Some of these applications use just the Huffman method, while others use it as one step in a multistep compression process. The Huffman method [Huffman 52] produces ideal compression (i.e., compression at the entropy of the data) when the probabilities of the symbols are negative powers of 2. The algorithm proceeds by constructing a code tree from the bottom up and then sliding down the tree to construct each individual code from right (least-significant bits) to left (most-significant bits). Since its development, in 1952, by D. Huffman, this method has been the subject of intensive research. (The last sentence of Section 3.3.2 shows that best variable-size codes can sometimes be obtained without this algorithm.)

The method starts by building a list of all the alphabet symbols in descending order of their probabilities. It then constructs a tree, with a symbol at every leaf, from the bottom up. This is done in steps, where at each step the two symbols with smallest probabilities are selected, added to the top of the partial tree, deleted from the list, and replaced with an auxiliary symbol representing both of them. When the list is reduced to just one auxiliary symbol (representing the entire alphabet), the tree is complete. The tree is then traversed to determine the codes of the symbols.

This is best illustrated by an example. Given five symbols with probabilities as shown in Figure 3.5a, the symbols are paired in the following order:

1. a_4 is combined with a_5 and both are replaced by the combined symbol a_{45}, whose probability is 0.2.
2. There are now four symbols left: a_1, with probability 0.4, and a_2, a_3, and a_{45}, with probabilities 0.2 each. We arbitrarily select a_3 and a_{45}, combine them, and replace them with the auxiliary symbol a_{345}, whose probability is 0.4.
3. Three symbols are now left: a_1, a_2, and a_{345}, with probabilities 0.4, 0.2, and 0.4, respectively. We arbitrarily select a_2 and a_{345}, combine them, and replace them with the auxiliary symbol a_{2345}, whose probability is 0.6.
4. Finally, we combine the two remaining symbols, a_1 and a_{2345}, and replace them with a_{12345} with probability 1.

The tree is now complete. It is shown in Figure 3.5a "lying on its side" with the root on the right and the five leaves on the left. To assign the codes, we arbitrarily assign a bit of 1 to the top edge and a bit of 0 to the bottom edge of every pair of edges. This results in the codes 0, 10, 111, 1101, and 1100. The assignments of bits to the edges is arbitrary.

The average size of this code is $0.4 \times 1 + 0.2 \times 2 + 0.2 \times 3 + 0.1 \times 4 + 0.1 \times 4 = 2.2$ bits/symbol, but even more importantly, the Huffman code is not unique. Some of the steps here were chosen arbitrarily, since there were more than two symbols with smallest probabilities. Figure 3.5b shows how the same five symbols can be combined differently to obtain a different Huffman code (11, 01, 00, 101, and 100). The average size of this code is $0.4 \times 2 + 0.2 \times 2 + 0.2 \times 2 + 0.1 \times 3 + 0.1 \times 3 = 2.2$ bits/symbol, the same as the previous code.

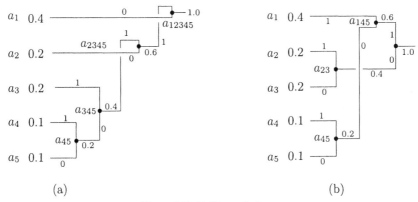

Figure 3.5: Huffman Codes.

⋄ **Exercise 3.2:** Given the eight symbols A, B, C, D, E, F, G, and H with probabilities 1/30, 1/30, 1/30, 2/30, 3/30, 5/30, 5/30, and 12/30, draw three different Huffman trees with heights 5 and 6 for these symbols and compute the average code size for each tree.

⋄ **Exercise 3.3:** Figure Ans.3d (see Answers to Exercises) shows another Huffman tree, with height 4, for the eight symbols introduced in Exercise 3.2. Explain why this tree is bad.

It turns out that the arbitrary decisions made in constructing the Huffman tree affect the individual codes but not the average size of the code. Still, we have to answer the obvious question, "Which of the different Huffman codes for a given set of symbols is best?" The answer, while not obvious, is simple: the code with the smallest variance. The variance of a code measures how much the sizes of the individual codes deviate from the average size (the concept of variance is explained in any text on statistics). The variance of code 3.5a is

$$0.4(1 - 2.2)^2 + 0.2(2 - 2.2)^2 + 0.2(3 - 2.2)^2 + 0.1(4 - 2.2)^2 + 0.1(4 - 2.2)^2 = 1.36,$$

while that of code 3.5b is

$$0.4(2 - 2.2)^2 + 0.2(2 - 2.2)^2 + 0.2(2 - 2.2)^2 + 0.1(3 - 2.2)^2 + 0.1(3 - 2.2)^2 = 0.16.$$

Code 3.5b is thus preferable (see below). A careful look at the two trees shows how to select the one we want. In the tree of Figure 3.5a, symbol a_{45} is combined with a_3, whereas in the tree of Figure 3.5b it is combined with a_1. The rule is this: when there are more than two smallest-probability nodes, select the ones that are lowest and highest in the tree and combine them. This will combine symbols of low probability with ones of high probability, thereby reducing the total variance of the code.

If the encoder simply writes the compressed file on a file, the variance of the code makes no difference. A small-variance Huffman code is preferable only in cases where the encoder *transmits* the compressed file, as it is being generated, over a communications line. In such a case, a code with large variance causes the encoder to generate bits at a rate that varies all the time. Since the bits have to be transmitted at a constant rate, the encoder has to use a buffer. Bits of the compressed file are entered into the buffer as they are being generated and are moved out of it at a constant rate to be transmitted. It is easy to see intuitively that a Huffman code with zero variance will enter bits into the buffer at a constant rate, so only a short buffer will be necessary. The larger the code variance, the more varied is the rate at which bits enter the buffer, requiring the encoder to use a larger buffer.

The following claim is sometimes found in the literature:

It can be shown that the size of the Huffman code of a symbol a_i with probability P_i is always less than or equal to $\lceil - \log_2 P_i \rceil$.

Even though it is correct in many cases, this claim is not true in general. I am indebted to Guy Blelloch for pointing this out and also for the example of Table 3.6. The second row of this table shows a symbol whose Huffman code is three bits long but for which $\lceil - \log_2 0.3 \rceil = \lceil 1.737 \rceil = 2$.

P_i	Code	$- \log_2 P_i$	$\lceil - \log_2 P_i \rceil$
.01	000	6.644	7
*.30	001	1.737	2
.34	01	1.556	2
.35	1	1.515	2

Table 3.6: A Huffman Code Example.

⋄ **Exercise 3.4:** Find an example where the size of the Huffman code of a symbol a_i is greater than $\lceil - \log_2 P_i \rceil$.

⋄ **Exercise 3.5:** It seems that the size of the Huffman code of symbol a_i must also depend on the number n of symbols (the size of the alphabet). A small alphabet requires just a few codes, so these can all be short; a large alphabet requires many codes, so some must be long. This being so, how can we say that the size of the code of symbol a_i depends just on its probability P_i?

Figure 3.7 shows a Huffman code for the 26 letters.

⋄ **Exercise 3.6:** Discuss the Huffman codes for symbols with equal probabilities.

Exercise 3.6 shows that symbols with equal probabilities don't compress under the Huffman method. This suggests that strings of such symbols are normally random. There may be special cases where strings of symbols with equal probabilities are not random and can be compressed. A good example is the string $a_1 a_1 \ldots a_1 a_2 a_2 \ldots a_2 a_3 a_3 \ldots$ in which each symbol appears in a long run. This string can be compressed with RLE but not with Huffman codes. (RLE stands for *run-length encoding*. This simple method is inefficient by itself but can be used as one step in a multistep compression method [Salomon 04].)

Notice that the Huffman method cannot be applied to a two-symbol alphabet. In such an alphabet, one symbol can be assigned the code 0 and the other the code 1. The

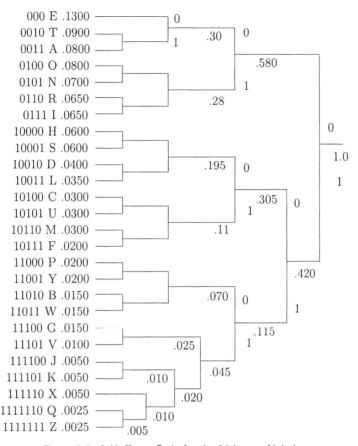

Figure 3.7: A Huffman Code for the 26-Letter Alphabet.

Huffman method cannot assign to any symbol a code shorter than one bit, so it cannot improve on this simple code. If the original data (the source) consists of individual bits, as in the case of a bi-level (monochromatic) image, it is possible to combine several bits (perhaps 4 or 8) into a new symbol and to pretend that the alphabet consists of these (16 or 256) symbols. The problem with this approach is that the original binary data may have certain statistical correlations between the bits, and some of these correlations may be lost when the bits are combined into symbols. When a typical bi-level image (a painting or a diagram) is digitized by scan lines, a pixel is more likely to be followed by an identical pixel than by the opposite one. We thus have a file that can start with either a 0 or a 1 (each has 0.5 probability of being the first bit). A zero is more likely to be followed by another 0 and a 1 by another 1. Figure 3.8 is a finite-state machine illustrating this situation. If these bits are combined into, say, groups of eight, the bits inside a group will still be correlated, but the groups themselves will not be correlated by the original pixel probabilities. If the input file contains, e.g., the two adjacent groups 00011100 and 00001110, these will be encoded independently, ignoring the correlation between the last 0 of the first group and the first 0 of the next group. Selecting larger groups improves this situation but increases the number of groups, which implies more storage for the code table and also a longer time to calculate the table.

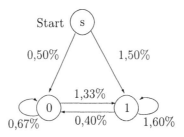

Figure 3.8: A Finite-State Machine

◇ **Exercise 3.7:** How does the number of groups increase when the group size increases from s bits to $s + n$ bits?

A more complex approach to image compression by Huffman coding is to create several complete sets of Huffman codes. If the group size is, e.g., 8 bits, then several sets of 256 codes are generated. When a symbol S is to be encoded, one of the sets is selected, and S is encoded using its code in that set. The choice of set depends on the symbol preceding S.

◇ **Exercise 3.8:** Imagine an image with 8-bit pixels, where half the pixels have values 127 and the other half 128. Analyze the performance of RLE on the individual bitplanes of such an image and compare it to what can be achieved with Huffman coding.

David Huffman (1925–1999)

David Huffman started his distinguished career as a brilliant student at MIT, where he developed his code in the early 1950s.

He joined the faculty at MIT in 1953. In 1967, he went to UC Santa Cruz as the founding faculty member of the Computer Science Department. He played a major role in the development of the department's academic programs and the hiring of its faculty and served as chair from 1970 to 1973. He retired in 1994 but remained active until 1999 as an emeritus professor, teaching information theory and signal analysis courses. He died in late 1999, at age 74.

Huffman made important contributions in many different areas, including information theory and coding, signal designs for radar and communications applications, and design procedures for asynchronous logical circuits. As an outgrowth of his work on the mathematical properties of "zero curvature" surfaces, Huffman developed his own techniques for folding paper into unusual sculptured shapes [Grafica 96].

3.5.1 Huffman Decoding

Before starting the compression of a data stream, the compressor (encoder) has to determine the codes. It does so based on the probabilities (or frequencies of occurrence) of the symbols. The probabilities or frequencies have to appear on the compressed file so that any Huffman decompressor (decoder) will be able to decompress the file (but see Sections 3.4 and 3.6 for different approaches). This is easy, since the frequencies are integers and the probabilities can be written as scaled integers, and it normally adds just a few hundred bytes to the compressed file. It is also possible to write the variable-size codes themselves on the file, but doing so may be awkward, since the codes have different sizes. It is also possible to write the Huffman tree on the file, but this tree may be longer than just the frequencies.

In any case, the decoder must know what's at the start of the file, read it, and construct the Huffman tree for the alphabet. Only then can it read and decode the rest of the file. The algorithm for decoding is simple. Start at the root and read the first bit off the compressed file. If it is zero, follow the bottom edge of the tree; if it is one, follow the top edge. Read the next bit and move another edge toward the leaves of the tree. When the decoder gets to a leaf, it finds the original uncompressed code of the symbol (normally, its ASCII code), and that code is emitted by the decoder. The process starts again at the root with the next input bit.

This process is illustrated for the five-symbol alphabet of Figure 3.9. The four-symbol input string $a_4 a_2 a_5 a_1$ is encoded into 1001100111. The decoder starts at the root, reads the first bit 1, and goes up. The second bit 0 sends it down, as does the third bit. This brings the decoder to leaf a_4, which it emits. It again returns to the root, reads 110, moves up, up, and down to reach leaf a_2, and so on.

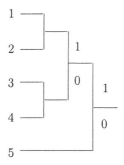

Figure 3.9: Huffman Codes for Equal Probabilities.

3.5.2 Average Code Size

Figure 3.12a shows a set of five symbols with their probabilities and a typical Huffman tree. Symbol A appears 55% of the time and is assigned a 1-bit code, so it contributes $0.55 \cdot 1$ bits to the average code size. Symbol E appears only 2% of the time and is assigned a 4-bit Huffman code, so it contributes $0.02 \cdot 4 = 0.08$ bits to the code size.

The average code size is therefore calculated to be

$$0.55 \cdot 1 + 0.25 \cdot 2 + 0.15 \cdot 3 + 0.03 \cdot 4 + 0.02 \cdot 4 = 1.7 \text{ bits per symbol.}$$

Surprisingly, the same result is obtained by adding the values of the four internal nodes of the Huffman codetree: $0.05 + 0.2 + 0.45 + 1 = 1.7$. This provides a way to calculate the average code size of a set of Huffman codes without any multiplications. Simply add the values of all the internal nodes of the tree. Table 3.10 illustrates why this works.

$0.05 =$	$= 0.02 + 0.03 + \cdots$
$a_1 \quad = 0.05 + \ldots = 0.02 + 0.03 + \cdots$	
$a_2 \quad = a_1 \quad + \ldots = 0.02 + 0.03 + \cdots$	
$\vdots \quad =$	
$a_{d-2} = a_{d-3} + \ldots = 0.02 + 0.03 + \cdots$	
$1.0 \quad = a_{d-2} + \ldots = 0.02 + 0.03 + \cdots$	

$.05 = \qquad\qquad .02 + .03$
$.20 = .05 + .15 = .02 + .03 + .15$
$.45 = .20 + .25 = .02 + .03 + .15 + .25$
$1.0 = .45 + .55 = .02 + .03 + .15 + .25 + .55$

Table 3.10: Composition of Nodes.

Table 3.11: Composition of Nodes.

(Internal nodes are shown in italics in Table 3.10.) The left column consists of the values of all the internal nodes. The right columns show how each internal node is the sum of some of the leaf nodes. Summing the values in the left column yields 1.7, and summing the other columns shows that this 1.7 is the sum of the four values 0.02, the four values 0.03, the three values 0.15, the two values 0.25, and the single value 0.55.

This argument can be extended to the general case. It is easy to show that, in a Huffman-like tree (a tree where each node is the sum of its children) the weighted sum of the leaves, where the weights are the distances of the leaves from the root, equals the sum of the internal nodes. (This property was communicated to me by John M. Motil.)

Figure 3.12b shows such a tree, where we assume that the two leaves 0.02 and 0.03 have d-bit Huffman codes. Inside the tree, these leaves become the children of internal node 0.05, which, in turn, is connected to the root by means of the $d - 2$ internal nodes a_1 through a_{d-2}. Table 3.11 has d rows and shows that the two values 0.02 and 0.03 are included in the various internal nodes exactly d times. Adding the values of all the internal nodes produces a sum that includes the contributions $0.02 \cdot d + 0.03 \cdot d$ from the two leaves. Since these leaves are arbitrary, it is clear that this sum includes similar contributions from all the other leaves, so this sum is the average code size. Since this sum also equals the sum of the left column, which is the sum of the internal nodes, it is clear that the sum of the internal nodes equals the average code size.

Notice that this proof does not assume that the tree is binary. The property illustrated here exists for any tree where a node contains the sum of its children.

> Statistics are no substitute for judgment.
> —Henry Clay

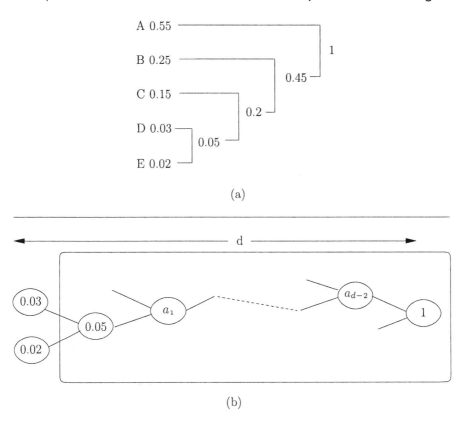

(a)

(b)

Figure 3.12: Huffman Code Trees.

3.6 Adaptive Huffman Coding

The Huffman method assumes that the frequencies of occurrence of all the symbols of the alphabet are known to the compressor. In practice, the frequencies are seldom, if ever, known in advance. One solution is for the compressor to read the original data twice. The first time it just calculates the frequencies. The second time, it compresses the data. Between the two passes, the compressor constructs the Huffman tree. Such a method is called *semiadaptive* (Section 3.4) and is normally too slow to be practical. The method used in practice is called *adaptive* (or *dynamic*) Huffman coding. This method is the basis of the UNIX `compact` program.

For more information on the adaptive method described here and on other adaptive Huffman algorithms, see [Lelewer and Hirschberg 87], [Knuth 85], and [Vitter 87].

The main idea is for the compressor and the decompressor to start with an empty Huffman tree and to modify it as symbols are being read and processed (in the case of the compressor, the word *processed* means *compressed*; in the case of the decompressor, it means *decompressed*). The compressor and decompressor should modify the tree in the same way, so at any point in the process they should use the same codes, although those codes may change from step to step. We say that the compressor and decompressor are synchronized, or that they work in *lockstep* (although they don't necessarily work together; compression and decompression usually take place at different times). The term *mirroring* is perhaps a better choice. The decoder mirrors the operations of the encoder.

Initially, the compressor starts with an empty Huffman tree. No symbols have been assigned codes. The first symbol being input is simply written on the output file in its uncompressed form. The symbol is then added to the tree and a code is assigned to it. The next time this symbol is encountered, its current code is written on the file and its frequency is incremented by one. Since this modifies the tree, it (the tree) is examined to see whether it is still a Huffman tree (best codes). If not, it is rearranged, which entails changing the codes (Section 3.6.2).

The decompressor mirrors the same steps. When it reads the uncompressed form of a symbol, it adds it to the tree and assigns it a code. When it reads a compressed (variable-size) code, it uses the current tree to determine what symbol the code belongs to, and it updates the tree in the same way as the compressor.

The only subtle point is that the decompressor needs to know whether the item it has just input is an uncompressed symbol (normally, an 8-bit ASCII code, but see Section 3.6.1) or a variable-size code. To remove any ambiguity, each uncompressed symbol is preceded by a special, variable-size *escape code*. When the decompressor reads this code, it knows that the next 8 bits are the ASCII code of a symbol that appears in the compressed file for the first time.

The trouble is that the escape code should not be any of the variable-size codes used for the symbols. Since these codes are being modified every time the tree is rearranged, the escape code should also be modified. A natural way to do this is to add an empty leaf to the tree, a leaf with a zero frequency of occurrence, that is always assigned to the 0-branch of the tree. Since the leaf is in the tree, it is assigned a variable-size code. This code is the escape code preceding every uncompressed symbol. As the tree is being rearranged, the position of the empty leaf—and thus its code—changes, but this escape code is always used to identify uncompressed symbols in the compressed file. Figure 3.13 shows how the escape code moves as the tree grows.

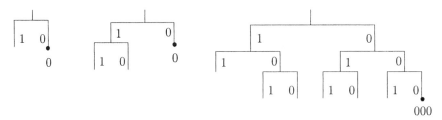

Figure 3.13: The Escape Code.

This method is used to compress/decompress data in the V.32 protocol for 14,400-baud modems.

3.6.1 Uncompressed Codes

If the symbols being compressed are ASCII characters, they may simply be assigned their ASCII codes as uncompressed codes. In the general case where there can be any symbols, uncompressed codes of two different sizes can be assigned by a simple method. Here is an example for the case $n = 24$. The first 16 symbols can be assigned the numbers 0 through 15 as their codes. These numbers require only 4 bits, but we encode them in 5 bits. Symbols 17 through 24 can be assigned the numbers $17 - 16 - 1 = 0$, $18 - 16 - 1 = 1$ through $24 - 16 - 1 = 7$ as 4-bit numbers. We end up with the sixteen 5-bit codes $00000, 00001, \ldots, 01111$, followed by the eight 4-bit codes $0000, 0001, \ldots, 0111$.

In general, we assume an alphabet that consists of the n symbols $a_1, a_2, \ldots, a_n$. We select integers m and r such that $2^m \leq n < 2^{m+1}$ and $r = n - 2^m$. The first 2^m symbols are encoded as the $(m + 1)$-bit numbers 0 through $2^m - 1$. The remaining symbols are encoded as m-bit numbers such that the code of a_k is $k - 2^m - 1$. This code is also called a *phased-in binary code*.

> A single death is a tragedy; a million deaths is a statistic.
> —Joseph Stalin

3.6.2 Modifying the Tree

The main idea is to check the tree each time a symbol is input. If the tree is no longer a Huffman tree, it should be updated. A glance at Figure 3.14a shows what it means for a binary tree to be a Huffman tree. The tree in the figure contains five symbols: A, B, C, D, and E. It is shown with the symbols and their frequencies (in parentheses) after 16 symbols have been input and processed. The property that makes it a Huffman tree is that if we scan it level by level, scanning each level from left to right and going from the bottom (the leaves) to the top (the root), the frequencies will be in sorted, nondescending order. Thus, the bottom-left node (A) has the lowest frequency, and the top-right one (the root) has the highest frequency. This is called the *sibling property*.

◇ **Exercise 3.9:** Why is the sibling property the criterion for a tree to be a Huffman tree?

Here is a summary of the operations necessary to update the tree. The loop starts at the current node (the one corresponding to the symbol just input). This node is a leaf that we denote by X, with frequency of occurrence F. Each iteration of the loop involves three steps:

1. Compare X to its successors in the tree (from left to right and bottom to top). If the immediate successor has frequency $F + 1$ or greater, the nodes are still in sorted order and there is no need to change anything. Otherwise, some successors of X have identical frequencies of F or smaller. In this case, X should be swapped with the last node in this group (except that X should not be swapped with its parent).

2. Increment the frequency of X from F to $F + 1$. Increment the frequencies of all its parents.

3. If X is the root, the loop stops; otherwise, the loop repeats with the parent of node X.

Figure 3.14b shows the tree after the frequency of node A has been incremented from 1 to 2. It is easy to follow the three rules to see how incrementing the frequency of A results in incrementing the frequencies of all its parents. No swaps are needed in this simple case because the frequency of A hasn't exceeded the frequency of its immediate successor B. Figure 3.14c shows what happens when A's frequency has been incremented again, from 2 to 3. The three nodes following A, namely, B, C, and D, have frequencies of 2, so A is swapped with the last of them, D. The frequencies of the new parents of A are then incremented and each is compared to its successor, but no more swaps are needed.

Figure 3.14d shows the tree after the frequency of A has been incremented to 4. Once we decide that A is the current node, its frequency (which is still 3) is compared to that of its successor (4), and the decision is not to swap. A's frequency is incremented, followed by incrementing the frequencies of its parents.

In Figure 3.14e, A is again the current node. Its frequency (4) equals that of its successor, so they should be swapped. This is shown in Figure 3.14f, where A's frequency is 5. The next loop iteration examines the parent of A, with frequency 10. It should be swapped with its successor E (with frequency 9), which leads to the final tree of Figure 3.14g.

> One that would have the fruit must climb the tree.
>
> —Thomas Fuller

3.6.3 Counter Overflow

The frequency counts are accumulated in the Huffman tree in fixed-size fields, and such fields may overflow. A 16-bit unsigned field can accommodate counts of up to $2^{16} - 1 = 65{,}535$. A simple solution is to watch the count field of the root each time it is incremented and, when it reaches its maximum value, to *rescale* all frequency counts by dividing them by 2 (integer division). In practice, this is done by dividing the count fields of the leaves and then updating the counts of the interior nodes. Each interior node gets the sum of the counts of its children. The problem is that the counts are integers, and integer division reduces precision. This may change a Huffman tree to one that does not satisfy the sibling property.

A simple example is shown in Figure 3.14h. After the counts of the leaves are halved, the three interior nodes are updated as shown in Figure 3.14i. The latter tree, however, is no longer a Huffman tree, since the counts are no longer in sorted order. The solution is to rebuild the tree each time the counts are rescaled, which does not happen very often. A Huffman data compression program intended for general use should thus have large count fields that would not overflow very often. A 4-byte count field overflows at $2^{32} - 1 \approx 4.3 \times 10^9$.

It should be noted that after rescaling the counts, the new symbols being read and compressed have more effect on the counts than the old symbols (those counted before the rescaling). This turns out to be fortuitous since it is known from experience that the probability of appearance of a symbol depends more on the symbols immediately preceding it than on symbols that appeared in the distant past.

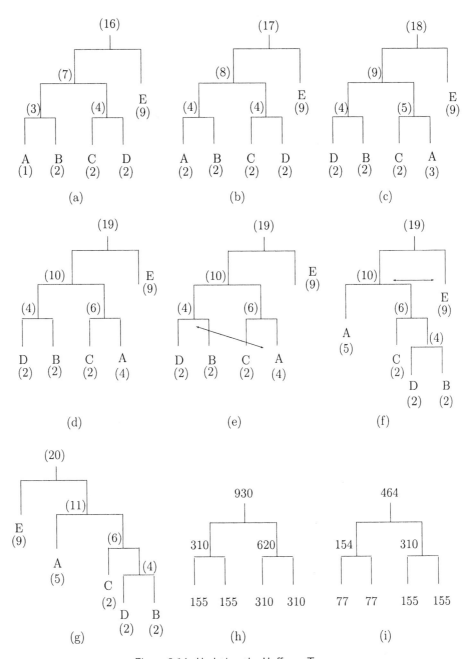

Figure 3.14: Updating the Huffman Tree.

3.6.4 Code Overflow

An even more serious problem is code overflow. This may happen when many symbols are added to the tree and it becomes tall. The codes themselves are not stored in the tree, since they change all the time, and the compressor has to figure out the code of a symbol X each time X is input. Here are the details:

- The encoder has to locate symbol X in the tree. The tree has to be implemented as an array of structures, each a node, and the array is searched linearly.
- If X is not found, the escape code is emitted, followed by the uncompressed code of X. X is then added to the tree.
- If X is found, the compressor moves from node X back to the root, building the code bit by bit as it goes along. Each time it goes from a left child to a parent, a 1 is appended to the code. Going from a right child to a parent appends a 0 bit to the code (or vice versa, but this should be consistent because it is mirrored by the decoder). Those bits have to be accumulated someplace, since they have to be emitted in the *reverse order* in which they are created. When the tree gets taller, the codes get longer. If they are accumulated in a 16-bit integer, then codes longer than 16 bits would cause a malfunction.

One solution is to accumulate the bits of a code in a linked list, where new nodes can be created, limited in number only by the amount of available memory. This is general but slow. Another solution is to accumulate the codes in a large integer variable (perhaps 50 bits wide) and document a maximum code size of 50 bits as one of the limitations of the program.

Fortunately, this problem does not affect the decoding process. The decoder reads the compressed code bit by bit and uses each bit to go one step left or right down the tree until it reaches a leaf node. If the leaf is the escape code, the decoder reads the uncompressed code of the symbol off the compressed file (and adds the symbol to the tree). Otherwise, the uncompressed code is found in the leaf node.

⋄ **Exercise 3.10:** Given the 11-symbol string "sir␣sid␣is", apply the adaptive Huffman method to it. For each symbol input, show the output, the tree after the symbol has been added to it, the tree after being rearranged (if necessary), and the list of nodes traversed left to right and bottom up.

3.6.5 A Variant

This variant of the adaptive Huffman method is simple but less efficient. The idea is to compute a set of n variable-size codes based on equal probabilities, to assign those codes to the n symbols at random, and to vary the assignments "on the fly," as symbols are being read and compressed. The method is inefficient because the codes are not based on the actual probabilities of the symbols in the input file. However, the variant is easier to implement and also faster than the adaptive method above, because it has to swap rows in a table, rather than update a tree, when updating the frequencies of the symbols.

The main data structure is an $n \times 3$ table where the three columns store the names of the n symbols, their frequencies of occurrence so far, and their codes. The table is always kept sorted by the second column. When the frequency counts in the second column change, rows are swapped, but only columns 1 and 2 are moved. The codes in column 3 never change. Figure 3.15 shows an example of four symbols and the behavior of the method when the string a_2, a_4, a_4 is compressed.

Figure 3.15a shows the initial state. After the first symbol a_2 is read, its count is incremented, and since it is now the largest count, rows 1 and 2 are swapped (Figure 3.15b). After the second symbol a_4 is read, its count is incremented and rows 2 and 4 are swapped (Figure 3.15c). Finally, after the last symbol a_4 is read, its count is the largest, so rows 1 and 2 are swapped (Figure 3.15d).

Name	Count	Code	Name	Count	Code	Name	Count	Code	Name	Count	Code
a_1	0	0	a_2	1	0	a_2	1	0	a_4	2	0
a_2	0	10	a_1	0	10	a_4	1	10	a_2	1	10
a_3	0	110	a_3	0	110	a_3	0	110	a_3	0	110
a_4	0	111	a_4	0	111	a_1	0	111	a_1	0	111
(a)			(b)			(c)			(d)		

Figure 3.15: Four Steps in a Huffman Variant.

The only point that can cause a problem with this method is overflow of the count fields. If such a field is k bits wide, its maximum value is $2^k - 1$, so it will overflow when incremented for the 2^kth time. This may happen if the size of the input file is not known in advance, which is very common. Fortunately, we do not really need to know the counts; we just need them in sorted order, making it easy to solve this problem.

One solution is to count the input symbols and, after $2^k - 1$ symbols are input and compressed, to (integer) divide all the count fields by 2 (or shift them one position to the right, if this is easier).

Another similar solution is to check each count field every time it is incremented and, if it has reached its maximum value (if it consists of all ones), to integer divide all the count fields by 2. This approach requires fewer divisions but more complex tests.

Whatever solution is adopted should be used by both the compressor and decompressor.

> Get your facts first, and then you can distort them as much as you please. (Facts are stubborn, but statistics are more pliable.)
>
> —Mark Twain

3.7 Facsimile Compression

Data compression is especially important when images are transmitted over a communications line, because the user is typically waiting at the receiving end, eager to see something quickly. Documents transferred between fax machines are sent as bitmaps, which is why a standard data compression method was needed when those machines became popular. Several methods were developed and proposed by the ITU-T and one has been selected and accepted by industry; see [Anderson et al. 87], [Hunter and Robinson 80], [Marking 90], and [McConnell 92] as examples of the many references available for this popular standard. Formal descriptions can be found in [RFC804 03].

The ITU-T is one of four permanent parts of the International Telecommunications Union (ITU) based in Geneva, Switzerland (`http://www.itu.ch/`). It issues recommendations for standards applying to telecommunications equipment. Although it has no power of enforcement, the standards it recommends are generally accepted and adopted by industry. Until March 1993, the ITU-T was known as the Consultative Committee for International Telephone and Telegraph (Comité Consultatif International Télégraphique et Téléphonique, or CCITT).

The first fax data compression standards developed by the ITU-T were T2 (also known as Group 1) and T3 (Group 2). These are now obsolete and have been replaced by T4 (Group 3) and T6 (Group 4). Group 3 is currently used by all fax machines designed to operate with the Public Switched Telephone Network (PSTN). These are the machines we have at home, and at the time of this writing, they operate at maximum speeds of 9,600 baud. Group 4 is used by fax machines designed to operate on a digital network, such as ISDN. They have typical speeds of 64K baud. Both methods can produce compression factors of 10:1 or better, reducing the transmission time of a typical page to about a minute with the former and a few seconds with the latter.

> The word facsimile comes from the Latin *facere* (make) and *similis* (like).

3.7.1 One-Dimensional Coding

A fax machine scans a document line by line, converting each scan line to small black and white dots called *pels* (from Picture ELement). The horizontal resolution is always 8.05 pels per millimeter (about 205 pels per inch). An 8.5-inch-wide scan line is therefore converted to 1728 pels. The T4 standard, though, recommends scanning only about 8.2 inches, thereby producing 1664 pels per scan line (these numbers, as well as those in the next paragraph, are all to within $\pm 1\%$ accuracy).

The vertical resolution is either 3.85 scan lines per millimeter (standard mode) or 7.7 lines/mm (fine mode). Many fax machines have also a very-fine mode, where they scan 15.4 lines/mm. Table 3.16 assumes a 10-inch-high page (254 mm) and shows the total number of pels per page and typical transmission times for the three modes without compression. The times are long, and they illustrate the importance of compression in fax transmissions.

To derive the Group 3 code, the ITU-T counted all the run lengths of white and black pels in a set of eight "training" documents that were felt to represent typical text and images sent by fax and applied the Huffman algorithm to assign a variable-size code

Scan lines	Pels per line	Pels per page	Time (sec)	Time (min)
978	1664	1.670M	170	2.82
1956	1664	3.255M	339	5.65
3912	1664	6.510M	678	11.3

Ten inches equal 254 mm. The number of pels is in the millions, and the transmission times, at 9600 baud without compression, are between 3 and 11 minutes, depending on the mode. However, if the page is shorter than 10 inches, or if most of it is white, the compression factor can be 10:1 or better, resulting in transmission times of between 17 and 68 seconds.

Table 3.16: Fax Transmission Times.

to each run length. (The eight documents are described in Table 3.17. They are not shown here because they are copyrighted by the ITU-T, but they can be downloaded; see [funet 03].) The most common run lengths were found to be 2, 3, and 4 black pixels, so these were assigned the shortest codes (Table 3.18). Next come run lengths of 2–7 white pixels, which were assigned slightly longer codes. Most run lengths were rare and were assigned long, 12-bit codes. Thus, the Group 3 standard uses a combination of RLE and Huffman coding.

◇ **Exercise 3.11:** A run length of 1664 white pels was assigned the short code 011000. Why is this length so common?

Image	Description
1	Typed business letter (English)
2	Circuit diagram (hand drawn)
3	Printed and typed invoice (French)
4	Densely typed report (French)
5	Printed technical article including figures and equations (French)
6	Graph with printed captions (French)
7	Dense document (Kanji)
8	Handwritten memo with very large white-on-black letters (English)

Table 3.17: The Eight CCITT Training Documents.

Since run lengths can be long, the Huffman algorithm was modified. Codes were assigned to run lengths of 1 to 63 pels (these are the termination codes in Table 3.18a) and to run lengths that are multiples of 64 pels (the makeup codes in Table 3.18b). Group 3 is thus a *modified Huffman code* (also called MH). The code of a run length

(a)

Run length	White code-word	Black code-word	Run length	White code-word	Black code-word
0	00110101	0000110111	32	00011011	000001101010
1	000111	010	33	00010010	000001101011
2	0111	11	34	00010011	000011010010
3	1000	10	35	00010100	000011010011
4	1011	011	36	00010101	000011010100
5	1100	0011	37	00010110	000011010101
6	1110	0010	38	00010111	000011010110
7	1111	00011	39	00101000	000011010111
8	10011	000101	40	00101001	000001101100
9	10100	000100	41	00101010	000001101101
10	00111	0000100	42	00101011	000011011010
11	01000	0000101	43	00101100	000011011011
12	001000	0000111	44	00101101	000001010100
13	000011	00000100	45	00000100	000001010101
14	110100	00000111	46	00000101	000001010110
15	110101	000011000	47	00001010	000001010111
16	101010	0000010111	48	00001011	000001100100
17	101011	0000011000	49	01010010	000001100101
18	0100111	0000001000	50	01010011	000001010010
19	0001100	00001100111	51	01010100	000001010011
20	0001000	00001101000	52	01010101	000000100100
21	0010111	00001101100	53	00100100	000000110111
22	0000011	00000110111	54	00100101	000000111000
23	0000100	00000101000	55	01011000	000000100111
24	0101000	00000010111	56	01011001	000000101000
25	0101011	00000011000	57	01011010	000001011000
26	0010011	000011001010	58	01011011	000001011001
27	0100100	000011001011	59	01001010	000000101011
28	0011000	000011001100	60	01001011	000000101100
29	00000010	000011001101	61	00110010	000001011010
30	00000011	000001101000	62	00110011	000001100110
31	00011010	000001101001	63	00110100	000001100111

(b)

Run length	White code-word	Black code-word	Run length	White code-word	Black code-word
64	11011	0000001111	1344	011011010	0000001010011
128	10010	000011001000	1408	011011011	0000001010100
192	010111	000011001001	1472	010011000	0000001010101
256	0110111	000001011011	1536	010011001	0000001011010
320	00110110	000000110011	1600	010011010	0000001011011
384	00110111	000000110100	1664	011000	0000001100100
448	01100100	000000110101	1728	010011011	0000001100101
512	01100101	0000001101100	1792	00000001000	same as
576	01101000	0000001101101	1856	00000001100	white
640	01100111	0000001001010	1920	00000001101	from this
704	011001100	0000001001011	1984	000000010010	point
768	011001101	0000001001100	2048	000000010011	
832	011010010	0000001001101	2112	000000010100	
896	011010011	0000001110010	2176	000000010101	
960	011010100	0000001110011	2240	000000010110	
1024	011010101	0000001110100	2304	000000010111	
1088	011010110	0000001110101	2368	000000011100	
1152	011010111	0000001110110	2432	000000011101	
1216	011011000	0000001110111	2496	000000011110	
1280	011011001	0000001010010	2560	000000011111	

Table 3.18: Group 3 and 4 Fax Codes: (a) Termination Codes. (b) Makeup Codes.

is either a single termination code (if the run length is short) or one or more makeup codes, followed by one termination code (if it is long). Here are some examples:

1. A run length of 12 white pels is coded as 001000.
2. A run length of 76 white pels ($= 64 + 12$) is coded as 11011|001000 (without the vertical bar).
3. A run length of 140 white pels ($= 128 + 12$) is coded as 10010|001000.
4. A run length of 64 black pels ($= 64 + 0$) is coded as 0000001111|0000110111.
5. A run length of 2561 black pels ($2560 + 1$) is coded as 000000011111|010.

⋄ **Exercise 3.12:** The length of a run cannot be zero. Why, then, were codes assigned to runs of zero black and white pels?

⋄ **Exercise 3.13:** An 8.5-inch-wide scan line results in only 1728 pels, so how can there be a run of 2561 consecutive identical pels?

Each scan line is coded separately, and its code is terminated by the special 12-bit EOL code 000000000001. Each line also gets one white pel appended to it on the left when it is scanned. This is done to remove any ambiguity when the line is decoded on the receiving end. After reading the EOL for the previous line, the receiver assumes that the new line starts with a run of white pels, and it ignores the first of them. Examples:

1. The 14-pel line ▮▮▮▮ ▮▮ is coded as the run lengths 1w 3b 2w 2b 7w EOL, which become 000111|10|0111|11|1111|000000000001. The decoder ignores the single white pel at the start.
2. The line ▮▮▮▮▮▮ ▮▮ is coded as the run lengths 3w 5b 5w 2b EOL, which becomes the binary string 1000|0011|1100|11|000000000001.

⋄ **Exercise 3.14:** The group 3 code for a run length of five black pels (0011) is also the prefix of the codes for run lengths of 61, 62, and 63 white pels. Explain this.

The Group 3 code has no error correction, but many errors can be detected. Because of the nature of the Huffman code, even one bad bit in the transmission can cause the receiver to get out of synchronization and to produce a string of wrong pels. This is why each scan line is encoded separately. If the receiver detects an error, it skips bits, looking for an EOL. This way, one error can cause at most one scan line to be received incorrectly. If the receiver does not see an EOL after a certain number of lines, it assumes a high error rate, and it aborts the process, notifying the transmitter. Since the codes are between 2 and 12 bits long, the receiver detects an error if it cannot decode a valid code after reading 12 bits.

Each page of the coded document is preceded by one EOL and is followed by six EOL codes. Because each line is coded separately, this method is a *one-dimensional coding* scheme. The compression ratio depends on the image. Images with large contiguous black or white areas (text or black and white images) can be highly compressed. Images with many short runs can sometimes produce negative compression. This is especially true in the case of images with shades of gray (such as scanned photographs). Such shades are produced by halftoning, a process that covers areas with many alternating black and white pels (runs of length one).

⬦ **Exercise 3.15:** What is the compression ratio of runs of length one (strictly alternating pels)?

Since the T4 standard is based on run lengths, it may result in poor compression or even in expansion when the document features only short lengths. An extreme (and unlikely) case is a hypothetical document where all the run lengths are of size 1. The code of a run length of one white pel is 000111, and that of one black pel is 010. Thus, two consecutive pels of different colors are coded into 9 bits. Since the uncoded data requires just two bits (01 or 10), the compression ratio is $9/2 = 4.5$ (the compressed file is 4.5 times longer than the uncompressed one, a large expansion).

The T4 standard also allows for fill bits to be inserted between the data bits and the EOL. This is done in cases where a pause is necessary or where the total number of bits transmitted for a scan line must be a multiple of 8. The fill bits are zeros.

Example: The binary string 000111|10|0111|11|1111|000000000001 becomes a bit longer, 000111|10|0111|11|1111|00|000000000001, after two zeros are added as fill bits, bringing the total length of the string to 32 bits ($= 8 \times 4$). The decoder sees the two zeros of the fill, followed by the eleven zeros of the EOL, followed by the single 1, so it knows that it has encountered a fill followed by an EOL.

> 98% of all statistics are made up.
> —Unknown

3.7.2 Two-Dimensional Coding

Two-dimensional coding was developed because one-dimensional coding does not produce good results for images with gray areas. Two-dimensional coding is optional on fax machines that use Group 3 but is the only method used by machines intended to work on a digital network. When a fax machine using Group 3 supports two-dimensional coding as an option, each EOL is followed by one extra bit to indicate the compression method used for the next scan line. That bit is 1 if the next line is encoded with one-dimensional coding, 0 if it is encoded with two-dimensional coding.

The two-dimensional coding method is also called MMR, for *modified modified READ*, where *READ* stands for *relative element address designate*. The term *modified modified* is used because this is a modification of one-dimensional coding, which itself is a modification of the original Huffman method. The two-dimensional coding method works by comparing the current scan line (called the *coding line*) to its predecessor (called the *reference line*) and recording the differences between them, the assumption being that two consecutive lines in a document will normally differ by just a few pels. The method assumes that there is an all-white line above the page, which is used as the reference line for the first scan line of the page. After coding the first line, it becomes the reference line, and the second scan line is coded. As in one-dimensional coding, each line is assumed to start with a white pel, which is ignored by the receiver.

The two-dimensional coding method is less reliable than one-dimensional coding, since an error in decoding a line will cause errors in decoding all its successors and will propagate through the entire document. This is why the T.4 (Group 3) standard includes a requirement that after a line is encoded with the one-dimensional method, at most $K - 1$ lines will be encoded with the two-dimensional coding method. The value of K for standard resolution is 2 and for fine resolution is 4. The T.6 standard (Group 4) does not have this requirement and uses two-dimensional coding exclusively.

Scanning the coding line and comparing it to the reference line results in three cases, or modes. The mode is identified by comparing the next run length on the reference line, $(b_1 b_2)$ in Figure 3.20, with the current run length $(a_0 a_1)$ and the next one $(a_1 a_2)$ on the coding line. Each of these three runs can be black or white. The three modes are as follows:

1. **Pass mode.** This is the case where $(b_1 b_2)$ is to the left of $(a_1 a_2)$ and b_2 is to the left of a_1 (Figure 3.20a). This mode does not include the case where b_2 is above a_1. When this mode is identified, the length of run $(b_1 b_2)$ is coded using the codes of Table 3.19 and is transmitted. Pointer a_0 is moved below b_2, and the four values b_1, b_2, a_1, and a_2 are updated.

2. **Vertical mode.** $(b_1 b_2)$ overlaps $(a_1 a_2)$ by not more than three pels (Figure 3.20b1, b2). Assuming that consecutive lines do not differ by much, this is the most common case. When this mode is identified, one of seven codes is produced (Table 3.19) and is transmitted. Pointers are updated as in case 1. The performance of the two-dimensional coding method depends on this case being common.

3. **Horizontal mode.** $(b_1 b_2)$ overlaps $(a_1 a_2)$ by more than three pels (Figure 3.20c1, c2). When this mode is identified, the lengths of runs $(a_0 a_1)$ and $(a_1 a_2)$ are coded using the codes of Table 3.19 and are transmitted. Pointers are updated as in cases 1 and 2.

Mode	Run length to be encoded	Abbreviation	Codeword
Pass	$b_1 b_2$	P	0001+coded length of $b_1 b_2$
Horizontal	$a_0 a_1, a_1 a_2$	H	001+coded length of $a_0 a_1$ and $a_1 a_2$
Vertical	$a_1 b_1 = 0$	V(0)	1
	$a_1 b_1 = -1$	VR(1)	011
	$a_1 b_1 = -2$	VR(2)	000011
	$a_1 b_1 = -3$	VR(3)	0000011
	$a_1 b_1 = +1$	VL(1)	010
	$a_1 b_1 = +2$	VL(2)	000010
	$a_1 b_1 = +3$	VL(3)	0000010
Extension			0000001000

Table 3.19: 2D Codes for the Group 4 Method.

When scanning starts, pointer a_0 is set to an imaginary white pel on the left of the coding line, and a_1 is set to point to the first black pel on the coding line. (Since a_0 corresponds to an imaginary pel, the first run length is $|a_0 a_1| - 1$.) Pointer a_2 is set to the first white pel following that. Pointers b_1, b_2 are set to point to the start of the first and second runs on the reference line, respectively.

After identifying the current mode and transmitting codes according to Table 3.19, a_0 is updated as shown in the flowchart, and the other four pointers are updated relative

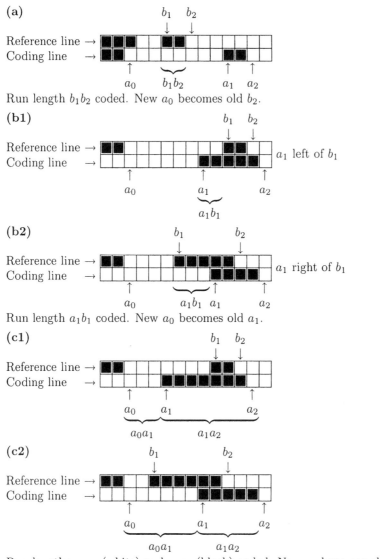

Figure 3.20: Five Run-Length Configurations: (a) Pass Mode. (b) Vertical Mode. (c) Horizontal Mode.

to the new a_0. The process continues until the end of the coding line is reached. The encoder assumes an extra pel on the right of the line, with a color opposite that of the last pel.

The extension code in Table 3.19 is used to abort the encoding process prematurely, before reaching the end of the page. This is necessary if the rest of the page is transmitted in a different code or even in uncompressed form.

⋄ **Exercise 3.16:** Manually figure out the code generated from the two lines

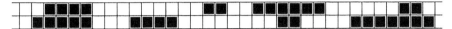

> The statistics on sanity are that one out of every four Americans is suffering from some form of mental illness. Think of your three best friends. If they're okay, then it's you.
> —Rita Mae Brown

3.8 Arithmetic Coding

The Huffman method is simple and efficient, and produces the best codes for the individual data symbols. However, Section 3.5 shows that the only case where it produces ideal variable-size codes (codes whose average size equals the entropy) is when the symbols have probabilities of occurrence that are negative powers of 2 (i.e., numbers such as $1/2$, $1/4$, or $1/8$). This is because the Huffman method assigns a code with an integral number of bits to each symbol in the alphabet. Information theory shows that a symbol with probability 0.4 should ideally be assigned a 1.32-bit code, since $-\log_2 0.4 \approx 1.32$. The Huffman method, however, normally assigns such a symbol a code of 1 or 2 bits.

Arithmetic coding overcomes the problem of assigning integer codes to the individual symbols by assigning one (normally long) code to the entire input file. The method starts with a certain interval, reads the input file symbol by symbol, and uses the probability of each symbol to narrow the interval. Specifying a narrower interval requires more bits, so the number constructed by the algorithm grows continuously. To achieve compression, the algorithm is designed such that a high-probability symbol narrows the interval less than a low-probability symbol, with the result that high-probability symbols contribute fewer bits to the output.

An interval can be specified by its lower and upper limits or by one limit and width. We use the latter method to illustrate how an interval's specification becomes longer as the interval narrows. The interval $[0, 1]$ can be specified by the two 1-bit numbers 0 and 1. The interval $[0.1, 0.512]$ can be specified by the longer numbers 0.1 and 0.412. The very narrow interval $[0.12575, 0.1257586]$ is specified by the long numbers 0.12575 and 0.0000086.

The output of arithmetic coding is interpreted as a number in the range $[0, 1)$. (The notation $[a, b)$ means the range of real numbers from a to b, including a but not including b. The range is "closed" at a and "open" at b.) Thus the code 9746509 is be interpreted as 0.9746509, although the 0. part is not included in the output file.

Before we plunge into the details, here is a bit of history. The principle of arithmetic coding was first proposed by Peter Elias in the early 1960s and was first described in [Abramson 63]. Early practical implementations of this method were developed by [Rissanen 76], [Pasco 76], and [Rubin 79]. The work of [Moffat et al. 98] and [Witten et al. 87] should especially be mentioned. These authors discuss both the principles and details of practical arithmetic coding and show examples.

The first step is to calculate, or at least to estimate, the frequencies of occurrence of each symbol. For best results, the exact frequencies are calculated by reading the entire input file in the first pass of a two-pass compression job. However, if the program can get good estimates of the frequencies from a different source, the first pass may be omitted.

The first example involves the three symbols a_1, a_2, and a_3, with probabilities $P_1 = 0.4$, $P_2 = 0.5$, and $P_3 = 0.1$, respectively. The interval $[0, 1)$ is divided among the three symbols by assigning each a subinterval proportional in size to its probability. The order of the subintervals is immaterial. In our example, the three symbols are assigned the subintervals $[0, 0.4)$, $[0.4, 0.9)$, and $[0.9, 1.0)$. To encode the string $a_2a_2a_2a_3$, we start with the interval $[0, 1)$. The first symbol a_2 reduces this interval to the subinterval from its 40% point to its 90% point. The result is $[0.4, 0.9)$. The second a_2 reduces $[0.4, 0.9)$ in the same way (see note below) to $[0.6, 0.85)$, the third a_2 reduces this to $[0.7, 0.825)$, and the a_3 reduces this to the stretch from the 90% point of $[0.7, 0.825)$ to its 100% point, producing $[0.8125, 0.8250)$. The final output of this method can be any number in this final range. (Note: The subinterval $[0.6, 0.85)$ is obtained from the interval $[0.4, 0.9)$ by $0.4 + (0.9 - 0.4) \times 0.4 = 0.6$ and $0.4 + (0.9 - 0.4) \times 0.9 = 0.85$.)

With this example in mind, it's easy to understand the following rules, which summarize the main steps of arithmetic coding:

1. Start by defining the current interval as $[0, 1)$.
2. Repeat the following two steps for each symbol s in the input file:
    2.1 Divide the current interval into subintervals whose sizes are proportional to the symbols' probabilities.
    2.2 Select the subinterval for s and make it the new current interval.
3. When the entire input file has been processed in this way, the output should be any number that uniquely identifies the current interval (i.e., any number inside the current interval).

For each symbol processed, the current interval gets smaller, so it takes more bits to express it, but the point is that the final output is a single number and does not consist of codes for the individual symbols. The average code size can be obtained by dividing the size of the output (in bits) by the size of the input (in symbols). Notice also that the probabilities used in step 2.1 may change all the time, since they may be supplied by an adaptive probability model (Section 3.9).

The next example is a little more involved. We show the compression steps for the short string SWISS␣MISS. Table 3.21 shows the information prepared in the first step (the *statistical model* of the data). The five symbols appearing in the input may be arranged in any order. For each symbol, its frequency is counted first, followed by its probability of occurrence (the frequency divided by the string size, 10). The range $[0, 1)$

is then divided among the symbols, in any order, with each symbol getting a chunk, or a subrange, equal in size to its probability. Thus S gets the subrange $[0.5, 1.0)$ (of size 0.5), whereas the subrange of I is of size 0.2 $[0.2, 0.4)$. The cumulative frequencies column is used by the decoding algorithm on page 103.

Char	Freq	Prob.	Range	CumFreq
		Total CumFreq=		10
S	5	$5/10 = 0.5$	$[0.5, 1.0)$	5
W	1	$1/10 = 0.1$	$[0.4, 0.5)$	4
I	2	$2/10 = 0.2$	$[0.2, 0.4)$	2
M	1	$1/10 = 0.1$	$[0.1, 0.2)$	1
⊔	1	$1/10 = 0.1$	$[0.0, 0.1)$	0

Table 3.21: Frequencies and Probabilities of Five Symbols.

The symbols and frequencies in Table 3.21 are written on the output file before any of the bits of the compressed code. This table will be the first thing input by the decoder.

The encoding process starts by defining two variables, Low and High, and setting them to 0 and 1, respectively. They define an interval [Low, High). As symbols are being input and processed, the values of Low and High are moved closer together to narrow the interval.

After processing the first symbol S, Low and High are updated to 0.5 and 1, respectively. The resulting code for the entire input file will be a number in this range $(0.5 \leq \text{Code} < 1.0)$. The rest of the input file will determine precisely where, in the interval $[0.5, 1)$, the final code will lie. A good way to understand the process is to imagine that the new interval $[0.5, 1)$ is divided among the five symbols of our alphabet using the same proportions as for the original interval $[0, 1)$. The result is the five subintervals $[0.5, 0.55)$, $[0.55, 0.60)$, $[0.60, 0.70)$, $[0.70, 0.75)$, and $[0.75, 1.0)$. When the next symbol W is input, the third of those subintervals is selected and is again divided into five subsubintervals.

As more symbols are being input and processed, Low and High are being updated according to

```
NewHigh:=OldLow+Range*HighRange(X);
NewLow:=OldLow+Range*LowRange(X);
```

where Range=OldHigh−OldLow and LowRange(X), HighRange(X) indicate the low and high limits of the range of symbol X, respectively. In the example, the second input symbol is W, so we update Low := $0.5+(1.0-0.5)\times0.4 = 0.70$, High := $0.5+(1.0-0.5)\times 0.5 = 0.75$. The new interval $[0.70, 0.75)$ covers the stretch $[40\%, 50\%)$ of the subrange of S. Table 3.22 shows all the steps involved in coding the string SWISS⊔MISS. The final code is the final value of Low, 0.71753375, of which only the eight digits 71753375 need be written on the output file (a modification of this statement is discussed later). Figure 3.23 shows how the input symbols are used to select the current subinterval.

Char.		The calculation of low and high
S	L	$0.0 + (1.0 - 0.0) \times 0.5 = 0.5$
	H	$0.0 + (1.0 - 0.0) \times 1.0 = 1.0$
W	L	$0.5 + (1.0 - 0.5) \times 0.4 = 0.70$
	H	$0.5 + (1.0 - 0.5) \times 0.5 = 0.75$
I	L	$0.7 + (0.75 - 0.70) \times 0.2 = 0.71$
	H	$0.7 + (0.75 - 0.70) \times 0.4 = 0.72$
S	L	$0.71 + (0.72 - 0.71) \times 0.5 = 0.715$
	H	$0.71 + (0.72 - 0.71) \times 1.0 = 0.72$
S	L	$0.715 + (0.72 - 0.715) \times 0.5 = 0.7175$
	H	$0.715 + (0.72 - 0.715) \times 1.0 = 0.72$
␣	L	$0.7175 + (0.72 - 0.7175) \times 0.0 = 0.7175$
	H	$0.7175 + (0.72 - 0.7175) \times 0.1 = 0.71775$
M	L	$0.7175 + (0.71775 - 0.7175) \times 0.1 = 0.717525$
	H	$0.7175 + (0.71775 - 0.7175) \times 0.2 = 0.717550$
I	L	$0.717525 + (0.71755 - 0.717525) \times 0.2 = 0.717530$
	H	$0.717525 + (0.71755 - 0.717525) \times 0.4 = 0.717535$
S	L	$0.717530 + (0.717535 - 0.717530) \times 0.5 = 0.7175325$
	H	$0.717530 + (0.717535 - 0.717530) \times 1.0 = 0.717535$
S	L	$0.7175325 + (0.717535 - 0.7175325) \times 0.5 = 0.71753375$
	H	$0.7175325 + (0.717535 - 0.7175325) \times 1.0 = 0.717535$

Table 3.22: The Process of Arithmetic Encoding.

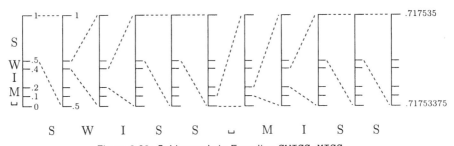

Figure 3.23: Subintervals in Encoding SWISS MISS.

The decoder works in the opposite way. It starts by inputting the symbols and their ranges and reconstructing Table 3.21. It then inputs the rest of the code. The first digit is 7, so the decoder immediately knows that the entire code is a number of the form $0.7\ldots$. This number is inside the subrange $[0.5, 1)$ of S, so the first symbol is S. The decoder eliminates the effect of S from the code by subtracting the lower limit 0.5 of S and dividing by the width of the subrange of S (0.5). The result is 0.4350675, which tells the decoder that the next symbol is W (since the subrange of W is $[0.4, 0.5)$).

To eliminate the effect of symbol X from the code, the decoder performs the operation `Code:=(Code-LowRange(X))/Range`, where `Range` is the width of the subrange of X. Table 3.24 summarizes the steps for decoding our example string.

The next example is of three symbols with probabilities as shown in Table 3.25a. Notice that the probabilities are very different. One is large (97.5%) and the others are much smaller. This is a case of *skewed probabilities.*

Encoding the string $a_2a_2a_1a_3a_3$ produces the strange numbers (accurate to 16 digits) in Table 3.26, where the two rows for each symbol correspond to the Low and High values, respectively.

At first glance, it seems that the resulting code is longer than the original string, but Section 3.8.3 shows how to figure out the true compression achieved by arithmetic coding.

The decoding of this string is shown in Table 3.27 and involves a special problem. After eliminating the effect of a_1, on line 3, the result is 0. Earlier, we implicitly assumed that this means the end of the decoding process, but now we know that there are two more occurrences of a_3 that should be decoded. These are shown on lines 4 and 5 of the table. This problem always occurs when the last symbol in the input file is the one whose subrange starts at zero.

In order to distinguish between such a symbol and the end of the input file, we need to define an additional symbol, the end-of-input (or end-of-file, eof). This symbol should be added, with a small probability, to the frequency table (see Table 3.25b), and it should be encoded at the end of the input file.

Tables 3.28 and 3.29 show how the string $a_3a_3a_3a_3$eof is encoded into the very small fraction 0.0000002878086184764172 and then decoded properly. Without the eof symbol, a string of all a_3s would have been encoded into a 0.

Notice how the low value is 0 until the eof is input and processed and how the high value quickly approaches 0. It has already been mentioned that the final code does not have to be the final low value but can be any number between the final low and high values. In the example of $a_3a_3a_3a_3$eof, the final code can be the much shorter number 0.0000002878086 (or 0.0000002878087 or even 0.0000002878088).

(Figure 3.30 lists the *Mathematica* code that computed Table 3.26.)

◇ **Exercise 3.17:** Encode the string $a_2a_2a_2a_2$ and summarize the results in a table similar to Table 3.28. How do the results differ from those of the string $a_3a_3a_3a_3$?

If the size of the input file is known, it is possible to do without an eof symbol. The encoder can start by writing this size (unencoded) on the output file. The decoder reads the size, starts decoding, and stops when the decoded file reaches this size. If the decoder reads the compressed file byte by byte, the encoder may have to add some zeros at the end to make sure the compressed file can be read in groups of 8 bits.

> Do not put faith in what statistics say until you have carefully considered what they do not say.
>
> —William W. Watt

Char.	Code − low	Range
S	$0.71753375 - 0.5 = 0.21753375$	$/0.5 = 0.4350675$
W	$0.4350675 - 0.4\ \ = 0.0350675$	$/0.1 = 0.350675$
I	$0.350675 - 0.2\ \ \ = 0.150675$	$/0.2 = 0.753375$
S	$0.753375 - 0.5\ \ \ = 0.253375$	$/0.5 = 0.50675$
S	$0.50675 - 0.5\ \ \ \ = 0.00675$	$/0.5 = 0.0135$
⊔	$0.0135 - 0\ \ \ \ \ \ \ = 0.0135$	$/0.1 = 0.135$
M	$0.135 - 0.1\ \ \ \ \ \ = 0.035$	$/0.1 = 0.35$
I	$0.35 - 0.2\ \ \ \ \ \ \ \ = 0.15$	$/0.2 = 0.75$
S	$0.75 - 0.5\ \ \ \ \ \ \ \ = 0.25$	$/0.5 = 0.5$
S	$0.5 - 0.5\ \ \ \ \ \ \ \ \ \ = 0$	$/0.5 = 0$

Table 3.24: The Process of Arithmetic Decoding.

Char	Prob.	Range		Char	Prob.	Range
a_1	0.001838	[0.998162, 1.0)		eof	0.000001	[0.999999, 1.0)
a_2	0.975	[0.023162, 0.998162)		a_1	0.001837	[0.998162, 0.999999)
a_3	0.023162	[0.0, 0.023162)		a_2	0.975	[0.023162, 0.998162)
				a_3	0.023162	[0.0, 0.023162)

(a)   (b)

Table 3.25: (Skewed) Probabilities of Three Symbols.

a_2	$0.0 + (1.0 - 0.0) \times 0.023162 = 0.023162$
	$0.0 + (1.0 - 0.0) \times 0.998162 = 0.998162$
a_2	$0.023162 + .975 \times 0.023162 = 0.04574495$
	$0.023162 + .975 \times 0.998162 = 0.99636995$
a_1	$0.04574495 + 0.950625 \times 0.998162 = 0.99462270125$
	$0.04574495 + 0.950625 \times 1.0 = 0.99636995$
a_3	$0.99462270125 + 0.00174724875 \times 0.0 = 0.99462270125$
	$0.99462270125 + 0.00174724875 \times 0.023162 = 0.994663171025547$
a_3	$0.99462270125 + 0.00004046977554749998 \times 0.0 = 0.99462270125$
	$0.99462270125 + 0.00004046977554749998 \times 0.023162 = 0.994623638610941$

Table 3.26: Encoding the String $a_2 a_2 a_1 a_3 a_3$.

Char.	Code − low		Range	
a_2	$0.99462270125 - 0.023162 = 0.97146170125/0.975$			$= 0.99636995$
a_2	$0.99636995 - 0.023162$	$= 0.97320795$	$/0.975$	$= 0.998162$
a_1	$0.998162 - 0.998162$	$= 0.0$	$/0.00138$	$= 0.0$
a_3	$0.0 - 0.0$	$= 0.0$	$/0.023162$	$= 0.0$
a_3	$0.0 - 0.0$	$= 0.0$	$/0.023162$	$= 0.0$

Table 3.27: Decoding the String $a_2a_2a_1a_3a_3$.

a_3	$0.0 + (1.0 - 0.0) \times 0.0 = 0.0$
	$0.0 + (1.0 - 0.0) \times 0.023162 = 0.023162$
a_3	$0.0 + .023162 \times 0.0 = 0.0$
	$0.0 + .023162 \times 0.023162 = 0.000536478244$
a_3	$0.0 + 0.000536478244 \times 0.0 = 0.0$
	$0.0 + 0.000536478244 \times 0.023162 = 0.000012425909087528$
a_3	$0.0 + 0.000012425909087528 \times 0.0 = 0.0$
	$0.0 + 0.000012425909087528 \times 0.023162 = 0.00000028780890628532$35
eof	$0.0 + 0.00000028780890628532$35 $\times 0.999999 = 0.00000028780861847641$72
	$0.0 + 0.00000028780890628532$35 $\times 1.0 = 0.00000028780890628532$35

Table 3.28: Encoding the String $a_3a_3a_3a_3$eof.

Char.	Code−low		Range	
a_3	$0.00000028780861847641$72-0	$=0.00000028780861847641$72	$/0.023162$	$=0.0000124258966616189$1247
a_3	$0.0000124258966616189$1247-0	$=0.0000124258966616189$1247	$/0.023162$	$=0.00053647770752$1756
a_3	$0.00053647770752$1756-0	$=0.00053647770752$1756	$/0.023162$	$=0.02316197683$8
a_3	$0.02316197683$8-0.0	$=0.02316197683$8	$/0.023162$	$=0.999999$
eof	0.999999-0.999999	$=0.0$	$/0.000001$	$=0.0$

Table 3.29: Decoding the String $a_3a_3a_3a_3$eof.

3.8.1 Implementation Details

The encoding process described earlier is not practical, since it assumes that numbers of unlimited precision can be stored in Low and High. The decoding process described on page 98 ("The decoder then eliminates the effect of the S from the code by subtracting... and dividing ...") is simple in principle but also impractical. The code, which is a single number, is normally long and may be very long. A 1 MB file may be encoded into, say, a 500 KB one that consists of a single number. Dividing a 500 KB number is complex and slow.

```
lowRange={0.998162,0.023162,0.};
highRange={1.,0.998162,0.023162};
low=0.; high=1.;
enc[i_]:=Module[{nlow,nhigh,range},
range=high-low;
nhigh=low+range highRange[[i]];
nlow=low+range lowRange[[i]];
low=nlow; high=nhigh;
Print["r=",N[range,25]," l=",N[low,17]," h=",N[high,17]]]
enc[2]
enc[2]
enc[1]
enc[3]
enc[3]
```

Figure 3.30: *Mathematica* Code for Table 3.26.

Any practical implementation of arithmetic coding should use just integers (because floating-point arithmetic is slow and precision is lost), and these should not be very long (preferably just single precision). We describe such an implementation here, using two integer variables Low and High. In our example they are four decimal digits long, but in practice they might be 16 or 32 bits long. These variables hold the low and high limits of the current subinterval, but we don't let them grow too much. A glance at Table 3.22 shows that once the leftmost digits of Low and High become identical, they never change. We therefore shift such digits out of the two variables and write one digit on the output file. This way, the two variables have to hold not the entire code, but just the most recent part of it. As digits are shifted out of the two variables, a zero is shifted into the right end of Low and a 9 into the right end of High. A good way to understand this is to think of each of the two variables as the left end of an infinitely long number. Low contains $xxxx00\ldots$, and High= $yyyy99\ldots$.

One problem is that High should be initialized to 1, but the contents of Low and High should be interpreted as fractions less than 1. The solution is to initialize High to $9999\ldots$, since the infinite fraction $0.999\ldots$ equals 1.

(This is easy to prove. If $0.999\ldots$ were less than 1, then their average $a = (1 + 0.999\ldots)/2$ would be a number between $0.999\ldots$ and 1, but there is no way to write a. It is impossible to give it more digits than to $0.999\ldots$ and it is impossible to make the digits any bigger. This is why the infinite fraction $0.999\ldots$ must equal 1.)

⋄ **Exercise 3.18:** Write the number 0.5 in binary.

Table 3.31 describes the encoding process of the string SWISS␣MISS. Column 1 shows the next input symbol. Column 2 shows the new values of Low and High. Column 3 shows these values as scaled integers, after High has been decremented by 1. Column 4 shows the next digit sent to the output file. Column 5 shows the new values of Low and High after being shifted to the left. Notice how the last step sends the four digits 3750

1	2	3	4	5
S	$L = 0+(1 - 0)\times 0.5 = 0.5$	5000		5000
	$H = 0+(1 - 0)\times 1.0 = 1.0$	9999		9999
W	$L = 0.5+(1 - .5)\times 0.4 = 0.7$	7000	7	0000
	$H = 0.5+(1 - .5)\times 0.5 = 0.75$	7499	7	4999
I	$L = 0 +(0.5 - 0)\times 0.2 = 0.1$	1000	1	0000
	$H = 0 +(0.5 - 0)\times 0.4 = 0.2$	1999	1	9999
S	$L = 0+(1 - 0)\times 0.5 = 0.5$	5000		5000
	$H = 0+(1 - 0)\times 1.0 = 1.0$	9999		9999
S	$L = 0.5+(1 - 0.5)\times 0.5 = 0.75$	7500		7500
	$H = 0.5+(1 - 0.5)\times 1.0 = 1.0$	9999		9999
⊔	$L = .75+(1 - .75)\times 0.0 = 0.75$	7500	7	5000
	$H = .75+(1 - .75)\times 0.1 = .775$	7749	7	7499
M	$L = 0.5+(.75 - .5)\times 0.1 = .525$	5250	5	2500
	$H = 0.5+(.75 - .5)\times 0.2 = 0.55$	5499	5	4999
I	$L = .25+(.5 - .25)\times 0.2 = 0.3$	3000	3	0000
	$H = .25+(.5 - .25)\times 0.4 = .35$	3499	3	4999
S	$L = 0.0+(0.5 - 0)\times 0.5 = .25$	2500		2500
	$H = 0.0+(0.5 - 0)\times 1.0 = 0.5$	4999		4999
S	$L = .25+(.5 - .25)\times 0.5 = .375$	3750	3750	
	$H = .25+(.5 - .25)\times 1.0 = 0.5$	4999		4999

Table 3.31: Encoding SWISS␣MISS by Shifting.

to the output file. The final output is 717533750.

Decoding is the opposite of encoding. We start with Low=0000, High=9999, and Code=7175 (the first four digits of the compressed file). These are updated at each step of the decoding loop. Low and High approach each other (and both approach Code) until their most significant digits are the same. They are then shifted to the left, which separates them again, and Code is also shifted at that time. An index is calculated at each step and is used to search the cumulative frequencies column of Table 3.21 to figure out the current symbol.

Each iteration of the loop consists of the following steps:

1. Calculate index:=((Code-Low+1)x10-1)/(High-Low+1) and truncate it to the nearest integer. (The number 10 is the total cumulative frequency in our example.)

2. Use index to find the next symbol by comparing it to the cumulative frequencies column in Table 3.21. In the following example, the first value of index is 7.1759, truncated to 7. Seven is between the 5 and the 10 in the table, so it selects the S.

3. Update Low and High according to

```
Low:=Low+(High-Low+1)LowCumFreq[X]/10;
High:=Low+(High-Low+1)HighCumFreq[X]/10-1;
```

where `LowCumFreq[X]` and `HighCumFreq[X]` are the cumulative frequencies of symbol X and of the symbol above it in Table 3.21.

4. If the leftmost digits of `Low` and `High` are identical, shift `Low`, `High`, and `Code` one position to the left. `Low` gets a 0 entered on the right, `High` gets a 9, and `Code` gets the next input digit from the compressed file.

Here are all the decoding steps for our example:

0. Initialize `Low`=0000, `High`=9999, and `Code`=7175.

1. index= $[(7175 - 0 + 1) \times 10 - 1]/(9999 - 0 + 1) = 7.1759 \rightarrow 7$. Symbol S is selected.
`Low` $= 0 + (9999 - 0 + 1) \times 5/10 = 5000$. `High` $= 0 + (9999 - 0 + 1) \times 10/10 - 1 = 9999$.

2. index= $[(7175 - 5000 + 1) \times 10 - 1]/(9999 - 5000 + 1) = 4.3518 \rightarrow 4$. Symbol W is selected.
`Low` $= 5000 + (9999 - 5000 + 1) \times 4/10 = 7000$. `High` $= 5000 + (9999 - 5000 + 1) \times 5/10 - 1 = 7499$.
After the 7 is shifted out, we have `Low`=0000, `High`=4999, and `Code`=1753.

3. index= $[(1753 - 0 + 1) \times 10 - 1]/(4999 - 0 + 1) = 3.5078 \rightarrow 3$. Symbol I is selected.
`Low` $= 0 + (4999 - 0 + 1) \times 2/10 = 1000$. `High` $= 0 + (4999 - 0 + 1) \times 4/10 - 1 = 1999$.
After the 1 is shifted out, we have `Low`=0000, `High`=9999, and `Code`=7533.

4. index= $[(7533 - 0 + 1) \times 10 - 1]/(9999 - 0 + 1) = 7.5339 \rightarrow 7$. Symbol S is selected.
`Low` $= 0 + (9999 - 0 + 1) \times 5/10 = 5000$. `High` $= 0 + (9999 - 0 + 1) \times 10/10 - 1 = 9999$.

5. index= $[(7533 - 5000 + 1) \times 10 - 1]/(9999 - 5000 + 1) = 5.0678 \rightarrow 5$. Symbol S is selected.
`Low` $= 5000 + (9999 - 5000 + 1) \times 5/10 = 7500$. `High` $= 5000 + (9999 - 5000 + 1) \times 10/10 - 1 = 9999$.

6. index= $[(7533 - 7500 + 1) \times 10 - 1]/(9999 - 7500 + 1) = 0.1356 \rightarrow 0$. Symbol ⊔ is selected.
`Low` $= 7500 + (9999 - 7500 + 1) \times 0/10 = 7500$. `High` $= 7500 + (9999 - 7500 + 1) \times 1/10 - 1 = 7749$.
After the 7 is shifted out, we have `Low`=5000, `High`=7499, and `Code`=5337.

7. index= $[(5337 - 5000 + 1) \times 10 - 1]/(7499 - 5000 + 1) = 1.3516 \rightarrow 1$. Symbol M is selected.
`Low` $= 5000 + (7499 - 5000 + 1) \times 1/10 = 5250$. `High` $= 5000 + (7499 - 5000 + 1) \times 2/10 - 1 = 5499$.
After the 5 is shifted out, we have `Low`=2500, `High`=4999, and `Code`=3375.

8. index= $[(3375 - 2500 + 1) \times 10 - 1]/(4999 - 2500 + 1) = 3.5036 \rightarrow 3$. Symbol I is selected.
`Low` $= 2500 + (4999 - 2500 + 1) \times 2/10 = 3000$. `High` $= 2500 + (4999 - 2500 + 1) \times 4/10 - 1 = 3499$.
After the 3 is shifted out, we have `Low`=0000, `High`=4999, and `Code`=3750.

9. index= $[(3750 - 0 + 1) \times 10 - 1]/(4999 - 0 + 1) = 7.5018 \rightarrow 7$. Symbol S is selected.
`Low` $= 0 + (4999 - 0 + 1) \times 5/10 = 2500$. `High` $= 0 + (4999 - 0 + 1) \times 10/10 - 1 = 4999$.

10. index= $[(3750 - 2500 + 1) \times 10 - 1]/(4999 - 2500 + 1) = 5.0036 \rightarrow 5$. Symbol S is selected.

Low $= 2500 + (4999 - 2500 + 1) \times 5/10 = 3750$. High $= 2500 + (4999 - 2500 + 1) \times 10/10 - 1 = 4999$.

⋄ **Exercise 3.19:** How does the decoder know to stop the loop at this point?

1	2			3	4	5
1	L=0+(1	−	0)×0.0	= 0.0	000000	0	000000
	H=0+(1	−	0)×0.023162	= 0.023162	023162	0	231629
2	L=0+(0.231629	−	0)×0.0	= 0.0	000000	0	000000
	H=0+(0.231629	−	0)×0.023162	= 0.00536478244	005364	0	053649
3	L=0+(0.053649	−	0)×0.0	= 0.0	000000	0	000000
	H=0+(0.053649	−	0)×0.023162	= 0.00124261813	001242	0	012429
4	L=0+(0.012429	−	0)×0.0	= 0.0	000000	0	000000
	H=0+(0.012429	−	0)×0.023162	= 0.00028788049	000287	0	002879
5	L=0+(0.002879	−	0)×0.0	= 0.0	000000	0	000000
	H=0+(0.002879	−	0)×0.023162	= 0.00006668339	000066	0	000669

Table 3.32: Encoding $a_3a_3a_3a_3a_3$ by Shifting.

> The greater danger for most of us lies not in setting our aim too high and falling short; but in setting our aim too low, and achieving our mark.
> —Michelangelo

3.8.2 Underflow

Table 3.32 shows the steps in encoding the string $a_3a_3a_3a_3a_3$ by shifting. This table is similar to Table 3.31, and it illustrates the problem of underflow. Low and High approach each other, and since Low is always 0 in this example, High loses its significant digits as it approaches Low.

Underflow may happen not just in this case but in any case where Low and High need to converge very closely. Because of the finite size of the Low and High variables, they may reach values of, say, 499996 and 500003 and from there, instead of reaching values where their most significant digits are identical, they reach the values 499999 and 500000. Since the most significant digits are different, the algorithm will not output anything, there will not be any shifts, and the next iteration will add digits only beyond the first six. Those digits will be lost, and the first six digits will not change. The algorithm will iterate without generating any output until it reaches the eof.

The solution is to detect such a case early and *rescale* both variables. In the example above, rescaling should be done when the two variables reach values of 49xxxx and 50yyyy. Rescaling should squeeze out the second most significant digits, end up with 4xxxx0 and 5yyyy9, and increment a counter cntr. The algorithm may have to rescale several times before the most significant digits become equal. At that point, the most significant digit (which can be either 4 or 5) should be output, followed by `cntr` zeros (if the two variables converged to 4) or nines (if they converged to 5).

3.8.3 Final Remarks

All the examples so far have been in decimal, since the computations involved are easier to understand in this number base. It turns out that all the algorithms and rules described here apply to the binary case as well, with only one change: every occurrence of 9 (the largest decimal digit) should be replaced by 1 (the largest binary digit).

The examples above don't seem to show any compression at all. It seems that the three example strings SWISS␣MISS, $a_2a_2a_1a_3a_3$, and $a_3a_3a_3a_3$eof are encoded into very long numbers. In fact, it seems that the length of the final code depends on the probabilities involved. The long probabilities of Table 3.25a generate long numbers in the encoding process, whereas the shorter probabilities of Table 3.21 result in the more reasonable Low and High values of Table 3.22. This behavior demands an explanation.

To figure out the kind of compression achieved by arithmetic coding, we have to consider two facts: (1) in practice, all the operations are performed on binary numbers, so we have to translate the final results to binary before we can estimate the efficiency of the compression; and (2) since the last symbol encoded is the eof, the final code does not have to be the final value of Low; it can be any value between Low and High. This makes it possible to select a shorter number as the final code that is being output.

Table 3.22 encodes the string SWISS␣MISS into Low and High values 0.71753375 and 0.717535 whose approximate binary values are 0.10110111101100000100101010111 and 0.101101111011000000101111111011. Thus, we can select 10110111101100000100 as our final, compressed output. The ten-symbol string has been encoded into a 20-bit number. Does this represent good compression?

The answer is yes. Using the probabilities of Table 3.21, it is easy to calculate the probability of the string SWISS␣MISS: it is $P = 0.5^5 \times 0.1 \times 0.2^2 \times 0.1 \times 0.1 = 1.25 \times 10^{-6}$. The entropy of this string is therefore $-\log_2 P = 19.6096$. Twenty bits is thus the minimum needed in practice to encode the string.

The symbols in Table 3.25a have probabilities 0.975, 0.001838, and 0.023162. These numbers require quite a few decimal digits, and as a result, the final Low and High values in Table 3.26 are the numbers 0.99462270125 and 0.994623638610941. Again, it seems that there is no compression, but an analysis similar to the one above shows compression that's very close to the entropy.

The probability of the string $a_2a_2a_1a_3a_3$ is $0.975^2 \times 0.001838 \times 0.023162^2 \approx 9.37361 \times 10^{-7}$, and $-\log_2 9.37361 \times 10^{-7} \approx 20.0249$.

The binary representations of the final values of Low and High in Table 3.26 are 0.11111110100111111001011111110011 and 0.1111111101001111110100111101. We can select any number between these two, so we select 1111111010011111100, a 19-bit number. (This should have been a 21-bit number, but the numbers in Table 3.26 have limited precision and are not exact.)

⋄ **Exercise 3.20:** Given the three symbols a_1, a_2, and eof, with probabilities $P_1 = 0.4$, $P_2 = 0.5$, and $P_{\mathrm{eof}} = 0.1$, encode the string $a_2a_2a_2$eof and show that the size of the final code equals the theoretical minimum.

The following argument shows why arithmetic coding can, in principle, be a very efficient compression method. We denote by s a sequence of symbols to be encoded and by b the number of bits required to encode it. As s gets longer, its probability $P(s)$ gets smaller and b gets larger. Since the logarithm is the information function, it is easy to see that b should grow at the same rate that $\log_2 P(s)$ shrinks. Their product should, therefore, be constant or close to a constant. Information theory shows that b and $P(s)$ satisfy the double inequality

$$2 \le 2^b P(s) < 4,$$

which implies

$$1 - \log_2 P(s) \le b < 2 - \log_2 P(s). \tag{3.1}$$

As s gets longer, its probability $P(s)$ shrinks, the quantity $-\log_2 P(s)$ becomes a large positive number, and the double inequality of Equation (3.1) shows that in the limit, b approaches $-\log_2 P(s)$. This is why arithmetic coding can, in principle, compress a string of symbols to its theoretical limit.

3.9 Adaptive Arithmetic Coding

Two features of arithmetic coding make it easy to extend:

1. The main encoding step is

```
Low:=Low+(High-Low+1)LowCumFreq[X]/10;
High:=Low+(High-Low+1)HighCumFreq[X]/10-1;
```

This means that in order to encode symbol X, the encoder should be given the cumulative frequencies of the symbol and of the one above it (see Table 3.21 for an example of cumulative frequencies). This also implies that the frequency of X (or, equivalently, its probability) could be changed each time it is encoded, provided that the encoder and the decoder agree on how to do this.

2. The order of the symbols in Table 3.21 is unimportant. The symbols can even be swapped in the table during the encoding process as long as the encoder and decoder do it in the same way.

With this in mind, it is easy to understand how adaptive arithmetic coding works. The encoding algorithm has two parts: the probability model and the arithmetic encoder. The model reads the next symbol from the input file and invokes the encoder, sending to it the symbol and the two required cumulative frequencies. The model then increments the count of the symbol and updates the cumulative frequencies. The point is that the symbol's probability is determined by the model from its *old* count, and the count is incremented only after the symbol has been encoded. This makes it possible for the decoder to mirror the encoder's operations. The encoder knows what the symbol is even before it is encoded, but the decoder has to decode the symbol in order to find out what it is. The decoder can therefore use only the old counts when decoding a symbol. Once the symbol has been decoded, the decoder increments its count and updates the cumulative frequencies in exactly the same way as the encoder.

The model should keep the symbols, their counts (frequencies of occurrence), and their cumulative frequencies in an array. This array should be kept in sorted order of the counts. Each time a symbol is read and its count is incremented, the model updates the cumulative frequencies and then checks to see whether it is necessary to swap the symbol with another one to keep the counts in sorted order.

It turns out that there is a simple data structure that allows for both easy search and update. This structure is a balanced binary tree housed in an array. (A balanced binary tree is a complete binary tree in which some of the bottom-right nodes may be missing.) The tree should have a node for every symbol in the alphabet, and since it is balanced, its height is $\lceil \log_2 n \rceil$, where n is the size of the alphabet. For $n = 256$ the height of the balanced binary tree is 8, so starting at the root and searching for a node takes at most eight steps. The tree is arranged such that the most probable symbols (the ones with high counts) are located near the root, which speeds up searches. Table 3.33a shows an example of a ten-symbol alphabet with counts. Table 3.33b shows the same symbols sorted by count.

a_1	a_2	a_3	a_4	a_5	a_6	a_7	a_8	a_9	a_{10}
11	12	12	2	5	1	2	19	12	8

(a)

a_8	a_2	a_3	a_9	a_1	a_{10}	a_5	a_4	a_7	a_6
19	12	12	12	11	8	5	2	2	1

(b)

Table 3.33: A Ten-Symbol Alphabet with Counts.

The sorted array "houses" the balanced binary tree of Figure 3.34a. This is a simple, elegant way to build a tree. A balanced binary tree can be housed in an array without the use of pointers. The rule is that the first array location (with index 1) houses the root, the two children of the node at array location i are housed at locations $2i$ and $2i+1$, and the parent of the node at array location j is housed at location $\lfloor j/2 \rfloor$. It is easy to see how sorting the array has placed the symbols with largest counts at and near the root.

In addition to a symbol and its count, another value is now added to each tree node, namely, the total counts of its left subtree. This will be used to compute cumulative frequencies. The corresponding array is shown in Table 3.35a.

Assume that the next symbol read from the input file is a_9. Its count is incremented from 12 to 13. The model keeps the array in sorted order by searching for the farthest array element to the left of a_9 that has a count smaller than that of a_9. This search can be a straight linear search if the array is short enough or a binary search if the array is long. In our case, symbols a_9 and a_2 should be swapped (Table 3.35b). Figure 3.34b shows the tree after the swap. Notice how the left subtree counts have been updated.

Finally, here is how the cumulative frequencies are computed from this tree. When the cumulative frequency for a symbol X is needed, the model follows the tree branches

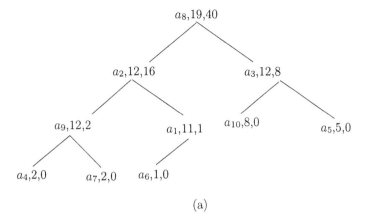

(a)

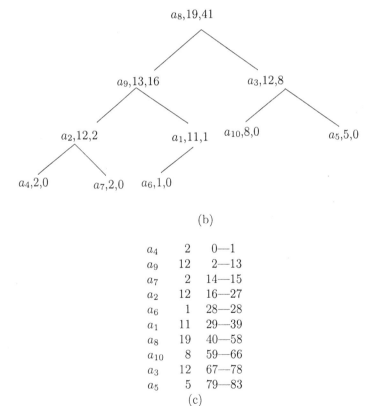

(b)

a_4	2	0—1
a_9	12	2—13
a_7	2	14—15
a_2	12	16—27
a_6	1	28—28
a_1	11	29—39
a_8	19	40—58
a_{10}	8	59—66
a_3	12	67—78
a_5	5	79—83

(c)

Figure 3.34: Adaptive Arithmetic Coding.

from the root to the node containing X while adding numbers into an integer af. Each time a right branch is taken from an interior node N, af is incremented by the two numbers (the count and the left-subtree count) found in that node. When a left branch is taken, af is not modified. When the node containing X is reached, the left-subtree count of X is added to af, and af then contains the quantity LowCumFreq[X].

a_8	a_2	a_3	a_9	a_1	a_{10}	a_5	a_4	a_7	a_6
19	12	12	12	11	8	5	2	2	1
40	16	8	2	1	0	0	0	0	0

(a)

a_8	a_9	a_3	a_2	a_1	a_{10}	a_5	a_4	a_7	a_6
19	13	12	12	11	8	5	2	2	1
41	16	8	2	1	0	0	0	0	0

(b)

Table 3.35: A Ten-Symbol Alphabet with Counts.

As an example, we trace the tree of Figure 3.34a from the root to symbol a_6, whose cumulative frequency is 28. A right branch is taken at node a_2, adding 12 and 16 to af. A left branch is taken at node a_1, adding nothing to af. When reaching a_6, its left-subtree count, 0, is added to af. The result in af is $12 + 16 = 28$, as can be verified from Figure 3.34c. The quantity HighCumFreq[X] is obtained by adding the count of a_6 (which is 1) to LowCumFreq[X].

To trace the tree and find the path from the root to a_6, the algorithm performs the following steps:

1. Find a_6 in the array housing the tree by means of a binary search. In our example, the node with a_6 is found at array location 10.
2. Integer-divide 10 by 2. The remainder is 0, which means that a_6 is the left child of its parent. The quotient is 5, which is the array location of the parent.
3. Location 5 of the array contains a_1. Integer-divide 5 by 2. The remainder is 1, which means that a_1 is the right child of its parent. The quotient is 2, which is the array location of a_1's parent.
4. Location 2 of the array contains a_2. Integer-divide 2 by 2. The remainder is 0, which means that a_2 is the left child of its parent. The quotient is 1, the array location of the root, so the process stops.

The PPM compression method (see [Cleary and Witten 84] and [Moffat 90]) is a good example of a statistical model that invokes an arithmetic encoder as described here.

Statistics are like bikinis. What they reveal
is suggestive, but what they conceal is vital.

—Aaron Levenstein, *Why People Work*

4
Dictionary Methods

Statistical compression methods use a statistical model of the data, so the quality of compression they achieve depends on how good that model is. Dictionary-based compression methods do not use a statistical model, nor do they use variable-size codes. Instead they select strings of symbols and encode each string as a *token* using a dictionary. The dictionary holds strings of symbols and it may be static or dynamic (adaptive). The former is permanent, sometimes allowing the addition of strings but no deletions, whereas the latter holds strings previously found in the input file, allowing for additions and deletions of strings as new input is read.

Perhaps the simplest example of a static dictionary is a dictionary of the English language used to compress English text. Imagine a dictionary containing perhaps half a million words (without their definitions). A word (a string of symbols terminated by a space or a punctuation mark) is read from the input file and the dictionary is searched. If a match is found, an index to the dictionary is written into the output file. Otherwise, the uncompressed word itself is written. This is an example of *logical compression.*

As a result, the output file consists of indexes and raw words, and it is important to distinguish between them. One way to do this is to add an extra bit to every item written. In principle, a 19-bit index is sufficient to specify an item in a $2^{19} = 524{,}288$-word dictionary. Thus, when a match is found, we can write a 20-bit token consisting of a flag bit (perhaps a zero) followed by a 19-bit index. When no match is found, a flag of 1 is written, followed by the size of the unmatched word, followed by the word itself.

Example: Assuming that the word `bet` is found in dictionary entry 1025, it is encoded as the 20-bit number 0|0000000010000000001. Assuming that the word `xet` is not found, it is encoded as 1|0000011|01111000|01100101|01110100. This is a 4-byte number where the 7-bit field 0000011 indicates that three more bytes follow.

Assuming that the size is written as a 7-bit number and that an average word size is five characters, an uncompressed word occupies, on average, 6 bytes (= 48 bits) in the output file. Compressing 48 bits into 20 is excellent, provided that it happens often enough. Thus, we have to answer the question "How many matches are needed in order to have overall compression?" We denote the probability of a match (the case where the word is found in the dictionary) by P. After reading and compressing N words, the size of the output file will be $N[20P + 48(1 - P)] = N[48 - 28P]$ bits. The size of the input file is (assuming five characters per word) $40N$ bits. Compression is achieved when $N[48 - 28P] < 40N$, which implies $P > 0.29$. A matching rate of 29% or better is therefore needed to achieve compression.

⋄ **Exercise 4.1:** What compression factor is obtained with $P = 0.9$?

As long as the input file consists of English text, most words will be found in a 500,000-word dictionary. Other types of data, however, may not do that well. A file containing the source code of a computer program may contain "words" such as cout, xor, and malloc that may not be found in an English dictionary. A binary file normally contains gibberish when viewed in ASCII, resulting in very few matches and in considerable expansion instead of compression.

These examples show that a static dictionary is not a good choice for a general-purpose compressor. It may, however, be a good choice for a special-purpose one. Consider a chain of hardware stores, for example. Their files may contain words such as nut, bolt, and paint many times, but words such as peanut, lightning, and painting will be rare. Special-purpose compression software for such a company may benefit from a small, specialized dictionary containing perhaps just a few hundred words. The computers in each branch would each have a copy of the dictionary, making it easy to compress files and send them between stores and offices in the chain.

In general, an adaptive dictionary-based method is preferable. Such a method can start with an empty dictionary or with a small, default dictionary, add words to it as they are found in the input file, and delete old words, since a big dictionary results in slow search. Such a method consists of a loop where each iteration starts by reading the input file and breaking it up (parsing it) into words or phrases. It then should search the dictionary for each word and, if a match is found, write a token on the output file. Otherwise, the uncompressed word should be written and also added to the dictionary. The last step in each iteration checks to see whether an old word should be deleted from the dictionary. This process may sound complicated, but it has two advantages:

1. It involves string search and match operations, rather than numerical computations. Many programmers prefer that.

2. The decoder is simple (thus, this is an asymmetric compression method). In statistical compression methods, the decoder is normally the exact opposite of the encoder (resulting in symmetric compression). In an adaptive dictionary-based method, however, the decoder has to read its input file, determine whether the current item is a token or uncompressed data, use tokens to obtain data from the dictionary, and output the final, uncompressed data. It does not have to parse the input file in a complex way, and it does not have to search the dictionary to find matches. Many programmers like that, too.

Having one's name attached to a scientific discovery, technique, or phenomenon is considered a special honor in science. Having one's name associated with an entire field of science is even more so. This is what happened to Jacob Ziv and Abraham Lempel. In the 1970s these two researchers developed the first methods, LZ77 and LZ78, for dictionary-based compression. Their ideas have been a source of inspiration to many researchers, who generalized, improved, and combined these ideas with RLE and statistical methods to form many commonly used lossless compression methods for text, images, and sound. The remainder of this chapter describes a few common LZ compression methods and shows how they were developed from the basic ideas of Ziv and Lempel.

4.1 LZ77 (Sliding Window)

The main idea of the LZ77 method (sometimes referred to as LZ1) [Ziv 77] is to use part of the previously seen input file as the dictionary. The encoder maintains a window to the input file and shifts the input in that window from right to left as strings of symbols are being encoded. Thus, the method is based on a *sliding window*. The window shown here is divided into two parts. The part on the left is called the *search buffer*. This is the current dictionary, and it always includes symbols that have recently been input and encoded. The part on the right is the *look-ahead buffer*, containing text yet to be encoded. In practical implementations, the search buffer is some thousands of bytes long, while the look-ahead buffer is only tens of bytes long. The vertical bar between the t and the e represents the current dividing line between the two buffers. Thus, we assume that the text "sir␣sid␣eastman␣easily␣t" has already been compressed, while the text "eases␣sea␣sick␣seals" still needs to be compressed.

← coded text... sir␣sid␣eastman␣easily␣t eases␣sea␣sick␣seals ... ← text to be read

The encoder scans the search buffer backward (from right to left), looking for a match to the first symbol e in the look-ahead buffer. It finds one at the e of the word easily. This e is at a distance (offset) of 8 from the right end of the search buffer. The encoder then matches as many symbols following the two e's as possible. The three symbols eas match in this case, so the length of the match is 3. The encoder then continues the backward scan, trying to find longer matches. In our case, there is one more match, at the word eastman, with offset 16, and it has the same length. The encoder selects the longest match or, if they are all the same length, the last one found and then prepares the token (16, 3, "e").

Selecting the last match rather than the first one simplifies the encoder, since it has to keep track of only the last match found. It is interesting to note that selecting the first match, while making the program somewhat more complex, also has an advantage. It selects the smallest offset. It would seem that this is not an advantage, since a token should have room for the largest possible offset. However, it is possible to follow LZ77 with Huffman or some other statistical coding of the tokens, where small offsets are assigned shorter codes. The LZH method, proposed by Bernd Herd, employs this idea. Having many small offsets improves the performance of LZH and similar methods.

⋄ **Exercise 4.2:** How does the decoder know whether the encoder selects the first match or the last match?

In general, an LZ77 token has three parts: offset, length, and next symbol in the look-ahead buffer (which, in our case, is the **second** e of the word teases). This token is written on the output file, and the window is shifted to the right (or, alternatively, the input file is moved to the left) four positions: three positions for the matched string and one position for the next symbol.

$$\dots\texttt{sir}_\sqcup\boxed{\texttt{sid}_\sqcup\texttt{eastman}_\sqcup\texttt{easily}_\sqcup\texttt{tease}}\boxed{\texttt{s}_\sqcup\texttt{sea}_\sqcup\texttt{sick}_\sqcup\texttt{seals}\dots}\dots$$

If the backward search yields no match, an LZ77 token with zero offset and length and with the unmatched symbol is written. For this reason, a token has to have a third component. Tokens with zero offset and length are common at the beginning of any compression job, when the search buffer is empty or almost empty. The first seven steps in encoding our example are the following:

sir$_\sqcup$sid$_\sqcup$eastman$_\sqcup$	$\Rightarrow$	$(0,0,\texttt{s})$
s|ir$_\sqcup$sid$_\sqcup$eastman$_\sqcup$e	$\Rightarrow$	$(0,0,\texttt{i})$
si|r$_\sqcup$sid$_\sqcup$eastman$_\sqcup$ea	$\Rightarrow$	$(0,0,\texttt{r})$
sir|$_\sqcup$sid$_\sqcup$eastman$_\sqcup$eas	$\Rightarrow$	$(0,0,_\sqcup)$
sir$_\sqcup$|sid$_\sqcup$eastman$_\sqcup$easi	$\Rightarrow$	$(4,2,\texttt{d})$

⋄ **Exercise 4.3:** What are the next two steps?

Clearly, a token of the form $(0,0,\dots)$, which encodes a single symbol, does not provide good compression. It is easy to estimate its length. The size of the offset is $\lceil\log_2 S\rceil$, where S is the length of the search buffer. In practice, the search buffer may be a few thousand bytes long, so the offset size is typically 10–12 bits. The size of the "length" field is similarly $\lceil\log_2(L-1)\rceil$, where L is the length of the look-ahead buffer (see the next paragraph for the -1). In practice, the look-ahead buffer is only a few tens of bytes long, so the size of the "length" field is just a few bits. The size of the "symbol" field is typically 8 bits, but in general it is $\lceil\log_2 A\rceil$, where A is the alphabet size. The total size of the 1-symbol token $(0,0,\dots)$ may typically be $11+5+8=24$ bits, much longer than the raw 8-bit size of the (single) symbol it encodes.

Here is an example showing why the "length" field may be longer than the size of the look-ahead buffer:

$$\dots\texttt{Mr.}_\sqcup\boxed{\texttt{alf}_\sqcup\texttt{eastman}_\sqcup\texttt{easily}_\sqcup\texttt{grows}_\sqcup\texttt{alf}}\boxed{\texttt{alfa}_\sqcup\texttt{in}_\sqcup\texttt{his}_\sqcup}\texttt{garden}\dots$$

The first symbol a in the look-ahead buffer matches the 5 a's in the search buffer. It seems that the two extreme a's match with a length of 3 and the encoder should select the last (leftmost) of them and create the token (28,3,a). In fact, it creates the token $(3,4,_\sqcup)$. The four-symbol string alfa in the look-ahead buffer is matched to the rightmost three symbols alf in the search buffer *and* the first symbol a in the look-ahead buffer. The reason for this is that the decoder can handle such a token naturally, without any modifications. It starts at position 3 of its search buffer and copies the next four symbols, one by one, extending its buffer to the right. The first three symbols are copies of the old buffer contents, and the fourth one is a copy of the first of those three. The next example is even more convincing (and only somewhat contrived):

···|alf␣eastman␣easily␣yells␣A|AAAAAAAAAA|AAAAAH...

The encoder creates the token (1,9,A), matching the first nine copies of A in the look-ahead buffer and including the tenth A. This is why, in principle, the length of a match can be up to the size of the look-ahead buffer minus 1.

The LZ77 decoder is much simpler than the encoder (thus, LZ77 is an asymmetric compression method). The decoder has to maintain a buffer equal in size to the encoder's window. The decoder inputs a token, finds the match in its buffer, writes the match and the third token field on the output file, and shifts the matched string and the third field into the buffer. This process implies that LZ77 or any of its variants is useful in cases where a file is compressed once (or just a few times) and is decompressed often. A heavily used archive of old compressed files is a good example.

At first it seems that this method does not make any assumptions about the input data. Specifically, it does not pay attention to symbol frequencies. A little thinking, however, shows that because of the nature of the sliding window, the LZ77 method always compares the look-ahead buffer to the recently input text in the search buffer, never to text that was input long ago (and has since been flushed out of the search buffer). The method therefore implicitly assumes that patterns in the input data occur close together. Data that satisfies this assumption will compress well.

The basic LZ77 method was improved in several ways by researchers and programmers during the 1980s and 1990s. One way to improve it is to use variable-size "offset" and "length" fields in the tokens. Another is to increase the sizes of both buffers. Increasing the size of the search buffer makes it possible to find better matches, but the tradeoff is increased search time. Obviously, a large search buffer requires a more sophisticated data structure that allows for fast search (Section 4.4.2). A third improvement has to do with sliding the window. The simplest approach is to move all the text in the window to the left after each match. A faster method is to replace the linear window with a *circular queue*, where sliding the window is done by resetting two pointers (Section 4.1.1). Yet another improvement is adding an extra bit (a flag) to each token, thereby eliminating the third field (Section 4.2).

4.1.1 A Circular Queue

The circular queue is a basic data structure. Physically, it is a linear array, but it is used circularly. Figure 4.1 illustrates a simple example. It shows a 16-byte array with characters being appended at the "end" and others being deleted from the "start." Both the start and end positions move, and two pointers, s and e, point to them all the time. In (a), there are the 8 characters sid␣east, with the rest of the buffer empty. In (b), all 16 bytes are occupied, and e points to the end of the buffer. In (c), the first letter s has been deleted and the l of easily inserted. Notice how pointer e is now located *to the left* of s. In (d), the two letters id have been deleted just by moving the s pointer; the characters themselves are still present in the array but have been effectively deleted. In (e), the two characters y␣ have been appended and the e pointer moved. In (f), the pointers show that the buffer ends at teas and starts at tman. Inserting new symbols into the circular queue and moving the pointers is therefore equivalent to shifting the contents of the queue. However, no actual shifting or moving is necessary.

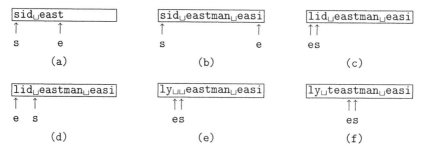

Figure 4.1: A Circular Queue.

More information on circular queues can be found in most texts on data structures.

4.2 LZSS

This version of LZ77 was developed by Storer and Szymanski in 1982 [Storer 82]. It improves LZ77 in three ways: (1) it holds the look-ahead buffer in a circular queue, (2) it holds the search buffer (the dictionary) in a binary search tree, and (3) it creates tokens with two fields instead of three.

A binary search tree is a binary tree where the left subtree of every node A contains nodes smaller than A and the right subtree contains nodes greater than A. Since the nodes of our binary search trees contain strings, we first need to know how to compare two strings and decide which one is "greater." This is easily understood by imagining that the strings appear in a dictionary or a lexicon, where they are sorted alphabetically. Clearly, the string rote precedes the string said, since r precedes s (even though o follows a), so we consider rote smaller than said. This is called *lexicographic order* (ordering strings lexicographically).

What about the string ␣abc? Most modern computers use ASCII codes to represent characters (although more and more support Unicode, discussed in Chapter 10, and some older IBM, Amdahl, Fujitsu, and Siemens mainframe computers use the old 8-bit EBCDIC code developed by IBM). The ASCII code of a blank space precedes the codes of the letters, so a string that starts with a space is considered smaller than any string that starts with a letter. In general, the *collating sequence* of the computer determines the sequence of characters arranged from small to large. Figure 4.2 shows two examples of binary search trees.

Notice the difference between the (almost) balanced tree in Figure 4.2a and the skewed one in Figure 4.2b. These trees contain the same 14 nodes, but they look and behave very differently. In the balanced tree, any node can be found in at most four steps. In the skewed tree, up to 14 steps may be needed. In either case, the maximum

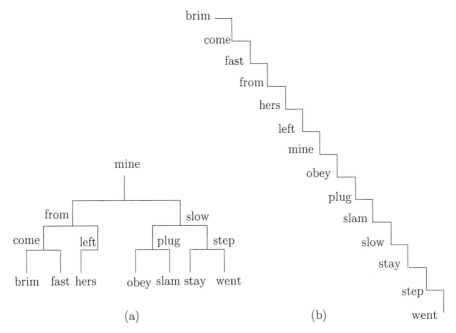

Figure 4.2: Two Binary Search Trees.

number of steps necessary to locate a node equals the height of the tree. For a skewed tree (which is really the same as a linked list), the height is the number of elements n; for a balanced tree, the height is $\lceil \log_2 n \rceil$, a much smaller number. More information on the properties of binary search trees may be found in any text on data structures.

Example: We show how a binary search tree can be used to speed up the search of the dictionary. The input file is sid␣eastman␣clumsily␣teases␣sea␣sick␣seals. To keep the example simple, we assume a window of a 16-byte search buffer followed by a 5-byte look-ahead buffer. After the first $16 + 5$ characters have been input, the sliding window is

sid␣eastman␣clum|sily␣|teases␣sea␣sick␣seals

with the string teases␣sea␣sick␣seals still waiting to be input.

The encoder scans the search buffer, creating the twelve five-character strings of Table 4.3 (twelve since $16 - 5 + 1 = 12$), which are inserted into the binary search tree, each with its offset.

The first symbol in the look-ahead buffer is s, so the encoder searches the tree for strings that start with an s. Two are found, at offsets 16 and 10, and the first of them, sid␣e (at offset 16), provides a longer match.

(We now have to sidetrack and discuss the case where a string in the tree completely matches that in the look-ahead buffer. In that case, the encoder should go back to the search buffer to attempt to match longer strings. In principle, the maximum length of a match can be $L - 1$.)

$$\text{sid}_\sqcup\text{e} \quad 16$$
$$\text{id}_\sqcup\text{ea} \quad 15$$
$$\text{d}_\sqcup\text{eas} \quad 14$$
$$_\sqcup\text{east} \quad 13$$
$$\text{eastm} \quad 12$$
$$\text{astma} \quad 11$$
$$\text{stman} \quad 10$$
$$\text{tman}_\sqcup \quad 09$$
$$\text{man}_\sqcup\text{c} \quad 08$$
$$\text{an}_\sqcup\text{cl} \quad 07$$
$$\text{n}_\sqcup\text{clu} \quad 06$$
$$_\sqcup\text{clum} \quad 05$$

Table 4.3: Five-Character Strings.

In our example, the match is of length 2, and the two-field token $(16, 2)$ is emitted. The encoder now has to slide the window two positions to the right and update the tree. The new window is

si│d␣eastman␣clumsi│ly␣te│ases␣sea␣sick␣seals

The tree should be updated by deleting strings sid␣e and id␣ea and inserting the new strings clums and lumsi. If a longer, k-letter string is matched, the window has to be shifted k positions, and the tree should be updated by deleting k strings and adding k new strings—but which ones?

A little thinking shows that the k strings to be deleted are the first ones in the search buffer before the shift, and the k strings to be added are the last ones in it after the shift. A simple procedure for updating the tree is to prepare a string consisting of the first five letters in the search buffer, find it in the tree, and delete it. Then slide the buffer one position to the right (or shift the data to the left), prepare a string consisting of the last five letters in the search buffer, and append it to the tree. This should be repeated k times. (End of example.)

Since each update deletes and adds the same number of strings, the tree size never changes. It always contains T nodes, where T is the length of the search buffer minus the length of the look-ahead buffer plus 1 ($T = S - L + 1$). The shape of the tree, however, may change significantly. As nodes are being added and deleted, the tree may change its shape between a completely skewed tree (the worst case for searching) and a balanced one, the ideal shape for searching.

The third improvement of LZSS over LZ77 is in the tokens created by the encoder. An LZSS token contains just an offset and a length. If no match is found, the encoder emits the uncompressed code of the next symbol instead of the wasteful three-field token $(0, 0, \ldots)$. To distinguish between tokens and uncompressed codes, each is preceded by a single bit (a flag).

In practice, the search buffer may be a few thousand bytes long, so the offset field would typically be 11–13 bits. The size of the look-ahead buffer should be selected such that the total size of a token would be 16 bits (2 bytes). For example, if the search buffer size is 2 Kb ($= 2^{11}$), then the look-ahead buffer should be 32 bytes long ($= 2^5$). The offset field would be 11 bits long and the length field 5 bits (the size of the look-ahead buffer). With this choice of buffer sizes, the encoder will emit either 2-byte tokens or 1-byte uncompressed ASCII codes. But what about the flag bits? A good practical idea is to collect eight output items (tokens and ASCII codes) in a small buffer and then output one byte consisting of the eight flags, followed by the eight items (which are 1 or 2 bytes-long each).

> The only place where success comes before work is in the dictionary.
> —Vidal Sassoon

4.2.1 LZ77 Deficiencies

Before we discuss LZ78, let's summarize the deficiencies of LZ77 and its variants. It has already been mentioned that LZ77 uses the built-in implicit assumption that patterns in the input data occur close together. Data files that don't satisfy this assumption compress poorly. A common example is text where a certain word, say economy, occurs often but is uniformly distributed throughout the text. When this word is shifted into the look-ahead buffer, its previous occurrence may have already been shifted out of the search buffer. A better algorithm would save commonly occurring strings in the dictionary and not simply slide the dictionary all the time.

Another disadvantage of LZ77 is the limited size L of the look-ahead buffer. The size of matched strings is limited to $L - 1$, but L must be kept small, since the process of matching strings involves comparing individual symbols. If L were doubled in size, compression would improve, since longer matches would be possible, but the encoder would be much slower when searching for long matches. The size S of the search buffer is also limited. A large search buffer produces better compression but slows down the encoder, since searching takes longer (even with a binary search tree). Increasing the sizes of the two buffers also means creating longer tokens, thereby reducing the compression ratio. With 2-byte tokens, compressing a 2-character string into one token results in 2 bytes plus 1 flag. Writing the two characters as two raw ASCII codes results in 2 bytes plus 2 flags, a very small difference in size. The encoder should, in such a case, use the latter choice and write the two characters in uncompressed form, saving time and wasting just one bit. We say that the encoder has a 2-byte *break-even* point. With longer tokens, the break-even point increases to 3 bytes.

4.3 LZ78

The LZ78 method (sometimes referred to as LZ2) [Ziv 78] does not use any search buffer, look-ahead buffer, or sliding window. Instead, there is a dictionary of previously encountered strings. This dictionary starts empty (or almost empty), and its size is limited only by the amount of available memory. The encoder outputs two-field tokens. The first field is a pointer to the dictionary; the second is the code of a symbol. Tokens do not contain the length of a string, since this length is implied in the dictionary. Each token corresponds to a string of input symbols, and that string is added to the dictionary after the token is written on the compressed file. Nothing is ever deleted from the dictionary, which is both an advantage over LZ77 (since future strings can match even strings seen in the distant past) and a liability (since the dictionary tends to grow fast).

The dictionary starts with the null string at position zero. As symbols are input and encoded, strings are added to the dictionary at positions 1, 2, and so on. When the next symbol x is read from the input file, the dictionary is searched for an entry with the one-symbol string x. If none is found, x is added to the next available position in the dictionary, and the token $(0, x)$ is output. This token indicates the string "null x" (a concatenation of the null string and x). If an entry with x is found (at, say, position 37), the next symbol y is read, and the dictionary is searched for an entry containing the two-symbol string xy. If none is found, then string xy is added to the next available position in the dictionary, and the token $(37, y)$ is output. This token indicates the string xy, since 37 is the dictionary position of string x. The process continues until the end of the input file is reached.

In general, the current symbol is read and becomes a one-symbol string. The encoder then tries to find it in the dictionary. If the symbol is found in the dictionary, the next symbol is read and is concatenated with the first to form a two-symbol string that the encoder then tries to locate in the dictionary. As long as those strings are found in the dictionary, more symbols are read and concatenated to the string. At a certain point, the string is not found in the dictionary, so the encoder adds it to the dictionary and outputs a token with the last dictionary match as its first field and the last symbol of the string (the one that caused the search to fail) as its second field. Table 4.4 shows the steps in encoding sir␣sid␣eastman␣easily␣teases␣sea␣sick␣seals.

Dictionary		Token		Dictionary		Token
0	null					
1	s	$(0,s)$		8	a	$(0,a)$
2	i	$(0,i)$		9	st	$(1,t)$
3	r	$(0,r)$		10	m	$(0,m)$
4	␣	$(0,␣)$		11	an	$(8,n)$
5	si	$(1,i)$		12	␣ea	$(7,a)$
6	d	$(0,d)$		13	sil	$(5,l)$
7	␣e	$(4,e)$		14	y	$(0,y)$

Table 4.4: First 14 Encoding Steps in LZ78.

⋄ **Exercise 4.4:** Complete Table 4.4.

In each step, the string added to the dictionary is the one being encoded, minus its last symbol. In a typical compression run, the dictionary starts with short strings, but as more text is being input and processed, longer and longer strings are added to it. The size of the dictionary can either be fixed or may be determined by the size of the available memory each time the LZ78 compression program is executed. A large dictionary may contain more strings and so allow for longer matches, but the tradeoff is longer pointers (and therefore bigger tokens) and slower dictionary search.

A good data structure for the dictionary is a tree, but not a binary one. The tree starts with the null string as the root. All the strings that start with the null string (strings for which the token pointer is zero) are added to the tree as children of the root. In the example, those are s, i, r, ⊔, d, a, m, y, e, c, and k. Each of these becomes the root of a subtree as shown in Figure 4.5. For example, all the strings that start with s (the four strings si, sil, st, and s(eof)) constitute the subtree of node s.

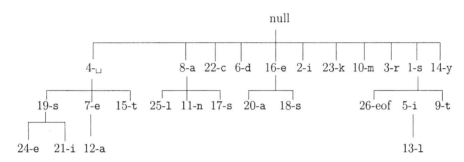

Figure 4.5: An LZ78 Dictionary Tree.

Given an alphabet with 8-bit symbols, there are 256 different symbols. In principle, each node in the tree could have up to 256 children. Adding a child to a tree node should therefore be a dynamic process. When the node is first created, it has no children and should not reserve any memory space for them. As a child is added to the node, memory space should be claimed for it. Since no nodes are ever deleted, there is no need to reclaim memory space, which simplifies the memory management task somewhat.

Such a tree makes it easy to search for a string and to add strings. To search for sil, for example, the program looks for the child s of the root, then for the child i of s, and so on, going down the tree. Here are some examples:

1. When the s of sid is input in step 5, the encoder finds node "1-s" in the tree as a child of "null". It then inputs the next symbol i, but node s does not have a child i (in fact, it has no children at all at this point), so the encoder adds node "5-i" as a child of "1-s", which effectively adds the string si to the tree.

2. When the blank space between eastman and easily is input in step 12, a similar situation occurs. The encoder finds node "4-⊔", inputs e, finds "7-e", inputs a, but "7-e" does not have "a" as a child, so the encoder adds node "12-a", which effectively adds the string "⊔ea" to the tree.

A tree of the type described here is called a *trie*. In general, a trie is a tree in which the branching structure at any level is determined by just part of a data item, not the entire item. In the case of LZ78, each string added to the tree effectively adds just one symbol and does so by adding a branch.

Since the total size of the tree is limited, it may fill up during compression. This, in fact, happens all the time except when the input file is unusually small. The original

LZ78 method does not specify what to do in such a case, so here are some possible solutions.

- The simplest solution is to freeze the dictionary when it fills up. No new nodes should be added and the tree becomes a static dictionary, but it can still be used to encode strings.
- Delete the entire tree once it fills up and start with a new, empty tree. This solution effectively breaks the input into blocks, each with its own dictionary. If the content of the input varies from block to block, this solution will produce good compression, since it will eliminate a dictionary with strings that are unlikely to be used in the future. We can say that this solution implicitly assumes that future symbols will benefit more from new data than from old (the same implicit assumption used by LZ77).
- The UNIX `compress` utility uses a more complex solution. This utility (also called LZC) uses LZW (Section 4.4) with a growing dictionary. It starts with a small dictionary of just $2^9 = 512$ entries (with the first 256 of them already filled up). While this dictionary is being used, 9-bit pointers are written onto the output file. When the original dictionary fills up, its size is doubled to 1024 entries, and 10-bit pointers are used from then on. This process continues until the pointer size reaches a maximum set by the user (it can be set to between 9 and 16 bits, with 16 as the default value). When the largest allowed dictionary fills up, the program continues without changing the dictionary (which then becomes static) but with monitoring of the compression ratio. If the ratio falls below a predefined threshold, the dictionary is deleted, and a new 512-entry dictionary is started. This way, the dictionary never gets too out of date.
- When the dictionary is full, delete some of the least recently used entries to make room for new ones. Unfortunately, there is no good algorithm to decide which entries to delete and how many.

The LZ78 decoder works by building and maintaining the dictionary in the same way as the encoder. It is therefore more complex than the LZ77 decoder.

> Words—so innocent and powerless as they are, as standing in a dictionary, how potent for good and evil they become in the hands of one who knows how to combine them.
>
> —Nathaniel Hawthorne

4.4 LZW

This is a popular variant of LZ78, developed by Terry Welch in 1984 (see [Welch 84] and [Phillips 92]). Its main feature is eliminating the second field of a token. An LZW token consists of just a pointer to the dictionary. To best understand LZW, we should temporarily forget that the dictionary is a tree and should think of it as an array of variable-size strings. The LZW method starts by initializing the dictionary to all the symbols in the alphabet. In the common case of 8-bit symbols, the first 256 entries of the dictionary (entries 0 through 255) are occupied before any data is input. Because the dictionary is initialized, the next input symbol will always be found in the dictionary. This is why an LZW token can consist of just a pointer and does not have to contain a symbol code as in LZ77 and LZ78.

(LZW has been patented. In the United States, this troublesome patent expired on 20 June 2003, but in many parts of the world it expires in 2004. The issue of software patents is discussed in [Salomon 04].)

The principle of LZW is that the encoder inputs symbols one by one and accumulates them in a string I. After each symbol is input and is concatenated to I, the dictionary is searched for string I. As long as I is found in the dictionary, the process continues. At a certain point, adding the next symbol x causes the search to fail; string I is in the dictionary, but string Ix (symbol x appended to I) is not. At this point, the encoder (1) outputs the dictionary pointer that points to string I, (2) saves string Ix (which is now called a *phrase*) in the next available dictionary entry, and (3) initializes string I to symbol x. To illustrate this process, we again use the text string sir␣sid␣eastman␣easily␣teases␣sea␣sick␣seals. The steps are as follows:

- Initialize entries 0–255 of the dictionary to all 256 8-bit bytes.
- The first symbol s is input and is found in the dictionary (in entry 115, since this is the ASCII code of s). The next symbol i is input, but si is not found in the dictionary. The encoder performs the following: (1) outputs 115, (2) saves string si in the next available dictionary entry (entry 256), and (3) initializes I to the symbol i.
- The r of sir is input, but string ir is not in the dictionary. The encoder (1) outputs 105 (the ASCII code of i), (2) saves string ir in the next available dictionary entry (entry 257), and (3) initializes I to the symbol r.

Table 4.6 summarizes all the steps of this process. Table 4.7 shows some of the original 256 entries in the LZW dictionary plus the entries added during encoding of the string above. The complete output file is as follows (only the numbers are output, not the strings in parentheses):

115 (s), 105 (i), 114 (r), 32 (␣), 256 (si), 100 (d), 32 (␣), 101 (e), 97 (a), 115 (s), 116 (t), 109 (m), 97 (a), 110 (n), 262 (␣e), 264 (as), 105 (i), 108 (l), 121 (y), 32 (␣), 116 (t), 263 (ea), 115 (s), 101 (e), 115 (s), 259 (␣s), 263 (ea), 259 (␣s), 105 (i), 99 (c), 107 (k), 280 (␣se), 97 (a), 108 (l), 115 (s), eof.

Figure 4.8 is a pseudocode listing of the algorithm. We denote by λ the empty string and by <<a,b>> the concatenation of strings a and b.

The line append <<di,ch>> to the dictionary is of special interest. It is clear that in practice, the dictionary may fill up. This line should therefore include a test for a full dictionary and certain actions for the case where it is full.

Since the first 256 entries of the dictionary are occupied right from the start, pointers to the dictionary have to be longer than 8 bits. A simple implementation would typically use 16-bit pointers, which allow for a 64K-entry dictionary (where $64K = 2^{16} = 65,536$). Such a dictionary will, of course, fill up very quickly in all but the smallest compression jobs. The same problem exists with LZ78, and any solutions used with LZ78 can also be used with LZW. Another interesting fact about LZW

I	in dict?	new entry	output	I	in dict?	new entry	output
s	Y			y	Y		
si	N	256-si	115 (s)	y	N	274-y	121 (y)
i	Y			␣	Y		
ir	N	257-ir	105 (i)	␣t	N	275-␣t	32 (␣)
r	Y			t	Y		
r	N	258-r	114 (r)	te	N	276-te	116 (t)
␣	Y			e	Y		
␣s	N	259-␣s	32 (␣)	ea	Y		
s	Y			eas	N	277-eas	263 (ea)
si	Y			s	Y		
sid	N	260-sid	256 (si)	se	N	278-se	115 (s)
d	Y			e	Y		
d	N	261-d	100 (d)	es	N	279-es	101 (e)
␣	Y			s	Y		
␣e	N	262-␣e	32 (␣)	s	N	280-s	115 (s)
e	Y			␣	Y		
ea	N	263-ea	101 (e)	␣s	Y		
a	Y			␣se	N	281-␣se	259 (␣s)
as	N	264-as	97 (a)	e	Y		
s	Y			ea	Y		
st	N	265-st	115 (s)	ea	N	282-ea	263 (ea)
t	Y			␣	Y		
tm	N	266-tm	116 (t)	␣s	Y		
m	Y			␣si	N	283-␣si	259 (␣s)
ma	N	267-ma	109 (m)	i	Y		
a	Y			ic	N	284-ic	105 (i)
an	N	268-an	97 (a)	c	Y		
n	Y			ck	N	285-ck	99 (c)
n	N	269-n	110 (n)	k	Y		
␣	Y			k	N	286-k	107 (k)
␣e	Y			␣	Y		
␣ea	N	270-␣ea	262 (␣e)	␣s	Y		
a	Y			␣se	Y		
as	Y			␣sea	N	287-␣sea	281 (␣se)
asi	N	271-asi	264 (as)	a	Y		
i	Y			al	N	288-al	97 (a)
il	N	272-il	105 (i)	l	Y		
l	Y			ls	N	289-ls	108 (l)
ly	N	273-ly	108 (l)	s	Y		
				s,eof	N		115 (s)

Table 4.6: Encoding sir␣sid␣eastman␣easily␣teases␣sea␣sick␣seals.

0	NULL	110	n	262	␣e	276	te
1	SOH	...		263	ea	277	eas
...		115	s	264	as	278	se
32	SP	116	t	265	st	279	es
...		...		266	tm	280	s
97	a	121	y	267	ma	281	␣se
98	b	...		268	an	282	ea
99	c	255	255	269	n	283	␣si
100	d	256	si	270	␣ea	284	ic
101	e	257	ir	271	asi	285	ck
...		258	r	272	il	286	k
107	k	259	␣s	273	ly	287	␣sea
108	l	260	sid	274	y	288	al
109	m	261	d	275	␣t	289	ls

Table 4.7: An LZW Dictionary.

```
for i:=0 to 255 do
  append i as a 1-symbol string to the dictionary;
append λ to the dictionary;
di:=dictionary index of λ;
repeat
  read(ch);
  if <<di,ch>> is in the dictionary then
    di:=dictionary index of <<di,ch>>;
  else
    output(di);
    append <<di,ch>> to the dictionary;
    di:=dictionary index of ch;
  endif;
until end-of-input;
```

Figure 4.8: The LZW Algorithm.

is that strings in the dictionary become only one character longer at a time. It therefore takes a long time to get long strings in the dictionary and thus provides a chance to achieve really good compression. We can say that LZW adapts slowly to its input data.

◊ **Exercise 4.5:** Apply LZW to encode the string alf␣eats␣alfalfa. Show the encoder output and the new entries added by it to the dictionary.

◊ **Exercise 4.6:** Analyze the LZW compression of the string "aaaa...".

4.4.1 LZW Decoding

In order to understand how the LZW decoder works, we should first recall the three steps the encoder performs each time it writes something on the output file: (1) it outputs the dictionary pointer that points to string I, (2) it saves string Ix in the next available entry of the dictionary, and (3) it initializes string I to symbol x.

The decoder starts with the first entries of its dictionary initialized to all the symbols of the alphabet (normally 256 symbols). It then reads its input file (which consists of pointers to the dictionary) and uses each pointer to retrieve uncompressed symbols from its dictionary and write them on its output file. It also builds its dictionary in the same way as the encoder (this fact is usually expressed by saying that the encoder and decoder are *synchronized*, or that they work in *lockstep*).

In the first decoding step, the decoder inputs the first pointer and uses it to retrieve a dictionary item I. This is a string of symbols, and it is written on the decoder's output file. String Ix needs to be saved in the dictionary, but symbol x is still unknown; it will be the first symbol in the next string retrieved from the dictionary.

In each decoding step after the first, the decoder inputs the next pointer, retrieves the next string J from the dictionary, writes it on the output file, isolates its first symbol x, and saves string Ix in the next available dictionary entry (after checking to make sure string Ix is not already in the dictionary). The decoder then moves J to I and is ready for the next step.

In our sir sid... example, the first pointer that is input by the decoder is 115. This corresponds to the string s, which is retrieved from the dictionary, gets stored in I, and becomes the first item written on the decoder's output file. The next pointer is 105, so string i is retrieved into J and is also written on the output file. J's first symbol is concatenated with I to form string si, which does not exist in the dictionary, and is therefore added to it as entry 256. Variable J is moved to I, so I is now the string i. The next pointer is 114, so string r is retrieved from the dictionary into J and is also written on the output file. J's first symbol is concatenated with I to form string ir, which does not exist in the dictionary, and is added to it as entry 257. Variable J is moved to I, so I is now the string r. The next step reads pointer 32, writes "␣" on the output file, and saves string "r␣".

◊ **Exercise 4.7:** Decode the string alf␣eats␣alfalfa by using the encoding results from Exercise 4.5.

◊ **Exercise 4.8:** Given a two-symbol alphabet with the symbols a and b, show the first few steps for encoding and decoding the string "ababab...".

4.4.2 LZW Dictionary Structure

Up until now we have assumed that the LZW dictionary is an array of variable-size strings. To understand why a trie is a better data structure for the dictionary, we need to recall how the encoder works. It inputs symbols and concatenates them into a variable I as long as the string in I is found in the dictionary. At a certain point the encoder inputs the first symbol x, which causes the search to fail (string Ix is not in the dictionary). It then adds Ix to the dictionary. This means that each string added to the dictionary effectively adds just one new symbol, x. (Phrased another way: for each dictionary string of more than one symbol, there exists a "parent" string in the dictionary that is one symbol shorter.)

A tree similar to the one used by LZ78 is therefore a good data structure, since adding string Ix to such a tree is done by adding one node with x. The main problem is that each node in the LZW tree may have many children (the tree is multiway, not binary). Imagine the node for the letter a in entry 97. Initially it has no children, but if the string ab is added to the tree, node 97 receives one child. Later, when, say, the string ae is added, node 97 receives a second child, and so on. The data structure for the tree should therefore be designed such that a node could have any number of children without having to reserve any memory for them in advance.

One way of designing such a data structure is to house the tree in an array of nodes, each a structure with two fields: a symbol and a pointer to the parent node. A node has no pointers to any child nodes. Moving down the tree from a node to one of its children is done by a *hashing process* in which the pointer to the node and the symbol of the child are hashed to create a new pointer.

Suppose that string abc has already been input, symbol by symbol, and has been stored in the tree in the three nodes at locations 97, 266, and 284. Following that, the encoder has just input the next symbol d. The encoder now searches for string abcd or, more specifically, for a node containing the symbol d whose parent is at location 284. The encoder hashes the 284 (the pointer to string abc) and the 100 (ASCII code of d) to create a pointer to some node, say, 299. The encoder then examines node 299. There are three cases:

1. The node is unused. This means that abcd is not yet in the dictionary and should be added to it. The encoder adds it to the tree by storing the parent pointer 284 and ASCII code 100 in the node. The result is the following:

Node				
Address	:	97	266	284	299
Contents	:	(-:a)	(97:b)	(266:c)	(284:d)
Represents:		a	ab	abc	abcd

2. The node contains a parent pointer of 284 and the ASCII code of d. This means that string abcd is already in the tree. The encoder inputs the next symbol, say e, and searches the dictionary tree for string abcde.

3. The node contains something else. This means that another hashing of a pointer and an ASCII code has resulted in 299, and node 299 already contains information from another string. This is called a *collision*, and it can be dealt with in several ways. The

simplest way to deal with a collision is to increment pointer 299 and examine nodes 300, 301,... until an unused node is found or until a node with (284:d) is found.

In practice, we build nodes that are structures with three fields, a pointer to the parent node, the pointer (or index) created by the hashing process, and the code (normally ASCII) of the symbol contained in the node. The second field is necessary because of collisions. A node can therefore be illustrated by the triplet

parent
index
symbol

Example: We illustrate this data structure using string `ababab...` (see Exercise 4.8). The dictionary is an array `dict` where each entry is a structure with the three fields `parent`, `index`, and `symbol`. We refer to a field by, e.g., `dict[pointer].parent`, where `pointer` is an index to the array. The dictionary is initialized to the two entries a and b. (To keep the example simple, we use no ASCII codes. We assume that a has code 1 and b has code 2.) The first few steps of the encoder are as follows:

Step 0: Mark all dictionary locations from 3 on as unused.

Step 1: The first symbol a is input into variable I. What is actually input is the code of a, which in our example is 1, so I = 1. Since this is the first symbol, the encoder assumes that it is in the dictionary and so does not perform any search.

Step 2: The second symbol b is input into J, so J = 2. The encoder has to search for string ab in the dictionary. It executes `pointer:=hash(I,J)`. Let's assume that the result is 5. Field `dict[pointer].index` contains "unused", since location 5 is still empty, so string ab is not in the dictionary. It is added by executing

```
dict[pointer].parent:=I;
dict[pointer].index:=pointer;
dict[pointer].symbol:=J;
```

with `pointer=5`. J is moved into I, so I = 2.

Step 3: The third symbol a is input into J, so J = 1. The encoder has to search for string ba in the dictionary. It executes `pointer:=hash(I,J)`. Let's assume that the result is 8. Field `dict[pointer].index` contains "unused", so string ba is not in the dictionary. It is added as before by executing

```
dict[pointer].parent:=I;
dict[pointer].index:=pointer;
dict[pointer].symbol:=J;
```

with `pointer=8`. J is moved into I, so I = 1.

```
/  /  /  /  1  /  /  2  /
1  2  -  -  5  -  -  8  -  ...
a  b        b        a
```

Step 4: The fourth symbol b is input into J, so J=2. The encoder has to search for string ab in the dictionary. It executes `pointer:=hash(I,J)`. We know from step 2 that the result is 5. Field `dict[pointer].index` contains 5, so string ab is in the dictionary. The value of `pointer` is moved into I, so I = 5.

Step 5: The fifth symbol a is input into J, so J = 1. The encoder has to search for string aba in the dictionary. It executes as usual `pointer:=hash(I,J)`. Let's assume that the result is 8 (a collision). Field `dict[pointer].index` contains 8, which looks good, but field `dict[pointer].parent` contains 2 instead of the expected 5, so the hash function knows that this is a collision and string aba is not in dictionary entry 8. It increments `pointer` as many times as necessary until it finds a dictionary entry with index=8 and parent=5 or until it finds an unused entry. In the former case, string aba is in the dictionary, and `pointer` is moved to I. In the latter case aba is not in the dictionary, and the encoder saves it in the entry pointed at by `pointer`, and moves J to I.

```
/  /  /  /  1  /  /  2  5  /
1  2  -  -  5  -  -  8  8  -  ...
a  b        b        a  a
```

Example: The 15 hashing steps for encoding the string alf␣eats␣alfalfa are shown here. The encoding process itself was illustrated in detail in Exercise 4.5. The results of the hashing are arbitrary; they are not the results produced by a real hash function. The 12 trie nodes constructed for this string are shown in Figure 4.9.

1. Hash(l,97) → 278. Array location 278 is set to (97, 278, l).
2. Hash(f,108) → 266. Array location 266 is set to (108, 266, f).
3. Hash(␣,102) → 269. Array location 269 is set to (102, 269, ␣).
4. Hash(e,32) → 267. Array location 267 is set to (32, 267, e).
5. Hash(a,101) → 265. Array location 265 is set to (101, 265, a).
6. Hash(t,97) → 272. Array location 272 is set to (97, 272, t).
7. Hash(s,116) → 265. A collision! Skip to the next available location, 268, and set it to (116, 265, s). This is why the index needs to be stored.
8. Hash(␣,115) → 270. Array location 270 is set to (115, 270, ␣).
9. Hash(a,32) → 268. A collision! Skip to the next available location, 271, and set it to (32, 268, a).
10. Hash(l,97) → 278. Array location 278 already contains index 278 and symbol l from step 1, so there is no need to store anything else or to add a new trie entry.
11. Hash(f,278) → 276. Array location 276 is set to (278, 276, f).
12. Hash(a,102) → 274. Array location 274 is set to (102, 274, a).
13. Hash(l,97) → 278. Array location 278 already contains index 278 and symbol l from step 1, so there is no need to do anything.
14. Hash(f,278) → 276. Array location 276 already contains index 276 and symbol f from step 11, so there is no need to do anything.
15. Hash(a,276) → 274. A collision! Skip to the next available location, 275, and set it to (276, 274, a).

265	266	267	268	269	270	271	272	273	274	275	276	277	278
/	/	/	/	/	/	/	/	/	/	/	/	/	97
-	-	-	-	-	-	-	-	-	-	-	-	-	278
													1

265	266	267	268	269	270	271	272	273	274	275	276	277	278
/	108	/	/	/	/	/	/	/	/	/	/	/	97
-	266	-	-	-	-	-	-	-	-	-	-	-	278
	f												1

265	266	267	268	269	270	271	272	273	274	275	276	277	278
/	108	/	/	102	/	/	/	/	/	/	/	/	97
-	266	-	-	269	-	-	-	-	-	-	-	-	278
	f			␣									1

265	266	267	268	269	270	271	272	273	274	275	276	277	278
/	108	32	/	102	/	/	/	/	/	/	/	/	97
-	266	267	-	269	-	-	-	-	-	-	-	-	278
	f	e		␣									1

265	266	267	268	269	270	271	272	273	274	275	276	277	278
101	108	32	/	102	/	/	/	/	/	/	/	/	97
265	266	267	-	269	-	-	-	-	-	-	-	-	278
a	f	e		␣									1

265	266	267	268	269	270	271	272	273	274	275	276	277	278
101	108	32	/	102	/	/	97	/	/	/	/	/	97
265	266	267	-	269	-	-	272	-	-	-	-	-	278
a	f	e		␣			t						1

265	266	267	268	269	270	271	272	273	274	275	276	277	278
101	108	32	116	102	/	/	97	/	/	/	/	/	97
265	266	267	265	269	-	-	272	-	-	-	-	-	278
a	f	e	s	␣			t						1

265	266	267	268	269	270	271	272	273	274	275	276	277	278
101	108	32	116	102	115	/	97	/	/	/	/	/	97
265	266	267	265	269	270	-	272	-	-	-	-	-	278
a	f	e	s	␣	␣		t						1

265	266	267	268	269	270	271	272	273	274	275	276	277	278
101	108	32	116	102	115	32	97	/	/	/	/	/	97
265	266	267	265	269	270	268	272	-	-	-	-	-	278
a	f	e	s	␣	␣	a	t						1

265	266	267	268	269	270	271	272	273	274	275	276	277	278
101	108	32	116	102	115	32	97	/	/	/	278	/	97
265	266	267	265	269	270	268	272	-	-	-	276	-	278
a	f	e	s	␣	␣	a	t				f		1

265	266	267	268	269	270	271	272	273	274	275	276	277	278
101	108	32	116	102	115	32	97	/	102	/	278	/	97
265	266	267	265	269	270	268	272	-	274	-	276	-	278
a	f	e	s	␣	␣	a	t		a		f		1

265	266	267	268	269	270	271	272	273	274	275	276	277	278
101	108	32	116	102	115	32	97	/	102	276	278	/	97
265	266	267	265	269	270	268	272	-	274	274	276	-	278
a	f	e	s	␣	␣	a	t		a	a	f		1

Figure 4.9: Growing an LZW Trie for alf␣eats␣alfalfa.

Readers who have carefully followed the discussion up to this point will be happy to learn that the LZW decoder's use of the dictionary tree array is simple and no hashing is needed. The decoder starts, like the encoder, by initializing the first 256 array locations. It then reads pointers from its input file and uses each pointer to locate a symbol in the dictionary.

In the first decoding step, the decoder inputs the first pointer and uses it to retrieve a dictionary item I. This is a symbol that is now written by the decoder on its output file. String Ix needs to be saved in the dictionary, but symbol x is still unknown; it will be the first symbol in the next string retrieved from the dictionary.

In each decoding step after the first, the decoder inputs the next pointer and uses it to retrieve the next string J from the dictionary and write it on the output file. If the pointer is, say, 8, the decoder examines field `dict[8].index`. If this field equals 8, then this is the right node. Otherwise, the decoder examines consecutive array locations until it finds the right one.

Once the right tree node is found, the **parent** field is used to go back up the tree and retrieve the individual symbols of the string *in reverse order*. The symbols are then placed in J in the right order (see point 2 of the string reversal discussion after the example) and the decoder isolates the first symbol x of J and saves string Ix in the next available array location. (String I was found in the previous step, so only one node, with symbol x, needs be added.) The decoder then moves J to I and is ready for the next step.

Retrieving a complete string from the LZW tree therefore involves following the pointers in the **parent** fields. This is equivalent to moving *up* the tree, which is why the hash function is no longer needed.

Example: The previous example describes the 15 hashing steps in the encoding of string `alf␣eats␣alfalfa`. The last step sets array location 275 to (276,274,a) and writes 275 (a pointer to location 275) on the compressed file. When this file is read by the decoder, pointer 275 is the last item that is input and processed by the decoder. The decoder finds symbol a in the **symbol** field of location 275 (this indicates that the string stored at 275 ends with an a) and a pointer to location 276 in the **parent** field. The decoder then examines location 276, where it finds symbol f and parent pointer 278. Examining location 278, the decoder finds symbol l and a pointer to 97. Finally, in location 97, the decoder finds symbol a and a null pointer. The (reversed) string is therefore `afla`. There is no need for the decoder to do any hashing or to use the **index** fields.

The last point to discuss is string reversal. Two commonly used approaches are outlined here:

Use a stack. A stack is a common data structure in modern computers. It is an array in memory that is accessed at one end only. At any time, the item that was last pushed into the stack will be the first one to be popped out (last-in-first-out, or LIFO). Symbols retrieved from the dictionary are pushed into the stack. When the last one has been retrieved and pushed, the stack is popped, symbol by symbol, into variable J. When the stack is empty, the entire string has been reversed. This is a common way to reverse a string.

Retrieve symbols from the dictionary and concatenate them into J *from right to left*. When done, the string will be stored in J in the right order. Variable J must be long enough to accommodate the longest possible string, but then it has to be long enough even when a stack is used.

◇ **Exercise 4.9:** What is the longest string that can be retrieved from the LZW dictionary during decoding?

4.4.3 LZW in Practice

The discussion and examples in this chapter have assumed that the data being compressed is text, but dictionary-based methods perform well on all types of data and come close to being general. The early dictionary methods were clumsy, but LZW is an efficient algorithm whose 1984 publication has caused a revolution. LZW has strongly affected the data compression community and has influenced many to come up with implementations and variants of this method. Some of the most important LZW spin-offs are described in [Salomon 04].

> [Ramsay] MacDonald has the gift of compressing the largest amount of words into the smallest amount of thoughts.
>
> —Winston Churchill

4.5 Summary

The dictionary-based methods presented here are different but are based on the same principle. They read the input file symbol by symbol and add phrases to the dictionary. The phrases are symbols or strings of symbols from the input. The main difference between the methods is in deciding what phrases to add to the dictionary. When a string in the input file matches a dictionary phrase, the encoder outputs the position of the match in the dictionary. Compression is achieved when that position requires fewer bits than the matched string.

In general, dictionary-based methods, when carefully implemented, give better compression than statistical methods. This is why many popular compression programs are dictionary based or involve a dictionary as one of several compression steps. More dictionary-based methods can be found in [Salomon 04].

> Luckily, he went on, you have come to exactly the right place with your interesting problem, for there is no such word as "impossible" in my dictionary. In fact, he added, brandishing the abused book, everything between "herring" and "marmalade" appears to be missing.
>
> —Douglas Adams, *Dirk Gently's Holistic Detective Agency*

5
Image Compression

The modern field of data compression is vast, encompassing many methods and approaches for the compression of different types of data, such as text, images, video, and audio. Of these types, image compression is special because (1) it was the first field where users routinely had large files that needed efficient compression and (2) it was the first field that allowed the development of *lossy* compression methods.

In ASCII, each character occupies one byte. A typical book of a quarter of a million words may consist of about a million characters and therefore occupies about 1 Mb. However, if one image is added to the book, its size may double, since the image file may easily be 1 Mb or even bigger.

Image files tend to be large because an image is two-dimensional and because present-day displays can handle many colors, requiring each dot (pixel) in the image to be represented by many (typically 24) bits.

Text compression is always lossless. There may be documents where some of the text is unimportant and may be omitted during compression, but no algorithms exist that allow a computer to independently decide what text can be dropped. In contrast, there are many efficient lossy algorithms for image compression. Such an algorithm may delete much image information when the image is compressed, thereby resulting in excellent compression. The test for the performance of such an algorithm is for a person to visually compare the original image to its decompressed (lossy) version. If the person cannot tell which is which, the lossy compression is acceptable. Sometimes a person can tell the difference but may still judge the decompressed image acceptable.

The discussion of image compression in this chapter is mostly general. Most of the chapter describes approaches to image compression. Of the few specific methods that are included, the most important one is JPEG (Section 5.9).

5.1 Introduction

Modern computers employ graphics extensively. Current operating systems display the disk's file directory graphically. The progress of many system operations, such as downloading a file, may also be displayed graphically. Many applications provide a graphical user interface (GUI), which makes it easier to use the program and to interpret displayed results. Computer graphics is used in many areas in everyday life to convert many types of complex information to images. Images are therefore important, but they tend to be big! Since modern hardware can display many colors, it is common to have a pixel represented internally as a 24-bit number, where the percentages of red, green, and blue occupy 8 bits each. Such a 24-bit pixel can specify one of $2^{24} \approx 16.78$ million colors. Thus, an image at a resolution of 512×512 that consists of such pixels occupies 786,432 bytes. At a resolution of 1024×1024 it becomes four times as big, requiring 3,145,728 bytes. Movies are also commonly used in computers, making for even bigger images. This is why image compression is so important. An important feature of image compression is that it can be lossy. An image, after all, exists for people to look at, so, when it is compressed, it is acceptable to lose image features to which the human eye is not sensitive. This is one of the main ideas behind the many lossy image compression methods developed in the past three decades.

In general, information can be compressed if it is redundant. It has been mentioned several times that data compression amounts to reducing or removing redundancy in the data. With lossy compression, however, we have a new concept, namely compressing by removing *irrelevancy*. An image can be lossy-compressed by removing irrelevant information even if the original image does not have any redundancy.

⬦ **Exercise 5.1:** It would seem that an image with no redundancy is always random (and therefore uninteresting). Is that so?

The idea of losing image information becomes more palatable when we consider how digital images are created. Here are three examples: (1) a real-life image may be scanned from a photograph or a painting and digitized (converted to pixels); (2) an image may be recorded by a video camera that creates pixels and stores them directly in memory; (3) an image may be painted on the screen by means of a paint program. In all these cases, some information is lost when the image is digitized. The fact that the viewer is willing to accept this loss suggests that further loss of information might be tolerable if done properly.

(Digitizing an image involves two steps: sampling and quantization. Sampling is dividing the two-dimensional original image into small regions: pixels. Quantization is the process of assigning an integer value to each pixel. Notice that digitizing sound involves the same two steps, with the difference that sound is one-dimensional.)

Here is a simple process to determine qualitatively the amount of data loss in a compressed image. Given an image A, (1) compress it to B, (2) decompress B to C, and (3) subtract $D = C - A$. If A was compressed without any loss and decompressed properly, then C should be identical to A and image D should be uniformly white. The more data that was lost in the compression, the further will D be from uniformly white.

How should an image be compressed? The main approaches to compression discussed so far are RLE, statistical methods, and dictionary-based methods. All three can be applied to image compression, but the differences between text and images suggest that special-purpose methods, developed specifically for the compression of images, may perform better. There are three main differences between text and images, as follows:

1. Text is one-dimensional while an image is two-dimensional. An entire text file may be considered as one long row of symbols. Each character of text has two neighbors, on its left and right, and there is very little correlation between the neighbors. In this paragraph, for example, the letter "i" is preceded by "d," "s," "h," "t," "f," and others, and it is followed by "m," "o," "l," "r," "d," and others. In other paragraphs, the same "i" may have different neighbors. In an image, a pixel has four immediate neighbors and eight near neighbors (except the pixels on the edges of the image; see Figure 5.1, where the near neighbors of pixel "∗" are shown in black), and there is strong correlation between them.

2. Text consists of a relatively small number of symbols. These are normally the 128 ASCII characters or the 256 8-bit bytes. In contrast, each pixel in an image may be represented by 24 bits, so there can be up to $2^{24} \approx 16.78$ different pixels. The number of elementary "symbols" in an image may therefore be very large.

3. There is no known algorithm to determine what parts of any given text are unimportant or irrelevant and can be deleted, but there are ways to automatically delete unimportant image information and thereby achieve high compression factors.

Figure 5.1: Four Immediate
and Eight Near Neighbors of
a Pixel.

Compression methods developed for files with individual symbols organized in one dimension are therefore unsatisfactory for image compression, which is why this chapter discusses different approaches. These approaches are all different, but they remove redundancy from an image by applying the following principle:

The Principle of Image Compression. If we select a pixel with color P at random, chances are that its near neighbors will have color P or very similar colors.

Image compression is therefore based on the fact that neighboring pixels are *highly correlated*. This correlation is also called *spatial redundancy*.

> The teeth and hair, the colour of the skin and of the hair, are more or less correlated.
> —Charles Darwin, *The Ascent of Man*

Here is a simple example that illustrates what can be done with correlated pixels. The following sequence of values gives the intensities of 24 adjacent pixels in a row of a continuous-tone image:

12, 17, 14, 19, 21, 26, 23, 29, 41, 38, 31, 44, 46, 57, 53, 50, 60, 58, 55, 54, 52, 51, 56, 60.

Only two of the 24 pixels are identical. Their average value is 40.3. Subtracting pairs of adjacent pixels results in the sequence

12, 5, −3, 5, 2, 4, −3, 6, 11, −3, −7, 13, 4, 11, −4, −3, 10, −2, −3, 1, −2, −1, 5, 4.

The two sequences are illustrated graphically in Figure 5.2.

Figure 5.2: Values and Differences of 24 Adjacent Pixels

The sequence of difference values has three properties that illustrate its compression potential: (1) The difference values are smaller than the original pixel values. Their average is 2.58. (2) They repeat. There are just 15 distinct difference values, so in principle they can be coded by 4 bits each. (3) They are *decorrelated*: adjacent difference values tend to be different. This can be seen by subtracting them, which results in the sequence of 24 second differences

12, −7, −8, 8, −3, 2, −7, 9, 5, −14, −4, 20, −11, 7, −15, 1, 13, −12, −1, 4, −3, 1, 6, 1.

They are larger than the differences themselves.

Figure 5.3 provides another illustration of the meaning of the words *correlated quantities*. A 32×32 matrix A is constructed of random numbers, and its elements are displayed in part (a) as shaded squares. The random nature of the elements is obvious. The matrix is then inverted and stored in B, which is shown in part (b). This time, there seems to be more structure to the 32×32 squares. A direct calculation using the Pearson correlation coefficient of Equation (5.1) shows that the cross-correlation between the top two rows of A is the small value 0.0412, whereas the cross-correlation between the top two rows of B is the large value −0.9831. The elements of B are correlated since each depends on *all* the elements of A.

$$R = \frac{n \sum x_i y_i - \sum x_i \sum y_i}{\sqrt{[n \sum x_i^2 - (\sum x_i)^2][n \sum y_i^2 - (\sum y_i)^2]}}. \tag{5.1}$$

◇ **Exercise 5.2:** Use mathematical software to illustrate the covariance matrices of (1) a matrix with correlated values and (2) a matrix with decorrelated values.

Once the concept of correlated quantities is familiar, we start looking for a correlation test. Given a matrix M, a statistical test is needed to determine whether its elements are correlated or not. The test is based on the statistical concept of covariance.

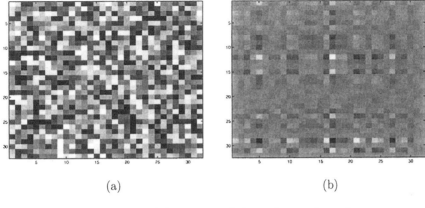

(a)   (b)

```
n=32; a=rand(n); imagesc(a); colormap(gray)
b=inv(a); imagesc(b)
```

Figure 5.3: Maps and Code of (a) a Random Matrix and (b) Its Inverse.

If the elements of M are decorrelated (i.e., independent), then the covariance of any two different rows and any two different columns of M will be zero (the covariance of a row or of a column with itself is always 1). As a result, the covariance matrix of M (whether covariance of rows or of columns) will be diagonal. If the covariance matrix of M is not diagonal, then the elements of M are correlated. The statistical concepts of variance, covariance, and correlation are basic and are discussed in any text (elementary or advanced) on statistics.

The principle of image compression has another aspect. We know from experience that the *brightness* of neighboring pixels is also correlated. Two adjacent pixels may have different colors: one may be mostly red and the other mostly green. Yet if the red component of the first is bright, the green component of its neighbor will, in most cases, also be bright. This property can be exploited by converting pixel representations from RGB to three other components, one of which is brightness and the other two (the chromatic components) of which represent color. One such format (or *color space*) is YCbCr, where Y (the *luminance* component) represents the brightness of a pixel, and Cb and Cr define its color. This format is discussed in Section 5.9.1, but its advantage is easy to understand. The eye is sensitive to small changes in brightness but not to small changes in color (this important fact is mentioned several times in this chapter). Thus, losing information in the Cb and Cr components compresses the image while introducing distortions to which the eye is not sensitive. Losing information in the Y component, on the other hand, is very noticeable to the eye.

5.2 Image Types

A digital image is a rectangular array of dots, or picture elements, arranged in m rows and n columns. The expression $m \times n$ is called the *resolution* of the image (although sometimes the term *resolution* refers to the number of pixels per unit length of the image), and the dots are called *pixels* (except in the cases of fax images and video compression, where they are referred to as *pels*). For the purpose of image compression, it is useful to distinguish the following types of images:

1. *Bi-level* (or monochromatic) image. This is an image where the pixels can have one of two values, normally referred to as black (binary 1, or foreground) and white (binary 0, or background). Each pixel in such an image is represented by 1 bit, so this is the simplest type of image.

2. *Grayscale* image. A pixel in such an image can have one of the n values 0 through $n - 1$, indicating one of 2^n shades of gray (or shades of some other color). The value of n is normally compatible with a byte size, i.e., it is 4, 8, 12, 16, 24, or some other convenient multiple of 4 or of 8. The set of the most significant bits of all the pixels is the most significant bitplane. Thus, a grayscale image with 2^n shades of gray has n bitplanes.

3. *Color* image. There are various methods for specifying colors, but each requires the use of three parameters. Therefore, a color image requires three-part pixels. Currently, it is common to have color images where each pixel consists of three bytes specifying the three parameters of the pixel's color. Typical color models are RGB, HLS, and CMYK. A detailed description of color models is outside the scope of this book, but there is a basic discussion of luminance and chrominance in Section 5.9.1.

4. *Continuous-tone* image. This type of image is normally a natural scene (natural as opposed to artificial) produced by taking a photograph with a digital camera or by scanning a photograph or a painting. Such an image has regions with colors that seem to vary continuously as the eye moves along the region. A region may therefore have a large number of similar colors, so the eye cannot tell when some of them are slightly modified. This feature is termed *image noise* and is the main characteristic of a continuous-tone image. Examples of regions are a cloud, a mountain, and the surface of a lake.

5. *Discrete-tone* image (also called a graphical image or a synthetic image). This is normally an artificial image. It may have few colors or many colors, but it does not have the noise and blurring of a natural image. Examples of this type of image are a photograph of an artificial object or machine, a page of text, a chart, a cartoon, and the contents of a computer screen. (Not every artificial image is discrete-tone. A computer-generated image that is meant to look natural is a continuous-tone image in spite of being artificially generated.) Artificial objects, text, and line drawings have sharp, well-defined edges and are therefore highly contrasted from the rest of the image (the background). Adjacent pixels in a discrete-tone image often either are identical or vary significantly in value. Such an image does not compress well with lossy methods, since the loss of just a few pixels may render a letter illegible or change a familiar pattern to an unrecognizable one. Compression methods for continuous-tone images often do not handle the sharp edges of a discrete-tone image very well, so special methods are

needed for efficient compression of these images. Notice that a discrete-tone image may be highly redundant, since the same character or pattern may appear many times in the image.

6. *Cartoon-like* image. This is a color image that consists of uniform areas. Each area has a uniform color, but adjacent areas may have very different colors. This feature may be exploited to obtain better compression.

It is intuitively clear that each type of image may feature redundancy, but they are redundant in different ways. This is why any given compression method may not perform well for all images and why different methods are needed to compress the different image types. There are compression methods for bi-level images, for continuous-tone images, and for discrete-tone images. There are also methods that try to break an image up into continuous-tone and discrete-tone parts and compress each separately.

> It's the weird color-scheme that freaks me. Every time you try to operate one of these weird black controls, which are labeled in black on a black background, a small black light lights up black to let you know you've done it!
>
> —Douglas Adams, *The Hitchhiker's Guide to the Galaxy* (1981)

5.3 Approaches to Image Compression

An image compression method is normally designed for a specific type of image, and this section lists various approaches to compressing images of different types. This section discusses only general principles; specific methods are described later in this chapter and in [Salomon 04].

Approach 1: For compressing a bi-level image. A pixel in such an image is represented by one bit. Applying the principle of image compression to a bi-level image therefore means that the immediate neighbors of a pixel P tend to be *identical* to P. Thus, it makes sense to use run length encoding (RLE) to compress such an image. A compression method for such an image may scan it in raster order (row by row) and compute the lengths of runs of black and white pixels. The lengths are encoded by variable-size (prefix) codes and are written on the compressed file. An example of such a method is facsimile compression (Section 3.7).

It should be stressed that this is just an approach to bi-level image compression. The details of specific methods vary. For instance, a method may scan the image column by column or in zigzag (Figure 5.4a), it may convert the image to a quadtree, or it may scan it region by region using a space-filling curve (see [Salomon 04] for these techniques).

Approach 2: Also for bi-level images. The principle of image compression tells us that the near neighbors of a pixel tend to resemble it. We can extend this principle and conclude that if the current pixel has color c (where c is either black or white), then pixels of the same color seen in the past (and also those that will be found in the future) tend to have the same immediate neighbors.

This approach looks at n of the near neighbors of the current pixel and considers them an n-bit number. This number is the *context* of the pixel. In principle there can

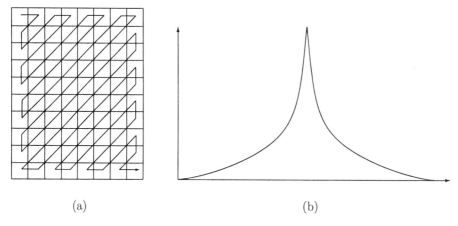

(a)   (b)

Figure 5.4: (a) Zigzag Scan of an Image. (b) Laplace Distribution.

be 2^n contexts, but because of image redundancy, we expect them to be distributed in a nonuniform way. Some contexts should be common, while the rest will be rare.

The encoder counts how many times each context has already been found for a pixel of color c and assigns probabilities to the contexts accordingly. If the current pixel has color c and its context has probability p, the encoder can use adaptive arithmetic coding to encode the pixel with that probability. This approach is used by JBIG [Salomon 04].

Next, we turn to grayscale images. A pixel in such an image is represented by n bits and can have one of 2^n values. Applying the principle of image compression to a grayscale image implies that the immediate neighbors of a pixel P tend to be similar to P but are not necessarily identical. Thus, RLE should not be used to compress such an image. Instead, two approaches are discussed.

Approach 3: Separate the grayscale image into n bi-level images and compress each with RLE and prefix codes. The principle of image compression seems to imply intuitively that two adjacent pixels that are similar in the grayscale image will be identical in most of the n bi-level images. This, however, is not true, as the following example makes clear. Imagine a grayscale image with $n = 4$ (i.e., 4-bit pixels, or 16 shades of gray). The image can be separated into four bi-level images. If two adjacent pixels in the original grayscale image have values 0000 and 0001, then they are similar. They are also identical in three of the four bi-level images. However, two adjacent pixels with values 0111 and 1000 are also similar in the grayscale image (their values are 7 and 8, respectively) but differ in all four bi-level images.

This problem occurs because the binary codes of adjacent integers may differ by several bits. The binary codes of 0 and 1 differ by one bit, those of 1 and 2 differ by two bits, and those of 7 and 8 differ by four bits. The solution is to design special binary codes where the codes of any two consecutive integers differ by one bit only. An example of such a code is the *reflected Gray codes* (Section 14.2.1).

Approach 4: Use the context of a pixel to *predict* its value. The context of a pixel consists of the values of some of its neighbors. We can examine some neighbors of a pixel P, compute an average A of their values, and predict that P will have the value A. The principle of image compression tells us that our prediction will be correct in most cases, almost correct in many cases, and completely wrong in a few cases. We can say that the predicted value of pixel P represents the redundant information in P. We now calculate the difference

$$\Delta \stackrel{\text{def}}{=} P - A$$

and assign variable-size (prefix) codes to the different values of Δ such that small values (which we expect to be common) are assigned short codes and large values (which are expected to be rare) are assigned long codes. If P can have the values 0 through $m - 1$, then values of Δ are in the range $[-(m-1), +(m-1)]$, and the number of codes needed is $2(m - 1) + 1$ or $2m - 1$.

Experiments with a large number of images suggest that the values of Δ tend to be distributed according to the Laplace distribution (Figure 5.4b), a well-known statistical distribution. Thus, a compression method can employ this distribution to assign a probability to each value of Δ and use arithmetic coding to encode the Δ values very efficiently. This is the principle of the MLP image compression method [Salomon 04].

The context of a pixel may consist of just one or two of its immediate neighbors, but better results are obtained when several neighbor pixels are included in the context. The average A in such a case should be weighted, with near neighbors assigned higher weights. Another important consideration is the decoder. In order for it to decode the image, it should be able to calculate the context of every pixel before it decodes that pixel. This means that the context should contain only pixels that have already been decoded. If the image is scanned in raster order (i.e., row by row from top to bottom and each row from left to right), the context should include only pixels located above the current pixel or on the same row and to its left.

> The best way to predict the future is to create it.
> —Peter Drucker, *Reader's Digest*, August 1997

Approach 5: Transform the values of the pixels, and encode the transformed values. The concept of a transform, as well as the most important transforms used in image compression, are discussed in Section 5.5. Recall that compression is achieved by reducing or removing redundancy. The redundancy of an image is caused by the correlation between pixels, so transforming the pixels to a representation where they are decorrelated eliminates the redundancy. Quantizing the transformed values can produce efficient lossy image compression. We want the transformed values to be independent because coding independent values makes it simpler to construct a statistical model.

We now turn to color images. A pixel in such an image consists of three color components, such as red, green, and blue. Most color images are either continuous-tone or discrete-tone.

Approach 6: The principle of this approach is to separate a continuous-tone color image into three grayscale images and compress each of the three separately, using approaches 3, 4, or 5.

For a continuous-tone image, the principle of image compression implies that adjacent pixels have similar, although perhaps not identical, colors. However, similar colors do not mean similar pixel values. Consider, for example, 12-bit pixel values where each color component is expressed in 4 bits. Thus, the 12 bits 1000|0100|0000 represent a pixel whose color is a mixture of eight units of red (about 50%, since the maximum is 15 units), four units of green (about 25%), and no blue. Now imagine two adjacent pixels with values 0011|0101|0011 and 0010|0101|0011. These have similar colors, since only their red components differ and only by one unit. However, when considered as 12-bit numbers, the two numbers 001101010011 = 851 and 001001010011 = 595 are very different, since they differ in one of their most significant bits.

An important feature of this approach is to use a luminance–chrominance color representation instead of the more common RGB. The concepts of luminance and chrominance are discussed in Section 5.9.1 and in [Salomon 99]. The advantage of the luminance–chrominance color representation is that the eye is sensitive to small changes in luminance but not in chrominance. This allows the loss of considerable data in the chrominance components, while making it possible to decode the image without a significant visible loss of quality.

Approach 7: A different approach is needed for discrete-tone images. Recall that such an image has uniform regions, and a region may appear several times in the image. A good example is a screen dump. Such an image consists of text and icons. Each character of text and each icon is a region, and any region may appear several times in the image. A possible way to compress such an image is to scan it, identify regions, and find repeating regions. If a region B is identical to an already-found region A, then B can be compressed by writing a pointer to A on the compressed file. The block decomposition method (FABD, [Salomon 04]) is an example of how this approach can be implemented.

Approach 8: Partition the image into parts (overlapping or not) and compress it by processing the parts one by one. Suppose that the next unprocessed image part is part number 15. Try to match it with parts 1–14 that have already been processed. If part 15 can be expressed, for example, as a combination of parts 5 (scaled) and 11 (rotated), then only the few numbers that specify the combination need be saved, and part 15 can be discarded. If part 15 cannot be expressed as a combination of already processed parts, it is declared processed and is saved in raw format.

This approach is the basis of the various *fractal* methods for image compression. It applies the principle of image compression to image parts instead of to individual pixels. Applied this way, the principle tells us that "interesting" images (i.e., those that are being compressed in practice) have a certain amount of *self-similarity*. Parts of the image are identical or similar to the entire image or to other parts.

Image compression methods are not limited to these basic approaches. [Salomon 04] discusses methods that use the concepts of finite-state automata, context trees, Markov models, and wavelets, among others. In addition, the concept of *progressive image compression* (Section 5.8) should be mentioned, since it adds another dimension to the compression of images.

> Art is a technique of communication. The image is the most complete technique of all communication.
>
> —Claes Thure Oldenburg

5.3.1 Error Metrics

Developers and implementers of lossy image compression methods need a standard metric to measure the quality of reconstructed images compared with the original ones. The better a reconstructed image resembles the original one, the bigger should be the value produced by this metric (which suggests that *similarity metric* may be a more appropriate name). Such a metric should also produce a dimensionless number, and that number should not be very sensitive to small variations in the reconstructed image. A common measure used for this purpose is the *peak signal-to-noise ratio* (PSNR). It is familiar to workers in the field, it is also simple to calculate, but it has only a limited, approximate relationship with the perceived errors noticed by the human visual system. This is why higher PSNR values imply closer resemblance between the reconstructed and the original images, but they do not provide a guarantee that viewers will like the reconstructed image.

Denoting the pixels of the original image by P_i and the pixels of the reconstructed image by Q_i (where $1 \leq i \leq n$), we first define the *mean square error* (MSE) between the two images as

$$\text{MSE} = \frac{1}{n} \sum_{i=1}^{n} (P_i - Q_i)^2. \tag{5.2}$$

It is the average of the square of the errors (pixel differences) of the two images. The *root mean square error* (RMSE) is defined as the square root of the MSE, and the PSNR is defined as

$$\text{PSNR} = 20 \log_{10} \frac{\max_i |P_i|}{\text{RMSE}}.$$

The absolute value is normally not needed, since pixel values are rarely negative. For a bi-level image, the numerator is 1. For a grayscale image with 8 bits per pixel, the numerator is 255. For color images, only the luminance component is used.

Greater resemblance between the images implies smaller RMSE and, as a result, larger PSNR. The PNSR is dimensionless, since the units of both numerator and denominator are pixel values. However, because of the use of the logarithm, we say that the PSNR is expressed in *decibels* (dB). The use of the logarithm also implies less sensitivity to changes in the RMSE. For example, dividing the RMSE by 10 multiplies the PSNR by 2. Notice that the PSNR has no absolute meaning. It is meaningless to say that a PSNR of, say, 25 is good. PSNR values are used only to compare the performance of different lossy compression methods or the effects of different parametric values on the performance of an algorithm. The MPEG committee, for example, uses an informal threshold of PSNR = 0.5 dB to decide whether to incorporate a coding optimization, since they believe that an improvement of that magnitude would be visible to the eye.

Typical PSNR values range between 20 and 40. Assuming pixel values in the range [0, 255], an RMSE of 25.5 results in a PSNR of 20, and an RMSE of 2.55 results in a PSNR of 40. An RMSE of zero (i.e., identical images) results in an infinite (or, more precisely, undefined) PSNR. An RMSE of 255 results in a PSNR of zero, and RMSE values greater than 255 yield negative PSNRs.

◇ **Exercise 5.3:** If the maximum pixel value is 255, can RMSE values be greater than 255?

Some authors define the PSNR as

$$\text{PSNR} = 10\log_{10}\frac{\max_i |P_i|^2}{\text{MSE}}.$$

In order for the two formulations to produce the same result, the logarithm is multiplied in this case by 10 instead of by 20, since $\log_{10} A^2 = 2\log_{10} A$. Either definition is useful, because only relative PSNR values are used in practice.

A related measure is *signal-to-noise ratio* (SNR). This is defined as (the numerator is the root mean square of the original image)

$$\text{SNR} = 20\log_{10}\frac{\sqrt{\frac{1}{n}\sum_{i=1}^{n} P_i^2}}{\text{RMSE}}.$$

Figure 5.5 is a Matlab function to compute the PSNR of two images. A typical call is PSNR(A,B), where A and B are image files. These must have the same resolution and have pixel values in the range $[0,1]$.

```
function PSNR(A,B)
if A==B
 error('Images are identical; PSNR is undefined')
end
max2_A=max(max(A)); max2_B=max(max(B));
min2_A=min(min(A)); min2_B=min(min(B));
if max2_A>1 | max2_B>1 | min2_A<0 | min2_B<0
    error('pixels must be in [0,1]')
end
differ=A-B;
decib=20*log10(1/(sqrt(mean(mean(differ.^2)))));
disp(sprintf('PSNR = +%5.2f dB',decib))
```

Figure 5.5: A Matlab Function to Compute PSNR.

Another cousin of the PSNR is the *signal-to-quantization-noise ratio* (SQNR). This is a measure of the effect of quantization on signal quality. It is defined as

$$\text{SQNR} = 10\log_{10}\frac{\text{signal power}}{\text{quantization error}},$$

where the quantization error is the difference between the quantized signal and the original signal.

Another approach to the comparison of an original and a reconstructed image is to generate the difference image and judge it visually. Intuitively, the difference image is

$D_i = P_i - Q_i$, but such an image is hard to judge visually because its pixel values D_i tend to be small numbers. If a pixel value of zero represents white, such a difference image would be almost invisible. In the opposite case, where pixel values of zero represent black, such a difference would be too dark to judge. Better results are obtained by calculating

$$D_i = a(P_i - Q_i) + b,$$

where a is a magnification parameter (typically a small number such as 2) and b is half the maximum value of a pixel (typically 128). Parameter a serves to magnify small differences, while b shifts the difference image from extreme white (or extreme black) to a more comfortable gray.

5.4 Intuitive Methods

It is easy to come up with simple, intuitive methods for compressing images. These are included here for the purpose of illustration, since much more sophisticated (and efficient) methods are used in practice.

5.4.1 Subsampling

Subsampling is perhaps the simplest way to compress an image. One approach to subsampling is simply to ignore some of the pixels. The encoder may, for example, ignore every other row and every other column of the image and write the remaining pixels (which constitute 25% of the image) on the compressed file. The decoder inputs the compressed data and uses each pixel to generate four identical pixels of the reconstructed image. This, of course, involves the loss of much image detail and is rarely acceptable. Notice that the compression ratio is known in advance.

A slight improvement is achieved when the encoder calculates the average of each block of four pixels and writes this average on the compressed file. No pixel is totally ignored, but the method is still primitive, since a good lossy image compression method should lose data to which the eye is not sensitive.

Better results (but worse compression) are obtained when the color representation of the image is transformed from the original (normally RGB) to luminance and chrominance. The encoder subsamples the two chrominance components of a pixel but not its luminance component. Assuming that each component uses the same number of bits, the two chrominance components make up 2/3 of the image size. Subsampling them reduces this to 25% of 2/3, or 1/6. The size of the compressed image is thus 1/3 (for the uncompressed luminance component) plus 1/6 (for the two chrominance components) or 1/2 of the original size.

5.4.2 Quantization

The term *quantization* as used in data compression means to truncate a real value to an integer or to transform an integer to a smaller integer. There are two types of quantization: scalar and vector. The former is an intuitive, lossy method where the information that is lost is not necessarily the least important. The latter can obtain better results, and a simple version of it is described here.

The image is partitioned into equal-size blocks (called *vectors*) of pixels, and the encoder has a list (called a *codebook*) of blocks of the same size. Each image block B is compared to all the blocks of the codebook and is matched with the "closest" one. If B is matched with codebook block C, then the encoder writes a pointer to C on the compressed file. If the pointer is smaller than the block size, compression is achieved. Figure 5.6 shows an example.

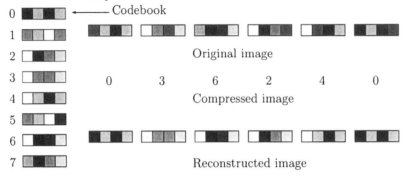

Figure 5.6: Intuitive Vector Quantization

The details of selecting and maintaining the codebook and of matching blocks are discussed in [Salomon 04], with an algorithm due to Linde [Linde et al. 80]. Notice that vector quantization is a method where the compression ratio is known in advance.

5.5 Image Transforms

The concept of a transform is familiar to mathematicians. It is a standard mathematical tool used to solve problems in many areas. The idea is to transform a mathematical quantity (a number, a vector, a function, or anything else) to another form, where it may look unfamiliar but may have useful properties. The transformed quantity is used to solve a problem or to perform a calculation, and the result is then transformed back to the original form.

A simple, illustrative example of how a transform can be useful is arithmetic operations on Roman numerals. The ancient Romans presumably knew how to operate on such numbers, but when we have to, say, multiply two Roman numerals, we may find it more convenient to transform them into modern (Arabic) notation, multiply, then transform the result back into a Roman numeral. Here is a simple example:

$$\text{XCVI} \times \text{XII} \to 96 \times 12 = 1152 \to \text{MCLII}.$$

An image can be compressed by transforming its pixels (which are correlated) to a representation where they are decorrelated. Compression is achieved if the new values are smaller, on average, than the original ones. Lossy compression can be achieved by quantizing the transformed values. The decoder inputs the transformed values from the compressed file and reconstructs the (precise or approximate) original data by applying the opposite transform. The image transforms discussed here are of two main types: orthogonal (Section 5.6) and subband (Section 5.7). (But see page 369 for a different type of pixel transform.)

The term *decorrelated* means that the transformed values are independent of one another. As a result, they can be encoded independently, which makes it simpler to construct a statistical model. An image can be compressed if its representation has redundancy. The redundancy in images stems from pixel correlation. If we transform the image to a representation where the pixels are decorrelated, we have eliminated the redundancy and the image has been fully compressed.

We start with a simple example of a transform, where an image is scanned in raster order and pairs of adjacent pixels are collected. Because the pixels are correlated, the two pixels (x, y) of a pair normally have similar values. Each pair of pixels is considered a point in two-dimensional space and is plotted. Points of the form (x, x) are located on the 45° line $y = x$, so we expect our points to be concentrated around this line. Figure 5.7a shows the results of plotting the pixels of a typical image—where a pixel has values in the interval $[0, 255]$—in such a way. Most points form a cloud around this line, and only a few points are located away from it. We now transform the image by rotating all the points 45° clockwise about the origin such that the 45° line becomes the x axis (Figure 5.7b). This is done by the simple transformation

$$(x^*, y^*) = (x, y) \begin{pmatrix} \cos 45° & -\sin 45° \\ \sin 45° & \cos 45° \end{pmatrix} = (x, y)\frac{1}{\sqrt{2}} \begin{pmatrix} 1 & -1 \\ 1 & 1 \end{pmatrix} = (x, y)\mathbf{R}, \qquad (5.3)$$

where the rotation matrix $\mathbf{R}$ is orthonormal (i.e., the dot product of a row with itself is 1, the dot product of different rows is 0, and the same is true for columns). The inverse transformation is

$$(x, y) = (x^*, y^*)\mathbf{R}^{-1} = (x^*, y^*)\mathbf{R}^T = (x^*, y^*)\frac{1}{\sqrt{2}} \begin{pmatrix} 1 & 1 \\ -1 & 1 \end{pmatrix}. \qquad (5.4)$$

(The inverse of an orthonormal matrix is its transpose.)

It is obvious that most points end up having y coordinates that are zero or close to zero, while the x coordinates don't change much. Figure 5.8a and b show the distributions of the x and y coordinates (i.e., the odd-numbered and even-numbered pixels) of the $128 \times 128 \times 8$ grayscale Lena image (a well-known test image used by researchers) before the rotation. It is clear that the two distributions don't differ by much. Figure 5.8c and d show that the distribution of the x coordinates stays about the same (with greater variance) but the y coordinates are concentrated around zero. The Matlab code that generated these results is also listed. (Figure 5.8d shows that the y coordinates are concentrated around 100, but this is because a few were as small as -101, so they had to be scaled by 101 to fit in a Matlab array, which always starts at index 1.)

Once the coordinates of points are known before and after the rotation, it is easy to measure the reduction in correlation. A simple measure is the sum $\sum_i x_i y_i$, also called the *cross-correlation* of points (x_i, y_i).

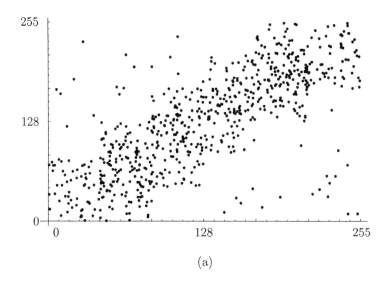

(a)

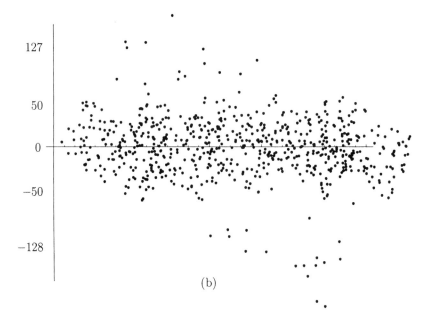

(b)

Figure 5.7: Rotating a Cloud of Points.

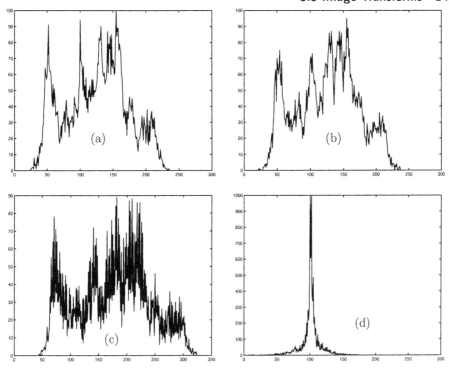

```
filename='lena128'; dim=128;
xdist=zeros(256,1); ydist=zeros(256,1);
fid=fopen(filename,'r');
img=fread(fid,[dim,dim])';
for col=1:2:dim-1
 for row=1:dim
  x=img(row,col)+1; y=img(row,col+1)+1;
  xdist(x)=xdist(x)+1; ydist(y)=ydist(y)+1;
 end
end
figure(1), plot(xdist), colormap(gray) %dist of x&y values
figure(2), plot(ydist), colormap(gray) %before rotation
xdist=zeros(325,1); % clear arrays
ydist=zeros(256,1);
for col=1:2:dim-1
 for row=1:dim
  x=round((img(row,col)+img(row,col+1))*0.7071);
  y=round((-img(row,col)+img(row,col+1))*0.7071)+101;
  xdist(x)=xdist(x)+1; ydist(y)=ydist(y)+1;
 end
end
figure(3), plot(xdist), colormap(gray) %dist of x&y values
figure(4), plot(ydist), colormap(gray) %after rotation
```

Figure 5.8: Distribution of Image Pixels Before and After Rotation.

⋄ **Exercise 5.4:** Given the five points $(5, 5)$, $(6, 7)$, $(12.1, 13.2)$, $(23, 25)$, and $(32, 29)$, we rotate them $45°$ clockwise and calculate their cross-correlations before and after the rotation.

```
p={{5,5},{6, 7},{12.1,13.2},{23,25},{32,29}};
rot={{0.7071,-0.7071},{0.7071,0.7071}};
Sum[p[[i,1]]p[[i,2]], {i,5}]
q=p.rot
Sum[q[[i,1]]q[[i,2]], {i,5}]
```

Figure 5.9: Code for Rotating Five Points.

We can now compress the image by simply writing the transformed pixels on the compressed file. If lossy compression is acceptable, then all the pixels can be quantized, resulting in even smaller numbers. We can also write all the odd-numbered pixels (those that make up the x coordinates of the pairs) on the compressed file, followed by all the even-numbered pixels. These two sequences are called the *coefficient vectors* of the transform. The latter sequence consists of small numbers and may, after quantization, have runs of zeros, resulting in even better compression.

It can be shown that the total variance of the pixels (defined as the sum $\sum_i x_i^2 + y_i^2$) does not change by the rotation, because a rotation matrix is orthonormal. However, since the variance of the new y coordinates is small, most of the variance is now concentrated in the x coordinates. The variance is sometimes called the *energy* of the distribution of pixels, so we can say that the rotation has concentrated (or compacted) the energy in the x coordinate and has created compression this way.

Concentrating the energy in one coordinate has another advantage. It makes it possible to quantize that coordinate more finely than the other coordinates. This type of quantization results in better (lossy) compression.

The following simple example illustrates the power of this basic transform. We start with the point $(4, 5)$, whose two coordinates are similar. Using Equation (5.3) the point is transformed to $(4, 5)\mathbf{R} = (9, 1)/\sqrt{2} \approx (6.36396, 0.7071)$. The energies of the point and its transform are $4^2 + 5^2 = 41 = (9^2 + 1^2)/2$. If we delete the smaller coordinate (4) of the point, we end up with an error of $4^2/41 = 0.39$. If, on the other hand, we delete the smaller of the two transform coefficients (0.7071), the resulting error is just $0.7071^2/41 = 0.012$. Another way to obtain the same error is to consider the reconstructed point. Passing $(9, 1)/\sqrt{2}$ through the inverse transform [Equation (5.4)] results in the original point $(4, 5)$. Doing the same with $(9, 0)/\sqrt{2}$ results in the approximate reconstructed point $(4.5, 4.5)$. The energy difference between the original and reconstructed points is the same small quantity

$$\frac{\left[(4^2 + 5^2) - (4.5^2 + 4.5^2)\right]}{4^2 + 5^2} = \frac{41 - 40.5}{41} = 0.012.$$

This simple transform can easily be extended to any number of dimensions. Instead of selecting pairs of adjacent pixels, we can select triplets. Each triplet becomes a point in three-dimensional space, and these points form a cloud concentrated around the line that forms equal (although not 45°) angles with the three coordinate axes. When this line is rotated such that it coincides with the x axis, the y and z coordinates of the transformed points become small numbers. The transformation is done by multiplying each point by a 3×3 rotation matrix, and such a matrix is, of course, orthonormal. The transformed points are then separated into three coefficient vectors, of which the last two consist of small numbers. For maximum compression, each coefficient vector should be quantized separately.

This process can be extended to more than three dimensions, with the only difference being that we cannot visualize spaces of dimensions higher than three. However, the mathematics can easily be extended. An important point is that the number of dimensions should not be too large because the performance of the rotation depends on the correlation between adjacent pixels. If we collect, say, 24 adjacent pixels and consider them a point in 24-dimensional space, that point would generally not be near the "45° line" because there is no correlation between a pixel and its far neighbors. When the point is rotated, its last 23 dimensions will not end up near their corresponding axes, so the last 23 numbers will generally not be small. Experience shows that a pixel is generally correlated with neighbors up to a distance of eight, but rarely further away.

The JPEG method of Section 5.9 divides an image into blocks of 8×8 pixels each and rotates each block twice by means of Equation (5.9), as shown in Section 5.6.2. This double rotation produces a set of 64 transformed values, of which the first—termed the *DC coefficient*—is large and the other 63 (called the *AC coefficients*) are normally small. Thus, this transform concentrates the energy in the first of 64 dimensions. The set of DC coefficients and each of the sets of 63 AC coefficients should, in principle, be quantized separately (JPEG does this a little differently, though; see Section 5.9.4).

5.6 Orthogonal Transforms

Image transforms are designed to have two properties: (1) to reduce image redundancy by reducing the sizes of most pixels and (2) to identify the less important parts of the image by isolating the various frequencies of the image. Thus, this section starts with a short discussion of frequencies. We intuitively associate a frequency with a wave. Water waves, sound waves, and electromagnetic waves have frequencies (the number of waves per second, or temporal frequency), but pixels in an image can also feature frequencies (spatial, not temporal). Figure 5.10 shows a small, 5×8 bi-level image that illustrates this concept. The top row is uniform, so we can assign it zero frequency. The rows below it have increasing pixel frequencies as measured by the number of color changes along a row. The four waves on the right roughly correspond to the frequencies of the four top rows of the image.

Image frequencies are important because of the following basic fact: Low frequencies correspond to the important image features, while high frequencies correspond to the details of the image, which are less important. Thus, if the various image frequencies can be isolated and identified, pixels that correspond to high frequencies can be quantized heavily, while pixels that correspond to low frequencies should be quantized lightly or

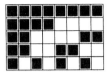 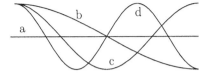

Figure 5.10: Image Frequencies.

not at all. This is how a transform that isolates pixel frequencies can compress an image very effectively by losing information, but only information associated with unimportant image details.

Practical image transforms should be fast and preferably also simple to implement. This suggests the use of *linear transforms*. In such a transform, each transformed value (or transform coefficient) c_i is a weighted sum of the data items (the pixels) d_j, where each item is multiplied by a weight (or a transform coefficient) w_{ij}. Thus, $c_i = \sum_j d_j w_{ij}$, for $i, j = 1, 2, \ldots, n$. For the case $n = 4$, this result is expressed in matrix notation:

$$
\begin{pmatrix} c_1 \\ c_2 \\ c_3 \\ c_4 \end{pmatrix} = \begin{pmatrix} w_{11} & w_{12} & w_{13} & w_{14} \\ w_{21} & w_{22} & w_{23} & w_{24} \\ w_{31} & w_{32} & w_{33} & w_{34} \\ w_{41} & w_{42} & w_{43} & w_{44} \end{pmatrix} \begin{pmatrix} d_1 \\ d_2 \\ d_3 \\ d_4 \end{pmatrix}.
$$

For the general case, we can write $\mathbf{C} = \mathbf{W} \cdot \mathbf{D}$. Each row of $\mathbf{W}$ is called a *basis vector*.

The only quantities that have to be computed are the weights w_{ij}. The guiding principles are as follows:

- Reducing redundancy. The first transform coefficient c_1 can be large, but the remaining values $c_2, c_3, \ldots$ should be small.
- Isolating frequencies. The first transform coefficient c_1 should correspond to zero pixel frequency, and the remaining coefficients should correspond to higher and higher frequencies.

The key to determining the weights w_{ij} is the fact that our data items d_j are not arbitrary numbers but pixel values, which are nonnegative and correlated.

The basic relation $c_i = \sum_j d_j w_{ij}$ suggests that the first coefficient c_1 will be large when all the weights of the form w_{1j} are positive. To make the other coefficients c_i small, it is enough to make half the weights w_{ij} positive and the other half negative. A simple choice is to assign half the weights the value $+1$ and the other half the value -1. In the extreme case where all the pixels d_j are identical, this will result in $c_i = 0$. When the d_j's are similar, c_i will be small (positive or negative).

This choice of w_{ij} satisfies the first requirement: to reduce pixel redundancy by means of a transform. In order to satisfy the second requirement, the weights w_{ij} of row i should feature frequencies that get higher with i. Weights w_{1j} should have zero frequency; they should all be $+1$s. Weights w_{2j} should have one sign change, i.e., they should be $+1, +1, \ldots + 1, -1, -1, \ldots, -1$. This process should continue until the last row of weights w_{nj}, which should have the highest frequency $+1, -1, +1, -1, \ldots, +1, -1$.

The mathematical discipline of vector spaces employs the term *basis vectors* for our rows of weights.

In addition to isolating the various frequencies of pixels d_j, this choice results in basis vectors that are orthogonal. The basis vectors are the rows of matrix $\mathbf{W}$, which is why this matrix and, by implication, the entire transform are also termed orthogonal.

These considerations are satisfied by the orthogonal matrix

$$\mathbf{W} = \begin{pmatrix} 1 & 1 & 1 & 1 \\ 1 & 1 & -1 & -1 \\ 1 & -1 & -1 & 1 \\ 1 & -1 & 1 & -1 \end{pmatrix}. \tag{5.5}$$

The first basis vector (the top row of $\mathbf{W}$) consists of all 1s, so its frequency is zero. Each of the subsequent vectors has two +1s and two −1s, so they produce small transformed values, and their frequencies (measured as the number of sign changes along the basis vector) get higher. This matrix is similar to the Walsh–Hadamard transform [Salomon 04].

To illustrate how this matrix identifies the frequencies in a data vector, we multiply it by four vectors as follows:

$$\mathbf{W}\cdot\begin{bmatrix}1\\0\\0\\1\end{bmatrix} = \begin{bmatrix}2\\0\\2\\0\end{bmatrix}, \quad \mathbf{W}\cdot\begin{bmatrix}0\\0.33\\-0.33\\-1\end{bmatrix} = \begin{bmatrix}0\\2.66\\0\\1.33\end{bmatrix}, \quad \mathbf{W}\cdot\begin{bmatrix}1\\0\\0\\0\end{bmatrix} = \begin{bmatrix}1\\1\\1\\1\end{bmatrix}, \quad \mathbf{W}\cdot\begin{bmatrix}1\\-0.8\\1\\-0.8\end{bmatrix} = \begin{bmatrix}0.4\\0\\0\\3.6\end{bmatrix}.$$

The results make sense when we realize that the four test vectors were determined as follows

$$(1,0,0,1) = 0.5(1,1,1,1) + 0.5(1,-1,-1,1),$$
$$(1,0.33,-0.33,-1) = 0.66(1,1,-1,-1) + 0.33(1,-1,1,-1),$$
$$(1,0,0,0) = 0.25(1,1,1,1) + 0.25(1,1,-1,-1) + 0.25(1,-1,-1,1) + 0.25(1,-1,1,-1),$$
$$(1,-0.8,1,-0.8) = 0.1(1,1,1,1) + 0.9(1,-1,1,-1).$$

The product of $\mathbf{W}$ and the first vector shows how that vector consists of equal amounts of the first and the third frequencies. Similarly, the transform $(0.4, 0, 0, 3.6)$ shows that vector $(1, -0.8, 1, -0.8)$ is a mixture of a small amount of the first frequency and nine times the fourth frequency.

It is also possible to modify this transform to conserve the energy of the data vector. All that's needed is to multiply the transformation matrix $\mathbf{W}$ by the scale factor $1/2$. Thus, the product $(\mathbf{W}/2) \times (a, b, c, d)$ has the same energy $a^2 + b^2 + c^2 + d^2$ as the data vector (a, b, c, d). An example is the product of $\mathbf{W}/2$ and the correlated vector $(5, 6, 7, 8)$. It results in the transform coefficients $(13, -2, 0, -1)$, where the first coefficient is large and the remaining ones are smaller than the original data items. The energy of both $(5, 6, 7, 8)$ and $(13, -2, 0, -1)$ is 174, but whereas in the former vector the first component accounts for only 14% of the energy, in the transformed vector this component accounts for 97% of the energy. This is how our simple orthogonal transform compacts the energy of the data vector.

Another advantage of $\mathbf{W}$ is that it also performs the inverse transform. The product $(\mathbf{W}/2) \cdot (13, -2, 0, -1)^T$ reconstructs the original data $(5, 6, 7, 8)$.

We are now in a position to appreciate the compression potential of this transform. We use matrix $\mathbf{W}/2$ to transform the (not very correlated) data vector $d = (4, 6, 5, 2)$. The result is $t = (8.5, 1.5, -2.5, 0.5)$. It's easy to transform t back to d, but t itself does not provide any compression. In order to achieve compression, we quantize the components of t, and the point is that even after heavy quantization, it is still possible to get back a vector very similar to the original d.

We first quantize t to the integers $(9, 1, -3, 0)$ and perform the inverse transform to get back $(3.5, 6.5, 5.5, 2.5)$. In a similar experiment, we completely delete the two smallest elements and inverse-transform the coarsely quantized vector $(8.5, 0, -2.5, 0)$. This produces the reconstructed data $(3, 5.5, 5.5, 3)$, still very close to the original values of d. The conclusion is that even this simple, intuitive transform is a powerful tool for "squeezing out" the redundancy in data. More sophisticated transforms produce results that can be quantized coarsely and still be used to reconstruct the original data to a high degree.

> Some painters transform the sun into a yellow spot; others transform a yellow spot into the sun.
>
> —Pablo Picasso

5.6.1 Two-Dimensional Transforms

Given two-dimensional data such as the 4×4 matrix

$$\mathbf{D} = \begin{pmatrix} 5 & 6 & 7 & 4 \\ 6 & 5 & 7 & 5 \\ 7 & 7 & 6 & 6 \\ 8 & 8 & 8 & 8 \end{pmatrix},$$

where each of the four columns is highly correlated, we can apply our simple one-dimensional transform to the columns of $\mathbf{D}$. The result is

$$\mathbf{C}' = \mathbf{W} \cdot \mathbf{D} = \begin{pmatrix} 1 & 1 & 1 & 1 \\ 1 & 1 & -1 & -1 \\ 1 & -1 & -1 & 1 \\ 1 & -1 & 1 & -1 \end{pmatrix} \cdot \mathbf{D} = \begin{pmatrix} 26 & 26 & 28 & 23 \\ -4 & -4 & 0 & -5 \\ 0 & 2 & 2 & 1 \\ -2 & 0 & -2 & -3 \end{pmatrix}.$$

Each column of $\mathbf{C}'$ is the transform of a column of $\mathbf{D}$. Notice how the top element of each column of $\mathbf{C}'$ is dominant, because the data in the corresponding column of $\mathbf{D}$ is correlated. $\mathbf{C}'$ is the first stage in a two-stage process that produces the two-dimensional transform of matrix $\mathbf{D}$. The second stage should transform each *row* of $\mathbf{C}'$, and this is done by multiplying $\mathbf{C}'$ by the transpose $\mathbf{W}^T$. Our particular $\mathbf{W}$, however, is symmetric, so we end up with $\mathbf{C} = \mathbf{C}' \cdot \mathbf{W}^T = \mathbf{W} \cdot \mathbf{D} \cdot \mathbf{W}^T = \mathbf{W} \cdot \mathbf{D} \cdot \mathbf{W}$ or

$$\mathbf{C} = \begin{pmatrix} 26 & 26 & 28 & 23 \\ -4 & -4 & 0 & -5 \\ 0 & 2 & 2 & 1 \\ -2 & 0 & -2 & -3 \end{pmatrix} \begin{pmatrix} 1 & 1 & 1 & 1 \\ 1 & 1 & -1 & -1 \\ 1 & -1 & -1 & 1 \\ 1 & -1 & 1 & -1 \end{pmatrix} = \begin{pmatrix} 103 & 1 & -5 & 5 \\ -13 & -3 & -5 & 5 \\ 5 & -1 & -3 & -1 \\ -7 & 3 & -3 & -1 \end{pmatrix}.$$

The top left element is dominant. It contains most of the energy in the original $\mathbf{D}$. The elements in the top column and the leftmost row are somewhat large, while the remaining elements are smaller than the original data items. The double-stage, two-dimensional transformation has reduced the correlation in both the horizontal and vertical dimensions. As in the one-dimensional case, excellent compression can be achieved by quantizing the elements of $\mathbf{C}$, especially those that correspond to higher frequencies (i.e., those located toward the bottom-right corner of $\mathbf{C}$).

The remainder of this section discusses the following important image transforms:

1. The discrete cosine transform (DCT, Sections 5.6.2 and 5.9.2) is a well-known, efficient transform used by popular compression methods such as JPEG and MPEG-1. Several fast algorithms for DCT calculation are known, making the use of this method even more attractive.

2. The Haar transform. This is a simple and fast subband, not orthogonal, transform. It is the simplest wavelet transform and is discussed in Section 5.7.

5.6.2 Discrete Cosine Transform

We first look at the one-dimensional DCT (in practice, the *two-dimensional* DCT is used to compress images, but the one-dimensional DCT is easier to understand, and it is based on the same principles). Figure 5.11 shows eight cosine waves, $w(f) = \cos(f\theta)$, for $0 \leq \theta \leq \pi$, with frequencies $f = 0, 1, \ldots, 7$. Each wave $w(f)$ is sampled at the eight points

$$\theta = \frac{\pi}{16}, \quad \frac{3\pi}{16}, \quad \frac{5\pi}{16}, \quad \frac{7\pi}{16}, \quad \frac{9\pi}{16}, \quad \frac{11\pi}{16}, \quad \frac{13\pi}{16}, \quad \frac{15\pi}{16} \tag{5.6}$$

to form one basis vector $\mathbf{v}_f$, and the resulting eight vectors $\mathbf{v}_f$, $f = 0, 1, \ldots, 7$ (a total of 64 numbers) are shown in Table 5.12. These serve as the basis of the one-dimensional DCT. Notice the similarity between this table and matrix $\mathbf{W}$ of Equation (5.5). In both cases the rows have increasing frequencies.

It can be shown that these $\mathbf{v}_i$ vectors are orthogonal (because of the particular choice of the eight sample points), and it is also easy, with appropriate mathematical software, to check this by direct calculations. This set of eight orthogonal vectors can therefore be considered an 8×8 transformation matrix. Since this matrix is orthogonal, it is a rotation matrix. Thus, we can interpret the one-dimensional DCT as a rotation. The two-dimensional DCT can also be interpreted as a (double) rotation, and this is discussed on page 160.

The one-dimensional DCT has another interpretation. Because of the similarity between matrix $\mathbf{W}$ of Equation (5.5) and the eight orthogonal vectors $\mathbf{v}_i$, these vectors

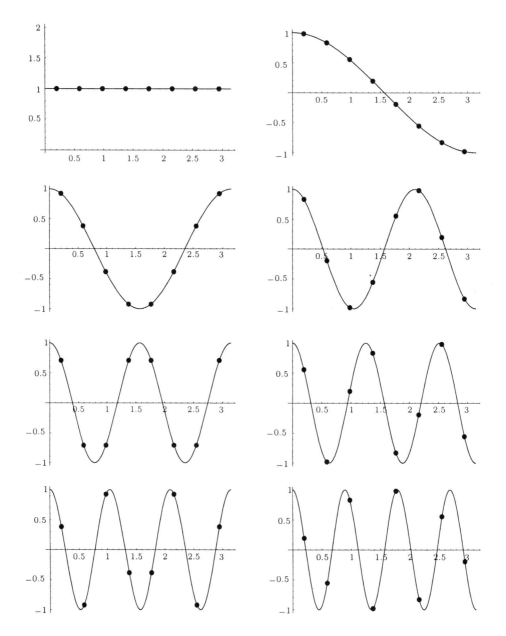

Figure 5.11: Calculating a One-Dimensional DCT.

```
dct[pw_]:=Plot[Cos[pw t], {t,0,Pi}, DisplayFunction->Identity,
  AspectRatio->Automatic];
dcdot[pw_]:=ListPlot[Table[{t,Cos[pw t]},{t,Pi/16,15Pi/16,Pi/8}],
  DisplayFunction->Identity]
Show[dct[0],dcdot[0], Prolog->AbsolutePointSize[4],
  DisplayFunction->$DisplayFunction]
...
Show[dct[7],dcdot[7], Prolog->AbsolutePointSize[4],
  DisplayFunction->$DisplayFunction]
```

Code for Figure 5.11.

θ	0.196	0.589	0.982	1.374	1.767	2.160	2.553	2.945
$\cos 0\theta$	1.	1.	1.	1.	1.	1.	1.	1.
$\cos 1\theta$	0.981	0.831	0.556	0.195	-0.195	-0.556	-0.831	-0.981
$\cos 2\theta$	0.924	0.383	-0.383	-0.924	-0.924	-0.383	0.383	0.924
$\cos 3\theta$	0.831	-0.195	-0.981	-0.556	0.556	0.981	0.195	-0.831
$\cos 4\theta$	0.707	-0.707	-0.707	0.707	0.707	-0.707	-0.707	0.707
$\cos 5\theta$	0.556	-0.981	0.195	0.831	-0.831	-0.195	0.981	-0.556
$\cos 6\theta$	0.383	-0.924	0.924	-0.383	-0.383	0.924	-0.924	0.383
$\cos 7\theta$	0.195	-0.556	0.831	-0.981	0.981	-0.831	0.556	-0.195

```
Table[N[t],{t,Pi/16,15Pi/16,Pi/8}]
dctp[pw_]:=Table[N[Cos[pw t]],{t,Pi/16,15Pi/16,Pi/8}]
dctp[0]
dctp[1]
...
dctp[7]
```

Table 5.12: Calculating a One-Dimensional DCT.

can be considered the basis of an 8-dimensional vector space. Any vector $\mathbf{p}$ in this space can be expressed as a linear combination $\sum w_i \mathbf{v}_i$ of the $\mathbf{v}_i$'s where the eight coefficients w_i indicate the magnitudes of the eight possible frequencies in $\mathbf{p}$. As an example, we select the eight (correlated) numbers $\mathbf{p} = (.6, .5, .4, .5, .6, .5, .4, .55)$ as our test data. We express vector $\mathbf{p}$ as a linear combination $\mathbf{p} = \sum w_i \mathbf{v}_i$ of the eight basis vectors $\mathbf{v}_i$ and compute the eight weights by solving a simple system of eight equations:

$$w_0 = 0.506, \quad w_1 = 0.0143, \quad w_2 = 0.0115, \quad w_3 = 0.0439,$$
$$w_4 = 0.0795, \quad w_5 = -0.0432, \quad w_6 = 0.00478, \quad w_7 = -0.0077.$$

Weight w_0 indicates a strong zero frequency in $\mathbf{p}$, and the other seven weights indicate much smaller higher frequencies. This is how the DCT offers the potential for compression. We can simply write the eight weights on the compressed file, where they will occupy less space than the eight components of $\mathbf{p}$. Quantizing the eight weights may increase compression considerably while resulting in just a small loss of data.

Figure 5.13 illustrates this linear combination graphically. Each of the eight $\mathbf{v}_i$'s is shown as a row of eight small, gray rectangles, where a value of $+1$ is painted white and -1 is black. Each of the eight elements of vector $\mathbf{p}$ is expressed as the weighted sum of eight grayscales.

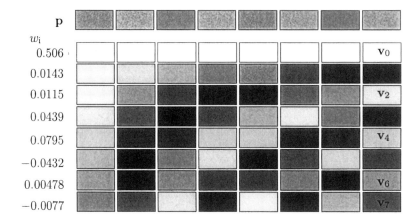

Figure 5.13: A Graphic Representation of the One-Dimensional DCT.

The simplest way to calculate the one-dimensional DCT in practice is by

$$G_f = \frac{1}{2} C_f \sum_{t=0}^{7} p_t \cos\left[\frac{(2t+1)f\pi}{16}\right],\tag{5.7}$$

$$\text{where } C_f = \begin{cases} \frac{1}{\sqrt{2}}, & f = 0, \\ 1, & f > 0, \end{cases} \quad \text{for } f = 0, 1, \ldots, 7.$$

This starts with a set of eight data values p_t (pixels, sound samples, or other data) and produces a set of eight DCT coefficients G_f. It is straightforward but slow (Section 5.9.3 discusses faster versions). The decoder inputs the DCT coefficients in sets of eight and uses the *inverse* DCT (IDCT) to reconstruct the original data values (also in groups of eight). The simplest way to calculate the IDCT is by

$$p_t = \frac{1}{2} \sum_{j=0}^{7} C_j G_j \cos\left[\frac{(2t+1)j\pi}{16}\right], \quad \text{for } t = 0, 1, \ldots, 7.\tag{5.8}$$

The following experiment illustrates the power of the DCT. We start with the set of eight correlated data items $\mathbf{p} = (12, 10, 8, 10, 12, 10, 8, 11)$, apply the one-dimensional DCT to them, and end up with the eight coefficients

28.6375, 0.571202, 0.46194, 1.757, 3.18198, -1.72956, 0.191342, -0.308709.

These can be used to precisely reconstruct the original data (except for small errors caused by limited machine precision). Our goal, however, is to improve compression by quantizing the coefficients. We quantize them to $28.6, 0.6, 0.5, 1.8, 3.2, -1.8, 0.2, -0.3$, and apply the IDCT to get back

$$12.0254,\ 10.0233,\ 7.96054,\ 9.93097,\ 12.0164,\ 9.99321,\ 7.94354,\ 10.9989.$$

We then quantize the coefficients even more, to $28, 1, 1, 2, 3, -2, 0, 0$, and apply the IDCT to get back

$$12.1883,\ 10.2315,\ 7.74931,\ 9.20863,\ 11.7876,\ 9.54549,\ 7.82865,\ 10.6557.$$

Finally, we quantize the coefficients to $28, 0, 0, 2, 3, -2, 0, 0$ and still get back from the IDCT the sequence

$$11.236,\ 9.62443,\ 7.66286,\ 9.57302,\ 12.3471,\ 10.0146,\ 8.05304,\ 10.6842,$$

where the largest difference between an original value (12) and a reconstructed one (11.236) is 0.764 (or 6.4% of 12). The code that does all that is listed in Figure 5.14.

```
p={12.,10.,8.,10.,12.,10.,8.,11.};
c={.7071,1,1,1,1,1,1,1};
dct[i_]:=(c[[i+1]]/2)Sum[p[[t+1]]Cos[(2t+1)i Pi/16],{t,0,7}];
q=Table[dct[i],{i,0,7}] (* use precise DCT coefficients *)
q={28,0,0,2,3,-2,0,0}; (* or use quantized DCT coefficients *)
idct[t_]:=(1/2)Sum[c[[j+1]]q[[j+1]]Cos[(2t+1)j Pi/16],{j,0,7}];
ip=Table[idct[t],{t,0,7}]
```

Figure 5.14: Experiments with the One-Dimensional DCT.

These simple experiments illustrate the power of the DCT. The set of coarsely quantized DCT coefficients $28, 0, 0, 2, 3, -2, 0, 0$ has four properties that make it ideal for compression, yet it also produces excellent lossy decompression. The four properties are (1) it consists of integers only, (2) only four of the eight coefficients are nonzero, (3) the zero coefficients are concentrated in runs, and (4) of the nonzero coefficients, only the first is large; the rest are smaller than the original data items. These properties can be exploited by applying RLE, Huffman codes, and other techniques (Sections 5.9.4 and 5.9.5) to further compress this set.

$\diamond$ **Exercise 5.5:** Calculate the one-dimensional DCT [Equation (5.7)] of the eight correlated values $11, 22, 33, 44, 55, 66, 77$, and 88. Show how to quantize the results, and calculate the IDCT of the quantized coefficients.

When reaching this point in the text, some readers tend to claim: "Amazing—reconstructing eight data items from just two numbers is magic." Those who understand the concept of a transform, however, know the simple explanation. The reconstruction is done not just by the two numbers 140 and −71 but also by their positions in the sequence of eight coefficients. Each position corresponds to a certain frequency. Also, the original data has been reconstructed to a high degree because it is correlated and therefore has redundancy.

An extreme case of redundant data is a sequence of identical data items. These are, of course, perfectly correlated, and we feel intuitively that only one number is needed to perfectly reconstruct them. Reconstructing a highly correlated sequence such as $20, 31, 42, 53, \ldots$ requires just two numbers. They can be the initial value (10) and the step size (11), but they can also be other values. In general, the less correlated a sequence is, the more numbers are required to reconstruct it.

Two-Dimensional DCT: We know from experience that the pixels of an image are correlated in two dimensions, not in just one dimension (a pixel is correlated with its neighbors on the left and right as well as above and below). This is why image compression methods use the two-dimensional DCT, given by

$$G_{ij} = \frac{1}{\sqrt{2n}} C_i C_j \sum_{x=0}^{n-1} \sum_{y=0}^{n-1} p_{xy} \cos\left[\frac{(2y+1)j\pi}{2n}\right] \cos\left[\frac{(2x+1)i\pi}{2n}\right] \qquad (5.9)$$

for $0 \leq i, j \leq n-1$. The image is broken up into blocks of $n \times n$ pixels p_{xy} (we use $n = 8$ as an example), and Equation (5.9) is used to produce a block of 8×8 DCT coefficients G_{ij} for each block of pixels. If lossy compression is required, the coefficients are quantized. The decoder reconstructs a block of (approximate or precise) data values by computing the inverse DCT (IDCT):

$$p_{xy} = \frac{1}{4} \sum_{i=0}^{7} \sum_{j=0}^{7} C_i C_j G_{ij} \cos\left[\frac{(2x+1)i\pi}{16}\right] \cos\left[\frac{(2y+1)j\pi}{16}\right], \qquad (5.10)$$

$$\text{where } C_f = \begin{cases} \frac{1}{\sqrt{2}}, & f = 0, \\ 1, & f > 0. \end{cases}$$

The two-dimensional DCT can be interpreted in two different ways: as a rotation (actually, two separate rotations) and as a basis of an $n \times n$-dimensional vector space. The first interpretation starts with a block of $n \times n$ pixels (Figure 5.15a, where the elements are labeled "L"). It first considers each row of this block a point $(p_{x,0}, p_{x,1}, \ldots, p_{x,n-1})$ in n-dimensional space, and it rotates the point by means of the innermost sum

$$G1_{x,j} = C_j \sum_{y=0}^{n-1} p_{xy} \cos\left[\frac{(2y+1)j\pi}{2n}\right]$$

of Equation (5.9). This results in a block $G1_{x,j}$ of $n \times n$ coefficients where the first element of each row is dominant (labeled "L" in Figure 5.15b) and the remaining elements are small (labeled "S" in that figure). The outermost sum of Equation (5.9) is

$$G_{ij} = \frac{1}{\sqrt{2n}} C_i \sum_{x=0}^{n-1} G1_{x,j} \cos \left[\frac{(2x+1)i\pi}{2n} \right].$$

Here, the *columns* of $G1_{x,j}$ are considered points in n-dimensional space and are rotated. The result is one large coefficient at the top left corner of the block ("L" in Figure 5.15c) and $n^2 - 1$ small coefficients elsewhere ("S" and "s" in that figure). This interpretation looks at the two-dimensional DCT as two sets of rotations in n dimensions. It is interesting to note that two rotations in n dimensions are faster than one rotation in n^2 dimensions, since the latter requires an $n^2 \times n^2$ rotation matrix.

```
L L L L L L L L          L S S S S S S S          L S S S S S S S
L L L L L L L L          L S S S S S S S          S s s s s s s s
L L L L L L L L          L S S S S S S S          S s s s s s s s
L L L L L L L L          L S S S S S S S          S s s s s s s s
L L L L L L L L          L S S S S S S S          S s s s s s s s
L L L L L L L L          L S S S S S S S          S s s s s s s s
L L L L L L L L          L S S S S S S S          S s s s s s s s
L L L L L L L L          L S S S S S S S          S s s s s s s s
```

(a)   (b)   (c)

Figure 5.15: The Two-Dimensional DCT as a Double Rotation.

The second interpretation (assuming $n = 8$) applies Equation (5.9) to create 64 blocks of 8×8 values each. The 64 blocks are then used as a basis of an 8×8-dimensional vector space (they are basis images). Any block B of 8×8 pixels can be expressed as a linear combination of the basis images, and the 64 weights of this linear combination are the DCT coefficients of B.

Figure 5.16 shows the graphic representation of the 64 basis images of the two-dimensional DCT for $n = 8$. A general element (i, j) in this figure is the 8×8 block obtained by calculating the product $\cos(i \cdot s) \cos(j \cdot t)$, where s and t are varied independently over the values listed in Equation (5.6). This figure can easily be generated by the *Mathematica* code shown with it. The alternative code shown is a modification of code in [Watson 94], and it requires the GraphicsImage.m package, which is not widely available.

⋄ **Exercise 5.6:** An 8×8 block of bits is given, where the odd-numbered rows contain 1s and the even-numbered rows are all zeros. The block is DCT transformed. Use Figure 5.16 to predict which of the 64 transform coefficients will be nonzeros.

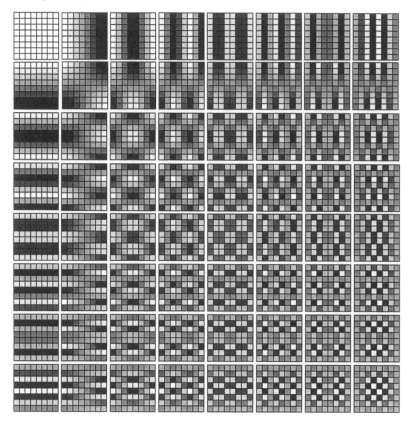

Figure 5.16: The 64 Basis Images of the Two-Dimensional DCT.

```
dctp[fs_,ft_]:=Table[SetAccuracy[N[(1.-Cos[fs s]Cos[ft t])/2],3],
 {s,Pi/16,15Pi/16,Pi/8},{t,Pi/16,15Pi/16,Pi/8}]//TableForm
dctp[0,0]
dctp[0,1]
...
dctp[7,7]
```

Code for Figure 5.16.

```
Needs["GraphicsImage'"] (* Draws 2D DCT Coefficients *)
DCTMatrix=Table[If[k==0,Sqrt[1/8],Sqrt[1/4]Cos[Pi(2j+1)k/16]],
 {k,0,7}, {j,0,7}] //N;
DCTTensor=Array[Outer[Times, DCTMatrix[[#1]],DCTMatrix[[#2]]]&,
 {8,8}];
Show[GraphicsArray[Map[GraphicsImage[#, {-.25,.25}]&,
 DCTTensor,{2}]]]
```

Alternative Code for Figure 5.16.

5.7 Subband Transforms

The transforms discussed in Section 5.5 are *orthogonal* because each is based on an orthogonal matrix. An orthogonal transform can also be expressed as an *inner product* of the data (pixel values or audio samples) with a set of *basis functions*. The result of an orthogonal transform is a set of transform coefficients that can be compressed with RLE, Huffman coding, or other methods. Lossy compression is obtained when the transform coefficients are quantized before being compressed.

The discrete inner product of the two vectors f_i and g_i is defined by

$$\langle f, g \rangle = \sum_i f_i \, g_i,$$

and Section 5.6 starts with a transform of the form $c_i = \sum_j d_j w_{ij}$, where d_j are the data items and w_{ij} are certain weights.

Many modern image compression methods are based on the *wavelet transform*. The details of this mathematically sophisticated transform are beyond the scope of this book, but one of its features can be discussed here. The wavelet transform [Stollnitz 92] is a *subband transform*, not an orthogonal transform. It is computed as a *convolution* of the data items (pixel values or audio samples) with a set of *bandpass filters*. Each resulting subband encodes a particular portion of the frequency content of the data.

The word *convolution* means coiling together. The discrete convolution of the two vectors f_i and g_i is denoted by $f \star g$. Each element $(f \star g)_i$ of the convolution is defined as the sum

$$(f \star g)_i = \sum_j f_j \, g_{i-j}, \tag{5.11}$$

taken over all valid values of j.

5.7.1 Averaging and Differencing

The wavelet transform is mathematically sophisticated, but there is a simple way to illustrate its chief properties. This section tries to convey the flavor of this transform by employing elementary operations such as averages and differences instead of filter coefficients.

We start with a one-dimensional array of N correlated values. In practice, these are neighboring pixels or adjacent audio samples. For simplicity, we assume that N is a power of 2. (We use this assumption throughout this discussion, but there is no loss of generality. If N has a different value, the data can be extended by appending zeros or by duplicating the last value as many times as needed. After decompression, the added items are removed.) An example is the array of eight values $(5, 7, 6, 5, 3, 4, 6, 9)$. We first compute the four averages $(5+7)/2 = 12/2$, $(6+5)/2 = 11/2$, $(3+4)/2 = 7/2$, and $(6+9)/2 = 15/2$. It is impossible to reconstruct the original eight values from these four averages, so we also compute the four differences $(5-7)/2 = -2/2$, $(6-5)/2 = 1/2$, $(3-4)/2 = -1/2$, and $(6-9)/2 = -3/2$. These differences are called *detail coefficients*, and in this section the terms *difference* and *detail* are used interchangeably. We can think of the averages as a coarse resolution representation of the original image and of the details as the data needed to reconstruct the original image from this coarse resolution. If the data items are correlated, the coarse representation will resemble the original items, while the details will be small.

The array $(12/2, 11/2, 7/2, 15/2, -2/2, 1/2, -1/2, -3/2)$ of four averages and four differences is sufficient to reconstruct the eight original values. This array has eight values, but its last four components, the differences, tend to be small numbers, which helps in compression. Encouraged by this, we repeat the process on the four averages, the large components of our array. They are transformed into two averages and two differences, yielding the array $(23/4, 22/4, 1/4, -8/4, -2/2, 1/2, -1/2, -3/2)$. The next and last iteration of this process transforms the first two components of the new array into one average (the average of the eight original data items) and one difference $(45/8, 1/8, 1/4, -8/4, -2/2, 1/2, -1/2, -3/2)$. The last array is the *Haar wavelet transform* of the original data items.

Because of the differences, the wavelet transform tends to have numbers smaller than the original pixel values, so it is easier to compress with quantization, run-length encoding, Huffman coding, and perhaps other methods such as move-to-front [Salomon 04]. Lossy compression can be obtained if some of the smaller differences are quantized or even completely deleted (changed to zero).

Before we continue, it is interesting (and also useful) to estimate the *complexity* of this transform, i.e., the number of arithmetic operations as a function of the size of the data. In our example, we needed $8+4+2 = 14$ operations (additions and subtractions), a number that can also be expressed as $14 = 2(8 - 1)$. In the general case, assume that we start with $N = 2^n$ data items. In the first iteration we need 2^n operations, in the second one we need 2^{n-1} operations, and so on, until the last iteration, where $2^{n-(n-1)} = 2^1$ operations are needed. Thus, the total number of operations is

$$\sum_{i=1}^{n} 2^i = \left(\sum_{i=0}^{n} 2^i\right) - 1 = \frac{1 - 2^{n+1}}{1 - 2} - 1 = 2^{n+1} - 2 = 2(2^n - 1) = 2(N - 1).$$

The Haar wavelet transform of N data items can therefore be performed with $2(N-1)$ operations, so its complexity is $\mathcal{O}(N)$, an excellent result.

It is useful to associate with each iteration a quantity called *resolution*, which is defined as the number of remaining averages at the end of the iteration. The resolutions after each of the three iterations above are $4(-2^?)$, $2(-2^1)$, and $1(= 2^0)$. Better results are obtained when each component of the wavelet transform is normalized by dividing it by the square root of the resolution. (This is referred to as the *orthonormal Haar transform*.) Thus, our example wavelet transform becomes

$$\left(\frac{45/8}{\sqrt{2^0}}, \frac{1/8}{\sqrt{2^0}}, \frac{1/4}{\sqrt{2^1}}, \frac{-8/4}{\sqrt{2^1}}, \frac{-2/2}{\sqrt{2^2}}, \frac{1/2}{\sqrt{2^2}}, \frac{-1/2}{\sqrt{2^2}}, \frac{-3/2}{\sqrt{2^2}}\right).$$

If the normalized wavelet transform is used, it can be shown that ignoring the smallest differences is the best choice for lossy image compression, since it corresponds to the highest pixel frequencies and therefore to the least important image information.

The two procedures of Figure 5.17 illustrate how the normalized wavelet transform of an array of n components (where n is a power of 2) can be computed. Reconstructing the original array from the normalized wavelet transform is illustrated by the pair of procedures of Figure 5.18.

These procedures seem at first to be different from the averages and differences discussed earlier. They don't compute averages, since they divide by $\sqrt{2}$ instead of by 2; the first one starts by dividing the entire array by $\sqrt{n}$, and the second one ends by doing the reverse. The final result, however, is the same as that shown above. Starting with array $(5, 7, 6, 5, 3, 4, 6, 9)$, the three iterations of procedure NWTcalc result in

$$\left(\frac{12}{\sqrt{2^4}}, \frac{11}{\sqrt{2^4}}, \frac{7}{\sqrt{2^4}}, \frac{15}{\sqrt{2^4}}, \frac{-2}{\sqrt{2^4}}, \frac{1}{\sqrt{2^4}}, \frac{-1}{\sqrt{2^4}}, \frac{-3}{\sqrt{2^4}} \right),$$

$$\left(\frac{23}{\sqrt{2^5}}, \frac{22}{\sqrt{2^5}}, \frac{1}{\sqrt{2^5}}, \frac{-8}{\sqrt{2^5}}, \frac{-2}{\sqrt{2^4}}, \frac{1}{\sqrt{2^4}}, \frac{-1}{\sqrt{2^4}}, \frac{-3}{\sqrt{2^4}} \right),$$

$$\left(\frac{45}{\sqrt{2^6}}, \frac{1}{\sqrt{2^6}}, \frac{1}{\sqrt{2^5}}, \frac{-8}{\sqrt{2^5}}, \frac{-2}{\sqrt{2^4}}, \frac{1}{\sqrt{2^4}}, \frac{-1}{\sqrt{2^4}}, \frac{-3}{\sqrt{2^4}} \right),$$

$$\left(\frac{45/8}{\sqrt{2^0}}, \frac{1/8}{\sqrt{2^0}}, \frac{1/4}{\sqrt{2^1}}, \frac{-8/4}{\sqrt{2^1}}, \frac{-2/2}{\sqrt{2^2}}, \frac{1/2}{\sqrt{2^2}}, \frac{-1/2}{\sqrt{2^2}}, \frac{-3/2}{\sqrt{2^2}} \right).$$

5.7.2 Extending to Two Dimensions

The one-dimensional Haar wavelet transform performed by averaging and differencing is easy to generalize to two-dimensional data. This is an important step, since in practice this transform has to be applied to images which are two-dimensional. This generalization can be done in several ways, as discussed in [Salomon 04]. Here we show two approaches, called the *standard decomposition* and the *pyramid decomposition*.

The former (Figure 5.20) starts by computing the wavelet transform of every row of the image. Each row goes through all the iterations until the leftmost data item of the row is transformed into an average and all the other data items are transformed into differences. This results in a transformed image where the first column contains averages and all the other columns contain differences. The standard algorithm then computes the wavelet transform of every column. This results in one average value at the top-left corner, with the rest of the top row containing averages of differences, the rest of the leftmost column containing differences of averages, and all other pixel values transformed into differences.

The latter method computes the wavelet transform of the image by alternating between rows and columns. The first step is to calculate averages and differences for all the rows (just one iteration, not the entire wavelet transform). This creates averages in the left half of the image and differences in the right half. The second step is to calculate averages and differences for all the columns, which results in averages in the top-left quadrant of the image and differences elsewhere. Steps 3 and 4 operate on the rows and columns of that quadrant, resulting in averages concentrated in the top-left subquadrant. Pairs of steps are repeatedly executed on smaller and smaller subsquares, until only one average is left, at the top-left corner of the image, and all other pixel values have been reduced to differences. This process is summarized in Figure 5.21.

```
procedure NWTcalc(a:array of real, n:int);
 comment n is the array size (a power of 2)
 a:=a/√n comment divide entire array
 j:=n;
 while j≥ 2 do
  NWTstep(a, j);
  j:=j/2;
 endwhile;
end;

procedure NWTstep(a:array of real, j:int);
 for i=1 to j/2 do
  b[i]:=(a[2i-1]+a[2i])/√2;
  b[j/2+i]:=(a[2i-1]-a[2i])/√2;
 endfor;
 a:=b; comment move entire array
end;
```

Figure 5.17: Computing the Normalized Wavelet Transform.

```
procedure NWTreconst(a:array of real, n:int);
 j:=2;
 while j≤n do
  NWTRstep(a, j);
  j:=2j;
 endwhile
 a:=a√n; comment multiply entire array
end;

procedure NWTRstep(a:array of real, j:int);
 for i=1 to j/2 do
  b[2i-1]:=(a[i]+a[j/2+i])/√2;
  b[2i]:=(a[i]-a[j/2+i])/√2;
 endfor;
 a:=b; comment move entire array
end;
```

Figure 5.18: Restoring from a Normalized Wavelet Transform.

The orthogonal transforms of Section 5.5 transform the original pixels into a few large numbers and many small numbers. Subband transforms, of which the Haar transform is an example, behave differently. They partition the image into regions (subbands) such that one region contains large numbers (averages in the case of the Haar transform) and the other regions contain small numbers (differences). The subbands, however, are more than just sets of large and small numbers. They reflect different geometrical features of the image. To illustrate this property, we examine a small, mostly uniform image with one vertical line and one horizontal line. Figure 5.19a shows an 8×8 image with pixel values of 12, except for a vertical line with pixel values of 14 and a horizontal line with pixel values of 16.

```
12 12 12 12 14 12 12 12        12 12 13 12│ 0 0 2 0        12 12 13 12│ 0 0 2 0
12 12 12 12 14 12 12 12        12 12 13 12│ 0 0 2 0        12 12 13 12│ 0 0 2 0
12 12 12 12 14 12 12 12        12 12 13 12│ 0 0 2 0        14 14 14 14│ 0 0 0 0
12 12 12 12 14 12 12 12        12 12 13 12│ 0 0 2 0        12 12 13 12│ 0 0 2 0
12 12 12 12 14 12 12 12        12 12 13 12│ 0 0 2 0         0  0  0  0│ 0 0 0 0
16 16 16 16 14 16 16 16        16 16 15 16│ 0 0 2 0         0  0  0  0│ 0 0 0 0
12 12 12 12 14 12 12 12        12 12 13 12│ 0 0 2 0         4  4  2  4│ 0 0 4 0
12 12 12 12 14 12 12 12        12 12 13 12│ 0 0 2 0         0  0  0  0│ 0 0 0 0
           (a)                          (b)                          (c)
```

Figure 5.19: An 8×8 Image and Its Subband Decomposition.

Figure 5.19b shows the results of applying the Haar transform once to the rows of the image. The right half of this figure (the differences) is mostly zeros, reflecting the uniform nature of the image. However, traces of the vertical line can easily be seen (the notation $\underline{2}$ indicates a negative difference). Figure 5.19c shows the results of applying the Haar transform once to the columns of Figure 5.19b. The upper right subband now contains traces of the vertical line, whereas the lower left subband shows traces of the horizontal line. These subbands are denoted by HL and LH, respectively (see Figure 5.22, although there is inconsistency in the use of this notation by various authors). The lower right subband, denoted by HH, reflects diagonal image artifacts (which our example image lacks). Most interesting is the upper left subband, denoted by LL, that consists entirely of averages. This subband is a one-quarter version of the entire image, containing traces of both the vertical and the horizontal lines.

◇ **Exercise 5.7:** Construct a diagram similar to Figure 5.19 to illustrate how subband HH isolates diagonal artifacts of the image.

Figure 5.22 shows four levels of subbands, where level 1 contains the detailed features of the image (also referred to as the high-frequency or fine-resolution wavelet coefficients) and the top level, level 4, contains the coarse image features (low-frequency or coarse-resolution coefficients). It is clear that the lower levels can be quantized coarsely without much loss of important image information, while the higher levels should be quantized finely or not at all. The subband structure is the basis of all the image compression methods that use the wavelet transform.

```
procedure StdCalc(a:array of real, n:int);
 comment array size is nxn (n = power of 2)
 for r=1 to n do NWTcalc(row r of a, n);
 endfor;
 for c=n to 1 do comment loop backwards
  NWTcalc(col c of a, n);
 endfor;
end;
procedure StdReconst(a:array of real, n:int);
 for c=n to 1 do comment loop backwards
  NWTreconst(col c of a, n);
 endfor;
 for r=1 to n do
  NWTreconst(row r of a, n);
 endfor;
end;
```

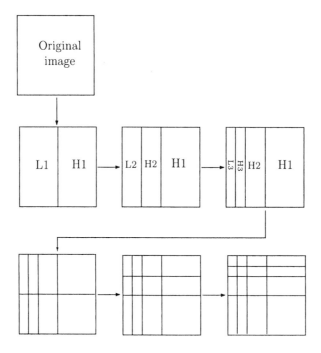

Figure 5.20: The Standard Image Wavelet Transform and Decomposition.

```
procedure NStdCalc(a:array of real, n:int);
 a:=a/√n comment divide entire array
 j:=n;
 while j> 2 do
  for r=1 to j do NWTstep(row r of a, j);
  endfor;
  for c=j to 1 do comment loop backwards
   NWTstep(col c of a, j);
  endfor;
  j:=j/2;
 endwhile;
end;
procedure NStdReconst(a:array of real, n:int);
 j:=2;
 while j≤n do
  for c=j to 1 do comment loop backwards
   NWTRstep(col c of a, j);
  endfor;
  for r=1 to j do
   NWTRstep(row r of a, j);
  endfor;
  j:=2j;
 endwhile
 a:=a√n; comment multiply entire array
end;
```

Figure 5.21: The Pyramid Image Wavelet Transform.

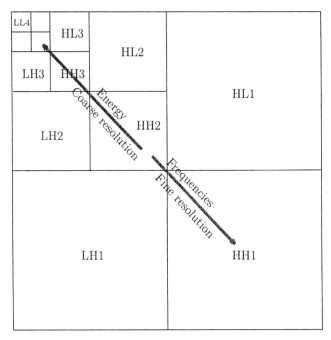

Figure 5.22: Subbands and Levels in Wavelet Decomposition.

Figure 5.23 shows typical results of the pyramid wavelet transform. The original image is shown in Figure 5.23a, and Figure 5.23c is a general pyramid decomposition. In order to illustrate how the pyramid transform works, this image consists only of horizontal, vertical, and slanted lines. The four quadrants of Figure 5.23b show smaller versions of the image. The top left subband, containing the averages, is similar to the entire image, while each of the other three subbands shows image details. Because of the way the pyramid transform is constructed, the top right subband contains vertical details, the bottom left subband contains horizontal details, and the bottom right subband contains the details of slanted lines.

Figure 5.23c shows the results of repeatedly applying this transform. The image is transformed into subbands of horizontal, vertical, and diagonal details, while the top left subsquare, containing the averages, is shrunk (if desired) all the way to a single pixel.

Either method, standard or uniform, results in a transformed—although not yet compressed—image that has one average at the top left corner and smaller numbers, differences, or averages of differences everywhere else. This can now be compressed using a combination of methods, such as RLE, move-to-front [Salomon 04], and Huffman coding. If lossy compression is acceptable, many of the smallest differences can be quantized or even set to zero (i.e., discarded), which creates run lengths of zeros, making the use of RLE even more attractive.

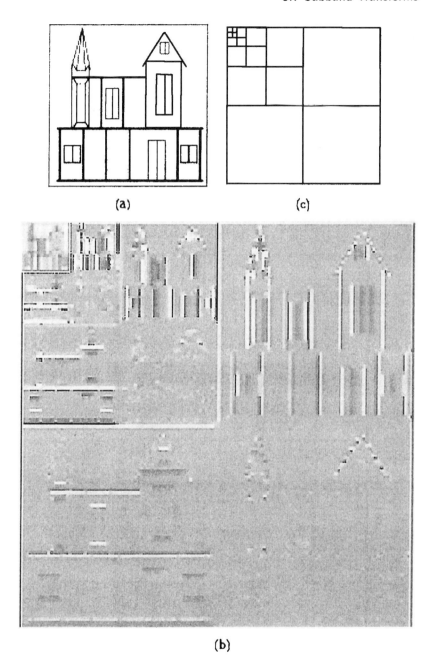

(a)

(c)

(b)

Figure 5.23: An Example of the Pyramid Image Wavelet Transform.

Discarding wavelet coefficients introduces a new compression measure termed *sparseness ratio*. It is defined as the number of nonzero wavelet coefficients divided by the number of coefficients left after some have been discarded. The higher the sparseness ratio, the fewer coefficients are left. Higher sparseness ratios lead to better compression but may result in poorly reconstructed images. The sparseness ratio is distantly related to the *compression factor*.

Color Images: So far we have assumed that each pixel is a single number (i.e., we have a single-component image, in which all pixels are shades of the same color, normally gray). Any compression method for single-component images can be extended to color (three-component) images by separating the three components and then transforming and compressing each individually. If the compression method is lossy, it makes sense to convert the three image components from their original color representation (often RGB) to the YIQ color representation. The Y component of this representation is called *luminance*, and the I and Q (chrominance) components are responsible for the color information [Salomon 99]. The advantage of this color representation is that the human eye is most sensitive to Y and least sensitive to Q. A lossy method should therefore leave the Y component alone and delete some data from the I and more data from the Q component, resulting in good compression and in a loss to which the eye is not that sensitive. Section 5.9.1 offers more information on luminance and chrominance.

It is interesting to note that U.S. color television transmission also takes advantage of the YIQ representation. Signals are broadcast with bandwidths of 4 MHz for Y, 1.5 MHz for I, and only 0.6 MHz for Q.

> Honesty is the best image.
> —Ziggy (Tom Wilson)

5.8 Progressive Image Compression

Most modern image compression methods are either progressive or optionally so. Progressive compression is an attractive choice when compressed images are transmitted over a communications line and are decompressed and viewed in real time (as is done, for example, in a Web browser). When such an image is received and decompressed, the decoder can very quickly display the entire image in a low-quality format and improve the display quality as more and more of the image is being received and decompressed. A user watching the image develop on the screen can normally recognize most of the image features after only 5–10% of it has been decompressed.

This process should be compared to raster-scan image compression. When an image is raster scanned and compressed, a user normally cannot tell much about the image when only 5–10% of it has been decompressed and displayed. Since images are supposed to be viewed by humans, progressive compression makes sense even in cases where it is slower or less efficient than nonprogressive.

Perhaps a good way to think of progressive image compression is to imagine that the encoder compresses the most important image information first, then compresses less important information and appends it to the compressed file, and so on. This explains why all progressive image compression methods have a natural lossy option; simply stop compressing at a certain point. The user can control the amount of loss by means of a parameter that tells the encoder how soon to stop the progressive encoding process. The sooner encoding is stopped, the better the compression ratio and the bigger the data loss.

Another advantage of progressive compression becomes apparent when the compressed file has to be decompressed several times and displayed with different resolutions. The decoder can, in each case, stop the decompression when the image has reached the resolution of the particular output device used.

Progressive image compression is supported by JPEG (page 180). JPEG uses the DCT to break the image up into its spatial frequency components, and it compresses the low-frequency components first. The decoder can therefore display these parts quickly, and it is these low-frequency parts that contain the general image information. The high-frequency parts contain image details. Thus, JPEG encodes spatial frequency data progressively.

> Education is a progressive discovery of our own ignorance.
>
> —Will Durant

It is useful to think of progressive decoding as the process of improving image features over time, and this can be done in three ways:

1. Encode spatial frequency data progressively. An observer watching such an image being decoded sees the image changing from blurred to sharp. Methods that work this way typically feature medium-speed encoding and slow decoding. This type of progressive compression is sometimes called *SNR progressive* or *quality progressive*.

2. Start with a gray image and add colors or shades of gray to it. An observer watching such an image being decoded will see all the image details from the start and will see them improve as more color is continuously added to them. Vector quantization methods use this kind of progressive compression. Such a method normally features slow encoding and fast decoding.

3. Encode the image in layers, where early layers consist of a few large low-resolution pixels, followed by later layers with smaller higher-resolution pixels. A person watching such an image being decoded will see more detail added to the image over time. Such a method therefore adds detail (or resolution) to the image as it is being decompressed. This way of progressively encoding an image is called *pyramid coding* or *hierarchical coding*. Pyramid coding is popular, and the remainder of this section discusses various ways for implementing it. Figure 5.25 illustrates the three principles of progressive compression mentioned here. It should be contrasted with Figure 5.24, which illustrates sequential decoding.

Assuming that the image size is $2^n \times 2^n = 4^n$ pixels, the simplest method that comes to mind in trying to do progressive compression is to calculate each pixel of layer $i-1$ as the average of a group of 2×2 pixels of layer i. Thus, layer n is the entire image (4^n pixels), layer $n-1$ contains $2^{n-1} \times 2^{n-1} = 4^{n-1}$ large pixels of size 2×2, and so on, down to layer 0, with $4^{n-n} = 1$ large pixel representing the entire image. If the image isn't too large, all the layers can be saved in memory. The pixels are then written on the compressed file in reverse order, starting with layer 0. The single pixel of layer 0

Figure 5.24: Sequential Decoding.

is the parent of the four pixels of layer 1, each of which is the parent of four pixels in layer 2, and so on. This process creates a progressive image file but results in expansion instead of compression, since the total number of pixels in the pyramid is

$$4^0 + 4^1 + \cdots + 4^{n-1} + 4^n = (4^{n+1} - 1)/3 \approx 4^n (4/3) \approx 1.33 \times 4^n = 1.33(2^n \times 2^n),$$

33% more than the original number!

A simple way to bring the total number of pixels in the pyramid down to 4^n is to include only three of the four pixels of a group in layer i and to compute the value of the fourth pixel using the parent of the group (from the preceding layer, $i - 1$) and its three siblings.

Example: Figure 5.26c shows a 4×4 image that becomes the third layer (layer 2) in its progressive compression. Layer 1 is shown in Figure 5.26b, where, for example, pixel 81.25 is the average of the four pixels 90, 72, 140, and 23 of layer 2. The single pixel of layer 0 is shown in Figure 5.26a.

The compressed file should contain just the numbers

$$54.125, \ 32.5, 41.5, 61.25, \ 72, 23, 140, 33, 18, 21, \ 18, 32, 44, \ 70, 59, 16$$

(properly encoded, of course) from which all the missing pixel values can easily be calculated. The missing pixel 81.25, for example, can be calculated from the equation $(x + 32.5 + 41.5 + 61.25)/4 = 54.125$.

A small complication with this method is that averages of integers may be nonintegers. If we want our pixel values to remain integers, we have to either lose precision or keep using longer and longer integers. Assuming that pixels are represented by 8 bits, adding four 8-bit integers produces a 10-bit integer. Dividing it by 4, to create the average, reduces the sum back to an 8-bit integer, but some precision may be lost. If

Figure 5.25: Progressive Decoding.

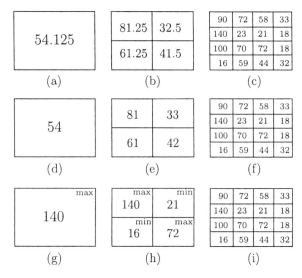

Figure 5.26: Progressive Image Compression.

we don't want to lose precision, we should represent our second-layer pixels as 10-bit numbers and our first-layer (single) pixel as a 12-bit number. Figure 5.26d,e,f shows the results of rounding off our pixel values and thus losing some image information. The contents of the compressed file in this case should be

$$54, 33, 42, 61, 72, 23, 140, 33, 18, 21, 18, 32, 44, 70, 59, 16.$$

The first missing pixel, 81, of layer 2 can be calculated from the equation $(x + 33 + 42 + 61)/4 = 54$, which yields the (slightly wrong) value 80.

⋄ **Exercise 5.8:** Show that the sum of four n-bit numbers is an $n + 2$-bit number.

A better method is to let the parent of a group help in calculating the values of its four children. This can be done by calculating the differences between the parent and its children and writing the differences (suitably encoded) in layer i of the compressed file. The decoder decodes the differences and then uses the parent from layer $i - 1$ to compute the values of the four pixels. Either Huffman or arithmetic coding can be used to encode the differences. If all the layers are calculated and saved in memory, then the distribution of difference values can be found and used to achieve the best statistical compression.

If there is no room in memory for all the layers, a simple adaptive model can be implemented. It starts by assigning a count of 1 to every difference value (to avoid the zero-probability problem; see [Salomon 04]). When a particular difference is calculated, it is assigned a probability and is encoded according to its count, and its count is then updated. It is a good idea to update the counts by incrementing them by a value greater than 1, since in this way the original counts of 1 become insignificant very quickly.

Some improvement can be achieved if the parent is used to help calculate the values of three child pixels, and then these three plus the parent are used to calculate the value of the fourth pixel of the group. If the four pixels of a group are a, b, c, and d, then their average is $v = (a + b + c + d)/4$. The average becomes part of layer $i - 1$, and layer i need contain only the three differences $k = a - b$, $l = b - c$, and $m = c - d$. Once the decoder has read and decoded the three differences, it can use their values, together with the value of v from the previous layer, to compute the values of the four pixels of the group. Calculating v by a division by 4 still causes the loss of two bits, but this 2-bit quantity can be isolated before the division and retained by encoding it separately, following the three differences.

The parent pixel of a group does not have to be its average. One alternative is to select the maximum (or the minimum) pixel of a group as the parent. This approach has the advantage that the parent is identical to one of the pixels in the group. The encoder has to encode just three pixels in each group, and the decoder decodes three pixels (or differences) and uses the parent as the fourth pixel to complete the group. When encoding consecutive groups in a layer, the encoder should alternate between selecting the maximum and the minimum as parents, since always selecting the same level creates progressive layers that are either too dark or too bright. Figure 5.26g,h,i shows the three layers in this case.

The compressed file should contain the numbers

$$140, \ (0), 21, 72, 16, \ (3), 90, 72, 23, \ (3), 58, 33, 18, \ (0), 18, 32, 44, \ (3), 100, 70, 59,$$

where the numbers in parentheses are two bits each. They tell where (in what quadrant) the parent from the previous layer should go. Notice that quadrant numbering is $\left(\begin{smallmatrix} 0 & 1 \\ 3 & 2 \end{smallmatrix}\right)$.

Selecting the median of a group is a little slower than selecting the maximum or the minimum, but it improves the appearance of the layers during progressive decompression. In general, the median of a sequence $(a_1, a_2, \ldots, a_n)$ is an element a_i such that half the elements (or as close to half as possible) are smaller than a_i and the other half are bigger. If the four pixels of a group satisfy $a < b < c < d$, then either b or c can serve as the median pixel of the group. The main advantage of selecting the median as the group's parent is that it tends to smooth large differences in pixel values that may occur because of one extreme pixel. In the group 1, 2, 3, 100, for example, selecting 2 or 3 as the parent is much more representative than selecting the average. Finding the median of four pixels requires a few comparisons, but calculating the average requires a division by 4 (or, alternatively, a right shift).

Once the median has been selected and encoded as part of layer $i-1$, the remaining three pixels can be encoded in layer i by encoding their (three) differences, preceded by a 2-bit code telling which of the four is the parent. Another small advantage of using the median is that once the decoder reads this 2-bit code, it knows how many of the three pixels are smaller and how many are bigger than the median. If the code says, for example, that one pixel is smaller and the other two are bigger than the median, and the decoder reads a pixel that is smaller than the median, it knows that the next two pixels decoded will be bigger than the median. This knowledge changes the distribution of the differences, and it can be taken advantage of by using three count tables to estimate probabilities when the differences are encoded. One table is used when a pixel is encoded that the decoder will know is bigger than the median. Another table is used to encode pixels that the decoder will know are smaller than the median, and the third table is used for pixels where the decoder will not know in advance their relations to the median. This improves compression by a few percent and is an example of how adding more features to a compression method brings diminishing returns.

Some of the important progressive image compression methods used in practice, such as SPIHT and EZW, are described in [Salomon 04].

5.9 JPEG

JPEG is a sophisticated lossy/lossless compression method for color or grayscale still images (not movies). It does not handle bi-level (black and white) images very well. It also works best on continuous-tone images, where adjacent pixels tend to have similar colors. One advantage of JPEG is the existence of many parameters that allow the user to adjust the amount of data lost (and thereby also the compression ratio) over a very wide range. Often, the eye cannot see any image degradation even at compression factors of 10 or 20. There are two main modes: lossy (also called baseline) and lossless (which isn't very efficient and typically produces compression factors of around 2). Most implementations support just the lossy mode. This mode includes progressive and hierarchical coding.

JPEG is a compression method, not a complete standard for image representation. This is why it does not specify image features such as pixel aspect ratio, color space, or interleaving of bitmap rows.

JPEG has been developed as a compression method for continuous-tone images. The main goals of JPEG compression are the following:

1. High compression ratios, especially in cases where the quality of the decompressed image is judged as very good to excellent.
2. The use of many parameters, allowing sophisticated users to experiment and achieve the desired compression/quality tradeoff.
3. Obtaining good results with any kind of continuous-tone image, regardless of image dimensions, color space, pixel aspect ratio, or other features.
4. A sophisticated but not too complex compression method, allowing software and hardware implementations on many platforms.
5. Several modes of operation: (a) sequential mode, where each color component is compressed in a single left-to-right, top-to-bottom scan; (b) progressive mode, where the image is compressed in multiple blocks (known as *scans*) to be decompressed and viewed from coarse to fine detail; (c) lossless mode: important for cases where the user decides that no pixels should be lost (the tradeoff is low compression ratio compared to the lossy modes); and (d) hierarchical mode: the image is compressed at multiple resolutions, allowing lower-resolution blocks to be viewed without first having to decompress the following higher-resolution blocks.

The term *JPEG* is an acronym that stands for Joint Photographic Experts Group. The JPEG project was a joint effort by the CCITT and the ISO (the International

Standards Organization) that started in June 1987 and produced the first JPEG draft proposal in 1991. The JPEG standard has proved successful and has become widely used for image compression, especially in Web pages.

The main JPEG compression steps are outlined here, and each step is then described in detail later.

1. Color images are transformed from RGB into a luminance/chrominance color space (Section 5.9.1; this step is skipped for grayscale images). The eye is sensitive to small changes in luminance but not in chrominance, so the chrominance parts can later lose much data and therefore be highly compressed without visually impairing the overall image quality much. This step is optional but important, since the remainder of the algorithm works on each color component separately. Without transforming the color space, none of the three color components will tolerate much loss, thereby resulting in little compression.

2. Color images are downsampled by creating low-resolution pixels from the original ones (this step is used only when hierarchical compression is needed; it is always skipped for grayscale images). The downsampling is not done for the luminance component. Downsampling (Figure 5.27) is done either at a ratio of 2:1 both horizontally and vertically (the so-called 2h2v or "4:1:1" sampling) or at ratios of 2:1 horizontally and 1:1 vertically (2h1v or "4:2:2" sampling). Since this is done on two of the three color components, 2h2v reduces the image to $1/3 + (2/3) \times (1/4) = 1/2$ its original size, while 2h1v reduces it to $1/3 + (2/3) \times (1/2) = 2/3$ its original size. Since the luminance component is not touched, there is no noticeable loss of image quality. Grayscale images don't go through this step.

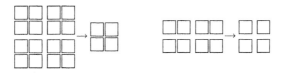

Figure 5.27: 2h2v and 2h1v Sampling.

3. The pixels of each color component are organized in groups of 8×8 pixels called *data units*. If the number of image rows or columns is not a multiple of 8, the bottom row and the rightmost column are duplicated as many times as necessary. In the noninterleaved mode (Figure 5.28a), the encoder handles all the data units of the first image component, then the data units of the second component, and finally those of the third component. In the interleaved mode (Figure 5.28b), the encoder processes the three top left (#1) data units of the three image components, then the three data units (#2) to their right, and so on.

4. The *discrete cosine transform* (DCT, Section 5.6.2) is then applied to each data unit to create an 8×8 data unit (or block) of frequency components (Section 5.9.2). These components indicate the frequency content of the pixels in the group. This process prepares the image data for the crucial step of losing information. Since DCT involves the cosine function, it must involve some loss of information due to the limited precision

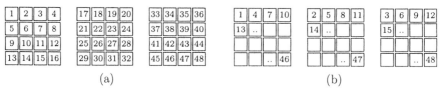

Figure 5.28: Order of Data Unit Processing.

of computer arithmetic. This means that even without the main lossy step (Step 5), there will be some loss of image quality, but this is normally very small.

5. Each of the 64 frequency components in a data unit is divided by a separate number called its *quantization coefficient* (QC) and then rounded to an integer (Section 5.9.4). This is where information is irretrievably lost. Large QCs cause more loss, which is why it makes sense to have larger QCs for the high-frequency components. Each of the 64 QCs is a JPEG parameter and can, in principle, be specified by the user. In practice, most JPEG implementations use the QC tables recommended by the JPEG standard for the luminance and chrominance image components (Table 5.30).

6. The 64 quantized frequency coefficients (which are now integers) of each data unit are encoded using a combination of RLE and Huffman coding (Section 5.9.5). An arithmetic coding variant known as the QM coder [Salomon 04] can be used instead of Huffman coding, but it is rarely used because it is patented.

7. The last step adds headers and the values of all the JPEG parameters used and outputs the result. The compressed file may be in one of three formats: (1) the *interchange* format, in which the file contains the compressed image and all the tables needed by the decoder (mostly quantization tables and tables of Huffman codes); (2) the *abbreviated* format for compressed image data, where the file contains the compressed image and may contain no tables (or just a few tables); and (3) the *abbreviated* format for table-specification data, where the file contains just tables and no compressed image. The second format makes sense in cases where the same encoder/decoder pair is used, and both the encoder and decoder have the same tables built in. The third format is used in cases where many images have been compressed by the same encoder, using the same tables. When those images need to be decompressed, they are sent to a decoder, preceded by one file with table-specification data.

The JPEG decoder performs the reverse steps. (Thus, JPEG is a symmetric compression method.)

The progressive mode is a JPEG option. In this mode, higher-frequency DCT coefficients are written on the compressed file in blocks called *scans*. Each scan read and processed by the decoder results in a sharper image. The idea is to use the first few scans to quickly create a low-quality, blurred preview of the image and then either to input the remaining scans or to stop the process and reject the image. The tradeoff is that the encoder has to save all the coefficients of all the data units in a memory buffer before they are sent in scans (this is because they are sent in scans in the reverse order in which they are generated; see page 173) and also go through all the steps for each scan, slowing down the progressive mode.

Figure 5.29a shows an example of an image with resolution 1024×512. The image is divided into $128 \times 64 = 8192$ data units, and each is DCT transformed, becoming a set of 64 8-bit numbers. Figure 5.29b is a block whose depth corresponds to the 8,192 data units, whose height corresponds to the 64 DCT coefficients (the DC coefficient is the top one, numbered 0), and whose width corresponds to the 8 bits of each coefficient.

After preparing all the data units in a memory buffer, the encoder writes them on the compressed file in one of two methods, *spectral selection* or *successive approximation* (Figure 5.29c,d). The first scan in either method is the set of DC coefficients. If spectral selection is used, each successive scan consists of several consecutive (a *band* of) AC coefficients. If successive approximation is used, the second scan consists of the four most significant bits of all AC coefficients, and each of the following four scans, numbers 3 through 6, adds one more significant bit (bits 3 through 0, respectively).

In the hierarchical mode, the encoder stores the image several times in the output file at several resolutions. However, each high-resolution part uses information from the low-resolution parts of the output file, so the total amount of information is less than that required to store the different resolutions separately. Each hierarchical part may use the progressive mode.

The hierarchical mode is useful in cases where a high-resolution image needs to be output in low resolution. Older dot-matrix printers may be a good example of a low-resolution output device sometimes still in use.

The lossless mode of JPEG (Section 5.9.6) calculates a "predicted" value for each pixel, generates the difference between the pixel and its predicted value for relative encoding, and encodes the difference using the same method (i.e., Huffman or arithmetic coding) as in step 5 above. The predicted value is calculated using values of pixels above and to the left of the current pixel (pixels that have already been input and encoded). The following sections discuss these steps in more detail.

> When in doubt, predict that the present trend will continue.
>
> —Merkin's Maxim

5.9.1 Luminance

The main international organization devoted to light and color is the International Committee on Illumination (Commission Internationale de l'Éclairage), abbreviated CIE. It is responsible for developing standards and definitions in this area. One of the early achievements of the CIE was its *chromaticity diagram* [Salomon 99], developed in 1931. It shows that no fewer than three parameters are required to specify color. Expressing a certain color by the triplet (x, y, z) is similar to denoting a point in three-dimensional space, hence the term *color space*. The most common color space is RGB, where the three parameters are the intensities of red, green, and blue in a color. When used in computers, these parameters are normally in the range 0–255 (8 bits) each.

The CIE defines color as the perceptual result of light in the visible region of the spectrum, having wavelengths in the region of 400 nm to 700 nm incident on the retina (a nanometer, nm, equals 10^{-9} meter). Physical power (or radiance) is expressed in a spectral power distribution (SPD), often in 31 components, each representing a 10 nm band.

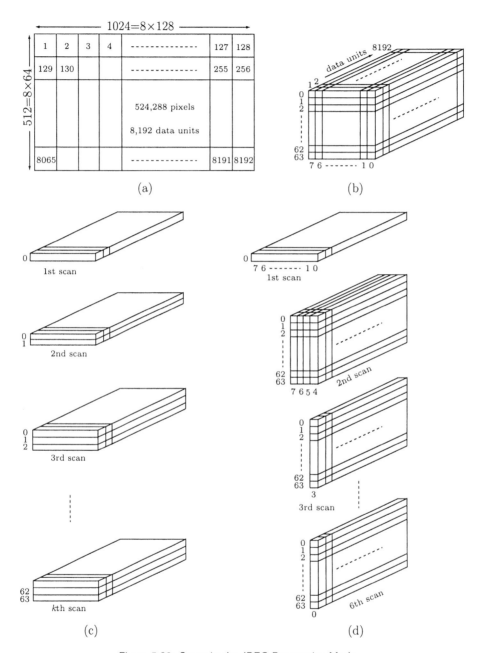

Figure 5.29: Scans in the JPEG Progressive Mode.

The CIE defines brightness as the attribute of a visual sensation according to which an area appears to emit more or less light. The brain's perception of brightness is impossible to define, so the CIE defines a more practical quantity called *luminance*. It is defined as radiant power weighted by a spectral sensitivity function that is characteristic of vision. The luminous efficiency of the standard observer is defined by the CIE as a positive function of the wavelength, which has a maximum at about 555 nm. When a spectral power distribution is integrated using this function as a weighting function, the result is CIE luminance, which is denoted by Y. Luminance is an important quantity in the fields of digital image processing and compression.

Luminance is proportional to the power of the light source. It is similar to intensity, but the spectral composition of luminance is related to the brightness sensitivity of human vision. Based on the results of many experiments, luminance is defined as a weighted sum of red, green, and blue, with weights 77/256, 150/256, and 29/256, respectively.

The eye is very sensitive to small changes in luminance, which is why it is useful to have color spaces that use Y as one of their three parameters. A simple way to create such a space is to subtract Y from the blue and red components of RGB and use the three components Y, Cb = B − Y, and Cr = R − Y as a new color space. The last two components are called chroma. They represent color in terms of the presence or absence of blue (Cb) and red (Cr) for a given luminance intensity.

Various number ranges are used in B − Y and R − Y for different applications. The YPbPr ranges are optimized for component analog video. The YCbCr ranges are appropriate for component digital video such as studio video, JPEG, JPEG 2000, and MPEG-1.

The YCbCr color space was developed as part of Recommendation ITU-R BT.601 (formerly CCIR 601) during the development of a worldwide digital component video standard. Y is defined to have a range of 16 to 235; Cb and Cr are defined to have a range of 16 to 240, with 128 equal to zero. There are several YCbCr sampling formats, such as 4:4:4, 4:2:2, 4:1:1, and 4:2:0, which are also described in the recommendation.

Conversions between RGB with a 16–235 range and YCbCr are linear and therefore simple. Transforming RGB to YCbCr is done by (notice the small weight assigned to blue)

$$Y = (77/256)R + (150/256)G + (29/256)B,$$
$$Cb = -(44/256)R - (87/256)G + (131/256)B + 128,$$
$$Cr = (131/256)R - (110/256)G - (21/256)B + 128,$$

while the opposite transformation is

$$R = Y + 1.371(Cr - 128),$$
$$G = Y - 0.698(Cr - 128) - 0.336(Cb - 128),$$
$$B = Y + 1.732(Cb - 128).$$

When performing YCbCr to RGB conversion, the resulting RGB values have a nominal range of 16–235, with possible occasional values in 0–15 and 236–255.

5.9.2 DCT

The discrete cosine transform (DCT) is discussed in Section 5.6.2. The JPEG committee elected to use the DCT because of its good performance, because it does not assume anything about the structure of the data being compressed, and because there are ways to speed up the DCT (Section 5.9.3).

The JPEG standard does not apply the DCT to the entire image but to data units (blocks) of 8×8 pixels each: (1) Applying the DCT to the entire image involves many arithmetic operations and is therefore slow. Applying the DCT to individual data units is faster. (2) Experience shows that, in a continuous-tone image, correlations between pixels are short range. A pixel in such an image has a value (color component or shade of gray) that is close to those of its near neighbors but has nothing to do with the values of far neighbors. Applying the DCT to the entire image may therefore not result in better compression.

It should be noted that the principle of transforming individual data units has its downside. Applying the DCT to the entire image produces a better-looking image after lossy compression and decompression. Applying the DCT to data units is faster, but when an image is compressed and then decompressed, it may feature blocky artifacts due to the way the various blocks respond to the quantization step that follows the DCT.

The JPEG DCT is computed by Equation (5.9), duplicated here:

$$G_{ij} = \frac{1}{4} C_i C_j \sum_{x=0}^{7} \sum_{y=0}^{7} p_{xy} \cos \left[\frac{(2x+1)i\pi}{16} \right] \cos \left[\frac{(2y+1)j\pi}{16} \right], \tag{5.9}$$

$$\text{where } C_f = \begin{cases} \frac{1}{\sqrt{2}}, & f = 0, \\ 1, & f > 0, \end{cases} \quad \text{and } 0 \le i, j \le 7,$$

The DCT is JPEG's key to lossy compression. JPEG "loses" unimportant image information by dividing each of the 64 DCT coefficients (especially the ones located toward the right bottom part of the data unit) by a quantization coefficient (QC). In general, each of the 64 DCT coefficients is divided by a different quantization coefficient, and all 64 QCs are parameters that can, in principle, be controlled by the user (Section 5.9.4).

The JPEG decoder computes the inverse DCT (IDCT) by Equation (5.10), duplicated here:

$$p_{xy} = \frac{1}{4} \sum_{i=0}^{7} \sum_{j=0}^{7} C_i C_j G_{ij} \cos \left[\frac{(2x+1)i\pi}{16} \right] \cos \left[\frac{(2y+1)j\pi}{16} \right], \tag{5.10}$$

$$\text{where } C_f = \begin{cases} \frac{1}{\sqrt{2}}, & f = 0; \\ 1, & f > 0. \end{cases}$$

It takes the 64 quantized DCT results and calculates 64 pixels p_{xy}. Mathematically, the DCT is a one-to-one mapping of 64-point vectors from the image domain to the frequency domain. The IDCT is the reverse mapping. If the DCT and IDCT could be calculated with infinite precision and if the DCT coefficients were not quantized, the original 64 pixels could be exactly reconstructed. In practice, quantization is often used, but if done carefully, the new 64 pixels will be very similar to the original ones.

5.9.3 Practical DCT

Equation (5.9) can be coded directly in any higher-level language. However, several improvements are possible, which speed it up considerably. Since this equation is the "heart" of JPEG, its fast calculation is essential. Here are some ideas.

1. Regardless of the image size, only 32 cosine functions are involved (see the next paragraph). They can be precomputed once and used repeatedly to calculate all the 8×8 data units. Calculating the expression

$$p_{xy} \cos\left[\frac{(2x+1)i\pi}{16}\right] \cos\left[\frac{(2y+1)j\pi}{16}\right]$$

now amounts to performing two multiplications. The double sum of Equation (5.9) thus requires $64 \times 2 = 128$ multiplications and 63 additions.

(The arguments of the cosine functions used by the DCT are of the form $(2x + 1)i\pi/16$, where i and x are integers in the range $[0, 7]$. Such an argument can be written in the form $n\pi/16$, where n is an integer in the range $[0, 15 \times 7]$. Since the cosine function is periodic, it satisfies $\cos(32\pi/16) = \cos(0\pi/16)$, $\cos(33\pi/16) = \cos(\pi/16)$, and so on. As a result, only the 32 values $\cos(n\pi/16)$ for $n = 0, 1, 2, \ldots, 31$ are needed. I am indebted to V. Saravanan for pointing out this feature of the DCT.)

2. A little algebraic tinkering shows that the double sum of Equation (5.9) can be written as the matrix product $\mathbf{C}\,\mathbf{P}\,\mathbf{C}^T$, where $\mathbf{P}$ is the 8×8 matrix of the pixels, $\mathbf{C}$ is the matrix defined by

$$C_{ij} = \begin{cases} \frac{1}{\sqrt{8}}, & i = 0, \\ \frac{1}{2} \cos\left(\frac{(2j+1)i\pi}{16}\right), & i > 0, \end{cases}$$

and $\mathbf{C}^T$ is the transpose of $\mathbf{C}$.

Calculating one matrix element of the product $\mathbf{C}\mathbf{P}$ thus requires eight multiplications and seven (but for simplicity let's say eight) additions. Multiplying the two 8×8 matrices $\mathbf{C}$ and $\mathbf{P}$ requires $64 \times 8 = 8^3$ multiplications and the same number of additions. Multiplying the product $\mathbf{C}\mathbf{P}$ by $\mathbf{C}^T$ requires the same number of operations, so the DCT of one 8×8 data unit requires 2×8^3 multiplications (and the same number of additions). Assuming that the entire image consists of $n \times n$ pixels, and that $n = 8q$, there are $q \times q$ data units, so the DCT of all the data units requires $2q^2 8^3$ multiplications (and the same number of additions). In comparison, performing one DCT for the entire image would require $2n^3 = 2q^3 8^3 = (2q^2 8^3)q$ operations. By dividing the image into data units, we reduce the number of multiplications (and also of additions) by a factor of q. Unfortunately, q cannot be too large, since that would mean very small data units.

We should remember that a color image consists of three components (normally RGB, but usually converted to YCbCr or YPbPr). Each is DCT-transformed separately, bringing the total number of arithmetic operations to $32q^28^3 = 3,072q^2$. For a 512×512-pixel image, this means $3,072\times64^2 = 12,582,912$ multiplications (and the same number of additions).

3. Another way to speed up the DCT is to perform all the arithmetic operations on fixed-point (scaled integer) rather than floating-point numbers. On many computers, operations on fixed-point numbers require (somewhat) sophisticated programming techniques but are considerably faster than floating-point operations (except in some supercomputers that are specifically designed for fast floating-point operations).

Arguably the best DCT algorithm is described in [Feig and Linzer 90]. It uses 54 multiplications and 468 additions and shifts. Today, there are also various VLSI chips that perform this calculation efficiently. The interested reader should also check [Loeffler et al. 89] for a fast one-dimensional DCT algorithm that uses 11 multiplications and 29 additions.

5.9.4 Quantization

After each 8×8 matrix of DCT coefficients G_{ij} is calculated, it is quantized. This is the step where the information loss (except for some unavoidable loss because of finite precision calculations in other steps) occurs. Each number in the DCT coefficients matrix is divided by the corresponding number from the particular "quantization table" used, and the result is rounded to the nearest integer. As has already been mentioned, three such tables are needed for the three color components. The JPEG standard allows for up to four tables, and the user can select any of the four for quantizing each color component. The 64 numbers constituting each quantization table are all JPEG parameters. In principle, they can all be specified and fine-tuned by the user for maximum compression. In practice, few users have the time or expertise to experiment with so many parameters, so JPEG software normally uses two approaches:

1. Default quantization tables. Two such tables, one for the luminance (grayscale) and one for the chrominance components, are the result of many experiments performed by the JPEG committee. They are included in the JPEG standard and are reproduced here as Table 5.30. It is easy to see how the QCs in the table generally grow as we move from the upper left corner to the bottom right one. This is how JPEG reduces the DCT coefficients with high spatial frequencies.

2. A simple quantization table Q is computed, based on one parameter R supplied by the user. A simple expression such as $Q_{ij} = 1 + (i + j) \times R$ guarantees that QCs start small at the upper left corner and get bigger toward the bottom right corner.

If the quantization is done right, very few nonzero numbers will be left in the DCT coefficients block, and these will typically be concentrated in the upper left part. These numbers are the output of JPEG, but they are further compressed before being written on the output file. In the JPEG literature, this compression is called *entropy coding*, and Section 5.9.5 shows in detail how it is done. Three techniques are used by entropy coding to compress the 8×8 matrix of integers:

1. The 64 numbers are collected by scanning the matrix in zigzags (Figure 5.4a). This produces a string of 64 numbers that starts with some nonzeros and typically ends with many consecutive zeros. Only the nonzero numbers are output (after further

16	11	10	16	24	40	51	61
12	12	14	19	26	58	60	55
14	13	16	24	40	57	69	56
14	17	22	29	51	87	80	62
18	22	37	56	68	109	103	77
24	35	55	64	81	104	113	92
49	64	78	87	103	121	120	101
72	92	95	98	112	100	103	99

17	18	24	47	99	99	99	99
18	21	26	66	99	99	99	99
24	26	56	99	99	99	99	99
47	66	99	99	99	99	99	99
99	99	99	99	99	99	99	99
99	99	99	99	99	99	99	99
99	99	99	99	99	99	99	99
99	99	99	99	99	99	99	99

Luminance   Chrominance

Table 5.30: Recommended Quantization Tables.

compressing them) and are followed by a special end-of-block (EOB) code. This way there is no need to output the trailing zeros (we can say that the EOB is the run-length encoding of all the trailing zeros).

⋄ **Exercise 5.9:** Table 5.31 lists 64 hypothetical DCT coefficients. What is their zigzag sequence?

1118	2	0	0	0	0	0	0
0	0	0	0	0	0	0	0
−2	0	0	−1	0	0	0	0
0	0	0	0	0	0	0	0
0	0	0	0	0	0	0	0
0	0	0	0	0	0	0	0
0	0	0	0	0	0	0	0
0	0	0	0	0	0	0	0

Table 5.31: 64 Quantized Coefficients.

⋄ **Exercise 5.10:** Suggest a practical way of writing a software loop to traverse an 8×8 matrix in zigzag.

2. The nonzero numbers are compressed using Huffman coding (Section 5.9.5).
3. The first of those numbers (the DC coefficient, page 151) is treated differently from the others (the AC coefficients).

5.9.5 Coding

We first discuss point 3 above. Each 8×8 matrix of quantized DCT coefficients contains one DC coefficient (at position $(0,0)$, the top left corner) and 63 AC coefficients. The DC coefficient is a measure of the average value of the 64 original pixels constituting the data unit. Experience shows that in a continuous-tone image, adjacent data units of pixels are normally correlated in the sense that the average values of the pixels in adjacent data units are close. We already know that the DC coefficient of a data unit is a multiple of the average of the 64 pixels constituting the unit. This implies that the

DC coefficients of adjacent data units don't differ much. JPEG outputs the first one (encoded), followed by *differences* (also encoded) of the DC coefficients of consecutive data units.

Example: If the first three 8×8 data units of an image have quantized DC coefficients of 1118, 1114, and 1119, then the JPEG output for the first data unit is 1118 (Huffman encoded; see below) followed by the 63 (encoded) AC coefficients of that data unit. The output for the second data unit will be $1114 - 1118 = -4$ (also Huffman encoded), followed by the 63 (encoded) AC coefficients of that data unit, and the output for the third data unit will be $1119 - 1114 = 5$ (also Huffman encoded), again followed by the 63 (encoded) AC coefficients of that data unit. This way of handling the DC coefficients is worth the extra trouble, since the differences are small.

Coding the DC differences is done using Table 5.32. This table uses the so-called *unary code*, defined as follows: The unary code of the nonnegative integer n consists of $n - 1$ ones followed by a single 0 or, alternatively, of $n - 1$ zeros followed by a single 1. The length of the unary code for the integer n is therefore n bits.

0:	0									0
1:	-1	1								10
2:	-3	-2	2	3						110
3:	-7	-6	-5	-4	4	5	6	7		1110
4:	-15	-14	...	-9	-8	8	9	10	... 15	11110
5:	-31	-30	-29	...	-17	-16	16	17	... 31	111110
6:	-63	-62	-61	...	-33	-32	32	33	... 63	1111110
7:	-127	-126	-125	...	-65	-64	64	65	... 127	11111110
⋮			⋮						
14:	-16383	-16382	-16381	...	-8193	-8192	8192	8193	... 16383	111111111111110
15:	-32767	-32766	-32765	...	-16385	-16384	16384	16385	... 32767	1111111111111110
16:	32768									1111111111111111

Table 5.32: Coding the Differences of DC Coefficients.

Each row of Table 5.32 has a row number (on the left), the unary code for the row (on the right), and several columns in between. Each row contains greater numbers (and also more numbers) than its predecessor but not the numbers contained in previous rows. Row i contains the range of integers $[-(2^i - 1), +(2^i - 1)]$ but is missing the middle range $[-(2^{i-1} - 1), +(2^{i-1} - 1)]$. The rows thus get very long, which means that a simple two-dimensional array is not a good data structure for this table. In fact, there is no need to store these integers in a data structure, since the program can figure out where in the table any given integer x is supposed to reside by analyzing the bits of x.

The first DC coefficient to be encoded in our example is 1118. It is found in row 11 column 930 of the table (column numbering starts at zero), so it is encoded as 111111111110|01110100010 (the unary code for row 11, followed by the 11-bit binary value of 930). The second DC difference is -4. It resides in row 3 column 3 of Table 5.32, so it is encoded as 1110|011 (the unary code for row 3, followed by the 3-bit binary value of 3).

⋄ **Exercise 5.11:** How is the third DC difference, 5, encoded?

Point 2 at the end of Section 5.9.4 has to do with the precise way the 63 AC coefficients of a data unit are compressed. This compression uses a combination of RLE and either Huffman or arithmetic coding. The idea is that the sequence of AC coefficients normally contains just a few nonzero numbers, with runs of zeros between them, and with a long run of trailing zeros. For each nonzero number x, (1) the encoder finds the number Z of consecutive zeros preceding x; (2) it finds x in Table 5.32 and prepares its row and column numbers (R and C); (3) the pair (R, Z)—that's (R, Z), not (R, C)—is used as row and column numbers for Table 5.33; and (4) the Huffman code found in that position in the table is concatenated to C (where C is written as an R-bit number) and the result is the code emitted by the JPEG encoder for the AC coefficient x and all the consecutive zeros preceding it. (Quite a mouthful.)

R Z:	0	1	. . .	15
0:	1010			11111111001(ZRL)
1:	00	1100	. . .	1111111111110101
2:	01	11011	. . .	1111111111110110
3:	100	1111001	. . .	1111111111110111
4:	1011	111110110	. . .	1111111111111000
5:	11010	11111110110	. . .	1111111111111001
⋮	⋮			

Table 5.33: Coding AC Coefficients.

The Huffman codes in Table 5.33 are arbitrary and are not the ones recommended by the JPEG standard. The standard recommends the use of Tables 5.34 and 5.35 and says that up to four Huffman code tables can be used by a JPEG codec, except that the baseline mode can use only two such tables. The reader should notice the EOB code at position $(0,0)$ and the ZRL code at position $(0,15)$. The former indicates end-of-block, and the latter is the code emitted for 15 consecutive zeros when the number of consecutive zeros exceeds 15. These codes are the ones recommended for the luminance AC coefficients of Table 5.34. The EOB and ZRL codes recommended for the chrominance AC coefficients of Table 5.35 are 00 and 1111111010, respectively.

Example: Consider again the sequence $1118, 2, 0, -2, \underbrace{0, \ldots, 0}_{13}, -1, \underbrace{0, \ldots, 0}_{46}$. The first AC coefficient 2 has no zeros preceding it, so $Z = 0$. It is found in Table 5.32 in row 2, column 2, so $R = 2$ and $C = 2$. The Huffman code in position $(R, Z) = (2, 0)$ of Table 5.33 is 01, so the final code emitted for 2 is 01|10. The next nonzero coefficient, -2, has one zero preceding it, so $Z = 1$. It is found in Table 5.32 in row 2 column 1, so $R = 2$ and $C = 1$. The Huffman code in position $(R, Z) = (2, 1)$ of Table 5.33 is 11011, so the final code emitted for 2 is 11011|01.

Z	R 1 6	R 2 7	R 3 8	R 4 9	R 5 A
0	00 1111000	01 11111000	100 1111110110	1011 1111111110000010	11010 1111111110000011
1	1100 1111111110000100	11011 1111111110000101	11110001 1111111110000110	111110110 1111111110000111	1111110110 1111111110001000
2	11100 111111110001010	11111001 111111110001011	1111110111 111111110001100	111111110100 111111110001101	111111110001001 111111110001110
3	111010 1111111110010001	111110111 1111111110010010	111111110101 1111111110010011	1111111110001111 1111111110010100	1111111110010000 1111111110010101
4	111011 1111111110011001	1111111000 1111111110011010	1111111110010110 1111111110011011	1111111110010111 1111111110011100	1111111110011000 1111111110011101
5	1111010 1111111110100001	11111110111 1111111110100010	1111111110011110 1111111110100011	1111111110011111 1111111110100100	1111111110100000 1111111110100101
6	1111011 1111111110101001	111111110110 1111111110101010	1111111110100110 1111111110101011	1111111110100111 1111111110101100	1111111110101000 1111111110101101
7	11111010 1111111110110001	111111110111 1111111110110010	1111111110101110 1111111110110011	1111111110101111 1111111110110100	1111111110110000 1111111110110101
8	111111000 1111111110111001	111111111000000 1111111110111010	1111111110110110 1111111110111011	1111111110110111 1111111110111100	1111111110111000 1111111110111101
9	111111001 1111111111000010	1111111110111110 1111111111000011	1111111110111111 1111111111000100	1111111111000000 1111111111000101	1111111111000001 1111111111000110
A	111111010 1111111111001011	1111111111000111 1111111111001100	1111111111001000 1111111111001101	1111111111001001 1111111111001110	1111111111001010 1111111111001111
B	1111111001 1111111111010100	1111111111010000 1111111111010101	1111111111010001 1111111111010110	1111111111010010 1111111111010111	1111111111010011 1111111111011000
C	1111111010 1111111111011101	1111111111011001 1111111111011110	1111111111011010 1111111111011111	1111111111011011 1111111111100000	1111111111011100 1111111111100001
D	11111111000 1111111111100110	1111111111100010 1111111111100111	1111111111100011 1111111111101000	1111111111100100 1111111111101001	1111111111100101 1111111111101010
E	1111111111101011 1111111111110000	1111111111101100 1111111111110001	1111111111101101 1111111111110010	1111111111101110 1111111111110011	1111111111101111 1111111111110100
F	11111111001 1111111111111001	1111111111110101 1111111111111010	1111111111110110 1111111111111011	1111111111110111 1111111111111101	1111111111111000 1111111111111110

Table 5.34: Recommended Huffman Codes for Luminance AC Coefficients.

Z	R = 1 / 6	2 / 7	3 / 8	4 / 9	5 / A
0	01 111000	100 1111000	1010 111110100	11000 1111110110	11001 111111110100
1	1011 111111110101	111001 111111110001000	11110110 1111111110001001	111110101 1111111110001010	1111110110 1111111110001011
2	11010 1111111110001100	11110111 1111111110001101	1111110111 1111111110001110	111111110110 1111111110001111	111111111000010 1111111110010000
3	11011 1111111110010010	11111000 1111111110010011	1111111000 1111111110010100	111111110111 1111111110010101	1111111110010001 1111111110010110
4	111010 1111111110011010	111110110 1111111110011011	1111111110010111 1111111110011100	1111111110011000 1111111110011101	1111111110011001 1111111110011110
5	111011 1111111110100010	1111111001 1111111110100011	1111111110011111 1111111110100100	1111111110100000 1111111110100101	1111111110100001 1111111110100110
6	1111001 1111111110101010	11111110111 1111111110101011	1111111110100111 1111111110101100	1111111110101000 1111111110101101	1111111110101001 1111111110101110
7	1111010 1111111110110010	11111111000 1111111110110011	1111111110101111 1111111110110100	1111111110110000 1111111110110101	1111111110110001 1111111110110110
8	11111001 1111111110111011	1111111110110111 1111111110111100	1111111110111000 1111111110111101	1111111110111001 1111111110111110	1111111110111010 1111111110111111
9	111110111 1111111111000100	1111111111000000 1111111111000101	1111111111000001 1111111111000110	1111111111000010 1111111111000111	1111111111000011 1111111111001000
A	111111000 1111111111001101	1111111111001001 1111111111001110	1111111111001010 1111111111001111	1111111111001011 1111111111010000	1111111111001100 1111111111010001
B	111111001 1111111111010110	1111111111010010 1111111111010111	1111111111010011 1111111111011000	1111111111010100 1111111111011001	1111111111010101 1111111111011010
C	111111010 1111111111011111	1111111111011011 1111111111100000	1111111111011100 1111111111100001	1111111111011101 1111111111100010	1111111111011110 1111111111100011
D	11111111001 1111111111101000	1111111111100100 1111111111101001	1111111111100101 1111111111101010	1111111111100110 1111111111101011	1111111111100111 1111111111101100
E	11111111100000 1111111111110001	1111111111101101 1111111111110010	1111111111101110 1111111111110011	1111111111101111 1111111111110100	1111111111110000 1111111111110101
F	111111111000011 1111111111111010	1111111111010110 1111111111111011	1111111111110111 1111111111111100	1111111111111000 1111111111111101	1111111111111001 1111111111111110

Table 5.35: Recommended Huffman Codes for Chrominance AC Coefficients.

◊ **Exercise 5.12:** What code is emitted for the last nonzero AC coefficient, -1?

Finally, the sequence of trailing zeros is encoded as 1010 (EOB), so the output for the sequence of AC coefficients is 0110110111011101010101010. We saw earlier that the DC coefficient is encoded as 11111111110|1110100010, so the final output for the entire 64-pixel data unit is the 46-bit number

$$11111111110011101000100110110111011101010101010.$$

These 46 bits encode one color component of the 64 pixels of a data unit. Let's assume that the other two color components are also encoded into 46-bit numbers. If each pixel originally consists of 24 bits, then this corresponds to a compression factor of $64 \times 24/(46 \times 3) \approx 11.13$; very impressive!

(Notice that the DC coefficient of 1118 has contributed 23 of the 46 bits. Subsequent data units code differences of their DC coefficient, and these may typically consist of fewer than 10 bits instead of 23. They may feature much higher compression factors as a result.)

The same tables (Tables 5.32 and 5.33) used by the encoder should, of course, be used by the decoder. The tables may be predefined and used by a JPEG codec as defaults, or they may be specifically calculated for a given image in a special pass preceding the actual compression. The JPEG standard does not specify any code tables, so any JPEG codec must use its own.

Some JPEG variants use a particular version of arithmetic coding, called the QM coder, that is specified in the JPEG standard. This version of arithmetic coding is adaptive, so it does not need Tables 5.32 and 5.33. It adapts its behavior to the image statistics as it goes along. Using arithmetic coding may produce 5–10% better compression than Huffman for a typical continuous-tone image. However, it is more complex to implement than Huffman coding and it is also patented, so in practice it is rarely implemented.

5.9.6 Lossless Mode

The lossless mode of JPEG uses differencing to reduce the values of pixels before they are compressed. This particular form of differencing is called *predicting*. The values of some near neighbors of a pixel are subtracted from the pixel to get a small number, which is then compressed further using Huffman or arithmetic coding. Figure 5.36a shows a pixel X and three neighbor pixels A, B, and C. Figure 5.36b shows eight possible ways (predictions) to combine the values of the three neighbors. In the lossless mode of JPEG, the user can select one of these predictions, and the encoder then uses it to combine the three neighbor pixels and subtract the combination from the value of X. The result is normally a small number, which is then entropy-coded in a way very similar to that described for the DC coefficient in Section 5.9.5.

Predictor 0 is used only in the hierarchical mode of JPEG. Predictors 1, 2, and 3 are called *one-dimensional*. Predictors 4, 5, 6, and 7 are *two-dimensional*.

It should be noted that the lossless mode of JPEG has never been very successful. It produces typical compression factors of 2 and is thus inferior to other lossless image compression methods. Because of this, popular JPEG implementations do not even

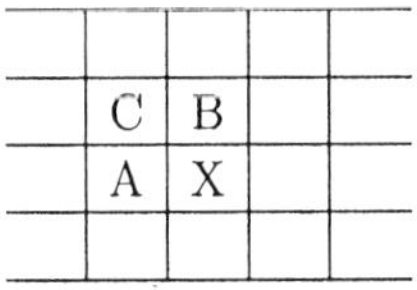

	Selection value	Prediction
	0	no prediction
	1	A
	2	B
	3	C
	4	$A + B - C$
	5	$A + ((B - C)/2)$
	6	$B + ((A - C)/2)$
	7	$(A + B)/2$

C B
A X

(a)   (b)

Figure 5.36: Pixel Prediction in the Lossless Mode.

implement this mode. Even the lossy (baseline) mode of JPEG does not perform well when asked to limit the amount of loss to a minimum. As a result, some JPEG implementations do not allow parameter settings that result in minimum loss. The strength of JPEG is in its ability to generate highly compressed images that when decompressed are indistinguishable from the original. Recognizing this, the ISO has decided to come up with another standard for lossless compression of continuous-tone images. This standard is now commonly known as JPEG-LS and is described in [Salomon 04].

5.9.7 The Compressed File

A JPEG encoder outputs a compressed file that includes parameters, markers, and the compressed data units. The parameters are either 4 bits (these always come in pairs), one byte, or two bytes long. The markers serve to identify the various parts of the file. Each is two bytes long, where the first byte is X'FF' and the second one is not 0 or X'FF'. A marker may be preceded by a number of bytes with X'FF'. Table 5.38 lists all the JPEG markers (the first four groups are start-of-frame markers). The compressed data units are combined into MCUs (minimal coded unit), where an MCU is either a single data unit (in the noninterleaved mode) or three data units from the three image components (in the interleaved mode).

Figure 5.37 shows the main parts of the JPEG compressed file (the parts in square brackets are optional). The file starts with the SOI marker and ends with the EOI marker. Between these markers, the compressed image is organized in frames. In the hierarchical mode there are several frames, and in all other modes there is only one frame. In each frame, the image information is contained in one or more scans, but the frame also contains a header and optional tables (which, in turn, may include markers). The first scan may be followed by an optional DNL segment (define number of lines), which starts with the DNL marker and contains the number of lines in the image that is represented by the frame. A scan starts with optional tables, followed by the scan header, followed by several entropy-coded segments (ECS), which are separated by (optional) restart markers (RST). Each ECS contains one or more MCUs, where an MCU is, as explained earlier, either a single data unit or three such units.

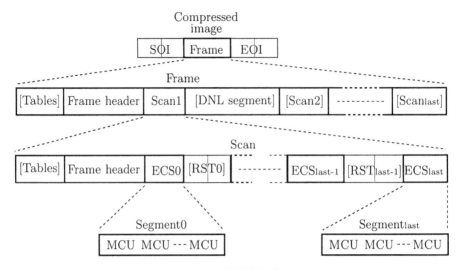

Figure 5.37: JPEG File Format.

5.9.8 JFIF

It has been mentioned earlier that JPEG is a compression method, not a graphics file format, which is why it does not specify image features such as pixel aspect ratio, color space, or interleaving of bitmap rows. This is where JFIF comes in.

JFIF (JPEG file interchange format) is a graphics file format that makes it possible to exchange JPEG-compressed images between computers. The main features of JFIF are the use of the YCbCr triple-component color space for color images (only one component for grayscale images) and the use of a *marker* to specify features missing from JPEG, such as image resolution, aspect ratio, and features that are application-specific.

The JFIF marker (called the APP0 marker) starts with the zero-terminated string JFIF. Following this, there is pixel information and other specifications (see below). Following this, there may be additional segments specifying JFIF extensions. A JFIF extension contains more platform-specific information about the image.

Each extension starts with the zero-terminated string JFXX, followed by a 1-byte code identifying the extension. An extension may contain application-specific information, in which case it starts with a different string, not JFIF or JFXX but something that identifies the specific application or its maker.

The format of the first segment of an APP0 marker is as follows:

1. APP0 marker (4 bytes): FFD8FFE0.
2. Length (2 bytes): Total length of marker, including the 2 bytes of the "length" field but excluding the APP0 marker itself (field 1).
3. Identifier (5 bytes): $4A46494600_{16}$. This is the JFIF string that identifies the APP0 marker.
4. Version (2 bytes): Example: 0102_{16} specifies version 1.02.
5. Units (1 byte): Units for the X and Y densities. 0 means no units; the Xdensity and

Value	Name	Description
\multicolumn{3}{c}{Nondifferential, Huffman coding}		
FFC0	SOF_0	Baseline DCT
FFC1	SOF_1	Extended sequential DCT
FFC2	SOF_2	Progressive DCT
FFC3	SOF_3	Lossless (sequential)
\multicolumn{3}{c}{Differential, Huffman coding}		
FFC5	SOF_5	Differential sequential DCT
FFC6	SOF_6	Differential progressive DCT
FFC7	SOF_7	Differential lossless (sequential)
\multicolumn{3}{c}{Nondifferential, arithmetic coding}		
FFC8	JPG	Reserved for extensions
FFC9	SOF_9	Extended sequential DCT
FFCA	SOF_{10}	Progressive DCT
FFCB	SOF_{11}	Lossless (sequential)
\multicolumn{3}{c}{Differential, arithmetic coding}		
FFCD	SOF_{13}	Differential sequential DCT
FFCE	SOF_{14}	Differential progressive DCT
FFCF	SOF_{15}	Differential lossless (sequential)
\multicolumn{3}{c}{Huffman table specification}		
FFC4	DHT	Define Huffman table
\multicolumn{3}{c}{Arithmetic coding conditioning specification}		
FFCC	DAC	Define arith coding conditioning(s)
\multicolumn{3}{c}{Restart interval termination}		
FFD0–FFD7	RST_m	Restart with modulo 8 count m
\multicolumn{3}{c}{Other markers}		
FFD8	SOI	Start of image
FFD9	EOI	End of image
FFDA	SOS	Start of scan
FFDB	DQT	Define quantization table(s)
FFDC	DNL	Define number of lines
FFDD	DRI	Define restart interval
FFDE	DHP	Define hierarchical progression
FFDF	EXP	Expand reference component(s)
FFE0–FFEF	APP_n	Reserved for application segments
FFF0–FFFD	JPG_n	Reserved for JPEG extensions
FFFE	COM	Comment
\multicolumn{3}{c}{Reserved markers}		
FF01	TEM	For temporary private use
FF02–FFBF	RES	Reserved

Table 5.38: JPEG Markers.

Ydensity fields specify the pixel aspect ratio. A 1 means that Xdensity and Ydensity are dots per inch; a 2 means that they are dots per centimeter.

6. Xdensity (2 bytes), Ydensity (2 bytes): Horizontal and vertical pixel densities (both should be nonzero).

7. Xthumbnail (1 byte), Ythumbnail (1 byte): Thumbnail horizontal and vertical pixel counts.

8. (RGB)n (3n bytes): Packed (24-bit) RGB values for the thumbnail pixels.
   $n = $ Xthumbnail $\times$ Ythumbnail.

   The syntax of the JFIF extension APP0 marker segment is as follows:

1. APP0 marker.

2. Length (2 bytes): Total length of marker, including the 2 bytes of the "length" field but excluding the APP0 marker itself (field 1).

3. Identifier (5 bytes): $4A46585800_{16}$ This is the **JFXX** string identifying an extension.

4. Extension code (1 byte): $10_{16} = $ Thumbnail coded using JPEG. $11_{16} = $ Thumbnail coded using 1 byte/pixel (monochromatic). $13_{16} = $ Thumbnail coded using 3 bytes/pixel (eight colors).

5. Extension data (variable): This field depends on the particular extension.

> When words become unclear, I shall focus with photographs. When images become inadequate, I shall be content with silence.
>
> —Ansel Adams

Part III:
Secure Codes

Part III of this book deals with the problem of securing information. Governments, armies, commercial organizations, and even individuals have sensitive information that must be kept secure. The traditional solution is to encrypt such information. In ancient times, cryptography was the domain of rulers, generals, spies, and a few scientists, philosophers, and alchemists who preferred to keep their knowledge to themselves. In modern times, cryptography has become the domain of governments. In the twentieth century, many countries had two governmental departments dedicated to secret information: one to develop strong ciphers and the other to break ciphers developed by other countries. It was not until the 1970s that cryptography became available to the general public. Today, with the advent of public-key cryptography, anyone has access to software that implements very safe, secure codes, thereby making it easy, even trivial, to send and receive private messages.

This part of the book starts with a short introduction in which the flavor of cryptography is introduced by discussing a few simple ciphers and the main principles of secure codes. Chapter 7 follows with a description of monoalphabetic substitution ciphers. These are ciphers where each symbol is replaced by another symbol and the replacement rule does not vary. Chapter 8 introduces transposition ciphers, where a piece of data is encrypted by replacing it with a permutation of itself. The topic of Chapter 9 is polyalphabetic substitution ciphers, where each symbol in the original data is replaced by another symbol and the replacement rule varies all the time. Stream ciphers are the topic of Chapter 10. Such a cipher encrypts a message (a string of bits) by encrypting each bit separately. In contrast, a block cipher (Chapter 11) divides the message into blocks and encrypts each block separately by substitution and transposition. The modern technique of public-key cryptography is the topic of Chapter 12.

Cryptography secures data by encrypting it. This hides the meaning of the data from prying eyes but does not hide the fact that there is a piece of encrypted data.

Anyone who intercepts encrypted data may try to decrypt it, with results that may affect the fates of individuals as well as world affairs in crucial ways. The new discipline of *data hiding* (steganography) looks for ways to hide the data itself, not just its meaning. A data file A may be hidden (or embedded) in "holes" that exist in another file B because of redundancy. File A is called the payload and file B is the cover.

Data hiding is described in three chapters. Chapter 13 is an introduction to data hiding, where basic methods are described. Methods for hiding data in image files are the topic of Chapter 14. Finally, Chapter 15 discusses other ways of hiding data.

> There are two kinds of cryptography in this world:
> cryptography that will stop your kid sister from reading your
> files, and cryptography that will stop major governments
> from reading your files. This book is about the latter.
>
> —Bruce Schneier, *Applied Cryptography* (1995)

6
Basic Concepts

Cryptology is the scientific discipline that deals with secret writing, messages that are processed in some manner to make them difficult or impossible for unauthorized persons to read. Cryptology is divided into the fields of cryptography (the science of writing secret messages, or the science of mathematical lock and key), cryptanalysis (the art and science of deciphering encrypted messages), steganography (the discipline of hiding information, Chapter 13) and steganalysis. Those active in the first two fields are known as *cryptographers* and *cryptanalysts* (or codebreakers), respectively.

Steganography hides information, while cryptography encrypts information and therefore hides the *meaning* of the information, not the information itself. We can think of cryptography as overt secret writing and of steganography as covert secret writing.

The terms *cryptography* and *cryptology* are derived from the Greek words $\kappa\rho\psi\pi\tau o\sigma$ (meaning *hidden*), $\gamma\rho\alpha\phi\iota\alpha$ (meaning *writing*), and $\lambda o\gamma o\sigma$ (*word* or *reason*). The term *cryptography* was coined in 1658 by Thomas Browne, an English physician.

The importance of cryptanalysis lies in one of the fundamental laws of cryptography, namely, that no code should be considered secure until it has gone through and passed extensive public tests and trials to expose all its weaknesses and faults.

Cryptography has four main components, as follows:

- Confidentiality. An encrypted message cannot be read by any unauthorized person.
- Integrity. Any attempt to alter or corrupt an encrypted message in storage or in transit is detectable.
- Nonrepudiation. The sender cannot later deny having generated or sent the encrypted message.
- Authentication. Sender and receiver can confirm each other's identities and the origin and destination of the message.

The four components are further discussed in Section 12.6.

Secure codes have always been important to, among others, merchants, tyrants, and generals and equally important to their opponents or competitors. Messages sent by a government to various parts of the country have to be encrypted as a precaution in case they fall into the wrong hands, and the same is true of orders issued by generals and memos sent by officers of a corporation. However, the "wrong hands" consider themselves the right side, not the wrong one, and always try to break secure codes. As a result, the development of secure codes has been a constant race between cryptographers (codemakers) and cryptanalysts (codebreakers). New codes have been developed throughout history and have consistently been broken, only for newer, more sophisticated encryption methods to be developed. This race has accelerated in the twentieth century, because of the two World Wars, advances in mathematics, and the development of computers.

Secure codes have become prevalent in modern life because of the rapid progress of telecommunications. Our telephone conversations are sometimes transmitted through communications satellites, and our email messages may pass through many computers before reaching their destination, thereby making our private conversations vulnerable to interception. Thus, we often wish we had a secure code for our private communications. Businesses and other commercial enterprises rely heavily on sending and receiving messages, so they also feel the need for secure communications. On the other hand, widespread use of secure codes worries law enforcement agencies, since criminals (organized or otherwise) and terrorists may also use secure codes if and when they become widely available.

There is a little-known connection between compression and cryptography. An old, traditional way to generate secret codes is a *codebook*. Such a document consists of a list of commonly used words and phrases, each associated with a short, secret word: its code. The code encrypts a message and at the same time also compresses it. The fact that a short word can replace a long word or even an entire phrase is significant. In the days of the telegraph, the cost of sending a telegram was normally determined by the number of words or letters it contained. A large commercial enterprise using a custom-made codebook could have saved significant amounts on telegrams. With the advent of computers, compression became even more important. Compressing a message before it is encrypted speeds up the transmission of the message and also makes it much harder for codebreakers to decipher. Even if a cryptanalyst knows or suspects how the message had been encrypted, and even if the right key is known or is guessed, the result of decrypting the message is still gibberish and may throw the would-be attacker off the right track.

Cryptography is divided into codes and ciphers (Figure 6.1). The term *code* refers to codes for words, phrases, or for entire messages, while *cipher* is a code for each individual symbol. For example, army units may agree on the codeword **green** to mean **attack at dawn** and on **red** to imply **retreat immediately**. The words **green** and **red** are codes. When carefully designed and used, a code may be impossible to break, but the use of codes is limited, because codes have to be agreed upon for every possible eventuality. Codes are used not just for secrecy and privacy. The ASCII code, for example, starts with a set of 128 characters and replaces each with an 8-bit code. Thus, letters, digits, and punctuation marks can be stored in a computer. An acronym such as SNAFU is also a code, since it replaces an entire phrase. This is an example of a code designed to save time. A cipher, on the other hand, is a rule that tells how to encode each letter in a message. Thus, for example, if we agree to replace each letter with the one two places following it in the alphabet, then the message `attack at dawn` will be encoded as `cvvcem cv fcyp` or, even more securely, as `cvvcemcvfcyp`. A cipher is general but is easier to break than a code. In practice, however, we use the terms *code* and *codebreaker* instead of the more accurate *cipher* and *cipherbreaker*.

| SNAFU: Situation Normal All Fouled Up (polite form). |

A text message sent between computers may first be coded into ASCII, then encrypted with a secure cipher that uses a key, and finally encoded with an error-correcting code for increased reliability. Thus, codes and ciphers are used in many real-life applications.

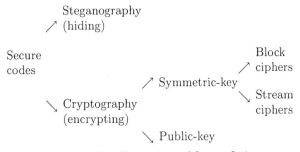

Figure 6.1: The Terminology of Secure Codes.

A combination of code and cipher, called *nomenclator*, is also possible. Parts of a message may be encrypted by codes, and the rest of the message, the parts for which codes do not exist, may be encrypted by a cipher.

Any encryption algorithm must allow for decryption. Moreover, decryption must be unique. Encryption is normally unique too, but there are exceptions, one of which is the homophonic substitution ciphers (Section 7.10).

The term *alphabet* refers to the set of symbols included in messages. This can be the set of bits (the two values 0 and 1), the set of 26 letters, the set of 26 letters plus a blank space, a set of letters, digits, and punctuation marks, the set of 128 ASCII codes, the set of 256 byte values, or any other sets.

An encryption algorithm inputs a message in *plaintext* and outputs it as *ciphertext*. The plaintext and ciphertext may use the same characters (they may be over the same alphabet) or different sets of characters (for example, the plaintext may be letters and the ciphertext may consist of numbers).

It is a tradition among users of codes to eliminate spaces and punctuation marks from the plaintext before encrypting it. Eliminating spaces may sometimes lead to ambiguities as in "week nights" and "wee knights" or "the rapists" and "therapists." Eliminating hyphens may often also lead to ambiguities as in the phrase "four thousand year old mummies" That can be interpreted as "four-thousand-year-old mummies," "four-thousand year-old mummies," and "four thousand-year-old mummies."

It is also traditional to write the ciphertext in groups of five symbols each. It seems that this tradition has its origin in some old telegraph systems that based their charges on groups of five characters.

In order to describe an encryption/decryption algorithm that involves sending secret messages, many authors use the generic names Alice and Bob instead of the cryptic A and B. When the algorithm involves protection from an eavesdropper, she is popularly referred to as Eve. This practice has become so common that one reference [Conceptlabs 04] provides a "biography" of Alice and Bob (see also box on page 312).

It is a popular saying that the First World War was the chemists' war, because of the large-scale use of poison gas for the first time. The Second World War was the physicists' war, because of the use of the atom bomb. Similarly, the Third World War (that we hope can be avoided) may turn out to be the mathematicians' war, because winning that war, if at all conceivable, may depend on the use, and the breaking, of secure codes.

Some of the development as well as the breaking of codes is done openly by researchers at universities and research institutes all over the world (see [Flannery 01] for an unusual example of this). It is generally agreed, however, that most of the work in this field is done in secret by government agencies. Two well-known such agencies are the National Security Agency (NSA) in the United States (purported to be the world's largest employer of mathematicians) and the Government Communications Headquarters (GCHQ) in the United Kingdom.

Encrypting a message involves two ingredients: an algorithm and a key. There are many known encryption algorithms, but the output of each depends on the choice of a key. Perhaps the simplest example of an encryption algorithm is letter shifting. The algorithm is simple. A message is encrypted by replacing each letter with the letter located n positions ahead of it (cyclically) in the alphabet. The key is the value of n. Here is an example for $n = 3$ (note how Y is replaced by A).

```
ABCDEFGHIJKLMNOPQRSTUVWXYZ␣
DEFGHIJKLMNOPQRSTUVWXYZ␣ABC
```

The top line is the *plain alphabet* and the bottom line is the *cipher alphabet*.

This was a contingency which neither Joam Dacosta nor his people could have anticipated. In fact, as those who have not forgotten the first scene in this story are aware, the document was written in a disguised form in one of the numerous systems used in cryptography.

But in which of them?

To discover this would require all the ingenuity of which the human brain was capable.

—Jules Verne, *Eight Hundred Leagues on the Amazon* (1881)

6.1 The Caesar Cipher

Such simple shifting is called the *Caesar cipher* because it is first described in Julius Caesar's book *Gallic Wars*. It is an example of a *substitution* algorithm, in which each letter is substituted by a different letter (or sometimes by itself). Most encryption algorithms are based on some type of substitution. A simple example of a substitution algorithm that can also be made very secure is the *book cipher*. A book is chosen and a page number is selected at random as the key. The words on the page are [1]numbered [2]and [3]a [4]table [5]is [6]prepared, [7]with [8]the [9]first [10]letter [11]of [12]each [13]word [14]and [15]the [16]word's [17]number. [18]This [19]code [20]table [21]is [22]later [23]used [24]to [25]encrypt [26]messages [27]by [28]replacing [29]each [30]letter [31]of [32]the [33]message [34]with [35]a [36]number [37]from [38]the [39]table. For example, the message NOT NOW may be encoded as 36|31|20|17|11|13 (but may also be encoded differently). If the messages are short, and if a different page is used for each message, then this simple code is very secure, but the various page numbers have to be agreed upon in advance, which makes this method impractical in many situations.

There exist also (letters from Caesar) to Cicero and acquaintances on topics on which he, when he had to transmit them confidentially, wrote in cipher. That is, he changed the order of the letters in such a way that no word could be made out. If somebody wanted to decipher it and understand the content, then he had to insert the fourth letter of the alphabet, that is D, for A, and so on.

—Seutonius, *Lives of the Caesars*, LVI

ROT13 (short for Rotate 13) is a Caesar cipher with the key 13, introduced to the Internet community in 1984 or 1985. It is used to temporarily hide answers to puzzles or to obfuscate objectionable material, such as dirty jokes in humor newsgroups. The reason for selecting 13 as the key is that 13 is half the size of the English alphabet. This implies that encrypting and decrypting Rot13 are identical.

Plain alphabet	ABCDEFGHIJKLMNOPQRSTUVWXYZ
Rot13 alphabet	NOPQRSTUVWXYZABCDEFGHIJKLM

The message AND THE ANSWER IS RED is encrypted by ROT13 to NAQ GUR NAFJRE VF ERQ.

/rot ther'teen/ [Usenet: from "rotate alphabet 13 places"], v. The simple Caesar-cypher encryption that replaces each English letter with the one 13 places forward or back along the alphabet, so that "The butler did it!" becomes "Gur ohgyre qvq vg!" Most Usenet news reading and posting programs include a rot13 feature. It is used to enclose the text in a sealed wrapper that the reader must choose to open - e.g. for posting things that might offend some readers, or spoilers. A major advantage of rot13 over rot(N) for other N is that it is self-inverse, so the same code can be used for encoding and decoding.

—From http://www.rot13.com/info.php

6.2 The Affine Cipher

The Caesar cipher can be considered an additive cipher because encoding a letter is done by adding (modulo 26) a constant a (the key) to its numeric value. It is also possible to have multiplicative ciphers, where a plainletter is transformed into a cipherletter by multiplying its value (modulo 26) by another key m.

It is easy to analyze the effect of m. We first assign the 26 letters numeric values from 0 (for A) to 25 (for Z). When each of the letters is multiplied by $m = 2$ (modulo 26), some letters are obtained twice while others are not obtained at all (Table 6.2). On the other hand, when each letter is multiplied by 3, the ciphertext includes each letter exactly once. Thus, 2 is a bad value for m but 3 is a good value. In general, the good values of m are those that are relatively prime to 26, i.e., the 12 numbers 1, 3, 5, 7, 9, 11, 15, 17, 19, 21, 23, and 25. (The term *relatively prime* means integers that don't have any common prime factors, or whose greatest common divisor (gcd) is 1.)

plaintext	a b c d	e	f	g	h	i	j	k	l	m	n	o	p	q	r	s	t	u	v	w	x	y	z
numeric	0 1 2 3	4	5	6	7	8	9	10	11	12	13	14	15	16	17	18	19	20	21	22	23	24	25
times 2	0 2 4 6	8	10	12	14	16	18	20	22	24	0	2	4	6	8	10	12	14	16	18	20	22	24
ciphertext	A C E G	I	K	M	O	Q	S	U	W	Y	A	C	E	G	I	K	M	O	Q	S	U	W	Y
times 3	0 3 6 9	12	15	18	21	24	1	4	7	10	13	16	19	22	25	2	5	8	11	14	17	20	23
ciphertext	A D G J	M	P	S	V	Y	B	E	H	K	N	Q	T	W	Z	C	F	I	L	O	R	U	X

Table 6.2: Letter Values Multiplied by 2 and by 3.

⋄ **Exercise 6.1:** It is obvious that any multiplicative cipher transforms "a" into "A." What other letter is transformed to itself by such a cipher and why?

Thus, we can denote a multiplicative cipher by $y = x \cdot m \bmod 26$ and there are 12 such ciphers (including the trivial one for $m = 1$). The next step is to combine additive and multiplicative ciphers into an *affine cipher*, which is defined as $y = [(x \cdot m) \bmod 26 + a] \bmod 26$ or, because of the properties of the modulo function, as $y = (x \cdot m + a) \bmod 26$. The additive key a can take 26 values, so the total number of affine ciphers is $12 \times 26 = 312$—not very large, but about enough for one cipher for each day of the year, excluding holidays. The key of an affine cipher is a pair (m, a).

(In geometry, an affine transformation of space transforms straight lines to straight lines, and the equation of a straight line is $y = mx + a$, which justifies the name *affine cipher*.)

If the prime factorization of an integer n is $P_1^{e_1} P_2^{e_2} \ldots P_k^{e_k}$, then the number of integers relatively prime to n is computed by the Euler function $\Phi(n)$:

$$\Phi(n) = \Pi_{i=1}^{k} \left(P_i^{e_i} - P_i^{e_i - 1} \right).$$

For example, the integer 126 has the prime factorization $2 \cdot 3^2 \cdot 7$, so for this number $\Phi(126) = (2^1 - 2^0)(3^2 - 3^1)(7^1 - 7^0) = 36$. Similarly, $\Phi(26) = (2^1 - 2^0)(13^1 - 13^0) = 12$.

Given a set of n symbols to be encrypted, the number of affine ciphers is therefore $n \cdot \Phi(n)$.

⋄ **Exercise 6.2:** A fixed-point affine cipher is one where some letters encrypt to themselves. Figure out the number of keys that generate affine ciphers (for the 26 letters) with no fixed point.

Modular arithmetic has many interesting and useful properties, one of which is the identity

$$([(x \times m + a) \bmod 26] \times n + b) \bmod 26 = [x(m \times n) + (a \times n + b)] \bmod 26,$$

which means that double encryption with two affine ciphers is only as good as single encryption. Affinely encrypting a piece of data twice generates the illusion of added security, and such illusion exists with regards to other cryptographic methods as well.

To decrypt an affine cipher, we start with Euclid's algorithm for computing the gcd of two integers. Given the two distinct integers r_0 and r_1, this algorithm computes $\gcd(r_0, r_1)$. This is easily demonstrated by means of an example. Given $r_0 = 20$ and $r_1 = 6$, the following steps are performed:

$$20 = 3 \cdot 6 + 2 \rightarrow \gcd(20, 6) = \gcd(6, 2),$$
$$6 = 3 \cdot 2 + 0 \rightarrow \gcd(6, 2) = \gcd(2, 0) = 2.$$

The algorithm can be summarized by the steps

$$\text{input } r_0, r_1,$$
$$r_0 = q_1 \times r_1 + r_2, \quad \gcd(r_0, r_1) = \gcd(r_1, r_2),$$
$$r_1 = q_2 \times r_2 + r_3, \quad \gcd(r_1, r_2) = \gcd(r_2, r_3),$$
$$\vdots$$
$$r_{m-2} = q_{m-1} \times r_{m-1} + r_m, \quad \gcd(r_{m-2}, r_{m-1}) = \gcd(r_{m-1}, r_m),$$
$$r_{m-1} = q_m \times r_m + 0, \quad \gcd(r_0, r_1) = \gcd(r_{m-1}, r_m) = r_m,$$

where a remainder of zero signals the last step.

Next, we examine the extension of this algorithm. The extended Euclidean algorithm solves the following problem. Given two integers r_0 and r_1, find two other integers s and t such that $s \cdot r_0 + t \cdot r_1 = \gcd(r_0, r_1)$. This employs Euclid's algorithm, where in each iteration the current remainder r_i is expressed in the form $r_i = s_i \cdot r_0 + t_i \cdot r_1$. The signal for the last iteration is $r_m = \gcd(r_0, r_1) = s_m \cdot r_0 + t_m \cdot r_1 = s \cdot r_0 + t \cdot r_1$. This algorithm can be expressed recursively as

$$s_0 = 1, \quad t_0 = 0,$$
$$s_1 = 0, \quad t_1 = 1,$$
$$\text{repeat}$$
$$s_i = s_{i-2} - q_{i-1} s_{i-1}, \quad t_i = t_{i-2} - q_{i-1} t_{i-1},$$
$$\text{for } i = 2, 3, \ldots.$$

As an example, we compute the extended Euclidean algorithm for $r_0 = 126$ and $r_1 = 23$.

$$126 = 5 \cdot 23 + 11, \quad t_0 = 0,$$
$$23 = 2 \cdot 11 + 1, \quad t_1 = 1,$$
$$11 = 11 \cdot 1 + 0, \quad t_2 = 0 - 5 \cdot 1 = -5,$$
$$t_3 = 1 - 2 \cdot (-5) = 11.$$

With this process in mind, decrypting an affine cipher is easy. From $y = (x \cdot m + b) \bmod 26$ we get $x = [m^{-1}(y - b)] \bmod 26 = [m^{-1} \bmod 26][(y - b) \bmod 26]$, where the extended Euclidean algorithm is used to compute $m^{-1} \bmod 26$.

⋄ **Exercise 6.3:** Find the decryption rule for $y = x \cdot 23 + 7 \bmod 126$.

Figure 6.3 lists a Matlab function for the affine cipher. The call `affine('home sweet home',3,1)` produces "`wrln dpnng wrln.`"

```
function msg=affine(msg,m,a)
l=length(msg);
for i=1:l,
  x=msg(i);
  if((x>='a')&(x<='z')),
    x=x-'a';
x=rem(x*m+a,26);
if(x<0) x=x+26; end;
msg(i)=x+'a';
  end
end
```

Figure 6.3: An Affine Cipher in Matlab.

6.3 The One-Time Pad

The one-time cipher is a perfect cipher in the sense that it is absolutely secure. Its use, however, is limited because of the difficulties in the distribution of its long key. Naturally, absolutely secure ciphers are important, so this section discusses the meaning of the words *absolutely secure*. We start with the concept of a cipher system.

A cipher system consists of an algorithm, all the possible keys for it, and all the possible plaintexts and their ciphertexts. In general, the number of plaintexts is infinite, but we can imagine a cipher system with a finite number of plaintexts. A simple example is the fixed-point affine cipher of Exercise 6.2 with its 168 keys. As plaintexts, we can choose all the books in our private library (rarely more than a few thousand volumes), where each book is one plaintext. For each plaintext there are 168 ciphertexts.

To focus our discussion, we imagine two parties, such as Alice and Bob, who communicate by sending each other two possible messages A and B (that may stand for "advance" and "retreat," "buy" and "sell," or "come to me" and "stay away"). The two parties agree on a key so that the messages may be sent in code. For the sake of an example, the key can be as short as one bit. Thus, if the key is 0, plaintext A is encrypted to itself and B is also encrypted to itself, whereas if the key is 1, A is encrypted to B and B is encrypted to A (Table 6.4).

	Plaintext	
Key	A	B
0	A	B
1	B	A

Table 6.4: A Simple Cipher System.

The security of this simple cipher lies in the key. A codebreaker or an eavesdropper Eve who knows the principle of the cipher but has no intercepted messages would, of course, know nothing about the real communications between Alice and Bob. At the same time, a codebreaker who is familiar with the cipher and has also intercepted many messages would be in the same situation and would know nothing about the real messages being transferred. We call such a cryptosystem *perfect* because intercepting any number of messages as well as trying all the possible keys (two) does not help the codebreaker in breaking the code.

(Such a simple cryptosystem with only two keys and two possible messages is, of course, easy to break. It is perfect only in principle and is described here only to illustrate the concept of a perfect cryptosystem. Eve may, for example, watch the actions of the receiver each time a message is received to deduce its meaning. A practical cryptosystem must have many keys and many different messages.)

This simple example can be extended to illustrate another important feature of cryptography, namely, authentication. An eavesdropper listening to the messages without understanding them may do damage just by stopping the original messages and passing on to the receiver the opposite messages or even random messages. It is therefore important for the receiver to be certain that the messages are authentic and came from the original sender and not from an eavesdropper.

	Plaintext	
Key	A	B
00	AA	AB
01	AB	BA
10	BA	BB
11	BB	AA

Table 6.5: Authentication Added.

A simple authentication protocol can be implemented by agreeing on a 2-bit key and using it to select one of four sets of messages (Table 6.5). Again, an eavesdropper who knows the algorithm cannot benefit from intercepting messages, so this version is as secure as the original method. Its greater complexity, however, results in increased authentication. If Eve tries to impersonate the sender, she will have to send messages from one of the rows of the table. If she sends AA and BA messages, the receiver will notice a break of security, because no row in the table has the message pair AA and BA. If Eve intercepts one message from the sender, say, AA, she still doesn't know the other message in the same row of the table. She can, of course, wait longer and intercept more messages, which is why the two parties should change keys very often. A cryptosystem with many keys, where the key is changed with every message, is perfect in practice.

With this introduction, the one-time pad is ready to be introduced. This was first proposed in 1917 by G. Vernam, so it is sometimes called the Vernam cipher. Historically, a writing pad was filled with random letters. Each page was used once to encrypt a message (and on the receiving side, to decrypt it) and was then torn up and destroyed. Encrypting was done by replacing an n-letter plaintext with the next available n random letters of the key. The remainder of the key was available to encrypt more plaintexts. This system was safe, but it required the safe distribution of large keys, rendering it impractical for many applications. The absolute security provided by the one-time pad has already been recognized by Shannon in his classical papers [Shannon 49] and [Shannon 51].

Nowadays, in the computer age, this cipher operates not on letters but on bits—a change that greatly simplifies the rules for encryption and decryption (Section 10.2).

> Human ingenuity cannot concoct a cipher which human ingenuity cannot resolve.
>
> —Edgar Allen Poe

6.4 Kerckhoffs' Principle

The entire field of cryptography is based on an important assumption, namely, that some information can be kept and disseminated securely, accessible only by authorized persons. This information is the *key* used by an encryption algorithm.

An important principle in cryptography, due to the Dutch linguist Auguste Kerckhoffs von Nieuwenhoff [Kerckhoffs 83], states that the security of an encrypted message must depend on keeping the key secret. It should not depend on keeping the encryption algorithm secret. This principle is widely accepted and implies that there must be many possible keys to an algorithm; the *key space* must be very large. The Caesar algorithm, for example, is very weak because it is limited to the 26 keys 1 through 26. Shifting the 27-symbol sequence (26 letters and a space) 27 positions returns it to its original position, and shifting it $27 + n$ positions is identical to shifting it just n positions. Notice that a large key space is a necessary but not a sufficient condition. An encryption algorithm may have an immense key space but may nevertheless be weak.

> Kerckhoffs' Principle
>
> One should assume that the method used to encipher data is known to the opponent, and that security must lie in the choice of key. This does not necessarily imply that the method should be public, just that it is considered public during its creation.
>
> —Auguste Kerckhoffs

It is possible to use a brute force approach to break a cipher. A would-be code-breaker can simply search the entire key space—every possible key! There are, however, two good reasons why this approach is impractical and has at best a limited value. One reason is the large number of keys, and the other is the problem of recognizing the correct plaintext once it has been obtained when the right key is guessed. Table 6.6 lists the times it takes to check all the keys, for several key sizes n. The table lists the times for the cases where one mega and one giga keys are checked each second (a mega is 2^{20}, about a million, and a giga is 2^{30}, about a billion). It is clear that doubling the key size more than doubles the total number of keys. In fact, for an n-bit key, the number of keys is 2^n, so it grows exponentially with n. Recognizing the plaintext is not easier. If the plaintext is text, it may be recognized by a computer program by looking up words in a dictionary. Even this can be defeated by artificially inserting many nonsense "words" in the text, but the plaintext may be compressed data, or a file containing executable machine code or image, video, or audio data. These types may be (practically) impossible to recognize.

n	Approx decimal	Time 1M tests/s		1G tests/s	
32	4.3×10^9	4096	sec	4	sec
40	1.1×10^{12}	291	hrs	1024	sec
56	72×10^{15}	2179	yrs	777	days
64	1.84×10^{19}	557845	yrs	545	yrs
128	3.4×10^{38}	10^{25}	yrs	10^{22}	yrs

Table 6.6: The Security Provided by Certain Key Sizes.

⋄ **Exercise 6.4:** Cryptographers often have to refute the following statement: "I can always crack an encrypted message by trying the entire key space. With a really fast computer, I can easily try all the possible 64-bit keys. Besides, I may succeed on the first try." Use real-life examples to illustrate the fallacy of this boast.

It should be mentioned that trying to break a code by searching the entire keyspace may fail even for short keys. Each time a key is tried on the ciphertext, the result should be checked to see whether it is the plaintext. If the plaintext is text, then a computer may use a dictionary to flag each result that contains a large percentage of valid words. If the plaintext is an image or an audio file, a computer may not be able to identify the correct result. The cryptographer may also defeat a search of the keyspace by simply compressing the plaintext before it is encrypted. A compressed file looks random, so anyone, a computer or a human, looking at all the results of the search may not be able to identify the correct result.

We conclude this introduction with lists of cryptographic and steganographic resources. The first is a list of books for the general reader. Most are general books on cryptography, while others concentrate on certain topics. Notice that there is currently a flood of books on cryptography and related subjects, so this short list represents the opinion of the author. In addition to the books listed here, one specialty publisher, [Aegean Park 01], should be mentioned because it specializes in books on cryptography.

[Kahn 96]: The most comprehensive survey of the history of cryptography from ancient times to the 1950s. The original book is out of print, but there is a new, revised edition with a short, cursory overview of the developments in this field since the 1950s.

[Bauer 02]: A general text on cryptography. It assumes only elementary mathematical knowledge and is interspersed with many exciting, amusing, and sometimes personal stories from the history of cryptology.

[Gaines 56]: A general reference for older (noncomputer-based) cryptography methods. It contains tips, examples, and many tables. There are tables of letter frequencies in various languages, initial and final letter frequencies, and an ordered list of the most-commonly used English words. This is a Dover reprint of the original, 1939 book.

[Hinsley and Stripp 92]: A set of 27 personal narratives by some of the codebreakers who worked at Bletchley Park during World War II. This book describes the human side of the codebreaking operations and is nontechnical.

[Johnson et al. 01]: Research contributions concerning data hiding and labeling techniques, attacks against steganography and watermarked information, and countermeasures against such attacks.

[Katzenbeisser et al. 00]: An excellent introduction to and reference on information hiding (steganography and watermarking). It covers the various aspects of the subject very well.

[Levy 01]: The story of modern cryptography. This nontechnical book is the result of many interviews with the movers and shakers of late twentieth century cryptography. Clearly written and easy to read, the book is a panorama of the entire field and its main players. Its description of the clashes between individual cryptographers and various governments is especially enlightening.

[Newton 97]: An encyclopedia. With 550 entries arranged alphabetically, this monograph surveys codes from ancient history through modern electronic media. The entries vary from a short sentence to several pages in length.

[Konheim 81]: A modest-sized book that provides a basic working knowledge of the state of the art of the huge field of cryptology as it was in 1981 to people with little or no previous knowledge.

[Savard 03]: A general online reference for secure codes.

[Schneier 95]: A comprehensive work that covers practically all topics of modern cryptography in detail. A big bonus is the detailed bibliography with over 1500 entries.

[Schneier 03]: A monthly newsletter on computer security and cryptography from Bruce Schneier, a leading security expert.

[Sinkov 80]: A discussion of the basics of cryptography in clear, easy-to-understand language. The examples and exercises accompanying each chapter provide the reader with hands-on practice of the concepts introduced.

[Stallings 98]: One of the better books on cryptography, concentrating on algorithms rather than codebreaking. It offers very detailed coverage of public-key encryption methods.

Some of the important government departments in charge of ciphers and cryptography are

- in the United Kingdom, Government Communications Headquarters [GCHQ 03];
- in the United States, National Security Agency [NSA 03];
- in Australia, Defence Signals Directorate [DSD 03];
- in Canada, Communications Security Establishment [CSE 03]; and
- in Russia, Academy of Federal Agency for Government [AFAC 03].

Other resources for the interested reader are

- National Cryptologic Museum [NCM 03], maintained by the NSA;
- The American Cryptogram Association [ACA 03], the crypto-enthusiast's society;
- *Cryptologia* [Cryptologia 03], a professional quarterly journal;
- *The Journal of Cryptology* [Cryptology 03], a professional quarterly journal; and
- (tongue in cheek.) *The Journal of Craptology* [Crap 03] is an electronic journal on cryptologic issues. Papers accepted for publication in *The Journal of Craptology* relate to cryptology and fall into one or several of the following categories: (1) it is funny; (2) it is controversial, or (3) it is crap.

> Gentlemen do not read each other's mail.
> —Henry L. Stimson

7
Monoalphabetic Substitution Ciphers

A substitution cipher is one where each symbol is replaced by another symbol. If the replacement rule does not vary, the cipher is a *monoalphabetic substitution* cipher.

A good monoalphabetic substitution algorithm matches the plain alphabet with a permutation of itself, a permutation determined by a key. (Notice that this is a substitution algorithm, not a transposition algorithm, because it replaces the plain alphabet, not the encrypted message, with a permutation. Transposition ciphers are the topic of Chapter 8.) If the alphabet consists of 26 symbols, there are $26! \approx 4 \times 10^{26}$ monoalphabetic substitution ciphers for the alphabet. In spite of this impressive number, these ciphers are not secure and are easily broken.

Here is a simple algorithm of this type. Start with a key that is a string from the alphabet, say, LAND␣AND␣TREE. Remove duplicate letters to obtain the key phrase LAND␣TRE. Use this as the start of the cipher alphabet, and append the rest of the plain alphabet in its natural order, starting where the key phrase ends (i.e., with the letter F). The result is

Plain alphabet	ABCDEFGHIJKLMNOPQRSTUVWXYZ␣
Cipher alphabet	LAND␣TREFGHIJKMOPQSUVWXYZBC

An alternative way to employ the key is to count its length (8 in our example), to place it under the plain alphabet starting at position 8 (i.e., starting under the I because the letters are numbered 0 to 25), and to follow with the rest of the alphabet starting from A (in our example, starting from B, since A is part of the key).

Plain alphabet	ABCDEFGHIJKLMNOPQRSTUVWXYZ␣
Cipher alphabet	QSUVWXYZLAND␣TREBCFGHIJKMOP

A relatively short key is easy to memorize and can produce good substitution (i.e., the chance that a letter would replace itself is negligible). Monoalphabetic substitution codes were extensively used throughout the first millennium A.D. but fell victims to the development of statistics and concepts of probability. Breaking such a code is easy and does not require the examination of many alternatives. It is based on the fact that in any language, each letter has a certain probability of appearing in texts (we say that the *distribution* of letters is nonuniform). Some letters are common while others are rare. The most common letters in English, for example, are E, T, and A (if a blank space is also included in the alphabet, then it is the most common), and the least common are Z and Q. If a monoalphabetic substitution code replaces E with, say, D, then D should be the most common letter in the ciphertext.

⋄ **Exercise 7.1:** Suggest a simple way to modify any monoalphabetic cipher such that it generates ciphertext where all symbols have equal probabilities.

7.1 Letter Distributions

The standard letter distribution in a language is computed by selecting documents that are considered typical in the language and then counting the number of times each letter appears in those documents. For reliable results, the total number of letters in all the documents should be in the hundreds of thousands. Table 7.1 lists the letter distribution computed from the 328,943 letters in three plays by Shakespeare. The Matlab code for this computation is also listed. Any single document may have a letter distribution very different from the standard. In a mathematical text, the words **quarter**, **quadratic**, and **quadrature** may be common, increasing the frequencies of Q and U, while a text on the (zilch) effects of ozone on zebras' laziness in Zaire and Zanzibar may have unusually many occurrences of Z. Also, any short text may have a letter distribution sufficiently different from the standard to defy simple analysis. The short story *The Gold Bug* by Edgar Allan Poe is an early example of breaking a monoalphabetic substitution code.

The Gold Bug

Here, then, we have, in the very beginning, the groundwork for something more than a mere guess. The general use which may be made of the table is obvious—but, in this particular cipher, we shall only very partially require its aid. As our predominant character is 8, we will commence by assuming it as the "e" of the natural alphabet. To verify the supposition, let us observe if the 8 be seen often in couples—for "e" is doubled with great frequency in English—in such words, for example, as "meet," "fleet," "speed," "seen," "been," "agree," etc. In the present instance we see it doubled no less than five times, although the cryptograph is brief.

—Edgar Allan Poe

Letter	Freq.	Prob.	Letter	Freq.	Prob.	Letter	Freq.	Prob.
A	25246	0.0767	J	238	0.0007	S	20843	0.0634
B	4890	0.0149	K	3566	0.0108	T	29912	0.0909
C	7196	0.0219	L	15348	0.0467	U	10839	0.0330
D	13409	0.0408	M	10080	0.0306	V	2977	0.0091
E	39334	0.1196	N	21236	0.0646	W	7802	0.0237
F	7201	0.0219	O	27290	0.0830	X	433	0.0013
G	6366	0.0194	P	4600	0.0140	Y	7615	0.0231
H	21164	0.0643	Q	406	0.0012	Z	163	0.0005
I	20680	0.0629	R	20109	0.0611			

Frequencies and probabilities of the 26 letters in *Hamlet*, *Macbeth*, and *King Lear* by Shakespeare, a total of 524,411 characters, of which 328,943 were letters (upper- and lowercase).

```
% Computes letter frequencies (UC & LC) in text files
% Each call to 'dofile' reads and analyzes one file
global buf gtot totl;
buf=zeros(26,1); totl=0; gtot=0;
dofile('hamlet')
dofile('macbeth')
dofile('lear')
 gtot % total # of chars input
 totl % total # of letters
 buf % Counts of occurrences of 26 letters
 buf=buf/totl % in percent
 sum(buf) % should be 1
      File "dofile.m"
function []=dofile(filename)
global buf gtot totl;
inp=zeros(128,1);
fid=fopen(filename,'r');
if fid==-1
 disp('file not found')
else
 while feof(fid)~=1
  [inp,c]=fread(fid,128,'char'); % input c chars
   gtot=gtot+c;
   for i=1:c
   if (inp(i)>=65)&(inp(i)<=90) % UC letters
     j=inp(i)-64; buf(j)=buf(j)+1; totl=totl+1;
     elseif (inp(i)>=97)&(inp(i)<=122) % LC letters
     j=inp(i)-96; buf(j)=buf(j)+1; totl=totl+1;
   end; % if
  end; % for i=1:c
 end; % while
end % if fid==-1
```

Table 7.1: Probabilities of English Letters and Matlab Code.

Group	Frequency of group	Range of frequencies
E	11.96	more than 12%
T,A,O,I,N,S,H,R	56.69	6–9%
D,L	8.75	4–5%
C,U,M,W,F,G,Y,P,B	20.25	1.5–3.5%
V,K,J,X,Q,Z	2.36	1% or less

Table 7.2: Groups of English Letters and Their Probabilities.

As can be seen from Table 7.2 (itself based on Table 7.1), a group of just **nine** letters accounts for close to 70% of all letters in "typical" sentences (of which this is one).

Another statistical property of letters in a language is the relation between pairs (and even triplets) of letters (digrams and trigrams). In English, a T is very often followed by H (as in this, that, then, and them) and a Q is almost always followed by a U. Thus, *digram frequencies* can also be used in deciphering a stubborn monoalphabetic substitution code. Notice that E is not always the most common letter; no português é A (in Portuguese it is A) while Auf Deutsch sind die zwei am meisten-allgemeinen Zeichen E und N (in German, the two most common letters are E and N).

◇ **Exercise 7.2:** Search the cryptographic literature for tables of digrams and trigrams in English and possibly other languages. Alternatively, write a program to input text files and compute such tables.

> Not everything that counts can be counted, and not everything that can be counted counts.
>
> —Albert Einstein

7.2 The Pigpen Cipher

This simple monoalphabetic cipher has been used for generations in the form presented here and in similar forms. It is a special favorite of children. It is an example of a substitution cipher where the source and destination alphabets are different. The source is the 26 letters and the destination is 26 simple geometric symbols. Figure 7.3 shows how the 26 letters are arranged in four simple grids.

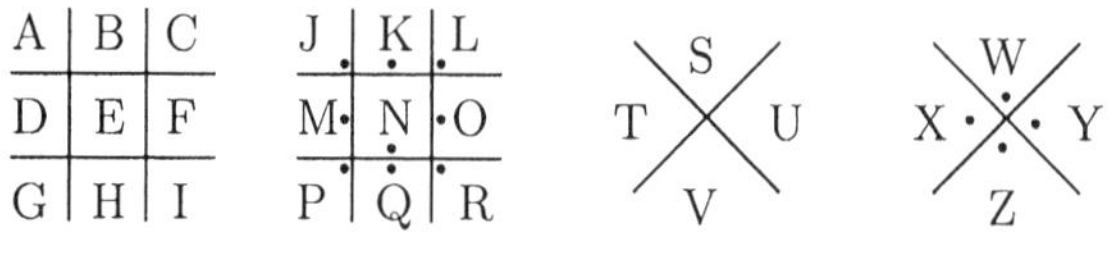

Figure 7.3: The Pigpen Cipher.

A letter is encrypted by replacing it with the part of the grid nearest it. Thus, for example, a = $\lrcorner$, b = $\sqcup$, ..., z = $\wedge$.

⋄ **Exercise 7.3:** Some people feel more comfortable drawing geometrical figures that have only horizontal and vertical segments. Develop a variant of the pigpen cipher that uses only such segments.

7.3 Polybius' Monoalphabetic Cipher

The second century B.C. Greek author and historian Polybius (or Polybios) had an interest in cryptography and developed the simple monoalphabetic cipher that today bears his name. The cipher is based on a small square of letters, so when applied to English text, the number of letters is artificially reduced from 26 to 25 by considering I and J identical. The 25 remaining letters are arranged in a 5×5 square (Figure 7.4a) where each letter is identified by its row and column (integers in the interval [1, 5]). Encrypting is done by replacing each plainletter with its coordinates in the Polybius square. Thus, the plaintext POLYBIUS⊔CIPHER is encrypted into the numeric sequence 35, 34, 31, 54, 12, 24, 45, 43, 13, 24, 35, 23, 15, and 42.

Even though the ciphertext consists of numbers, this cipher is still monoalphabetic and can easily be broken. An experienced cryptanalyst will easily discover that the ciphertext consists of 2-digit integers where each digit is in the interval [1, 5], and that the integer 15 appears about 12% of the time. The ciphertext may be written as a sequence of digits, such as 3 5 3 4 3 1 5 4 1 2 2 4 4 5 4 3 1 3 2 4 3 5 2 3 1 5 4 2, but this does not significantly strengthen the method. A key may be added to the basic cipher, in accordance with Kerckhoffs' principle (in the Introduction). The key polybius⊔cipher becomes, after the removal of spaces and duplicate letters, the string polybiuscher. The rest of the alphabet is appended to this string, and the result is the Polybius square of Figure 7.4b.

⋄ **Exercise 7.4:** Suggest another way to extend the short key polybius⊔cipher to the complete set of 25 letters.

	1	2	3	4	5
1	a	b	c	d	e
2	f	g	h	i/j	k
3	l	m	n	o	p
4	q	r	s	t	u
5	v	w	x	y	z

(a)

	1	2	3	4	5
1	p	o	l	y	b
2	i/j	u	s	c	h
3	e	r	a	d	f
4	g	k	m	n	q
5	t	v	w	x	z

(b)

Figure 7.4: The Polybius Monoalphabetic Cipher.

The monoalphabetic Polybius cipher is sometimes called the *nihilistic cipher* or a *knock cipher* because it was used by the Russian Nihilists, the opponents of the Czar, to communicate in prison by knocking the numbers on the walls between cells. They naturally used the old 35-letter Cyrillic alphabet, and so had a 6×6 Polybius square. Each letter was transmitted by tapping its two coordinates (each an integer in the interval $[1, 6]$) on the wall.

Another variant embeds the digits 6–9 in the ciphertext randomly, to act as nulls or placebos, to confuse any would-be codebreakers or listening jailers.

The monoalphabetic Polybius cipher rearranges the one-dimensional string of letters in a two-dimensional square. The method can therefore be extended by increasing the number of dimensions. Since $3^3 = 27$, it makes sense to have a three-dimensional box of size $3 \times 3 \times 3$ and to store 27 symbols in it. Each symbol can be encrypted to a triplet of digits, each in the interval $[0, 2]$ (these are ternary digits, or trits). If the original Polybius method, using a square, can be called *bipartite*, its three-dimensional extension may be called *tripartite*. Similarly, since $2^8 = 256$, it is possible to construct an eight-dimensional structure with 256 symbols, where each symbol can be coded with eight bits. This may be termed *octopartite* encryption and it is the basis of the EBCDIC (extended BCD Interchange code) used in IBM mainframe computers.

Today, the monoalphabetic Polybius cipher is used mostly to convert letter sequences to numeric sequences. Section 9.14 discusses a polyalphabetic version of this cipher.

7.4 Extended Monoalphabetic Ciphers

As soon as it became easy for cryptanalysts to break monoalphabetic ciphers, cryptographers started developing extensions of these simple ciphers. The following sections describe a few simple extensions that are much more secure than just plain monoalphabetic substitution codes.

7.5 The Playfair Cipher

This extension of the basic monoalphabetic cipher is not fair in any sense. It is named after Lyon Playfair, first Baron Playfair of St. Andrews. It was actually developed, in 1854, by the English physicist and inventor Sir Charles Wheatstone, who is better known for the Wheatstone bridge (which was improved by him but had actually been invented by one Samuel Christie in 1833). Playfair promoted the cipher, which became popular and was used, among others, by the British forces in the Boer War and in World War I.

The cipher is based on a 5×5 square with 25 letters that is constructed by a key (the letter J is omitted and messages substitute either I or II for J). All spaces, all occurrences of J, and all multiple copies of letters are deleted from the key, and the remainder of the alphabet is appended to it in its natural order. The resulting string of 25 letters is rearranged in a square (either row by row, column by column, or in a spiral) and messages are encrypted and decrypted with the square. Obviously, a long key with few or no repeating letters is preferable. As an example, we select the key WHEATSTONE, which produces the square shown in Figure 7.5a.

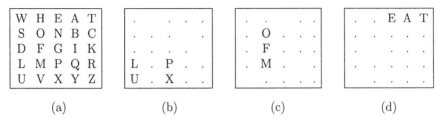

| (a) | (b) | (c) | (d) |

Figure 7.5: The Playfair Cipher.

The plaintext is divided into pairs of letters. If the two letters of a pair are identical, an X is inserted between them, and the pairs are recreated (or one of the two identical letters is simply removed). Each pair x, y is encrypted by first locating x and y in the square. They are considered the two opposite corners of a rectangle, and are replaced by the letter pair at the opposite corners of the rectangle. For example, the plaintext FOLLOW ME EARLY becomes the eight pairs FO, LX, LO, WM, EX, EA, RL, and YX. The second pair LX defines the rectangle shown in Figure 7.5b, so it is replaced by the pair PU (P is first, since it is on the same row as L, the first letter of the original pair). There are extra rules for pairs that do not form a rectangle. The first pair FO in our example is located on the same column, so it is replaced by MF (each letter is replaced by the one below it; see Figure 7.5c). The pair EA is on the same row, so it is replaced by the pair AT (each letter is replaced by the one following it; see Figure 7.5d). These rules explain why the two letters of a pair must be different.

(The words *below* and *following* are used here in a cyclic sense. Thus, the pair FV is replaced by MH and the pair MR is replaced by PL. Alternatively, we can think of the Playfair square as a double torus, where the leftmost column is also located on the right of the rightmost column and the top row is also located below the bottom row; see Figure 7.6a.)

⋄ **Exercise 7.5:** Complete the encryption of FOLLOW ME EARLY.

The reverse rules are used to decrypt the message. If the two letters of a ciphertext pair are in different rows and columns, select the letters in the opposite corners of the rectangle thus generated. If they are in the same row, select the letters one place to the left. If they are in the same column, select the letters above each of them.

The rules of the Playfair cipher imply that a letter cannot be encrypted to itself. Also, if a pair XY is encrypted to AB, then its reverse YX is encrypted to the reverse BA. These two features make the Playfair cipher relatively easy to break. It can also be broken by looking for pairs of letters that occur frequently in the ciphertext and trying to match them to common digrams in English.

```
        ⋮
  Z  U  V  X  Y  Z  U
  T  W  H  E  A  T  W              1  2  3  4  5
  C  S  O  N  B  C  S          1 │ W  H  E  A  T
...K  D  F  G  I  K  D ...      2 │ S  O  N  B  C        L  X
  R  L  M  P  Q  R  L          3 │ D  F  G  I  K       41  53
  Z  U  V  X  Y  Z  U          4 │ L  M  P  Q  R         ✕
  T  W  H  E  A  T  A          5 │ U  V  X  Y  Z       43  51
        ⋮                                                P  U
```

| (a) | (b) | (c) |

Figure 7.6: The Playfair Cipher. (a) Double Torus. (b,c) Fractionating Method.

This cipher has an unexpected aspect. If we number the rows and columns of the 5×5 Playfair square as in Figure 7.6b, it becomes clear that there is a simple relationship, illustrated in Figure 7.6c, between a pair of plainletters and the corresponding pair of cipherletters. Using this relation, a pair of plainletters can be encrypted by taking the two coordinates of the pair, separating them, crossing them as shown in the figure, and attaching the crossed digits. Thus, the coordinate pair 41 and 53 becomes the pair 43 and 51. This is an example of a *fractionating* encryption method.

7.6 The Double Playfair Cipher

A more sophisticated version of Playfair, known as *double Playfair* (or *double box*), was used by the Germans in World War II. Two keys are used, to construct two 5×5 squares, as in the original Playfair. The two squares resulting from the keys WHEATSTONE and PLAYFAIR are shown in Figure 7.7a.

```
W H E A T │ P L A Y F      W H E A T │ P L A Y F      W H E A T │ P L A Y F
S O N B C │ I R B C D      S O N B C │ I R B C D      S O N B C │ I R B C D
D F G I K │ E G H K M      D F G I K │ E G H K M      D F G I K │ E G H K M
L M P Q R │ N O Q S T      L M P Q R │ N O Q S T      L M P Q R │ N O Q S T
U V X Y Z │ U V W X Z      U V X Y Z │ U V W X Z      U V X Y Z │ U V W X Z
```

| (a) | (b) | (c) |

Figure 7.7: The Double Playfair Cipher.

The plaintext is arranged in an even number of equal-sized lines (where several random letters may have to be added to pad the bottom line or the two bottom lines). The length of the lines is a parameter that has to be agreed upon in advance. This divides the plaintext into letter pairs in a simple, obvious way. Using the plaintext FOLLOW ME EARLY, we end up with the two 7-letter lines

$$
\begin{array}{ccccccc}
F & O & L & L & O & W & M \\
E & E & A & R & L & Y & X
\end{array}
$$

The third pair LA is encrypted in two steps. In the first step, the L is located in the first square, the A is located in the second square, and the other two opposite corners QW of the rectangle thus defined are selected (the first letter Q is taken from the second square and the second letter W is from the first square; see Figure 7.7b). In the second step, the rectangle defined by Q in the first square and W in the second square is identified (Figure 7.7c), and its other opposite corners, QY are selected. Thus, the pair LA is encrypted by replacing it with QY.

The first pair FE of plaintext letters does not define a rectangle. If we consider it a thin rectangle, then the first step would select EF and the second step would result in the original pair FE. An additional rule is therefore needed for this case. In step 1 of this rule, we select the letter pair located to the left of FE. This turns out to be KD. (E has no left neighbor in its square, so its left neighbor K from the first square is chosen. D is also from the first square.) The pair KD (where K is in the first square and D is in the second square) defines a rectangle whose other opposite corners are MC. Thus, the pair FE is encrypted to MC. If the pair KD had turned out to be on the same row, it would have been encrypted to DK.

For added safety, the two lines of ciphertext are merged with a perfect shuffle before they are transmitted. This cipher is more secure than basic Playfair because it requires two keys plus a parameter (the length of the lines of plaintext).

From Mr. Hetherington, the Master of the Hounds, who was up at no one knows what hour, to go down to the kennel and see that the men did their work well and thoroughly, to stern old Sir Lionel Playfair, the upright magistrate, the thoughtful, conscientious landlord—they did their work according to their lights; there were few laggards among those with whom Mr. Wilkins associated in the field or at the dinner table.

—Elizabeth Gaskell, *A Dark Night's Work* (1864)

7.7 Delastelle Fractionation

This simple variation of the basic Playfair method, due to Félix M. Delastelle, performs the fractionation differently, as illustrated in Figure 7.8. Instead of fractionating 41 and 53 to 43 and 51, they are fractionated to 45 and 31. This method also requires special rules to deal with the cases where the letters to be encrypted are in the same row or column.

	1	2	3	4	5
1	W	H	E	A	T
2	S	O	N	B	C
3	D	F	G	I	K
4	L	M	P	Q	R
5	U	V	X	Y	Z

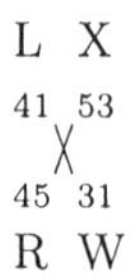

L X

41 53

X

45 31

R W

Figure 7.8: The Delastelle Cipher.

7.8 Ohaver Encryption: Fractionated Morse

The simple method described here is one of many developed by M. E. Ohaver. It is mentioned as an example of a fractionating algorithm. A more detailed description of this and similar methods can be found in [Gaines 56].

The Morse codes have different lengths, but they don't satisfy the prefix rule (Section 9.13). There must therefore be special codes for the spaces between letters (three wait units) and between words (five wait units). Table 8.12 shows that the 26 letters are assigned codes of lengths 1 to 4. There is a total of $2 + 4 + 8 + 16 = 30$ such codes, so four of them are not assigned to any characters. For Morse fractionation, every code of 1 to 4 dots and dashes should be assigned to a symbol, so four codes can be assigned to certain punctuation marks or accented letters.

A message to be encrypted is first converted to Morse code. Next, the operator (or a computer) prepares a list of the lengths of the Morse codes in the message. This is a list of numbers in the range $[1, 4]$. When this list is available, there is no longer any need for letter and word spaces, and the message consists only of dots and dashes. The message is encrypted in several steps as follows: (1) the list of numbers is partitioned into segments of size n (where n is a key of this method); (2) each segment is reversed; and (3) using the numbers in a reversed segment, the next available dots and dashes are converted back into letters. This is possible because any combination of between 1 and 4 dots and dashes has a symbol (letter or punctuation mark) assigned to it.

The Plaintext MEET␣ME␣AT␣TEN is used as an example. After eliminating the blank spaces, this 11-letter string is Morse coded to become --|.|.|-|--|.|.-|-|-|.|.-., and it results in the sequence of code lengths 21112121112 that is partitioned into sequences of six codes each. Reversing the first six codes yields 121112, which is used to create the Morse codes -|-.|.|-|-|-. that become the cipher string TNETTN. Reversing the remaining five code lengths yields 21112, which is used to create the Morse codes .-|-|-|.|-. that become the cipher string ATTEN. Thus, the complete ciphertext is TNETTNATTEN. Notice that 21112 is symmetric, so the last five characters of the ciphertext are identical to the last five characters of the plaintext.

7.9 Delastelle Trifid Fractionation

This simple cipher is somewhat similar to fractionated Morse. Each letter is assigned a 3-digit code (Table 13.3, duplicated here). There are $3^3 = 27$ such codes, so one punctuation mark ("&" in the table) can be included in the alphabet, in addition to the 26 letters. The simple encryption steps are as follows: (1) replace each plainletter with its 3-digit code; (2) partition the numeric string thus obtained into $3n$ segments; (3) reverse each segment; (4) concatenate the segments into a single numeric string; and (5) decrypt the string into a string of letters using Table 13.3.

Alternatively, encryption can be done as follows: (1) write the 3-digit code of each plainletter vertically, in three rows; (2) read the resulting matrix (three rows and many columns) row by row, to become a numeric string; and (3) decrypt the string into letters with the help of Table 13.3, duplicated here.

A 111	D 121	G 131	J 211	M 221	P 231	S 311	V 321	Y 331
B 112	E 122	H 132	K 212	N 222	Q 232	T 312	W 322	Z 332
C 113	F 123	I 133	L 213	O 223	R 233	U 313	X 323	& 333

Table 13.3: Three-Digit Codes for the Letters.

In general, a fractionating cipher requires a cipher alphabet of the *multifid* type, where each cipher symbol consists of several parts. It is those parts that are broken up during encryption and combined in a different way. Each cipher symbol in the method described here consists of three digits, which is the reason for the name *trifid fractionation*.

From the Dictionary

fid.
1. Suffix: Divided into parts or lobes: pinnatifid.
2. Etymology: Latin -fidus, from findere, fid-, to split.

7.10 Homophonic Substitution Ciphers

The family of *homophonic substitution* ciphers is an example of ciphers that combine features of monoalphabetic and polyalphabetic ciphers. Perhaps the earliest example of this type of cipher is the one used by officials in the city of Mantua (pronounced *manchoo*, the capital of the province of Lombardy in northern Italy) in the early 1400s. They did not know the letter frequencies that are so well known today, but they felt intuitively that certain letters occur more often than others and they exploited this feature to design a code that is more secure than a simple monoalphabetic cipher. They constructed a code table, similar to Table 7.9, where the common letters were assigned several alternative symbols. Encrypting with such a table produces ciphertext where no single symbol dominates, so frequency analysis cannot by itself break this code. The Mantua homophonic cipher is far more advanced than the Cæsar cipher, but is still primitive compared to modern ciphers.

a	b	c	d	e	f	g	h	i	j	k	l	m	n	o	p	q	r	s	t	u	v	w	x	y	z
3	t	s	p	g	u	r	d	f	e	4	w	m	l	k	a	y	v	q	c	z	k	2	h	i	n
b		7		5				8									o								
j				6													1								
				l																					
				x																					

Table 7.9: A Mantua Homophonic Cipher.

A better homophonic substitution cipher replaces each letter with a number, taking into account letter frequencies. Table 7.1 shows that the probability of the letter B in English is about 2% (i.e., B accounts for roughly 2% of all letters in English texts), so two numbers should be assigned to encode B. Similarly, the probability of D is close to 3%, so three numbers should be assigned to encode D. The result is that 100 numbers are assigned, each counting for roughly 1% of the encrypted text. A possible assignment of 100 numbers to the 26 letters is shown in Table 7.10 with an alternative representation in Table 7.11a. Table 7.11b is a simple variant modeled after the monoalphabetic Polybius cipher (Section 7.3). (The reason for the term *homophonic*, meaning *same sound*, is that we can consider each of the numbers assigned to D the sound of that letter.) The encryption method is simple. Each time the letter D is encountered in the plaintext, one of the three numbers is selected at random and is appended to the ciphertext. Thus, the message TENNESSEE may be encrypted to 66|01|26|77|63|21|99|32|19. Notice that in a homophonic cipher, encryption is not unique. Decryption is trivial.

The advantage of the homophonic substitution cipher is that the distribution of the 100 numbers in the ciphertext of a long message is uniform (i.e., each of the 100 numbers occurs roughly the same number of times). It seems that a homophonic substitution cipher cannot be broken by frequency analysis, but it is still vulnerable to digram analysis. Breaking a ciphertext, once it is known (or suspected) that it has been encrypted

a	b	c	d	e	f	g	h	i	j	k	l	m	n	o	p	q	r	s	t	u	v	w	x	y	z
90	70	62	18	76	89	61	83	71	44	91	94	52	81	67	43	31	46	13	72	60	87	07	28	79	51
03	84	82	14	32	53	64	37	27			36	96	77	00	22		98	93	17	65		45		38	
23		75	54	01		20	12				69		08	97			57	10	80	73					
09		95	63			74	56				58		26	29			92	21	66							
55			33			25	05						48	11			02	39	59							
40			68			15	41						34	85			78	99	86							
49			47										16							04					
88			06																	35					
			19																	50					
			24																						
			30																						
			42																						

Table 7.10: A Homophonic Substitution Cipher.

	0	1	2	3	4	5	6	7	8	9
0	o	e	r	a	t	i	e	w	n	a
1	s	o	i	s	d	h	o	t	d	e
2	h	s	p	a	e	h	n	i	x	o
3	e	q	e	e	n	t	l	h	y	s
4	a	i	e	p	j	w	r	e	n	a
5	t	z	m	f	d	a	i	r	l	t
6	u	g	c	e	g	u	t	o	e	l
7	b	i	t	u	h	c	e	n	r	y
8	t	n	c	h	b	o	t	v	a	f
9	a	k	r	s	l	d	m	o	r	s

	1	2	3	4	5	6	7	8	9
0123456	e	t	a	o	i	n	s	h	r
78	d	l	u	m	w	y	f	c	g
9	b	p	k	v	x	q	j	z	

(a)   (b)

Table 7.11: (a) An Alternative Representation of Table 7.10. (b) A Variant.

with a homophonic substitution code, can start, for example, with the letter Q. Since this letter is rare, there is a good chance that only one number had been assigned to it. We know that Q is almost always followed by U, and that U appears 2–3% of the time, so it has been assigned 2 or 3 numbers. Thus, we can look for a number that is always followed by one of the same 2 or 3 numbers (as always when using statistical methods, there must be enough data).

◊ **Exercise 7.6:** Such cryptanalysis can be defeated by assigning two or three codes even to rare letters. This can be done, for example, by using 200 instead of 100 numbers. Suggest a practical way to select 200 numbers for this application.

◊ **Exercise 7.7:** The homophonic cipher requires random integers in various ranges. When a D is encountered, a random integer in the range $[1, 3]$ is needed, but enciphering an E requires a random integer in the range $[1, 12]$. Suggest a way to produce such integers, assuming that a random number generator is available that produces integers in the range $[a, b]$.

There are other ways to construct codes that are easy to use and are more secure than straightforward monoalphabetic substitution codes. Numbers can be assigned to the individual letters and also to many common syllables. When a common syllable is encountered in the plaintext, it is replaced by its code number. When a syllable is found that has no code assigned, its letters are encrypted individually by replacing each letter with its code. Certain codes may be assigned as traps, to throw any would-be cryptanalyst off the track. Such a special code may indicate, for example, that the following (or the preceding) number is spurious and should be ignored.

> He [Jan Tschichold] created a "monoalphabet," including a phonetic
> version which took into account proposals for a reform of German,
> and Saskia and Transito, which were more decorative typefaces.
> —Jean-François Porchez, *A Small History of Type*

8
Transposition Ciphers

In a substitution cipher, each letter in the plaintext is replaced by another letter. In a transposition cipher, the entire plaintext is replaced by a permutation of itself. If the plaintext is long, then each sentence is individually replaced by a permutation of itself. Permutations have been introduced in Section 2.8. The number of permutations of n objects is $n!$ (Exercise 2.7), a number that grows much faster than n. However, the permutation being used has to be chosen such that the receiver will be able to decipher the message. A single-column transposition cipher is described in [Barker 92].

It is important to understand that in a transposition cipher the plainletters are not replaced. An E in the plaintext does not become another letter in the ciphertext; it is just moved from its original position to another place. Frequency analysis of the ciphertext will reveal the normal letter frequencies, thereby serving as a hint to the cryptanalyst that a transposition cipher was used. A digram frequency analysis should then be performed in order to draw detailed conclusions about the cipher. Common digrams, such as th and an, would be torn apart by a substitution cipher, reinforcing the suspicion that this type of cipher was used.

Transposition ciphers are therefore weak, but there is a simple way to make such ciphers more secure. The plaintext can be divided into segments and each segment encrypted by a different permutation. The various permutations can be chosen by different keys, but it is also possible to start with a single long key and extract from it subkeys to choose a permutation for each segment. (See methods for generating permutations in Section 9.8.)

8.1 Simple Examples

We start with a few simple transposition ciphers. These are easy to break, but they illustrate the potential of this type of cipher.

A	D	E	H	I	L	M	P
B	C	F	G	J	K	N	O

Figure 8.1: 2×2 Blocks for a Transposition Cipher.

1. Break the plaintext into fixed-size blocks and apply the same permutation to each block. As an example, the plaintext ABCDE... can be broken into blocks of four letters each and one of the 4! = 24 permutations applied to each block. The ciphertext can be generated by either collecting the four letters of each block, or by collecting the first letter of each block, then the second letter, and so on. Figure 8.1 shows a graphic example of some 4-letter blocks. The resulting ciphertext can be either ACBD EGFH IKJL MONP... or AEIM...CGKO...BFJN...and DHLP....

2. A square or a rectangle with n cells is filled with the integers from 1 to n in some order. The first n plainletters are placed in the cells according to these integers, and the ciphertext is generated by scanning the rectangle in some order (possibly rowwise or columnwise) and collecting letters. An alternative is to place the plainletters in the rectangle in rowwise or columnwise order and to generate the ciphertext by scanning the rectangle according to the integers, collecting letters. If the plaintext is longer than n letters, the process is repeated. Some null letters, such as X or Q, may have to be appended to the last block. Figure 8.2a–c shows three 8×8 squares: the first with integers arranged in a knight's tour, the second a magic square, and the third a self-complementary magic square (where if the integer i is replaced by $65 - i$, the result is the same square, rotated).

47	10	23	64	49	2	59	6		52	61	4	3	20	29	36	45		1	62	5	59	58	12	61	2
22	63	48	9	60	5	50	3		14	3	62	51	46	35	30	19		57	14	50	48	19	45	18	9
11	46	61	24	1	52	7	58		53	60	5	12	21	28	37	44		10	27	34	25	41	36	33	54
62	21	12	45	8	57	4	51		11	6	59	54	43	38	27	22		49	30	26	23	37	22	21	52
19	36	25	40	13	44	53	30		55	58	7	10	23	26	39	42		13	44	43	28	42	39	35	16
26	39	20	33	56	29	14	43		9	8	57	56	41	40	25	24		11	32	29	24	40	31	38	55
35	18	37	28	41	16	31	54		50	63	2	15	18	31	34	47		56	47	20	46	17	15	51	8
38	27	34	17	32	55	42	15		16	1	64	49	48	33	32	17		63	4	53	7	6	60	3	64

(a)	(b)	(c)

Figure 8.2: Three 8×8 Squares For Transposition Ciphers.

In addition to row and column scanning, such a square can be scanned in zigzag, by diagonals, or in a spiral (Figure 8.3a–c, respectively).

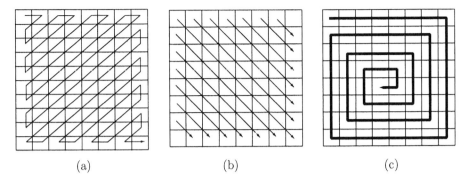

Figure 8.3: Three Ways to Scan an 8×8 Square.

⋄ **Exercise 8.1:** Show how to apply common space-filling curves to scan such a square.

3. The plaintext is arranged in a zigzagging rail fence whose height is the key of the cipher. Assuming the plaintext ABCDEFGHIJK and a key of 3, the rail fence is

$$
\begin{array}{ccccccccc}
A &   &   &   & E &   &   &   & I &   &   \\
  & B &   & D &   & F &   & H &   & J \\
  &   & C &   &   &   & G &   &   &   & K
\end{array}
$$

The fence is scanned row by row to form the ciphertext AEI.BDFHJ.CGK, where the dots are special symbols needed for decryption. This is an example of an irregular transposition cipher.

4. A related structure is the Greek cross (also known as *Four Winds*) where the plaintext is rearranged in three rows in the form of rectangles and is then read row by row to form the ciphertext. If the plaintext is the 24-letter string (in the normal alphabetical order)

$$
\begin{array}{ccccccccccc}
b &   & f &   & k &   & o &   & s &   & w \\
a & c & e & g & i & l & n ˎ p & r & t & v & x \\
d &   & h &   & m &   & q &   & u &   & z
\end{array}
$$

then the ciphertext is the permuted string BFKOSWACEGILNPRTVXDHMQUZ.

5. The plaintext is divided into groups of $n \times n$ letters, and each group is placed into an $n \times n$ square as shown in Figure 8.4, which illustrates the plaintext PLAINTEXT IN A SQUARE. The ciphertext is obtained by scanning the square in rows PLNIR IATNE TXEAX AUQSX XXXXX.

6. Start with a rectangle of m rows and n columns. In each column, select half the rows at random. This creates a template of $m \times n$ cells, half of which have been selected. All authorized users of the cipher must have this template. The plaintext is written in rows and is collected by columns to form the ciphertext. Figure 8.5 shows an example where the plaintext is the letters A through R and the ciphertext is CFLGK MADPH NQEIR BJO.

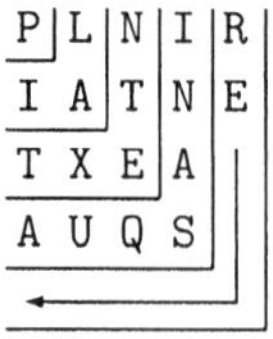

Figure 8.4: Transposition Cipher in a 5×5 Square.

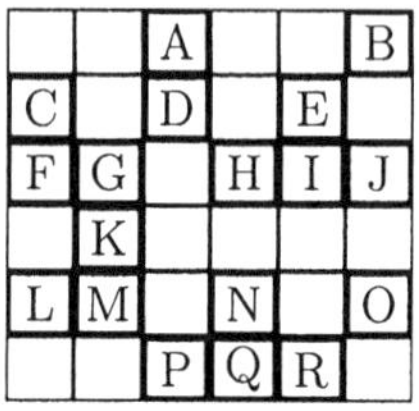

Figure 8.5: A 6×6 Template with Plaintext.

7. Select a key k whose decimal digits are $k_1 k_2 \ldots k_n$. Write the plaintext in an n-row rectangle row by row. On row i, start the text at position k_i. The ciphertext is generated by collecting the letters in columns from left to right. Figure 8.6 is an example. It illustrates how the plaintext ABCD...X is enciphered into NAOBG PCHQU DIRVE JLSWF KMTX by means of the key 23614. This type of transposition cipher is irregular and thus somewhat more secure, but involves a long key.

◇ **Exercise 8.2:** It is simple and natural to form the ciphertext by collecting the plaintext by columns. Suggest other ways to collect the plaintext.

Figure 8.6: An Irregular Rectangle with Plaintext.

8. A simple example of a substitution cipher is to reverse every string of three letters, while keeping the positions of all blank spaces. For example, the message ATTACK AT DAWN becomes TTAKCA DT ANWA. Another elementary transposition is to break a message up into two strings, one with the odd-numbered letters of the message and the other with the even-numbered letters, and then concatenate the two strings. The following is a simple, typical example.

```
WAIT␣FOR␣ME␣AT␣MIDNIGHT
W I ␣ O ␣ E A ␣ I N G T
A T F R M ␣ T M D I H
WI␣O␣EA␣INGTATFRM␣TMDIH
```

This method can be extended by selecting a key n, breaking the message up into n strings (where the first string contains letters $1, n + 1, 2n + 1, \ldots$), and concatenating the strings. A close variant is the perfect shuffle, where the plaintext is broken into two halves that are then merged together.

◇ **Exercise 8.3:** Encrypt the string `WAIT␣FOR␣ME␣AT␣MIDNIGHT` with the perfect shuffle.

9. An anagram is a rearrangement of the letters of a word or a phrase. Thus, for example, `red code` is an anagram of `decoder` and `strict union` is an anagram of `instruction`. It is possible to encrypt a message by scrambling its letters to generate an anagram (meaningful or not). A simple way to create nonsense anagrams is to write the letters of a message in alphabetical order. Thus `I came, I saw, I conquered` becomes the pile of letters `AACCDEEEIIIMNOQRSUW`. This kind of cipher is practically impossible for a receiver (even an authorized one) to decipher (and can also be ambiguous; see box below), but has its applications.

In past centuries, scientists sometimes wanted to keep a discovery secret and at the same time maintain their priority claim. Writing a report of the discovery in anagrams was an acceptable means to achieve both aims. No one could decipher the code, yet when someone else claimed to have made the same discovery, the original discoverer could always produce the original report in plaintext and prove that this text generates the published anagram.

◇ **Exercise 8.4:** It is possible to combine two or more of the transposition methods described here. Would such a combination be more secure than any of the individual methods included in it?

In response to Leibniz's request for further details [about the newly discovered calculus), Newton, after much prodding from Oldenburg and Collins, replied in a manner that was common at the time: he sent Leibniz an anagram—a coded message of garbled letters and numbers—that no one could possibly decode but that could later serve as "proof" that he was the discoverer

$$6accdae13eff7i3l9n4o4qrr4s8t12vx.$$

This famous anagram gives the number of different letters in the Latin sentence "Data aequatione quotcunque fluentes quantitates involvente, fluxiones invenire: et vice versa" (given an equation involving any number of fluent quantities, to find the fluxions, and vice versa).

—Eli Maor, *e, The Story of a Number* (1994)

8.2 Cyclic Notation and Keys

Mathematicians use the *cyclic notation* to describe permutations. This notation is easy to understand by means of an example. The cyclic notation of the permutation

abcdefghijklmnopqrstuvwxyz
QPALZMWOSKXEDCHRIFJVNTUGYB

is (aqisjkxgwunc)(bprfmdlez)(ho)(tv)(y). We start with the top-left symbol a. It corresponds to Q, q corresponds to I, i corresponds to S, and so on, up to c, which corresponds to A. This completes the first cycle. The second cycle starts with the first letter (in alphabetical order) not included in the first cycle. This is b, which corresponds to P, and so on, up to z, which corresponds to B, thereby completing the second cycle. The last cycle is (y), expressing the fact that y corresponds to Y in this particular permutation.

An *involutary permutation* is a permutation that is its own inverse. An involutary permutation is expressed in cyclic notation as a set of pairs. For example, the ROT13 permutation (Section 6.1), where the entire alphabet is rotated cyclically 13 positions, is expressed by

abcdefghijklmnopqrstuvwxyz
NOPQRSTUVWXYZABCDEFGHIJKLM

or cyclically as (an)(bo)(cp)...(zm). (This material is also discussed in Section 2.8.)

⋄ **Exercise 8.5:** Find a permutation of the 26 letters whose cyclic expression has one cycle.

It is possible to specify a permutation by means of a key. After removing spaces and duplicates from the key, the remaining alphabet is appended to it. Thus, the key PERMUTATIONS␣BY␣KEY yields the permutation

abcdefghijklmnopqrstuvwxyz
PERMUTAIONSBYKCDFGHJLQVWXZ

and such a permutation can be used as a simple monoalphabetic cipher. Obviously, a good key should be long and should contain few duplicates. Section 8.4 discusses other ways to construct permutations from a key.

The fundamental problem of transposition ciphers is how to specify a permutation by means of a short, easy-to-remember key. A detailed description of a permutation can be as long as the message itself, or even longer. It should contain instructions such as "swap positions 54 and 32, move position 27 to position 98," and so on. The following sections discuss several ways to implement transposition ciphers.

> As he sat on the arm of a leather-covered arm chair, putting his face through all its permutations of loathing, the whole household seemed to spring into activity around him.
>
> —Kingsley Amis, *Lucky Jim*, 1953

8.3 Transposition by Turning Template

The number of permutations of 36 objects is $36! \approx 3.72 \cdot 10^{41}$, an immense number. Many, albeit not all, of these permutations can be specified by means of a small, 6×6 template with some holes cut in it. This old method, which goes back to at least the mid-eighteenth century, was popularized in 1881 by the Austrian Colonel Eduard Fleissner von Wostrowitz and is easy to describe and to implement. A square piece of cardboard is prepared whose size equals the width of six letters, and nine square holes are cut in it (the gray squares in Figure 8.7a), turning it into a grille or a template. The first 36 letters of the plaintext are arranged in a 6×6 square and the template placed over it (Figure 8.7b). The nine letters seen through the holes are collected by rows and become the first nine letters ACEHPTWY6 of the ciphertext. The template is then rotated 90° (clockwise or counterclockwise, but encoder and decoder have to agree on the direction and use it consistently), and the nine letters now showing through the holes are appended to the ciphertext. The holes are arranged such that after four such readings, all 36 letters under the table have been seen through the holes and included in the ciphertext. The process is repeated for segments of 36 plaintext letters, and some random letters may have to be added to the last segment to complete its length to 36.

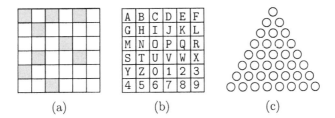

(a) (b) (c)

Figure 8.7: Three Turning Templates.

◇ **Exercise 8.6:** Rotate the template of Figure 8.7a clockwise over the plaintext of Figure 8.7b and collect the remaining three ciphertext groups of nine characters each.

Naturally, the opposite process is also possible. The first nine letters of the plaintext are written through the template holes, the template is rotated, and the process is repeated three more times, for a total of 36 letters arranged in a 6×6 square. The ciphertext is prepared by reading the 36 letters row by row.

The template is normally a square where the number of cells is divisible by 4 (so each of the four template orientations will require the same number of holes). However, the template can also be an equilateral triangle where the number of cells is divisible by 3 (Figure 8.7c) or a square with an odd number of cells, such as 7×7), in which case the central row and column can simply be ignored.

Decrypting is the reverse of encrypting, but breaking this code, even though not especially difficult, is tricky and requires intuition. The length of the ciphertext provides a clue to the size of the template (in the case of a 6×6 template, the length of the ciphertext is a multiple of 36). Once the codebreaker knows (or guesses or suspects) the size of the template, further clues can be found from the individual letters of common digrams. If it is suspected that the template size is 6×6, the ciphertext is broken up into 36-letter segments, and each segment is written as a 6×6 square. Any occurrences of the letters T and H in a square could be due to the digram TH or the trigram THE that were broken apart by the encryption. If the codebreaker discovers certain hole positions that would unite the T and H in one square, then other squares (i.e., other ciphertext segments) may be tried with these holes, to check whether their T and H also unite. This is a tedious process, but it can be automated to some degree. A computer program can try many hole combinations and display several squares of ciphertext partly decrypted with those holes. The user may reject some hole combinations and ask for further tests (perhaps with another common digram) with other combinations.

It is very easy to determine hole positions in such a square template. Figure 8.8a shows a 6×6 template divided into four 3×3 templates rotated with respect to each other. The nine cells of each small template are numbered in the same way. The rule for selecting cells is: If cell 3 is selected for a hole in one of the 3×3 templates, then cell 3 should not be a hole in any of the other three templates. This rule is easy to implement. We start by selecting cell 1 in one of the four templates (there are four choices for this). In the next step, we select cell 2 in one of the four templates (there are again four choices). This is repeated nine times, so the total number of possible hole configurations is $4^9 = 262{,}144$. This number is not large enough to prohibit current computers from trying all the possible templates and is, of course, much smaller than the total number 36! of permutations of 36 objects.

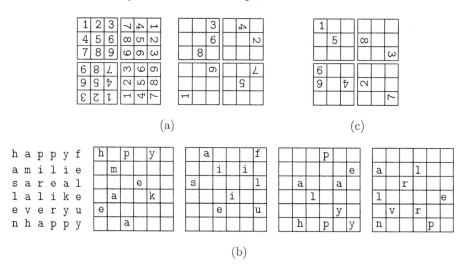

Figure 8.8: Turning Template Method.

◊ **Exercise 8.7:** How many hole configurations are possible in an 8×8 template?

We illustrate this method with the plaintext happy families are all alike every unhappy family is unhappy in its own way. The first 36 letters are arranged in a 6×6 square

```
h a p p y f
a m i l i e
s a r e a l
l a l i k e
e v e r y u
n h a p p y
```

Figure 8.8b shows how the same template is placed over this square four times while rotating it each time. The resulting cipher is HPYMEAKEA AFIISLIEU PEAALYHPY ALRLEVRNP.

It is also possible to use a key to determine the hole positions. The advantage is that the users don't have to keep the actual template (which may be difficult to destroy in a sudden emergency). Consider, for example, the key FAKE CIPHER. The first key letter, F, is the sixth letter of the alphabet, which implies that the square should be of size 6×6. Such a square has 36 cells, so 36/4 = 9 hole positions are needed, where each position is determined by one of the key's letters. The key should therefore be nine letters long. If it is shorter, it is repeated as needed, and if it is longer, only the first nine letters are used. The letters are numbered according to their alphabetic order. A is numbered 1. The next key letter in alphabetical order is C, so it is numbered 2. The next one is E, so its two occurrences are numbered 3 and 4. Thus, the key becomes the nine digits 518327964. These are divided into the four groups 51, 83, 27, and 964 for the four quadrants. The first group corresponds to holes 5 and 1 in the first quadrant. The second group corresponds to holes 8 and 3 in the second quadrant, and so on (Figure 8.8c).

◇ **Exercise 8.8:** Construct the template that results from the key DO GOOD.

This method can be made more secure by double encryption. Once the ciphertext is generated, it is encrypted by means of a mirror image of the template or even by a completely different template. However, even with this enhancement, the turning template method is unsafe and the template itself adds an extra complication. The template has to be kept safe, because it is the encryption key. A key that is a character string can be memorized, but a template is a physical object.

8.4 Columnar Transposition Cipher

A template requires constant protection, so it is preferable to specify a permutation by means of a key, without the need for a template. Here is a simple way of doing this. To specify a permutation of, say, 15 letters, we start with a key whose length is at least 15 letters (not counting spaces), eliminate the spaces, leave the first 15 letters, and discard the rest. Thus, if the key is the phrase TRANSPOSITION CIPHERS, we first generate the 15-letter string TRANSPOSITIONCI. The 15 letters are then numbered as follows: The A is numbered 1. There are no B's, so the C is numbered 2. The next letter (alphabetically) is I. There are three I's, so they are numbered 3, 4, and 5. The final result is

$$
\begin{array}{ccccccccccccccc}
T & R & A & N & S & P & O & S & I & T & I & O & N & C & I \\
14 & 11 & 1 & 6 & 12 & 10 & 8 & 13 & 3 & 15 & 4 & 9 & 7 & 2 & 5
\end{array}
$$

The sequence 14, 11, 1, 6, 12, 10, 8, 13, 3, 15, 4, 9, 7, 2, and 5 specifies the permutation. After the permutation, the third plainletter should be in position 1, the fourteenth plainletter should be in position 2, and so on. The plaintext is now arranged as the rows of a rectangle with 15 columns, the columns swapped according to the permutation, and the ciphertext collected column by column. Figure 8.9 shows an example.

T	R	A	N	S	P	O	S	I	T	I	O	N	C	I
14	11	1	6	12	10	8	13	3	15	4	9	7	2	5
h	a	p	p	y	f	a	m	i	l	i	e	s	a	r
e	a	l	l	a	l	i	k	e	e	v	e	r	y	u
n	h	a	p	p	y	f	a	m	i	l	y	i	s	u
n	h	a	p	p	y	i	n	i	t	s	o	w	n	w
a	y	e	v	e	r	y	t	h	i	n	g	w	a	s
i	n	c	o	n	f	u	s	i	o	n	i	n	t	h
e	o	b	l	o	n	s	k	y	s	h	o	u	s	e
t	h	e	w	i	f	e	h	a	d	d	i	s	c	o
v	e	r	e	d	t	h	a	t	t	h	e			
p	a	i	i	r	p	s	a	e	f	a	y	m	h	l
l	y	e	v	u	l	r	i	e	l	a	a	k	e	e
a	s	m	l	u	p	i	f	y	y	h	p	a	n	i
a	n	i	s	w	p	w	i	o	y	h	p	n	n	t
e	a	h	n	s	v	w	y	g	r	y	e	t	a	i
c	t	i	n	h	o	n	u	i	f	n	n	s	i	o
b	s	y	h	e	l	u	s	o	n	o	o	k	e	s
e	c	a	d	o	w	s	e	i	f	h	i	h	t	d
r		t	h		e		h	e	t	e	d	a	v	t

PLAAECBER AYSNATSC IEMIHIYAT IVLSNNHDH
RUUWSHEO PLPPVOLWE SRIWWNUS AIFIYUSEH
EEYOGIOIE FLYYRFNFT AAHHYNOHE YAPPENOID
MKANTSKHA HENNAIETV LEITIOSDT

Figure 8.9: Transposition Cipher with a Key.

This transposition cipher does not require a template, and the key is easy to memorize and replace, but the method isn't very secure. If the codebreaker can guess the number of columns (or try many guesses), then the permutation, or parts of it, can be guessed from the positions of the members of common digrams. Thus, if the codebreaker arranges the ciphertext in a rectangle of the right size, then columns can be moved around until all or most occurrences of H follow T's. If the result starts making sense, more digrams can be tried, leading to better decipherment.

As is true with many encryption methods, this cipher can be strengthened by performing double encryption. After the ciphertext is obtained by reading the 15 columns and collecting letters, it can be written in rows and reencrypted with the same key. An alternative is to reencrypt the ciphertext before it is read from the 15 columns. This is done by using another key on the rows. There are nine rows in our example, and they can be swapped according to a secondary key.

Replacing a key or even two keys as often as possible is the key (no pun intended) to good security. This can easily be done once the authorized users agree (or are being told) how to do this. The users may agree on a book and on a formula. The formula converts a date to a page number in the book, and the key consists of the last letters of the first 15 lines on that page. Every day, all users apply the formula to the current date and construct a new key from the new page. A possible formula may start with a 6-digit date of the form $d_1d_2m_1m_2y_1y_2$ and compute

$$\big((50d_1 + 51d_2 + 52m_1 + 53m_2 + 54y_1 + 55y_2) \bmod k\big) + 1,$$

where k is the number of pages in the book. This formula (which is a weighted sum; see the similar formula for ISBN in Section 2.1) depends on all six digits of the date in such a way that changing any digit almost always changes the sum. The result of computing any integer modulo k is a number in the interval $[0, k - 1]$, so adding 1 to it produces a valid page number.

⋄ **Exercise 8.9:** Assuming a 190-page book, compute the page number for today.

8.5 Double Transposition

Even more secure than double Playfair (Section 7.6), the double transposition cipher was one of the manual ciphers used in World War II by both sides of the conflict.

The cipher consists of two rounds of column transposition, using different keys. In the first round, a key, for example, DOUBLE, is chosen, and the plaintext is written under it in rows as in Figure 8.10a. The letters of the key are then numbered in alphabetical order, and the plaintext is read column by column according to the numbers. (The key may contain multiple letters and the direction they are numbered, left-to-right or right-to-left, has to be decided in advance. It should be considered a parameter of this method.) The resulting string of text is encrypted in the second round in the same way, but using another key (TRIPLE in Figure 8.10b). The resulting cipher text is then divided into blocks of five letters each, for easy transmission. The process is illustrated here for the plaintext this should be encrypted with caution.
The result of the first round is the string

sdrwu toetho hepti sbyit hunecn ilcda

and the result of the second round is

thbnc rtttn uosul whihi depica soeyed

```
2  5  6  1  4  3        6  5  2  4  3  1
D  O  U  B  L  E        T  R  I  P  L  E
t  h  i  s  s  h        s  d  r  w  u  t
o  u  l  d  b  e        o  e  t  h  o  h
e  n  c  r  y  p        e  p  t  i  s  b
t  e  d  w  i  t        y  i  t  h  u  n
h  c  a  u  t  i        e  c  n  i  l  c
o  n                    d  a
```

(a)   (b)

Figure 8.10: A Double Transposition Example.

which is transmitted as the quintets `thbnc rtttn uosul whihi depic asoey ed`.

Decryption is straightforward and is done in the following steps.

1. Start with the second key. Denote its length by k and the length of the ciphertext by c. Perform the integer division $c \div k$. Denote the quotient and remainder of this division by q and r, respectively.

2. Prepare a rectangle with k columns and $q+1$ rows. Only the leftmost r columns will be full; the rest will have q rows each.

3. Write the key (letters and numbers) above the rectangle.

4. Find the column labeled 1 and place the beginning of the ciphertext in it. If this column is one of the leftmost r columns, it should be full (i.e., have $q + 1$ rows); otherwise, it should have only q rows. Next, find the column labeled 2 and place the next q or $q + 1$ cipherletters in it. Continue until the entire ciphertext has been placed in the rectangle.

5. Read the text off the rectangle in rows. The resulting string becomes the new ciphertext.

6. Repeat steps 1–5 with the first key. The resulting string is the plaintext.

◇ **Exercise 8.10:** Apply these rules to decrypt the example above.

Even though very secure, the double transposition cipher has two weaknesses. If two or more messages of the same length are sent using the same key, they can be decrypted by *multiple anagramming*, a tedious but straightforward process. The cipher is also susceptible to encrypting mistakes. A mistake made at a sensitive point during encryption may lead to many decryption errors.

For a more detailed approach to the solution of this cipher, see [Kullback 90] and [Barker 96].

Through a sudden transposition, the preferred of the former regime had become the disgraced, while the disgraced of the former regime had become the preferred; unjust favor and unjust disfavor still subsisted, but with a change of object.

—Hippolyte A. Taine, *The Origins of Contemporary France* (1876–1894)

8.5.1 The Myszkowsky Cipher

This method, due to E. Myszkowsky, is a variation on the general columnar transposition cipher. The key is replicated as many times as needed to bring it to the size of the plaintext. Each key letter is replaced by a number according to its alphabetic position, and the plainletters are collected according to these numbers to form the ciphertext. The example shown here uses the key QUALITY, that is duplicated four times to cover the entire 28-letter plaintext Come home immediately. All is lost.

```
Q  U  A  L  I  T  Y  Q  U  A  L  I  T  Y  Q  U  A  L  I  T  Y  Q  U  A  L  I  T  Y
13 21 1  9  5  17 25 14 22 2  10 6  18 26 15 23 3  11 7  19 27 16 24 4  12 8  20 28
C  O  M  E  H  O  M  E  I  M  M  E  D  I  A  T  E  L  Y  A  L  L  I  S  L  O  S  T
```

The ciphertext is MMESH EYOEM LLCEA LODAS OITIM ILT. Since the extended key contains duplicate letters, the original key may also contain duplicates, as in the word INSTINCT.

8.5.2 The AMSCO Cipher

The AMSCO cipher, due to A. M. Scott, is a columnar transposition cipher where the plaintext is placed in the columns such that every other column receives a pair of plainletters. The example presented here uses the same key and plaintext as in Section 8.5.1.

```
Q  U  A  L  I  T  Y
4  6  1  3  2  5  7
----------------------
C  OM E  HO M  EI M
ME D  IA T  EL Y  AL
L  IS L  OS T
```

The ciphertext is EIALM ELTHO TOSCM ELEIY OMDIS MAL.

⋄ **Exercise 8.11:** Design a cipher very similar to AMSCO and name it the way AMSCO was named.

8.6 A 2-Step ADFGVX Cipher

Another way to strengthen a transposition cipher is to combine it with a substitution cipher into a two-step encryption algorithm. As an example, the Polybius monoalphabetic cipher (Section 7.3) can be the first step, followed by the columnar transposition cipher of Section 8.4 as the second step. The first step replaces each letter with a number pair, while the second step tears each pair apart. This defeats any attempt at decryption by means of letter frequency analysis.

Table 8.12 lists the well-known Morse code. Today, this code is rarely used, but just a generation ago it was very popular with, among others, radio amateurs. Anyone who has used Morse code for a while knows that some codes are hard to distinguish, while others are very different. The codes for A, D, F, G, V, and X belong to the latter category,

	A	D	F	G	V	X
A	a	b	c	d	e	f
D	g	h	i	j	k	l
F	m	n	o	p	q	r
G	s	t	u	v	w	x
V	y	z	1	2	3	4
X	5	6	7	8	9	0

Figure 8.11: A 6×6 Polybius Square.

so in a Morse-based encrypted communications network it makes sense to use these letters, or some of them, instead of digits, to label the rows and columns of a Polybius square. Such a 6×6 square containing letters and digits is shown in Figure 8.11.

Combining such a Polybius square with the transposition method of Section 8.4 yields ciphertext with just six different letters ADFGVX. This may lead the knowledgeable codebreaker in the right direction toward easy breaking of the code, so one more step should be added to strengthen this method. Random letters other than the six ones may be generously sprinkled in the ciphertext, to throw any would-be cryptanalyst off the right track. The random letters may be added such that the final ciphertext has uniform letter frequencies (so it looks random), or they may be added to create ciphertext that resembles a monoalphabetic substitution code, i.e., where one letter has the frequency of E (11–12%), another has the frequency of T, and so on. This increases the size of the ciphertext significantly, but may prevent decryption or at least delay it considerably.

The ADFGVX cipher was used by the Germans near the end of World War I. It was broken by the French cryptanalyst Lieutenant Georges Painvin, whose work was crucial in defending France from Germany. (See [Childs 00] for a detailed solution of this cipher.)

> With birds there has sometimes been a complete transposition of the ordinary characters proper to each sex; the females having become the more eager in courtship, the males remaining comparatively passive, but apparently selecting the more attractive females, as we may infer from the results.
>
> —Charles Darwin, *The Descent of Man* (1871)

8.7 Conclusions

Transposition ciphers are simple and have been used in the past, before the computer age, to encrypt messages sent between individuals. Their use on a large scale, such as for messages in a war or in a large organization, was never popular because this type of cipher has certain drawbacks.

1. An ideal transposition cipher performs a permutation of the entire text. Most practical transposition ciphers divide the plaintext into blocks and transpose each block

A	.-	N	-.	1	.----	Period	.-.-.-
B	-...	O	---	2	..---	Comma	--..--
C	-.-.	P	.--.	3	...--	Colon	---...
Ch	----	Q	--.-	4	....-	Question mark	..--..
D	-..	R	.-.	5	.....	Apostrophe	.----.
E	.	S	...	6	-....	Hyphen	-....-
F	..-.	T	-	7	--...	Dash	-..-.
G	--.	U	..-	8	---..	Parentheses	-.--.-
H	....	V	...-	9	----.	Quotation marks	.-..-.
I	..	W	.--	0	-----		
J	.---	X	-..-				
K	-.-	Y	-.--				
L	.-..	Z	--..				
M	--						

If the duration of a dot is taken to be one unit, then that of a dash is three units. The space between the dots and dashes of one character is one unit, between characters it is three units, and between words six units (five for automatic transmission). To indicate that a mistake has been made and for the receiver to delete the last word, send "........" (eight dots).

Table 8.12: The Morse Code.

individually. The larger the block, the better the encryption, but any error in encrypting a block or in transmitting its ciphertext may prevent (or at least delay) the decryption of the block. The longer the block, the more serious each error becomes.

2. A large-scale use of transposition ciphers encrypted with the same key leads to repetitions, and we know that avoiding repetitions is one of the most important rules in cryptography. If hundreds of messages are sent during a single day, all using the same key, then there are bound to be quite a few messages of the same length. Such messages are all transposed in the same way. If the first letter of an n-letter message is moved to, say, position k, then the first letter of every n-letter message is moved to the same position. With this in mind, the codebreaker writes all the n-letter ciphertexts vertically in an n-column rectangle, and tries several permutations. Once a codebreaker is able to partially decrypt one such n-letter message, all other n-letter messages can be partially decrypted in the same way, and serve as a check. If a permutation creates a chunk of meaningful text in one row only, it is probably a coincidence. If it generates readable text in all or in most of the rows, then the codebreaker can assume that this permutation is the beginning of a successful decryption. We propose some ideas on how to try certain permutations.

Idea. Check for common digrams. If a Q is found in position j in a certain row, and there is a U in position i of the same row, the codebreaker checks the letters in positions i and j of each row for common digrams.

Idea. Check for initial letters. We know that English words tend to start with TAOSWCIHBD. If a single column contains just these letters, chances are that this is the first column of the plaintext.

Idea. If a rare letter, such as Z, appears in the messages more often than statistically expected, it may indicate that a word containing it, such as ZIGZAGGING, appears often in those messages.

Transposition lost its importance with the surge of mechanical cipher machines at the beginning of the 20th century, since it is hard for a mechanical device to store a great number of letters. Things have changed since then. Semiconductor technology now offers enough storage to encrypt effectively with transposition, and tiny chips provide millions of bits, with very short access time, for the price of a bus ticket. The 21st century will see transposition regain its true importance.

—Friedrich L. Bauer, *Decrypted Secrets,* 2nd ed. (2000)

9
Polyalphabetic Substitution Ciphers

Perhaps the simplest way to extend the basic monoalphabetic substitution codes is to define two cipher alphabets and use them alternately. In the example below, the first letter S of the plain message SURRENDER is replaced by a letter (D) from cipher alphabet 1, and the second letter U is replaced by a letter (which also happens to be a D) from cipher alphabet 2. The same cipher letter D replaces two plaintext letters. Similarly, the two cipher letters Q and L stand for the plain letter A. This primitive *polyalphabetic substitution cipher*, developed by the Renaissance figure Leon Battista Alberti, is already much safer than any monoalphabetic cipher.

Plain alphabet	abcdefghijklmnopqrstuvwxyz␣
Cipher alphabet 1	QWERTYUIOPLKJH␣GFSDAZXCVBNM
Cipher alphabet 2	LASKM␣JFHGQPWOEIRUTYDZXNCBV

◇ **Exercise 9.1:** Suggest a way to add a key to this cipher.

I believe that the arts which aim at imitating the creations of nature originated in the following way: in a tree trunk, a lump of earth, or in some other thing were accidentally discovered one day certain contours that needed only a very slight change to look strikingly like some natural object. Noticing this, people tried to see if it were not possible by addition or subtraction to complete what still was lacking for a perfect likeness. Thus by adjusting and removing outlines and planes in the way demanded by the object itself, men achieved what they wanted, and not without pleasure.

—Leon Battista Alberti, *De Statua,* (1436)

9.1 Self-Reciprocal Ciphers

We start this chapter with a simple, albeit weak, polyalphabetic cipher that is self-reciprocal. A digram is a pair of consecutive letters or other symbols. The elements of a self-reciprocal digram table have the following property: If the element at row i, column j, is XY, then the element at row x, column y, is IJ (Table 9.1). This results in a polyalphabetic, symmetric cipher. The cipher is polyalphabetic because a given plainletter, such as A, is encrypted to different letters depending on its immediate plaintext neighbor. It is symmetric because the same table is used for encryption and decryption.

	a	b	c	d	e	f	g	h	i	j	k	...
a	BD	DK	CE	JH	NS	OM	PA	OE	MV	US	HN	
b	EG	UB	WG	AA	SF	DD	ML	SO	UV	BR	YV	
c	FH	WC	FR	QA	AC	CN	DH	SX	ZM	NB	WD	
d	FG	DE	EK	BF	DB	FF	WI	CG	NE	EL	AB	
e	DX	GS	TC	MP	ON	FU	BA	HH	US	NK	DC	
⋮												

Table 9.1: A Self-Reciprocal Digram Table.

A good design for such a table is a Latin square (Section 10.7), where for each row, each of the 26 letters occurs exactly once as the first letter of a digram and exactly once as the second letter of a digram (and the same is true for the columns). However, a self-reciprocal digram table produces weak encryption because digram frequencies in the various languages are well known. In English, for example, the most common digram is th. If the entry in row t, column h, of the table is XY, then the ciphertext would contain many occurrences of the digram XY, thereby providing the codebreaker with a clue.

Better security can be obtained with a self-reciprocal trigram table. Such a table has $26^3 = 17{,}576$ entries, where each entry is a trigram. (In practice, the table can be printed or stored as 26 separate tables, each with 26×26 trigrams, which occupy several pages.) Even trigram frequencies are well known but are statistically less significant than digram frequencies (especially since there are so many trigrams).

9.2 The Porta Polyalphabetic Cipher

The Renaissance figure Giambattista Della Porta is responsible for this early polyalphabetic cipher. In its original version, it was limited to 22 letters and consisted of 11 alphabets. Figure 9.2a shows the modern version, with 13 alphabets, (each an involutary permutation; see Section 8.2) that can encipher all 26 letters. Notice that each of these permutations is simply a shifted version of its predecessor. The cipher is based on an alphabetic key where each key letter specifies one of the 13 alphabets and that alphabet is used to encrypt the current plainletter.

key	a	b	c	d	e	f	g	h	i	j	k	l	m
AB	N	O	P	Q	R	S	T	U	V	W	X	Y	Z
CD	O	P	Q	R	S	T	U	V	W	X	Y	Z	N
EF	P	Q	R	S	T	U	V	W	X	Y	Z	N	O
GH	Q	R	S	T	U	V	W	X	Y	Z	N	O	P
IJ	R	S	T	U	V	W	X	Y	Z	N	O	P	Q
KL	S	T	U	V	W	X	Y	Z	N	O	P	Q	R
MN	T	U	V	W	X	Y	Z	N	O	P	Q	R	S
OP	U	V	W	X	Y	Z	N	O	P	Q	R	S	T
QR	V	W	X	Y	Z	N	O	P	Q	R	S	T	U
ST	W	X	Y	Z	N	O	P	Q	R	S	T	U	V
UV	X	Y	Z	N	O	P	Q	R	S	T	U	V	W
WX	Y	Z	N	O	P	Q	R	S	T	U	V	W	X
YZ	Z	N	O	P	Q	R	S	T	U	V	W	X	Y

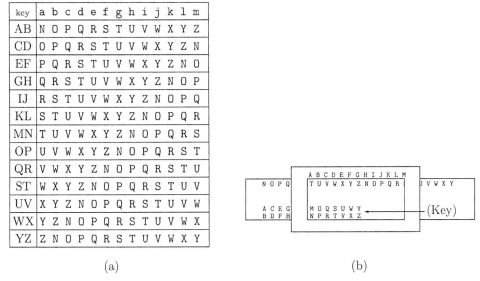

(a)   (b)

Figure 9.2: The Porta Cipher.

The top row of the cipher lists the first 13 plainletters. Each subsequent row corresponds to two key letters (in the leftmost column) and lists an involutary permutation. The current key letter selects a row, and the current plainletter is encrypted by the permutation in that row. Thus, the key lock encrypts the plaintext come to the rescue into UHNW BH FZW KSAUAS. Decryption is the exact opposite of encryption because the permutations are involutary. Thus, the key letter l encrypts c to U and decrypts U to c. The Porta cipher is therefore self-reciprocal.

◇ **Exercise 9.2:** Explain why the plaintext come is encrypted to UHNW under the key lock.

It is intuitively clear that this cipher, even though polyalphabetic, is weak. One reason for this is the special permutations that the cipher employs. They encrypt a letter in one half of the alphabet to a letter in the other half, and this may provide the codebreaker with an important clue. Suppose, for example, that we have the ciphertext fragment ABC. It is immediately clear that this fragment cannot represent the plaintext the, because B must represent a plainletter in the range n–z.

The cryptographer M. E. Ohaver, the originator of many interesting ciphers and cipher puzzles, noticed that the Porta cipher can be implemented by means of a sliding device (Figure 9.2b, after [Gaines 56]).

9.3 The Beaufort Cipher

This old polyalphabetic cipher originated in the early 1700s and was reinvented in 1857 by Admiral Sir Francis Beaufort, who also introduced the wind force scale, still in widespread use today.

The cipher is based on a 27×27 square, where each row is a cyclic shift of its predecessor (Table 9.3). The top and bottom rows are identical, as are also the leftmost and rightmost columns. Each corner has the letter A. Encryption is done by a key that is placed over the plaintext and is repeated as many times as necessary to cover the entire plaintext. Each plainletter is encrypted by the key letter above it in the following way. Suppose that the current plainletter is x and the current key letter is y. Find x on any of the four square sides. Proceed either horizontally or vertically along the row or column that starts with x until you run into letter y. Make a 90° turn in any direction and continue to the end of the row (or column). The last letter is the cipherletter that substitutes x. For example, if the current plainletter is P and the current key letter is F, we can start at the P on the top row, slide down to the F, turn right (or left) and slide to the end, finding Q. It is now obvious that decryption is the exact reverse of encryption, making this a self-reciprocal cipher.

```
A  B C D E F G H I J K L M N O P Q R S T U V W X Y Z  A
B  C D E F G H I J K L M N O P Q R S T U V W X Y Z A  B
C  D E F G H I J K L M N O P Q R S T U V W X Y Z A B  C
D  E F G H I J K L M N O P Q R S T U V W X Y Z A B C  D
E  F G H I J K L M N O P Q R S T U V W X Y Z A B C D  E
F  G H I J K L M N O P Q R S T U V W X Y Z A B C D E  F
G  H I J K L M N O P Q R S T U V W X Y Z A B C D E F  G
H  I J K L M N O P Q R S T U V W X Y Z A B C D E F G  H
I  J K L M N O P Q R S T U V W X Y Z A B C D E F G H  I
J  K L M N O P Q R S T U V W X Y Z A B C D E F G H I  J
K  L M N O P Q R S T U V W X Y Z A B C D E F G H I J  K
L  M N O P Q R S T U V W X Y Z A B C D E F G H I J K  L
M  N O P Q R S T U V W X Y Z A B C D E F G H I J K L  M
N  O P Q R S T U V W X Y Z A B C D E F G H I J K L M  N
O  P Q R S T U V W X Y Z A B C D E F G H I J K L M N  O
P  Q R S T U V W X Y Z A B C D E F G H I J K L M N O  P
Q  R S T U V W X Y Z A B C D E F G H I J K L M N O P  Q
R  S T U V W X Y Z A B C D E F G H I J K L M N O P Q  R
S  T U V W X Y Z A B C D E F G H I J K L M N O P Q R  S
T  U V W X Y Z A B C D E F G H I J K L M N O P Q R S  T
U  V W X Y Z A B C D E F G H I J K L M N O P Q R S T  U
V  W X Y Z A B C D E F G H I J K L M N O P Q R S T U  V
W  X Y Z A B C D E F G H I J K L M N O P Q R S T U V  W
X  Y Z A B C D E F G H I J K L M N O P Q R S T U V W  X
Y  Z A B C D E F G H I J K L M N O P Q R S T U V W X  Y
Z  A B C D E F G H I J K L M N O P Q R S T U V W X Y  Z
A  B C D E F G H I J K L M N O P Q R S T U V W X Y Z  A
```

Table 9.3: The Beaufort Cipher.

⋄ **Exercise 9.3:** How was Table 9.3 constructed?

Francis Beaufort was born in Ireland in 1774. He entered the Royal Navy at the age
of 13 and was a midshipman aboard the *Aquilon*. Beaufort is said to have had an
illustrious career on the seas and by 1800 had risen to the rank of Commander. In the
summer of 1805 Beaufort was appointed to the command of the *Woolwich*, a 44-gun
man-of-war. It was at this time that he devised his wind force scale. By 1838 the
Beaufort wind force scale was made mandatory for log entries in all ships of the Royal
Navy. Beaufort last served as Hydrographer to the Admiralty. He died in 1857, two
years after his retirement.

9.4 The Trithemius Cipher

A slightly more complex and impressive-looking (although not much more secure)
polyalphabetic cipher was developed by the fifteenth-century German author and monk
Johannes Trithemius (who was from the town of Trittenheim on the Moselle River and
is thus known in German as von Trittenheim). He came up with the letter-square de-
picted in Figure 9.4. The square consists of a top row with the 26 plain letters, followed
by 26 rows, each shifted one position to the left relative to its predecessor. In fact, the
26 rows constitute 26 different Caesar ciphers. The principle is to encrypt consecutive
letters of the plaintext with consecutive rows of the square. Thus, the plaintext `let`
`me`...is encrypted (after removing the space) with the first five rows of the square to
become the ciphertext `LFVPI`....

This cipher removes the natural letter frequencies from the ciphertext, thereby
producing ciphertext that looks random. However, if the codebreaker knows or suspects
that the Trithemius method was used to encrypt a message, breaking it becomes easy.
The codebreaker simply applies consecutive rows of the Trithemius square to decrypt
the ciphertext letter by letter. The reason this cipher is so vulnerable to attack is the
lack of a key. The Trithemius cipher breaks one of cryptography's most sacred rules,
namely, Kerckhoffs' principle.

Trithemius' algorithm was published shortly after his death (in his book *Polygraphiae Libri Sex*, 1518), and was quickly taken up and improved by several enthu-
siasts. Two well-known Renaissance figures who showed interest in this method were
Giambattista (Giovanni Battista) Della Porta and Girolamo Cardano. The former was
an all-around genius, while the latter (who is also known as Geronimo or Hieronymus)
is mostly known as a mathematician. Although the details of their methods differ,
these methods are based on a key that is added to the basic Trithemius algorithm. The
improved methods no longer scan the Trithemius letter-square row by row but select
the next row based on the secret key. The key makes these methods secure but at the
same time introduces the problem of key distribution. Everyone authorized to send and
receive messages has to agree on the same key and keep it secret, or to securely receive
the key from a central person or group. As long as the number of people involved is

```
abcdefghijklmnopqrstuvwxyz
ABCDEFGHIJKLMNOPQRSTUVWXYZ
BCDEFGHIJKLMNOPQRSTUVWXYZA
CDEFGHIJKLMNOPQRSTUVWXYZAB
DEFGHIJKLMNOPQRSTUVWXYZABC
EFGHIJKLMNOPQRSTUVWXYZABCD
FGHIJKLMNOPQRSTUVWXYZABCDE
GHIJKLMNOPQRSTUVWXYZABCDEF
HIJKLMNOPQRSTUVWXYZABCDEFG
IJKLMNOPQRSTUVWXYZABCDEFGH
JKLMNOPQRSTUVWXYZABCDEFGHI
KLMNOPQRSTUVWXYZABCDEFGHIJ
LMNOPQRSTUVWXYZABCDEFGHIJK
MNOPQRSTUVWXYZABCDEFGHIJKL
NOPQRSTUVWXYZABCDEFGHIJKLM
OPQRSTUVWXYZABCDEFGHIJKLMN
PQRSTUVWXYZABCDEFGHIJKLMNO
QRSTUVWXYZABCDEFGHIJKLMNOP
RSTUVWXYZABCDEFGHIJKLMNOPQ
STUVWXYZABCDEFGHIJKLMNOPQR
TUVWXYZABCDEFGHIJKLMNOPQRS
UVWXYZABCDEFGHIJKLMNOPQRST
VWXYZABCDEFGHIJKLMNOPQRSTU
WXYZABCDEFGHIJKLMNOPQRSTUV
XYZABCDEFGHIJKLMNOPQRSTUVW
YZABCDEFGHIJKLMNOPQRSTUVWX
ZABCDEFGHIJKLMNOPQRSTUVWXY
```

Figure 9.4: The Trithemius Letter-Square.

small, especially if they are located in the same geographical area, distribution may not present a problem. The users may get together periodically and decide on a new key. With many users, a safe key distribution may be impractical. An example of a large group of users is an army. The key has to be delivered to many units, possibly located over a wide area. New keys have to be issued and delivered periodically, as well as every time someone loses or misplaces a copy of the key. In a war situation, this is at best a tough logistical problem and at worst might lead to defeat.

It had been two long, exhausting days since the arrival of the parcel from London. Simon knew from the irregular script that announced his name on the wrapping that it was from his mentor and colleague, Dr. John Dee, court astrologer to Her Majesty Queen Elizabeth. Dr. Dee had often confided in Simon on matters about which both the Court and the Church would rather have been kept ignorant. The parcel contained hundreds of pages encrypted in a strange code. Indeed, Simon knew that only Dr. Dee, a student of Giovanni della Porta and the abbot Trithemius, could devise such a cunning cipher. Each character was a mathematical puzzle, to be solved with the result being a whole number. The number was then taken by the root of its square to reveal a Latin letter. It had been two days since its arrival, and Simon finally finished decoding the first page. It was a letter of introduction from Dr. Dee.

—Mike Lotstein, *The Mirror's Desire*, 1997

Michael.Lotstein@asu.edu

9.5 The Vigenère Cipher

The most important extension of Trithemius' polyalphabetic substitution algorithm is the method of Blaise de Vigenère, who in 1586 published it in his book *Traicté des Chiffres*. The Vigenère system is generally regarded as the most secure of the simpler polyalphabetic substitution ciphers. It is based on a letter-square (Figure 9.5) very similar to Trithemius', but it adds a key.

```
Plain   ABCDEFGHIJKLMNOPQRSTUVWXYZ

  1     BCDEFGHIJKLMNOPQRSTUVWXYZA
  2     CDEFGHIJKLMNOPQRSTUVWXYZAB
  3     DEFGHIJKLMNOPQRSTUVWXYZABC
  4     EFGHIJKLMNOPQRSTUVWXYZABCD
  5     FGHIJKLMNOPQRSTUVWXYZABCDE
  6     GHIJKLMNOPQRSTUVWXYZABCDEF
  7     HIJKLMNOPQRSTUVWXYZABCDEFG
  8     IJKLMNOPQRSTUVWXYZABCDEFGH
  9     JKLMNOPQRSTUVWXYZABCDEFGHI
 10     KLMNOPQRSTUVWXYZABCDEFGHIJ
 11     LMNOPQRSTUVWXYZABCDEFGHIJK
 12     MNOPQRSTUVWXYZABCDEFGHIJKL
 13     NOPQRSTUVWXYZABCDEFGHIJKLM
 14     OPQRSTUVWXYZABCDEFGHIJKLMN
 15     PQRSTUVWXYZABCDEFGHIJKLMNO
 16     QRSTUVWXYZABCDEFGHIJKLMNOP
 17     RSTUVWXYZABCDEFGHIJKLMNOPQ
 18     STUVWXYZABCDEFGHIJKLMNOPQR
 19     TUVWXYZABCDEFGHIJKLMNOPQRS
 20     UVWXYZABCDEFGHIJKLMNOPQRST
 21     VWXYZABCDEFGHIJKLMNOPQRSTU
 22     WXYZABCDEFGHIJKLMNOPQRSTUV
 23     XYZABCDEFGHIJKLMNOPQRSTUVW
 24     YZABCDEFGHIJKLMNOPQRSTUVWX
 25     ZABCDEFGHIJKLMNOPQRSTUVWXY
 26     ABCDEFGHIJKLMNOPQRSTUVWXYZ
```

Figure 9.5: The Vigenère Cipher System.

A message is encrypted by replacing each of its letters using a different row, selecting rows by means of the key. The key (a string of letters with no spaces) is written above the plaintext and is repeated as many times as necessary to cover the entire plaintext. For example, the key LAND AND TREE corresponds (after removing the spaces) to rows 11, 26, 13, 3, 26, 13, 3, 19, 17, 4, and 4 of the Vigenère letter-square. Thus, the first letter of the plaintext is replaced using the row that starts with L (row 11). If the first letter is, say, E, it is replaced by P. The second letter is replaced by a letter from the row indicated by the A of the key (row 26), and so on up to the eleventh letter, which is replaced using row 4. The twelfth letter is replaced, like the first letter, by means of row 11.

It is obvious that the strength of this simple algorithm lies in the key. A sufficiently long key with many different letters uses most of the rows in the Vigenère square and results in a secure encrypted string. A short key or a key with identical letters produces weak ciphertext. A key such as AAAAA should be avoided, because it reduces this polyalphabetic method to a simple, monoalphabetic Caesar cipher. (It also breaks another important rule of cryptography, namely, to avoid repetition.) The number of possible keys is enormous, since a key can be between 1 and 26 letters long. The knowledge that a message has been encrypted with this method helps little in breaking it. Simple frequency analysis does not work, since a letter in the ciphertext, such as S, is replaced by different letters each time it occurs in the plaintext.

After remaining secure for more than three hundred years, the Vigenère cipher was broken, first in the 1850s by Charles Babbage, then in the 1860s independently by Friedrich W. Kasiski, a retired officer in the Prussian army. Babbage was the first to break the Vigenère code, but he never published his findings. Kasiski, on the other hand, described his method in a slim volume *Die Geheimschriften und die Dechiffrierkunst* (*Secret Writings and the Art of Deciphering*) published in Berlin in 1863. The full story of these achievements is told in [Salomon 03].

9.6 A Variation on Vigenère

One reason why the Vigenère cipher is relatively easy to break is that the 26 rows of the letter-square are closely related; they are shifts of the top row. A secure variant of the basic Vigenère cipher is based on a letter-square with independent rows. Each row contains a different permutation (preferably random) of the 26 letters (Figure 9.6).

On the left of Figure 9.6 are the key letters, and on top are the plaintext letters. Thus, if the current key letter is F, then row 6 is used to encipher the current plainletter. If that is A, it becomes E. If it is B, it is enciphered to W.

One advantage of the original Vigenère cipher is that the letter-square can be generated automatically. With the new variant, however, the square has to be distributed with the key and also changed periodically for increased security. This variant, however, is more secure. Let's assume that a codebreaker knows the size of the key (n letters), breaks the ciphertext up into n substrings, computes the letter frequencies of the first substring, and finds that X is the most common letter by far in that substring. The codebreaker knows (with some certainty) that X stands for E, but this knowledge is not sufficient to identify the row that was used to encipher the first substring.

⋄ **Exercise 9.4:** There is a way to fully specify such a square by specifying just one string of 26 letters. What is this based on?

This variant is more secure than the original Vigenère cipher but is not absolutely secure. It can be broken because the ciphertext still contains the rhythm of the key and therefore reflects the letter distribution in the plaintext.

```
       Plain   ABCDEFGHIJKLMNOPQRSTUVWXYZ
   Key 1  A    WGRFVAHTKBSQXDOPEYMINJZUCL
       2  B    EHBNDMOCFZSARGVWPKILUXTJYQ
       3  C    RZUMHVPOKTCSEWGJQBDILXAYFN
       4  D    JOMSGITRNPYZVEKACFUXBQHWDL
       5  E    ILAJTMQPWNXRVCFKUBHZGSEDYO
       6  F    EWDXNKJGFYBHOPMZULTVCRQSAI
       7  G    DLRHOGKTJASCZQNFEMVPXBYWUI
       8  H    SGLBRNJKEFXTVUWPCHDZMIOYQA
       9  I    ZFXBTLMUPHDRKEOWGYCQIJSVAN
      10  J    QPVGJZYRCMUWNKHALESDOTXIBF
      11  K    QXSMPCEBLZVFRYWTDINJAGHOUK
      12  L    WEDNBAKSLJPZUXHVMFQTCGIOYR
      13  M    BIMNXELGUZOKFHRJDYTACVWPQS
      14  N    XJDYURFMNWBHGAEZQIKSLPCOTV
      15  O    GJUBKFCWEZAQNSHYOIMRLXPDVT
      16  P    XAOTLZQMFDSBUPRWJEGHICNVYK
      17  Q    PKDFIUONQTJGVMSLBEHWYRACXZ
      18  R    XDGKSRZHUYWVBMJEPITOALNCFQ
      19  S    ELTUJZFQDHCYMIXSKPONVRGBWA
      20  T    HFIKCLTWSMADNEVOXPQBUGJYZR
      21  U    QMNPXTIRWYBAJUDKHLGSOFVEZC
      22  V    VYWQEZFRMXODJPSHBIANLCGTKU
      23  W    VHEKWGPZMIUCOTNJYADXFLSRBQ
      24  X    NZAXILSEDKMBJFOWUTHPCRQGVY
      25  Y    QXHNKVGWJAOIDZSELPTMRCUYBF
      26  Z    MRQZXFHUWJIDCGKAOVSNTEYLPB
           for k=1:26
           p=randperm(26)+64;
           ls(k,:)=char(p);
           end; ls
```

Figure 9.6: A Nonshift Vigenère Letter-Square and Matlab Code.

9.7 The Gronsfeld Cipher

This simple polyalphabetic cipher can be viewed both as an extension of the (monoalphabetic) Caesar cipher and as a limited version of the Vigenère cipher. It uses a numeric key and encrypts each plainletter with one of the key digits. If the plainletter is L and the current key digit is d, then the cipherletter is the letter at distance d (cyclically) from L. Here is an example.

```
3 1 4 8 5  3 1 4 8 5  3 1 4 8 5
c o m e t  o t h e r  e s c u e
F P Q M Y  R U L M W  H T G C J
```

The plainletter c is encrypted to the letter F, three positions away, while the u is encrypted to C, eight positions (cyclically) ahead.

It is easy to see that the Gronsfeld cipher with the key 31485 produces the same encryption as the Vigenère cipher with key `cadhe`. Thus, the Gronsfeld cipher is a Vigenère cipher limited to 10 alphabets.

The cipher was attributed to Count Gronsfeld by Gaspari Schotti in his book *Schola Steganographica* (1665) [Schotti 65].

"You seem fond of that particular book."

"One copy is for you."

"But I've read it," Wormold said, "years ago, and I don't like Lamb."

"It's not meant for reading. Have you never heard of a book code?"

"As a matter of fact, no."

"In a minute I'll show you how to work it. I keep one copy. All you have to do when you communicate with me is to indicate the page and line where you begin the coding. Of course it's not so hard to break as a machine code, but it's hard enough for the mere Hasselbachers."

"I wish you'd get Dr. Hasselbacher out of your head."

"When we have your office here properly organized, with sufficient security—a combination safe, radio, trained staff, all the gimmicks—then of course we can abandon a primitive code like this, but except for an expert cryptologist it's damned hard to break without knowing the name and edition of the book."

—Graham Greene, *Our Man In Havana* (1958)

9.8 Generating Permutations

Automatic generation of permutations is a topic related to the Vigenère cipher. Given a set A of n symbols—an alphabet—the problem is to generate easily and automatically many (at least n) permutations of A. This section considers alphabets that consist of the 26 letters. Given a key, it is possible to generate a permutation of the 26 letters in several ways, the simplest of which is to remove spaces and duplicates from the key, to use the resulting string as the start of the new permutation, and to append to it the remaining letters in alphabetical order. Thus, keys such as "Melvin Schwartzkopf" (where no letter repeats) should be avoided, as should also sentences such as "Quick zephyrs blow, vexing daft Jim" (a pangram that has all the 26 letters in its 30 letters). Another feature to avoid in a good key is words where letters repeat, such as "caucasus" (where every letter repeats). In contrast, the string NOW␣I␣KNOW␣WHY␣SHE␣ENCRYPTS␣DOUBLE is a good key. It is short and easy to memorize, and it produces the 17-letter random (or randomlike) string NOWIKHYSECRPTDUBL. Appending the nine remaining letters AFGJMQVXZ to this string results in the permutation

```
abcdefghijklmnopqrstuvwxyz
NOWIKHYSECRPTDUBLAFGJMQVXZ
```

◇ **Exercise 9.5:** Come up with another good key.

We propose a few simple ways to produce 25 more permutations starting with
```
abcdefghijklmnopqrstuvwxyz
NOWIKHYSECRPTDUBLAFGJMQVXZ
```

1. It is possible to create *powers* of a permutation by multiplying it by itself. Our permutation changes **a** to **N** and **n** to **D**, so its second power substitutes **D** for **a**. Similarly, **b** becomes **O** and **o** becomes **U**, so the second power substitutes **U** for **b**. The result is

```
abcdefghijklmnopqrstuvwxyz
DUQERSXFKWABGIJOPNHYCTLMVZ
```

2. A permutation can be extended vertically in alphabetical order. The first letter in our permutation is **N**, so we write **OPQRS**... vertically under it. The second letter is **O**, so the string **PQRS**... is placed vertically under it. The result is the square in Table 9.7a.

3. A somewhat similar idea results in the 26-permutation square of Table 9.7b, where each letter of the top permutation NOWIKHYSECRPTDUBLAFGJMQVXZ is extended diagonally.

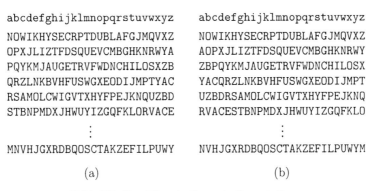

(a)   (b)

Table 9.7: Two Ways to Generate Permutations.

4. A completely different approach is based on skipping symbols. We start with a string of the 26 letters (either in alphabetical order or in an order determined by a key). We select the first letter, then select the letter h positions (cyclically) following it, and continue in this way. This method will select every letter exactly once if (and only if) h is relatively prime to 26 (i.e., if it is one of the 12 numbers 1, 3, 5, 7, 9, 11, 15, 17, 19, 21, 23, and 25). Thus, this method can generate 12 permutations of the 26 letters.

◇ **Exercise 9.6:** Find the four integers h relatively prime to 8, and illustrate the four permutations generated in this way.

The number of integers relatively prime to n (see affine ciphers in Section 6.2) is given by the Euler function,

$$\Phi(n) = \Pi_{i=1}^{k} \left(P_i^{e_i} - P_i^{e_i - 1} \right)$$

9.9 The Eyraud Cipher

Designed by the French cryptographer Charles Eyraud, this encryption method is more complex than the basic Vigenère cipher, but seems to offer more security, if for no other reason than its use of two keys. Encryption is done in the following steps.

1. Select two keys and use each to generate a string with the 26-letter alphabet. We illustrate this method by selecting the key but␣she␣will␣decrypt␣more␣afghan, which generates the string butshewildcrypmoafgnjkqvxz and also the 27-letter key NOW␣I␣KNOW␣WHY␣SHE␣ENCRYPTS␣DOUBLE, which produces the 26-letter alphabet permutation NOWIKHYSECRPTDUBLAFGJMQVXZ.

2. Select two integers $c1$ and $c2$ (we select 3 and 9), and write the first string (duplicated as many times as necessary) as a $c1$-column table and the second string (also duplicated) as a $c2$-column table (Figure 9.8a,b). $c1$ and $c2$ must be selected such that the tables will have the same size; i.e., $\alpha \cdot c1 \bmod 26 = \alpha \cdot c2 \bmod 26$ for some integer α.

3. Select a start letter in each table. We select the first occurrences of i and P in the two tables, respectively.

4. Collect the 26 consecutive letters that start with i in the first table. This produces the string ildcrypmoafgnjkqvxzbutshew (Figure 9.8a).

5. Collect the P from the second table and the 25 letters located under it (cyclically) in the same column. This produces the string PJITMKDQHUVYBXSLZEANCFORGW (Figure 9.8a).

6. Combine the two strings into the permutation

$$
\begin{array}{c}
\texttt{ildcrypmoafgnjkqvxzbutshew} \\
\texttt{PJITMKDQHUVYBXSLZEANCFORGW}
\end{array}
\tag{9.1}
$$

and use it to encrypt the first plainletter. Thus, if the plaintext starts with **plain**, the first letter p is encrypted to D.

Decryption is done in similar steps.

1. Generate the two tables and select the start letters as in steps 1–3 above.

2. Collect the i from the first table, followed cyclically by the 25 letters in its column. This results in the string icpanqztelrmfjvbswdyogkxuh (Figure 9.8b).

3. Collect the P in the second table together with the 25 letters that follow it cyclically. This produces the string PTDUBLAFGJMQVXZNOWIKHYSECR (Figure 9.8b).

4. Combine the two strings into the permutation

$$
\begin{array}{c}
\texttt{PTDUBLAFGJMQVXZNOWIKHYSECR} \\
\texttt{icpanqztelrmfjvbswdyogkxuh}
\end{array}
\tag{9.2}
$$

and use it to decrypt the first cipherletter. If it is D, it will be decrypted to p.

This looks like magic. Why did permutation (9.2) come out as the inverse of permutation (9.1)? Before answering that, here is the last detail needed to complete this elegant algorithm. As described here, it is a monoalphabetic method, the same permutation is used to encrypt the entire plaintext. To turn it into a polyalphabetic encryption

but	N O W I K H Y S E	but	N O W I K H Y S E
s h e	C R **P** T D U B L A	s h e	C R **P** T D U B L A
w **i** l	F G **J** M Q V X Z N	w **i** l	F G **J** M Q V X Z N
d c r	O W **I** K H Y S E C	d **c r**	O W **I** K H Y S E C
y pm	R **P** T D U B L A F	y **p**m	R **P** T D U B L A F
o a f	G J M Q V X Z N O	o a f	G J M Q V X Z N O
g n j	W I K H Y S E C R	g n j	W I K H Y S E C R
k q v	P T D U B L A F G	k q v	P T D U B L A F G
x z b	J M Q V X Z N O W	x z b	J M Q V X Z N O W
u t s	I K H Y S E C R P	u t s	I K H Y S E C R P
h e w	T D U B L A F G J	h e w	T D U B L A F G J
i l d	M Q V X Z N O W I	i l d	M Q V X Z N O W I
c r y	K H Y S E C R P T	c r y	K H Y S E C R P T
pmo	D U B L A F G J M	pmo	D U B L A F G J M
a f g	Q V X Z N O W I K	a f g	Q V X Z N O W I K
n j k	H Y S E C R P T D	n j k	H Y S E C R P T D
q v x	U B L A F G J M Q	q v x	U B L A F G J M Q
z b u	V X Z N O W I K H	z b u	V X Z N O W I K H
t s h	Y S E C R P T D U	t s h	Y S E C R P T D U
e w i	B L A F G J M Q V	e w i	B L A F G J M Q V
l d c	X Z N O W I K H Y	l d c	X Z N O W I K H Y
r y p	S E C R P T D U B	r y p	S E C R P T D U B
mo a	L A F G J M Q V X	mo a	L A F G J M Q V X
f gn	Z N O W I K H Y S	f gn	Z N O W I K H Y S
j k q	E C R P T D U B L	j k q	E C R P T D U B L
v x z	A F G J M Q V X Z	v x z	A F G J M Q V X Z

(a)	(b)

Figure 9.8: The Eyraud Cipher: An Example.

algorithm, a different pair of start letters should be selected for each plainletter. Thus, in our example, to encrypt the second plainletter l, select the two letters l and T that follow i and P in the two tables, and use them as the new start letters. This requires more table manipulations, but results in a new permutation for each plainletter.

To understand why the method generates a permutation and its inverse, we examine the way the encryption permutation (9.1) was generated. Consecutive letters were picked up from the first table, starting with i. Those letters were l, d, c, r,..., which we can denote by $i + 1$, $i + 2$, and so on. Letters from the second table were selected at intervals of 9, so the successors of P were J, I, T,..., which can be denoted by $P + 9$, $P + 18$, $P + 27$, and so on. Thus, we can say that letter $i + x$ in the first table is associated with letter $P + 9x$ in the second table. In general, we can write the association in the form

$$i + 3x \leftrightarrow P + 27x. \tag{9.3}$$

However, the letter at position $P + 27$ is T or $P + 1$, because the second table consists of repetitions of the same 26-letter string. Thus, we can rewrite Equation (9.3) in the form

$$\texttt{i} + 3x \leftrightarrow \texttt{P} + x. \tag{9.4}$$

We now consider how the decrypting permutation was selected. Letters were picked up from the same column in the first table. There is therefore a distance of 3 between them. These letters were associated with consecutive letters from the second table, but this is the association given by Equation (9.4). This is why the two permutations generated by this method, for encryption and decryption, are the inverse of each other.

According to *Precis de Cryptographie Moderne* by the French cryptographer Charles Eyraud (1953), the initial break into the ADFGVX cipher came during early April 1918 when the French intercepted two messages, each of three parts, which they soon determined to be retransmissions of the same basic information, since there were only slight differences in the ciphertexts of the two messages. One of the French cryptographers, Georges Painvain, was able to exploit this case of retransmission and recovered both the transposition key and the digraphic substitution employed in the messages. With the keys recovered from these two messages, the French cryptanalysts were able to read all the other messages sent by the Germans during the same period. This is a classic example of the result of breaking one of cryptography's basic rules.

9.10 The Hill Cipher

The Hill cipher [Hill 29] is an example of a polyalphabetic cipher that employs the modulus function and techniques of linear algebra. The key K used by this cipher is an $n{\times}n$ matrix of integers. Encryption is done by transforming a group P of n symbols over the plain alphabet (of m symbols) into another group C of n symbols over the cipher alphabet (the same or a different alphabet, but of the same size m). The encryption rule is $C = K \cdot P \bmod m$. If a group G is encrypted into a group H, then other occurrences of G will also be encrypted to the same H. However, two different groups containing the letter A in position 3 will generally be encrypted to two different groups containing different letters in position 3. This is why the Hill cipher is polyalphabetic.

Given an alphabet with m symbols, they are assigned integer values from 0 to $m - 1$. A value for n is then selected, and the key K is constructed as an $n{\times}n$ matrix whose elements are also integers in the interval $[0, m-1]$. The first n plaintext symbols are converted to a column vector P of integers, and the first n ciphertext integer values are obtained as a vector C by the (modular) matrix multiplication $C = A \cdot P \bmod m$. These integers are then converted to ciphertext symbols.

As an example, we select the 26 letters A through Z and assign them the integer values 0 through 25, respectively (m is therefore 26). We also select $n = 2$ and select the key $K = \left(\begin{smallmatrix} 9 & 10 \\ 2 & 5 \end{smallmatrix}\right)$. The plaintext NOT␣ME is encrypted by removing the space, appending another E (to make the plaintext's length an integer multiple of n), and dividing it into the three n-letter groups NO, TM, and EE. The groups are replaced by their numerical values $(14, 15)$, $(20, 13)$, and $(05, 05)$ and the key is multiplied by each group to yield

$$\begin{bmatrix} 9 & 10 \\ 2 & 5 \end{bmatrix} \begin{bmatrix} 14 \\ 15 \end{bmatrix} \bmod 26 = \begin{bmatrix} 16 \\ 25 \end{bmatrix}, \quad K \begin{bmatrix} 20 \\ 13 \end{bmatrix} \bmod 26 = \begin{bmatrix} 24 \\ 1 \end{bmatrix}, \quad K \begin{bmatrix} 5 \\ 5 \end{bmatrix} \bmod 26 = \begin{bmatrix} 17 \\ 9 \end{bmatrix}.$$

The three groups $(16, 25)$, $(24, 01)$, and $(17, 09)$ are replaced by their letter equivalents to produce the ciphertext PZXAQI.

Decryption is done by $P = K^{-1} \cdot C \bmod m$. In our example, the inverse of K is $K^{-1} = \begin{pmatrix} 21 & 10 \\ 2 & 17 \end{pmatrix}$, so decrypting the group $(16, 25)$ is done by $K^{-1}(16, 25) \bmod 26 = (14, 15)$.

Thus, decryption requires the inverse (modulo m) of the original key, which raises the question of how to compute the inverse of a matrix, modulo a given integer, and also implies that the key matrix must be invertible. The general derivation of the inverse of a matrix, modulo a given integer m is beyond the scope of this book, but the special case $n = 2$ is simple and is given here. The inverse, modulo m of the 2×2 matrix $\begin{pmatrix} a & b \\ c & d \end{pmatrix}$, is given by

$$(ad - bc)^{-1} \begin{bmatrix} d & -b \\ -c & a \end{bmatrix} \bmod m, \tag{9.5}$$

where $(ad - bc)^{-1}$ is the multiplicative inverse, modulo m, of $(ad - bc)$.

The multiplicative inverse, modulo m, of an integer a is another integer b such that $a \times b \bmod m = 1$. The multiplicative inverses, modulo 26, of the 26 integers 0 through 25 are as follows:

a	1	3	5	7	9	11	15	17	19	21	23	25
a^{-1}	1	9	21	15	3	19	7	23	11	5	17	25

Notice that 0 does not have a multiplicative inverse modulo 26 (this is true for numbers in general). Also, the even numbers 4, 8, 10, 12, 14, 16, 18, 20, 22, and 24 are missing from the table above. They don't have multiplicative inverses because each has the prime number 2 as a common factor of itself and 26. Also, 13 and 26 have 2 as a common factor, implying that 13 does not have a multiplicative inverse modulo 26.

Armed with this knowledge, we can invert our key $K = \begin{pmatrix} 9 & 10 \\ 2 & 5 \end{pmatrix}$. Equation (9.5) implies

$$K^{-1} = (45 - 20)^{-1} \begin{bmatrix} 5 & -10 \\ -2 & 9 \end{bmatrix} \bmod 26 = 25 \begin{bmatrix} 5 & 16 \\ 24 & 9 \end{bmatrix} \bmod 26$$

$$= \begin{bmatrix} 125 & 400 \\ 600 & 225 \end{bmatrix} \bmod 26 = \begin{bmatrix} 21 & 10 \\ 2 & 17 \end{bmatrix}.$$

Notice that $-2 \bmod 26 = 24$ because $24 + 2 = 26$. Similarly, $-10 \bmod 26 = 16$.

⋄ **Exercise 9.7:** Compute the inverse of $\begin{pmatrix} 1 & 0 \\ 2 & 3 \end{pmatrix}$ modulo 26.

The Hill cipher is generally more secure than the Vigenère cipher (Section 9.5) but becomes progressively weaker (closer to monoalphabetic) as n gets smaller. The examples here employ $n = 2$, and it is easy to see that our key encrypts the letter E to either Q or I, which helps a codebreaker who is trying to break the code by a frequency analysis.

There is also a known attack on the Hill cipher for cases where enough plaintext and its corresponding ciphertext are known. If n consecutive groups $P_1, P_2, \ldots, P_n$ of plaintext are known, together with the corresponding groups C_i of ciphertext, then a codebreaker can construct the two $n \times n$ matrices P and C, whose columns are P_i and C_i, respectively, and compute the sequence of elementary operations that reduce C^T to the identity matrix. It can be shown that when those operations are applied to P^T, they reduce it to the key matrix K.

"You know I'm not supposed to be doing this," Tyrone said as he pecked at the keyboard.

"Nonsense. You do it all the time."

"Not as a public service." The screen darkened and then announced that Tyrone had been given access to the CHiP computers.

"So suppose I could do that, I suppose you'd want a copy of it."

"Only if the switch on the right side of the printer is turned ON and if the paper is straight. Otherwise, I just wouldn't bother." Scott stared at the ceiling while the dot matrix printer sang a high pitched song as the head traveled back and forth.

—Winn Schwartau, *Terminal Compromise* (1993)

9.11 The Jefferson Multiplex Cipher

Designed and built in the 1790s by Thomas Jefferson, this mechanical cipher is easy to construct and use. It is a polyalphabetic substitution cipher, and improved versions of it were used as late as World War II by various individuals and organizations, including the United States Navy. William Friedman named this type of cipher *multiplex*.

The device (Figure 9.9, where the plaintext starts with "PLAIN...") consists of 36 disks, each with a different permutation of the 26 letters engraved on its edge. Each disk has a hole at its center and a rod is inserted through the 36 disks, turning the device into a cylinder. Each disk can still be rotated about the rod. A wire is also positioned parallel to the rod, to serve as a reference bar. The plaintext is divided into blocks of 36 letters, and each block is individually encrypted. To encrypt a block, each of the 36 disks is rotated until the corresponding plainletter is positioned at the reference bar. The ciphertext can then be read from any of the remaining 25 disk positions. In the figure, the ciphertext can be YPGSK... or CKOZB... or any of 23 other strings. Notice that the ciphertext is not unique. Each message can be encrypted into one of 25 ciphertexts, a feature termed *polyphonic encryption* (Section 9.13).

The receiver must have a device with the same 36 disks, positioned along the center rod in the same order. To decrypt a cipherblock, the disks are rotated until the 36 cipherletters of the block are positioned along the reference bar. The remaining 25 disk positions are then examined until a position is found with a 36-letter string that makes

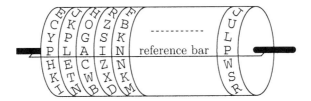

Figure 9.9: The Jefferson Cipher Wheel.

sense. There is a chance that two of the 26 disk positions will make sense, which is a disadvantage of any polyphonic encryption algorithm, but this chance depends heavily on the nature of the plaintext. If the plaintext is in a natural language, which always has high redundancy, then the chance of two or more rows having text that makes sense is extremely small. If, on the other hand, the plaintext is in an artificial language that has little or no redundancy, such as numbers, there is no way to select the right row based on its "sense," and the key has to contain information on how to select the row with the plaintext.

◇ **Exercise 9.8:** Think of a case where this chance is not small.

Each disk can be numbered and all the parties using the device must agree on a 36-number key that indicates the order of the disks. The size of the key space is therefore $36! \approx 3.72 \times 10^{41}$, a staggeringly large number.

The Jefferson cipher wheel was reinvented, in 1891, by the eminent French cryptographer Étienne Bazeries, who called it a cylinder and used 20 disks with 25 letters each (omitting the letter Q). Notwithstanding his knowledge of cryptanalysis and his rich experience, Bazeries was convinced that this simple device offered absolute security. However, the cylinder code was broken in 1893, just two years after its introduction, by Gaëtan de Viaris (and later, in 1918, by William F. Friedman). Nevertheless, considering its mechanical simplicity, the device offers reasonably good security.

The de Viaris method assumes that the codebreaker has access to a cylinder with the same disks used by the authorized encryptor and decryptor, and also to some plaintext. All that the codebreaker needs to find is the order of the disks, and this becomes possible if the 26 letters are placed on each disk randomly and without attention to possible weaknesses. In Figure 9.9 we see that the letter following E (clockwise) is C in the first disk and T in the second disk. If E is followed on the disks by several Cs and Ts and is never followed by certain other letters, a cryptanalyst with access to the disks may be able to deduce information about the placement of the individual disks on the cylinder.

Another weakness of the device is that a plainletter cannot be encrypted to itself, thus enabling the cryptanalyst to reduce the number of cases that have to be examined. The device has this property because a disk contains each letter exactly once.

Thus, we conclude that E should be followed on each disk by a different letter. In general, when the alphabets on the disks are written as the rows of a table, the table should be a Latin square. In such a square, each row contains each letter exactly once, and the same is true for the columns.

Table 9.11a,b shows the alphabets in the 20 disks used by Bazeries and the 25 disks designed by Joseph Mauborgne in his M-94 encryption device (which was used by the United States Navy in World War II). It is easy to see how the bottom 14 rows (rows 7 through 20) of the former have been constructed. Row 19, for example, starts with the phrase *ride a horse* (in French, *montez à cheval*, where spaces and duplicate letters are removed), and continues with the remaining letters bdfgi... in alphabetical order. As a result of this construction, the letter a appears three times and the letter b appears twice in the first column. The latter table, in contrast, is a Latin square (with the unexplained exceptions of the three underlined letters in row 16), so it is much more secure.

Notice that just having a Latin square does not guarantee security. The squares of Figure 9.10 are all Latin but are cryptographically weak, since all the disks are identical.

An ideal Latin square for multiplex encryption should have the following property. Imagine a 25-disk cylinder with the 26 letters engraved on each disk. Select a letter and align the disks to get a row of 25 occurrences of the letter. The remaining 25 letters on the 25 disks should form a Latin square. This should happen when any of the 26 letters is selected. Anyone discovering such a disk configuration is invited to communicate it to the author.

```
1 2 3 4 5    4 5 1 2 3    5 4 3 2 1
2 3 4 5 1    1 2 3 4 5    4 3 2 1 5
3 4 5 1 2    2 3 4 5 1    3 2 1 5 4
4 5 1 2 3    5 1 2 3 4    2 1 5 4 3
5 1 2 3 4    3 4 5 1 2    1 5 4 3 2
```

Figure 9.10: Weak Latin Squares.

9.12 Strip Ciphers

Any cylinder cipher can be converted to a strip cipher by unrolling each disk into a narrow strip of plastic, wood, cardboard, or other suitable material. To compensate for the cyclic nature of a disk, each strip should contain two copies of its alphabet. (If each strip has just one copy of the alphabet, it may be necessary to slide a strip up to 25 positions to align the desired letter at the right position. This may sometimes result in shifted strips that have only one full column. If a strip has two copies of the alphabet, the maximum shift needed is 13 positions.)

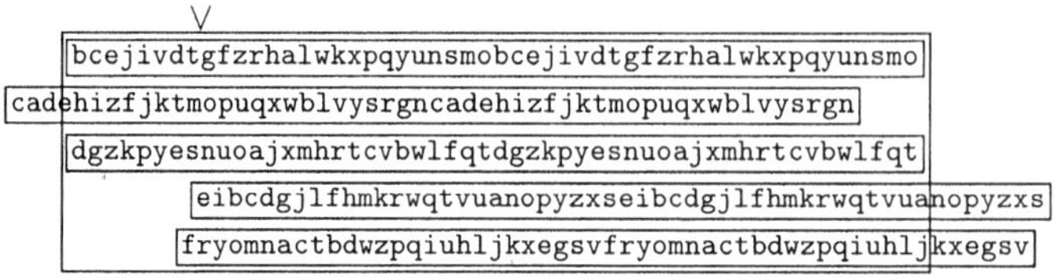

```
              v
  bcejivdtgfzrhalwkxpqyunsmobcejivdtgfzrhalwkxpqyunsmo
 cadehizfjktmopuqxwblvysrgncadehizfjktmopuqxwblvysrgn
  dgzkpyesnuoajxmhrtcvbwlfqtdgzkpyesnuoajxmhrtcvbwlfqt
        eibcdgjlfhmkrwqtvuanopyzxseibcdgjlfhmkrwqtvuanopyzxs
      fryomnactbdwzpqiuhljkxegsvfryomnactbdwzpqiuhljkxegsv
```

1	a b c d e f g h i j k l m n o p q r s t u v x y z
2	b c d f g h j k l m n p q r s t v x z a e i o u y
3	a e b c d f g h i o j k l m n p u y q r s t v x z
4	z y x v u t s r q p o n m l k j i h g f e d c b a
5	y u z x v t s r o i q p n m l k e a j h g f d c b
6	z x v t s r q p n m l k j h g f d c b y u o i e a
7	a l o n s e f t d p r i j u g v b c h k m q x y z
8	b i e n h u r x l s p a v d t o y m c f g j k q z
9	c h a r y b d e t s l f g i j k m n o p q u v x z
10	d i e u p r o t g l a f n c b h j k m q s v x y z
11	e v i t z l s c o u r a n d b f g h j k m p q x y
12	f o r m e z l s a i c u x b d g h j k n p q t v y
13	g l o i r e m t d n s a u x b c f h j k p q v y z
14	h o n e u r t p a i b c d f g j k l m q s v x y z
15	i n s t r u e z l a j b c d f g h k m o p q v x y
16	j a i m e l o g n f r t h u b c d k p q s v x y z
17	k y r i e l s o n a b c d f g h j m p q t u v x z
18	l h o m e p r s t d i u a b c f g j k n q v x y z
19	m o n t e z a c h v l b d f g i j k p q r s u x y
20	n o u s t e l a c f b d g h i j k m p q r v x y z

1	b c e j i v d t g f z r h a l w k x p q y u n s m o
2	c a d e h i z f j k t m o p u q x w b l v y s r g n
3	d g z k p y e s n u o a j x m h r t c v b w l f q t
4	e i b c d g j l f h m k r w q t v u a n o p y z x s
5	f r y o m n a c t b d w z p q i u h l j k x e g s v
6	g j i y t k p w x s v u e d c o f n q a r m b l z h
7	h n f u z m s x k e p c q i g v t o y w l r a j d b
8	i w v x r z t p h o c q g s b j e y u d m f k a n l
9	j x r s f h y g v d q p b l i m o a k z n t c w u e
10	k d a f l j h o c g e b t m n r s q v p x z i y w u
11	l e g i j b k u z a r t s o h n p f x m w q d v c y
12	m y u v w l c q s t x h n f a z g d r b j e o i p k
13	n m j h a e x b l i g d k c r f y p w s z o q u v t
14	o l t w g a n z u v j e f y d k h s m x q i p b r c
15	p v x r n q u i y z s j a t w b d l g c e h f o k m
16	q t s e o p i d m n f x w u k y j v h g b l z c a r
17	r k w p u t q e b x l n y v f c i m z h s a g d o j
18	s o n m q u v a w r y g c e z l b k d f i j x h t p
19	t s m z k x w v r y u f i g j d a b e o p c h n l q
20	u p k g s c f j o w a y d h v e l z n r t b m q i x
21	v f l q y s o r p m h z u k x a c g j i d n t e b w
22	w h o l b d m k e q n i x r t u z j f y c s v p a g
23	x z p t v o b m q c w s l j y g n e i u f d r k h a
24	y q h a c r l n d p b o v z s x w i t e g k u m j f
25	z u q n x w r y a l i v p b e s m c o k h g j t f d

Table 9.11: (a, top) Bazeries' Disks. (b, bottom) Mauborgne's Latin Square.

The United States Navy started using the M-138 strip cipher in 1934 and later replaced it with the M-138-A and other improved models. Such a cipher has many (perhaps around 100) strips available, of which perhaps 30 are selected by the key and are arranged vertically. The encryptor slides strips horizontally until the plaintext appears on one of the columns. The ciphertext is then read from any of the other complete (in our example, 5-row) columns. The figure shows how the plaintext `goner` can be encrypted into `fpuiy`, `zuobo`, and so on, up to `unwwq`.

9.13 Polyphonic Ciphers and Ambiguity

Polyphonic encryption is the case where two ciphersymbols stand for the same plainsymbol. A simple example is a cipher where each of the 26 letters is encrypted by a single digit. Since there are only 10 digits, each digit must be used to encrypt 2 or 3 letters. A possible assignment of the 10 digits to the 26 letters may be to assign each digit to one common letter and to one rare letter. We may end up with a table similar to the following:

```
ETAOINSHRDLUMWYFCGBPKVXQJZ
01234567890123456789012345
```

where each of the digits 0–5 is assigned to three letters and each of 6–9 is assigned to two letters. The nine-letter message `POLYPHONY` is encrypted to the 9-digit string 930497354, but this string can be decrypted in several ways, as shown here.

9	3	0	4	9	7	3	5	4
D	O	E	I	D	H	O	N	I
P	W	L	Y	P	G	W	F	Y
Q	K	J		Q	Z	J		

An authorized decryptor would only rarely be faced by a choice of more than one meaningful decryption, but a cryptanalyst trying to break such a cipher would be faced, at least initially, with the polyalphabetic nature of the cipher. The digit 0 is assigned to the common letter `E` but also to the less frequently used letters `L` and `K`.

From the Dictionary

Polyphony: music whose texture is formed by the interweaving of several melodic lines. The lines are independent but sound together harmonically. Contrasting terms are *homophony*, wherein one part dominates while the others form a basically chordal accompaniment, and *monophony*, wherein there is but a single melodic line.

◇ **Exercise 9.9:** Suggest a more balanced way to assign the 10 codes to the letters.

When this type of cipher is implemented on a computer, it is natural to assign binary codes to the 26 letters. Since there are only 2 bits, the codes assigned to the letters have to be longer than 1 bit. With 5-bit codes, it is possible to have $2^5 = 32$ codes, but such a cipher is strictly monoalphabetic and easy to break. It is better to select 26 codes of different sizes: variable-size codes. Such a cipher is also monoalphabetic but is safer because the codebreaker has to read the ciphertext and break it up into the individual codes before attempting to decrypt it. Regardless of the particular way the codes are assigned to the letters, there is the question of how to decrypt a message coded in this way. Imagine that the codes 0, 01, 101, and 110 are assigned to the letters M, E, T, and O, respectively. The message ME␣TOO is easy to encrypt and results in 0|01|101|110|110 (without the vertical bars). Decrypting the binary string 001101110110, however, is ambiguous. The first 0 is decrypted to M because it is followed by a 0 and no code starts with 00. The next 0 is followed by 110, so it could be either an MO or an E followed by 10 and by more bits—an ambiguity.

It is clear that such a code has to be designed to allow for unambiguous reading and decryption, and this is easy to do once the reason for its ambiguity is understood. In our example, the reason for the ambiguity is that 01 (the code of E) starts with a 0 (the code of M). The code of M is a prefix of the code of E. Removing the ambiguity from such codes can therefore be done by following the *prefix rule*, which says: Once a certain bit pattern has been selected as the code of a letter, no other code should start with that pattern (see also Section 3.3 for these codes). The pattern should not be the prefix of any other code. Thus, once 0 has been assigned as the code of M, no other codes should start with 0; they should all start with 1.

The four codes above can be modified to the unambiguous (prefix) set 0, 10, 110, and 111 or to one of many other such sets. The message ME␣TOO is now encrypted to 0|10|110|111|111, which is easily read and decrypted in only one way.

There remains the question of assigning the codes to the letters. Assigning the shorter codes to the most common letters results in short encrypted messages but may provide the codebreaker with important clues. A better assignment may be to alternate between short and long codes. The most common letter (E) may be assigned the shortest code and the next most common (T) may be assigned the longest code. Alternating this way between short and long codes may be a good way to confuse a codebreaker but may also prove to be an illusory complication.

9.14 Polybius' Polyalphabetic Cipher

The simple Polybius monoalphabetic cipher of Section 7.3 can be extended to a polyalphabetic cipher. A long key is chosen (normally text from a book) and is encrypted by the Polybius square of Figure 7.4a, duplicated here. The result is a sequence of two-digit numbers.

	1	2	3	4	5
1	a	b	c	d	e
2	f	g	h	i/j	k
3	l	m	n	o	p
4	q	r	s	t	u
5	v	w	x	y	z

The Polybius Monoalphabetic Cipher (Figure 7.4a).

The plaintext is also encrypted by the same square, resulting in another sequence of 2-digit numbers. The two sequences are combined by adding corresponding numbers, but the addition is done without propagating any carries. Assuming that the plaintext is POLYBIUS␣CIPHER, and the key is the text happy families are all alike..., the two sequences and their (carryless) sum are

Plaintext	35	34	31	54	12	24	45	43	13	24	35	23	15	42
Key	23	11	35	35	54	21	11	32	24	31	24	15	43	11
Ciphertext	**58**	**45**	**66**	**89**	**66**	**45**	**56**	**75**	**37**	**55**	**59**	**38**	**58**	**53**

The digits of the two numbers added are in the interval $[1, 5]$, so each digit of the sum is in the interval $[2, 10]$, where 10 is written as a single 0.

Decrypting is done by subtracting the key from the ciphertext. In our example, this operation is summarized by the three lines

Ciphertext	**58**	**45**	**66**	**89**	**66**	**45**	**56**	**75**	**37**	**55**	**59**	**38**	**58**	**53**
Key	23	11	35	35	54	21	11	32	24	31	24	15	43	11
Plaintext	35	34	31	54	12	24	45	43	13	24	35	23	15	42

The carryless addition simplifies the subtraction. Each digit of the ciphertext is greater than the corresponding digit of the key, except for cipherdigits that are zero. If a cipherdigit is zero, it should be replaced by the number 10 before subtraction.

⋄ **Exercise 9.10:** In a 6×6 Polybius square, each digit is in the interval $[1, 6]$. When two digits are added, the sum is in the interval $[2, 12]$, where 10, 11, and 12 are considered 0, 1, and 2, respectively. Is it still possible to add two numbers without propagating carries?

Even though this cipher employs numbers, it is similar to any other polyalphabetic cipher because the numbers are related to letters and the letter frequencies are reflected in the numbers. The resulting ciphertext can be broken with methods very similar to those used to break the Vigenère code. As with the Vigenère cipher, absolute security can be obtained if the key is as long as the plaintext, is random, and is used just once.

9.15 The Index of Coincidence

The index of coincidence is a statistical measure used to identify text encrypted with a monoalphabetic substitution cipher. It is also very helpful in determining the length of a Vigenère key. This measure was developed by William F. Friedman and published in the 1920s (see reprint in [Friedman 96]) in a book that has been called by [Kahn 96] "the most important single publication in cryptology." Notwithstanding its importance, the index is easy to compute. The text in question is written as a long string, and a copy of the text is placed under it and is circularly shifted n positions (where n is a parameter, not the length of the text). The two rows of text are checked position by position, looking for coincidences (positions where both rows have the same letter). The index is simply the percentage of coincidences. An example of 154 letters is shown here.

```
Happyfamiliesareallalikeeveryunhappyfamilyisunhappyinitsownwayeverythingwasin
itsownwayeverythingwasinHappyfamiliesareallalikeeveryunhappyfamilyisunhappyin
       x              x    x                                              xx
Confusionintheoblonskyshousethewifehaddiscoveredthatthehusbandwascarryingonan
hehusbandwascarryingonanConfusionintheoblonskyshousethewifehaddiscoveredthatt
          x                                     xxx     x  xx
```

There are 12 coincidences for the 154 characters of text, so the index is approximately 7.8%.

> Riverbank Publication No. 22, written in 1920 when Friedman was 28, must be regarded as the most important single publication in cryptography.
>
> —David Kahn, 1967

Imagine a random string of letters with a shifted copy below it. When we examine a certain position in the top row, it can have any of the 26 letters with equal probability. When we look at the same position in the bottom row, there is a probability of $1/26 \approx 0.038$ that it will have the *same* letter. Thus, the index of coincidence for random text is 3.8%, independent of the amount n of the shift! Friedman, however, has shown that typical English text, with the letter probabilities of Table 7.1, has an index of coincidence of about 0.066 (or 6.6%). This simple fact can be used to easily identify a monoalphabetic substitution cipher. In such ciphertext, the probabilities of letters are the same as in a typical text (but are associated with different letters), so its index of coincidence is about 0.066.

(The number 0.066 is derived as follows. Imagine that the 26 letters a through z occur in typical English with probabilities p_1 through p_{26}, respectively. We randomly select two different letters in a given English text. The probability that both will happen to be as is p_1^2 [strictly speaking, this would be the probability if we could select the same letter twice, but for long text the correct probability is very close to p_1^2]. Similarly, the probability that both letters will happen to be bs is p_2^2. Thus, we conclude that the probability of finding the same letter in two different, randomly selected positions is the sum $p_1^2 + p_2^2 + \cdots + p_{26}^2$. When the actual probabilities are substituted, this sum becomes 0.066 or very close to this value.)

◇ **Exercise 9.11:** Explain why the sum $\sum_1^{26} p_i^2$ is a probability.

It is now easy to see how this simple measure can help in determining the length of a Vigenère key. We split the ciphertext into n segments and compute the index of coincidence of each. If the key length is n, then each of the n segments will be a monoalphabetic substitution string, and its index will be about 0.066. Otherwise, the indexes will be those of random text, about 0.038. All that the cryptanalyst has to do is try various values of n (probably starting at $n = 3$, because $n = 2$ provides hardly any security).

Figure 9.12 lists Matlab code to compute the index of coincidence of a given text file (`vigenere` in the example).

```
% Computes index of coincidence.
% inputs data from file 'vigenere'
% and calculates for 6 values of n
fid=fopen('vigenere','r');
if fid==-1 error('file not found'); end;
c=fread(fid,'char'); % input entire file
lc=length(c);
for n=1:6
 indx=0;
 for k=1:lc
  l=k+n; if l>lc l=l-lc; end;
  if c(k)==c(l) indx=indx+1; end;
 end; % for k
 indx/lc
end; % for n
```

Figure 9.12: Matlab Code for the Index of Coincidence.

The Kasiski–Babbage method and the index of coincidence help in breaking the Vigenère cipher, but only in cases where the key is short. These methods cannot be applied to long keys, and this becomes especially obvious when we consider a key as long as the message itself. It therefore seems that the use of very long keys makes this cipher very secure, but long keys are difficult to distribute. A practical way to distribute very long keys is to agree on a book and to distribute a page number. The key will be the text starting at the top of that page. Such a key can be very long, but because it is meaningful text, it is not random, so its statistical properties "rub off" on the ciphertext. Ideally, a very long key that is also random is very secure and generates ciphertext that cannot be distinguished from random. Such a key is called a *one-time pad* and is discussed in the Introduction. The importance of the one-time pad is that it can lead to ciphers that are perfectly (or absolutely) secure.

William (Wolfe) Frederick Friedman, 1891–1969

Wolfe Frederick Friedman was born on 24 September 1891 in Kishinev, then part of imperial Russia, now Chisinau, capital of Moldova. His father, an interpreter for the Czar's postal service, emigrated to the United States the following year to escape increasing anti-Semitic regulations; the family joined him in Pittsburgh in 1893. Three years after that, when the elder Friedman became a United States citizen, Wolfe's name was changed to William.

After receiving a B.S. and doing some graduate work in genetics at Cornell University, William Friedman was hired by Riverbank Laboratories—what would today be termed a think tank—in Geneva, Illinois, outside Chicago. Colonel George Fabyan founded Riverbank with laboratories for biology, chemistry, and acoustics, and also hired cryptographers in a futile attempt to prove that Shakespeare's works were actually written by Sir Francis Bacon.

At Riverbank, Friedman became interested in the study of codes and ciphers as well as in Elizebeth Smith (the rare spelling of her name is attributed to her mother, a Quaker, who held a strong passion against Elizebeth ever being called "Eliza"), who was doing cryptanalytic research there. Friedman left Riverbank to become a cryptologic officer during World War I, the beginning of a distinguished career in government service.

Friedman's contributions thereafter are well known—prolific author, teacher, and practitioner of cryptology. He coined the term *cryptanalysis*. Perhaps his greatest achievements were introducing mathematical and scientific methods into cryptology and producing training materials used by several generations of pupils. His work affected for the better both signals intelligence and information systems security, and much of what is done today at NSA may be traced to William Friedman's pioneering efforts.

====

There are two major products that came out of Berkeley: LSD and UNIX. We don't believe this to be a coincidence.

—Jeremy S. Anderson

10
Stream Ciphers

The encryption methods discussed in previous chapters assume that the plaintext consists of letters and digits. With the development of the modern digital computer, which uses binary numbers, secure codes had to be based on bits. If the plaintext is text, then it is represented internally either in ASCII, with eight bits per character (seven code bits and one parity bit), or in Unicode, with 16 bits per character. Any transposition or substitution algorithms should be redesigned to operate on bits, a normally easy task. The ASCII codes of the plaintext string MASTER are

$$1001101|1000001|1010011|1010100|1000101|1010010.$$

It is very easy to come up with simple permutations that will make a transposition cipher for such a string. Some possible permutations are (1) swap every pair of consecutive bits; (2) reverse the seven bits of each code and then swap consecutive codes; and (3) perform a perfect shuffle as shown here:

$$1001101100000110100011|10101001000101101010010$$
$$1\ 0\ 0\ 1\ 1\ 0\ 1\ 1\ 0\ 0\ 0\ 0\ 0\ 1\ 1\ 0\ 1\ 0\ 0\ 1\ 1$$
$$1\ 0\ 1\ 0\ 1\ 0\ 0\ 1\ 0\ 0\ 0\ 1\ 0\ 1\ 1\ 0\ 1\ 0\ 0\ 1\ 0$$
$$11000110110010110000000100111100110000111 0$$

Unicode

The ASCII character code was developed in the 1960s. It assigns 7-bit codes to characters, so it supports $2^7 = 128$ characters. (ASCII codes are always 8 bits long, where the 8th bit can be used, as parity, to make the code more reliable. However, its function is not defined in the ASCII standard.) With the rapid development of computers, high-resolution printers, and large databases from the 1970s onward, users have felt the need for a larger character set, including foreign characters, accents, and mathematical and other symbols. At the same time, capacities of memories, disk drives, and other data storage devices have rapidly increased, while costs have plummeted, so a long character code is no longer prohibitively expensive—hence Unicode. Unicode is often referred to as a 16-bit system, which allows for only 65,536 characters, but by reserving certain codes as escape codes for mapping into additional 32-bit codes, it has the potential to cope with over a million unique characters. The Unicode organization [Unicode 03] describes the code as follows.

The Unicode Worldwide Character Standard is a character coding system designed to support the interchange, processing, and display of the written texts of the diverse languages of the modern world. In addition, it supports classical and historical texts of many written languages.

In version 3.2.0, the Unicode standard contains 95,156 distinct coded characters derived from the supported scripts. These characters cover the principal written languages of all the major regions on earth.

Some modern written languages are not yet supported or only partially supported due to a need for further research into the encoding needs of certain scripts. The Unicode standard is described in detail in [Unicode Standard 96].

Note: The above is intended as a concise source of information about the Unicode Standard. It is neither a comprehensive definition of, nor a technical guide to, the Unicode Standard. For the authoritative source of information, see [Unicode Standard 96].

The Unicode Standard is the international standard used to encode text for computer processing. It is a subset of the International Standard ISO/IEC 10646-1,1993, whose 32-bit values can represent 4,294,967,296 characters. Its design is based on the simplicity and consistency of ASCII, but goes far beyond ASCII's limited ability to encode only the Latin alphabet. The Unicode Standard provides the capacity to encode all of the characters used for the major written languages of the world.

To accommodate the many thousands of characters used in international text, the Unicode Standard adopts a 16-bit codeset, thereby providing codes for 65,536 characters, enough to represent all the characters/symbols used by all of the world's major languages. To keep character coding simple and efficient, the Unicode Standard assigns each character a unique 16-bit value and does not use complex modes or escape codes.

Unicode provides a consistent coding format for international character sets and brings order to a chaotic state of affairs that has made it difficult to exchange text files across language borders. Computer users who deal with multilingual text—international business people, linguists, researchers, scientists, and others—will find that the Unicode Standard greatly simplifies their work. Mathematicians and technicians, who regularly use mathematical symbols and other technical characters, will also find the Unicode Standard valuable.

10.1 Symmetric Key and Public Key

Modern encryption methods are classified into symmetric key and public key. The former class uses the same key for encryption and decryption and is further divided into stream ciphers and block ciphers. The latter class (Section 12.2) employs different keys for encryption and decryption and thereby solves the key distribution problem. It is sometimes referred to as asymmetric-key cryptography.

Stream ciphers (Section 10.2) encrypt a message (a string of bits) by encrypting each bit independently. A block cipher (Section 11.1), on the other hand, divides the message into blocks and encrypts each block separately by substitution and transposition.

Symmetric-key cryptography has the following advantages.

1. The encryption and decryption algorithms can be fast in both software and hardware.
2. The keys are relatively short.
3. The ciphers can be used to generate pseudorandom numbers, hash functions, and digital signatures.
4. The ciphers can be combined to create very secure encryption. An example is the triple data encryption standard (TDEA, Section 11.3.3).
5. This class has an extensive history, and many types of algorithms are known. Therefore it is easy (at least in principle) to develop new methods.

Symmetric-key cryptography also has disadvantages. The main ones are the following.

1. The key-distribution problem. This is a problem even in the simplest case where only two parties communicate. With a large organization, where many individuals must have the key, this problem may dictate the use of a public-key cipher.
2. The key must be replaced very often, even in situations where the number of participants is small. This issue is an aspect of the key-distribution problem.
3. Digital signature algorithms using symmetric-keys require large keys, which complicates the key-distribution problem even further.

Public-key cryptography has the following advantages.

1. It solves the key-distribution problem.
2. The key does not have to be replaced often.
3. When used in a large network, only a small number of keys are needed.
4. Public-key encryption methods tend to support efficient digital signature algorithms.

Public-key cryptography also has its drawbacks. The principal ones are the following.

1. Encryption algorithms are normally much slower than symmetric-key ciphers.
2. The keys are much longer (typically around 1000 bits) than those in symmetric-key (which are typically in the range 64–128). This increase in length is necessary to prevent easy factoring of the key.
3. Security is based on the difficulty of factoring large numbers, but this difficulty may be temporary if an efficient factoring algorithm is discovered.

10.2 Stream Ciphers

Stream ciphers constitute an important class of encryption methods for bits (although the principle of a stream cipher can also be applied to other symbols). Such a cipher encodes the bits of a binary string one at a time, using a very simple rule. Stream ciphers are faster and also easier to implement than block ciphers, especially in hardware. They are a natural choice in cases where the binary string has to be encrypted and transmitted at a constant rate. Imagine ciphertext received bit by bit from a communications line and decrypted. If a cipherbit is corrupted, then it is decrypted incorrectly, but the error is not propagated by the decryption algorithm. This property makes stream ciphers ideal in cases where ciphertexts are transmitted on an unreliable communications channel.

Much is currently known about this class of ciphers, and many individual algorithms have been proposed, implemented, and analyzed. However, most of the encryption methods commonly used in practice are block ciphers

The principle of a stream cipher is to create a random string of bits, called the *keystream*, and to combine the bits of the plaintext with those of the keystream. The resulting bit string is the ciphertext. The combiner is normally the exclusive-or (XOR) operation, but Section 10.6 illustrates a different approach. Decrypting is done by XORing the ciphertext with the same keystream. Thus, a stream cipher is based on the following property of the XOR operation (Table 10.1): If $B = A \oplus K$, then $A = B \oplus K$. As an example, the plaintext MASTER is enciphered with the keystream KEY ($= 1001011|1000101|1011001$ and repeats as necessary).

Key   1001011100010110110011001011100010110110011

Text   1001101100000110100111010100100010110100010

XOR   0001110000010000010100011111000000000001011

The resulting ciphertext can then easily be deciphered by performing an XOR between it and the keystream.

B\A	0	1
0	0	1
1	1	0

Table 10.1: Truth Table of XOR.

⋄ **Exercise 10.1:** What other logical operation on bits has this useful property of the XOR?

The main advantage of stream ciphers is their high speed for both encryption and decryption. A stream cipher is easily implemented in software, but special hardware can also be constructed to generate the keystream and perform the encryption and decryption operations. There are two main types of stream ciphers: *synchronous* and *self-synchronizing*. The former uses a keystream that is independent of the plaintext and of the ciphertext; this is the common type. The latter uses a keystream that depends on the plaintext and may also depend on that part of the ciphertext that has been generated so far.

The simplest (and also most secure) type of stream cipher is the one-time pad (mentioned in the Introduction), sometimes called the *Vernam cipher*. Given the plaintext (a string of n bits), the keystream is selected as a random string of n bits that is used only once. The resulting ciphertext is also a random bit string, even if the plaintext wasn't random. The ciphertext has no regularities or patterns that a codebreaker can exploit. A codebreaker who knows or suspects that this method was used to encrypt a message can try to break it by generating *every* random string of n bits and using each as a keystream. The original plaintext would eventually be produced this way, but the cryptanalyst would have to examine every plaintext generated—an impossible task given the immense number of random strings of n bits, even for modest values of n. There is also a slight chance that several meaningful plaintexts would be generated, making it even harder to decide which one is *the* real plaintext.

This interesting and important cipher was developed by Gilbert S. Vernam in 1917, and United States patent #1310719 was issued to him in 1918.

⋄ **Exercise 10.2:** Show that if the keystream of a Vernam cipher is a random sequence of bits, then the ciphertext is random even if the plaintext isn't random.

⋄ **Exercise 10.3:** The chance that a wrong key would produce meaningful plaintext is very small. Advance arguments to support this claim.

In order to achieve good security, the one-time pad should be used just once. The Venona project [NSA 04] run by the United States Army's signal intelligence service during 1943–1980 is a good, practical example of a case where this rule was broken, with significant results. Using the one-time pad more than once breaks one of the cherished rules of cryptography, namely, to avoid repetitions, and may provide enough clues to a would-be codebreaker to reconstruct the random key and use it to decipher messages. Here is how such deciphering can be done.

We assume that two ciphertexts are given and it is known or suspected that they were encrypted with the same random keystream. We select a short, common word, such as **the**. We can assume that the first message contains some occurrences of this word, so we start by assuming that the *entire* first message consists of copies of this word. We then figure out the random keystream needed to encrypt a series of **the** into the first ciphertext, and try to decrypt the second ciphertext with this key (a key that we can consider *the first guess*). Any part of this first-guess key that corresponds to an actual **the** in the first message would decrypt a small part of the second message correctly. Applying the first-guess key to the second ciphertext may therefore result in plaintext with some meaningful words and fragments.

The next step is to guess how to expand those fragments in the second plaintext and use the improved plaintext to produce a second-guess key. This key is then applied to the first ciphertext to produce a first plaintext that has some recognizable words and fragments and is therefore a little better than just a series of **the**. Using our knowledge of the language, we can expand those fragments and use the improved plaintext to construct a third-guess key.

After a few iterations, both plaintexts may have so much recognizable material that the rest can be guessed with more certainty, thereby leading to complete decipherment.

Even though it offers absolute security, the one-time pad is generally impractical, because the one-time pads have to be generated and distributed safely to every member of an organization that may be very large (such as an army division). This method can be used in only a limited number of situations, such as exchanging top-secret messages between a government and its ambassador abroad or between world leaders.

(In principle, the one-time pad can be used, or rather abused, in cases where the sender wants to remain unaccountable. Once an encrypted message A is decrypted to plaintext B and the one-time pad is destroyed, there is no way to redecrypt A and thus to associate it with B. The sender may deny sending B and may claim that decrypting A had to result in something else.)

In practice, stream ciphers are used with keystreams that are *pseudorandom* bit strings. Such a bit string is generated by repeatedly applying a recursive relation, so it is deterministic and therefore not truly random. Still, if a sequence of n pseudorandom bits does not repeat itself, it can be used as the keystream for a stream cipher with relative safety.

10.3 Linear Shift Registers

One way to generate pseudorandom bits is with a *linear feedback shift register* (LFSR, [Barker 84] and [Golomb 82]), most often used in hardware stream ciphers. Another is a pseudorandom number generator (PRNG, a very common piece of software), usually implemented in software. Figure 10.2a shows a simple shift register with 10 stages, each a flip-flop (such as an SR latch). Bits are shifted from left to right, and the new bit entered on the left is the XOR of bits 6 and 10. Such a shift register is said to correspond to the polynomial $x^{10} + x^6 + 1$. The latches at stages 6 and 10 are said to be *tapped*. Before encryption starts, the register is initialized to a certain, agreed-upon 10-bit number (this is its initial state, the key). The register is then shifted repeatedly, and the bits output from the rightmost stage are used as the keystream to encrypt the plaintext.

From the Dictionary

Tap (noun).
1. A cylindrical plug or stopper for closing an opening through which liquid is drawn, as in a cask; spigot.
2. A faucet or cock.
3. A connection made at an intermediate point on an electrical circuit or device.
4. An act or instance of wiretapping.

The term *linear* is used because the input that is fed back to the register is the XOR of the tapped stages, and this is simply the sum modulo 2 of those stages.

The bit string output by the register depends, of course, on the initial state and on the corresponding polynomial. If the initial state of the register is reached after s

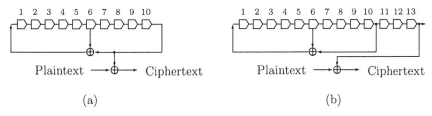

Figure 10.2: Linear Feedback Shift Registers.

steps, there will be a cycle, and the same s states will repeat over and over. Repetition, as is well known, is a major sin in cryptography and should be avoided. A shift register should therefore be designed to go through the maximum number of states before it cycles. In a 10-stage shift register, there can be $2^{10} = 1024$ different 10-bit states. Of those, the special state of all zeros should be avoided because it degenerates the output to a stream of all zeros. Thus, it is clear that the best that can be achieved in a 10-stage shift register is a sequence of $2^{10} - 1 = 1023$ different states. It can be shown that this can be achieved if the polynomial associated with the register is *primitive*.

(A polynomial $P(x)$ of degree n is primitive if it satisfies (1) $P(0) \neq 0$, (2) $P(x)$ is of order $2^n - 1$, and (3) $P(x)$ is irreducible. The order of a polynomial is the smallest e for which $P(x)$ divides $x^e + 1$. For example, the polynomial $x^2 + x + 1$ has degree 2. It has order $e = 3 = 2^2 - 1$ because $(x^2 + x + 1)(x + 1) = x^3 + 1$. A polynomial is irreducible if it cannot be written as the product of lower-degree polynomials. For example, $x^2 + x + 1$ is irreducible, but $x^2 - 1$ is not because it equals the product $(x + 1)(x - 1)$. We therefore conclude that $x^2 + x + 1$ is primitive.)

Also, a shift register with the maximum number of states must have an even number of taps and the rightmost stage (the oldest bit) must be a tap. The latter property is illustrated in Figure 10.2b. It is easy to see that the output bit string generated by this 13-stage register is identical to that generated by the similar 10-stage register, except that it is delayed.

⋄ **Exercise 10.4:** Design a four-stage shift register where a nonzero state is followed by a state of all zeros.

Selecting the right polynomial is important. We never use our initials, our address, or our phone number as a password. Similarly, certain polynomials have been adopted for use in various international standards, such as CRC (Appendix C). These polynomials should be avoided in a shift register. Some well-known examples are $x^{16} + x^{12} + x^5 + 1$, which is used by the CCITT; $x^{12} + x^3 + x + 1$ and $x^{16} + x^{15} + x^2 + 1$ which generate the common CRC-12 and CRC-16 cyclic redundancy codes; and $x^{10} + x^3 + 1$ and $x^{10} + x^9 + x^8 + x^6 + x^3 + x^2 + 1$, which are used by the GPS satellites.

⋄ **Exercise 10.5:** Given the four-stage shift register defined by the polynomial $x^4 + x + 1$, show the states that follow state 1000.

The linear shift registers described here are simple. The input to the register is a linear function (an XOR) of some of its states. Even though the output of such a register passes the statistical tests for randomness, the register itself is still vulnerable to cryptanalysis because of its simple structure. To understand how a linear shift register can be analyzed, imagine an n-stage register where every stage is a tap. The input is the XOR of all n stages. The simple response of the XOR makes it possible to completely analyze the behavior of this device and express the future state of each stage as a recursive function of the present state of the register. Once this is done, it is possible to deduce the precise structure of the register (i.e., which stages are taps), if a short output string is known.

We illustrate this approach for $n = 4$. Figure 10.3 shows a four-stage linear shift register where the four stages are numbered 4, 3, 2, 1, from left to right and are initially set to the string $b_4 b_3 b_2 b_1$. We know that any stage may be a tap, so we tentatively connect each stage to an XOR gate through an AND gate that is controlled by a binary input c_i. If $c_i = 1$, then stage i affects the input that is fed back to the shift register. If $c_i = 0$, then stage i is not a tap and does not affect the input. The problem is to determine which stages are taps, or equivalently, which c_i's are 1s.

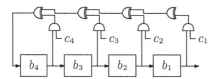

Figure 10.3: A Four-Stage Shift Register.

After the first shift, stages 3, 2, and 1 contain bits $b_4 b_3 b_2$. Bit b_1 is gone, but it has affected the state of stage 4 (the leftmost stage), which is now

$$b^{(1)} \stackrel{\text{def}}{=} (b_4 \cdot c_4) \oplus (b_3 \cdot c_3) \oplus (b_2 \cdot c_2) \oplus (b_1 \cdot c_1)$$

(where the multiplication stands for the logical AND operation). After another shift, stages 3, 2, and 1 contain bits $b^{(1)} b_4 b_3$. Bit b_2 is gone, but it has affected the state of stage 4, which is now

$$b^{(2)} \stackrel{\text{def}}{=} (b^{(1)} \cdot c_4) \oplus (b_4 \cdot c_3) \oplus (b_3 \cdot c_2) \oplus (b_2 \cdot c_1).$$

After two more shifts, the shift register contains the string $b^{(4)} b^{(3)} b^{(2)} b^{(1)}$, where

$$b^{(1)} = (b_4 \cdot c_4) \oplus (b_3 \cdot c_3) \oplus (b_2 \cdot c_2) \oplus (b_1 \cdot c_1),$$
$$b^{(2)} = (b^{(1)} \cdot c_4) \oplus (b_4 \cdot c_3) \oplus (b_3 \cdot c_2) \oplus (b_2 \cdot c_1),$$
$$b^{(3)} = (b^{(2)} \cdot c_4) \oplus (b^{(1)} \cdot c_3) \oplus (b_4 \cdot c_2) \oplus (b_3 \cdot c_1),$$
$$b^{(4)} = (b^{(3)} \cdot c_4) \oplus (b^{(2)} \cdot c_3) \oplus (b^{(1)} \cdot c_2) \oplus (b_4 \cdot c_1).$$

This may be considered a system of four linear algebraic equations with the four unknowns c_1, c_2, c_3, and c_4. It can easily be solved if the 8-bit string $b^{(4)} b^{(3)} b^{(2)} b^{(1)} b_4 b_3 b_2 b_1$ is known.

Thus, it is clear that an n-stage linear shift register can be completely analyzed if an output string of $2n$ bits is known. Such a string can be deduced from two known strings of $2n$ plainbits and $2n$ cipherbits. The maximum length of a nonrepeating output string is 2^n, which for large values of n is much greater than $2n$. For $n = 20$, for example, 2^n is more than a million, but $2n$ is only 40.

10.4 Nonlinear Shift Registers

Since linear feedback shift registers are easy to analyze, practical stream ciphers must use nonlinear feedback shift registers (NFSR) to generate the pseudorandom key bits they need. Figure 10.4 shows the general structure of such a register. Note that the longest nonrepeating output string is 2^n bits, the same as that of a linear shift register.

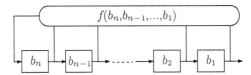

Figure 10.4: A Nonlinear Feedback Shift Register.

The figure implies that all the stages are used to determine the input, but in practice only some of the stages are tapped. The states of the tapped stages become the inputs of a Boolean function $f(b_n, b_{n-1}, \ldots, b_1)$ whose output is fed back to the leftmost stage of the register. Such a function consists of several logic gates feeding each other and ending with a single output.

⋄ **Exercise 10.6:** How many Boolean functions with n inputs are there?

In practice, nonlinear shift registers are based on linear shift registers because the latter type is well understood and easy to construct. There are several ways to combine a number of LFSRs to form a nonlinear shift register. Such combinations can be used to construct a nonlinear shift register with a large period, increased complexity, and output that passes the statistical tests for randomness. One design principle is always to use maximal-length LSFRs. Several such methods are shown here.

1. Several LFSRs are used, and their outputs are combined by a nonlinear Boolean function to form one output. This is called a *nonlinear combination generator*.
2. A single LFSR is employed, and its content is filtered by a nonlinear Boolean function. This is known as a *nonlinear filter generator*.
3. The outputs of one or several LFSRs are used to control the clocks of the main LFSR (there can be several main LFSRs). This is a *clock-controlled generator*.

Nonlinear Combination Generators. A general design for this type of shift register is shown in Figure 10.5a. Figure 10.5b shows the *Geffe generator*, which is constructed by three maximum-length LFSRs with lengths L_1, L_2, and L_3. The lengths must be pairwise relatively prime, i.e., $\gcd(L_1, L_2) = \gcd(L_2, L_3) = \gcd(L_1, L_3) = 1$. The nonlinear combining function is

$$f(x_1, x_2, x_3) = x_1 x_2 \oplus (1 \oplus x_2) x_3 = x_1 x_2 \oplus x_2 x_3 \oplus x_3.$$

The keystream generated has period $(2^{L_1} - 1)(2^{L_2} - 1)(2^{L_3} - 1)$.

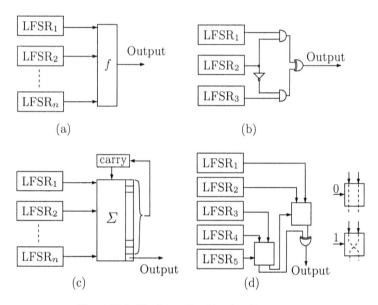

(a)   (b)

(c)   (d)

Figure 10.5: Nonlinear Combination Generators.

Figure 10.5c depicts the *summation generator*. This device is constructed from n maximum-length LFSRs whose lengths L_i are pairwise relatively prime. The secret key consists of the initial states of the LFSRs, and an initial carry c_0 that is an integer, not just a single bit. In step i, the LFSRs are shifted one position and their outputs are fed into the summation function as n individual bits x_i. Those bits are arithmetically added and are also added to the carry c_{i-1} from the previous step. The result is an integer S. The bit output by the summation generator in step i is the least significant bit of S, and the new carry c_i is the remaining bits of S. The period of the output stream is

$$\prod_{i=1}^{n} \left(2^{L_i} - 1\right),$$

which can be very large.

More complex versions of this type of shift register are easily designed. Figure 10.5d shows an extension of the Geffe generator that employs five LFSRs (denoted here by R1 through R5). R5 determines which of R3 and R4 will be used for the output and which for mixing the outputs of R1 and R2. The final output is the XOR of (R1 or R2) and (R3 or R4). This design uses a simple switch with two inputs. The switch either passes its two inputs straight through or swaps them, depending on its control input.

Nonlinear Filter Generators. This type of nonlinear shift register is based on a single linear shift register whose content is fed to a nonlinear Boolean function f. The output of f is the output of the nonlinear filter generator (Figure 10.6). The Gifford cipher is an example of the use of this type of nonlinear shift register.

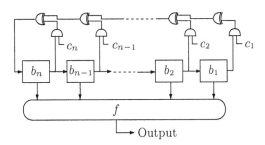

Figure 10.6: A Nonlinear Filter Generator.

The Gifford PRNG [Gifford 85] is based on a nonlinear shift register where each element is a byte (Figure 10.7). The initial content of the register is the 64-bit encryption key of this cipher. Bytes 0, 2, 4, and 7 are used to form one byte of pseudorandom output that is XORed with one byte of plaintext to form a byte of ciphertext. Bytes 0 and 2 are concatenated to form a 16-bit integer that is multiplied by the 16-bit integer formed from bytes 4 and 7. The output consists of bits 8 through 15 (the second least significant byte) of the 32-bit product (bits are normally numbered from right to left, from 0 to 31).

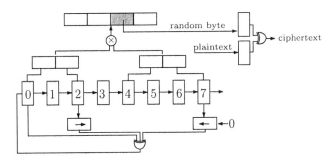

Figure 10.7: The Gifford Cipher.

After the output byte is generated and used to encrypt a byte of plaintext, the register is shifted to the right by byte; i.e., each of the seven leftmost bytes is shifted to the right, and the rightmost byte is discarded. A new byte (prepared before the shift) is input on the left. This byte (the filtered state of the shift register) is the XOR of byte 0, byte 1 (arithmetically shifted one position to the right), and byte 7 (logically shifted one position to the left). (An arithmetic shift to the right extends the leftmost bit. A logical shift to the left sets the rightmost bit to zero.)

This cipher was originally developed by David K. Gifford [Gifford 85] to encrypt wire reports from *The New York Times* and The Associated Press to subscribers in the Boston area. It was eventually broken by [Cain and Sherman 97].

Clock-Controlled Generators. The principle of this type of shift register is to have the output of one LFSR control the stepping (clocking) of another LFSR. The irregular stepping of the second LFSR introduces an element of nonlinearity that makes this type of shift register much harder to analyze.

A common type of clock-controlled generator is the *alternating step generator* (Figure 10.8a). This device employs one primary LFSR (R_1 in Figure 10.8a) whose output is used to select one of the two secondary LFSRs R_2 and R_3. The final output is the XOR of R_2 and R_3. In more detail, the same clock pulse is sent to all three LFSRs but may be blocked to the secondary ones by AND gates. If the output of R_1 is 1, then R_2 is clocked but R_3 is not, so its output does not change. (Its output bit is the same as its previous output, and for the first step it is zero.) If the output of R_1 is 0, then R_3 is clocked but R_2 is not. The output bits of R_2 and R_3 are XORed to form the output of the alternating step generator.

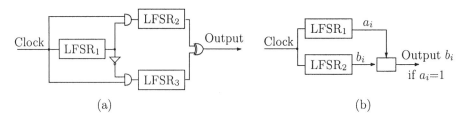

Figure 10.8: Clock-Controlled Generators.

For maximum security, the lengths of the three LFSRs should be pairwise relatively prime and should not differ much.

⬦ **Exercise 10.7:** Construct (on paper) the alternating step generator defined by $R_1 = x^3 + x^2 + 1$ with an initial state of 001, $R_2 = x^4 + x^3 + 1$ with an initial state of 1011, and $R_3 = x^5 + x^4 + x^3 + x + 1$ with an initial state of 01001. Show (1) the output sequence of R_1, (2) the output sequences of R_2 and R_3 (affected by the output of R_1), and (3) the final output string.

A different clock-controlled generator is the *shrinking generator* (Figure 10.8b). This is a simple device whose properties are well understood. It consists of a primary LFSR R_1 whose output stream a_i controls the output stream b_i of the secondary LFSR R_2. The output stream consists of all the b_i bits for which $a_i = 1$. All the b_i bits for which $a_i = 0$ are discarded (or decimated). The output therefore consists of a shrunken version of the b_i sequence.

⋄ **Exercise 10.8:** Construct a shrinking generator with a primary LFSR $R_1 = x^3 + x + 1$ and a secondary LFSR $R_2 = x^5 + x^3 + 1$. Assume that the initial states of the two LFSRs are 100 and 00101, respectively, and compute the output sequences of the device.

If R_1 and R_2 are maximum-length LFSRs of lengths L_1 and L_2, respectively, and if L_1 and L_2 are relatively prime, then the output of the shrinking generator with a primary R_1 and a secondary R_2 has period $2^{L_1-1}(2^{L_2} - 1)$. The output of the shrinking generator has good statistical properties if the polynomials for R_1 and R_2 are chosen randomly from the set of all primitive polynomials of degrees L_1 and L_2.

10.5 Other Stream Ciphers

The feedback shift registers are ideal for hardware implementations. They are constructed from simple building blocks (flip-flops for the individual stages and logic gates for the Boolean functions) and require a small number of connections between the parts. In cases where an efficient software implementation is needed, other ciphers may be more suitable. Three such ciphers—dynamic substitution, the Latin square combiner, and SEAL—are described next.

10.6 Dynamic Substitution

All the stream ciphers discussed earlier use an XOR to do the actual encryption. One bit of plaintext is XORed with a bit of the key to generate one bit of ciphertext. We can consider the XOR a *combiner* of the plaintext and key. The XOR is its own inverse, which makes it a natural candidate for encryption. However, it is linear and is therefore a weak combiner (it is equivalent to addition modulo 2). If a codebreaker knows or guesses strings of plaintext and the corresponding ciphertext, it is relatively easy to break a cipher that uses the XOR as a combiner. This is why a substitution method may be preferable to the XOR. Such a method uses a table (or several tables) to substitute ciphertext for the plaintext. The tables must be reversible in order to allow decryption. They should also be modified all the time (dynamic substitution) because static tables (and in general, anything that is static) make the codebreaker's task easier.

The dynamic substitution method developed by [Ritter 90] uses a dynamic table instead of an XOR as a combiner. The table has many entries and is constantly shuffled during encryption, which makes it a nonlinear combiner. The method is, of course, reversible in order to allow decryption. It encrypts the plaintext in bytes and is fast and simple to implement.

It starts by initializing a 256-byte table T to all 256 possible byte values. Each byte b of plaintext is used as a pointer to T, and the byte at T[b] becomes the ciphertext. The next byte r of a pseudorandom sequence is then also used as a pointer, and table entries T[b] and T[r] are swapped. If b = r, no swapping takes place. The example shown here uses 2-bit quantities instead of bytes to illustrate this operation. Thus, T has $2^2 = 4$ entries. We assume that the current state of T is

$$\begin{array}{|c|c|c|c|} \hline 01 & 10 & 11 & 00 \\ \hline \end{array}$$
$$\ \ 00\ \ \ 01\ \ \ 10\ \ \ 11$$

If the next plaintext pair of bits is 01, it is encrypted to T[01] = 10. Assuming that the next pair of key bits is 11, table entries 01 and 11 are swapped and the table becomes

$$\begin{array}{|c|c|c|c|} \hline 01 & 00 & 11 & 10 \\ \hline \end{array}$$
$$\ \ 00\ \ \ 01\ \ \ 10\ \ \ 11$$

Decrypting requires both T and its inverse I. If T[a] = b, then the inverse table satisfies I[b] = a. An example is

forward $\begin{array}{|c|c|c|c|} \hline 01 & 10 & 00 & 11 \\ \hline \end{array}$
$\qquad\quad\ \ 00\ \ \ 01\ \ \ 10\ \ \ 11$
inverse $\begin{array}{|c|c|c|c|} \hline 10 & 00 & 01 & 11 \\ \hline \end{array}$
$\qquad\quad\ \ 00\ \ \ 01\ \ \ 10\ \ \ 11$

Examining the forward table, we see that plaintext 10 should be encrypted to 00. Therefore, given ciphertext 00, it is obvious that it should be decrypted to I[00] = 10. In general, ciphertext c should be decrypted to I[c], and this should be followed by swapping certain entries in both tables to keep them synchronized. If we denote the next random number by r, then entries I[c] and I[T[r]] are swapped in the inverse table, and entries T[I[c]] and T[r] should be swapped in the forward table.

If c = 00 and r = 11, then entries I[c] = I[00] = 10 and I[T[r]] = I[11] = 11 are first swapped, followed by a swap of entries T[I[c]] = T[10] and T[r] = T[11]. Notice that the latter swap uses the "old" value 10 of I[c]. The result is

forward $\begin{array}{|c|c|c|c|} \hline 01 & 10 & 11 & 00 \\ \hline \end{array}$
$\qquad\quad\ \ 00\ \ \ 01\ \ \ 10\ \ \ 11$
inverse $\begin{array}{|c|c|c|c|} \hline 11 & 00 & 01 & 10 \\ \hline \end{array}$
$\qquad\quad\ \ 00\ \ \ 01\ \ \ 10\ \ \ 11$

Thus, both encryption and decryption are simple and fast. The complete key of this algorithm consists of the seed of the PRNG and the information needed to construct the inverse table. Since the table has 256 entries, the key may have to be long, which provides increased security. On the other hand, certain users may prefer an initial table that is regular, which is somewhat less secure but requires only a short key.

⋄ **Exercise 10.9:** What information is needed to construct the inverse table if the original table is set to T[a] = a?

This method is more secure than a simple XOR. Each time a table entry is used for encryption, it is relocated at random, which means that identical plaintext bytes are encrypted from the same table location to different values. This process tends to erase and randomize any patterns in the plaintext and in the random numbers. Notice that the random numbers are used only to shuffle the table, not to encrypt the plaintext. Other substitution methods may modify the entire table each time it is used, but this approach seems unnecessary and is also slow. Modifying just one element is faster and perhaps only slightly less secure.

Another advantage of this method is the many ways it can be extended. A simple extension uses two tables S and T for encryption. A plaintext byte b is first encrypted to S[b] (and table S is shuffled using a random byte) and then to T[S[b]] (and table T is shuffled using the next random byte). The two tables should be initialized differently. We know that combining two XOR encryptions does not increase security, but combining two (or more) dynamic substitution tables does increase security because this method is based on nonlinear operations. A variation of this idea is to encipher a plaintext byte twice with the same table. Thus, b is encrypted to T[T[b]], which is followed by swapping T[T[b]] and T[r].

An extension of the basic substitution method uses an array of tables and uses a random byte to select a table in the array to encrypt the next plaintext.

On the downside, if some plaintexts and their corresponding ciphertexts are known, certain conclusions can be drawn about the PRNG used (recall that with an XOR, such knowledge reveals the structure of the shift register). Also, this method is somewhat slower than using an XOR because of the extra work needed for swapping entries.

This method is not popular because it has been patented (United States patent 4,979,832) and because it is vulnerable to errors. The encryption of a plaintext byte depends to some extent on the preceding bytes (because they determine how the table is shuffled), and the same is true for decryption. If the ciphertext is transmitted and one bit in a cipher byte becomes corrupted, that byte will not be decrypted correctly, and the wrong swapping that follows will cause bad decryption of many of its successors. A possible solution is to add an error-correcting code to the ciphertext when it is transmitted (and even when it is written on a disk).

10.7 The Latin Square Combiner

A Latin square of order n is an $n \times n$ table with n distinct symbols drawn from a source alphabet. Each symbol appears in the table n times, once in each row and once in each column. Here is an order-4 example with the four 2-bit symbols 0, 1, 2, and 3.

$$
\begin{array}{cccc}
1 & 0 & 3 & 2 \\
2 & 1 & 0 & 3 \\
3 & 2 & 1 & 0 \\
0 & 3 & 2 & 1
\end{array}
$$

A Latin square combiner is an example of a cryptographic combining algorithm. In a simple combiner algorithm, two consecutive plaintext symbols A and B are used to select a third symbol C, and the resulting ciphertext consists of a combination of either A and C or B and C. In the Latin square above, the next two pairs of input bits are used to select a row and a column of the square. The symbol thus selected from the square is combined with one of the pairs to form the ciphertext for the four input bits.

For example, we can use the four input bits 00|11 as pointers to the symbol 2 located in row 0 and column 3 of the square, and replace the four input bits with 00|10. Decrypting is done by searching row 00 for symbol 10. It is found in column 3, so ciphertext 00|10 is decrypted to 00|11.

A Latin square can be viewed as a set of substitution tables. The plaintext selects a table and a location in the table. The ciphertext selects a table and searches for an item in it. This process also explains why the method is secure. If we denote the two pairs of input bits by r and c, and the two pairs of cipherbits by r and x, then r and c are correlated by the statistical properties of the plaintext, but r and x are not.

Decryption involves searching one row of the square for a given symbol. Since the square may be large, it is possible to speed up decryption by preparing the inverse of the Latin square and using it for decryption. If row r of the original square contains symbol x in column c, then row r of the inverse square should contain symbol c in column x. The Latin square above is its own inverse. This particular square is also easy to generate because each row is a circular shift of the row above it. This feature is handy for large squares, since only the top row has to be stored, but it is undesirable because its regularity weakens the encryption.

In practice, a Latin square may be of order 256. Each of its 256 rows and each of its 256 columns contains each of the 256 possible byte values once.

A Latin square can strengthen a stream cipher. Recall that a stream cipher uses an XOR to combine a plainbit a and a key bit b to the cipherbit $a \oplus b$. Employing an order-n Latin square, such a cipher can combine n plainbits and n key bits to form n cipherbits. A detailed description of this method can be found in [Ritter 04].

1	3	2	5	6	4
5	1	4	6	3	2
4	3	1	5	2	6
5	3	2	1	4	6
2	1	4	3	5	6
4	2	1	5	3	6

A 6×6 Latin Square.

10.8 SEAL Stream Cipher

SEAL (software-optimized encryption algorithm) is a stream cipher that was specifically designed for efficient software implementation on 32-bit processors [Coppersmith and Rogaway 94, 95]. SEAL is a length-increasing pseudorandom function that employs a 160-bit encryption key a to map a 32-bit sequence number n to an L-bit output. In the preprocessing stage (step 1 of Figure 10.9), the key is stretched into larger tables using the table-generation function $Ga(i)$ specified in Figure 10.10. This function is based on the secure hash algorithm SHA-1 [Salomon 03]. Following the preprocessing, each byte of generated output requires about five machine instructions. SEAL is an order of magnitude faster than DES (Section 11.3). Version 2 of SEAL has a modified table-generation function that is based on the modified SHA-1. The following notation is used in SEAL for the 32-bit quantities A, B, C, D, X_i, and Y_j.

- $\overline{A}$: bitwise complement of A.

- $A \wedge B$, $A \vee B$, $A \oplus B$: bitwise AND, OR, and XOR.

- $A \leftarrow s$: rotating the 32-bit A to the left s positions.

- $A \rightarrow s$: rotating the 32-bit A to the right s positions.

- $A + B$: the sum (modulo 2^{32}) of the unsigned integers A and B.

SEAL(a, n)

INPUT: a 160-bit encryption key a, a nonsecret integer n, $0 \leq n < 2^{32}$ (the sequence number), and the desired bitlength L of the output.

OUTPUT: bitstream y of length L', where L' is the smallest multiple of 128 that is still $\geq L$.

1. *Table generation.* Generate tables T, S, and R, with 32-bit entries.
   Define $Fa(i) = H_{i \bmod 5}^i$, where $H_0^i H_1^i H_2^i H_3^i H_4^i = Ga(\lfloor i/5 \rfloor)$.

   1.1 For i from 0 to 511 do: $T[i] \leftarrow F_a(i)$.

   1.2 For j from 0 to 255 do: $S[j] \leftarrow F_a(0x00001000 + j)$.

   1.3 For k from 0 to $4 \cdot \lceil (L-1)/8192 \rceil - 1$ do: $R[k] \leftarrow F_a(0x00002000 + k)$.

2. *Initialization procedure.* The following is a description of subroutine
   Initialize$(n, l, A, B, C, D, n_1, n_2, n_3, n_4)$, which takes as input a 32-bit word n and an integer l, and outputs eight 32-bit words A, B, C, D, n_1, n_2, n_3, n_4. This subroutine is used in Step 4.

   $A \leftarrow n \oplus R[4l]$, $\ B \leftarrow (n \rightharpoonup 8) \oplus R[4l+1]$, $\ C \leftarrow (n \rightharpoonup 16) \oplus R[4l+2]$,
   $D \leftarrow (n \rightharpoonup 24) \oplus R[4l+3]$.

   For j from 1 to 2 do:
   $\quad P \leftarrow A \wedge 0x000007fc$, $\ B \leftarrow B + T[P/4]$, $\ A \leftarrow (A \rightharpoonup 9)$,
   $\quad P \leftarrow B \wedge 0x000007fc$, $\ C \leftarrow C + T[P/4]$, $\ B \leftarrow (B \rightharpoonup 9)$,
   $\quad P \leftarrow C \wedge 0x000007fc$, $\ D \leftarrow D + T[P/4]$, $\ C \leftarrow (C \rightharpoonup 9)$,
   $\quad P \leftarrow D \wedge 0x000007fc$, $\ A \leftarrow A + T[P/4]$, $\ D \leftarrow (D \rightharpoonup 9)$.
   $(n_1, n_2, n_3, n_4) \leftarrow (D, B, A, C)$.
   $P \leftarrow A \wedge 0x000007fc$, $\ B \leftarrow B + T[P/4]$, $\ A \leftarrow (A \rightharpoonup 9)$.
   $P \leftarrow B \wedge 0x000007fc$, $\ C \leftarrow C + T[P/4]$, $\ B \leftarrow (B \rightharpoonup 9)$.
   $P \leftarrow C \wedge 0x000007fc$, $\ D \leftarrow D + T[P/4]$, $\ C \leftarrow (C \rightharpoonup 9)$.
   $P \leftarrow D \wedge 0x000007fc$, $\ A \leftarrow A + T[P/4]$, $\ D \leftarrow (D \rightharpoonup 9)$.

3. Initialize y to the empty string, and l to 0.

4. Repeat the following:

   4.1 Execute procedure Initialize$(n, l, A, B, C, D, n_1, n_2, n_3, n_4)$.

   4.2 For i from 1 to 64 do:
   $P \leftarrow A \wedge 0x000007fc$, $\ B \leftarrow B + T[P/4]$, $\ A \leftarrow (A \rightharpoonup 9)$, $\ B \leftarrow B \oplus A$,
   $Q \leftarrow B \wedge 0x000007fc$, $\ C \leftarrow C \oplus T[Q/4]$, $\ B \leftarrow (B \rightharpoonup 9)$, $\ C \leftarrow C + B$,
   $P \leftarrow (P + C) \wedge 0x000007fc$, $\ D \leftarrow D + T[P/4]$, $\ C \leftarrow (C \rightharpoonup 9)$, $\ D \leftarrow D \oplus C$,
   $Q \leftarrow (Q + D) \wedge 0x000007fc$, $\ A \leftarrow A \oplus T[Q/4]$, $\ D \leftarrow (D \rightharpoonup 9)$, $\ A \leftarrow A + D$,
   $P \leftarrow (P + A) \wedge 0x000007fc$, $\ B \leftarrow B \oplus T[P/4]$, $\ A \leftarrow (A \rightharpoonup 9)$,
   $Q \leftarrow (Q + B) \wedge 0x000007fc$, $\ C \leftarrow C + T[Q/4]$, $\ B \leftarrow (B \rightharpoonup 9)$,
   $P \leftarrow (P + C) \wedge 0x000007fc$, $\ D \leftarrow D \oplus T[P/4]$, $\ C \leftarrow (C \rightharpoonup 9)$,
   $Q \leftarrow (Q + D) \wedge 0x000007fc$, $\ A \leftarrow A + T[Q/4]$, $\ D \leftarrow (D \rightharpoonup 9)$,
   $y \leftarrow y \| (B + S[4i-4]) \| (C \oplus S[4i-3]) \| (D + S[4i-2]) \| (A \oplus S[4i-1])$.
   If $y \geq L$ bits in length then return(y) and stop.
   If i is odd, set $(A, C) \leftarrow (A + n_1, C + n_2)$. Otherwise, $(A, C) \leftarrow (A + n_3, C + n_4)$.

   4.3 Set $l \leftarrow l + 1$.

Figure 10.9: SEAL Main Algorithm.

Function $Ga(i)$
INPUT: a 160-bit string a and an integer i, $0 \leq i < 2^{32}$.
OUTPUT: a 160-bit string, denoted by $Ga(i)$.

1. *Definition of constants.* Four 32-bit constants: $y_1 = 5a827999_{16}$,
   $y_2 = 6ed9eba1_{16}$, $y_3 = 8f1bbcdc_{16}$, $y_4 = ca62c1d6_{16}$.

2. *Table-generation function.*
   (*initialize 80 32-bit words $X_0, X_1, \ldots, X_{79}$*)
   Set $X_0 \leftarrow i$. For j from 1 to 15 do: $X_j \leftarrow 00000000_{16}$.
   For j from 16 to 79 do: $X_j \leftarrow ((X_{j-3} \oplus X_{j-8} \oplus X_{j-14} \oplus X_{j-16}) \hookleftarrow 1)$.
   (*initialize working variables*)
   Break up the 160-bit string a into five 32-bit words: $a = H_0 H_1 H_2 H_3 H_4$.
   $(A, B, C, D, E) \leftarrow (H_0, H_1, H_2, H_3, H_4)$.
   (*execute four rounds of 20 steps, then update; t is a temporary variable*)
   (*Round 1*) For j from 0 to 19 do:
   $t \leftarrow ((A \hookleftarrow 5) + f(B, C, D) + E + X_j + y_1)$,
   $(A, B, C, D, E) \leftarrow (t, A, B \hookleftarrow 30, C, D)$.
   (*Round 2*) For j from 20 to 39 do:
   $t \leftarrow ((A \hookleftarrow 5) + h(B, C, D) + E + X_j + y_2)$,
   $(A, B, C, D, E) \leftarrow (t, A, B \hookleftarrow 30, C, D)$.
   (*Round 3*) For j from 40 to 59 do:
   $t \leftarrow ((A \hookleftarrow 5) + g(B, C, D) + E + X_j + y_3)$,
   $(A, B, C, D, E) \leftarrow (t, A, B \hookleftarrow 30, C, D)$.
   (*Round 4*) For j from 60 to 79 do:
   $t \leftarrow ((A \hookleftarrow 5) + h(B, C, D) + E + X_j + y_4)$,
   $(A, B, C, D, E) \leftarrow (t, A, B \hookleftarrow 30, C, D)$.
   (*update chaining values*)
   $(H_0, H_1, H_2, H_3, H_4) \leftarrow (H_0 + A, H_1 + B, H_2 + C, H_3 + D, H_4 + E)$.

(*completion*) The value of $Ga(i)$ is the 160-bit string $H_0 \| H_1 \| H_2 \| H_3 \| H_4$.

Figure 10.10: SEAL Table-Generation Function $Ga(i)$.

- $f(B, C, D) \stackrel{\text{def}}{=} (B \wedge C) \vee (\overline{B} \wedge D)$.

- $g(B, C, D) \stackrel{\text{def}}{=} (B \wedge C) \vee (B \wedge D) \vee (C \wedge D)$.

- $h(B, C, D) \stackrel{\text{def}}{=} B \oplus C \oplus D$.

- $A \| B$: concatenation of A and B.

- $(X_1, \ldots, X_j) \leftarrow (Y_1, \ldots, Y_j)$: assignment $(X_i \leftarrow Y_i)$, where $(Y_1, \ldots, Y_j)$ is evaluated prior to the assignment.

  Note: Step 2 of Figure 10.10 (table generation) uses the compression function of SHA-1 to expand the encryption key a into tables T, S, and R. These tables can be precomputed once the key a has been chosen. Tables T and S are 2 K bytes and 1 K bytes long, respectively. The size of table R depends on the desired bitlength L of the output. Each 1 K bytes of output requires 16 bytes of R.

In most applications of SEAL 2.0, it is expected that $L \le 2^{19}$. Larger values of L are possible, but they increase the size of table R. A longer nonrepeating output can be generated without increasing R by concatenating the outputs of SEAL$(a, 0)$, SEAL$(a, 1)$,.... Since the sequence number satisfies $n < 2^{32}$, an output string of length up to 2^{51} bits can be obtained in this manner with $L = 2^{19}$.

The man who is swimming against
the stream knows the strength of it.
—Woodrow Wilson

11
Block Ciphers

A block cipher encrypts a message by breaking it up into (normally equal-size) blocks, encrypting each block independently of the other blocks, and turning each block of plaintext (plainblock) into a block of ciphertext (cipherblock) that has the same size. The same algorithm is used to encrypt all the blocks, and this algorithm should preferably be symmetric (or reversible). A reversible algorithm simplifies any implementations (software or hardware) because the same processes used to encrypt a block can also be used to decrypt it. It is possible to generate cipherblocks that are shorter than the plainblocks by simply using a compression method to compress the ciphertext once it has been created. It is also possible to end up with cipherblocks longer than the plainblocks by adding parity bits or employing any error-detection or error-correction code. However, cryptography, compression, and reliable codes are three separate disciplines, so modern cryptography limits itself to securing data.

Modern block ciphers are widely used today to secure many different types of data. These ciphers are well understood, are easy to implement in both software and hardware, and can be designed to use simple operations and therefore be fast in both encryption and decryption. Block ciphers are symmetric because they use a single private key shared by sender and receiver to both encrypt and decrypt. The main block cipher methods currently in use are DES (Section 11.3), Blowfish, IDEA, RC5, and Rijndael (also known as AES). The last four methods are described in [Salomon 03].

A simple block cipher that operates on 64-bit blocks can be designed as a substitution table. A block of plaintext is used as an index to the table and is encrypted by substituting it with the table entry to which it points. Each table entry is a random, 64-bit number. To decrypt a 64-bit cipherblock, the table is searched for the block, and the table index becomes the plainblock. Searching the table is inefficient, which is why a practical block cipher should be more sophisticated. Also, the table is very large because the number of 64-bit blocks is $2^{64} \approx 1.8 \times 10^{19}$ and each table entry has to be 64 bits or eight bytes. A practical approach must use smaller tables, and current algorithms use the principles developed by [Shannon 49 and 51].

⋄ **Exercise 11.1:** The security of an encryption algorithm is in the key. What is the key of the simple block cipher with a single substitution table?

Another way to design a simple block cipher is to permute each plainblock. A block of, say, 64 bits is scrambled by permuting its bits. Decoding is done with the reverse permutation, so it makes sense to use a permutation that is its own inverse—an involutary permutation.

Better block ciphers employ both substitution and permutation, or even several steps of substitution and permutation. Thus, they are substitution–permutation (SP) ciphers.

11.1 Substitution–Permutation Ciphers

Shannon's theory of secrecy systems showed that the Vernam cipher (Section 6.3) is the only absolutely secure cipher, provided that the key is random and is used only once. It also showed that a book cipher is not secure because the book is written in a certain language and the statistical properties of the language are reflected in the ciphertext.

Shannon introduced the substitution–permutation (SP) ciphers in 1949, and these techniques serve as the basis of modern block ciphers. An SP cipher is based on combining two simple operations, substitution and permutation, in a complex way, using the bits of the key and perhaps also using several layers or rounds in order to completely scramble the bits of the plaintext and eliminate any possible patterns that may have existed in them.

A substitution is done with a table (commonly referred to as an S-box). The plainblock is divided into small groups of k bits each, where k is typically in the range 4 (for old algorithms) to 12 (for new methods, reflecting the increased power of recent computers), and each group is used as an index (or a pointer) to an S-box with 2^k entries. The group is then replaced (substituted) by the content of the box entry it has selected. Thus, if the S-box, the group, and the result are denoted by S, G, and C, respectively, then $C = S[G]$. If a block consists of g groups, then each group should be substituted with a different S-box, for added security. An alternative is to have a small number of different boxes, and in each round use some of the key bits to select a box for each group.

In the simplest case, each S-box entry is the same size as G, so the substitution replaces a group G of k bits with a result C of the same size. Figure 11.1a shows an example of an S-box with $2^3 = 8$ entries, each three bits wide. A group $110(= 6)$ selects entry 6 in this S-box, and outputs 011. It is also possible to have S-boxes with 2^k entries, where each entry is fewer than k bits. The DES algorithm (Section 11.3), for example, uses S-boxes with 64 entries each (requiring 6-bit pointers), where each entry has 4 bits. Each S-box replaces 6 bits of plaintext with 4 bits, so 8 S-boxes are needed in order to generate a 32-bit block. These require a total of $8 \times 6 = 48$ bits of pointer, and those bits are generated by duplicating some bits in the 32-bit plainblock (Figure 11.10).

S-boxes are easy to implement in software (where each box is an array) as well as in hardware (where a box is a small ROM). However, partitioning the plainblock into groups, using each group as a pointer, and combining the individual outputs of the S-boxes are all easier and faster to implement in hardware.

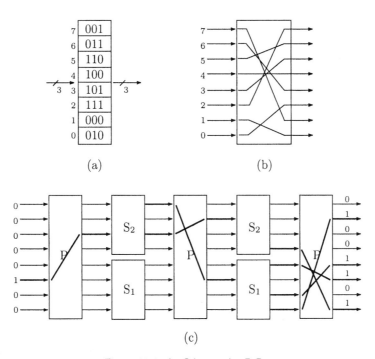

Figure 11.1: An S-box and a P-Box.

A permutation (naturally called a P-box, or just P) reorders the bits of a group. Figure 11.1b shows an example where bit 0 is moved to position 2 and bit 1 is moved to position 0. A permutation is easy to implement in hardware by simply running a wire from each input to one of the outputs. In software, a permutation can be implemented with a series of logical operations that isolate the individual bits and move each to a new position, a slow process. The number of permutations of n objects is $n!$, a number that grows very fast with n.

Conquering the past, the word gives legitimacy to explanations that presume it. Thus it implies some carrying device, i.e., a system of notation as a built-in memory and as a mechanism for associations, permutations, and substitutions.

—Mihai Nadin, *The Civilization of Illiteracy* (1997)

A substitution–permutation (SP) network as envisioned by Shannon (who called it *mixing transformation*) consists of alternating P-boxes and S-boxes as shown in Figure 11.1c. The figure shows how one bit of the input affects several output bits (four in the figure) of the network. An SP network is an example of a *product cipher*, a cipher consisting of several stages, where the output of each stage becomes the input of its successor. Not every product cipher increases security. Two consecutive substitutions are just one complex substitution. Similarly, two consecutive transpositions are just one complex transposition. However, a product cipher with one substitution stage and one transposition stage is more secure than a single-stage cipher. Modern block ciphers are therefore product ciphers, alternating between stages (rounds) of substitution and permutation.

◇ **Exercise 11.2:** Is it possible for one bit of the input block to affect all the bits of the output block?

Notice that a P-box can have a large number of inputs, but the number of input bits to an S-box is small. Thus, a single P-box can feed several S-boxes. In order to be practical, an SP network has to be reversible. Ideally, decrypting a cipherblock should be done by passing it through the network in the reverse direction. An important step in this direction is the *Feistel cipher*, developed by Horst Feistel at IBM in the late 1960s and early 1970s.

Horst Feistel

Born in Germany in 1915, Dr. Horst Feistel found himself emigrating to the United States in 1934, an unfortunate time both politically (with the Nazis in power in Germany) and economically (with the worldwide great depression at its peak) for immigrants from Europe and especially from Germany. In 1941, while he was trying to obtain United States citizenship, the country entered World War II. Feistel was investigated as a possible spy and placed under house arrest until 1944. To avoid provoking the authorities, he kept quiet about his interest in cryptography until after the war, when he went to work for the United States Air Force, pursuing his interest in developing new ciphers.

Ciphers were the NSA's domain, and this newly established agency didn't want the Air Force to do independent work on secret codes. Under pressure from the NSA, Feistel had to give up his research. He went to work for the Mitre Corporation in the 1960s and again worked on ciphers. Once more the NSA intervened with his superiors to stop his work. The NSA did not object to his German background, nor did they suspect him of being a spy. They simply wanted to keep the field to themselves. Finally, Feistel went to work for IBM and was able to work on ciphers more or less unmolested by the NSA. He came up with the principles of Feistel ciphers in the late 1960s and with Lucifer in the early 1970s. Among the data encryption patents issued to Feistel are 3,768,359, 3,768,360 and 4,316,055.

After developing Lucifer, Feistel was left with no major projects to work on and was eased out of IBM a few years later. He died in 1990.

The encryption process of a Feistel cipher is to (1) partition the input block into two halves, L and R, (2) perform several rounds to scramble the bits of each half, (3) modify only R in each round, and (4) exchange the two halves. Thus, the new R becomes the XOR of the previous L and the previous (scrambled) R, while the new L is just a copy of the old R. One round is illustrated in Figure 11.2.

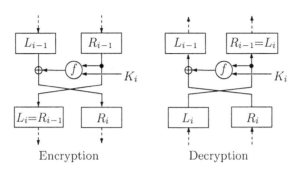

Encryption   Decryption

Figure 11.2: One Round of a Feistel Cipher.

Function f is used to scramble the bits of R. It consists of one stage of the SP network and also employs a subset K_i of the key K, a subset known as a subkey. This design makes it easy to decrypt. Decryption is done by performing the rounds in reverse order, from last to first, and reversing the operations in each round, as shown in Figure 11.2. Thus, an encryption round consists of the steps $L_i = R_{i-1}$ and $R_i = L_{i-1} \oplus f(R_{i-1}, K_i)$. Similarly, a decryption round is done by $R_{i-1} = L_i$ and $L_{i-1} = R_i \oplus f(L_i, K_i)$. The only difference between encryption and decryption is the order in which the subkeys have to be generated. This illustrates how a Feistel cipher adopts the principles of Shannon's SP network and employs them in an easily inverted structure.

⋄ **Exercise 11.3:** What property of the XOR is exploited in a Feistel cipher to make it reversible?

To see how decryption works, we start with R_{i-1}. During decryption, this quantity is set to L_i, but L_i was originally set, during encryption, to R_{i-1}. Thus, decryption restores R_{i-1} to its original value. On the other side, L_{i-1} is set during decryption to $R_i \oplus f(L_i, K_i)$, but R_i was originally set, during encryption, to $L_{i-1} \oplus f(R_{i-1}, K_i)$. This results in

$$L_{i-1} \leftarrow R_i \oplus f(L_i, K_i) \leftarrow \big(L_{i-1} \oplus f(R_{i-1}, K_i)\big) \oplus f(L_i, K_i) = L_{i-1}.$$

(The last equality is true because decryption sets R_{i-1} to L_i.)

A good block cipher should have the following properties.

1. It should create confusion of input bits by means of the S-boxes.
2. P-boxes should create diffusion across S-box inputs.

Diffusion and Confusion

The aim in a block cipher, as in any other cipher, is to eliminate any statistically significant features that may exist in the plaintext and to create ciphertext that cannot be distinguished from random. Shannon has coined the terms *diffusion* and *confusion* for two general approaches used to achieve this aim. Diffusion is a general name for any encryption technique that spreads (or smears) the statistical properties of the plaintext over a range of bits of the ciphertext. Diffusion causes each small part of plaintext to affect a large part of the ciphertext, thereby diffusing the statistical properties of the plaintext. In block ciphers, diffusion is achieved by the various permutations (P-boxes). Each permutation spreads the outputs of the S-boxes preceding it widely into the next stage. (Note that P-boxes by themselves are not enough; S-boxes are also needed to create diffusion.) Confusion is a term referring to any method that makes the statistical relationship between the ciphertext and the key as difficult as possible. This is achieved mainly by a complex, nonlinear substitution operation. In block ciphers, confusion is created by the S-boxes.

---

3. Switching the value of one bit in a plainblock should result in a cipherblock where approximately half the bits are switched. This is termed the *avalanche effect*. In a block cipher with good avalanche, small changes to the plaintext cause significant changes to the ciphertext. An attacker who obtains or guesses a good approximation to the plaintext would still end up with a key that is very different from the correct one.

4. Each ciphertext bit should be a function of all the plaintext bits and this function should be as complex as possible. This is the *completeness effect*. Completeness ensures that an attacker would be unable to successfully perform a "divide and conquer" attack on the ciphertext.

5. The design parameters should be chosen carefully. Those parameters include the block size (large sizes increase security but slow down both encryption and decryption), the key size (large key size slows execution but improves security because it makes a brute-force approach less practical), number of rounds (a larger number slows down algorithm execution but increases security because the input bits are scrambled more thoroughly), subkey computation (complex computations of the subkeys make it harder to cryptanalyze the cipher), and the function f that provides diffusion and confusion. Thus, a good block cipher design involves compromises or tradeoffs in selecting these parameters.

These properties are important in any type of cipher, but they are generally not found in classical ciphers.

We end this discussion of block ciphers with a few details about avalanche and completeness. We assume a block size of 64 bits. Avalanche can be measured by selecting a bit b in a plainblock and then varying the remaining 63 bits in every one of the 2^{63} possible ways and encrypting the block. This results in 2^{63} cipherblocks. Next, negate (complement) b; then repeat the process. This results in another set of 2^{63} cipherblocks. Now compare every pair of corresponding cipherblocks. For each of the

2^{63} pairs, record the number of bits by which they differ. The average of this number should be 32. This process should be repeated for each of the 64 bits b in the plainblock.

Completeness can be measured by first selecting a bit c in a cipherblock. Now go over all 64 bits of the plainblock, and, for each bit, try to find two plainblocks that differ in that bit and whose encryptions result in two cipherblocks where only bit c differs. If this is successful, repeat for another cipherbit c. If this process is successful for all 64 cipherbits c, then the algorithm has perfect completeness.

> Truth emerges more readily from error than from confusion.
>
> —Francis Bacon

11.2 Lucifer

After developing the principles of block ciphers over several years, IBM cryptographer Horst Feistel designed an actual block cipher. Both the program for developing a block cipher and the actual cipher were named Lucifer. Feistel hoped to incorporate Lucifer in various pieces of IBM equipment. Even though very certain of his algorithm, he kept most of its details secret when he first published it [Feistel 73]. A much later publication [Sorkin 84] includes the details.

Lucifer uses 128-bit blocks, 16 rounds, and a 128-bit key. Each round extracts the 64 leftmost bits of the key as the current subkey and then rotates the key to the left 56 positions. The result is that all the key bits are used in various subkeys in the 16 rounds, but in different positions. This simple way of computing the subkeys was later shown to be a design deficiency. Figure 11.3a shows the main steps in each round.

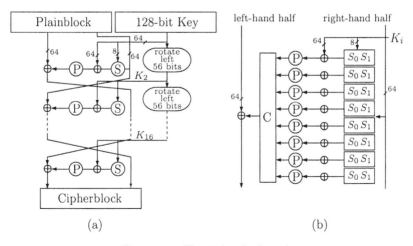

Figure 11.3: The 16 Lucifer Rounds.

In each round, the current subkey and the right-hand half are input to an SP network function (Figure 11.3b) whose output is XORed with the left-hand half before the two halves are exchanged. The SP function feeds the 64-bit right-hand input into eight identical pairs (i.e., a total of 16), 4-bit S-boxes where the order of the two boxes of a pair is determined by one bit of the subkey. As a result, the eight leftmost bits of the subkey are fed into the S-boxes in order to determine the order of the two boxes in each of the eight pairs. (Each pair of S-boxes can therefore be visualized as one S-box with nine inputs and eight outputs.) The output of the S-boxes is then XORed with the 64 bits of the current subkey and the result fed into a P-box. This box is a combination of small 8-bit P-boxes and one large 128-bit permutation.

Lucifer has never been extensively used, and its security has been shown to be an illusion. It is now known that Lucifer can be broken by differential cryptanalysis [Schneier 93]. Consequently, its main claim to fame is for being the basis for the development of the data encryption standard (DES, Section 11.3).

11.3 The Data Encryption Standard

The data encryption standard (DES) has been a popular encryption method since the mid-1970s and has resisted attacks by many cryptanalysts armed with faster and faster computers. Other names for DES are DEA (data encryption algorithm) and DEA-1.

In the late 1960s, with computers becoming more commonly used by industry, more and more nongovernment users started to feel a need for a fast, secure, and widespread encryption standard that would be implemented on many computers (and perhaps also in special hardware) and would allow easy and secure exchange of sensitive messages. At the time, several encryption algorithms and cipher machines were available, but no one could ascertain their security, and they were incompatible. Therefore, the National Bureau of Standards (NBS, now NIST) issued in 1972 a request for proposals for a standard encryption/decryption algorithm. The request specified the following set of design criteria.

1. The cryptographic algorithm must be secure to a high degree.
2. The details of the algorithm should be described in an easy-to-understand language.
3. The security of the algorithm must depend on the key, not on keeping the method itself (or parts of it) secret.
4. The details of the algorithm must be publicly available so that anyone could implement it in software or hardware.
5. The method must be adaptable for use in many applications.
6. Hardware implementations of the algorithm must be practical (i.e., not prohibitively expensive or extremely slow).
7. The method must be efficient (i.e., fast and with reasonable memory requirements).
8. It should be possible to test and validate the algorithm under real-life conditions.
9. The algorithm should be exportable (for a discussion of the importance of this feature, see [Levy 01]).

A number of proposals were very quickly submitted, but none came close to meeting all the requirements. This proved to the NBS that there was an interest in such a standard, but not the necessary knowledge. A second request was issued in 1974 and resulted in the submission of one promising algorithm, developed by a team at IBM and based on a previous IBM design developed in the early 1970s, mostly by Horst Feistel and known as Lucifer (Section 11.2). The NBS sent this algorithm to the NSA for its evaluation, received a response with requests for changes (mostly in cutting the key size from 128 to 56 bits and in the design of the S-boxes; see Section 11.3.1), and eventually also received a free, nonexclusive license from IBM to publish the algorithm and to implement it in hardware. The details of the method were published in 1975, along with a request for comments from the public. The comments, when they came, were mainly concerns about the NSA adding a trapdoor to the algorithm so that the agency would be able to decipher messages easily. Today, it seems that the changes proposed by the NSA made the algorithm more efficient but not vulnerable. After debating the algorithm in two NBS-sponsored workshops, the DES was adopted, in 1976, as a United States federal encryption standard to become effective in July 1977. It has been reaffirmed since in five-year intervals in 1983, 1988, 1993, and 1999.

In 1981, the American National Standards Institute (ANSI) adopted DES as an encryption standard in the private sector. It became known as DEA or ANSI X3.92. The International Standards Organization (ISO) adopted DES as its standard in 1987 and called it DEA-1.

The description in this section is based on [DES 99], a United States government publication titled *The Federal Information Processing Standard (FIPS) 46-3*. This publication describes both DES and Triple DES (TDEA, Section 11.3.3). The latter method is an extension of DES, developed to keep DES secure in the face of advances in computing power during the 1990s. Currently, the complete data encryption standard consists of the data encryption algorithm (DES) and the triple data encryption algorithm (TDEA). Detailed analyses of DES can be found in [Simovits 96] and [Barker 89].

DES is a symmetric algorithm. The same operations are performed for encryption and decryption, with the exception of computing the subkeys. In accordance with Kerckhoffs' principle, the DES algorithm has been published in detail, and the security of DES encryption depends entirely on the key. The key is a 64-bit (or 8-byte) number, of which 56 bits constitute the actual key and the remaining 8 bits are used for error detection. Each of those bits is odd parity for one of the 8 bytes of the key. Before the key is used to encrypt or decrypt, the parity bits are verified and discarded. The total number of keys is therefore $2^{56} \approx 7.2 \times 10^{16}$. This is a huge number (see Exercise 6.4), but certain keys are weak and should be avoided (Section 11.3.1).

DES operates on blocks of 64 bits, where the bits are numbered from left (1) to right (64). A block of 64 plaintext bits is encrypted into a block of 64 ciphertext bits.

The encryption of a block starts with an initial permutation IP, followed by 16 rounds of involved computations that employ the key, and ends with a final permutation IP^{-1} that is the inverse of IP. The key-dependent computation is defined in terms of two functions, the cipher function, denoted by f, and the key schedule function KS. The main steps are shown in Figure 11.4, where the quantities K_i are derived by function KS from the key.

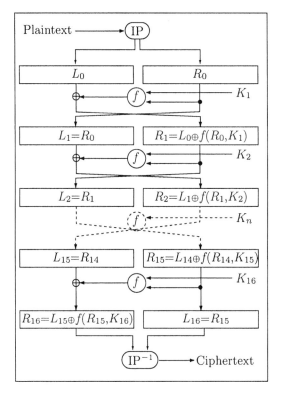

Figure 11.4: The 16 DES Rounds.

The initial permutation is listed in Table 11.5, which should be read left-to-right, top-to-bottom. The table shows, for example, that bit 58 of the block should be moved to position 1, bit 50 should be moved to position 2, and bit 7 should be moved to position 64. The combination of initial and final permutations does not add any security to DES, and these permutations, which are time consuming when performed by software, are left out by many software implementations of DES (although, strictly speaking, such implementations should not be called DES). It is easy, however, to perform these permutations in hardware, which may be the reason for their inclusion in the standard. (Notice how IP brings bits 64, 56, 48, 40, 32, 24, 16, and 8 together to form the fourth byte [from the left] of the new block. These bits are the least significant bits of the eight bytes that constitute the original block. Similarly, bits 57, 49, 41, 33, 25, 17, 9, and 1 are collected and concatenated to form the fifth byte. These are the most significant bits of the eight bytes of the original block. It seems that IP was designed this way for easy operation on 8-bit-based hardware, because such hardware was common in the 1970s.)

When round 1 starts, the IP-permuted block of 64 plaintext bits is broken up into two 32-bit halves L_0 and R_0. Function f is applied to R_0 and the subkey K_1, and

58	50	42	34	26	18	10	2	60	52	44	36	28	20	12	4
62	54	46	38	30	22	14	6	64	56	48	40	32	24	16	8
57	49	41	33	25	17	9	1	59	51	43	35	27	19	11	3
61	53	45	37	29	21	13	5	63	55	47	39	31	23	15	7

Table 11.5: The Initial Permutation (IP).

the result is XORed with L_0 to become R_1. The name of R_0 is changed to L_1, and the next round is performed in a similar fashion on L_1 and R_1 with subkey K_2. This process continues for 16 rounds and results in R_{16} and L_{16}, which are concatenated (with R_{16} on the left, as in Figure 11.4) and permuted according to IP^{-1} to obtain a 64-bit block of ciphertext. Thus, the two main steps of round i are $L_i = R_{i-1}$ and $R_i = L_{i-1} \oplus f(R_{i-1}, K_i)$.

Function KS is described next. It is responsible for generating the 16 subkeys K_i. The original 64-bit key consists of eight bytes whose least significant bits are parity bits for error detection. After the eight parities have been verified, the parity bits are stripped off, and the remaining 56 bits are permuted and divided into two 28-bit halves denoted by C_0 and D_0, as shown in Table 11.6 (this is designated *key permutation 1*).

C_0 57 49 41 33 25 17 9 1 58 50 42 34 26 18 10 2 59 51 43 35 27 19 11 3 60 52 44 36
D_0 63 55 47 39 31 23 15 7 62 54 46 38 30 22 14 6 61 53 45 37 29 21 13 5 28 20 12 4

Table 11.6: The 56-Bit Key Permutation 1.

For each round, a 48-bit subkey K_i (where $i = 1, 2, \ldots, 16$) is obtained (Figure 11.9) in the following steps.

1. Rotate C_{i-1} and D_{i-1} to the left the number of positions determined by Table 11.7.

1	2	3	4	5	6	7	8	9	10	11	12	13	14	15	16
1	1	2	2	2	2	2	2	1	2	2	2	2	2	2	1

Table 11.7: Sixteen Key Rotations.

2. Concatenate the two rotated parts and select the 48 bits specified by Table 11.8 (this is designated *key permutation 2*).

14 17 11 24 1 5 3 28 15 6 21 10 23 19 12 4 26 8 16 7 27 20 13 2
41 52 31 37 47 55 30 40 51 45 33 48 44 49 39 56 34 53 46 42 50 36 29 32

Table 11.8: Key Permutation 2.

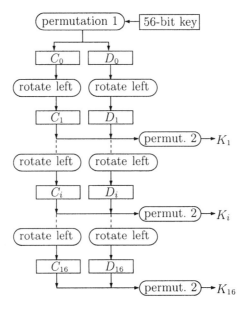

Figure 11.9: Subkey Computation.

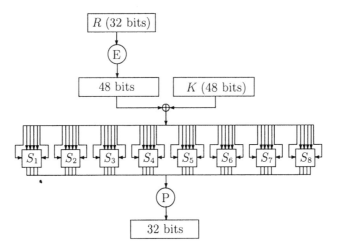

Figure 11.10: Function f.

These steps yield a 48-bit subkey computed from the 56-bit key, which is why function KS is called a *compression permutation*.

The main steps of function f are as follows (Figure 11.10).

1. The 32 bits of R_i are expanded to 48 bits by the expansion permutation E.
2. The resulting 48 bits are XORed with the 48 bits of the current subkey K_{i+1}.
3. The 48 bits created by step 2 are separated into eight groups of 6 bits each, and each group is used as the input of an S-box, which outputs 4 bits.
4. The 32 bits output by the eight S-boxes are permuted by the P-box. The result is the output of function f.

32	1	2	3	4	5	4	5	6	7	8	9	8	9	10	11	12	13	12	13	14	15	16	17
16	17	18	19	20	21	20	21	22	23	24	25	24	25	26	27	28	29	28	29	30	31	32	1

Table 11.11: Bit Positions For the E-Box.

The expansion permutation E is illustrated in Table 11.11 and Figure 11.12. Thus, the three leftmost bits of E are the bits in positions 32, 1, and 2 of R_i, while the rightmost two bits of E are the bits in positions 32 and 1. The main point here is that some of the bits output from the E-box are identical. As a result, the same bit from R_i goes into two different S-boxes. This spreads out the dependence of the cipherbits on the plainbits. Recall that the main aim of an encryption algorithm is to create ciphertext that looks random and lacks any patterns that may exist in the plaintext. One reason why DES is so secure is that every bit of the final ciphertext depends on every bit of the input plaintext and on every bit of the key. This feature is obtained by the bit duplication in the E-box as well as by the many rounds.

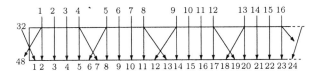

Figure 11.12: Operation of the E-Box.

The 48 bits produced by the E-box are divided into eight groups of 6 bits each, and each group becomes the input of one of the eight S-boxes shown in Figure 11.10 (where "S" stands for "substitution"). An S-box is a 4×16 array of 4-bit numbers and the contents of all eight S-boxes are listed in Table 11.13. The two extreme inputs to an S-box select one of its four rows (numbered 0 through 3 from top to bottom), and the four middle inputs select one of the 16 columns. The output of the S-box is the number found at that position. For example, if the 6-bit input to S_5 is 101110, then row 10 and column 0111 are selected, and 8 is output. This stage outputs $8 \times 4 = 32$ bits.

Conceptually, an S-box is a two-dimensional structure, which requires two indexes to access. In practice, it can be implemented as a one-dimensional array with 64 locations, where the entire 6-bit input is used as a single index. An S-box is visualized

S_1

14	4	13	1	2	15	11	8	3	10	6	12	5	9	0	7
0	15	7	4	14	2	13	1	10	6	12	11	9	5	3	8
4	1	14	8	13	6	2	11	15	12	9	7	3	10	5	0
15	12	8	2	4	9	1	7	5	11	3	14	10	0	6	13

S_2

15	1	8	14	6	11	3	4	9	7	2	13	12	0	5	10
3	13	4	7	15	2	8	14	12	0	1	10	6	9	11	5
0	14	7	11	10	4	13	1	5	8	12	6	9	3	2	15
13	8	10	1	3	15	4	2	11	6	7	12	0	5	14	9

S_3

10	0	9	14	6	3	15	5	1	13	12	7	11	4	2	8
13	7	0	9	3	4	6	10	2	8	5	14	12	11	15	1
13	6	4	9	8	15	3	0	11	1	2	12	5	10	14	7
1	10	13	0	6	9	8	7	4	15	14	3	11	5	2	12

S_4

7	13	14	3	0	6	9	10	1	2	8	5	11	12	4	15
13	8	11	5	6	15	0	3	4	7	2	12	1	10	14	9
10	6	9	0	12	11	7	13	15	1	3	14	5	2	8	4
3	15	0	6	10	1	13	8	9	4	5	11	12	7	2	14

S_5

2	12	4	1	7	10	11	6	8	5	3	15	13	0	14	9
14	11	2	12	4	7	13	1	5	0	15	10	3	9	8	6
4	2	1	11	10	13	7	8	15	9	12	5	6	3	0	14
11	8	12	7	1	14	2	13	6	15	0	9	10	4	5	3

S_6

12	1	10	15	9	2	6	8	0	13	3	4	14	7	5	11
10	15	4	2	7	12	9	5	6	1	13	14	0	11	3	8
9	14	15	5	2	8	12	3	7	0	4	10	1	13	11	6
4	3	2	12	9	5	15	10	11	14	1	7	6	0	8	13

S_7

4	11	2	14	15	0	8	13	3	12	9	7	5	10	6	1
13	0	11	7	4	9	1	10	14	3	5	12	2	15	8	6
1	4	11	13	12	3	7	14	10	15	6	8	0	5	9	2
6	11	13	8	1	4	10	7	9	5	0	15	14	2	3	12

S_8

13	2	8	4	6	15	11	1	10	9	3	14	5	0	12	7
1	15	13	8	10	3	7	4	12	5	6	11	0	14	9	2
7	11	4	1	9	12	14	2	0	6	10	13	15	3	5	8
2	1	14	7	4	10	8	13	15	12	9	0	3	5	6	11

Table 11.13: The Eight S-Boxes.

as having two dimensions because of the design criteria for those boxes. These criteria were determined by the developers of DES in the 1970s, and they are listed below.

1. An S-box should have six inputs and four outputs. (This small size was the largest that could be built on a single DES chip with 1970s technology.)

2. None of the four output bits of an S-box should be a linear function (or even close to a linear function) of the six input bits. (A linear function of bits is obtained by passing the bits through logic gates.)

3. If the two extreme input bits of an S-box are fixed and the four middle bits are varied, each of the 16 numbers 0 through 15 should be output exactly once. (This is why it is convenient to think of an S-box as a two-dimensional structure.)

4. If two inputs to an S-box differ by one bit, the corresponding outputs should differ by at least two bits.

5. If two inputs to an S-box differ in their two middle bits, the corresponding outputs should differ by at least two bits.

6. If two inputs to an S-box differ in their two leftmost bits and have identical two rightmost bits, the corresponding outputs should be different.

7. The 6-bit integers vary from $100000_2 = 32$ to $111111_2 = 63$. Imagine two 6-bit inputs to two different S-boxes. When these are arithmetically subtracted, the difference can be 0 (if the inputs are identical), 1 (if they differ slightly), 2 (if they differ more), and so on, up to a 6-bit difference. A 6-bit difference between two 6-bit integers is obtained in the following 32 cases: $32 - 0, 33 - 1, \ldots, 63 - 31$. Thus, this criterion says: If two S-boxes are fed one of the 32 pairs of those inputs, then at most 8 of the possible 32 output pairs may have the same difference (i.e., when each of the 32 pairs of outputs is subtracted, at most 8 differences will be the same).

8. This is similar to criterion 7 but for three S-boxes.

The S-boxes are another feature of DES that is easier to implement in hardware than in software. A hardware implementation uses a 6-bit input group as an address to a small read-only memory with 64 4-bit locations. In software, the concept is the same, but the S-box is an array. The 6-bit input is used as an index to the array, and the content of the location selected is the output of the S-box.

The 32 bits output by the S-boxes go through the P permutation, which is listed in Table 11.14. This is a regular permutation that places the 16th bit of its input in position 1, the 7th bit in position 2, and so on until the 25th bit of the input is placed in position 32.

$$16\ 7\ 20\ 21\ 29\ 12\ 28\ 17\ \ 1\ 15\ 23\ 26\ \ 5\ 18\ 31\ 10$$
$$2\ 8\ 24\ 14\ 32\ 27\ \ 3\ \ 9\ 19\ 13\ 30\ \ 6\ 22\ 11\ \ 4\ 25$$

Table 11.14: The P Permutation.

The criteria for the design of the P permutation are as follows.

1. The four output bits of each S-box in round n must be distributed such that two of them will affect the middle input bits of S-boxes in round $n + 1$ and the other two will affect the extreme input bits.

2. p The four outputs from an S-box should affect six different S-boxes in the next round, but no two output bits should affect the same S-box.
3. If an output bit from a box S_i affects (in the next round) one of the four middle input bits of another box S_j, then no output bit from S_j should affect any of the middle bits of S_i.

The final permutation IP^{-1} (Table 11.15) is the inverse of IP. Note in Figure 11.4 that the left and right halves are not swapped following round 16, so the 64-bit input to the final permutation is the block $R_{16}L_{16}$ and not $L_{16}R_{16}$.

40	8	48	16	56	24	64	32	39	7	47	15	55	23	63	31
38	6	46	14	54	22	62	30	37	5	45	13	53	21	61	29
36	4	44	12	52	20	60	28	35	3	43	11	51	19	59	27
34	2	42	10	50	18	58	26	33	1	41	9	49	17	57	25

Table 11.15: The Final Permutation (IP^{-1}).

DES Decryption. Even though DES completely scrambles the bits of the plaintext in its 16 rounds, which combine permutations, shifting, and XOR, its individual steps are designed to be reversible. Thus, DES decryption is the opposite of encryption, which makes DES easy to implement. Recall that the two encryption steps of round i are $L_i = R_{i-1}$ and $R_i = L_{i-1} \oplus f(R_{i-1}, K_i)$. The two steps for decryption are $R_{i-1} = L_i$ and $L_{i-1} = R_i \oplus f(L_i, K_i)$. Decryption therefore starts with the final permutation IP^{-1} and then performs 16 rounds where i is decremented from 16 to 1. The only difference between encryption and decryption is that decryption requires the subkeys K_i in reverse order, from K_{16} to K_1. As a result, when function KS is used for decryption, it performs a right rotation and the number of positions to rotate in the 16 reverse rounds is 0, 1, 2, 2, 2, 2, 2, 2, 1, 2, 2, 2, 2, 2, 2, and 1.

Modes of DES. DES can be used in four different modes as follows: the Electronic Codebook (ECB) mode, the Cipher Block Chaining (CBC) mode, the Cipher Feedback (CFB) mode, and the Output Feedback (OFB) mode. ECB is a direct application of the DES algorithm to encrypt and decrypt data. CBC is an enhanced mode of ECB that chains together blocks of ciphertext. CFB uses previously generated ciphertext as input to the DES to generate pseudorandom outputs that are combined with the plaintext to produce cipher, thereby chaining together the resulting cipher. OFB is an extension of CFB where the previous output of the DES is used as input in OFB while the previous cipher is used as input in CFB. OFB does not chain the cipher.

11.3.1 DES Security Issues

This short section discusses certain weaknesses that are either suspected to lurk in DES or have already been proved to exist.

Weak Keys. Certain keys are weak and should be avoided. Obviously, a key consisting of all zeros or all ones is weak because it is not affected by any rotation and therefore yields identical subkeys. Also, because the key is split in two and each half is shifted independently, each half should not be all zeros or all ones. There are also some keys that yield just two different subkeys and employ each subkey in eight rounds. Such keys are called *semiweak* and are listed in pairs in Table 11.16. Each pair consists of two keys that encrypt in the same way. A block of plaintext encrypted by one of these keys can be decrypted by the other key.

01FE	01FE	01FE	01FE	and	FE01	FE01	FE01	FE01
1FE0	1FE0	0EF1	0EF1	and	E01F	E01F	F10E	F10E
01E0	01E0	01F1	01F1	and	E001	E001	F101	F101
1FFE	1FFE	0EFE	0EFE	and	FE1F	FE1F	FE0E	FE0E
011F	011F	010E	010E	and	1F01	1F01	0E01	0E01
E0FE	E0FE	F1FE	F1FE	and	FEE0	FEE0	FEF1	FEF1

Table 11.16: The Semiweak DES Keys.

◇ **Exercise 11.4:** The 56-bit values of the four weak keys are (in hex) 0000000 0000000, 0000000 FFFFFFF, FFFFFFF 0000000, and FFFFFFF FFFFFFF. Compute the values of the parity bits of those keys and write the four keys as 64-bit hexadecimal numbers.

There are keys that yield only four different subkeys, each employed in four rounds of the algorithm. Such keys are called *possibly weak* and should also be avoided. They are listed in Table 11.17.

There is also the question of *complement keys*. If key K' is the 1s complement of K (every bit is flipped), then K and K' are complementary in the sense that if K encrypts a block of plaintext P to a block of ciphertext C, then K' encrypts block P' to C'. This happens because in each round the subkey is XORed with R_i after the expansion permutation. It is not clear whether complementary keys constitute a security risk, but their use can be avoided. This reduces the number of keys from 2^{56} to 2^{55}, still an unimaginably large number.

The Key Length. The original IBM proposal envisioned a 128-bit key. The 56-bit key length of DES has been suspected and criticized from the moment DES was announced as a standard. (Today, we know that the inherent robustness of DES is 56 bits, so the NSA simply adjusted the key length to the algorithm's strength.) Initially, researchers proposed many theoretical designs for special-purpose machines intended to crack DES by brute force. In the early years of DES, these machines were considered possible but prohibitively expensive for anyone except perhaps the NSA. At the time of this writing (late 2003), however, such machines are becoming more and more affordable and practical. Special machines that use brute force to search the entire 56-bit key space in a few hours may even now be routinely used by governments and other large entities.

The 16 Rounds. Research has shown that already after five rounds, every bit of ciphertext is a function of every plaintext bit and of every key bit. Defining DES with five rounds instead of 16 would have speeded it up but would also have made it easier to attack. Today, it is known that DES with fewer than 16 rounds can be cracked with differential cryptanalysis (if some plaintext is known) much more efficiently than with a brute force attack. This is a good justification for the large number of rounds. DES's

```
1F 1F 01 01 0E 0E 01 01        E0 01 01 E0 F1 01 01 F1
01 1F 1F 01 01 0E 0E 01        FE 1F 01 E0 FE 0E 0E F1
1F 01 01 1F 0E 01 01 0E        FE 01 1F E0 FE 01 0E F1
01 01 1F 1F 01 01 0E 0E        E0 1F 1F E0 F1 0E 0E F1
E0 E0 01 01 F1 F1 01 01        FE 01 01 FE FE 01 01 FE
FE FE 01 01 FE FE 01 01        E0 1F 01 FE F1 0E 01 FE
FE E0 1F 01 FE F1 0E 01        E0 01 1F FE F1 01 0E FE
E0 FE 1F 01 F1 FE 0E 01        FE 1F 1F FE FE 0E 0E FE
FE E0 01 1F FE F1 01 0E        1F FE 01 E0 0E FE 01 F1
E0 FE 01 1F F1 FE 01 0E        01 FE 1F E0 01 FE 0E F1
E0 E0 1F 1F F1 F1 0E 0E        1F E0 01 FE 0E F1 01 FE
FE FE 1F 1F FE FE 0E 0E        01 E0 1F FE 01 F1 0E FE
1F 1F 01 01 0E 0E 01 01        01 01 E0 E0 01 01 F1 F1
01 1F 1F 01 01 0E 0E 01        1F 1F E0 E0 0E 0E F1 F1
1F 01 01 1F 0E 01 01 0E        1F 01 FE E0 0E 01 FE F1
01 01 1F 1F 01 01 0E 0E        01 1F FE E0 01 0E FE F1
01 E0 E0 01 01 F1 F1 01        1F 01 E0 FE 0E 01 F1 FE
1F FE E0 01 0E FE F0 01        01 1F E0 FE 01 0E F1 FE
1F E0 FE 01 0E F1 FE 01        01 01 FE FE 00 01 FE FE
01 FE FE 01 01 FE FE 01        1F 1F FE FE 0E 0E FE FE
1F E0 E0 1F 0E F1 F1 0E        FE FE E0 E0 FE FE F1 F1
01 FE E0 1F 01 FE F1 0E        E0 FE FE E0 F1 FE FE F1
01 E0 FE 1F 01 F1 FE 0E        FE E0 E0 FE FE F1 F1 FE
1F FE FE 1F 0E FE FE 0E        E0 E0 FE FE F1 F1 FE FE
```

Table 11.17: The Possibly Weak DES Keys.

designers knew about differential cryptanalysis (they called it the T-attack) and tested DES to make sure it could resist this type of attack.

The S-Boxes. Originally, the content of the S-boxes was determined by the IBM design team, but they changed it later to comply with a request from the NSA. Potential users immediately suspected that the NSA had changed the S-boxes in order to leave themselves a trapdoor, but today it seems that the changes were proposed by the NSA in order to optimize the S-boxes against differential cryptanalysis attack. (Differential cryptanalysis was not published until 1990, but it is now virtually certain that the NSA experts had known about it much earlier.)

11.3.2 The DES Challenges

DES has been in common use since the 1970s and has been reevaluated and reaffirmed five times. In spite of this success, DES users have always been uncomfortable. Advances in computing, especially the increased speed of individual computers and the increased sophistication of distributed computing (solving a problem with a network of computers) have led many DES users to suspect that the effectiveness and security of DES have been eroded and that somewhere, someone may be able to break DES and guess any 56-bit key in reasonable time by a brute force approach involving perhaps thousands of fast computers working in parallel and communicating among themselves. (See discussion in Section 6.4 on how to defeat an exhaustive search of the keyspace.) Responding to these fears, RSA Laboratories Inc. has sponsored three public challenges to DES. These challenges, run from 1997 to 1999, became progressively more difficult, requiring the participants to find the encryption key in a challenge in less time than was achieved in the previous challenge. All three challenges have been met successfully, and the third one was cracked in a record 22 hours and 15 minutes by a worldwide network of nearly 100,000 personal computers, assisted by a special piece of hardware (a "DES cracker"). At the point in time when the correct key was found, this system was trying 245 billion keys each second!

The first RSA challenge to DES was announced in early 1997. The prize was $10,000, and it proved sufficiently large to attract several qualified contestants. It took this team only 90 days to develop specialized software that used thousands of computers to work collectively, trying keys until the right one was found. When the results were announced, DES users felt even more vulnerable, but some experts argued that the typical hacker does not have access to a large network of computers and that DES can be broken only by a concentrated effort involving a large group with access to immense computing power.

In response, RSA announced its second challenge in early 1998. A 56-bit key was randomly generated, used just twice to encrypt two messages, then destroyed. One encrypted message was then posted on the World Wide Web in January and the other one was posted in July. This challenge carried a prize whose amount was to be determined by the time it took to find the key. For the winner to receive any prize at all, this time would have to be shorter than 75% of the 90 days it had taken to meet the first challenge. If the time was improved by 25%, the prize was to be only $1000. The prize for solving the challenge in half the time (45 days) of challenge I was $5000, and any solution obtained in 22.5 days or less carried a prize of $10,000.

The first message of this second challenge (challenge II-1) was cracked in 41 days (13 January to 23 February 1998) by the same team (Distributed.Net) that cracked challenge I. The correct key was 76 9E 8C D9 F2 2F 5D EA and the plaintext was "Many hands make light work."

The second message (challenge II-2) was cracked in July 1998, taking only 56 hours, by "Deep Crack," a special computer built by the Electronic Frontier Foundation (EFF). It should be noted that "Deep Crack" took less than a year to construct and cost less than $250,000. Flying in the face of earlier predictions and estimates, this machine had proved that the security provided by DES is being eroded quickly and that the time had come to either increase the size of the key or develop a new encryption standard (to be called, naturally, the Advanced Encryption Standard (AES)).

The third RSA challenge was issued in early 1999. A maximum prize of $10,000 was to be determined by the following rules: Up to 24 hours to crack, win $10,000. Up to 48 hours, a prize of $5,000. Up to 56 hours, only $1,000. More than 56 hours brings no prize. The challenge was met by the combined teams of Distributed.Net and EFF, the latter using its "Deep Crack" computer. Using a large network of computers, they were able to try 245 billion keys a second and met the challenge in 22 hours 15 minutes (less than half of the previously recorded time). The plaintext of this challenge was "see you in Rome" (referring to the second AES conference that took place in Rome in late March 1999).

The attack on this challenge was well coordinated and involved thousands of volunteers who ran client programs on their (mostly personal) computers. Several servers handled all the clients, assigning a block of work to each client to test. Success was due to the fact that this type of problem (cracking a code by brute force) is an ideal candidate for a solution by a distributed network of computers (another, well-known application that lends itself well to this type of computing is SETI, the search for extraterrestrial intelligence).

These challenges and the fact that they were met in short times and by a simple, brute force approach helped convince all the parties involved—users, cryptographers, bureaucrats, and administrators—that the 56-bit key length can no longer resist a concerted attack. As a result, NIST recommended in 1997 that DES be retired and replaced with a stronger cryptographic algorithm to be called the Advanced Encryption Standard (AES). It has recently been announced that the winning entry is Rijndael [Salomon 03], a block cipher employing a key of between 128 and 256 bits and having absolutely no trapdoors.

11.3.3 Triple Data Encryption Algorithm

In response to the growing computing power available to the general public, the DES has been strengthened in a simple way, by passing each 64-bit block through DES three times. The result was a new encryption standard (ANSI standard X9.52), popularly known as the triple data encryption algorithm (TDEA).

A TDEA key consists of three 64-bit DES keys K_a, K_b, and K_c (for a total of 168 bits plus 24 parity bits). This multipart key is sometimes referred to as a *key bundle*. A 64-bit block of plaintext is encrypted by TDEA in several steps: (1) the block is DES-encrypted with K_a, (2) the result is then *decrypted* with K_b, and (3) the result of step 2 is further DES-encrypted with K_c. TDEA decryption is done by (1) decrypting with K_c, (2) encrypting the result with K_b, and (3) decrypting the result of step 2 with K_a. Such an algorithm is said to operate in the *encrypt–decrypt–encrypt* (EDE) mode. The method is easy to describe, but a better understanding requires answers to the following two questions.

Question 1. Why encrypt–decrypt–encrypt and not encrypt–encrypt–encrypt? The answer is that the EDE mode reduces to simple DES when all three keys are identical and also when $K_a = K_b$ or $K_b = K_c$.

Question 2. What is the added security provided by the three keys? More specifically, is there a fourth key K_d such that performing DES with K_d on a block of plaintext and performing TDEA on the same block with K_a, K_b, and K_c would produce the same ciphertext? The answer is no. Technically, this is equivalent to saying that DES is not a mathematical group (see discussion of groups in the next paragraph). Thus, the three keys do increase security but not by as much as naively expected. A naive assumption is that the 168 bits of the three keys create a key space of size $2^{168} \approx 3.7 \times 10^{50}$, but there is an efficient attack on TDEA, described in [Merkle and Hellman 81], that limits its security to that of a key space of 112 bits (equivalent to two DES keys and still an immense keyspace).

(In a nutshell, a mathematical group is a collection of mathematical entities plus a 2-operand operation on them. Among other requirements, a group must be closed under the operation, which means that the result of operating on two elements in the group is also an element in the group. In DES, the 64-bit blocks of plaintext and ciphertext play the role of group elements, and the encryption plays the role of the operation. It has been proved by [Campbell and Wiener 93] that the set of 64-bit blocks is not closed under DES encryption.)

TDEA has various modes of operation, all part of the X9.52 standard. The modes are (1) the TDEA Electronic Codebook Mode of Operation (TECB) mode, (2) the TDEA Cipher Block Chaining Mode of Operation (TCBC), (3) the TDEA Cipher Block Chaining Mode of Operation—Interleaved (TCBC-I), (4) the TDEA Cipher Feedback Mode of Operation (TCFB), (5) the TDEA Cipher Feedback Mode of Operation—Pipelined (TCFB-P), (6) the TDEA Output Feedback Mode of Operation (TOFB), and (7) the TDEA Output Feedback Mode of Operation—Interleaved (TOFB-I). The TECB, TCBC, TCFB, and TOBF modes are based on the ECB, CBC, CFB, and OFB modes, respectively, obtained by substituting the DES encryption/decryption operation with the TDEA encryption/decryption operation.

> Laughter is the cipher key wherewith we decipher the whole man.
> —Thomas Carlyle

12
Public-Key Cryptography

The problem of key distribution has been mentioned several times in this part of the book. For many years it was strongly believed that this problem has no satisfactory solution, but in the 1970s, an ideal, simple solution was found and has since become the foundation upon which much of modern cryptography is based.

The following narrative illustrates the nature of the solution. Suppose that Alice wants to send Bob a secure message. She places the message in a strong box, locks it with a padlock, and mails it to Bob. Bob receives the box safely, but then realizes that he does not have the key to the padlock. This is a simplified version of the key distribution problem, and it has a simple, unexpected solution. Bob simply adds another padlock to the box and mails it back to Alice. Alice removes her padlock and mails the box to Bob, who removes his lock, opens the box, and reads the message.

◇ **Exercise 12.1:** (Easy.) When restricted to physical boxes and keys, this problem has a simpler solution. Once Bob verifies receipt of the box, Alice can mail him the key under a separate envelope. Explain why this solution cannot be used when the messages and keys are files sent between computers.

The cryptographic equivalent is similar. We start with a similar, albeit unsatisfactory, approach. Imagine a group of users of a particular encryption algorithm, where each user has a private key that is unknown to anyone else. Also imagine a user, Alice, who wants to send an encrypted message to another user, Bob. Alice encrypts the message with her private key (a key unknown to Bob) and sends it. Bob receives the encrypted message, encrypts it again, with his key, and sends the doubly-encrypted message back to Alice. Alice now decrypts the message with her key, but the message is still encrypted with Bob's key. Alice sends the message again to Bob, who decrypts it with his key and can read it.

The trouble with this simple scenario is that most ciphers must obey the LIFO (last in first out) rule. The last cipher used to encrypt a doubly-encrypted message must be the first one used to decipher it. This is easy to see in the case of a monoalphabetic cipher. Suppose that Alice's key replaces D with P and L with X and Bob's key replaces P with L. After encrypting a message twice, first with Alice's key and then with Bob's key, any D in the message becomes an L. However, when Alice's key is used to decipher the L, it replaces it with X. When Bob's key is used to decipher the X, it replaces it with something different from the original D. The same happens with a polyalphabetic cipher.

> The paper was also notable for a more whimsical touch. Instead of what had been the standard form of delineating the recipient and sender of a message by alphabetic notation—**A** for the sender, **B** for the recipient, for instance—Rivest personified them by giving them gender and identity. Thus the RSA paper marks the first appearance of a fictional "Bob" who wants to send a message to "Alice." As trivial as this sounds, these names actually became a de facto standard in future papers outlining cryptologic advances, and the cast of characters in such previously depopulated mathematical papers would eventually be widened to include an eavesdropper dubbed Eve and a host of supporting actors including Carol, Trent, Wiry, and Dave. The appearance of these dramatic personae, however nerdy, would be symbolic of the iconoclastic personality of a brand-new community of independent cryptographers, working outside of government and its secrecy clamps.
>
> —Steven Levy, *Crypto* (2001)

12.1 Diffie–Hellman–Merkle Keys

However, there is a way out, a discovery made in 1976 by Whitfield Diffie, Martin Hellman, and Ralph Merkle. Their revolutionary Diffie–Hellman–Merkle key exchange method makes it possible to securely exchange a cryptographic key (or any piece of data) over an unsecure channel. It involves the concept of a *one-way function*, a function that either does not have an inverse or whose inverse is not unique. Most functions have simple inverses. The inverse of the exponential function $y = e^x$, for example, is the natural logarithm $x = \log_e y$. However, modular arithmetic provides an example of a simple and useful one-way function. The value of the modulo function $f(x) = x \bmod p$ is the remainder of the integer division $x \div p$ and is an integer in the interval $[0, p - 1]$. Table 12.1 illustrates the one-way nature of modular arithmetic by listing values of $3^x \bmod 7$ for 10 values of x. It is easy to see, for example, that the number 3 is the value of $3^x \bmod 7$ for $x = 1$ and $x = 7$. The point is that the same number is the value of this function for infinitely more values of x, effectively making it impossible to reverse this simple function.

x	1	2	3	4	5	6	7	8	9	10
3^x	3	9	27	81	243	729	2187	6561	19683	59049
$3^x \bmod 7$	3	2	6	4	5	1	3	2	6	4

Table 12.1: Ten Values of $3^x \bmod 7$.

◇ **Exercise 12.2:** Find some real-world processes that are one-way either in principle or in practice.

Based on this interesting property of modular arithmetic, the three researchers came up with an original and unusual scheme for distributing keys. The process is summarized in Figure 12.2. The process requires the modular function $L^x \bmod P$, whose two parameters P (a large prime, about 512 bits) and L should satisfy $L < P$. The two parties have to select values for L and P, but these values don't have to be secret.

	Alice	**Bob**
Step 1	Selects a secret number a, say, 4	Selects a secret number b, say, 7
Step 2	Computes $\alpha = 5^a \bmod 13 = 624 \bmod 13 = 1$ and sends α to Bob	Computes $\beta = 5^b \bmod 13 = 78125 \bmod 13 = 8$ and sends β to Alice
·Step 3	Computes the key by $\beta^a \bmod 13 = 4096 \bmod 13 = 1$	Computes the key by $\alpha^b \bmod 13 = 1 \bmod 13 = 1$

Notice that knowledge of α, β, and the function is not enough to compute the key. Either a or b is needed, but these are kept secret.

Figure 12.2: Three Steps to Compute the Same Key.

Careful study of Figure 12.2 shows that even if the messages exchanged between Alice and Bob are intercepted, and even if the values $L = 5$ and $P = 13$ that they use are known, the key still cannot be derived, since the values of either a or b are also needed, but both are kept secret by the two parties.

This breakthrough has proved that cryptographic keys can be securely exchanged through unsecure channels, and users no longer have to meet personally to agree on keys or to trust couriers to deliver them. However, the Diffie–Hellman–Merkle key exchange method described in Figure 12.2 is inefficient. In the ideal case, where both users are online at the same time, they can go through the process of Figure 12.2 (select the secret numbers a and b, compute and exchange the values of α and β, and calculate the key) in just a few minutes. If they cannot be online at the same time (for example, if they live in very different time zones), then the process of determining the key may take a day or more.

⋄ **Exercise 12.3:** Show why the steps of Figure 12.2 produce the same key for Alice and for Bob.

⋄ **Exercise 12.4:** Why should P be large and why should L be less than P?

The following analogy may explain why a one-way function is needed to solve the key distribution problem. Imagine that Bob and Alice want to agree on a certain paint color and keep it secret. Each starts with a container that has one liter of paint of a certain color, say, R. Each adds one liter of paint of a secret color. Bob may add a liter of paint of color G and Alice may add a liter of color B. Neither knows what color was added by the other one. They then exchange the containers (which may be intercepted and examined). When each gets the other's container, each adds another liter of his or her secret paint. Thus, each container ends up having one liter each of paints of colors R, G, and B. Each container contains paint of the same color. Intercepting and examining the containers on their ways is fruitless, because one cannot unmix paints. Mixing paints is a one-way operation.

The Venetian adventurer and autobiographer Giacomo Casanova was given an encrypted manuscript by a Madame d'Urfé, which he deciphered. Later, upon learning this, Madame d'Urfé was incredulous, believing he must have known the keyword to do so. He relates this in Volume 6 of his autobiography [Casanova 57]:

"I then told her the keyword, which belonged to no language, and I saw her surprise. She told me that it was impossible, for she believed herself the only possessor of that word which she kept in her memory and which she had never written down.

I could have told her the truth—that the same calculation which had served me for deciphering the manuscript had enabled me to learn the word—but on a caprice it struck me to tell her that a genie had revealed it to me. This false disclosure fettered Madame d'Urfé to me. That day, I became the master of her soul, and I abused my power. Every time I think of it, I am distressed and ashamed, and I do penance now in the obligation under which I place myself of telling the truth in writing my memoirs."

12.2 Public-Key Cryptography

In 1975, a little after the Diffie–Hellman–Merkle key exchange was published, Whitfield Diffie came up with the concept of an *asymmetric key*. Traditionally, ciphers use symmetric keys. The same key is used to encipher and decipher a message. Deciphering is the exact reverse of enciphering. Cryptography with an asymmetric key requires two keys, one for enciphering and the other for deciphering. This seems a trivial concept but is in fact revolutionary. In an asymmetric cipher, there is no need to distribute keys or to compute them by exchanging data as in the Diffie–Hellman–Merkle key exchange scheme. Alice could decide on two keys for her secret messages, make the encryption key public, and keep the decryption key secret (this is her private key). Bob could then use Alice's public key to encrypt messages and send them to Alice. Anyone intercepting such a message would not be able to decipher it because this requires the secret decryption key that only Alice knows.

Whitfield Diffie took cryptography out of the hands of the spooks and made privacy possible in the digital age—by inventing the most revolutionary concept in encryption since the Renaissance.

—*Wired*, November 1994

12.3 RSA Cryptography

It was clear to Diffie that a cipher based on an asymmetric key would be the ideal solution to the troublesome problem of key distribution and would completely revolutionize cryptography. Unfortunately, he was unable to actually come up with such a cipher. The first, simple, practical, and secure public-key cipher, known today as RSA cryptography, was finally developed in 1977 by Ronald Rivest, Adi Shamir, and Leonard Adleman. RSA was a triumphal achievement, an achievement based on the properties of prime numbers.

A prime number, as most know, is a number with no divisors. More accurately, it is a positive integer N whose only divisors are 1 and itself. (Nonprime integers are called composites.) For generations, prime numbers and their properties (the mathematical discipline of number theory) were of interest to mathematicians only and had no practical applications whatsoever. RSA cryptography found an interesting, original, and very practical application for these numbers. This application relies on the most important property of prime numbers, the property that justifies the name *prime*. Any positive integer can be represented as the product of prime numbers (its prime factors) *in one way only*. In other words, any integer has a unique prime factorization. For example, the number 65,535 can be represented as the product of integers in many ways, but there is only one set of primes, namely 3, 5, 17, and 257, whose product equals 65,535.

The main idea behind RSA is to choose two large primes p and q that together constitute the private key. The public key N is their product $N = p{\times}q$ (naturally, it is a composite). The important (and surprising) point is that multiplying large integers is a one-way function! It is relatively easy to multiply integers, even very large ones, but it is practically impossible, or at least extremely time consuming, to find the prime factors of a large integer, with hundreds of digits. Today, after millennia of research (primes have been known to the ancients), no efficient method for factoring numbers has been discovered. All existing factoring algorithms are slow and may take years to factor an integer consisting of a few hundred decimal digits. The factoring challenge (with prizes) offered by RSA laboratories [RSA 01] testifies to the accuracy of this statement.

To summarize, we know that the public key N has a unique prime factorization and that its prime factors constitute the private key. However, if N is large enough, we will not be able to factor it, even with the fastest computers, which makes RSA a secure cipher. That said, however, no one has proved that a fast factorization method does not exist. It is not inconceivable that someone will come up with such an algorithm that would render RSA (impregnable for more than two decades) useless and would stimulate researchers to discover a different public-key cipher.

(Recent declassifying of secret British documents suggests that a cipher very similar to RSA had been developed by James Ellis and his colleagues starting in 1969. They worked for the British government communications headquarters, GCHQ, and so had to keep their work secret. See [Singh 99].

The following is a comment made by an anonymous reviewer: "Another reason why the GCHQ work was never applied was because no one there believed it to be useful. It took private industry to recognize its worth. In other words, it wasn't just secrecy that prevented its use until it was reinvented in the open literature.")

And now, to the details of RSA. These are deceptively simple, but the use of large numbers requires special arithmetic routines to be implemented and carefully debugged. We assume that Alice has selected two large primes p and q as her private key. She has to compute and publish two more numbers as her public key. They are $N = p \cdot q$ and e. The latter can be any integer, but it should be relatively prime to $(p-1)(q-1)$, a number denoted by ϕ. Notice that N must be unique (if Joe has selected the same N as his public key, then he knows the values of p and q), but e does not have to be. To encrypt a message M (an integer) intended for Alice, Bob gets her public key (N and e), computes $C = M^e \bmod N$, and sends C to Alice through an open communications channel. To decrypt the message, Alice starts by computing the decryption key d from $e \times d = 1 \bmod \phi$, then uses d to compute $M = C^d \bmod N$.

The security of the encrypted message depends on the one-way nature of the modulo function. Since the encrypted message C is $M^e \bmod N$, and since both N and e are public, the message can be decrypted by inverting the modulo function. However, as mentioned earlier, this function is impossible to invert (or, rather has too many inverses) for large values of N. It is important to understand that polyalphabetic ciphers, block ciphers, and stream ciphers can be as secure as RSA, are easier to implement, and are faster to execute, but they are symmetric and therefore suffer from the problem of key distribution.

The use of large numbers requires special routines for the arithmetic operations. Specifically, the operation M^e may be problematic, since M may be a large number. One way to simplify this operation is to break the message M up into small segments. Another option is to break up e into a sum of terms and use each term separately. For example, if $e = 7 = 1 + 2 + 4$, then

$$M^e \bmod N = [(M^1 \bmod N) \times (M^2 \bmod N) \times (M^4 \bmod N)] \bmod N.$$

James Ellis, a mathematician and computer scientist, joined GCHQ (then at Eastcote, West London) in 1952, having previously worked for the Admiralty.
— From `http://www.gchq.gov.uk/`

RSA in Two Lines of Perl

Adam Back (aba@dcs.exeter.ac.uk) has created an implementation of RSA in just two lines of Perl. It uses dc, an arbitrary-precision arithmetic package that ships with most UNIX systems. Here's the Perl code:

```
print pack"C*",split/\D+/,'echo "16iII*o\U@{$/=$z;[(pop,pop,unpack"H*",<>
)]}\EsMsKsN0[lN*llK[d2%Sa2/d0<X+d*lMLa^*lN%0]dsXx++lMlN/dsM0<J]dsJxp"|dc'
```

Here is an example of RSA encryption and decryption using small parameters. We select the two small primes $p = 137$ and $q = 191$ as our private key and compute $N = p \cdot q = 26{,}167$ and $\phi = (p-1)(q-1) = 25{,}840$. We also select $e = 3$ and, using the extended Euclidean algorithm, find a value $d = 17{,}227$ such that $e \cdot d = 1 \bmod \phi$. The public key is the pair $(N, e) = (26167, 3)$, and the decryption key is $d = 17{,}227$. For the plaintext M, we select the 4-character string abcd whose ASCII codes are 97, 98, 99, and 100, or in binary 01100001, 01100010, 01100011, and 01100100. These are grouped into the two 16-bit blocks $0110000101100010_2 = 24{,}930$ and $0110001101100100_2 = 25{,}444$. Encrypting the blocks is done by

$$C = M^e \bmod N = 24{,}930^3 \bmod 26{,}167 = 23{,}226,$$
$$C = M^e \bmod N = 25{,}444^3 \bmod 26{,}167 = 23{,}081.$$

Decrypting the two blocks C of ciphertext is done by

$$C^d \bmod N = 23{,}226^{17227} \bmod 26{,}167 = 24{,}930,$$
$$C^d \bmod N = 23{,}081^{17227} \bmod 26{,}167 = 25{,}444.$$

The security of RSA depends on the infeasibility of factoring large numbers, and this paragraph shows that this problem is equivalent to keeping the private quantity d secret. It turns out that knowledge of d can lead to an efficient factoring of N in the following way. We know that $e \cdot d = 1 \bmod \phi$, which implies that there is an integer k such that $e \cdot d - 1 = k\phi$. From this it follows (by one of the many theorems proved by the great Leonhard Euler) that $a^{ed-1} = 1 \bmod \phi$ for all integers a in the interval $[0, n-1]$. If we now use the notation $ed - 1 = 2^s t$, where t is odd, then it can be shown that there is an integer $b \in [1, s]$ such that $a^{2^{b-1}t} \neq \pm 1 \bmod N$ and $a^{2^b t} = 1 \bmod N$ for at least half of the integers a. We therefore conclude that if such a and b are known, then the greatest common divisor of $a^{2^{b-1}t} - 1$ and N is a factor of N. Factoring N may therefore be done by selecting a random integer a in the proper range and looking for an integer $b \in [1, s]$ that satisfies the property above. With the computing power currently available, this can be achieved quickly and easily.

The value of parameter e is also important. Encryption requires the computation of M^e, so small e implies faster encryption. However, small values of e may also lead to a weaker ciphertext, as the following example illustrates. Suppose that Alice wants to encrypt a message M and send it to three recipients whose public keys are N_1, N_2, and N_3. Suppose also that all three recipients use the same small e, say, $e = 3$ as in our example. Alice can then compute $C_i = M^3 \bmod N_i$ for $i = 1, 2, 3$ and send the three ciphertexts C_i to their recipients. If Eve intercepts the ciphertexts, however, she may have an easy way to decrypt them. She may use Gauss's algorithm to solve the three modular equations $x = C_i \bmod N_i$ for $i = 1, 2, 3$. The solution x will be in the interval $[0, N_1 N_2 N_3)$. We know that $M^3 < N_1 N_2 N_3$, so from the Chinese remainder theorem we conclude that x must equal M^3. Hence, Eve can decrypt the message by computing $\sqrt[3]{x}$. This vulnerability can be avoided by using large values for e or, in cases where the same message is sent to several recipients, by appending a random string to each message in order to make the plaintexts different.

The Chinese remainder theorem states that if the integers n_1 through n_k are pairwise relatively prime, then the system of equations

$$x = a_1 \bmod n_1, \quad x = a_2 \bmod n_2, \ldots, x = a_k \bmod n_k,$$

has a unique solution modulo the quantity $n = n_1 n_2 \ldots n_k$.

Gauss's theorem states that the solution to the system of equations in the Chinese remainder theorem can be expressed as the sum $x = \sum_{i=1}^{k} a_i N_i M_i \bmod n$, where $N_i = n/n_i$ and $M_i = N_i^{-1} \bmod n_i$.

Another potential vulnerability of RSA is its *multiplicative property*. We denote by $\mathcal{Z}_N$ the set of integers modulo N, i.e., $\{0, 1, \ldots, N-1\}$. We similarly denote by $\mathcal{Z}_N^*$ the set of integers $\{a \in \mathcal{Z}_n \mid \gcd(a, N) = 1\}$. In the special case where N is prime, $\mathcal{Z}_N^* = \{1, 2, \ldots, N-1\}$. It can be shown that $\mathcal{Z}_N$ is closed under multiplication and constitutes a multiplicative group.

Assume that $C_i = M_i^e \bmod N$ for $i = 1, 2$ (i.e., two messages use the same N). This implies that $(M_1 M_2)^e = C_1 C_1 \bmod N$. The RSA multiplicative property can now be stated as follows. The ciphertext C that corresponds to the plaintext $M = M_1 M_2 \bmod N$ is $C = C_1 C_2 \bmod N$. An attack by Eve on messages decrypted by Alice is possible if Alice has a certain amount of trust in Eve and is willing to encrypt certain messages for her. Suppose that Eve wants to decrypt a message $C = M^e \bmod N$ that she has intercepted on its way to Alice. Eve can select a random integer $x \in \mathcal{Z}_N^*$, compute $C' = C \cdot X^e \bmod N$, and ask Alice to encrypt C'. If Alice complies, she will compute $M' = (C')^d \bmod N$ and send M' to Eve, who can then use the relation

$$M' = (C')^d \bmod N = C^d (X^e)^d = M \cdot X \bmod N$$

to compute $M = M' X^{-1} \bmod N$.

The *cycling attack* poses another threat to RSA security. Given a plaintext M in the interval $[0, N-1]$, it is encrypted to $C = M^e \bmod N$. The ciphertext C is therefore also an integer in the same interval. Thus, M and C are *permutations* of each other. Because of this, there must be a positive integer k such that $C^{e^k} \bmod N = C$ and $C^{e^{k-1}} \bmod N = M$. The cycling attack uses the public key (N, e) and an intercepted ciphertext C to compute the sequence $C^e \bmod N$, $C^{e^2} \bmod n$, $C^{e^3} \bmod N$, and so on, until one of those numbers, $C^{e^k} \bmod n$, equals C. This reveals the value of k and makes it possible to decrypt C by computing $M = C^{e^{k-1}} \bmod N$. Special software has to be used in these calculations, since the quantities C^{e^k} grow very quickly.

Regardless of the key used, some plaintexts are encrypted by RSA to themselves. Thus, M^e mod N may sometimes equal M. Such messages are referred to as *unconcealed* and are rare. Nevertheless, RSA encryption software should compare every ciphertext C to its plaintext M and alert the user when an unconcealed message is detected.

The various problems mentioned here are eliminated by the Public-Key Cryptography Standards (PKCS) developed by RSA Laboratories. The interested reader should consult especially PKCS #1 [PKCS 04].

RSA stands for "resists serious attack."

12.4 Pretty Good Privacy

The computations required for RSA encryption and decryption are straightforward but require special software. In a software package intended for general use, both accuracy and speed are important. Special routines, optimized for speed, must be implemented to perform the arithmetic operations on large numbers without any loss of accuracy. With the right software, anyone could access the power of RSA and exchange messages confidentially. Without such software, RSA remains a largely unused resource. Such software was implemented in the late 1980s by Phil Zimmermann, who named it *pretty good privacy* or PGP for short. Certain versions of PGP are free, while others are commercial products. In the United States, PGP software is available from `http://www.pgp.com/`. Outside the United States it is available from `http://www.pgpi.org/`. The source code of PGP has been published in [Zimmermann 95] (currently out of print). For a detailed description of Zimmermann's background and the events that led to the development of PGP, see [Levy 01].

To overcome the speed problem, PGP was designed in a special way [Garfinkel 95]. The software (version 2) uses IDEA, a symmetric block cipher [Salomon 03] to encrypt the actual message. The RSA method and the receiver's public key are used by PGP only to encrypt the IDEA key (i.e., the key used by IDEA to encrypt the message). IDEA is patented by Ascom Systec of Switzerland but is free for noncommercial use.

Nowadays, many PGP users use OpenPGP, a nonproprietary protocol for encrypting email [OpenPGP 04], based on TDES or AES instead of IDEA. Many also use the free GnuPG [GnuPG 04]. The following is quoted from [GNUPG 04]:

> GnuPG is a complete and free replacement for PGP. Because it does not use the patented IDEA algorithm, it can be used without any restrictions. GnuPG is a RFC2440 (OpenPGP) compliant application.

> Version 1.0.0 has been released on September 7th, 1999. The current (late 2004) stable version is 1.2.5.

> GnuPG is Free Software. It can be freely used, modified and distributed under the terms of the GNU General Public License.

> PGP, on which OpenPGP is based, was originally developed by Philip Zimmermann in the early 1990s.

Project Aegypten provides Sphinx-Clients (Mutt, KMail, ...), which are compatible with S/MIME within a GnuPG framework. Within this project a few new tools have been developed, most notably "gpgsm" as the S/MIME counterpart of "gpg."

PGP also has several features that make it especially user friendly and easy to use. It can automatically generate private and public keys for the user. The user just wiggles the mouse randomly, and the software uses this movement to generate a unique key. PGP can also digitally authenticate encrypted messages. Authentication is needed in cases where the identity of the sender is important and is in doubt. Imagine a bank receiving an encrypted message signed "Bob" that asks them to transfer all of Bob's assets to a Swiss numbered bank account. Authentication would show whether the message really came from Bob. Bob can authenticate his message by including a short "signature message" in his main message. The main message is, of course, encrypted with the bank's public key, so only the bank can decipher it. The signature is simply a short, agreed-upon message encrypted with *Bob's private key*. Anyone in possession of Bob's public key (i.e., anyone at all) can decrypt this message and read it, but only Bob can encrypt it (with his private key). The signature is not secure, but it verifies that it was Bob who sent the message.

In 1993, after PGP became widely used all over the world, the United States government made Zimmermann the target of a three-year criminal investigation. The government claimed that United States export restrictions for cryptographic software were violated when PGP spread all over the world. This investigation was dropped in early 1996, and today PGP is a widely used, important encryption tool. For more details, see [Zimmermann 01].

12.5 Sharing Secrets: Threshold Schemes

The well-known soft drink known as Coca-Cola was invented (concocted?) by the pharmacist John Styth Pemberton in May of 1886. The name *Coca-Cola* was registered as a trademark in the United States Patent Office in 1893, but the recipe for this drink has never been patented (which would have made it public knowledge) and is still kept secret. Clearly, someone has to know this secret, and it better be more than one person. It is possible to trust the secret to a small number of trusted persons such that each knows the entire recipe. It is safer, however, to divide such a secret among n individuals such that they have to meet and combine their parts in order to produce the complete recipe. It is even safer to divide a secret among n persons such that any k of the n can combine their parts and generate the complete secret but any $k - 1$ of the n cannot achieve this goal. Such a method is called a (k, n) threshold scheme.

There are many similar situations where a secret should be shared among several persons such that any subset of them could retrieve the secret by combining their parts. One common example is safe deposit boxes in banks. Each box has two keys, one held by the box owner and the other kept by the bank. Both keys are needed to open the box. (The main reason why the bank insists on keeping one key is to reduce the chance of the box owner being robbed. A robber knows that the single key held by the owner is not sufficient.) Another example is the launch of a nuclear missile. Two operators are needed and both have to push buttons simultaneously. A third example is a group of scientists working on a secret project. Documents are kept in a safe that can be opened only by three keys (or combinations) such that any combination of a scientist, a security officer, and an administrator (a political commissar?) can open the safe, but any other combination cannot.

In cryptography, an efficient threshold scheme can be indispensable for safe keeping of the key. Data can be secured by encrypting it, but how do we secure the encryption key? It is pointless to encrypt the key, because another key would have to be kept in such a case. The most secure place for it is in someone's head or in a safe, but keeping a key in a single location is vulnerable to accidents, theft, and sabotage. Storing multiple copies of the key in different locations reduces the chance of key loss but increases vulnerability to attack by robbers, hackers, or corrupt employees or officials. A (k, n) threshold scheme, where k pieces of information are stored in different locations or trusted to different individuals, offers an ideal compromise, especially when k is chosen such that $n = 2k - 1$. Consider the following. The key can be extracted even if half the pieces (specifically, if $\lfloor n/2 \rfloor = k - 1$ pieces) are missing, and on the other hand, an enemy that has obtained half of the pieces (again, $k - 1$) wouldn't be able to retrieve the secret key.

These examples make it clear that threshold schemes are an ideal solution in cases where a group of individuals who have conflicting interests and are mutually suspicious must cooperate. Once n is given, a proper choice of k can give a sufficiently large majority the authority to make an important decision while giving any sufficiently large minority the power to oppose it.

Perhaps the simplest idea that comes to mind, when considering how to share a secret, is multiple encryption. This is similar to the two-padlock technique described in Section 12.1. We denote by $E(k_i, X)$ a function that encrypts message X with a key k_i. A secret message X can be encrypted n times to become

$$Y = E(k_1, E(k_2, E(k_3, \ldots E(k_n, X) \ldots))).$$

If each person has one of the n keys and all have access to the result Y, then all n individuals can cooperate and decrypt the original secret X.

This is a simple approach, but its use is limited to cases where all the participants can be trusted and each has to have part of the key. Also, it is not clear how secure this approach is. The encryption function E may be very secure, but applying it several times may introduce unexpected weaknesses in the resulting ciphertext (this is a general problem in cryptography).

An even simpler approach, and one that appears very secure, is the use of the exclusive-OR operation (denoted by XOR or by $\oplus$), similar to its use in the steganographic file system (Section 15.7). We denote the secret by X and assume, with no loss of generality, that X is a number (because any type of data, text, images, video, or audio stored in a computer is represented in bits). We choose $n-1$ random numbers X_1, $X_2, \ldots, X_{n-1}$, each the same size as X, and compute $X_n = X_1 \oplus X_2 \oplus \cdots \oplus X_{n-1} \oplus X$.

The n numbers X_i are distributed to the n participants in the scheme, who can easily compute the secret number X as the XOR of their n individual numbers (see Exercise 11.3 about the XOR being its own inverse).

As an example, we use $n = 5$, the 10-bit secret $X = 1111000110$ and four random 10-bit numbers $X_1 = 0100101100$, $X_2 = 1111001100$, $X_3 = 1011000101$, and $X_4 = 1111110110$. The XOR of X and the four X_i produces $X_5 = 0000010101$, and it is easy to verify that the XOR of the five X_i retrieves the original secret X. Notice that X_n is as random as the $n - 1$ random numbers X_i.

Because the random numbers X_i are chosen freshly for each new secret X, this technique is as safe as a one-time pad, i.e., theoretically unbreakable. Another point to consider is: Even if the secret X is a nonrandom number (say, all zeros or all ones), it does not cause X_n to be nonrandom. (If X is zeros, then X_n is simply the XOR of the X_i. If X is all ones, then X_n is the complement of that XOR.)

This technique also offers *deniability*. Imagine a hacker, Henry, who wants to post a malicious message on the Internet. Henry selects three images of the same size, one each from CNN, from a respected member of parliament, and from a known hacker site. Henry extracts the least-significant bits from each image and uses them as the three strings X_1, X_2, and X_3. He then computes the XOR of those strings with his secret message X to obtain string X_4 which he embeds in the least significant bits of one of his images (this embedding technique is described in Section 14.1).

Henry then anonymously advertises the fact that the four images contain important information (this can be done by means of anonymous messages to many news groups). Anyone can download the four images, extract the least significant bits of each, and XOR the four resulting binary strings to produce the secret message, but the point is that Henry is now only one of four entities that are suspect. Many people are employed by CNN, and several of them could have posted the first image. Even a respected member of parliament may decide to leak information from time to time and may be responsible for the second image (see box on page 347). Henry can deny any wrongdoing, and it may be difficult or even impossible to prove anything against him, especially if he uses many images for his scheme.

Next, we consider techniques to share a secret among n persons such that any k of them can obtain it. We start with a few geometric approaches. Given a secret $p \neq 0$, select another number $q \neq 0$ at random (but make sure that $q \neq p$, because this may unnecessarily provide the codebreaker with a clue) and consider the pair (p, q) a point in two-dimensional space (since $p \neq 0$ and $q \neq p$, the point can be located anywhere except on the coordinate axes or on the line $y = x$). Randomly select two distinct, nonparallel straight lines that pass through this point. It is intuitively clear that knowing one line that passes through (p, q) is not enough to identify p but knowing two lines is enough, since two lines intersect at a point (parallel lines don't intersect at all and identical lines intersect at infinitely many points, so such pairs of lines should be avoided).

The equation of a straight line is $y = ax + b$ where a is the slope and b is the y intercept. To select a line that passes through (p, q), we first select an arbitrary value for a (this can be any real number), then compute b by $q = ap + b$. If we select two different values a_1 and a_2, then the two pairs (a_1, b_1) and (a_2, b_2) identify the two lines and b_1 and b_2 will also be different, because neither p nor q are zero. On the decoding side, given the two pairs of line parameters, the intersection point (p, q) can be found by solving the two equations $q = a_1 p + b_1$ and $q = a_2 p + b_2$.

Sharing the secret p between two individuals A and B can now be done by giving one line pair (a_1, b_1) to A and the other line pair (a_2, b_2) to B. Neither individual can obtain p without the other, but together they can easily compute it.

◇ **Exercise 12.5:** Given the secret $p = 5$, show how to share it between two individuals.

So far we have considered the basic case where each of two individuals has partial information and the two have to cooperate to obtain the secret. This case can easily be extended to three or more participants by computing more lines that pass through (p, q). The lines have to have different slopes because otherwise some lines may be identical. When n different lines are available, any two can be used to calculate the intersection point and to obtain the secret p.

This approach takes care of the case $k = 2$. Certain information can be given to each of n persons such that any two of them can cooperate to obtain the secret. Before this approach is extended to $k = 3$ and beyond, a subtle point and also a variant should be mentioned. The subtle point involves the use of the extra number q. Our approach is based on a randomly chosen q. When point (p, q) is eventually calculated by two individuals, q is discarded. This may seem a waste. After all, given a secret number s, it is possible to partition it into two numbers p and q, and there is no need to select q randomly as an extra number, to be eventually discarded. Some may also be tempted to hide two related secrets p and q in one point (p, q).

These ideas, however, compromise the security of the method. Anyone given a line pair (a_i, b_i) knows that p and q are related by the expression $q = a_i p + b_i$. This equation is not sufficient to determine p and q, but it expresses a relationship between them, a relationship that might be exploited by an unscrupulous participant in the scheme. An attacker who has the expression $q = a_i\, p + b_i$ *and* also knows something else about p and q, for example, that q is about twice p, can obtain at least approximate values for the two quantities.

The conclusion is that q should be selected at random, even if this seems a waste (avoiding repetition is important in cryptography, but it is also associated with waste).

◇ **Exercise 12.6:** Show how this approach works and what restrictions, if any, are placed on the n points.

And now, to the case $k = 3$. This is handled by extending the geometry from two to three dimensions. Instead of lines through a two-dimensional point, we calculate planes that pass through a three-dimensional point. Given a secret p, select two random numbers q and r to create the triplet (p, q, r) that is considered a point in three-dimensional space. A plane that passes through this point is computed. Knowing the equation of the plane is not enough to obtain the point because there are infinitely many points on a plane. A second, different, plane that passes through (p, q, r) is also computed, but even knowing two planes that pass through a point is not enough, since the intersection of two planes is in general a straight line. The intersection of three different planes is a single point (except for some special cases), so three different planes are needed to obtain the secret $p.$. The approach is as before. n different planes that contain (p, q, r)

are computed, and each of the n participants receives the four parameters of a plane. In this way, any three persons can obtain the point of intersection and thereby be in possession of the secret p.

The line equation $y = ax + b$ is called the *explicit representation* of a line. It is limited because it cannot express a vertical line (for which the slope is infinite). A more general equation is the *implicit representation* $ax + by + c = 0$. This equation can be extended to the three-dimensional case, where $Ax + By + Cz + D = 0$ becomes the equation of a flat plane. A plane can therefore be identified by the 4-tuple (A, B, C, D) of coefficients. Two planes are identical if they have the same four coefficients and are parallel if they share (A, B, C) and differ by D only.

Given a point (p, q, r), we can determine one plane that contains it by the equation $Ap + Bq + Cr + D = 0$. This is one equation in four unknowns, so three unknowns— perhaps (A, B, C)—have to be selected at random and the fourth one, D, computed.

⋄ **Exercise 12.7:** Given the secret $p = 5$, show how to share it among three individuals.

This approach can be extended to any k (i.e., more than three dimensions). We cannot visualize spaces with more than three dimensions, but the mathematics can easily be extended to any number of dimensions. One slight problem is that each participant has to keep $k + 1$ numbers, which makes it somewhat cumbersome for large values of k.

The geometric techniques proposed here are simple but not very practical. They use real numbers, and it is well known that arithmetic operations on real (i.e., floating-point) numbers in different computers generally produce slightly different results. In many applications this makes little or no difference, because the user expects approximate results. In the case of a hidden secret, though, it is important to obtain the exact result. A change in even one bit may produce a completely different secret as, for example, in the case where the secret is the key to decrypting a certain file. Changing even one bit in the key may produce a decrypted file very different from the original. It is therefore important to develop secret-sharing techniques that use only integers. Such methods were first developed in 1979 (two important references are [Shamir 79] and [Blakley 79]), and they use polynomials with integer coefficients (although any functions that are easy to calculate and interpolate can be used).

We denote the secret data (an integer) by s, and we assume that two positive integers n and k are given. We construct a polynomial $P(x)$ of degree $k - 1$ by selecting its (integer) coefficients at random except the first coefficient a_0, which we set to the secret s. The polynomial is

$$P(x) = \sum_{j=0}^{k-1} a_j x^j.$$

We then compute the n values $s_1 = P(1)$, $s_2 = P(2), \ldots, s_n = P(n)$, and distribute the pairs (i, s_i) to n individuals. Each pair is a two-dimensional point (with integer coordinates) through which the polynomial passes. An advantage of this method is that each participant has to keep only two numbers, namely i and s_i, and those numbers are integers. Recall that the geometric method requires each individual to keep several real numbers, depending on the value of k.

Given any k of the (i, s_i) pairs, we can write k equations, solve them, and find the values of all k coefficients a_j, specifically the value of a_0, that is the hidden secret. As an example, we assume that the values of the first k pairs are given. The equations are

$$s_1 = a_0 + a_1 \times 1 + a_2 \times 1^2 + \cdots + a_{k-1} \times 1^{k-1},$$
$$s_2 = a_0 + a_1 \times 2 + a_2 \times 2^2 + \cdots + a_{k-1} \times 2^{k-1},$$
$$\vdots$$
$$s_k = a_0 + a_1 \times k + a_2 \times k^2 + \cdots + a_{k-1} \times k^{k-1}.$$

This is a system of k linear equation in k unknowns, so it has a unique solution. However, if only $k - 1$ pairs (i, s_i) are known, there will not be enough equations to solve for the k coefficients.

Since the coefficients are integers, the value of the polynomial at any point is an integer, all the equations have integer coefficients, and the solutions, which are the original polynomial coefficients, are also integers. The main advantages of this method are as follows.

1. Each participant has to keep information whose size is small and does not depend on k.
2. As long as k is kept constant, pairs (i, s_i) can be added and deleted. If a participant loses or forgets his pair (or suspects that his pair has been leaked to his opponents/competitors), that pair may be deleted and another pair generated.
3. It is possible to replace all the pairs (i, s_i) by simply choosing another polynomial (i.e., selecting a different set of k random integer coefficients a_j). In fact, this should be done periodically to enhance security.
4. Because of human nature, some participants may be considered more important or more trustworthy than others. Such individuals may be given several pairs to reflect their relative importance (pecking order) in the organization. For example, the party secretary may be given three pairs, each undersecretary may be given two pairs, and each member of the central committee (politburo) may be given just one pair. Using a $(3, n)$ threshold scheme under these conditions will allow important decisions to be made by any three central committee members, or by any two committee members plus an undersecretary, or by the party secretary alone.

> All animals are equal, but some animals are more equal than others.
> —George Orwell, *Animal Farm*

More complex threshold schemes are possible for cases where the participants belong to several groups. Imagine, for example, a two-chamber legislative system such as the one used in the United States with a 100-member Senate and a 540-member House of Representatives (as in the 107th Congress). A bill requires majorities in both the House and the Senate in order to become a law. It is therefore wrong to divide the secret (total votes, in this case) into 640 parts and give each senator and each member of the House one part. The secret s has first to be divided into two parts sa for the Senate and sb for the House; then a $(51, 100)$ threshold scheme should be applied to sa and a $(271, 540)$ threshold scheme should be applied to sb. Successful votes in both chambers would obtain both sa and sb and, through them, the majority vote needed.

Problem: Share the sentence
"US 1 south to Port Street, Lucie Boulevard, u-turn at intersection 2nd drive on right" among 21 parties.

Solution: Give each party a column number c and the four (or five) letters in column c.

```
123456789012345678901
US␣1␣south␣to␣Port␣St
reet,␣Lucie␣Boulevard
,␣u-turn␣at␣intersect
ion␣2nd␣drive␣on␣righ
```

12.6 The Four Components

As mentioned in the Introduction, cryptography has four main components, as follows:
- **Confidentiality**. An encrypted message should be unreadable by any unauthorized party.
- **Integrity**. Any attempt to alter or corrupt an encrypted message in storage or in transit is detectable.
- **Nonrepudiation**. The sender cannot later deny having generated or sent the encrypted message, and similarly, the receiver cannot deny receiving it.
- **Authentication**. Sender and receiver can confirm each other's identities and the origin and destination of the message.

These components are now discussed in some detail.

Confidentiality (also termed *secrecy*) is achieved by strong cryptography, but the important cryptographic element here is the key, not the encryption algorithm. Common methods for key management are the Diffie–Hellman–Merkle key exchange (Section 12.1), public-key cryptography (Section 12.2), and the (k, n) threshold schemes discussed in Section 12.5.

Authentication is needed to make sure that both receiver and sender are who they claim to be. When Alice receives a message from Bob, she somehow has to be certain that the message was sent by Bob and not by someone pretending to be Bob. Similarly, before Bob sends a message to Alice, he has to satisfy himself that it is Alice, and not someone else, who is on the receiving end. Authentication has to be done automatically by the computers on both sides, even in the simple case of just two individuals exchanging only a few messages from time to time and sharing a common encryption key.

Imagine a case where Alice's computer receives a request stating that her friend, Bob, wants to upload a file. Alice's operating system has to make sure that the file is in fact coming from Bob, because otherwise it may be a dangerous computer virus. Bob may identify himself by sending a secret password, but the password may be intercepted by Eve and is therefore good for one use only. A better choice is for the two computers to execute a fast and simple *authentication protocol*. Section 12.7 discusses authentication protocols, but here is a simple example.

Alice's computer draws a random number a and sends it, as a challenge, to Bob's computer. That computer encrypts a with the common key and sends the result b, as its response, to Alice's computer which decrypts it and compares the result to a. The challenge a has to be random because Eve may have intercepted both a and the response. Eve may then pretend to be Bob, hoping that the same a would be sent as a challenge, so she would have the response ready. Also, if consecutive challenges are dependent, Eve may discover their dependence, which may provide her with clues to the key. A complete authentication protocol does not stop at this point, because Bob's computer has to satisfy itself that it is really talking to Alice's computer, so it also sends a challenge, waits for a response, and verifies it.

A similar protocol, using public keys, is discussed in Section 12.4.

A special case of authentication is the *digital signature*. For centuries, information had been recorded and stored on paper. In the last few decades, however, more and more information is recorded, stored, and transmitted digitally, which makes it easy to copy and alter. Forging or even just faithfully copying a handwritten document is a job for "experts," while copying and modifying a data file is done by most of us all the time. This is why it is important to have a way to verify the authenticity, validity, authorship, or ownership of a data file: a digital signature. One aspect of digital signatures, namely, *watermarking*, has been researched extensively in the last decade. Watermarking is discussed in Chapter 13.

Integrity is another important component of cryptography. Alice may be able to authenticate Bob as the sender of the message, but Eve can still tamper with the message on its way to Alice. Even a small modification such as adding a word or changing it may seriously affect the message. Adding the word "no" to a sentence reverses its meaning. Tampering with a virus detection program may render it useless. It is therefore important to have a test or a check that will discover any modifications made to a message while on its way through the communications channel from sender to receiver.

Integrity can be achieved by a simple checksum or by its more sophisticated relative, the CRC (cyclic redundancy code, Appendix C). A CRC for a file can be considered the fingerprint of the file. With four CRC bytes (32 bits) per file, there are $2^{32} \approx 4.3$ billion different CRCs, and because of the way the CRC is calculated, any small change in the file is very likely to change the CRC.

To ensure integrity, a CRC of any length can be computed by the sender of a message and sent as a separate message to the receiver. A successful verification of the CRC amounts to a proof of integrity. If it is important to send just one message, instead of the main message and the CRC, then the CRC can be embedded in the message. This can be done by (1) appending the CRC to the message, (2) chopping the message and the CRC into n parts each and merging the chunks, or (3) applying any steganographic method (Chapter 13) to embed the CRC in the file and using the encryption key as a stego-key.

Nonrepudiation is necessary because a person may deny or may even forget that an important message has been received. A general issuing important commands during a battle wants to make sure not only that the commands have been received by the proper officers but also that no officer can deny (or *repudiate*) that a command had been received. This can be done either by using an escrow (a third, trusted party) or by using the public-key idea.

In the first approach, the receiver, Lieutenant Bob, sends an encrypted receipt stating that the message had been received. The receipt is sent to the sender, Colonel Alice, but also to an escrow. In case of a dispute, it is the escrow, not Alice, who presents the decrypted receipt to prove that the original message had in fact been received by Bob.

In the second approach, Bob receives the original message and immediately sends Alice a receipt encrypted with his private key. Anyone, including Alice, can decrypt the receipt, but only Bob could have encrypted it, since he is the only one who has his private key.

12.7 Authentication

In addition to encrypting and decrypting messages, cryptography is concerned with the problem of authentication, i.e., confirming the identities of any individuals sending and receiving messages. Authentication is one of the four main components of cryptography (Section 12.6). Like other topics in cryptography, authentication may at first seem impossible. How can the identity of another person be confirmed by sending messages back and forth, especially through an unsecure line where any eavesdropper may listen and even corrupt the messages or send a forged one? We normally identify a person by sight (seeing the person), sound (hearing a familiar voice), by asking personal questions, or by examining identification papers, but how can this be done by computers?

In order to better understand the protocols described here, we start with a question, follow it with a story, and then describe a simple mathematical game. The question is: How can a person convince others that he possesses a secret without giving it away? In many cases this may be impossible, but there are examples where this is easy to do. One such example is the story of the solution to the cubic equation.

Solving equations (and the question of which equations have solutions and which ones do not) was one of the fundamental problems in mathematics until its final solution by Evariste Galois and Niels Abel in the 1820s. A linear (first-degree) equation is trivial to solve. The solution of $ax + b = 0$ is $x = -b/a$. A quadratic (degree-2) equation is also easy to solve, but the solutions may be complex numbers. Even high-school students learn that $ax^2 + by + c = 0$ has the two solutions

$$x = \frac{-b \pm \sqrt{b^2 - 4ac}}{2a}.$$

In contrast, the cubic (degree-3) equation $ax^3 + bx^2 + cx + d = 0$ baffled mathematicians for generations. In 1535, however, the Italian Niccolo Fontana, known as Tartaglia (the stammerer), announced that he had a formula to solve such equations. According to the fashion of the times, however, he refused to publish his formula and kept it secret. Obviously, it was easy for him to convince others that he really knew how to solve the cubic. Anyone giving him four numbers, such as $a = 1$, $b = -2$, $c = -5$, and $d = 6$, would receive, after a while, the three solutions of the equation $x^3 - 2x^2 - 5x + 6 = 0$ (they are, by the way, 1, -2, and 3). For the full story, see [Dunham 90]. (The use of anagrams in Section 8.1 for encryption is a related topic.)

A procedure whereby someone can convince others that he possesses a secret without disclosing the secret is called a *zero-knowledge protocol.*

And now, for the promised game. This is a simple, albeit not very interesting, mathematical game whose principle is later applied to an authentication protocol. We assume that the game is played by Alice and Bob. Alice claims that she knows a number s that satisfies $s^2 \bmod 45 = 36$, and her task is to convince Bob that she really knows such a number without actually telling him what the number is. (We assume that her choice is $s = 6$, but $s = 9$ and many nonintegers also satisfy this relation. Bob can easily figure that out, so the real protocol has to use very large numbers, making it impractical to find a solution.) The game is played in steps. In the first step, Alice selects a number r at random and sends Bob the value $x = r^2 \bmod 45$ (if, for example, $r = 7$, then $x = 4$). In the second step, Bob selects a bit b at random. If $b = 0$, Bob asks Alice for the value of r. If $b = 1$, Bob asks for the value of $(r \cdot s) \bmod 45$ (which in our example is $(7 \cdot 6) \bmod 45 = 42$). In step 3, Alice sends Bob the value he asked for, and in step 4 Bob verifies that value.

Verification is simple and can be done without knowing the value of s. If Alice sent the value of r, Bob verifies that $r^2 \bmod 45$ (which is $7^2 \bmod 45 = 4$) is the value x that Alice sent him in step 1. If Alice sent the value of $(r \cdot s) \bmod 45$ (i.e., 42), Bob uses the identity $(r \cdot s)^2 \bmod 45 = [(r^2 \bmod 45)(s^2 \bmod 45)] \bmod 45$ to verify the 42. He knows that $r^2 \bmod 45$ is supposed to be 4 and $s^2 \bmod 45$ is supposed to be 36. He first computes $42^2 \bmod 45$, then $(4 \cdot 36) \bmod 45$, and finds that both expressions equal 9. All this can be done without knowing the value of s.

Bob can verify that Alice knows what she is doing, while at the same time he cannot figure out the value of s because the modulo function is one-way. Bob can also ask for several rounds of this game, to make sure Alice sends him consistent, verifiable data each time.

This game becomes more interesting when Alice does not know such an s and is trying to convince Bob that she does. In step 1, she can select any r and send Bob the value $r^2 \bmod 45$ as her x. In step 3, she can easily send r to Bob, if he asks for it, and he has no reason to become suspicious. However, if Bob asks for $(r \cdot s) \bmod 45$, then Alice is in trouble because she does not have s. She can, of course, send a random number a and claim that this is $(r \cdot s) \bmod 45$, but Bob wouldn't be able to verify this number and would become suspicious. Recall that Bob already has two numbers, the value of $s^2 \bmod 45$ (36, which is a bluff, since Alice does not know s) and the value of $r^2 \bmod 45$. When Bob computes $[(r^2 \bmod 45)(s^2 \bmod 45)] \bmod 45$, he will find that the result does not equal $a^2 \bmod 45$.

The cheating Alice has another choice. She may claim that she knows a number s such that $s^2 \bmod 45 = 36$, and in step 1 she can find a suitable value that can pass Bob's verification, declare it to be $r^2 \bmod 45$, and send it to Bob as her x. Unfortunately for Alice, if Bob asks for r in step 2, she won't be able to send it in step 3. Knowing r, it is easy to compute $r^2 \bmod 45$, but knowing $r^2 \bmod 45$, one cannot compute the value of r because this involves a square root modulo 45, and the computation of the square root modulo n of an integer r is impractical for very large values of r. If Bob now asks for r in step 2, the best that Alice can do is send him a random number. Such a number will not pass verification in step 4 and will raise Bob's suspicion.

The conclusion is that if Alice does not know s, she can select either an r or a suitable value for $r^2 \bmod 45$. In the former case, she will fail if Bob asks for $(r \cdot s) \bmod 45$, and in the latter case she will fail if Bob asks for r. Her chance of cheating Bob successfully is therefore 0.5. When this game is played n times, Alice's chance of cheating Bob every time is 0.5^n, a number that gets smaller for large values of n.

A practical authentication protocol, similar to the one presented in the next section, can be based on this game and on the fact that finding various values of s when $s^2 \bmod n$ is given may be easy for small values of n but computationally infeasible for very large ones (hundreds of decimal digits long). There is another point to consider. It is relatively easy to compute s from $s^2 \bmod n$ if the prime factors of n are known, but it is practically impossible to calculate the prime factors of a large integer n.

Because of this, an actual authentication protocol should include a third, trusted party, a key-distribution center. This center selects two large prime numbers p and q, and multiplies them to obtain a nonsecret very large product n that is sent to both Alice and Bob. In addition, the center sends Alice a second, secret number s (her private key) and a third number $v = s^2 \bmod n$ that is her public key. (If Alice already has a public key v, she can send it to the center, where the factors of n will be used to determine s.) When Alice wants to identify herself to Bob, she (1) selects a random number r that is relatively prime to n, (2) computes $x = r^2 \bmod n$, and (3) sends x to Bob. On receiving this number, Bob randomly selects a bit b and sends it to Alice. Alice examines b. If b is zero, Alice computes $y = (r \cdot s) \bmod n$; otherwise, she computes $y = r \bmod n$. She then sends y to Bob, who verifies it. He first verifies that y is relatively prime to n; then, if $b = 0$, he verifies that $y^2 \bmod n$ equals x, and if $b = 1$, he verifies that $y^2 \bmod n$ equals $(x \cdot v) \bmod n$. If Bob is not satisfied, this protocol can be repeated with a different r.

The advantages of this protocol are as follows.

1. All the computations involved are simple and very few modulo n calculations are needed.
2. Bob (and any eavesdroppers) cannot discover the value of the private key s.
3. The probability of someone who doesn't possess s convincing Bob that she is Alice is 2^{-t}, where t is the number of rounds (number of times the protocol is repeated).

12.7.1 The Feige–Fiat–Shamir Protocol

This identification protocol [Feige et al. 88] employs a parallel construction to increase reliability and decrease computations. The first step is to compute a large integer n as a product of two large primes p and q. Based on this n, k random values r_i are chosen, all relatively prime to n, and the public key $v_i = r_i^2 \bmod n$ is computed for $i = 1, 2, \ldots k$.

This key is a set of k numbers. A private key is then computed as the set of k values s_i such that s_i is the smallest value that satisfies $s_i = \sqrt{1/v_i} \bmod n$. The identification protocol itself is done in the following steps.

1. Alice selects a random r that is less than n, computes $x = r^2 \bmod n$, and sends x to Bob.
2. Bob selects a random binary string $b_1 b_2 \ldots b_k$ and sends it to Alice.
3. Alice computes $y = r \cdot (s_1^{b_1} \times s_2^{b_2} \times \cdots \times s_k^{b_k}) \bmod n$ and sends it to Bob (the product consists of those s_i for which b_i is 1).
4. Bob verifies that $x = y \cdot (v_1^{b_1} \times v_2^{b_2} \times \cdots \times v_k^{b_k}) \bmod n$ (he also multiplies only those v_i for which b_i is 1).

After these steps are repeated t times, the chance of a cheater (someone who doesn't have Alice's private key, the k values s_i) to successfully convince Bob that she is Alice is 2^{-kt}. The parallel structure employing k values has reduced the chance of wrong identification considerably, while adding at most $k-1$ multiplications.

12.7.2 The Guillou–Quisquater Protocol

The Feige–Fiat–Shamir identification protocol is practical but may require many rounds for secure identification. Certain applications, such as identifying a smartcard to a computer, can benefit from an identification protocol that uses few exchanges and very little memory. The Guillou–Quisquater identification protocol discussed here [Guillou and Quisquater 88] employs one round of four steps and is therefore fast. However, it is not provably secure. In the description that follows, it is best to think of Alice as a smartcard and of Bob as a computer trying to identify the card.

Both Alice and Bob share public information in the form of an exponent v and a modulus n, which is a large number obtained by multiplying two large prime numbers. Alice (the smartcard) contains a set of credentials that consist of the card's issuer, serial number, expiration date, and possibly other items. This set is a long binary string that is denoted by B. Alice also has a private key K computed to satisfy the relation $B \cdot K^v = 1 \bmod n$.

Alice sends her credentials B to Bob and still has to convince him that she knows her private key without divulging that key. The protocol steps are as follows.

1. Alice selects a random integer r in the interval $[1, n-1]$, computes $T = r^v \bmod n$, and sends T to Bob.
2. Bob selects a random integer d in the range $[0, v-1]$ and sends it to Alice.
3. Alice computes $D = r \cdot K^d \bmod n$ and sends it to Bob.
4. Bob computes $D^v B^d$ and compares it to T. Positive identification is assumed if the two quantities are equal.

Keeping in mind that $B \cdot K^v = 1 \bmod n$, the chain of computations is

$$D^v B^d = (r \cdot K^d)^v B^d = r^v K^{dv} B^d = r^v (B \, K^v)^d = r^v \equiv T \bmod n.$$

12.7.3 The Schnorr Identification Protocol

The Schnorr protocol starts when a key authentication center (KAC) selects two primes p and q such that q is a prime factor of $p - 1$, and then selects an $a \neq 1$ such that $a^q = 1 \bmod p$. The three quantities a, p, and q don't have to be secret, and they are used by the KAC to generate a pair of keys, public and private. The private key s is any number less than q, and the public key is computed as $v = a^{-s} \bmod p$. In addition, there is also a security parameter t that controls the difficulty of breaking the method. The developer of the method [Schnorr 91] recommends that p be about 512 bits, q be about 140 bits, and t be set to 72. The protocol then consists of steps as follows.

1. Alice selects a random $r < q$, computes $x = a^r \bmod p$, and sends x to Bob.
2. Bob selects a random number e in the range $[0, 2^t - 1]$ and sends it to Alice.
3. Alice computes $y = (r + se) \bmod q$ and sends y to Bob.
4. Bob verifies that x equals $a^y v^e \bmod p$.

The algorithm uses exponentiation, so breaking it must be done with logarithms, and discrete logarithms are difficult to compute. For $p \geq 2^{512}$ and $q \geq 2^{140}$, known methods for computing a discrete logarithm require at least 2^{72} steps, which is why the security parameter t should be set to at least 72.

The discrete logarithm problem is to find x in the expression $B^x = P \bmod m$.

12.8 SSL: Secure Socket Layer

The following is a dramatization. Alice is hunched over her computer, browsing the Internet. Her wedding to Bob is in a week, and she is still looking for a wedding dress. She has just found a beautiful cream-colored layered chiffon dress that is exactly her size (36–24–36) and is within her price range. It is sold online by ChiffonDresses.com. Alice takes out her credit card, ready to send her number and order the dress, but her hand suddenly freezes in midair. She has just remembered that important transactions on the Internet require special security. She checks the bottom-left corner of her screen and yes, there is a small lock, similar to the one shown here, that assures her that the transaction she is about to perform is secure (the URL also changes to https instead of http). She can order her dress with confidence, being reasonably certain that no one can intercept and steal her credit card number.

This scenario is common. Most of us perform sensitive transactions over the Internet, and we expect them to be private. Online purchasing is one example. Online banking, where a bank account can be reviewed by a customer after a PIN is sent, is another.

This section describes the SSL (secure socket layer) protocol employed by all major Web browsers, as well as by other software, to secure messages sent over the Internet. First, a disclaimer. SSL provides secure communications but cannot guarantee total security. A credit card number or other sensitive information sent over the Internet by the SSL protocol is encrypted and cannot be compromised while in transit. When it arrives at its destination, however, the security provided by SSL ceases and the information may become vulnerable. A dishonest employee may steal it. An insecure data base may be taken over by a hacker and its content copied and misused. The conclusion is simple. Don't trust SSL all the way. Trust it only for communicating your sensitive data. If there is any reason to doubt the integrity of the receiver, don't send the data. The Better Business Bureau [BBB 03] is one source that can be employed to evaluate the integrity of a commercial organization.

SSL was developed at Netscape Communications, Inc. in 1994 in response to users' demand for secure Internet communications. It has since evolved and been strengthened considerably by several organizations. Today, the SSL protocol that is mostly used in the transport layer security (TLS), and there are other versions of SSL, such as an open version (openssl) and a version for wireless communications (WTLS).

Two recommended references are [Rescorla 00] and [Thomas 00].

As before, we assume two protagonists, Alice and Bob. Alice plays the part of a consumer trying to purchase an item online. Bob is the seller. The SSL protocol proceeds in the following steps:

1. An authentication protocol is executed by Alice to make sure that Bob is really who he claims to be. Bob's public key is sent to Alice as part of the protocol. This protocol is based on the public-key concept and employs RSA encryption and also a trusted third party.

2. Alice selects a random key for encrypting her sensitive information. This key is encrypted with Bob's public key and is sent to Bob.

3. Alice uses this key to encrypt her sensitive data with DES or another strong encryption algorithm. Bob uses the same key and algorithm to decrypt the data. Several messages can be exchanged this way between the two parties in complete privacy.

It is obvious that step 1 is the most important part of SSL. It provides secure communications over an insecure channel. This step is complex and slow, which is why it is used only for communicating a short (normally 128-bit) key. The sensitive data itself is encrypted with a fast cipher. This step depends on a basic property of the RSA encryption algorithm. Data encrypted with a public key can be decrypted only with the corresponding private key, but data can also be encrypted with the private key and decrypted only with the corresponding public key. With this in mind, we start with a simple authentication protocol. (We use the notation "<message> key" to indicate a message encrypted with a certain key.) If Alice wants to authenticate Bob, she can send him a short message and have Bob encrypt it with his private key and return the result.

Alice → Bob: `Authenticate this.`
Bob → Alice: `<Authenticate this> Bob's private key.`

Alice now decrypts this result with Bob's public key. If the result matches her original message, she has authenticated Bob. This simple protocol has two drawbacks, as follows:

1. Alice must know Bob's public key. If Alice and Bob are members of a group— say, both are scientists and have been communicating by email for a while—then their

public keys are known to all the group's members because they are included in each email message. However, if Bob is an organization, such as a new online store, Alice may not have the public key. Even if Bob sends his public key to Alice, she cannot be sure that it really came from Bob's store; it could have been sent by Eve pretending to be Bob and trying to steal Alice's card number.

2. Encrypting a message with your private key and sending it to Alice leads to weak security. Remember that Alice has the original message. If she also has its private-key encryption, she may use both to pretend to be Bob.

Our simple protocol needs improvements. The first one eliminates the need to encrypt Alice's message with Bob's private key. Instead, Bob selects a new message, computes its *message digest*, encrypts the digest with his private key, and sends the (plain) message and the encrypted digest to Alice.

Alice → Bob: `Looking for Bob.`
Bob → Alice: `I'm Bob, <Digest[I'm Bob]> Bob's private key.`

The digest of a message is a function of the message with the following useful properties: (1) it is practically infeasible to compute the original message from its digest and (2) the chance of finding another message that will produce the same digest is extremely small. In practice, a digest is a hash function that hashes text of any length to a small (typically 128-bit) number. The SHA-1 hash function is currently popular as a digest generator. It has replaced the (somewhat similar) MD5 function, which is described below.

With this protocol, Bob still has to send a message (`I'm Bob`) and the encrypted version of its digest (this is known as a digital signature), but now he can select the message, which gives him more protection from an unscrupulous Alice. The protocol constitutes authentication because Alice has a plain message and the private-key encryption of its digest. She can decrypt the digest, digest the message, and compare the two digests. There is still the problem of having Bob's public key and being certain that it is Bob's, and no one else's public key. Here is what may happen if Eve pretends to be Bob.

Alice → Bob: `I'm looking for Bob.`
Eve → Alice: `I'm Bob, Eve's-public-key.`
Alice → Bob: `Are you?`
Eve → Alice: `Of course I am, <Digest[Of course I am]> Eve's private key.`

The solution to this dilemma involves a third, trusted party, an escrow, that issues *certificates*. When Bob opens his store, he applies for a certificate from an escrow. The escrow company sends an inspector to check Bob and his facilities and to look at their operations and identification. If all is satisfactory, a certificate is issued, but it has an expiration date and has to be renewed periodically. Admittedly, this solution is not elegant. In principle, we would like a protocol that involves just the two communicating parties, but in practice a third party is needed. A certificate contains the following fields Figure 12.3:

1. The name of the certificate issuer (the escrow)
2. A digital signature of the certificate issuer

3. The name of the subject, Bob (the entity for which the certificate is issued)
4. The subject's public key
5. The certificate's expiration date

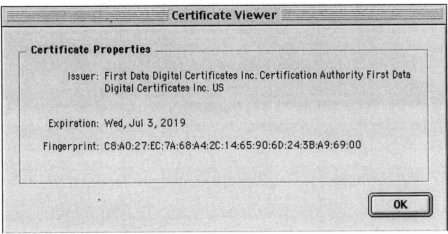

Figure 12.3: A Certificate.

Figure 12.5 is a detailed listing of the fields of a typical certificate.

Many organizations apply for certificates, so there must be many certificate issuers. Alice doesn't know all of them. She can be expected to know only a few. There is therefore a need for root certificate issuers. Every leading Web browser comes with a list of root certificates preinstalled. A root certificate (also known as a *CA* or *certificate authority*) belongs to a trusted authority that can issue certificates to other, smaller certificate issuers after checking each to make sure it can be trusted. The encryption preferences (or security preferences) menu of the browser can display the list of CA certificates it knows. If the certificate has expired, the browser displays a dialog box similar to Figure 12.4 that gives the user a choice to continue the sensitive web session or terminate it.

With certificates, the SSL protocol proceeds as follows:

Alice → Bob: I'm looking for Bob.
Bob → Alice: I'm Bob, Bob's certificate.
Alice → Bob: Are you really?
Bob → Alice: Definitely, <Digest[Definitely]> Bob's private key.

It is the certificate that provides Alice (or, in practice, her Web browser) with Bob's public key. To verify that this is really Bob's certificate, Alice's browser reads the certificate's issuer name (say, Y) and signature from the certificate. The digital signature contains the issuer's own certificate, which has been issued by one of the root issuers (call it X). The browser has a list of the root certificate issuers, and it communicates

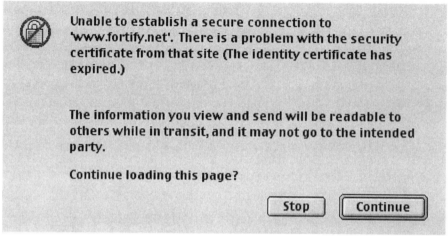

Figure 12.4: An Expired Certificate.

with root issuer X to verify the certificate of issuer Y. This is a slow, tedious process, so it is used as little as possible.

Eve may try to impersonate Bob in this protocol, so we have to keep her in mind. She can execute step 2 in the protocol, because she may have Bob's certificate from a past transaction with him, but she cannot execute step 4 because she doesn't have Bob's private key.

The protocol above is the first and most important step in the complete, three-step SSL protocol. Once it has been executed, Alice is confident that she is dealing with Bob and that she has his public key. In the second step, Alice (or rather her browser) selects a random number to serve as a secret key and sends it to Bob, encrypted with his public key, as a short message. Only Bob can decrypt this message, but again we have to place ourselves in Eve's shoes. What can she do? She cannot decrypt this short message, but she can damage it on its way to Bob. This may be useful to Eve, so the SSL protocol must have a way for Bob to identify damaged messages. One way of verifying a message is to append to it a message authentication code (MAC) that consists of a digest of the message and of the secret key. Eve doesn't know the secret key, so she cannot generate the MAC. Here is the revised protocol

Alice → Bob: Is this Bob?
Bob → Alice: I'm Bob, Bob's certificate.
Alice → Bob: Are you really?
Bob → Alice: Definitely, <Digest[Definitely]> Bob's private key.
Alice → Bob: You have been authenticated.
Alice → Bob: Here is our new key <secret-key> Bob's public key.
Alice computes: MAC=Digest[My CC # is 12345, secret-key].
Alice → Bob: <My CC # is 12345, MAC> secret-key.

Bob knows to expect two-part messages, where the second part consists of the MAC of the first part. Any corrupted message can easily be identified by Bob. Once Bob has received the new secret key (normally, 40, 56, or 128 bits) from Alice, the two can exchange messages with confidence. The messages are encrypted with this key by a secure, fast algorithm, such as DES or RC4.

As noted earlier, SSL was developed at Netscape Communications in 1994. Just a year later, several hackers discovered a weakness in the Netscape implementation of the first SSL version. It turned out that the secret key was selected by a pseudorandom number generator (PRNG) whose seed was a combination of the current time (just the seconds and microseconds) and the process id. Netscape programmers believed that such a combination was sufficiently random and would lead to pseudorandom numbers that could be used as secure keys. However, someone intercepting information packets sent by a browser can have a good idea of the time (in seconds) when the packets were generated. Also, someone with access to any account on the operating system where the Netscape browser is running can find the id of any process. The microseconds part of the seed can then be found by trying the million values between 0 and 999,999. It seems that Netscape has since improved the way the seed of the PRNG is computed.

12.8.1 Example of a Certificate

Figure 12.5 is a detailed listing of the fields of a typical certificate. The issuer part and the subject part have the fields C (two-letter international country code), ST (state or province), L (locality), O (organization name), and OU (organizational unit).

12.9 MD5 Hashing

MD5 (short for *message digest 5*) is a hash function developed by Ronald Rivest in 1992 ([Rivest 92] and [rfc1321 03]) to serve as a fast and secure message digest for digital signature applications. MD5 inputs a message of any length and hashes it to a 128-bit number that can serve as a fingerprint of the message. MD5 was designed to be especially fast on 32-bit machines. MD5 is an extension of the similar MD4 algorithm [Rivest 91]. It is somewhat slower than MD4 but is deemed more secure. Based on the experience of the algorithm's developer, it is conjectured (although not proved) that it is computationally infeasible to generate a message whose MD5 digest will equal a given 128-bit number or to find two nontrivial messages that have the same MD5 digest. Specifically, it is conjectured that the difficulty of coming up with two messages that will have the same MD5 output is on the order of 2^{64} operations, and the difficulty of finding a message that has a given MD5 digest is on the order of 2^{128} operations.

Computations in MD5 are based on 32-bit words. Thus, the symbol "+" indicates modulo 2^{32} addition of 32-bit words, and other symbols also correspond to operations on 32 bits.

We start with a b-bit message, where b is an arbitrary nonnegative integer. It can be zero and doesn't have to be a multiple of 8 or of any other number. The bits are denoted by m_0 through m_{b-1}. Hashing the message is done by scrambling its bits in five steps as follows:

```
Certificate:
Data:
Version: 1 (0x0)
Serial Number: 0 (0x0)
Signature Algorithm: md5WithRSAEncryption
Issuer:
  C=US,
  ST=NC,
  L=Cary,
  O=My New Outfit, Inc.,
  OU=Sales,
  CN=ntbox.somewhere.com/Email=me@somewhere.com

Validity
  Not Before: Oct 7 04:19:24 1999 GMT
  Not After : Oct 6 04:19:24 2000 GMT

Subject:
  C=US,
  ST=NC,
  L=Cary,
  O=My New Outfit, Inc.,
  OU=Sales,
  CN=ntbox.somewhere.com/Email=me@somewhere.com

Subject Public Key Info:
Public Key Algorithm: rsaEncryption
RSA Public Key: (1024 bit)
Modulus (1024 bit):

00:c9:dd:68:31:ca:1c:ab:74:7c:21:a8:de:71:22:
25:ec:48:dd:54:34:b5:b8:be:ad:96:cf:56:ad:a2:
7d:9f:81:d5:62:3a:f1:c2:03:4d:8d:73:a3:cb:ac:
f8:f4:d7:95:0d:3f:9e:2c:8f:5f:d3:40:91:09:79:
21:c4:8b:f6:0a:3b:2c:c7:42:3d:2c:c3:5b:17:68:
58:2e:47:42:1e:24:41:1d:59:ba:57:0c:26:63:2e:
46:55:72:e5:1e:61:6c:6e:c2:73:ad:e0:68:ed:70:
a9:43:73:69:b5:c3:9f:64:54:d6:12:11:f3:10:38:
42:e8:54:82:23:f7:20:26:03

Exponent: 65537 (0x10001)

Signature Algorithm: md5WithRSAEncryption

4f:27:7b:c5:f1:52:33:bc:f8:50:19:b9:98:e6:3b:08:9b:4b:
7b:24:f8:80:10:18:a4:25:6a:39:b1:75:35:05:64:54:ec:5e:
e4:c1:88:fb:7f:72:d1:32:f4:8c:0d:08:28:7e:7e:a5:5f:61:
9c:cc:b4:5c:13:f0:71:a8:d0:56:58:11:e6:b8:35:0a:01:b7:
72:7f:e8:a7:b6:82:aa:52:5d:05:29:d8:48:ba:26:8e:ed:41:
38:86:b8:62:2e:9a:f1:be:99:3c:20:76:57:0f:70:4b:a6:18:
82:aa:90:0c:1f:18:05:c3:98:b8:20:9e:e5:64:02:0d:01:4e:
c4:4e
```

Figure 12.5: A Detailed Certificate.

Step 1. Append padding bits. The message is extended by appending bits until its length becomes 64 bits less than the next multiple of 512. We say that the extended message size is congruent to 448 modulo 512. Padding is always done, even if the original length b of the message satisfies the above condition. This implies that at least one bit and at most 512 bits are appended. The first bit appended is a 1 and the remaining bits are zeros.

Step 2. Append length. The value of b (the original length of the message) is now appended to the extended message as a 64-bit number. If b is greater than 2^{64}, only the 64 least-significant bits of b are appended (the message length cannot be deduced from its 64 least-significant bits, but there is no need to deduce it). The message length at this point is a multiple of 512, so it is also a multiple of 16×32. We denote the number of 32-bit words in the message by N (N is a multiple of 16) and the words themselves by $M(0)$ through $M(N-1)$.

Step 3. Initialize buffer. A four-word buffer denoted by A, B, C, and D is allocated. These are initialized to the following values

$$A \leftarrow 01234567_{16}, \quad B \leftarrow 89abcdef_{16}, \quad C \leftarrow fedcba98_{16}, \quad D \leftarrow 76543210_{16}.$$

The final 128-bit result will be computed in these four 32-bit words.

Step 4. Process message. The hashing of the message involves four functions denoted by F, G, H, and I, a 16-word array X, a 64-word table T, four words denoted by AA, BB, CC, and DD, and shifts and logical operations. Each of the four functions receives three 32-bit words as input parameters and computes one word. The definitions of the four functions are

$$\mathtt{F}(X,Y,Z) = (X \times Y) \vee (\mathrm{not}(X) \times Z), \quad \mathtt{G}(X,Y,Z) = (X \times Z) \vee (Y \times \mathrm{not}(Z)),$$
$$\mathtt{H}(X,Y,Z) = X \text{ xor } Y \text{ xor } Z, \quad \mathtt{I}(X,Y,Z) = Y \text{ xor } (X \vee \mathrm{not}(Z)),$$

where $\times$, $\vee$, and, xor indicate logical AND, OR and XOR, respectively.

A table T of 64 constants is first computed, such that element T[i] (for i values 1 through 64) becomes the integer part of the product of abs(sin(i)) (where i is in radians) and the constant 4294967296. This table serves to further scramble the bits of the message.

The computations consist of steps where each step processes a block of 16 non-consecutive words from the message. Each step consists of four rounds. Each round starts by initializing array X to a block of 16 different words from the message and then scrambles the values of A, B, C, and D by means of T, X, and one of the four functions. Here are the details (the notation X <<< s denotes an s position, left-circular shift of X).

```
for i=0 to N/16-1 do {loop on blocks}
 for j=0 to 15 do
  X[j]:=M[i*16+j]
 endfor {j}
 AA:=A; BB:=B; CC:=C; DD:=D;
```

```
{Round 1. We denote by [abcd k s i] the operation
  a=b+((a+F(b,c,d)+X[k]+T[i])<<<s).
  Round 1 consists of the following 16 operations}
[ABCD  0  7  1]    [DABC  1 12  2]  [CDAB  2 17  3]  [BCDA  3 22  4]
[ABCD  4  7  5]    [DABC  5 12 16]  [CDAB  6 17  7]  [BCDA  7 22  8]
[ABCD  8  7  9]    [DABC  9 12 10]  [CDAB 10 17 11]  [BCDA 11 22 12]
[ABCD 12  7 13]    [DABC 13 12 14]  [CDAB 14 17 15]  [BCDA 15 22 16]
{Round 2. We denote by [abcd k s i] the operation
  a=b+((a+G(b,c,d)+X[k]+T[i])<<<s).
  Round 2 consists of the following 16 operations}
[ABCD  1  5 17]    [DABC  6  9 18]  [CDAB 11 14 19]  [BCDA  0 20 20]
[ABCD  5  5 21]    [DABC 10  9 22]  [CDAB 15 14 23]  [BCDA  4 20 24]
[ABCD  9  5 25]    [DABC 14  9 26]  [CDAB  3 14 27]  [BCDA  8 20 28]
[ABCD 13  5 29]    [DABC  2  9 30]  [CDAB  7 14 31]  [BCDA 12 20 32]
{Round 3. We denote by [abcd k s i] the operation
  a=b+((a+H(b,c,d)+X[k]+T[i])<<<s).
  Round 3 consists of the following 16 operations}
[ABCD  5  4 33]    [DABC  8 11 34]  [CDAB 11 16 35]  [BCDA 14 23 36]
[ABCD  1  4 37]    [DABC  4 11 38]  [CDAB  7 16 39]  [BCDA 10 23 40]
[ABCD 13  4 41]    [DABC  0 11 42]  [CDAB  3 16 43]  [BCDA  6 23 44]
[ABCD  9  4 45]    [DABC 12 11 46]  [CDAB 15 16 47]  [BCDA  2 23 48]
{Round 4. We denote by [abcd k s i] the operation
  a=b+((a+I(b,c,d)+X[k]+T[i])<<<s).
  Round 4 consists of the following 16 operations}
[ABCD  0  6 49]    [DABC  7 10 50]  [CDAB 14 15 51]  [BCDA  5 21 52]
[ABCD 12  6 53]    [DABC  3 10 54]  [CDAB 10 15 55]  [BCDA  1 21 56]
[ABCD  8  6 57]    [DABC 15 10 58]  [CDAB  6 15 59]  [BCDA 13 21 60]
[ABCD  4  6 61]    [DABC 11 10 62]  [CDAB  2 15 63]  [BCDA  9 21 64]
{final operations}
A:=A+AA; B:=B+BB; C:=C+CC; D:=D+DD;
endfor {i}
```

Step 5. Output. The final output is the four words A, B, C, and D, each read as four bytes from right to left. Thus, the most-significant byte of the 128-bit output is the least-significant byte of A, and the output ends with the most-significant byte of D.

The MD5 algorithm is based on the long experience of its creator. It has been used extensively since its inception about a decade ago, and no weaknesses have been discovered.

> Symmetry is what we see at a glance.
>
> —Blaise Pascal

13
Data Hiding

Today, in the digital age, any type of data, such as text, images, and audio, can be digitized, stored indefinitely, and transmitted at high speeds. Notwithstanding these advantages, digital data also has a downside. It is easy to access illegally, tamper with, and copy for purposes of copyright violation.

There is, therefore, a need to hide secret identification inside certain types of digital data. This information can be used to prove copyright ownership, to identify attempts to tamper with sensitive data, and to embed annotations. Storing, hiding, or embedding secret information in all types of digital data is one of the tasks of the field of steganography.

Steganography is the art and science of data hiding. In contrast with cryptography, which secures data by transforming it into another, unreadable format, steganography makes data invisible by hiding (or embedding) it in another piece of data, known alternatively as the *cover*, the *host*, or the *carrier*. The modified cover, including the hidden data, is referred to as a *stego object*. It can be stored or transmitted. We can think of cryptography as overt secret writing and of steganography as covert secret writing.

Secret data can be embedded in various types of cover. If the data is embedded in a text file (covertext), the result is a stego-text (or stegotext) object. Thus, it is possible to have coverimage and stegoimage, coveraudio and stegoaudio, covervideo and stegovideo, etc. This terminology was agreed upon at the First International Workshop on Information Hiding [Pfitzmann 96].

The word *steganography* is derived from the Greek στεγανος γραφεν, meaning *covered writing*. The term was coined by Johannes Trithemius, whose *Steganographia* [Trithemius 06], the first treatise on this subject, was published in 1606, long after his death. Another old book on steganography and cryptography is *Schola Steganographica* by Gaspari Schotti (1665) [Schotti 65]. Four hundred pages in this book are devoted to steganography.

Notice that the term *steganography* (spelled with *stega*, meaning *covered*) is not related to stegosauruses (spelled with *stego*, meaning *roof*), although one may claim, as a pun, that *roof* and *cover* are semantically related.

Steganography is useful even in cases where cryptographic tools are available and provide adequate security. The reason is psychological. When a file is examined or intercepted and is found to be encrypted, it may raise suspicion in the mind of the interceptor, who may presume that the sender is performing or planning malicious or illegal acts. Someone who does not want to risk raising suspicion and prefers not to attract attention may opt to use steganography to hide sensitive data (perhaps after encrypting it, to feel even safer) in an innocuous cover.

Embedding data in a cover is a technological challenge. The embedded data should not increase the size of the cover, because this would be noticeable to an attacker familiar with the original cover. Secret data should therefore be embedded in "holes" in the cover (places where the cover data has redundancies). Unfortunately for the steganographer, lossy compression techniques operate by removing redundancy from the cover, thereby destroying any data hidden in such holes. Thus, steganography faces the additional challenge of embedding the secret data in a robust way to make it impervious to lossy compression and other operations that may modify the cover.

Figure 13.1 shows the main steps in a typical steganographic method. The encoding algorithm receives three inputs: the secret data to be embedded, the cover data, and an optional steganographic key. The algorithm then produces a stegocover that can be stored and/or transmitted. The decoding algorithm receives the stegocover and the (optional) stego-key and extracts the secret data. In some algorithms, the decoder cannot actually extract the data and can only answer the question, "Is this data really embedded in the file being examined?" This makes sense in cases where the hidden data is a watermark, originally placed in the cover to prove ownership or simply for pride of ownership. Also note that certain decoders need the original cover in order to extract the data embedded in the stegocover.

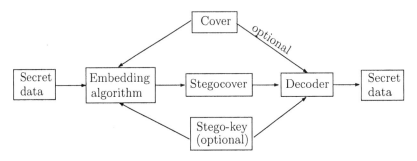

Figure 13.1: The Main Steps of Data Hiding and Extracting.

Fabien Petitcolas maintains a data hiding Web page that includes an annotated bibliography [Petitcolas 03] on the field of information hiding and digital watermarking. Some popular steganography programs are available at [cypherpunks 04].

Watermarking World [WatermarkingWorld 03] is an international meeting point for scientists, researchers, and organizations active in digital watermarking (one of the areas of steganography). It is the first nonprofit organization dedicated to digital watermarking. It provides means and services to the digital watermarking community. Its goal is to facilitate communication among those active in this field and to contribute to research and implementation efforts.

The organization of this chapter is as follows. Following a discussion of basic features, applications of steganography, the concepts of watermarking and fingerprinting, and intuitive methods, the remainder of the chapter is devoted to text steganography (data hiding in text files) starting at Section 13.6.

13.1 Basic Features

The various steganographic methods described in this chapter have different strengths and weaknesses, and this short section discusses the main attributes of a data hiding algorithm.

Embedding Capacity: Data is hidden (or embedded) in a larger volume of data called a *cover* or a *carrier*. The cover is a computer file, such as text, image, audio, or video. Embedding capacity (also known as *payload*) is the amount of data that can be hidden in a cover, compared with the size of the cover. This feature can be measured numerically in units of bit-per-bit (bpb). A steganographic algorithm with small embedding capacity may have other positive features such as robustness, so it may be the ideal choice when only a small amount of data, such as a short message, has to be hidden.

Invisibility: Any data hidden in a cover causes the cover to be modified. Invisibility (also termed *perceptual transparency* or *algorithm quality*) is a measure of the amount of distortion to the cover. A large embedding capacity is useless if it causes large distortions to the cover. Invisibility is a qualitative feature. It cannot be measured numerically, and the best way to measure it is to present several observers with the cover before and after the embedding. If no one can tell the difference between the covers, the steganographic algorithm is judged highly invisible. Invisibility is therefore tied to human visual or auditory perception.

Undetectability: An attacker may be able to detect the presence of hidden data in a given file by computing certain statistical properties of the file and comparing them with what is expected in that type of file. For example, the errors in the predictions of pixels in a color or grayscale image are many times distributed according to the Laplace distribution (this is explained in the next paragraph). If a particular image is examined and is found to have a significantly different pixel distribution, it may raise suspicion and trigger further scrutiny. Thus, a good steganographic method should not modify the statistical properties of the cover file. This property is termed *undetectability* and is distinct from invisibility because it does not depend on human perception.

(The pixels of an image are not independent. When we select a pixel at random, we normally find that it is similar in color to its near neighbors. Thus, it makes sense to *predict* the value of a pixel by computing an average of its near neighbors. This should be a weighted average with smaller weights assigned to nonimmediate neighbors. When the prediction is subtracted from the actual value of the pixel, the result is the error of the prediction. This is normally a small number but may sometimes be as large as the maximum pixel value and may also be negative. The prediction errors in the entire image are many times distributed according to the well-known Laplace statistical distribution, whose shape resembles the normal, Gaussian distribution somewhat.)

Robustness: This is a measure of the ability of the algorithm to retain the data embedded in the cover even after the cover has been subjected to various modifications as a result of lossy compression and decompression or of certain types of processing such as conversion to analog and back to digital. Most steganographic algorithms embed data in an image, and images may be subject to image processing operations such as filtering, color changes, rotating, cropping, resampling, and sharpening. Robustness is especially important when the hidden data consists of copyright or ownership information (the so-called watermark). A user may compress such an image with a lossy compression method, then decompress it in an attempt to destroy any hidden watermarks.

⋄ **Exercise 13.1:** There is a close relationship between compression and steganography. The two are often mentioned together here and elsewhere. Explain why.

Tamper Resistance: An attacker may try to alter the data embedded in a cover rather than destroy it. A tamper-resistant steganographic algorithm makes it extremely hard to alter the hidden data or to erase it and embed a different message. Especially vulnerable is copyright information embedded in a cover. Such information should stay intact for years (70 years after the author's death for text and 50 years for audio) and should resist attempts to modify it using future technologies.

Long experience in other areas of the computing field has shown that there is always a tradeoff. Improving a feature of an algorithm normally involves some downgrading of other features. In steganography, there is a tradeoff between embedding capacity and robustness (and also tamper resistance). The more robust an algorithm is, the less data it can embed in a given cover.

Notice that the data should be hidden in the *body* of the cover, not in a header, trailer, or footer. The principle is that the hidden data should stay intact even after the cover is converted to a different file format and its headers changed or removed.

However, long experience shows that anything done by a person may be undone (if not forbidden by a law of nature) by another person. It is therefore obvious that even the most sophisticated methods cannot always defeat attacks by knowledgeable, determined persons. In fact, such a person may regard sophisticated protection as a personal challenge and devote much time and effort attempting to break it.

Signal-to-Noise Ratio (SNR): This quantity serves as a measure of invisibility (or its opposite, detectability). In general, high SNR is desirable in communications systems, but a low SNR is ideal for steganography. This is because in steganography, the cover is the noise, while the embedded data is the signal. As a result, low SNR corresponds to low perceptibility.

Cover Escrow vs. Blind Cover: In some steganographic methods, the original cover is needed in order to retrieve the embedded data. Such a method is said to use *escrow cover*. Where the embedded data can be extracted without the need for the original cover, the cover is said to be *blind* or *oblivious*.

Some of these requirements conflict, so any specific algorithm can satisfy only one or two of them. In particular, embedding capacity, robustness, and undetectability are mutually conflicting and cannot all be achieved by the same algorithm. Figure 13.2 is a graphical description of the relationships between these three requirements. It shows that naive steganographic methods can achieve large embedding capacity, but at the expense of robustness and undetectability. Advanced algorithms can achieve a high degree of undetectability but offer small embedding capacity and insufficient robustness. Methods for embedding a watermark are normally designed to be robust but result in small embedding capacity and questionable undetectability.

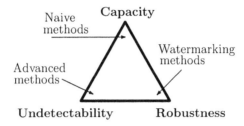

Figure 13.2: Conflicting Requirements for Data Hiding.

Other Features: Like any other discipline that uses computers, steganography has many other "digital" features, a few of which are listed here.

- Much as encryption methods use an encryption key, steganographic algorithms can use a stego-key to increase security.

Kerckhoffs' principle (Section 6.4), applies to steganography as well. When applied to steganography, this principle, due to the Dutch linguist Auguste Kerckhoffs von Nieuwenhoff [Kerckhoffs 83], states that the security of a hidden message must depend on keeping the stego-key secret. It must not depend on keeping the hiding algorithm secret.

- The complexity of the algorithm is also an important feature. A computationally intensive method may result in greater invisibility and robustness, which may justify the extra time needed to embed and retrieve the hidden data. The execution time of an algorithm may often be less important than its other features. An example is a music CD with copyright information embedded. The copyright has to be embedded into the music just once, following which the digital information (music plus copyright) can be recorded on as many CDs as needed without any extra computations.

- Asymmetric hiding of data may be a desirable feature. A slow encoding algorithm may many times be acceptable if the decoding algorithm is simple and fast.

- The use of error-correcting codes is an advantage. Many types of processing may modify the cover and thus corrupt the hidden data. An ideal steganographic algorithm may be able to detect and even correct the embedded data after such a process.

- Certain attacks on hidden data may destroy part of the cover. Ideally, it should be possible to retrieve that part of the embedded data that is hidden in the remaining part of the cover.
- A parallel steganographic algorithm is one that can be executed by several processors simultaneously, each embedding (or retrieving) part of the data. Such an algorithm may be important to steganalysts trying to break a steganographic algorithm.

13.2 Applications of Data Hiding

The first and most obvious application of data hiding is simply to hide private, sensitive data in a cover. The data is embedded either in its original, raw format or is encrypted first. Since the amount of data to be hidden may be large, it makes sense to compress it prior to its encryption and embedding. This enables several parties to exchange messages without communicating directly. Sender and receiver do not even have to exchange email, use instant messaging, or log into specific computers or accounts. All that a sender has to do is post a cover (text, image, or audio file) in a public forum under a pseudonym known to the receiver. The cover is then downloaded by the receiver (as well as by any other curious party) and the secret data extracted with the use of a stego-key. A text file with a hidden message may, for example, be placed in a newsgroup site. An image file may be placed in an Internet auction site by the sender pretending to be a seller.

Another important application of data hiding is to place a digital identification or signature, commonly known as a *watermark*, in the cover. The watermark is normally a small amount of data that indicates ownership, authorship, or another kind of relationship between the cover and a person or an organization. A suitable algorithm for this application can have low embedding capacity but has to be immune to removing or damaging the watermark. A watermark is usually placed in a cover so the owner could answer the question, "Is this cover mine?" Sometimes the aim is for anyone to be able to answer the question, "Whose file is this?" A common example is an artist who tries to sell pictures by placing them in a Web page. The pictures should be watermarked and part of the watermark should be visible so as to deter pirating. The hidden part of the watermark should not be affected even when the visible part is removed.

Watermarking is an important application for the publishing and broadcasting industries because any advance in multimedia technologies brings with it new markets but also new opportunities for illicit copying and pirating.

Fingerprinting is a variant of watermarking, where each watermark is different. Fingerprinting is useful in cases where many copies of the same product have to be tagged. When a fingerprint is hidden in a music CD, any illegal copies discovered and seized can be traced back to the original from which they were made.

Another variant of watermarking is *traitor tracing*. Before copies of an important document are disseminated to those in need to know it, each is fingerprinted differently.

Rumor has it that when Margaret Thatcher was the British prime minister in the 1980s, leaks of secret cabinet meetings to the press were so rife that she ordered the word processors of her cabinet ministers reprogrammed such that each generated slightly different spaces, to identify the origin of a document. No word as to whether the culprit had been unmasked this way.

If the document finds its way to the general public, the person responsible for the leak can easily be identified.

A third application is tamper-proofing the cover. Data can be hidden in such a way that any modification to the cover would be reflected in the hidden data. The purpose of this application is to be able to answer the question, "Has this file been modified?" If the cover is an audio file, tamper-proofing should be able to detect whether some words have been erased or modified but should forgive modifications such as stereo left–right balance. If the cover is an image, tamper-proofing should be able to detect whether an object has been removed from the image but should ignore small modifications such as change of color space or gamma correction.

Sealing a file is a special case of tamper-proofing. A checksum of the file is prepared and is hidden in the file. The file creator can then easily test the file for a broken seal.

Laws enacted by governments to restrict the encryption capabilities of private citizens are the source of the fourth important application of data hiding. Anyone concerned with privacy and unable to legally use strong encryption should consider data hiding. Also, as more lawmakers come to appreciate the power of steganography, they may relent and remove any archaic, useless, and unproductive restrictions on cryptography.

Methods of hiding data in audio files may have their own applications. Caller ID information can be embedded in a telephone conversation, enabling the receiver to identify the caller. A client contracting with a radio station to broadcast commercials can hide identifying information (a signature) in the commercial. A computer can then listen to the radio station continuously, looking for the signature. This can tell the client when, how often, and how many times the commercial had been broadcast. It can also identify cases where the commercial was only partly broadcast.

The last important application of steganography is feature location (or feature tagging). It may be desirable to hide items in the cover such as captions, annotations, names of persons or places associated with the cover, and dates (of creation and modification of parts of the cover). This application may require a large embedding capacity but not as much robustness as watermarking.

The value of many men and books rests solely on their faculty for compelling all to speak out the most hidden and intimate things.

Talking much about oneself may be a way of hiding oneself.

—Friedrich Nietzsche

13.3 Watermarking

The term *watermarking* refers to any technique used to embed ownership information in important digital data. The watermark can be a signature of the author, placed in the data for pride of authorship—the same reason that painters sign their work. The watermark can also be used to mark an important digital creation (mostly image, video, audio, but even text) before it is released externally (posted on the Web, sent to a magazine or a museum, or sold to a collector). In such cases, the watermark can later be used to identify digital data that has been illegally copied, stolen, or altered in any way. A typical example is a map. It takes time, money, and effort to create a road map of a city or a region. Once such a map is digitized, it becomes easy for anyone to copy it, make slight modifications, and sell it as an original product. A watermark hidden in the map can help the original developer of the map identify any attempts to steal the work. The watermark itself should not increase the size of the original data significantly and must also be robust, so it does not get destroyed by operations such as filtering, compressing, and cropping.

Watermarking can be achieved by steganographic methods. The watermark may be a string with, for example, the name of the owner, repeated as many times as needed. This string is hidden in the original data (image or audio) and can be extracted by the original owner by means of a secret key.

There is, however, a fundamental difference between hiding data and watermarking. In the former, the hidden data is important, while the cover image is not. The embedding capacity of the algorithm is important, but the hidden data may be fragile (it may be destroyed by transforming or compressing the cover image). In watermarking, the cover image is valuable, while the hidden data is not (it can be any identifying data). The embedding capacity is unimportant, but the hidden data has to be robust. As a result, watermarking should use specialized steganographic techniques.

The related concept of *fingerprinting* should also be mentioned. Fingerprinting refers to embedding a secret serial number in each copy of some important digital data. A commercially sold computer program, for example, is easy to copy illegally. By embedding a secret serial number in each copy of the program sold, the manufacturer can identify each buyer with a serial number, and so identify pirated copies.

For general references about watermarking, see [Cox 02] and [Arnold et al. 03].

13.4 Intuitive Methods

We start with a few elementary and tentative methods, most of which are implemented manually, although some can benefit from a computer. These are mostly of historical interest.

1. Write a message on a wooden tablet and cover it with a coat of wax on which another, innocuous message is written. This method is related by Greek historians. Modern variations include hiding a message in a hollow heel or in a false bottom of a suitcase.

2. Choose a messenger, shave his head, tattoo the message on his head, wait for the hair to grow, and send him to his destination, where his head is shaved again. This method is attributed to Histiaeus.

3. Use invisible ink, made of milk, vinegar, fruit juice, or even urine, and hide the message between the lines of a seemingly innocent letter. When the paper is heated up, the text of the hidden message slowly appears. This is a particular favorite of children.

4. The letters constituting the data are concealed in the second letter of every word of a specially constructed *cover text*, or in the third letter of the first word of each sentence. An example is the data "coverblown" that can be hidden in the specially contrived cover text "Accepted you over Neil Brown. About ill Bob Ewing, encountered difficulties." A built-in computer dictionary can help in selecting the words, but such specially constructed text often looks contrived and may raise suspicion. A variation on this method starts by writing the words of the secret message vertically. Each word becomes the first word of a line and the steganographer (writer or originator of the message) has to complete each line by adding more text. The following is an example of how the message "Come to our place at midnight" can be hidden in this way.

> Come see how the swallows fly
> to the south island helped by
> our fine weather. They locate the
> place in the immense ocean by navigating
> at night, following the clouds which form around
> midnight above the shore.

5. An ancient method to hide data uses a large piece of text where small dots are placed under the letters that are to be hidden. For example, this paragraph has dots placed under certain letters that together spell the message "i am hidden." A variation of this method slightly perturbs certain letters from their original positions to indicate the hidden data.

6. A series of lists of alternative phrases from which a paragraph can be built can be used, where each choice of a phrase from a list conceals one letter of a message. This method was published in 1518 in *Polygraphiae* by Johannes Trithemius and was still used during World War II.

◇ **Exercise 13.2:** Show examples of such phrases.

7. Check digits. This idea is used mostly to verify the validity of important data, such as bank accounts and credit card numbers (Chapter 2), but can also be considered a method for hiding validation information in a number. A simple example is the check digit used in the well-known *International Standard Book Number* (ISBN, Section 2.1), assigned to every book published. This number has four parts: a country code, a publisher code, a book number assigned by the publisher, and a check digit, for a total of 10 digits. For example, ISBN 0-387-95045-1 has country code 0, publisher code 387, book number 95045, and check digit 1. The check digit is computed by multiplying the leftmost digit by 10, the next digit by 9, and so on, up to the ninth digit from the left, which is multiplied by 2. The products are then added, and the check digit is determined as the smallest integer that when added to the sum will make it a multiple

of 11. The check digit is therefore in the range $[0, 10]$. If it happens to be 10, it is replaced by the Roman numeral X in order to make it a single symbol.

⋄ **Exercise 13.3:** What is the check digit for the 9-digit ISBN 0-387-98682?

8. It is possible to assign 3-digit codes to the letters of the alphabet as listed in Table 13.3. Once this is done, each letter can be converted into three words of cover text according to its 3-digit code. A code digit of 1 is converted into a word with 1, 4, or 7 syllables, a code digit of 2 is converted into a word with 2 or 5 syllables, and a code digit of 3 is converted into a word with 3 or 6 syllables. This way, there is a large selection of words for each word in the cover text.

A 111	D 121	G 131	J 211	M 221	P 231	S 311	V 321	Y 331
B 112	E 122	H 132	K 212	N 222	Q 232	T 312	W 322	Z 332
C 113	F 123	I 133	L 213	O 223	R 233	U 313	X 323	

Table 13.3: Three-Digit Codes for the Letters.

⋄ **Exercise 13.4:** Convert the two letters MO to innocuous text in this way.

9. Similarly, each of the 26 letters can be assigned a 5-bit code (there are 32 such codes, so six more symbols can be coded in addition to the 26 letters). Thus, any message to be hidden becomes a binary string. To hide the string, select some innocuous text and hide each bit in a letter of this text. A bit of zero, for example, may be hidden by changing the letter to lowercase or to italics. Thus, the bits 011000011 may be hidden in the text to be or not by changing it to tO Be or nOT. This type of information hiding is sometimes referred to as Bacon's biliteral cipher.

10. Select a keyword, such as blah. Find the serial numbers, 2, 12, 1, and 8 of its letters. Construct a grid with 12 columns (or even more than 12) and several rows, and mark columns 1, 2, 8, and 12 of each row. The letters of the message are inserted in those positions, four letters per row, and are hidden by filling the grid up with other letters, trying to come up with meaningful text.

11. Assign a letter to each of 26 musical notes, then write your message in the form of musical notes and hope that no one will try to play the music. This idea is due to Gaspari Schotti, who published it in his *Schola Steganographica* [Schotti 65].

12. Write or print the data on paper and then photograph it and shrink it to the size of a dot, like the one at the end of this sentence. Send an innocuous letter to the receiver and paste the dot at the end of one of the sentences. The receiver can identify the microdot by holding the letter to the light, looking for a shiny dot.

⋄ **Exercise 13.5:** Try to guess the data hidden in the sentence "I'm feeling really stuffy. Emily's medicine wasn't strong enough without another nembotil."

> Microphotography. You see, if there's anything really urgent that you can't put in a telegram, London wants us to communicate direct and save all the time it takes to Kingston. We can send a microphotograph in an ordinary letter. You stick it on as a full stop and they float the letter in water until the dot comes unstuck. I suppose you do write letters home sometimes. Business letters. . . ?
>
> —Graham Greene, *Our Man In Havana* (1958)

13.5 Simple Digital Methods

Modern steganography methods are more sophisticated than the ones presented so far and are based on the use of computers and on the binary nature of computer data. They can be classified into *naive steganography* (methods where no key is used), secret steganography (methods where a secret key is used), and public-key steganography (methods where an asymmetric key is used, similar to public key in cryptography). All three classes of steganographic methods are based on the fact that every communications process is accompanied by some natural randomness. A steganographic method replaces this randomness by the hidden data without changing the nature of the process. The hidden data ends up being *embedded* in the process.

A modern personal computer may have tens of thousands of files on one hard disk. Many files are part of the operating system and are unfamiliar to the computer owner or even to an expert user. Each time a large application is installed on the computer, it may install several system files, such as libraries, extensions, and preference files. A data file may therefore be hidden by making it look like a library or a system extension. Its name may be changed to something like `MsProLibMod.DLL` and its icon modified. When placed in a folder with hundreds of similar-looking files, it may be difficult to identify as something special.

Camouflage is the name of a steganography method that hides a data file D in a cover file A by scrambling D and then appending it to A. The original file A can be of any type. The camouflaged A looks and behaves like a normal file and can be stored or emailed without attracting attention. Camouflage is not very safe, since the large size of A may raise suspicion.

When files are written on a storage device (zip, flash, or other types), the operating system modifies the device's directory, which also includes information about the free space on the device. Special software can write a file on the device and then reset the directory to its previous state. The file is now hidden in space that is declared free, and only special software can read it. This method is risky, because any data written on the device may destroy the hidden file. Section 15.10.3 describes an example of such a method.

13.6 Data Hiding in Text

Text has less noise than an image, so hiding data in text normally results in low embedding capacity. Nevertheless, there are several methods, some of them ingenious, for hiding bits of data in a text file. This section discusses three general approaches and is followed by several detailed algorithms that hide data in text.

Modifying Spaces: Data can be hidden in a cover text by modifying blank spaces. A word processor can modify (1) the interword spaces in a sentence, (2) the spaces at the end of each line, and (3) the spaces following punctuation marks. Normally, spaces are automatically adjusted by the word processor in order to justify the right margin; they cannot be explicitly controlled by the user. Such a word processor should be modified to (1) allow the user a certain degree of control over spaces and (2) list the precise sizes of the blank spaces in a document, so that the hidden bits could be retrieved.

In a primitive word processor where spaces have fixed size, a bit can be hidden at the end of each sentence by appending one or two spaces to the sentence, where one space indicates a hidden 0 and two spaces indicate a hidden 1. Since a sentence ends with a period, every period in the text, even those in a context such as "Mr. Smith," hides one data bit and must be followed by one or two spaces.

Appending one or two spaces to the end of each line is also a simple data hiding method. Such spaces do not show up when the text is printed, but can be easily identified by the word processor. A potential problem may arise when the text is processed by programs that remove extra blank spaces.

A word processor using fixed-size spaces justifies the right margin of the text by placing more than one space between certain words, and this can be exploited for hiding data bits. Either one or two spaces are placed between successive words in order to hide a 0 or a 1, respectively. A potential problem with this method may be a case where the last two words on a line must have just one space between them (to right-justify the line), but the current bit to be hidden is a 1, requiring two spaces. A better algorithm hides bits by interpreting spaces as follows.

1. A single space followed by a word followed by a double space is interpreted as a bit of 0.
2. A double space followed by a word followed by one space is interpreted as a 1.
3. A single space followed by a word followed by a single space is interpreted as no data hidden.
4. A double space followed by a word followed by a double space is also interpreted as no data hidden.

◇ **Exercise 13.6:** Figure out the bits hidden by this method in the text

```
happy␣families␣␣are␣all␣␣alike␣every␣unhappy␣␣family␣is␣unhappy
in␣its␣␣own␣way␣every␣␣thing␣was␣in␣␣confusion␣in␣the␣oblonskys
house␣the␣␣wife␣␣had␣discovered␣that␣the␣␣husband␣␣was␣carrying
on␣an␣␣intrigue␣␣with␣a␣french␣girl
```

The TEX typesetting software [Knuth 84] permits very fine control over the interword spaces and the spaces following certain punctuation marks. The smallest dimension that TEX can use is called a *scaled point* (sp). One inch equals 72.27 printers' points (pt), and one pt equals 65,536 scaled points. Thus, the length of an sp is about the wavelength of visible light, and changing the normal interword space by 1 sp is invisible. TEX can also list the precise values of all the components of text (dimensions of letters and spaces). Because of these features, TEX may be an ideal tool for hiding data in spaces, although it was originally designed as a high-quality typesetting system for the production of books.

Syntactic Methods: These methods are based on ambiguous punctuation or on modifying the text such that its meaning is preserved. The former approach is vulnerable to attack, because inconsistent use of punctuation is noticeable, especially to an observer predisposed to being suspicious. The latter approach is safer but harder to implement because computers are notoriously bad at "understanding."

As an example of ambiguous punctuation, consider the phrases "a common, boring, but responsible task" and "a common, boring but responsible task." The latter phrase omits one comma and may be considered syntactically wrong by certain editors and linguists. The point is that one bit may be hidden in each of the two types of phrases. This method has low embedding capacity, since only one bit can be hidden for each phrase of the form "A, B, and/or/but not C" in the cover text.

Another example of applying ambiguous punctuation is slight modification of abbreviations. We normally write "see, e.g., page 100" but the phrase "see e.g. page 100" is only slightly different. These two forms of "e.g." may be used to hide bits.

Modifying text while preserving its meaning is a subtle way to hide data bits in text. It is easy to hide one bit in each of the phrases "when you finish this, you can go" and "you can go when you finish this." Such a method has low embedding capacity and must involve at least some manual adjustments to the text, but it is reliable because it is difficult to detect the two types of phrases mechanically (by computer). An attacker would have to actually read the message and manually identify the relevant phrases and extract the data bits.

Semantic Methods: These methods embed data in text by special word usage. The sender and receiver using such a method may agree on the use of a certain online thesaurus. This is a data set that contains synonyms for many words. The decoder reads the cover text word by word and searches the thesaurus for the first occurrence of each word as a synonym. If a word, such as `godchild`, is not the synonym of any other word, the decoder assumes that no data are hidden in it. Now suppose that the word `child` is input. The thesaurus is searched and the first occurrence of `child` in the thesaurus is as a synonym for `youngster`. Suppose that `youngster` has the five synonyms `bud`, `chick`, `child`, `kid`, and `minor`. This list is considered to hide two bits (because its length is between 4 and 7) and `child` (being the third word in the list, where word count starts from 0) is interpreted as hiding the 2-bit number 2 (01 in binary).

Encoding is not trivial but can be done mostly mechanically. The encoder inputs the next word of the cover text. Suppose it is `child`. It searches the thesaurus and finds that the first occurrence of `child` as a synonym is as the third word (i.e., word number 2) of the list of synonyms for `youngster`. If the next two bits of data to be hidden happen to be 01, then `child` can be used as is. Otherwise, the encoder tries to replace `child` in the input file with `bud`. It searches the thesaurus for the first occurrence of bud as a synonym and proceeds as with child. If bud cannot be used, the encoder tries to replace child with chick, and so on. If none of the five synonyms in the list can be used, the encoder may ask for a person's help in finding a replacement for child.

Another approach to semantic data hiding in text is to define a function that reduces a sentence to one bit. A possible choice is the parity (odd or even) of all the ASCII codes of the characters in the sentence. In a practical implementation of this method, the word processor should be modified as follows.

1. It first inputs the secret data and stores it as a string of bits.
2. It computes the function each time a period is typed in the artificial text and compares its result to the next bit to be hidden.
3. If the parity of all the ASCII codes in the current sentence corresponds to a bit opposite that to be hidden, the word processor beeps and refuses to take any more input. The only choice for the user is to back up and rewrite the sentence.

In the future, meaningful artificial text may be generated and revised by computers. At present, this task must be performed manually.

13.7 Innocuous Text

A government authority such as the NSA that intercepts a huge number of messages every day must use computers to analyze them and identify a small number of suspect messages, to be further checked by humans. A computer program looking for suspect messages checks first for randomness. If the message consists of random data, it may be enciphered and is therefore potentially suspect, but it may also be innocent and look random simply because it is compressed. The next test may be for a plain text message. Such a test starts by computing letter and digram frequencies. If these seem normal, then the program looks for words that are not in a dictionary (while doing this, the program may flag suspect words, such as *smuggling*, *FBI*, and *bomb*). If most of the words are in a dictionary, the program tries to identify invalid syntax (sentence structure). If a text file passes all these tests, it will be considered "clean" by the computer. Thus, one approach to steganography is to hide information (binary data) by creating a text message that has only valid words (i.e., words drawn from some dictionary) and where the words are generated in a special order so they constitute syntactically valid sentences. Such a text message contains nonsense text but may fool any computer algorithm designed to detect suspicious messages. The method used to transform pieces of binary data to words must, of course, be reversible, so a receiver will be able to read any hidden messages received.

This approach to steganography is different from hiding data in an image or an audio file. The data is not hidden in a cover image. Instead, pieces of data are replaced by words. Some may consider this approach a form of cryptography rather than steganography.

This section is based on two actual implementations: the NICETEXT program, by Mark Chapman and George Davida [Nicetext 04], and *Steganosaurus* by John Walker [Steganosaurus 04]. The former reads binary data and uses a dictionary and a style source to generate an innocuous text file that can later be converted back, with the help of the dictionary, to the original data. The dictionary contains valid words, classified according to type. The latter is similar but does not use syntax rules.

The example dictionary shown here has five grammatical types of words.

```
Article (4): the, a, this, your.
Noun    (16): dog, ball, woman, spring, John, Mary, house, man,
              car, soil, brush, animal, place, sentence, cup, food.
Verb    (16): hit, took, saw, spring, longed, sees, runs, played,
              hates, hear, knew, guesses, liked, walked, believes, work.
Adj.    (8): big, little, blue, green, long, wide, bright, dull.
Prep.   (4): to, in, by, which.
```

Notice that a word may have more than one meaning and may therefore appear more than once in the dictionary. To avoid ambiguity, such a word should always appear in the same position in all its types, and those types should have the same sizes. In our example dictionary, the word `spring` is both a noun and a verb, but it appears in position 3 in both lists (positions are numbered from 0). Also, both lists are 16 words long. The word `long` is both a verb and an adjective, but these types have different lengths, so the verb `long` had to be changed (to `longed`). Because of this feature, the decoder does not need the style rules.

Another solution to the problem of multiple dictionary words is to merge types. If the word `spring` is a noun and a verb, a new type, `Noun-Verb`, may be created, with `spring` (and possibly other words) included in it.

The style source provides syntax rules for several types of sentences. A basic sentence may have the syntax `Article, Noun, Verb, Article, Noun`, whereas a more complex sentence may be expressed by the rule

  `Article, (Adj), Noun, Verb, Article, Noun, (Prep, Article, Noun)`
where the parentheses indicate repetition. More complex style rules may include options. For example, the square brackets in

 `Article, (Adj), Noun, [Verb, Noun-Verb], Article, Noun, (Prep, Article, Noun)`
indicate either a verb or a noun-verb.

Imagine the 17-bit binary data 01011101001010101. The Nicetext encoder randomly selects one of the style rules and uses the input bits to select appropriate words from the dictionary for a sentence. If the first syntax rule is selected, the first word the encoder has to generate is of type `Article`. There are four such words, so the encoder uses the first two bits 01 of the input as a pointer and selects word 1 (the second word) of type `Article`. This is the word `a`. The next syntactic element of this syntax rule is `Noun`. There are 16 nouns, so the encoder uses the next four bits 0111 of the input as a pointer to select word 7 (`man`) of this type. The next four input bits 0100 are used to select `longed` (in type `Verb`), the following two bits 10 select the article `this`, and the next four bits 1010 select the noun `brush`. The 16-bit input string 01|0111|0100|10|1010 ends up being encoded as the sentence `a man longed this brush`. The encoder may generate a period and a space, then randomly select another style rule and encode more input bits. The random numbers used to select style rules may be uniformly distributed, or may have a distribution that prefers certain rules, thereby generating text dominated by certain types of sentences.

Since fragments of the input are used as pointers, the number of words included in each dictionary type must be a power of 2 (2^n for $n \geq 1$).

A problem arises if too few input bits remain, such that no style rule can be used. In our example, only one input bit remains, namely the bit 1. Our dictionary does not have a type with just two rules, so this single bit cannot be used as a pointer. A possible solution is to measure the length of the binary data before the encoding process starts and to prepare a string consisting of (1) the length of the data as a fixed-size number, (2) the binary data itself, and (3) many random bits. In our example, the binary data are 17 bits long, so we can prepare the string

$$0000010001|01011101001010101|1100\ldots$$

where the length 17 is written as a 10-bit number and the 17-bit data is followed by some random bits. When the encoder arrives at the end of the data, it uses as many of the random bits as needed to select the last word. The decoder starts by decoding the fixed-size length, so it knows how many bits remain to be decoded.

◇ **Exercise 13.7:** Suggest another solution.

Decoding is simple because the decoder does not need the style rules. When the decoder inputs the first word a, it searches the dictionary and finds a at position 1 (second position) of type `Article`. Since this type consists of four words, the a is decoded to the two bits 01. If the word `spring` is input by the decoder, it is found either in the word list for type `Noun` or in the list for type `Verb`. In either case, it is decoded to the four bits 0011.

The types in the dictionary may be more than just grammatical. There may be, for example, the types `MaleName`, `FemaleName`, and `SportVerb`. The latter type should include verbs such as `run`, `kicks`, and `jumped`. If the user wants to generate output text that seems to discuss sports, then instead of the style rule `Article`, `Noun`, `Verb`, `Article`, `Noun`, there may be the rule `Article`, `MaleName`, `SportVerb`, `Article`, `Noun`.

A syntax rule in the style source may also include punctuation marks, such as commas and question marks. Those are inserted by the encoder into the text and are ignored by the decoder. It is also possible to have several dictionaries and style sources, and any compatible pair may be used. A style source and a dictionary are compatible if every type mentioned in the syntax rules exists in the dictionary and any punctuation marks in the style are not words in the dictionary.

The syntax rule `do-verb name verb article noun prepos name?` is an example of a rule that may generate nonsense but seemingly correct sentences such as `will Henry gave my brush to Janet?`.

This basic method may be extended and generalized in various ways to provide greater security. In one such variant, the encoder and decoder use different dictionaries. In the encoder's dictionary, several extra words have been appended to each type. From time to time, the encoder selects one of those words at random and embeds it, as an extra word, in the text being generated. The decoder cannot find those words in its dictionary, so it simply ignores them and decodes the rest of the words. The advantage of this variant is that an eavesdropper who has access to the encoder's dictionary will not be able to use it to decode messages.

Another variant of the basic method embeds chunks of the innocuous text in real text. It is relatively easy to embed a few innocuous sentences (identified by special key words preceding and following them) in every other paragraph of some real text. This may fool even a person looking for suspicious messages. The decoder reads the text, looking for the key words to identify the important parts, and ignoring the rest.

We next describe ways to create a large dictionary with types. Collecting words is very easy because there are large collections on the Internet. One such file of English words can be found at [FreeBSD Words 03]. Another is the Gutenberg collection of books, located at [Gutenberg 04]. It is trivial to write a program that will delete all duplicate words, but the main problem is to associate a type with each word. There are several approaches.

1. Do it manually (preferably by an experienced user). This approach should be taken as a last resort after types have been assigned to most words automatically (i.e., by a computer program).

2. Use an online dictionary that has a type (such as noun, verb, or adjective) already assigned to each word. A program may be written that goes over the dictionary word by word and extracts each word and its type.

3. Use morphological analysis on root words. The root word `compartment` can be the source of derived forms such as `compartmented`, `compartmentalize`, `compartmentalization`, `recompartmentalize`, `noncompartmentalize`, and others. This is a complex process that does not work on many words.

Figure 13.4 shows a possible dictionary organization. Each type is assigned a number (article, noun, verb, adjective, and prep are assigned the numbers 1–5), so a syntax rule is a set of numbers (1, 2, 3, 1, 2 in the figure). The numbers point to an array of five structures (one of each type) where each structure contains the number of dictionary words for this type and a pointer to the start of the type in the dictionary array. The dictionary array itself is a dense array of characters, where each word is terminated by a special ASCII code.

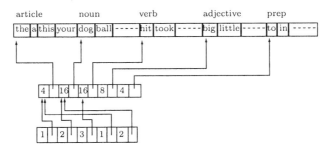

Figure 13.4: Dictionary Organization for Nicetext.

A full implementation of this approach to steganography should contain tools to create custom dictionaries from a variety of sources so as to simulate many different writing styles by example, and to alternatively use context-free grammars to control writing style.

Data expansion is an inherent problem with this type of steganography. To get an idea of the numbers involved, we assume a typical word size of four bytes. A typical grammatical type in a large dictionary should contain at least 1000 words, so a pointer to such a type is about 10 bits (because $2^{10} = 1024$). Thus, the algorithm replaces 10 bits of original data with about five bytes (a 4-byte word followed by a space, a total of 40 bits), resulting in an expansion factor of 4—very large. The solution is to use compression. The original data should be compressed, then enciphered (for added security), encoded as innocuous text, and the resulting text file (which is nonrandom) compressed again before being transmitted. As an example, a 1 Mbyte file may be reduced to 500 Kbytes by compression. Encryption may increase this to, say, 600 Kbytes, and encoding may multiply this by four, resulting in a 2.4 Mbyte file. After further compression, this may become a 1.2 Mbyte file, only about 20% bigger than the original.

Figure 13.5 lists some innocuous text in the style of Shakespeare, generated by Nicetext.

Which subtext so cold that is not remounted here? Would import above bran once think it? Hansom, I will. You lid me mistake it generally and yeah, Gaining to the pension and the rhyme. You may not, my lord, disguise her inertial jute. HOW, My lord! The ame oneself doeth reek Before equivalent parody. Hark you, sir. The Formant House Girlish. ZOUNDS, the mud more occurs To rouse a baron than to sort a mare! INSURGENT Good, i faith! I have referred my father blame him. Precon- tently, niobium, imaginatively. Thence, pack! Now shine it like a comet above infringe, A packet to the shawl above all our shows! Sorghum, your Sovereignty istoomuch sad. Good sparrow, groceries. IN Rearming whichever was furthest, we shall part up another. A background valves! Strut my lace, Lillian, strum! Vestally, naturedly: Therefore acquiesce thee studiously of thy pin, For to deny each marble ere oath Cannot re- move nor stoke the prolong permission That I do moan unright. Pester Johnnie. Now remit down, now omit down; come, margin. Adieu; be happy! While I uoresce mushrooming it by topple. The raven himself is sparse That wednesdays the managerial entrance of Jamison Neath my...

Figure 13.5: A Shakespeare-Like Nicetext.

13.8 Mimic Functions

Hiding data in artificially generated text must result in text that can pass any mechanical tests. Such text has to satisfy at least the following requirements.

1. The letter frequencies in the text must resemble those of a natural language. If the text is supposed to resemble English, then E and T should be the most common letters and Z and Q should be the rarest.

2. Most words in the text must be found in a good dictionary. Any text may include some words, such as proper names, slang, and scientific terms, that may not be found in a given dictionary, but if a computerized check finds too many such words, it should flag the text as suspicious.

3. The sentences in the text must be syntactically correct. If an automatic syntax checker finds, for example, two consecutive verbs in the text, it should become suspicious.

Just generating artificial text does not hide any data in it. One way to hide data in artificial text is to develop a method where a decision has to be made each time a word or a phrase is added to the newly generated text. Imagine a method where one of two options has to be chosen each time the next syntactic element is added to a sentence. The next data bit to be hidden can drive those decisions, resulting in text that can pass many computerized tests and also contain hidden data. An even better algorithm would have to select one of four options at each step, thereby hiding two data bits at a time.

The method described in this section does just that. It uses a context-free grammar to generate artificial text that mimics real text (i.e., has the same statistical properties), and uses several bits from the data being hidden in order to select one of several options at each step. The method is due to Peter Wayner [Wayner 92 and 02], who published the source code of his implementation, along with many examples, in [Wayner 02]. The method is based on the concept of *context-free grammars*, so we start with a short description of this important technique.

When I did him at this advantage take,
An ass's nole I fixed on his head.
Anon his Thisby must be answered,
And forth my mimic comes.

Puck's monologue in Shakespeare's
A Midsummer Night's Dream,
Act III, Scene ii

A context-free grammar (CFG) is a set of rewriting rules (also referred to as *production rules* or *productions*) that can be explicit or recursive. The rules are used to generate strings of various patterns. The set of all strings generated by a particular CFG is the *language* generated by the CFG. This set may be finite or (if the rules are recursive) infinite. The strings are considered as sentences in the language. The concept of formal grammars was originated in the 1950s by Noam Chomsky [Chomsky and Miller 58].

A CFG consists of the following.

1. A set of *terminal* symbols. These are the characters and words (the alphabet) that constitute the sentences generated by the grammar.
2. A set of *nonterminal* symbols. These are placeholders for patterns of terminal and nonterminal symbols. In our examples, the nonterminals are typeset in boldface.
3. A set of *productions*. These are rules for replacing (or rewriting) nonterminal symbols in a string with other nonterminal or terminal symbols. A production has the form $L \rightarrow R$, where L is the nonterminal symbol that is replaced by the string R of nonterminal or terminal symbols.
4. A *start* symbol—a special nonterminal. The process of generating a string by the grammar should start with a production that has this symbol on its left-hand side.

The following rules specify how to generate a string (of terminal symbols) from a given CFG.

1. Use the start symbol as the initial nonterminal.
2. Select a production that has the start symbol on the left-hand side and use it to replace the start symbol with the right-hand side of the production. This is the text generated so far.
3. Select a nonterminal symbol in the text, find a production that has this nonterminal on the left side, and replace the nonterminal with the right-hand side of the production.
4. Repeat Step 3 until the resulting text consists of just terminal symbols.

Here is a simple example of a CFG where the nonterminal symbols are typeset in boldface and the terminals are typeset in a Roman font.

Start → **noun verb**
noun → Alice | Bob
verb → is sending | is receiving

The four rules above can be applied as follows.

1. Select **Start**.
2. Replace with **noun verb**.
3. Replace **noun** with "Alice" to obtain "Alice **verb**."
4. Replace **verb** with "is sending" to obtain "Alice is sending."

This generates the sentence "Alice is sending," but it is obvious that the three sentences "Alice is receiving," "Bob is sending," and "Bob is receiving" can also be generated by this CFG if we select the productions and terminals in different orders. The four sentences that can be generated by this CFG constitute the language generated by the CFG.

The reason for the name *context-free* is that productions can be selected in any order. It is also possible to have context-sensitive grammars, where the choice of a production at each step is limited by certain rules.

◇ **Exercise 13.8:** Find the language generated by the following CFG.

Start → **noun verb**
noun → Alice | Bob
verb → is sending **what** | is receiving **what**
what → **type** | data | clothes
type → clean | dirty

The productions can also be recursive, which results in an infinite number of sentences that can be generated. A simple example is a CFG to generate simple arithmetic expressions. An expression consists of unsigned integers, the two arithmetic operations "+" and "−," and parentheses.

Start → **expression**
expression → **number** | (**expression**)
expression → **expression** + **expression** | **expression** − **expression**
number → **digit** | **number digit**
digit → 0 | 1 | ... | 9

The first rule states that a sentence is an expression. The second production says that an expression is a **number** (a nonterminal to be defined later) or any valid expression in parentheses (a recursive choice). The third production adds two recursive choices to **expression**. The fourth production defines **number** as either a single **digit** or (recursively) as any **number** with a **digit** appended to it. The last rule defines the nonterminal **digit** in terms of 10 terminals. The resulting sentences can have any length because the depth of the recursion is unlimited.

Once the basic concept of a CFG is clear, it is easy to see how data can be hidden in the sentences generated by the grammar. The idea is to associate each element (terminal or nonterminal) in the right-hand side of a production with a binary string. Thus, the four choices in the production **something** $\rightarrow$ A | B | **C** | D (notice that **C** is a nonterminal) correspond to the four bit strings 00, 01, 10, and 11. If the next pair of bits to be hidden is 01, the encoder should choose B at this point. An obvious conclusion is that each production should have 2^n choices in its right-hand side. If a production contains five choices, then the fifth one will never be used. Here is an example of a CFG used to hide the string 0100110.

> **Start** $\rightarrow$ **adjective noun tense verb**
> **adjective** $\rightarrow$ the **size** | a **size**
> **size** $\rightarrow$ tiny | small | large | big
> **noun** $\rightarrow$ saw | ladder | truth | boy
> **tense** $\rightarrow$ is | was
> **verb** $\rightarrow$ waiting | standing

The first nonterminal is **adjective**. The production for this nonterminal has two choices, so one bit can be hidden by picking the right choice. The first bit to be hidden is 0, so the first choice (the **size**) is selected. The terminal "the" is appended to the text and the nonterminal **size** is replaced next. There are four choices, so two bits can be hidden. The next two bits are 10, so the third choice, "large," is selected. The next nonterminal is **noun**. Again, there are four choices and the next bit pair to be hidden is 01, so "ladder" is selected. The choice for **tense** is "was" (directed by the next bit, 1), and the choice for **verb** is "waiting," since the last bit is 0. The resulting sentence is "the large ladder was waiting." It may raise eyebrows if read by a human, but can easily pass many computerized tests. The encoder can easily end each sentence (i.e., follow the choice of **verb**) with a period and start each sentence with a capital letter, thereby adding more realism to the artificial text that is generated.

It is clear that a large CFG with many choices can hide many bits and may produce realistic-looking sentences. The CFG listed in [Wayner 02] is based on baseball terminology, has hundreds of productions with thousands of choices, and produces mostly meaningful sentences (although a baseball expert may find the generated text somewhat limited, repetitive, and incomplete).

The decoder starts with the definition of the nonterminal **Start**. The first symbol in this definition is the nonterminal **adjective**, which has two choices. The decoder uses the input (the word "the") to decode a zero, since "the **size**" is the first choice. The nonterminal **size** has four choices, so the decoder uses the next input "large" to generate the two bits 10. This process is called *parsing* and is straightforward if the CFG has been carefully constructed. Two principles should be followed when constructing a CFG for mimicry; it has to be unambiguous and it should be in *Greibach normal form*.

A CFG is ambiguous if the same sentence can be generated by selecting productions in different orders. A simple example makes this clear.

> **Start** → **name action** | **who does**
> **name** → Alice | Bob
> **action** → is here | was there
> **who** → Alice is | Bob was
> **does** → here | there

The sentence "Alice is here" can be generated by replacing the nonterminals **name action** with "Alice" and "is here" but also by replacing **who does** by "Alice is" and "here." Obviously, such a CFG generates text that can be decoded in more than one way. This CFG is therefore useless for hiding data.

A CFG is in Greibach normal form (GNF) if the nonterminals are always the last choices in each option of a production. Thus, the production **something** → A **B** | C **D** is in GNF, but "**blah** → the **size** sum | a **size** bell" is not. It can, however, be modified to GNF by adding more productions as follows.

> **adjective** → the **sizesum** | a **sizebell**
> **sizesum** → tiny sum | small sum | large sum | big sum
> **sizebell** → tiny bell | small bell | large bell | big bell

Using a CFG in GNF simplifies the parsing, a task which is the main job of the decoder, as the following example shows.

> **Start** → **noun verb**
> **noun** → Alice | Bob
> **verb** → sent mail **to** | sent email **to**
> **to** → to **rel recipient**
> **rel** → all | some
> **recipient** → friends | relatives

To hide the binary string 01010, the encoder selects "Alice" for the first bit (0) and "sent email **to**" for the second bit (1). Nothing is hidden when the fourth production is applied (because there are no choices), but the encoder generates the terminal "to," uses the production for **rel** to select "all" for the third bit (0) and then uses the production for **recipient** to select "relatives" for the fourth bit (1). To hide the fifth bit, the encoder starts the next sentence. The reader is encouraged to decode the sentence "Alice sent email to all relatives" manually to see how easy it is for the decoder to identify the syntactic elements of a sentence and determine the hidden bits.

Those who have followed the examples so far will realize that this steganographic method is not very efficient. The last example has hidden just four bits in the sentence `Alice␣sent␣email␣to␣all␣relatives`, that is 33 characters long (including spaces). The hiding capacity of this example is $4/(33 \cdot 8) \approx 0.015$ hidden bits per each bit of text generated. The method can be made much more efficient if each production has many options on the right. A production with 2^n options can hide n bits. If an option is a four-letter (i.e., 32-bit) word and there are $1024 = 2^{10}$ options in a production, then

10 bits can be hidden in each 32 bits of generated text, leading to a hiding capacity of $10/32 = 0.3125$ bits per bit (bpb).

In principle, it is possible to construct a CFG with a hiding ratio of 1 bpb, although in practice, the text generated by such a CFG may be less convincing than the examples shown in this section. Here is the main idea.

1. The CFG has 256 terminals, T_0 through T_{255}, each a single character (i.e., 8 bits).

2. There are n nonterminals N_0 through N_n.

3. There are 256 productions for each nonterminal N_i. They are of the form $N_i \rightarrow T_j N_{a_1} \ldots N_{a_k}$ for $j = 0, 1, \ldots, 255$. Each production replaces the nonterminal N_i by one terminal T_j and by k nonterminals (k has different values for the various productions). The total number of productions is $256n$.

For each nonterminal N_i there are 256 productions, so it takes 8 bits to select one production. The production selected adds one terminal (i.e., 8 bits) to the text being generated, which leads to a hiding capacity of 1 bpb.

This method has been implemented and tested extensively by its creator, Peter Wayner, who also published its source code and prepared a large set of production rules for testing purposes. Compared to other steganographic algorithms, this method is well documented and tested.

> To know how to hide one's ability is great skill.
>
> —François de la Rochefoucauld

14
Data Hiding in Images

Virtually all sophisticated steganographic methods hide a message by embedding it as low-level noise in an image or audio file, which then becomes the *cover file*. This approach has two disadvantages: the information-hiding capacity of a cover file is small, so a large cover file is needed to hide a substantial amount of data; and once data is hidden in an image or audio file, any lossy compression destroys the embedded data. It seems that such an image should be compressed with lossless compression only, but this chapter shows how secret data can be hidden even in a lossily compressed image.

This chapter start with the description of methods for hiding data in the spatial domain of images. Starting with Section 14.6, several methods for transform-domain steganography are listed. Data hiding in binary images is the next topic, starting with Section 14.13. The data-hiding methods described here are mathematically simple. For more sophisticated methods, see [Salomon 03].

14.1 LSB Encoding

Data can be hidden in a grayscale or color image because slight changes to the colors of pixels are many times imperceptible to the eye (after all, changing the original pixels is the basis of all lossy image compression methods [Salomon 04]). The principle of LSB (least significant bit) encoding is to hide data bits by storing them in the least significant bits of the pixels of an image. The modified image is referred to as a *stegoimage*. One of the first implementations of LSB encoding was due to Romana Machado [Stego 04].

Given a color image A with three bytes per pixel, each of the three color components, typically red, green, and blue, is specified by one byte, so it can indicate one of 256 shades. The data to be hidden is a stream of bits, each of which is hidden by storing it as the least significant bit (LSB) of the next byte of image A, replacing the original bit. Obviously, the least significant bit of the next byte of A is either a 0 or a 1. The next bit to be hidden is also a 0 or a 1. This means that, on average, only half the least significant bits have to be modified by the bits being hidden. Each color pixel is represented by three bytes, so changing half the bytes means changing 1 or 2 least significant bits per pixel, on average.

Small changes in the color of a few isolated pixels may be noticeable if the pixels are located in large uniform areas or on sharply defined boundaries. It is therefore important to choose the cover image A carefully. It should contain a large number of small details with many different colors. Such an image is termed *busy*. An improvement to the basic LSB method is to hide a bit in a pixel only if the pixel satisfies certain conditions. If the variance of the luminances of the immediate neighbors of a pixel is very high (an indication that the pixel may be on a boundary) or very low (an indication that it is located in a uniform region), the pixel should be skipped. If a pixel passes these tests and is modified, it is important to verify that it passes the same tests after modification, since otherwise the decoder would not be able to reliably identify the pixels that have been skipped. If a pixel does not pass the tests after being modified, it should be returned to its original value.

A comparison of the original cover image and the stegoimage would show an attacker which bits have been modified and may serve as the basis of a successful attack on the hidden data. This is why the original image should be destroyed right after the stegoimage has been prepared.

⋄ **Exercise 14.1:** Suggest another obvious precaution.

If image A is to be compressed later, the compression should, of course, be lossless. If the owner forgets this, or if someone else compresses image A with a lossy compression algorithm, some of the hidden data will be lost during the compression. Thus, this basic method is not robust.

The hiding capacity of this method is low. If one data bit is hidden in a byte, then the amount of data hidden is $1/8 = 12.5\%$ of the cover image size. As an example, only 128 K bytes can be hidden in a 1 Mbyte cover image. *Stego*, a widely available implementation of this method, is described in Section 15.10.1.

It is easy to come up with sophisticated variants of this method that use a stego-key and are therefore more difficult to break. Here are a few ideas.

1. If the key is, say, 1011, then data bits are hidden in the least significant bits of bytes 1, 3, and 4 but not of byte 2, then in bytes 5, 7, and 8, but not in byte 6, and so on.

2. Bits are stored in selected bytes as in variant 1 but are stored alternately in the least-significant position and in the second least-significant position of bytes of the cover image.

3. The stego-key is used as the seed of a pseudorandom number generator that generates a random sequence of small positive integers r_i. The image pixels are numbered P_i, and bits are hidden in pixels P_1, P_{1+r_1}, $P_{1+r_1+r_2}$, and so on. Only certain pixels are affected, which reduces the data-embedding capacity of the cover image. This variant is more secure but can be used for hiding only small quantities of information.

4. The stego-key is again used as the seed of a pseudorandom number generator, and a random sequence of small positive integers r_i is generated. Data bits are hidden in pixels as in variant 3, but when an index $1 + r_1 + r_2 + \cdots + r_j$ exceeds the size of the image, it is computed modulo this size. The result is that data bits are hidden in pixels located farther and farther away from the start of the cover image, and following bits are hidden in bytes close to the start. It is easy to have a collision (a pixel that has already been modified is selected again), so this variant has to maintain a list of pixels that have been modified. When the algorithm arrives at such a pixel, the next pseudorandom number is drawn, and another pixel is selected for hiding the next bit. Notice that the decoder can mirror this operation.

5. Proceed as in the previous method but without maintaining a list of pixels that have been modified. Some of the embedded bits will be corrupted by bits stored "on top" of them, but these errors can be corrected by adding an error-correcting code to the data before it is hidden. The Hide and Seek software (Section 15.10.2) uses this method but with no error correction.

6. This variant is distantly related to BPCS steganography (Section 14.2). The stego-key is used to partition the cover image into disjoint regions. If the key is the single digit n, the image is partitioned into n equal-size strips (where the last strip may be shorter than the rest). If the key is the pair (r, c), the image is partitioned into rectangles, each with r rows and c columns (where the rectangles on the right edge and on the bottom of the image may be smaller). The stego-key may be the seed of a pseudorandom number generator, and the random integers thus generated are used to specify the regions.

A parity bit b_i is computed for each region i as the parity of the least-significant bits of the region's pixels. One data bit d_i is hidden in the region. If b_i is different from d_i, then b_i is made equal to d_i by changing the least significant bit of one pixel in the region.

The decoder simply computes the parity bit of each region and concatenates the parity bits to form the string of hidden data.

Only a small amount of data can be hidden in this variant, but this method has the advantage that the encoder may be able to select, in each region, the pixel whose modification will change the region's statistics the least. A pixel that is very similar to its immediate neighbors should not be modified, since it is located in a uniform (or almost uniform) region, where any small change may be noticeable. Similarly, a pixel that is very different from its immediate neighbors should not be modified, since this change may also be very perceptible. The encoder should therefore select a pixel according to the following steps: (1) compute the difference between a pixel and the average of its (four or eight) near neighbors; (2) repeat for all the pixels in the region; (3) let s and l be the smallest and largest differences; and (4) select a pixel whose difference is the closest to $(s + l)/2$.

7. No stego-key is used. This variant scans the image pixel by pixel along a complex path, not row by row, and hides one bit of the data in each pixel visited. For example, the pixels may be visited in the order defined by a space-filling curve, such as the Peano curve or the Hilbert curve (Section 8.1). Such curves visit each point of a square area exactly once.

8. The idea of this variant was published by [Aura 96], who also implemented it. A stego-key and a secure hash function H are used to generate a sequence of unique pixel addresses. One data bit is hidden in the LSB of each of those pixels. Hash functions are discussed in most texts on data structures. A secure hash function H has some useful properties: (1) if $z = H(x)$, then it is computationally infeasible to find a $y \neq x$ such that $z = H(y)$; and (2) collisions are extremely rare (i.e., it is also computationally infeasible to find two different arguments x and y that will hash to the same z). We assume that an image of dimensions $x \times y$ is given, where x is the horizontal dimension, i.e., the number of columns. A stego-key K is selected and is partitioned into three parts K_1, K_2, and K_3. To find the image location (X, Y) where the ith data bit is to be hidden, compute the following (where $\circ$ and $\div$ indicate concatenation and integer division, respectively):

$$Y = i \div x,$$
$$X = i \bmod x,$$
$$Y = \big(Y + H(K_1 \circ X)\big) \bmod y,$$
$$X = \big(X + H(K_2 \circ Y)\big) \bmod x,$$
$$Y = \big(Y + H(K_3 \circ X)\big) \bmod y,$$
$$\text{return } Y \times x + X.$$

For example, assume that the image has dimensions 800×600 (again, 800 is the horizontal dimension, i.e., the number of columns) and the stego-key is the integer 123,456,789. To find the location where the 1001st data bit should be hidden, perform

$$Y = 1001 \div 800 = 1,$$
$$X = 1001 \bmod 800 = 201,$$
$$Y = \big(1 + H(123 \circ 201)\big) \bmod 600 = (1 + 7377) \bmod 600 = 178,$$
$$X = \big(201 + H(456 \circ 178)\big) \bmod 800 = (201 + 3854) \bmod 800 = 55,$$
$$Y = \big(178 + H(789 \circ 55)\big) \bmod 600 = (178 + 1124) \bmod 600 = 102,$$
$$\text{return } Y \times x + X = 102 \cdot 800 + 55.$$

Thus, the value returned is $Y \times x + X = 102 \cdot 800 + 55 = 81{,}655$ or $(X, Y) = (55, 102)$. (End of variant 8.)

⋄ **Exercise 14.2:** Propose a way to make the above eight approaches more secure.

A marked improvement is achieved by considering the sensitivity of the eye to various colors. Of the three colors red, green, and blue, the eye is most sensitive to green and least sensitive to blue. Thus, hiding bits in the blue part of a pixel results in image modification that is less noticeable to the eye. The price for this improvement is reduced hiding capacity from 12.5% to 4.17%, since one bit is hidden in each group of three image bytes.

Figure 14.1a shows the well-known Lena image at a resolution of 128×128. Figure 14.1b–d shows the results of embedding text in bits 3, 5, and 7, respectively, of each pixel. (Bit positions are numbered from 1, the least significant bit, to 8, the most significant one.) It is clear that embedding foreign bits in most significant positions can significantly degrade the quality of the cover image. Figure 14.2 lists simple Matlab code to embed text in an image.

How can we identify a given image as a cover image? Figure 14.1e,f shows the distributions of pixel values (in the range [0, 255]) of the same Lena image before and after embedding foreign data. It is clear that the distributions are somewhat different and that embedding the data has created a "rougher" distribution. It turns out that the difference in pixel distributions can be magnified by transforming the pixels in a special way.

We know from experience that an image tends to have areas that are uniform or close to uniform. When moving from pixel to pixel in such an area, the pixels' colors don't vary much. In general, a pixel in an image tends to be similar to its immediate neighbors. If we select the four immediate neighbors of a pixel P and compute their average, the result will, in most cases, be very similar to P. If we subtract the average from P, we can expect to end up with a small number. Such a difference will be large (positive or negative) only when P and some of its neighbors differ much, a fairly rare case. Since the average of integers may be a noninteger, a more practical way of computing the transform is

$$P[x, y] = P[x - 1, y] + P[x + 1, y] + P[x, y - 1] + P[x, y + 1] - 4P[x, y].$$

After the 128×128 pixels of the Lena image are transformed in this way (by the Matlab code of Figure 14.4), their distribution is shown in Figure 14.3a. It is similar to the well-known Laplace distribution, so this transformation is known as a Laplace transform or Laplace filtering.

The point is that changing the pixel values by embedding data (even though only the least significant bits of the pixels are affected) may sometimes change the colors of neighbor pixels enough to affect the Laplace transform significantly. Thus, a good, quick test for a suspect image is to compute the Laplace transform of its pixels and plot the distribution of the transformed pixels (Figure 14.3b). If the distribution is significantly different from a Laplace distribution, the image should be suspect of being a cover (or of having been modified in some way).

The approach described in this section can fail if the cover image is subjected to manipulations such as lossy compression (and decompression), filtering, sharpening, and cropping. This is why *redundancy* is important in steganography. If the same bit is hidden several times in the cover, the decoder has a better chance of recovering it even after the stegoimage has been modified. The Patchwork method of Section 14.5 is a good example of the application of redundancy to steganography.

⋄ **Exercise 14.3:** What are practical methods of storing each data bits several times in an image?

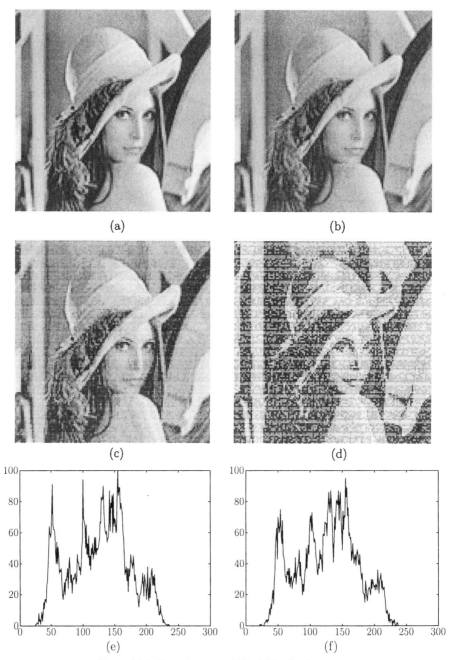

Figure 14.1: Lena Image and Pixel Distributions.

```
% Embed bits of text 'herring' in any bit position
% of pixels of image 'lena'
gmap=gray(256); % colormap for 8-bit pixels
filename='lena128'; dim=128;
fid=fopen(filename,'r');
if fid==-1 disp('image file not found'); end;
img=fread(fid,[dim,dim])';
status=fclose(fid);
figure(1), image(img), colormap(gmap), axis off, axis square
filename='herring';
fid=fopen(filename,'r');
if fid==-1 disp('data file not found'); end;
[hide,count]=fread(fid,[dim,dim],'ubit1');
count; % input text file bit by bit into 'hide'
status=fclose(fid);
pdist=zeros(256,1);
for row=1:dim
 for col=1:dim
  img(row,col)=bitset(img(row,col),1,hide(row,col));
% 2nd param of bitset is bit position to embed data
  p=img(row,col)+1;
  pdist(p)=pdist(p)+1;
 end
end
figure(2), image(img), colormap(gmap), axis off, axis square
figure(3), plot(pdist) % dist of pixel values in embedded image
```

Figure 14.2: Matlab Code to Embed Data in a Cover Image.

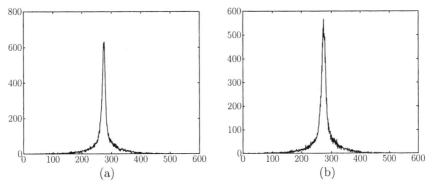

Figure 14.3: Distributions of Laplace-Transformed Pixels of the Lena Image Before and After Embedding.

```
% Matlab file 'LaplaceTransf.m'
% Embed bits of text 'herring' in image 'lena'
filename='lena128'; dim=128;
fid=fopen(filename,'r'); % open cover image
if fid==-1 disp('image file not found'); end;
img=fread(fid,[dim,dim])';
status=fclose(fid);
dumy=LaplaceProc(1,img,dim); % Transform pixels before embed
filename='herring';
fid=fopen(filename,'r'); % open text to be hidden
if fid==-1 disp('data file not found'); end;
[hide,count]=fread(fid,[dim,dim],'ubit1');
count; % input text file bit by bit into 'hide'
status=fclose(fid);
for row=1:dim % double loop to embed 'hide' in
 for col=1:dim % the cover image 'img'
  img(row,col)=bitset(img(row,col),1,hide(row,col));
 end
end
dumy=LaplaceProc(2,img,dim); % Transform pixels after embed

% Matlab file 'LaplaceProc.m'
function dumy=LaplaceProc(i,img,dim);
dumy=0; min=0; max=0; nimg=zeros(dim,dim);
for col=2:dim-1 % store transformed pixels in
 for row=2:dim-1 % nimg
  nimg(row,col)=img(row-1,col)+img(row+1,col)    ...
   +img(row,col-1)+img(row,col+1)-4*img(row,col);
  p=nimg(row,col);
  if p<min % find minimum and maximum
   min=p; % of transformed values
  end;
  if p>max
   max=p;
  end;
 end % for row
end % for col
pdist=zeros(max-min+1,1);
for col=2:dim-1
 for row=2:dim-1
  p=nimg(row,col)-min+1;
  pdist(p)=pdist(p)+1;
 end
end
figure(i), plot(pdist) % dist of transformed pixel values
```

Figure 14.4: Matlab Code for Figure 14.3.

> Steganography—putting encrypted messages in electronic files—is widely used by terrorist groups. A recent government report indicated that terrorists have been hiding pictures and maps of targets in sports chat rooms, on pornographic bulletin boards and on Web sites.
>
> —Jerry Freese

14.1.1 A Color Lookup Table

A modern computer displays an image on a screen by means of pixels. The process starts when a program constructs the image in a buffer, termed the *bitmap*, in memory. Each pixel of the image has an entry in the bitmap, indicating its color. The size of the entry depends on the number of colors of the image and normally ranges from 1 bit (two colors) to 24 bits ($2^{24} \approx 16.8$ million colors). If the screen resolution is high, the bitmap can become large.

⬦ **Exercise 14.4:** What is the size of the bitmap for a $1K \times 1K \times 24$ image?

A memory buffer of several megabytes is not excessively large, but the point is that an image with a resolution of $1K \times 1K$ has about a million pixels, so it cannot have more than a million different colors. Experience shows that a typical image may have just a few hundred (or at most, a few thousand) colors, which is why an image is normally represented in memory by means of a small bitmap combined with a *color lookup table*.

A typical color lookup table may have 256 rows (allowing for an image with 256 distinct colors) and three columns (allowing for three bytes or 24 bits to specify each color). Each pixel occupies one byte in the bitmap, so the bitmap size equals the image resolution in bytes. Each entry (byte) in the bitmap contains a pointer to one of the 256 entries of the lookup table (Figure 14.5). The three bytes of the entry are the three components of the color (normally RGB or YCbCr).

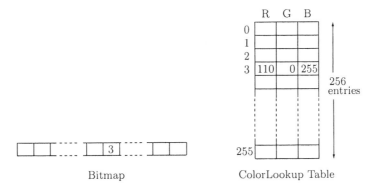

Figure 14.5: A Bitmap and a Color Lookup Table.

> Palette—board on which paints are laid and mixed.

When an image is written on a file, both the bitmap and the lookup table have to be included. The well-known GIF and BMP graphics file formats use this convention.

Data can be hidden in such an image file either in the lookup table or in the bitmap. The simplest way to hide data in the lookup table is to store data bits in the least significant positions of the color definitions in the table. In a typical lookup table of size 256×3, it is possible to hide $256 \times 3 = 768$ bits (or 96 bytes)—not much data. Each group of three bits stored in the least significant bits of three bytes of a table entry slightly modifies the color defined by that entry.

A more sophisticated approach makes use of the fact that the entries of the lookup table don't have to be sorted in any way. If we decide, for example, to swap entries i and j, all we need to do is scan the bitmap and change all occurrences of i to j and all occurrences of j to i. If the bits to be hidden are $b_1 b_2 b_3 \ldots$, we simply move items in the lookup table until the leftmost bit of entry i equals b_i. In a lookup table with 256 entries, it may normally be possible to hide about 200 bits this way. A drawback of this method is that a malicious attacker can easily destroy the hidden data by moving entries around in the lookup table.

Data can also be hidden in the bitmap, but the reader should notice that when a color lookup table is used, the bitmap contains pointers and not color specifications. Thus, adjacent bitmap entries may point to lookup table entries with very different colors. Changing the least significant bit of a bitmap entry from, say, 4 to 5, may significantly change the color of the corresponding pixel, because entries 4 and 5 of the lookup table may contain different color specifications.

A simple solution to this problem is to sort the lookup table such that adjacent entries specify similar colors. If each entry specifies the RGB components of a color, then the entries may be sorted according to their Euclidean norm

$$N = \sqrt{R^2 + G^2 + B^2}.$$

This approach can be improved by switching to a luminance–chrominance color representation (Section 5.9.1). The eye is more sensitive to luminance than to chrominance, so the lookup table can be sorted by the luminance values of its entries. When the least significant bit of a bitmap entry P is changed, it points to lookup table entry $P + 1$ or $P - 1$, and these entries contain color specifications with similar luminance values.

In cases where the lookup table should not be sorted, the following approach, although more complex, may produce good results. Suppose that a 0 bit should be hidden in a bitmap entry with an odd pointer P (i.e., a number with a least significant bit of 1). The algorithm starts with the color specified by entry P of the lookup table and searches for similar colors located in a lookup table entry whose address Q is even. The bitmap entry is then changed from the odd value P to the even value Q, thereby hiding a 0 bit and changing the color by the smallest possible amount.

14.2 BPCS Steganography

BPCS (bit-plane complexity segmentation) is the brainchild of Eiji Kawaguchi. Developed in 1997, this steganography method hides data in a cover image (color or grayscale) and its main feature is large hiding capacity [BPCS 03]. The size of the hidden data is typically 50–70% of the size of the cover image, and hiding the data does not increase the size of the cover image.

Figure 14.7 shows a grayscale image of parrots, together with five of the image's bitplanes (bitplane 8, the most significant one, bitplane 1, the least significant one, and bitplanes 3, 5, and 7). It is clear that the most significant bitplane is somewhat similar to the full image, the least significant bitplane is random (or at least seems random), and, in general, as we move from the most significant bitplanes to least significant ones, they become more random. However, each bitplane has some parts that look random. (BPCS converts the pixels of the cover image from binary to *Gray codes*, which are discussed in Section 14.2.1. When an image is represented by Gray codes, there is less difference between the least significant and most significant bitplanes; the randomness, or redundancy, in the image is distributed more uniformly.)

The principle of BPCS is to separate the image into individual bitplanes, check every 8×8-bit square region in each bitplane for randomness, and replace each random region with 64 bits of hidden data. Regions that are not random (*shape-informative* regions in BPCS terminology) are not modified. A special complexity measure α is used to determine whether a region is random. A color image, where each pixel is represented by 24 bits, has 24 bitplanes (8 bitplanes per color component). A grayscale image with 8 bits/pixel has eight bitplanes. The complexity measure α of an 8×8 block of bits is defined as the number of adjacent bits that are distinct. This measure (see note below) is normalized by dividing it by the maximum number of adjacent bits that can be different, so α is in the range $[0, 1]$.

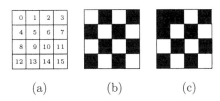

(a)   (b)   (c)

Figure 14.6: BPCS Image Complexity Measure.

An important feature of BPCS is that there is no need to identify those regions of the cover image that have been replaced with hidden data because the hidden data itself is transformed, before it is hidden, to a random representation. The BPCS decoder identifies random regions by performing the same tests as the encoder, and it extracts the 64 data bits of each random region. The hidden data is made to look random by first compressing it. It is known (see, for example, [Salomon 04]) that compressed data has little or no redundancy and therefore looks random. If a block of 64 bits (after compression) does not pass the BPCS randomness test, it goes through a *conjugation operation* that increases its randomness. The conjugation operation computes the exclusive-OR of the 64-bit block (which is regrouped as an 8×8 square) with an 8×8 block that has a checkerboard pattern and whose upper-left corner is white. This transforms a simple pattern to a complex one and changes the complexity measure of the block from α to $1 - \alpha$. The encoder has to keep a list of all the blocks that have gone through the conjugation operation, and this list (known as the conjugation map) is also hidden in the cover image as shown below.

Figure 14.6 shows how the BPCS image complexity measure α is defined. Part (a) of the figure shows a 4×4 image with the 16 pixels (1 bit each) numbered. The complexity of the image depends on how many adjacent bits differ. The first step is to compare each bit in the top row (row 1) to its neighbor below and count how many pairs differ. Then the four pairs of bits of rows 2 and 3 are compared, followed by the pairs in rows 3 and 4. The maximum number of different pairs is 4×3. The next step is to compare adjacent bits horizontally, starting with the four pairs in columns 1 and 2. This can also yield a maximum of 4×3 different bit pairs. The image complexity measure α is defined as the actual number of bit pairs that differ, divided by the maximum number, which for a 4×4 block is $2 \cdot 4(4 - 1) = 24$ and for an 8×8 block is $2 \cdot 8(8 - 1) = 112$.

Figure 14.6b shows a checkerboard pattern, where every pair of adjacent bits differs. The value of α for such a block is 1. Figure 14.6c shows a slightly different block, where the value of α is

$$\alpha = \frac{(3 + 4 + 4) + (3 + 4 + 4)}{2 \cdot 4 \cdot 3} = 0.917.$$

BPCS considers a block random if its complexity measure α is greater than or equal to a certain threshold. Experiments indicate that a threshold value of about 0.3 provides large embedding capacity without noticeably degrading the visual quality of the cover image. (The value 0.3 also equals $0.5 - 4\sigma$, where $\sigma = 0.047$ is a constant. The value of σ was determined by computing α values for many 8×8 blocks and plotting them. The distribution of the α values was found to be Gaussian with mean 0.5 and standard deviation 0.047.)

The simplest way to organize the conjugation map is to include in it one bit for each block of secret data. However, if the complexity measure α of a data block is in the interval [threshold, $1 -$ threshold], then the block does not have to be conjugated, and the BPCS decoder *can figure out this fact*. The conjugation map does not have to have a bit for such a data block. If the map is organized this way, the decoder has to compute the complexity measures α of each data block and its conjugate. If both are in the interval [threshold, $1 -$ threshold], then the decoder knows that the block is not conjugated and the conjugation map has no bit for the block. This can reduce the size of the map significantly

The last point to consider is how to hide the conjugation map itself in the image without increasing the image size. The map is hidden just like the rest of the hidden data; each block of the conjugation map is embedded in a random image block. However, some blocks of the conjugation map may not be random and may have to be conjugated. To avoid having a conjugation map of the conjugation map, we can place a conjugation indicator inside each block of the conjugation map. Each 8×8 block of the conjugation map contains 64 bits, of which only 63 are used for conjugation information and the

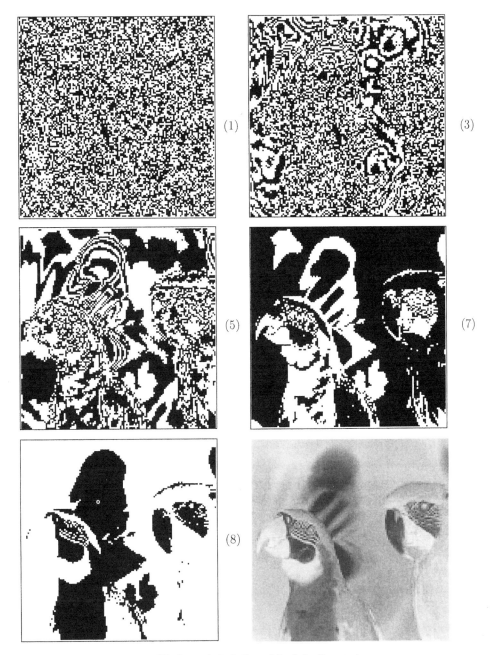

Figure 14.7: Bitplanes 1, 3, 5, 7, and 8 of the Parrots Image.

remaining one is used as an indicator. The indicator is a bit located in a position that gets complemented during conjugation. The bit is set to zero before the conjugation block is hidden. If the block ends up being conjugated, the bit becomes a 1. The decoder knows what blocks make up the conjugation map, and it conjugates those that have an indicator bit of 1 (and then ignores or deletes the indicator bit). Note that the entire conjugation map can be prepared while the secret data is being embedded in the image, because the map depends on the data, not on the image. Once prepared, the conjugation map can be embedded in the image, following the blocks of the secret data—ingenious!

14.2.1 Gray Codes

We are familiar with the standard binary representation of integers, where the value of a bit depends on its position in the number. Thus, the binary integer 1101_2 equals $2^3 + 2^2 + 2^0 = 13$. This is similar to the well-known decimal representation and makes it easy to operate on binary integers. However, there are other ways to represent integers with bits, and one of them, namely Gray codes, has advantages for the representation of images.

Imagine a grayscale image where each pixel is represented by four bits $b_3 b_2 b_1 b_0$. Thus, a pixel can have one of 16 grayscales. We now separate the image into four bitplanes, where bitplane i consists of bits b_i of all the pixels. What can we say about the four bitplanes? In principle, they can be anything, but in practice there is a difference between them because of the nonrandom nature of digital images. An image that we store in our computers is not random. Random images are generally useless, uninteresting, and unimportant; we don't keep such an image. If an image is important and interesting, then it is nonrandom and therefore has an important property. Neighboring pixels in such an image tend to be similar. If we select a pixel at random in an image, chances are that its immediate neighbors will be similar to it, and even its near (not immediate) neighbors will mostly be similar. We say that the pixels of an image are *correlated*.

When the image is separated into individual bitplanes, we find, however, that the least significant bitplanes are random, or almost so, while the most significant bitplanes look like black-and-white versions of the original image. The following experiment illustrates this behavior. We write the 16 4-bit integers 0–15 right next to each other in descending order. The difference between any of these numbers and its immediate neighbors is 1.

1111 1110 1101 1100 1011 1010 1001 1000 0111 0110 0101 0100 0011 0010 0001 0000.

When we separate these numbers into four "bitplanes," we immediately see the difference between them. The bits of the leftmost bitplane are highly correlated, they change only once. The bits of the rightmost (least significant) bitplane, on the other hand, alternate all the time:

1111111100000000, 1111000011110000, 1100110011001100, 1010101010101010.

This behavior of the bitplanes is a result of a basic feature of binary numbers. Consecutive binary numbers always differ in their least significant bits but rarely differ in their most significant bits. If we want to separate an image into bitplanes that are similar, we should use a different binary representation for the pixels.

The Gray binary representation (RGC, *Gray codes*, or reflected Gray codes), has the advantage that the codes of consecutive integers differ by exactly one bit.

This code is easy to generate with the following recursive construction (see also [Press and Flannery 88]). Start with the two 1-bit codes $(0, 1)$. Construct two sets of 2-bit codes by duplicating $(0, 1)$ and appending, either on the left or on the right, first a zero, then a one, to the original set.

The result is $(00, 01)$ and $(10, 11)$. Now reverse (reflect) the second set, and concatenate the two. The result is the 2-bit RGC $(00, 01, 11, 10)$: a binary code of the integers 0 through 3, where consecutive codes differ by exactly one bit. Applying the rule again produces the two sets $(000, 001, 011, 010)$ and $(110, 111, 101, 100)$, which are concatenated to form the 3-bit RGC. Note that the first and last codes of any RGC also differ by one bit.

Here are the first three steps for computing the 4-bit RGC:

$$\text{Add a zero } (0000, 0001, 0011, 0010, 0110, 0111, 0101, 0100),$$
$$\text{Add a one } (1000, 1001, 1011, 1010, 1110, 1111, 1101, 1100),$$
$$\text{reflect } (1100, 1101, 1111, 1110, 1010, 1011, 1001, 1000).$$

Table 14.8 shows how individual bits change when moving through the binary codes of the first 32 integers. The 5-bit binary codes of these integers are listed in the odd-numbered columns of the table, with the bits of integer i that differ from those of $i - 1$ shown in boldface. It is easy to see that the least significant bit (bit b_0) changes all the time, bit b_1 changes for every other number, and, in general, bit b_k changes every k integers. The even-numbered columns list one of the several possible reflected Gray codes for these integers. The table also lists a recursive Matlab function to compute RGC.

43210	Gray	43210	Gray	43210	Gray	43210	Gray
00000	00000	0**1**000	10010	**1**0000	00011	11000	10001
0000**1**	00100	0100**1**	10110	1000**1**	00111	11001	10101
000**1**0	01100	010**1**0	11110	100**1**0	01111	11010	11101
0000**1**1	01000	0101**1**	11010	1001**1**	01011	11011	11001
00**1**00	11000	01**1**00	01010	10**1**00	11011	11**1**00	01001
0010**1**	11100	0110**1**	01110	1010**1**	11111	11101	01101
001**1**0	10100	011**1**0	00110	101**1**0	10111	11110	00101
0011**1**	10000	0111**1**	00010	1011**1**	10011	11111	00001

```
function b=rgc(a,i)
[r,c]=size(a);
b=[zeros(r,1),a; ones(r,1),flipud(a)];
if i>1, b=rgc(b,i-1); end;
```

Table 14.8: First 32 Binary and Reflected Gray Codes.

⋄ **Exercise 14.5:** It is also possible to generate the reflected Gray code of an integer
n with the following nonrecursive rule: Exclusive-OR n with a copy of itself that is
logically shifted one position to the right. In the C programming language, this is
denoted by n^(n>>1). Use this expression to calculate a table similar to Table 14.8.

14.3 Lossless Data Hiding

The data hiding methods described so far distort the coverimage permanently. The
distortion can be made imperceptible to the eye, but it is still present in the stegoimage.
Following the terminology used in data compression, such steganographic methods can
be termed *lossy* or *irreversible*. In most applications, the coverimage is irrelevant to
both sender and receiver (encoder and decoder), so the stegoimage is discarded by the
receiver after the hidden data has been extracted. In certain applications, however, the
coverimage is important, and the receiver would like to restore the stegoimage to the
original coverimage after the hidden data has been extracted. A data hiding method
that allows a complete reconstruction of the coverimage is referred to as lossless (or
reversible, invertible, or distortion-free).

A lossless steganographic algorithm can be implemented in the following steps: (1)
identify the part of the coverimage that is going to be modified by the data-embedding
process; (2) compress this part; (3) append the compressed part to the secret data; and
(4) embed the secret data and the compressed part. Decoding is the exact opposite
of encoding. After the hidden data is recovered, the compressed part is extracted,
decompressed, and used to replace that part of the stegoimage that had been modified
by the encoder. This results in the original, unmodified coverimage.

Following are three situations where lossless data hiding is important.

1. Medical applications. A watermark is hidden in an X-ray image. The watermark
may consist of the names of the patient, doctor, and hospital, as well as confidential
medical information. In an X-ray image, any pixel may be significant, so it is important
to completely reconstruct the image after the watermark has been extracted.

2. An image taken by a spy satellite is examined by experts by filtering or under
high magnification. Individual pixels are scrutinized and may often be the source of
important information or may provide important clues. It makes sense to watermark
such an image (with the date the image was taken, the place shown in the image, the
date it was examined, the name of the examiner, and various notes), and this kind of
watermarking should obviously be lossless.

3. Artists displaying and selling images over the Internet want to watermark their
images as protection against theft and as a means to legally identify pirated images.
Some artists are picky and object to even a single pixel being modified in their images,
even when the modifications are visually imperceptible. Such artists can also benefit
from lossless data embedding.

The main problem facing a lossless data-hiding algorithm is that the secret data
is embedded in an image component that is visually unimportant, such as the LSB
(least significant bit) of certain pixels. Because of its unimportance, such a component

is normally random or close to random and therefore hard or impossible to compress. A lossless steganographic algorithm should therefore be more sophisticated than simple LSB embedding.

This section describes two lossless data embedding methods for raw images. Other, more sophisticated methods are described in [Salomon 03].

The first method described here is called *RS lossless data embedding*. It starts with a coverimage V, and it is based on selecting a component (or a part or a feature) B of V. B is extracted, losslessly compressed, concatenated with the secret data, and the result embedded in V, replacing the original B. In order for this method to work, component B has to satisfy the following: (1) it is compressible (i.e., is not random), and (2) it can be modified and replaced by other data without affecting important image features. If B satisfies these two requirements, then decoding the image is the opposite of encoding and restores image V to its original form.

Here is this method in more detail. We assume that image V has $M \times N$ pixels, each with values in a certain set P (for example, $P = (0, 1, \ldots, 255)$). The image is partitioned into groups G of n adjacent pixels $p_1, p_2, \ldots, p_n$ each. Examples of such groups are n pixels in a row, n pixels in a column, and a square consisting of n pixels. The number of groups is $M \times N/n$. A *discrimination function* $f(G)$ is defined for the groups $G = (p_1, p_2, \ldots, p_n)$ in order to measure the smoothness or regularity of the group members. An example of such a function is

$$f(p_1, p_2, \ldots, p_n) = \sum_{i=1}^{n-1} |p_{i+1} - p_i|,$$

but other functions are possible. The next step is to define an involutary "flipping" permutation F on the set P of pixel values. (An involutary permutation is a permutation that is its own inverse [Section 8.2].) For example, F may be the permutation $0 \leftrightarrow 1$, $2 \leftrightarrow 3$, up to $254 \leftrightarrow 255$. If we consider P a set of grayscale values, then this particular F corresponds to flipping the LSBs of these values. We can therefore denote it by F_{LSB} and say that it has an amplitude of 1.

⋄ **Exercise 14.6:** An involutary permutation that flips the values of the second LSB can be considered to have a bigger "amplitude." What is this permutation?

There may be flipping permutations with bigger amplitudes and also permutations where more than one bit is flipped. Thus, we define the *amplitude* A of a given flipping permutation F as the average change of values induced by applying F:

$$A = \frac{1}{|P|} \sum_{v \in P} |v - F(v)|.$$

For the F_{LSB} permutation, each difference $|v - F(v)|$ is 1, so A is always 1, regardless of the size of P. For the permutation of Exercise 14.6, A is 2.

The discrimination function f and the flipping permutation F are used to define the three types R, S, and U (for regular, singular, and unusable) of pixel groups as follows: Group G is of type R if it satisfies $f(F(G)) > f(G)$. Similarly, S is the type of all groups G that satisfy $f(F(G)) < f(G)$, and U is the type of all the groups for which $f(F(G)) = f(G)$.

In a typical image, adjacent pixels are correlated. We therefore expect $f(G)$ to be small for most groups G. Once permutation F has been applied to the pixels of a group G, they (the pixels) become perturbed and therefore less correlated. When the discrimination function f is applied to $F(G)$, it therefore results in a larger value. This is why most groups in an image are of type R.

We denote by N_R, N_S, and N_U the numbers of groups of type R, S, and U, respectively. Thus, $N_R + N_S + N_U = M \times N/n$, and for "regular" images $N_R > N_S$. It is this difference between the numbers of R and S groups that is exploited to hide the secret data. This is also the reason why this method is called RS lossless data embedding. Notice that the following relations hold:

If G is of type R, $F(G)$ is of type S.

If G is of type S, $F(G)$ is of type R.

If G is of type U, $F(G)$ is of type U.

These relations can be denoted by $F(R) = S$, $F(S) = R$, and $F(U) = U$. We can also say that the flipping permutation F flips the two types R and S but leaves type U unchanged.

We are now ready for the details of RS lossless embedding. The image is scanned in a certain order and an RS bitstring is constructed. For each group of type R encountered in the scan, a 0 is appended to RS, and for each type-S group, a 1 is appended to it. Groups of type U are rare and do not participate in the data embedding (that is done later). Such groups are simply skipped and do not affect RS. At the end of the scan, RS is complete, its size is $N_R + N_S$, and it is compressed. RS compresses well because each R group contributes a 1 and each S group contributes a 0 to it and there are more R than S groups. Thus, RS has more 1s than 0s, so it is *sparse* (or close to sparse), and sparse binary strings can be highly compressed (see, for example, [Salomon 04], page 761).

The secret data to be embedded is now appended to RS, and the extended RS is embedded in the R and S groups. (The extended RS string must start with a count or a pointer in order to enable the decoder to break it up into its two constituents.)

Embedding the extended RS string is done by scanning the image as before, looking for R and S groups. When the next such group is encountered, the next bit from the extended RS string is embedded in the group. If the group is of type R and the next bit is 1, no change is needed. If the next group G is of type R and the next bit is 0, the group is flipped to $F(G)$, whose type is S. This process can be summarized by saying that type-R groups are assigned to secret bits 1 and type-S groups are assigned to secret bits 0. If the next group and the next bit are mismatched, the group is flipped.

Decoding is simple. The stegoimage is scanned in the same order, and a bitstring is generated by appending a 1 bit for each R-type group of pixels encountered and a 0 bit for each group of type S. The string is then broken up into the compressed RS string and the secret data. The RS string is decompressed and is used to reconstruct the original image. This is done by scanning the image again, in the same order, looking for groups of types R and S. Each such group encountered corresponds to the next bit in RS. If the group type and the bit are mismatched, the group is flipped.

Since bits are embedded in the R and S groups, the total number of bits that can be embedded (the raw data capacity of the image) is $N_R + N_S = M \times N/n - N_U$ bits. If we denote the size of the compressed RS string by $|RS|$, then the net data capacity (the payload) is $D = N_R + N_S - |RS|$. The magnitude of $|RS|$ depends on the efficiency of the compression method used and also on the difference between R and S. If R and S are about equal, then string RS is not sparse and may be close to random; it will not compress well. If, on the other hand, there is a big difference between R and S, the string RS (whose size is $N_R + N_S$) will compress well. The best possible compression (the so-called *entropy compression*) will compress RS to

$$-N_R \log_2 \left(\frac{N_R}{N_R + N_S} \right) - N_S \log_2 \left(\frac{N_S}{N_R + N_S} \right) \quad \text{bits.}$$

The payload is therefore

$$D = N_R + N_S + N_R \log_2 \left(\frac{N_R}{N_R + N_S} \right) + N_S \log_2 \left(\frac{N_S}{N_R + N_S} \right) \quad \text{bits.}$$

It is easy to see that $N_R = N_S$ implies $D = 0$, while a big difference between N_R and N_S results in large D. The difference between N_R and N_S depends on the size and shape of the pixel groups G, on the discrimination function f, on the amplitude A of the flipping permutation F, and on the nature of the original image V. The difference increases with large group size n and with large amplitudes. Also, smooth, quiet images tend to result in bigger differences and therefore in increased payload capacity.

Experiments performed by the originators of this method on various images (all using $n = 4$) indicate that the number of secret bits embedded on average in one image pixel varies from 0.019 (for flipping permutation with amplitude 1) to 0.12 (for amplitude 7). Another result was that even the small group size $n = 4$ and the amplitude 1 F_{LSB} permutation performed well on many images.

The next method described in this section is based on the idea of locating in image V subsets (of pixels) with specific properties. We denote by $S(x)$ the set of all pixels in V whose value is x. We start by identifying two sets $S(x)$ and $S(y)$ that satisfy the following conditions.

1. The values x and y are similar.
2. The two sets $S(x)$ and $S(y)$ can be compressed; i.e., the pixels that constitute those sets are correlated.

Image V is scanned in some order (perhaps rowwise), and a binary string Z is prepared. For each x pixel found during the scan, a 0-bit is appended to Z. For each y pixel found, a 1-bit is similarly appended. Bitstring Z is then losslessly compressed and concatenated with the secret data to form bitstring W. Notice that W must start with a tag or a pointer that will make it possible for the decoder to identify its two parts (string Z and the secret data). The last step is to embed W in V by modifying some of the x and y pixels. Embedding is done by hiding each 0 bit of W as an x pixel and each 1 bit as a y pixel. If the next bit to be hidden is a 0, the algorithm scans the image until the next x or y pixel is encountered. If that pixel is y, it is changed to an x. If that bit is an x, there is no need for any changes.

Notice that bitstring Z is compressible if the sizes of sets $S(x)$ and $S(y)$ are very different. In such a case, Z has either many 0s and a few 1s or vice versa. In either case, Z would be sparse and therefore highly compressible.

Decoding is done by first extracting W from the stegoimage. The image is scanned in the same order as in encoding. Each x pixel encountered appends a 0 to the extracted bitstring, and each y pixel encountered appends a 1 to it. The resulting string W is then broken up into the secret data and bitstring Z. The latter is decompressed and is used to restore the original x and y pixels. This is done by scanning the image, looking for x or y pixels. When such a pixel is encountered, the next bit of Z determines whether its value should be switched.

An important feature of the method is that changing x pixels into y and vice versa does not affect the image much because we require the x and y values to be close.

This approach can be used for raw or compressed images, but has proved effective for palette images, of which the GIF format is a well-known example.

14.4 Data Hiding by Quantization

Data can be embedded in an image while the image is being compressed. A common approach to image compression, an approach used by several image compression algorithms, employs prediction and quantization combined with arithmetic coding. The approach is based on the fact that the pixels of a typical image are correlated. If we select a pixel at random in an image, chances are it will be similar to its near neighbors. A typical lossy image compression algorithm may therefore proceed as follows.

1. The image is scanned row by row. For each pixel P_{ij}, the algorithm computes an average of its neighbors. Figure 14.9 illustrates various ways of selecting the neighbors. The average may also be computed as a weighted sum, where neighbor pixels that are slightly more distant receive smaller weights. In general, the average is a noninteger. Notice that only neighbors that have already been seen by the algorithm are used for computing the average. This is because the decompressor has to compute the same average in order to decompress P_{ij}, but when the decompressor is working on P_{ij}, it hasn't yet decompressed the pixels below P_{ij} or to its right.

Figure 14.9: Various Neighbors (N) of Current Pixel (P).

2. The average is subtracted from P_{ij} to produce a (noninteger) pixel difference $\Delta_{ij} = P_{ij} -$ average, that is normally zero or very small. In rare cases, where P_{ij} differs significantly from its neighbors, Δ_{ij} may be very large (positive or negative). For

most images, the difference values are distributed according to the Laplace distribution (Figure 14.3).

3. This is the lossy step, where information is irretrievably lost. The difference Δ_{ij} is quantized. Quantization changes the value of Δ_{ij} to an integer. Fine quantization may simply round Δ_{ij} to the nearest integer, while coarse quantization may convert small Δ_{ij} values to zero. When the image is decompressed, the decompressor cannot reverse this step, with the result that the decompressed image differs from the original one.

4. The quantized difference values Δ_{ij} are now compressed by arithmetic coding (Section 3.8) or by replacing each with a variable-size code (Section 3.3).

Hiding data bits in the compressed image is done in step 3. When a difference value Δ_{ij} is quantized, its quantized value may be changed a little in order to reflect a hidden data bit. Difference values and hidden bits may, for example, be related by the table

$$
\begin{array}{lccccccccc}
\Delta_{ij} & -4 & -3 & -2 & -1 & 0 & 1 & 2 & 3 & 4 \\
\text{bit} & 0 & 1 & 0 & 1 & 1 & 1 & 0 & 0 & 1
\end{array}
$$

If a certain Δ_{ij} is quantized to -2 and a data bit of 1 should be hidden in it, then Δ_{ij} is quantized instead to -3 or -1.

14.5 Patchwork

This steganographic method, due to [Bender et al. 96], uses a stego-key to embed one bit of data in an image. The data-embedding capacity is very low, but the method has an important feature: it is practically impossible to remove this bit without disrupting the image in a major way. It seems that embedding one bit in an image isn't very useful, but because of the special way this bit is embedded, the modifications to the image can be used as a signature to verify that the image belongs to the owner of the stego-key. The image is modified such that a certain statistical property of the pixels is changed significantly. It is easy to discover that this property has been changed, but it is extremely hard to modify the pixels to restore the property back to its original value. The owner of the stego-key, however, can modify the original image to obtain the new value of the statistical property and thus prove ownership.

Patchwork is based on slightly changing the brightness values of many pixels. The pixels should therefore be represented in a luminance–chrominance color space such as YCbCr (Section 14.1.1). Experiments suggest that the eye can detect small, but not very small, changes in brightness. In a high-noise (random) region of an image, the eye cannot detect changes in brightness of less than 1 in 30. In uniform areas, the smallest changes detectable by the eye are approximately 1 in 240. Thus, Patchwork makes only small modifications of 1–5 units in 256 to the brightness of many pixels. The main encoding steps are the following.

1. The stego-key is used as the seed of a pseudorandom number generator.
2. Two pseudorandom numbers are drawn to select two pixels a_i and b_i.

3. The brightness of a_i is increased and the brightness of b_i is decreased by the value of a parameter δ, normally in the range 1–5.
4. Steps 2–3 are repeated n times (for $n = 10,000$ typically).

If δ is small enough, no changes are visible in the image. However, the quantity

$$S_n = \sum_{i=1}^{n}(a_i - b_i)$$

has been changed significantly. It is easy to see intuitively (and to prove rigorously) that S_n was zero before the brightness modifications (because for every positive difference $(a_i - b_i)$ there is a corresponding negative difference). The new value S'_n of S_n is

$$S'_n = \sum_{i=1}^{n}\big((a_i + \delta) - (b_i - \delta)\big) = 2\delta n + \sum_{i=1}^{n}(a_i - b_i) = 2\delta n + S_n \approx 2\delta n.$$

The parameter δ is relatively small, but n can be large.

An improvement to the original method performs Step 3 on the pixels of two small regions (patches) centered on a_i and b_i. This has the effect of shifting the image noise introduced by the brightness modifications to the lower frequencies, where it is more likely to survive lossy image compression. The patches can be square, hexagonal, or random (Figure 14.10).

Patchwork is robust against many types of image modifications, including cropping. However, geometrical changes such as scaling, rotation, and shearing may affect the value of S'_n adversely.

Figure 14.10: Square, Hexagonal, and Random Patches.

There is, hidden or flaunted, a sword between the sexes till an entire marriage reconciles them.

—C. S. Lewis

A lie hides the truth. A story tries to find it.

—Paula Fox

14.6 Transform Domain Methods

Steganographic techniques that hide data in the least significant bits of an image are simple and effective but very fragile. Any operations that modify the image, such as lossy compression, sharpening, or contrast adjustments, can modify the values of many pixels and thus destroy much of the hidden data. A useful, practical steganographic method should therefore be robust. It should retain the hidden data even after many pixel values have been modified. One approach to this problem is to transform the image and embed the data in the transformed pixels. We say that the original image exists in the spatial domain and the transformed image is in the transform domain. The data is then embedded in the transformed pixels and the image is transformed back to the spatial domain. The idea is that the image may now be exposed to various operations that will change the pixels, but when this modified image is transformed again, the hidden data will still be embedded in the transformed pixels. Section 14.7 shows how this can be done in the special case of the *discrete cosine transform* (DCT), so the reader should first review Section 5.6.2 for the details of this important technique.

Data can be hidden in a block of DCT coefficients by computing the DCT of the image, slightly modifying some of the DCT coefficients depending on the bits to be hidden, then computing the inverse DCT with the modified coefficients. The data is now embedded in the image, but it cannot be extracted by examining the pixels. Instead, the image has to be transformed, and the decoder should check the relationships between the modified DCT coefficients. These relationships determine the hidden data. Recall that the DCT coefficients near the top-left corner of an image block represent the lowest pixel frequencies which correspond to the important image information. Thus, these coefficients should not be modified. In addition, the coefficients near the bottom-right corner of the block are mostly zeros, so they should not be modified either.

14.7 Robust Data Hiding in JPEG Images

Embedding data bits in the least significant positions of image pixels is simple and effective, but it has a serious drawback. The embedded data becomes seriously damaged and may even become completely unreadable when the image is modified as a result of image processing or lossy compression. Digital image processing techniques for sharpening images, increasing contrast, and filtering change the values of many pixels. Lossy image compression methods, such as the popular JPEG (Section 5.9), have the same effect. JPEG compression may shrink an image to a small percentage of its original size. After decompression, an observer may not detect any changes from the original image, but a direct check will reveal that many pixel values have changed.

The attribute of color images that makes such lossy compression possible is called *noise*. A color image may have many pixels with similar colors, and the eye cannot tell when some of them (or even many of them) have been slightly modified. In contrast, a monochromatic image (i.e., an image with one foreground color on a uniform background) has very little noise, so it is much harder to change pixel colors without visually modifying such an image.

This section follows the ideas proposed by [Zhao and Koch 95]. The method discussed here can embed data in a color or a grayscale image such that the data are retained even after the image is compressed in JPEG. Section 14.14 shows how the same ideas can be applied to embedding data in monochromatic images.

The JPEG image compression method is discussed in detail in [Pennebaker and Mitchell 92] and [Salomon 04]. Here, only the main steps are listed.

Step 1. The color representation of the pixels is changed from RGB to a luminance-chrominance color space, such as YCbCr (Section 5.9.1). The remaining steps are executed on each color component separately.

Step 2. The image is partitioned into blocks of 8×8 pixels each and the remaining steps are executed on each block separately.

Step 3. The 64 pixel values of a block are transformed by the discrete cosine transform (DCT) to become 64 transform coefficients. The DCT has the following advantages. (1) Many of the coefficients are zero or small numbers, (2) the nonzero coefficients are concentrated at the top-left corner of the block, and (3) small changes to the nonzero coefficients do not affect the inverse DCT much.

Step 4. The nonzero coefficients are quantized. This is the lossy step, where image information is irretrievably lost. Quantization is done by dividing each coefficient by a *quantization coefficient* (QC, an integer taken from a quantization table) and rounding the result. The JPEG standard recommends certain quantization tables for the luminance and chrominance components, based on human factors studies.

Step 5. The 64 DCT coefficients are collected by scanning the block in zigzag (Figure 8.3a). Because of the nature of the DCT, the nonzero coefficients are mostly concentrated at the start of the resulting sequence and are followed by runs of zeros interspersed by a few nonzero coefficients.

Step 6. Each nonzero coefficient and each run of zero coefficients is replaced by a Huffman code. The codes are written on a file, and they (plus the values of certain parameters used in the preceding steps) constitute the compressed image.

The method discussed here embeds a single bit of data in each valid 8×8 block of pixels (the discussion later in this paragraph explains when a block is considered valid). The embedding capacity is therefore small (see note at end of this section). The method does not actually compress the image, but it performs (temporarily) the first four steps on every block. After quantizing the transform coefficients of a block (with the quantization factor QF, discussed later), the method prepares the block for the eventual hiding of the next data bit by selecting three coefficients and further modifying them, if needed, so that certain relations hold between them. Certain relations among the three chosen coefficients express a hidden 0, while other relations imply that a 1-bit is hidden in the block. If the correct relations already exist among the coefficients, there is no need for any modifications. If modifying the three coefficients would change the image too much, the block is declared invalid. Its coefficients are not modified and nothing is hidden in it.

The three coefficients are then dequantized, and the inverse DCT applied to the modified block, to recreate the pixels. If the transform coefficients have been modified, the recreated pixels are different from the original. The point is that the three chosen coefficients are never modified much, so the recreated pixels are not much different from the original ones and the modified image is indistinguishable from the original.

After all the valid blocks have been modified in this way, the image is compressed by any JPEG compressor. Because of the way the pixels have been changed by our method prior to compression, the valid blocks of DCT transform coefficients in the compressed image contain the hidden bits.

The image is eventually decompressed and viewed or stored. Retrieving the hidden bits is similar to the process of writing them in the first place. Blocks of 8×8 pixels are temporarily DCT transformed and checked. If a block is invalid, there is no hidden bit in it. Otherwise, the relation among the three chosen coefficients is checked in order to reveal the hidden bit.

Rather than selecting the 8×8 image blocks in raster order (row by row), it is possible to select them pseudorandomly, using a stego-key as the seed of a pseudorandom number generator. Retrieving the hidden data requires knowledge of the key.

Experiments with various color images indicate that the best three transform coefficients to use for hiding a bit in a block should be selected from among the eight coefficients in positions 2, 3, 9, 10, 11, 16, 17, and 18 (Figure 14.11, where coefficients are numbered rowwise from 0 at the top left to 63 at the bottom right). These coefficients are normally nonzero, are smaller than the coefficients in positions 0, 1, and 8, and are bigger than the other nonzero coefficients. Selecting 3 out of 8 objects can be done in $\binom{8}{3} = 56$ ways, but Table 14.12 lists only 18 recommended sets of three coefficients A, B, and C each. The algorithm uses a stego-key as the seed of a pseudorandom number generator to select one of the 18 sets for each block.

Once a set of three coefficients A, B, C has been selected, the coefficients are modified, if needed, to either reflect a hidden bit or indicate that the current block is invalid. They are modified such that one of the following four relations holds.

1. One of the three is the largest and another one is the smallest (this is indicated in Table 14.13 by the letters H, M, and L, standing for High, Medium, and Low).
2. Two coefficients are equal and the third is smaller (this is indicated by H, H, L).
3. Two coefficients are equal and the third is larger (this is indicated by L, L, H).
4. All three coefficients are equal (this is indicated by M, M, M).

The specific relations indicating an invalid block, a block containing a hidden bit of 1, and a block with a hidden 0-bit are listed in Table 14.13.

The responsiveness of this method, specifically, its robustness versus quality, is controlled by adjusting the values of two parameters: the maximum distance MD and the quantization factor QF. (The term *quality* refers to the appearance of the image after embedding the data. *High quality* is the case where the eye cannot distinguish between the modified image and the original one.) The distance parameter MD controls the maximum allowed difference among the values of the triplet A, B, and C of selected coefficients. A large value of MD produces robust data embedding (i.e., the image could tolerate very lossy JPEG compression before the embedded data is damaged or destroyed) but decreases the quality (the modified image may be visibly different from the original one). The default value of MD is 1. The quantization factor QF is used to temporarily quantize the three selected coefficients in step 4 above. It is expressed as a percentage and its default value is 75%. Large values of QF result in small quantized

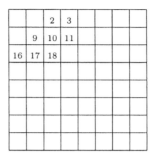

Figure 14.11: Recommended
Positions for Coefficients.

No.	A	B	C	No.	A	B	C		A	B	C	
1	2	9	10	10	9	2	16		H	M	L	⎫
2	9	2	10	11	10	17	3		M	H	L	⎬ patterns for "1"
2	3	10	11	12	17	10	3		H	H	L	⎭
4	10	3	11	13	10	3	17		M	L	H	⎫
5	9	2	10	14	3	10	17		L	M	H	⎬ patterns for "0"
6	2	9	10	15	9	16	17		L	L	H	⎭
7	9	16	2	16	16	9	17		H	L	M	⎫
8	16	9	2	17	10	17	18		L	H	M	⎬ invalid patterns
9	2	9	16	18	17	10	18		M	M	M	⎭

Table 14.12: 18 Recommended Sets.   Table 14.13: Nine Patterns.

coefficients, and small numbers require smaller changes to bring them to the desired relationship. Thus, large values of QF result in fewer modifications to the original image pixels, but the embedded data becomes less robust.

The remainder of this section lists the algorithms for embedding and reading the data. The main program for embedding the data requires the three parameters key, n (number of bits of data), and D (the data to be hidden). For each of the n data bits, the program calls Boolean procedure check_write(Bj,Di) to check whether block Bj is valid for hiding bit Di. If so, the program calls procedure write(Bj,Di) to actually embed bit Di in the block. There is the implied assumption that the image contains enough valid blocks to embed all n data bits.

```
1 program embed(D,n,key); % D=n bits of data to hide
2 randomseed(key);
3 i:=1; % 'i' is index of data bits
4 if i≥n then stop;
5 j:=random(); % select block Bj
6 if Bj has already been selected then goto 5;
7 if check_write(Bj,Di) else goto 5;
```

```
 8 % boolean proc to check whether Bj is valid
 9 write(Bj,Di); % embed bit Di in block Bj
10 i++; goto 4;
```

Procedure `check_write(Bj,Di)` checks image block `Bj` for validity. Its main steps are the following.

1. A pseudorandom number is drawn (using the stego-key as the seed) to select one triplet A, B, and C of transform coefficients from Table 14.12. Only the positions of the coefficients (in the range $[0, 63]$) are selected in this step, since the coefficients themselves will be computed in the next step.

2. The DCT is applied to the 64 pixel values of block `Bj`. The three coefficients A, B, and C are quantized with the quality factor QF to produce the quantized values a, b, and c.

3. The current bit to be hidden in the block is `Di`. This step is performed when `Di = 1`. If $\min(|a|, |b|) + \text{MD} < |c|$, then the block is invalid. Trying to modify the three quantized coefficients to any of the three patterns for "1" in Table 14.13 would change the original pixels too much. The algorithm then performs the substeps:

   3.1 Modify the three quantized coefficients to any of the three invalid patterns in Table 14.13.

   3.2 Dequantize the modified a, b, and c to obtain new values for A, B, and C, and then perform the inverse DCT on the entire block of transform coefficients to obtain a block of pixels, some of which will be different from the original.

   3.3 Return False.

4. This step is performed when `Di = 0`. If $\max(|a|, |b|) > |c| + \text{MD}$, then the block is invalid. The algorithm performs the three substeps 3.1, 3.2, and 3.3.

5. In any other case, the block is valid. Return True.

Procedure `write(Bj,Di)` embeds bit `Di` in block `Bj` by modifying three of the 64 transform coefficients. The modifications are then reflected in the pixels. The procedure is called only for valid blocks. Its main steps are the following.

1. A pseudorandom number is drawn (using the stego-key as the seed) to select the positions of A, B, and C from Table 14.12.

2. The DCT is applied to the 64 pixel values of block `Bj`. The three coefficients A, B, and C are quantized with the quality factor QF to produce the quantized values a, b, and c.

3. If `Di = 1`, modify a, b, and c such that they satisfy $a > c + \text{MD}$ and $b > c + \text{MD}$. The three modified coefficients now form one of the patterns for "1" of Table 14.13.

4. If `Di = 0`, modify a, b, and c such that they satisfy $a + \text{MD} < c$ and $b + \text{MD} < c$. The three modified coefficients now form one of the patterns for "0" of Table 14.13.

5. Dequantize a, b, and c and perform the inverse DCT on the block of coefficients to obtain a block of (modified) pixels.

The main program for retrieving the data requires the three parameters `key`, `n` (number of bits of data), and `D` (the embedded data). For each of the `n` data bits, the program calls Boolean procedure `check_read(Bj,Di)` to check whether block `Bj` is valid. If so, the program calls procedure `read(Bj,Di)` to identify bit `Di` in the block.

```
1 program read(D,n,key); % retrieve n data bits Di
2 randomseed(key);
3 i:=1; % 'i' is index of data bits
4 if i≥n then stop;
5 j:=random(); % select block Bj
6 if Bj has already been selected then goto 5;
7 if check_read(Bj,Di) else goto 5;
8 % boolean proc to check whether Bj is valid
9 read(Bj,Di); % retrieve bit Di from block Bj
10 i++; goto 4;
```

Procedure `check_read(Bj,Di)` checks image block `Bj` for validity. Its main steps are the following.

1. A pseudorandom number is drawn (using the stego-key as the seed) to select one triplet A, B, and C of transform coefficients from Table 14.12. Only the positions of the coefficients (in the range $[0, 63]$) are selected at this step, since the coefficients themselves will be computed in the next step.
2. The DCT is applied to the 64 pixel values of block `Bj`. The three coefficients A, B, and C are quantized with the quality factor QF to produce the quantized values a, b, and c.
3. If a, b, and c form any of the invalid patterns of Table 14.13, return False. Otherwise return True.

Procedure `read(Bj,Di)` returns bit `Di` embedded in block `Bj`. It selects the correct three transform coefficients and identifies the hidden bit by checking the relation between them. The procedure is called only for valid blocks. Its main steps are the following:

1. A pseudorandom number is drawn (using the key as the seed) to select the positions of A, B, and C from Table 14.12.
2. The DCT is applied to the 64 pixel values of block `Bj`. The three coefficients A, B, and C are quantized with the quantization factor QF to produce the quantized values a, b, and c.
3. If $a > c + \text{MD}$ and $b > c + \text{MD}$, then return 1.
4. If $a + \text{MD} < c$ and $b + \text{MD} < c$, then return 0.
5. If neither of the relations in 3 and 4 above is found, the block has been damaged and the embedded bit cannot be identified.

Note: It should be noted that the embedding capacity of this method is small. A $1\text{K} \times 1\text{K}$ image has 16 K blocks of 8×8 pixels, so at most 16 K bits (or 2048 bytes) can be embedded in it. Thus, the method is ideal for embedding small quantities of data, such as copyright information or the name of the image owner. The name and address of the person who created the image may be embedded in the image as a way to prove authorship. When copies of an image are sold, the name of the buyer (or a serial number) may be embedded by the seller in each copy as a means of identifying buyers who illegally distribute copies of the image.

14.8 Robust Frequency Domain Watermarking

We normally associate the term *frequency* with a wave, but Section 5.6 shows how this term can be applied to pixels in an image. The frequencies inherent in an image can be identified and isolated by means of a frequency domain transform, such as the discrete cosine transform (DCT). Even a little experience with such a transform shows that the low image frequencies correspond to the main image features and should therefore be preserved, while the high frequencies correspond to the fine image details and are therefore less important. This is why image processing techniques normally modify the high-frequency transform coefficients of an image and leave the low-frequency coefficients unchanged. Lossy image compression methods, for example, often work by quantizing (i.e., chopping off) the high-frequency transform coefficients of the image. Steganographic methods may also find it natural to hide data in the high-frequency transform coefficients.

The data-hiding method described here (due to [Cox et al. 96]) is unusual in that it hides data in the low-frequency coefficients. The method was developed specifically to hide a watermark and to be robust. The aim is to be able to identify the presence or absence of the watermark with a high degree of probability (but not to retrieve its individual bits) even after the image has been modified by many operations. The assumption is that image processing techniques tend to operate on the high-frequency transform coefficients, so hiding data in the low-frequency coefficients would preserve the hidden data during many types of image processing and therefore result in a robust steganographic algorithm. Any image processing that changes the low-frequency coefficients results in severe image degradation long before the watermark is destroyed.

The main problem is that the watermark being hidden should be invisible, but modifying the low-frequency coefficients affects the main image features and may result in visible changes to the image. The solution adopted by this method is to create the watermark automatically, as a large set of random numbers with the $N(0,1)$ distribution (the normal, Gaussian, distribution with zero mean and a standard deviation of 1). Each random number (these are called the *watermark components*, and they are real numbers, not bits) is scaled and is used to slightly modify one of the low-frequency transform coefficients. The originators of the method show that this special distribution of the watermark components is one reason for the robustness of this method.

The large number of the watermark components is another reason for the robustness of the method. It implies that each component can be small. This is in accordance with the principle of spread spectrum commonly used in communications. A strong, narrowband watermark is diluted and distributed among many transform coefficients. Detection of the watermark is done by identifying and collecting all the small modifications to the transform coefficients and then combining and concentrating them into a strong signal.

The method is secure because the watermark owner knows the watermark components (the random numbers), but an attacker does not. An attacker trying to destroy the watermark would randomly modify the transform coefficients. If the random modifications are small, the watermark would still be identified with a high degree of probability. If the modifications are large, they would result in noticeable changes to the image itself.

Because of this special choice of watermark components, the method is not suitable for cases where a specific watermark (such as a manufacturer's name or an owner identification) is required.

Encoding the watermark starts with an $N \times N$ cover image D and a watermark X that consists of n watermark components $x_1, \ldots, x_n$. The DCT is applied to the entire image (not to small blocks as in JPEG), resulting in $N \times N$ transform coefficients v_i. The n largest transform coefficients (excluding the DC coefficient) are selected, and each is added to one watermark component according to the rule $v_i(1 + \alpha x_i)$, where α is a scale factor. Other ways to add the watermark are $v_i + \alpha x_i$ and $v_i(e^{\alpha x_i})$. The inverse DCT is then applied to the $N \times N$ transform coefficients, resulting in the watermarked cover image D'. The scale factor α is important because the watermark is embedded in the largest (i.e., lowest-frequency) transform coefficients that contain the important image information and should not be modified much. Ideally, each coefficient v_i should have its own scale factor α_i, but experiments indicate that $\alpha = 0.1$ works well in most cases.

Since the watermark should be robust, we assume that a watermarked image D' will be modified to an image D^* as a result of image processing operations or even an attack on the watermark. The modified image D^* is tested for the presence of the watermark by extracting the (possibly corrupted) watermark X^* from it and comparing X^* statistically to the original watermark X.

The size n of the watermark X affects the degree to which the watermark components pervade the transform coefficients of the image. Generally, n should be large, but the developers of the method show that increasing n produces diminishing returns and conclude that the choice of n should be image specific. For example, if an image turns out to be sensitive to small changes of its DCT coefficients, a smaller scale factor α should be used, and n should be increased to compensate for this. The actual experiments with this method have used $n = 1000$.

Extracting watermark X^* from D^* requires the original image D. The DCT is applied to both images, resulting in two sets of DCT coefficients v_i and v_i'. Since $v_i' = v_i(1 + \alpha x_i)$, it is easy to compute x_i. Comparing X^* to the original watermark X can in principle be done by computing the correlation coefficient between the two arrays of numbers. The correlation coefficient of two arrays is a number in the range $[-1, +1]$ that is calculated by normalizing the elements of the arrays (such that the mean and variance of each array are 0 and 1, respectively) and then computing the dot product of the normalized arrays. However, the result of comparing X and X^* is not limited to the range $[-1, +1]$ and should be allowed to vary in a wider interval. It therefore makes sense to use the dot product $X^* \cdot X$ as the basis of this comparison. The developers of the method have decided to use as the measure of similarity the expression

$$\text{sim}(X, X^*) = \frac{X^* \cdot X}{\sqrt{X^* \cdot X^*}},$$

because this results in values $\text{sim}(X, X^*)$ that are distributed according to $N(0, 1)$.

In summary, encoding a watermark X in a cover image D results in a stegoimage D' that may be modified, by processing or by an attack, to an image D^*. Verifying the presence of the watermark of D in an image starts when an image M is presented for testing. The test for the presence of the watermark of D in M requires the original cover image D and its watermark X. These are used to extract the watermark X^* from M. The similarity $\text{sim}(X, X^*)$ is then computed. If the result is large, the conclusion is that image M is image D, perhaps modified by image processing or by an attack on the watermark.

The method has been implemented by its developers and tested on one image with a watermark consisting of 1000 numbers. The following tests were performed, with impressive results.

Test 1. The original image was copied 1000 times. The original was then watermarked, and each of the 1000 copies was also watermarked with a random watermark. Each of the 1000 random watermarks X^* was then extracted and compared to the original watermark X. The similarity measures yielded values in the range $[-4, +4]$, whereas the similarity measure of the original watermark with itself was 32.

Test 2. A watermark was embedded in the image. The image was then shrunk to one-quarter its size and scaled back to its original size by duplicating each pixel four times. Much detail was lost in the resulting image, but the similarity measure of the original watermark and the one after rescaling was 13.4.

Test 3. The image was JPEG compressed with medium compression ratio and then decompressed. Comparing the original and decompressed images resulted in a similarity measure of 22.8. The process was repeated with a high compression ratio such that the decompressed image was noticeably degraded. Comparing the watermarks of the original and decompressed images in this case yielded a similarity measure of 13.9.

Test 4. The image was dithered. The similarity measure was 5.2, still higher than the similarity measures between the original and random watermarks in test 1.

Test 5. The watermarked image was clipped such that only its center (one-quarter of the image area) remained. The missing parts were then replaced by pixels from the original, unwatermarked, image. The similarity measure in this case was 10.6.

Test 6. The image was watermarked, printed, xeroxed, scanned at the low resolution of 300 dpi, and rescaled to 256×256 pixels. The resulting image was distorted, but the similarity measure yielded 7—still significantly above random.

Test 7. The original image was watermarked and then watermarked again (with different random numbers) four more times. The five-times watermarked image was then tested against 1000 random watermarks that included the five "true" ones. The results are shown in Figure 14.14a, where the five spikes stand out against the background of 995 other tests.

Test 8. The original image was copied five times and one watermark embedded in each copy. The five watermarked copies were averaged to form one image. Testing the watermark in this image against 1000 random watermarks (which included the five original watermarks) resulted in the spectrum of Figure 14.14b, where the five spikes again stand out against the background of the 995 random ones.

This method has been improved by [Podilchuk and Zeng 97] who included the properties of the human visual system in the improved algorithm.

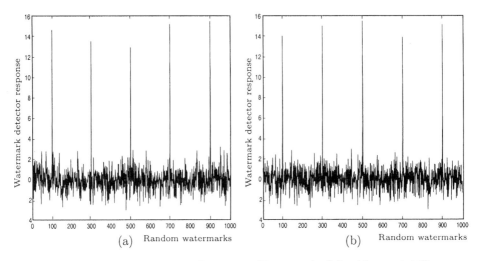

Figure 14.14: Watermark Detector Response in Tests 7 and 8 (after [Cox et al. 96]).

14.9 Detecting Malicious Tampering

Section 13.1 lists robustness and tamper resistance among the most desirable features of a steganographic method, especially a watermarking method. These features are mutually exclusive to some degree because robustness means reduced sensitivity to modification of the stegocover, whereas tamper resistance implies increased sensitivity to such modifications. There is also the problem of innocent modifications. An attempt to change the brightness, contrast, or color mixture of a stegoimage should be considered innocent tampering and should be ignored by a good tamper-resistant algorithm. On the other hand, an attempt to replace a person's face in a watermarked image should be detected and reported as tampering when the watermark is checked. Such degree of tamper resistance is especially important in view of the wide availability of sophisticated image processing software such as Adobe Photoshop and Paintshop Pro.

A tamper-resistant watermarking algorithm of this type is discussed here. It follows the descriptions in [Fridrich 98 and 99]. The watermark consists of a sequence of pseudorandom numbers that are added to the middle 30% of the DCT coefficients of the watermarked image. Thus, this method is somewhat similar to the spread spectrum algorithm of Section 14.8. The main difference is in the way the random numbers that make up the watermark are obtained.

The image is partitioned into blocks of 64×64 pixels each, and a different watermark (i.e., a different sequence of pseudorandom numbers) is embedded in each block. The seed of the pseudorandom number generator depends on the block number and on the content of the block. The reason for the particular block size is that many malicious attempts at image tampering try to modify a person's face in the image, and a (recognizable) face normally occupies more than 32×32 pixels.

Before transforming the image or embedding anything, the method uses the stego-key as the seed of a PRNG to construct M patterns P_i of 64×64 pseudorandom bits each, where M is typically in the range 30–50. The patterns are then smoothed using a lowpass filter and are made DC-free.

The main idea of this method is to use the M patterns to generate (in the first encoding step) M bits b_i from each image block in a special way and use them as part of the seed of the PRNG for the block's watermark. The method should be robust, which implies that generating M bits in the same way from the block after it has been modified should produce the same (or mostly the same) bits. To generate bit b_i ($i = 1, \ldots, M$), the image block is compared with pattern P_i, and those image pixels that correspond to bits of 1 in the pattern are selected and added together. If the sum is greater than a certain threshold, then b_i is set to 1; otherwise, it is set to 0. Experiments with many images have indicated that a threshold of 2500 results in approximately half of the b_i being 1s.

The point is that the M bits generated this way are immune to innocent modifications but sensitive to malicious tampering with the block's pixels. This is therefore the main strength of this watermarking algorithm. Experiments with the well-known Lena image have generated 50 bits per block, then subjected the image to various image processing operations, and generated 50 bits from each modified block. The following results were noticed. After blurring the image four times, at least 47 bits were correctly generated (in some blocks, all 50 bits were correct). Changing the brightness by $\pm 25\%$ resulted in at least 44 correct bits. Adding white Gaussian noise with standard deviation of 36 gray levels resulted in at least 46 correct bits. Other operations, including sharpening, decreasing color depth, histogram equalization, and very lossy JPEG compression and decompression, produced similar results. On the other hand, when part of a block was replaced (as in an attempt to replace some of the image), the bits generated from the modified block were very different from the original ones.

The conclusion is that by using error correction (by adding perhaps 20 parity bits), it is possible to generate 30–50 bits from each block and regenerate the same bits after the block is subjected to certain, innocent operations.

In the second encoding step, each block is DCT transformed and the middle 30% of the DCT coefficients are modulated by adding one watermark component (a pseudorandom number) to each coefficient. Assuming that D pseudorandom numbers are needed, these are generated by a PRNG whose seed depends on the stego-key, block number, and the M bits generated for the block. The pseudorandom numbers are in an interval $[0, \alpha]$, where α can be adjusted in order to obtain a stegoimage that is visually imperceptible from the original, while maintaining robustness.

In the third and last step, the modified blocks are inverse DCT transformed to create the stegoimage.

Detecting the watermark is done for each block individually. M bits are generated by the same method used by the encoder and are used (with the stego-key and block number) to generate the pseudorandom numbers of the watermark. The stegoimage is DCT transformed, the watermark is subtracted from the DCT coefficients, and the resulting coefficients are compared with those of the original image.

14.10 Robust Wavelet-Based Watermarking

The many image steganography methods can be divided into two classes: methods that hide the data in the spatial domain (i.e., in the pixels) and methods that hide data in the transform domain (by modifying the coefficients obtained after the image has been transformed). Section 14.6 describes the discrete cosine transform (DCT), and Section 14.7 shows how this transform can be applied to hide data in the transform domain of an image. The method described here is by [Xia et al. 98] and is designed for embedding a robust watermark in the wavelet coefficients (Section 5.7) of an image. The method is somewhat similar to the DCT-based Cox–Kilian method of Section 14.8 in that the watermark is a set of normally distributed pseudorandom numbers that are embedded by adding them to certain wavelet transform coefficients. The method has several advantages over the Cox–Kilian algorithm.

1. The Cox–Kilian method is computationally intensive. Identifying the presence of a watermark requires a computation (similar to a correlation coefficient) that involves the entire image. The wavelet-based method has multiresolution characteristics and is hierarchical. Most of the time, the presence or absence of the watermark can be ascertained by computing a correlation with just one subband (one-fourth of the image). If the image has been heavily modified by processing or by an attack on the watermark, the calculation should involve more subbands.

2. The wavelet transform concentrates the fine image details in the HH, HL, and LH subbands. Specifically, information about edges and textures is concentrated in those subbands. It is known that the eye is sensitive to small changes in a uniform area. If even one pixel is modified in an otherwise uniform area, it sticks out and is easily visible. On the other hand, if one pixel in a sharp edge is modified, it is harder for the eye to notice it. This means that adding the watermark components to the wavelet coefficients in subbands HH, HL, and LH (Figure Ans.13 in the Answers to Exercises section) affects mostly image features such as edges and can be made visually imperceptible.

3. Modern image compression methods, such as JPEG 2000, are based on the wavelet transform, so our method, which is also wavelet based, is especially robust to wavelet image compression. A watermarked image can be wavelet compressed (with much loss of image data) and decompressed several times without loss of the watermark.

The details of encoding and decoding a watermark with this method are described next. We assume that an $N \times N$ image with pixels $x[i, j]$ is given. The first step is to draw n pseudorandom numbers r_k that are $N(0, 1)$ distributed (i.e., have a normal distribution with zero mean and a variance of 1). The discrete wavelet transform (DWT) is then applied to the image, resulting in a pyramid decomposition with s levels of subbands, where s is a parameter of the method. The LL subband is ignored and the n largest DWT coefficients $y[i, j]$ in the remaining subbands are identified. Each is modified to a coefficient $y'[i, j]$ by

$$y'[i, j] = y[i, j] + \alpha y^2[i, j] \, r_k,$$

where r_k is the next pseudorandom number and α is a scale factor, to be determined experimentally. The inverse DWT is then applied to create an image with pixels $x'[i,j]$. The pixels of the new image are then modified according to

$$x'[i,j] = \min\big(\max(x[i,j]), \max\{x'[i,j], \min(x[i,j])\}\big).$$

This guarantees that the new image will have the same dynamic range as the old one. The entire process is summarized in Figure 14.15a.

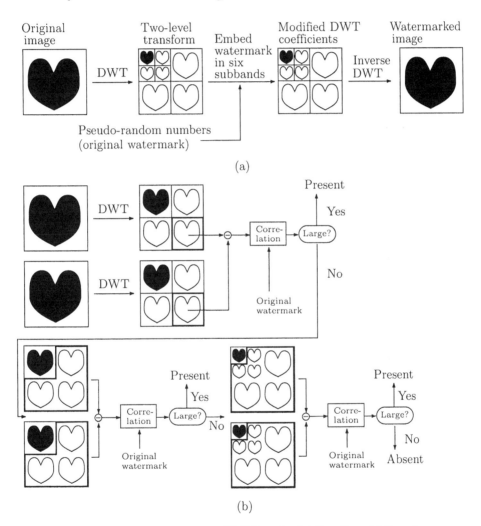

Figure 14.15: Watermarking in the DWT Domain: (a) Encoding: (b) Decoding.

Decoding is a hierarchical, multistep process. Given an image to be tested for the presence of the watermark, the DWT is applied to both the original image and the image being tested. Only one level (i.e., four subbands) is calculated. The coefficients of the HH subband of the original image are subtracted from the corresponding coefficients of the image being tested, and the result is correlated with the original pseudorandom numbers of the watermark. A large value (close to $+1$) indicates the presence of the watermark. If the result of the correlation is not large enough, the process is repeated on the three subbands HL, LH, and HH. If even this correlation is not large enough to indicate the presence of the watermark with any certainty, the DWT is applied again to the LL subbands of the two images in order to compute another level of four subbands, and the process is repeated with six subbands (HL, LH, and HH in each of the two subbands). More steps of DWT can be performed, each adding three subbands, until the number of levels reaches s (the number of levels computed in the encoding).

Several experiments have been performed with the method using two 512×512 images, the Haar wavelet transform, and a two-step DWT (i.e., two levels of subbands, for a total of seven subbands). The images were subjected to several types of distortions, similar to the tests described in Section 14.8. The results were as expected. With large distortions, more subbands must be included in the correlations in order to identify the presence of the watermark with high probability.

14.11 Kundur–Hatzinakos Watermarking: I

Here is a different approach to watermarking an image in the transform domain. This method, due to [Kundur and Hatzinakos 98], computes the pyramid wavelet transform of the cover image and embeds each bit of the watermark by examining three wavelet coefficients located at the same position in three subbands and modifying one of the three. Verifying the presence of the watermark requires the key and the watermark but not the original cover image. The method is easy to understand and seems to be robust enough to justify its use in practice.

The cover image is denoted by f. The watermark is a binary string generated by the user. An L-level pyramid wavelet decomposition of f is computed. The parameter L and the bank of filter coefficients are permanent parts of the encoder. The wavelet transform results in $3L$ subbands of horizontal, vertical, and diagonal image details. Certain coefficients in these subbands, chosen by the stego-key, are modified to hide the watermark. The low-level coefficients are not changed in any way.

At the lth resolution level, there are three subbands that are denoted by h, v, and d (for horizontal, vertical, and diagonal). A wavelet coefficient at position (m, n) in any of these subbands is denoted by $f_{kl}(m, n)$, where $k = h$, v, or d and $l = 1, 2, \ldots, L$. For each level l, triplets of coefficients are examined and some are selected by the stego-key.

The key is used as the seed of a pseudorandom number generator to generate pseudorandom bits. One such bit is generated for each triplet examined. If the bit is 1, one bit of the watermark is embedded in the triplet. If the watermark is short, several copies of it may be embedded in the image, which helps the decoder in identifying the presence or absence of the watermark.

In order to embed one bit in a trio of wavelet coefficients $f_{kl}(m, n)$, the three coefficients are sorted such that $f_{k1,l}(m, n) \leq f_{k2,l}(m, n) \leq f_{k3,l}(m, n)$, where $k1$, $k2$, and $k3$ are distinct and each is one of h, v, and d. The interval from $f_{k1,l}(m, n)$ to $f_{k3,l}(m, n)$ is divided into subintervals of width

$$\Delta = \frac{f_{k3,l}(m, n) - f_{k1,l}(m, n)}{2Q - 1},$$

where Q is a user-controlled parameter (whose value is typically around 4). To embed a watermark bit of 1 (or of 0), coefficient $f_{k2,l}(m, n)$ is modified to the nearest value shown in bold (or in dashes) in Figure 14.16.

Figure 14.16: Embedding One Bit in a Triplet of Coefficients.

Once all the coefficients in the $3L$ pyramid levels have been examined and modified in this way, the inverse wavelet transform is applied, resulting in the watermarked image. The parameter Q controls the tradeoff between robustness (small Q) and visual imperceptibility (large Q). A larger value of Q results in smaller Δ, which in turn results in less image degradation but more susceptibility to image processing (i.e., weaker robustness).

The decoder has to compute a reliable estimate of the original watermark from a given image r. Notice that r may be a distorted version of the watermarked image. The decoder starts by computing the L-level pyramid wavelet decomposition of r using the same filter bank and the same L as the encoder. The $3L$ low levels of subbands are then scanned one by one, and the stego-key is used to generate pseudorandom bits that indicate which triplets $r_{kl}(m, n)$ of wavelet coefficients should be examined. A triplet to be examined is sorted such that $r_{k1,l}(m, n) \leq r_{k2,l}(m, n) \leq r_{k3,l}(m, n)$, where $k1$, $k2$, and $k3$ are distinct and each is h, v, or d. The position of $r_{k2,l}(m, n)$ is noted relative to $r_{k1,l}(m, n)$ and $r_{k3,l}(m, n)$, which gives the value of the embedded bit. The same parameter Q must, of course, be used during this process. If the watermark has been embedded several times in the cover image, all the copies are extracted and compared. If a certain bit differs in the multiple copies, the voting principle is used to decide what value to assign to it.

Once the entire watermark has been extracted, the Pearson correlation coefficient is computed between the original and the extracted watermarks. If the result is greater than a predefined threshold T, the decoder reports positively (the watermark is present in image r).

Results obtained by the developers of the method indicate medium-to-good robustness of the method against various types of image distortions.

14.12 Kundur–Hatzinakos Watermarking: II

Any image processing algorithm should take into account the properties of the human visual system (HVS), and this is the main feature of the method described here [Kundur and Hatzinakos 97]. The algorithm computes the pyramid wavelet transforms of both the cover image and the watermark, and embeds the watermark in the image by adding the wavelet coefficients of the watermark to the wavelet coefficients of the cover image. The main point is that the wavelet coefficients of the watermark are scaled, before they are added, by a quantity called *salience*, which measures the perceptual importance of small blocks of the image. The result is a very robust *fusion* of the watermark into the image, a fusion that can be detected even after image processing operations have practically destroyed the watermarked image.

We assume that the watermark elements are random (noiselike), bits where each 0 has been changed to a -1. The watermark itself should be a rectangle of size $2x \times 2y$ that is smaller than the image by a factor of 2^M (where M is any positive integer). As an example, the image may be of size 256×256 and the watermark may be a 32×32 square. The value of M in this case is 3. The notation $f(m, n)$ is used to indicate the pixels of the cover image, while $w(m, n)$ indicates the elements of the watermark.

In the first encoding step, an L-level pyramid wavelet transform is applied to the cover image, where $L \leq M$. In our example, L can be 1, 2, or 3. This produces $3L$ subbands of detail coefficients, corresponding to the horizontal, vertical, and diagonal features of the image. In our example, assuming $L = 3$, the three subbands at level 1 are of size 128×128 each, those at level 2 are 64×64 each, and each of the three subbands at level 3 has a size of 32×32. The wavelet coefficients at level l are denoted by $f_{kl}(m, n)$, where $k \in (h, v, d)$ and $l = 1, 2, \ldots, L$. The watermark is also wavelet transformed, but only one level is computed. This results in three subbands of detail coefficients and one subband (at the top-left corner) of gross image features. Each subband is of size $x \times y$ (16×16 in our example). The detail coefficients are denoted by $w_k(m, n)$.

In step 2, the encoder segments each of the $3L$ detail subbands of the image pyramid transform into rectangles of size $x \times y$. In our example, each of the three 128×128 subbands of level 1 is segmented into 8×8 rectangles. Each of the three 64×64 subbands of level 2 is segmented into 4×4 rectangles, and each of the three subbands at level 3 is segmented into 2×2 rectangles. The number of rectangles on level l is $2^{2(M-l)}$ and the ith one is denoted by $f_{kl}^i(m, n)$.

A quantity S called *salience* is computed for each rectangle by

$$
S\big(f_{kl}^i(m, n)\big) = \sum_{\text{all } (u,v)} C(u, v) \left| F_{kl}^i(u, v) \right|^2,
$$

where u and v range over all the spatial frequencies of the rectangle, $F_{kl}^i(u, v)$ is the discrete Fourier transform of the elements of rectangle $f_{kl}^i(m, n)$, and $C(u, v)$ is the *contrast sensitivity* of the eye for frequencies u and v. This quantity is defined by

$$
C(u, v) = 5.05 e^{-0.178(u+v)} \left(e^{0.1(u+v)} - 1 \right).
$$

(The spatial frequency of pixels in an image row is defined as the number of times the pixels change color as we move along the row. In order for the eye to distinguish individual colors in a row with high spatial frequency, the contrast between the colors must be high. Contrast sensitivity is defined as the reciprocal of the contrast needed for a given spatial frequency to be perceived by the eye.)

Embedding the watermark is done by adding a rectangle of watermark wavelet coefficients $w_k(m,n)$ to each rectangle $f_{kl}^i(m,n)$ of image wavelet coefficients according to

$$g_{kl}^i(m,n) = f_{kl}^i(m,n) + \gamma_{kl}\sqrt{S(f_{kl}^i(m,n))}\,w_k(m,n),$$

where γ_{kl} is a scale factor that controls the tradeoff between robustness of the watermark to image distortions and visual imperceptibility of the watermarked image. This factor depends on the level l and on the value of k (h, v, or d). For best results, the values of γ_{kl} should be selected by the user for each individual image by experimentation. The following rule of thumb may help in this process

$$\gamma_{kl} = \frac{\alpha}{\max_{\text{all }(u,v)}\sqrt{S(f_{kl}^i(m,n))}},$$

where α equals 10% to 20% of the average value of the pixels of the original cover image.

Step 3 computes the inverse wavelet transform using rectangles $g_{kl}^i(m,n)$ instead of $f_{kl}^i(m,n)$, to obtain the watermarked image.

The decoder requires the original cover image. It performs the reverse operations and extracts the watermark components by subtracting the wavelet coefficients of the original cover from the wavelet coefficients of the image being tested. The set of extracted watermark components is compared to the set of original watermark components by computing the Pearson correlation coefficient between them. If the result is greater than a certain threshold, the algorithm returns a positive result (i.e., the image being tested is watermarked).

Experiments carried out with an implementation of this algorithm have indicated that the method is highly robust to lossy compression and to additive noise. In some cases, the watermark was extracted successfully from images that have been almost destroyed by these operations.

Banyak orang yang tidak tahu bahwa Babbage juga seorang ahli cryptanalysis yang berhasil memecahkan Vigenere cipher (polyalphabet cipher). Kepandaiannya ini sebetulnya sudah dimilikinya sejak tahun 1854, setelah dia berhasil mengalahkan tantangan Thwaites untuk memecahkan ciphernya. Akan tetapi penemuannya ini tidak dia terbitkan sehingga baru ketahuan di abad 20 ketika para ahli memeriksa notes-notes (tulisan, catatan) Babbage.

—Bahan bacaan, *Ensiklopedia Komputer Dan Internet*

14.13 Data Hiding in Binary Images

The JPEG compression method was designed to efficiently compress color images and does not do a good job on a monochromatic (binary) image. Such images, however, can also be manipulated by digital image processing techniques or by converting the images from one graphics file format to another. This is why a robust steganographic method is needed if data is to be hidden in such an image. The main problem in hiding data in a binary image is that such images have little or no "noise." Switching the values of even a few pixels may be noticeable, may arouse suspicion, and may invite an attack that involves switching the noticeable pixels back.

Several methods for hiding data in binary images (including fax) are discussed in the following subsections.

14.14 The Zhao–Koch Method

This section follows the ideas proposed by [Zhao and Koch 95] to embed data in a binary image and retrieve the data reliably even after many pixel values have been modified. The method is robust (i.e., retains the embedded data even after the original image is modified) but is not very efficient. A binary image has just two colors, white (or background) and black (or foreground), so such an image has less "noise" than a color or a grayscale image, which is why embedding data may sometimes result in noticeable changes to the original image.

The main idea behind the method is to partition the image into blocks of 8×8 pixels each and to modify the pixels of a block, if necessary, such that a single data bit can be hidden in the block and its value can later be determined by checking the percentage of black pixels in the block. A block where more than half the pixels are black is assumed to contain a hidden 1. Similarly, a 0-bit is assumed to be hidden in a block if less than half its pixels are black. (A block where exactly half the pixels are black is considered invalid and has to be modified in order for a bit to be hidden in it.) If a block has to be modified too much in order to hide the current data bit, the block is declared invalid. An important feature of the method is its robustness. A block is modified to hide a 1-bit in such a way that even after λ% of its pixels have been modified accidentally or by an attack (where λ is a user-controlled robustness parameter), the block still has more than 50% black pixels (and the same is true for a block hiding a 0-bit).

We denote the percentage of black pixels in a block B by $P_1(\text{B})$. There are 64 pixels in a block, so

$$P_1(\text{B}) = \frac{\text{number of black pixels in B}}{64},$$

and the percentage of white pixels is $P_0(\text{B}) = 1 - P_1(\text{B})$. In addition to λ (whose default value is 5%), the method uses two threshold parameters, R_0 and R_1. To understand their use, we consider two extreme cases.

Case 1. The current bit to be hidden is a 1, and the current block B satisfies $P_1(\text{B}) = 0.51$. According to our convention, such a block already hides a 1-bit. However, because of the robustness requirement, the block would have to be modified so that $P_1(\mathtt{B}) > 0.5 + \lambda$. As a result, we change our requirements to (1) a 1-bit is embedded in a block B if $P_1(\mathtt{B}) > R_1$ and (2) a 1 is read from B if $P_1(\mathtt{B}) > 0.5$. Similarly, a 0-bit is embedded in a block B if $P_1(\mathtt{B}) < R_0$ and a 0 is read from B if $P_1(\mathtt{B}) < 0.5$.

Case 2. The current bit to be hidden is a 0 and the current block B satisfies $P_1(\mathtt{B}) > R_1 + 3\lambda$. In order to hide the bit, we have to reduce $P_1(\mathtt{B})$ from $R_1 + 3\lambda$ to less than R_0, a process that requires changing too many pixels. The block is therefore declared invalid. The procedure that retrieves the data bits has to know which blocks are invalid, so the rule is that any block where $P_1(\mathtt{B}) > R_1 + 3\lambda$ (and similarly, any block where $P_1(\mathtt{B}) < R_0 - 3\lambda$) is always declared invalid, regardless of the current data bit.

The default values of R_0 and R_1 are 45% and 55%, respectively. The figure above shows how a 1-bit is embedded by bringing the value of $P_1(\mathtt{B})$ to the interval $[R_1, R_1 + \lambda]$. If pixels are later switched in the block such that $P_1(\mathtt{B})$ is increased or decreased by less than λ, then $P_1(\mathtt{B})$ is still greater than 50% and less than $R_1 + 2\lambda$. Similarly, a 0-bit is embedded by bringing the value of $P_1(\mathtt{B})$ to the interval $[R_0 - \lambda, R_0]$.

A block that is declared invalid by setting $P_1(\mathtt{B}) > R_1 + 3\lambda$ is also robust. If pixels are switched such that $P_1(\mathtt{B})$ decreases by less than λ or increases by any amount, the block would still be considered invalid because $P_1(\mathtt{B})$ of a valid block is always less than $R_1 + 2\lambda$.

An important feature of the method is the way it decides which pixels should be modified in a block. Once a block is found to be valid, the algorithm computes the color and the number n of pixels that should be modified (this depends on $P_1(\mathtt{B})$ and on the particular data bit being embedded). The modification strategy depends on the type of the block. If the black pixels are distributed throughout the block more or less uniformly (a dithered monochromatic image), then the candidates for modification are those pixels that have the largest number of same-color immediate neighbors. This strategy is illustrated in Figure 14.17a, where four white pixels have been switched. If, on the other hand, the block has large uniform areas (a sharply contrasted image), then the first candidates for modification are those pixels that are located along a boundary and that have the most opposite-color immediate neighbors (Figure 14.17b, where again four white pixels have been modified).

The main programs for hiding and retrieving data bits are identical to those of Section 14.7. The procedures for hiding, reading, and checking a block for validity are listed here.

Procedure `check_write(Bj,Di)` checks image block `Bj` for validity. Its main steps are the following.

1. If $P_1(\mathtt{B}) > R_1 + 3\lambda$ or $P_1(\mathtt{B}) < R_0 - 3\lambda$, return False.
2. Assuming that `Di = 1`, if $P_1(\mathtt{B}) < R_0$, modify block `Bj` such that $P_1(\mathtt{B}) < R_0 - 3\lambda$; then return False.
3. Assuming that `Di = 0`, if $P_1(\mathtt{B}) > R_1$, modify `Bj` such that $P_1(\mathtt{B}) > R_1 + 3\lambda$; then return False.

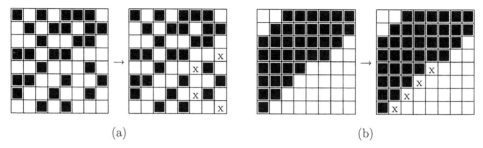

Figure 14.17: Modifying Pixels in (a) a Dithered Image and (b) a Uniform Image.

4. In all other cases, the block is valid. Return True.

Procedure write(Bj,Di) embeds bit Di in block Bj by modifying some of the black or white pixels. The procedure is called only for valid blocks. Its main steps are the following.

1. If Di = 1, modify block Bj such that $P_1(B) \geq R_1$ and $P_1(B) \leq R_1 + \lambda$.
2. If Di = 0, modify Bj such that $P_1(B) \leq R_0$ and $P_1(B) \geq R_0 - \lambda$.

Procedure check_read(Bj,Di) checks image block Bj for validity. Its only step is

1. If $P_1(B) > R_1 + 2\lambda$ or $P_1(B) < R_0 - 2\lambda$, return False; else, return True.

Procedure read(Bj,Di) returns the value of data bit Di that is hidden in block Bj. It simply compares $P_1(B)$ to 50%. The procedure is called only for valid blocks.

1. If $P_1(B) > 0.5$, return 1.
2. If $P_1(B) < 0.5$, return 0.
3. If $P_1(B) = 0.5$, return error (block has been damaged).

Step 3 of procedure check_write(Bj,Di) is one reason why this method is sometimes inefficient. Assume that the default values $R_1 = 0.55$ and $\lambda = 0.05$ are used. If an 8×8 block has 36 black pixels, then $P_1(B) = 36/64 = 0.5625$, so $P_1(B) > R_1$. Modifying the block such that $P_1(B) > R_1 + 3\lambda = 0.55 + 0.15 = 0.7$ requires changing the values of nine white pixels to black. Changing nine out of 64 pixels means changing 14% of the pixels in the block, and this may many times result in visible changes to the block. A similar problem exists in step 2 of the same procedure.

> He was unfamiliar with Latin (like all generals) but terrific in maths, a science indispensable to high officers who must be able to calculate (without paper or pencil) the number of men, rations, cartridges, kilometers, enemies, prisoners, dressings, decorations, and even coffins, that may be required at any moment by the hazards of war.
>
> —Marcel Pagnol, *The Time of Secrets*

14.15 The Wu–Lee Method

The novel features of this method [Wu and Lee 98] are the use of a key K for added security and the use of logical operations. The image is partitioned into blocks B of $m \times n$ pixels each, and the key, which is also an $m \times n$ block of bits, is used to embed at most one data bit d in each block. For simplicity, we assume that the image size is an integer multiple of the block size. The main advantage of the method is that the data bit is embedded in the block by changing the value of at most one pixel.

We use the symbol $\wedge$ to indicate a logical AND on two blocks of bits. The notation $SUM(\text{B})$ is used for the sum of all the $m \times n$ bits of block B.

Bit d is hidden in block B by establishing the relation $SUM(\text{B} \wedge \text{K}) \bmod 2 = \text{d}$. If this relation does not already exist between B, K, and d, then it is achieved by changing the value of one pixel in block B. The logical AND of B and K varies from zero to $m \times n$ (when the pixels of B and K are all 1s). The expression $n \bmod 2$ equals 0 for even n and 1 for odd n, so its value can be switched between 0 and 1 by incrementing or decrementing n by 1. There are, however, two problem cases.

Case 1. Block B is all zeros (or mostly zeros). Changing one bit of B from 0 to 1 would be noticeable. Moreover, such a change must be done in a position where the key K has a bit of 1, so it would provide an attacker with an important clue about the 1-bits in K. (It may be impossible to change one bit of B from 1 to 0 because B has few 1s and such a change must be made in a position where K has a 1.)

Case 2. The logical AND of any two blocks X and Y may contain at most as many 1s as Y. Therefore, if $SUM(\text{B} \wedge \text{K})$ already equals $SUM(\text{K})$, then B has at least as many 1s as K (and possibly more), and the only possible change in B is to switch a 1 to a 0. This would again be noticeable and would provide clues about the positions of 1-bits in the key K.

Because of these two problem cases, only blocks that satisfy $0 < SUM(\text{B} \wedge \text{K}) < SUM(\text{K})$ are candidates for hiding bits. Other blocks are declared invalid. Furthermore, the rules for embedding a bit should be such that the above inequality would still hold after the bit has been embedded in the block. Thus, the bit embedding rules are as follows:

1. **if** $0 < SUM(\text{B} \wedge \text{K}) < SUM(\text{K})$ **then** perform step 2, **else** select next block.

2. **if** $SUM(\text{B} \wedge \text{K}) \bmod 2 = \text{d}$ **then** keep B intact.
   else if $SUM(\text{B} \wedge \text{K}) = 1$ **then**
       randomly pick a bit $\text{B}_{ij} = 0$ such that $\text{K}_{ij} = 1$ and change B_{ij} to 1.
   else if $SUM(\text{B} \wedge \text{K}) = SUM(\text{K}) - 1$ **then**
       randomly pick a bit $\text{B}_{ij} = 1$ such that $\text{K}_{ij} = 1$ and change B_{ij} to 0.
   else randomly pick a bit B_{ij} such that $\text{K}_{ij} = 1$ and complement B_{ij}.
   endif;

Figure 14.18 shows an example of four 3×3 blocks where the three bits 011 are hidden. Block B_1 is invalid because $SUM(\text{B}_1 \wedge \text{K}) = SUM(\text{K}) = 5$. Block B_2 satisfies $SUM(\text{B}_2 \wedge \text{K}) = 3$, so it is valid. The first bit to be embedded is a 0, so one 0 bit in B_2 is switched to 1 (in boldface) in order to change $SUM(\mathsf{B}_2 \wedge \mathsf{K})$ to an even number. Block B_3 satisfies $SUM(\mathsf{B}_3 \wedge \mathsf{K}) = 3$, so it is valid, and since we need to embed a 1, there is no need for any changes. Block B_4 is also valid and is modified by changing a 1 to a 0 in order to hide a data bit of 1.

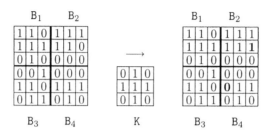

Figure 14.18: Hiding Bits in Four 3×3 Blocks.

The method is not very secure. An attacker who has access to the original image can gain information about the key by comparing the original blocks to the modified ones. A pixel location that hasn't been changed in any block implies a 0-bit in the key. Any pixel location that has changed in any of the blocks implies a 1-bit in the key.

The key K must be carefully selected. A key with few 1s has a small $SUM(\mathsf{K})$ and will render many blocks invalid. A key with many 1s is easier to compromise. Similarly, a cover image with many zeros may produce many zero blocks that are invalid.

14.16 The CPT Method

The Wu–Lee method of Section 14.15 can embed at most one data bit d in each image block B. The principle of that method is to equate a certain sum modulo 2 (which involves B) by changing at most one bit in B. Since the value of $(n \bmod 2)$ for any integer n is either 0 or 1, the modulo function can be used to embed one bit in the block.

The CPT method described in this section, originally developed by [Chen, Pan, and Tseng 00], partitions a binary image into blocks B of size $m \times n$ each and uses the modulo function to embed r data bits $d_1, d_2, \ldots, d_r$ in each block. The principle is to equate a certain sum (which involves B) modulo 2^r to the r-bit integer $d_1 d_2 \ldots d_r$ by switching the values of very few pixels in B. (Notice that an r-bit integer is always in the interval $[0, 2^r - 1]$.) In fact, the developers of the method prove that the result can always be achieved by switching the values of at most two pixels in B.

The number r of hidden data bits depends, of course, on the block size $m \times n$, and the relation is

$$2^r - 1 \le mn, \quad \text{or} \quad r \le \lfloor \log_2(mn + 1) \rfloor. \tag{14.1}$$

We use the symbols $\wedge$, $\vee$, and $\oplus$ to indicate the logical AND, OR, and Exclusive-OR (XOR) operations on two blocks of bits. The symbol $\otimes$ indicates pairwise multiplication of two blocks of numbers (not just bits). The notation $SUM(\mathrm{B})$ indicates the sum of all the $m \times n$ bits of block B.

A little thinking shows that it is always possible to equate $(SUM(\mathrm{B}) \bmod 2^r)$ to any number in the interval $[0, 2^r - 1]$ (and specifically, to the integer $d_1 d_2 \ldots d_r$) by switching pixels in B. However, up to $2^r/2$ pixels may have to be switched (either from 0 to 1 or from 1 to 0), which may often result in noticeable visual changes to the block.

In order to minimize the number of pixel switchings, the method uses a weight matrix W of size $m \times n$. Matrix W is the same for all the image blocks, its elements must be integers in the range $[1, 2^r - 1]$, and each integer in this range must appear in W at least once.

$\diamond$ **Exercise 14.7:** How many such matrices are possible?

Because of the relation $(m \cdot n \geq 2^r - 1)$ imposed by Equation (14.1), matrix W always has room for at least $(2^r - 1)$ integers, and therefore can always be constructed. As an example of how W is used, we assume $m = n = 3$. This allows for r values of up to 3. We therefore select $r = 3$ and assume the following:

$$\mathrm{B} = \begin{bmatrix} 1 & 1 & 0 \\ 1 & 0 & 0 \\ 1 & 1 & 0 \end{bmatrix} \quad W = \begin{bmatrix} 1 & 2 & 3 \\ 1 & 2 & 3 \\ 1 & 2 & 3 \end{bmatrix}.$$

A pairwise multiplication yields

$$\mathrm{B} \otimes W = \begin{bmatrix} 1 & 1 & 0 \\ 1 & 0 & 0 \\ 1 & 1 & 0 \end{bmatrix} \otimes \begin{bmatrix} 1 & 2 & 3 \\ 1 & 2 & 3 \\ 1 & 2 & 3 \end{bmatrix} = \begin{bmatrix} 1 & 2 & 0 \\ 1 & 0 & 0 \\ 1 & 2 & 0 \end{bmatrix}.$$

The sum of the elements of this product is $SUM(\mathrm{B} \otimes W) = 1 + 2 + 1 + 1 + 2 = 7$. To increment this sum by 2, we can switch the single element B_{22}. To increment it by 3, element B_{13} can be switched. To decrement it by 3, the two elements at positions $(1, 1)$ and $(1, 2)$ can be switched.

For increased security, the CPT method uses a key K that is also an $m \times n$ matrix of bits. Instead of multiplying B by W, the method multiplies the XOR $(\mathrm{B} \oplus \mathrm{K})$ by W. If we assume the inputs

$$\mathrm{B} = \begin{bmatrix} 1 & 1 & 0 \\ 1 & 0 & 0 \\ 1 & 1 & 0 \end{bmatrix} \quad \mathrm{K} = \begin{bmatrix} 0 & 1 & 1 \\ 1 & 1 & 0 \\ 0 & 1 & 1 \end{bmatrix} \quad W = \begin{bmatrix} 1 & 2 & 3 \\ 1 & 2 & 3 \\ 1 & 2 & 3 \end{bmatrix},$$

a pairwise multiplication yields

$$(\mathrm{B} \oplus \mathrm{K}) \otimes W = \begin{bmatrix} 1 & 1 & 0 \\ 1 & 0 & 0 \\ 1 & 1 & 0 \end{bmatrix} \oplus \begin{bmatrix} 0 & 1 & 1 \\ 1 & 1 & 0 \\ 0 & 1 & 1 \end{bmatrix} \otimes \begin{bmatrix} 1 & 2 & 3 \\ 1 & 2 & 3 \\ 1 & 2 & 3 \end{bmatrix} = \begin{bmatrix} 1 & 0 & 3 \\ 0 & 2 & 0 \\ 1 & 0 & 3 \end{bmatrix}.$$

The sum of the elements of this expression is $SUM(\mathrm{B} \oplus \mathrm{K}) \otimes W = 1 + 3 + 2 + 1 + 3 = 10$. In order to hide the three bits $d_1 d_2 d_3$ in block B, this sum (modulo 2^3) should be modified so that it equals $d_1d_2d_3$, and the developers of the method prove that this can always be achieved by following the three steps below, which involve switching the values of at most two pixels.

Step 1. Compute $SUM((\text{B} \oplus \text{K}) \otimes W)$.

Step 2. Compute the $2^r - 1$ sets S_w for $w = 1, 2, \ldots, 2^r - 1$ such that set S_w contains all the index pairs (i, j) that satisfy: If we complement pixel B_{ij}, the sum of step 1 will be incremented by w. In order for a pair (i, j) to be included in set S_w, either of the following conditions must be satisfied.

2.1 $W_{ij} = w$ and $\text{B}_{ij} = 0$. Switching B_{ij} will increment the sum by w.

2.2 $W_{ij} = 2^r - w$ and $\text{B}_{ij} = 1$. Switching B_{ij} will decrement the sum by $2^r - w$, which is equivalent to increasing it by $(w \bmod 2^r)$.

The formal definition of set S_w is

$$S_w = \{(i, j) \mid (W_{ij} = w \wedge [\text{B} \oplus \text{K}]_{ij} = 0) \vee (W_{ij} = 2^r - w \wedge [\text{B} \oplus \text{K}]_{ij} = 1)\}. \quad (14.2)$$

Step 3. Using the sets computed in step 2, this step shows which pixels should be switched in order to equate the sum of step 1 with $d_1d_2 \ldots d_r$. The quantity

$$\Delta = (d_1d_2 \ldots d_r) - [SUM((\text{B} \oplus \text{K}) \otimes W) \pmod{2^r}]$$

is computed. The sum will have to be increased by Δ to bring it to the required value. If $\Delta = 0$, there is no need to change anything. Otherwise, we select two nonempty sets $S_{h\Delta}$ and $S_{-(h-1)\Delta}$. These sets include the indexes of all the pixels B_{ij} whose switching will increase the sum by $h\Delta$ and $-(h-1)\Delta$, respectively. The total effect is to increase the sum by Δ. The following substeps constitute the formal description of this process, and the developers also prove that these steps can always be carried out.

3.1 Randomly select an h in the range $0 \leq h \leq 2^r - 1$, such that $S_{h\Delta} \neq \emptyset$ and $S_{-(h-1)\Delta} \neq \emptyset$.

3.2 Randomly select a pair $(i, j) \in S_{h\Delta}$ and switch the value of pixel B_{ij}.

3.3 Randomly select a pair $(i, j) \in S_{-(h-1)\Delta}$ and switch the value of pixel B_{ij}.

Steps 3.2 and 3.3 create the impression that two pixels have to be switched, but this is not the case. The formal definition of sets S_w [Equation (14.2)] implies that S_0 (and similarly, all sets S_r, S_{2r}, $S_{3r}, \ldots$) are undefined. From the intuitive definitions of those sets, we conclude that S_0 is the set of all pairs (i, j) such that switching pixel B_{ij} will increase the sum by 0. Increasing the sum by 0 can, of course, be achieved by doing nothing, so we add one more rule to steps 3.2 and 3.3: When a pair (i, j) is selected in set S_0, don't switch pixel B_{ij}. Thus, in some cases, only one pixel need be switched.

Retrieving the hidden data is trivial. The image is scanned block by block. For each block, the quantity $SUM((\text{B} \oplus \text{K}) \otimes W) \bmod 2^r$ is computed to yield the next set of r hidden data bits.

Figure 14.19 is an example of four 4×4 blocks that are modified to hide the 12 data bits 001010000001. Block B_1 satisfies $SUM((\text{B}_1 \oplus \text{K}) \otimes W) = 0 \bmod 8$. In order to hide bits 001, the sum should equal $1 \bmod 8 = 1$, so the sum has to be incremented by 1, which can be done by switching pixel $(2, 4)$. Block B_2 satisfies $SUM((\text{B}_2 \oplus \text{K}) \otimes W) = 2 \bmod 8$, so no change is required in order to hide bits 010. Block B_3 satisfies

$SUM((\mathsf{B}_3 \oplus \mathsf{K}) \otimes W) = 2 \bmod 8$. The data bits to be hidden are 000, so the sum has to be increased by 6, which can be done by switching the pixel at $(4,4)$. Block B_4 satisfies $SUM((\mathsf{B}_4 \oplus \mathsf{K}) \otimes W) = 4 \bmod 8$. The data bits to be hidden are 001, so the sum has to be increased by 5. There is no single pixel in this block whose complementing would increase the sum by 5, so we have to switch the values of two pixels. One way to do this is to select the sets $S_{10} = S_2 = \{(2,2)\}$ and $S_{-3} = S_3 = \{(1,3),(2,1),(3,2),(3,4)\}$. In our example, the pixels at $(2,2)$ and $(3,2)$ have been switched.

Figure 14.19: Hiding 12 Bits in Four 4×4 Blocks with the CPT Method.

The method is extremely secure against a brute force attack because there are 2^{mn} ways to select the key and a huge number of ways (see Exercise 14.7) to select the weight matrix. As a result, even an opponent who knows the algorithm and has the original cover image, the modified image, and the values of r, m, and n, would not be able to retrieve the hidden data by simply trying all the possible keys and weights.

14.17 The TP Method

The CPT method of Section 14.16 has been improved by two of the three original authors and is described in [Tseng and Pan 01]. Its principles are explained in this section, where it is referred to as the *TP method*. (For a full understanding of the TP method, please read Section 14.16 first.) The main innovation of TP is the way pixels are selected for switching. In CPT, one or two pixels are randomly selected and their values flipped. This may sometimes lead to visible changes in the block, as illustrated in Figure 14.20. The flipped pixel in boldface is much less noticeable than the one in italics.

Thus, one principle of the TP method is to flip a pixel P from b to b' only if one (or more) of the eight near neighbors of P have values b'. If this is impossible to achieve in a block, the block is declared invalid and no data bits are hidden in it (one pixel may have to be modified in such a block, so the TP decoder will identify it as invalid). Also, a uniform block (one that is completely white or completely black) is considered invalid and is left intact. In some rare cases, modifying one or two pixels in a block in order to hide bits in it may render it uniform. In such a case, the block is left uniform and the

1	1	1	1	0	0
1	1	1	0	0	0
1	1	0	0	0	0
1	0	0	0	0	0
0	0	0	0	0	0
0	0	0	0	0	0

1	1	1	1	0	0
1	1	1	0	0	0
1	1	0	0	0	0
1	1	0	0	0	0
0	0	0	0	0	0
0	0	0	0	0	0

1	1	1	1	0	0
1	1	1	0	0	0
1	1	0	0	0	0
1	0	0	0	*1*	0
0	0	0	0	0	0
0	0	0	0	0	0

Figure 14.20: Switching a Pixel with Different Neighbors.

data bits already hidden in it are hidden again in the next block. The decoder always ignores uniform blocks.

The first concept developed by the TP method is that of the distance of a pixel from its nearest complementary neighbor. For each $m \times n$ block, a distance matrix of the same size is computed, where each location (i, j) contains the quantity $\text{dist}B_{ij}$ defined by

$$\text{dist}B_{ij} = \min_{xy}(\sqrt{|i - x|^2 + |j - y|^2}, \text{ for all } B_{xy} \neq B_{ij}).$$

Intuitively, $\text{dist}B_{ij}$ is the Euclidean distance between pixel B_{ij} and the nearest pixel with the opposite color. Figure 14.21 shows an example (where the overbar signifies a square root).

1	1	0	0	0
1	1	0	0	0
1	0	0	0	0
1	0	0	0	0
1	0	0	0	0

2	1	1	2	3
$\sqrt{2}$	1	1	2	3
1	1	$\sqrt{2}$	$\sqrt{5}$	$\sqrt{10}$
1	1	2	$\sqrt{8}$	$\sqrt{13}$
1	1	2	3	4

Figure 14.21: Minimum Distances Between Differing Pixels.

The relation between the block size $m \times n$ and the number r of bits that can be embedded in a block is slightly different from that of the CPT method [Equation (14.1)] and is expressed by

$$r \leq \lfloor \log_2(mn + 1) \rfloor - 1 \tag{14.3}$$

(i.e., r is smaller by 1 compared to CPT).

The r bits are embedded in block B by modifying pixels such that the modified block B' satisfies

$SUM((B' \oplus K) \otimes W)$ is even, and divided by 2 and taken modulo 2^r it equals $d_1 d_2 \ldots d_r$.

If the encoder cannot embed any bits in the block, it modifies the block such that the sum above is odd, which indicates an invalid block.

The weight matrix W is also different from that used in the CPT scheme. Its elements must be integers in the range $[1, 2^{r+1} - 1]$, and there must be at least one odd

$$
\begin{bmatrix}
o & e & o & e & o & e \\
e & o & e & o & e & o \\
o & e & o & e & o & e \\
e & o & e & o & e & o \\
o & e & o & e & o & e \\
e & o & e & o & e & o
\end{bmatrix}
\quad
\begin{bmatrix}
o & o & o & o & o & o \\
e & e & e & e & e & e \\
o & o & o & o & o & o \\
e & e & e & e & e & e \\
o & o & o & o & o & o \\
e & e & e & e & e & e
\end{bmatrix}
\quad
\begin{bmatrix}
e & o & e & o & e & o \\
o & e & o & e & o & e \\
e & o & e & o & e & o \\
o & e & o & e & o & e \\
e & o & e & o & e & o \\
o & e & o & e & o & e
\end{bmatrix}
$$

Figure 14.22: Three Weight Matrices for the TP Method.

integer in each of its 2×2 subblocks. Figure 14.22 (where e and o stand for even and odd, respectively) shows three possible ways to construct such a matrix.

The following steps list the details of the TP encoder.

Step 1. If block B is uniform, perform step 1 with the next block.

Step 2. Compute $SUM((\text{B} \oplus \text{K}) \otimes W)$.

Step 3. Use matrix $\text{B} \oplus \text{K}$ to compute sets S_w for $w = 1, 2, \ldots, 2^{r+1} - 1$ according to the rule

$$
S_w = \Big\{ (i,j) \mid \big(W_{ij} = w \wedge [\text{B} \oplus \text{K}]_{ij} = 0 \wedge \big[\text{dist}\text{B}_{ij} \leq \sqrt{2}\big]\big) \vee
$$
$$
\big(W_{ij} = 2^r - w \wedge [\text{B} \oplus \text{K}]_{ij} = 1 \big) \wedge \big[\text{dist}\text{B}_{ij} \leq \sqrt{2}\big] \Big\}. \tag{14.4}
$$

Equation (14.4) is similar to Equation (14.2) but includes the distance between pixel (i,j) and its nearest opposite-color neighbor. Intuitively, set S_w contains all the index pairs (i,j) that satisfy: If we complement pixel B_{ij}, the sum of step 2 will be incremented by w. In order for a pair (i,j) to be included in set S_w, either of the following conditions must be satisfied.

3.1 $W_{ij} = w$, and $\text{B}_{ij} = 0$, and at least one of the eight near neighbors of B_{ij} has the opposite color. Switching B_{ij} will increment the sum by w.

3.2 $W_{ij} = 2^r - w$, and $\text{B}_{ij} = 1$, and at least one of the eight near neighbors of B_{ij} has the opposite color. Switching B_{ij} will decrement the sum by $2^r - w$, which is equivalent to increasing it by $(w \bmod 2^r)$.

Step 4. Compute the quantity

$$
\Delta = (d_1 d_2 \ldots d_r 0) - [SUM((\text{B} \oplus \text{K}) \otimes W) \quad (\bmod \ 2)^{r+1}].
$$

If $\Delta = 0$, the sum already has the right value and there is no need for any changes. Otherwise, the nested **if** below either flips (one or two) pixels to hide the r bits or declares the block invalid (which may necessitate the flipping of one pixel).

if there exists an h such that $S_{h\Delta} \neq \emptyset$ and $S_{-(h-1)\Delta} \neq \emptyset$
then % hide data
Randomly choose such an h.
Randomly choose a pair (i,j) from set $S_{h\Delta}$ and complement bit B_{ij}.
Randomly choose a pair (i,j) from set $S_{-(h-1)\Delta}$ and complement bit B_{ij}.

else % no data can be hidden
  if $SUM((\mathsf{B} \oplus \mathsf{K}) \otimes W)$ is even
  then % make the sum odd to indicate an invalid block
    Select a pair (i,j) such that B_{ij} is odd and distB_{ij} is the smallest.
    Complement B_{ij}.
  endif;
endif;

Step 4 is supplemented by the following rules.

1. If modifying B results in a uniform block, consider this block invalid, select the next block and go to Step 1 to hide the same data.

2. When a pair (i,j) is selected in set S_0, don't complement pixel B_{ij}. Thus, in some cases, only one pixel need be complemented (CPT has an identical rule).

The TP decoder is simple. It ignores uniform blocks and blocks where $SUM((\mathsf{B} \oplus \mathsf{K}) \otimes W)$ is odd. When a nonuniform block is found where this sum is even, the data bits are retrieved by dividing the sum by 2 and taking it modulo 2^r. Thus,

$$d_1 d_2 \ldots d_r = \frac{SUM((\mathsf{B} \oplus \mathsf{K}) \otimes W)}{2} \bmod 2^r.$$

The main advantage of this method is the way pixels are selected for complementing. A pixel is complemented only if one (or more) of its eight near neighbors has the opposite color. This prevents the appearance of new, isolated pixels in the modified block and helps make the embedded data invisible. If pixels are complemented in order to hide data (i.e., by the outer **if** of Step 4), then the definitions of sets S_w guarantee this property. If a pixel is complemented (by the inner **if** of step 4), in order to force the sum to be odd, then the way W is constructed (where each 2×2 submatrix has at least one odd element) guarantees that the switched pixel will not be isolated.

In a practical implementation, both encoder and decoder (sender and receiver) must have the same key and the same weight matrices, but the values of m, n, and r can be different for each cover image. They can be selected by the encoder and hidden (by means of the TP method) at the top of the cover image. Each of these three quantities can be hidden as a fixed-size integer in a fixed-size image block. The decoder needs to know only the fixed sizes. It starts by retrieving the values of the three parameters, then uses them to retrieve the rest of the embedded data.

Another point to consider in an implementation is that the values of K and W may be generated from a single seed (one long stego-key) by means of a special program that draws pseudorandom numbers in the right intervals (bits for K and integers in the interval $[1, 2^{r+1} - 1]$ for W).

"I thought binary was simpler than spoken languages," said Miro.
"It is, when it's programs and numerical data," said Jane. "But what if it's digitized visuals?"

— Orson Scott Card, *Ender's Saga* (1986)

14.18 Data Hiding in Fax Images

Facsimile (fax) machines for the transfer of documents by telephone have long been prevalent. The operation of those machines and the compression algorithm they use are described in Section 3.7. The short discussion here shows how to hide data in a document that is being faxed.

Data bits can be hidden in a fax image by changing certain run lengths by one unit. A simple convention is to associate a data bit of 0 with an even run length. If the current data bit to be hidden is 0 and the current run length is odd, the run length is made even by decreasing it by 1 (and increasing the following run by 1). If this run is the last one of a scan line, it is increased by 1, thereby adding one pel to the current line. A small problem exists when the current run length is already 1, and a possible solution is to eliminate such short runs by concatenating three run lengths into one. Thus, the sequence of five run lengths 4, 7, 1, 13, and 8 becomes the three numbers 4, 21, and 8. If the current data bit to be hidden is 1 and the current run length is even, the run length is made odd by increasing it by 1 (and decreasing the following run, if any, by 1).

The resulting image can be sent to another fax machine, decompressed, and printed without any noticeable effects. This is because the low resolution of a fax degrades the image quality even if no run lengths are modified. The hidden data can be read by intercepting the fax transmission and storing it as a file for later processing by computer.

A major drawback of this method is that the Group 3 compression method does not specify any parity bits for error detection. An error introduced during transmission over a noisy telephone line can corrupt the rest of the scan line and thereby lead to corruption of several hidden bits.

A Picture of many colors proclaims images of many Thoughts.
—Donna A. Favors

15
Data Hiding:
Other Methods

Starting with Section 15.2, this chapter discusses data hiding in an MPEG-2 video file, followed by a discussion of audio steganography. Starting with Section 15.3, the basics of digital audio and the properties of the human auditory system are described, followed by audio steganography in the time domain. Next, the chapter introduces (in Section 15.7) the concept of the steganographic file system. The last part of the chapter is a short discussion of the limits of steganography (Section 15.8) and the prospect of public-key steganography (Section 15.9).

15.1 Protecting Music Scores

Most watermarking algorithms are designed to protect image, audio, or video files. The work described here (currently being developed by a group at the Fraunhofer Institute [Fraunhofer 01]) is concerned with protecting music scores. A publisher producing music scores on paper is concerned with illegal copying of the product and should therefore be interested in protecting it with a watermark. Such a watermark should be robust because each time a copy is itself copied, the print quality degrades, making it harder to detect the watermark.

This problem has two aspects. If the score is generated by special software, the software should be modified to produce a watermarked image, which is then printed. If the score is old and exists only on paper, it should be scanned and the resulting image file modified and printed. In the latter case, it is an image (specifically, a binary image) that should be modified, but this image is not a general binary image. It is the image of music notes, so it consists of a set of symbols and therefore resembles scanned text. Data can be embedded in a general binary image (Section 14.13) by reversing the values of certain pixels, but the image of music notes should be modified by either slightly changing the position, orientation, or appearance of certain symbols, such as notes and stem lines, or by changing the spaces between symbols. Such modifications are similar to those done in text (Section 13.6), and the problem is to decide which elements of the score to modify and how.

The method is therefore interesting because it combines aspects of both image and text steganography.

The main consideration in modifying music scores is readability. The musician should be able to play from the modified score as easily as from the original one. The second consideration is visual perception. A person examining the music score should not notice any suspicious or unusual features. The third consideration is robustness. The modifications to the document should persist even after several generations of photocopying.

A music score contains many symbols that can be modified in different ways. Some examples are the following.

1. The dots above and below notes (indicating a 50% increase in the duration of the note) can be slightly displaced.
2. The angle and thickness of bars (such as stems, double bars, repeat bars, and final bars) can be modified.
3. The thickness of beams, slurs, and ties can be controlled to reflect hidden bits.
4. The lengths of note stems can be modulated according to the bits being embedded.
5. The angles of clefs, beams, notes, stems, and pause signs can be slightly changed.

Each proposed modification has to be checked on several real scores, because the results of even slight modifications may be unanticipated and noticeable. Changing the length of note stems, for example, is generally innocuous, but may be very noticeable if the notes belong to a group. Changing the angles of certain vertical bars may normally go undetected but becomes noticeable if the tilted bar happens to be next to an unchanged bar. Figure 15.1a shows this effect. Twelve vertical bars are identified, and the binary string 010010 is hidden in them by rotating certain bars to the left (to hide a 0) or to the right (to hide a 1). Two rotations, by 3° and 5°, are shown. When the original bars are replaced by the 5°-rotated bars, the results are noticeable, especially when adjacent bars are tilted in different directions or when a rotated bar is part of a group of notes. (A stego-key is used as the seed of a pseudorandom number generator so as to determine which bars to rotate.)

In practice, the software sees only the pixels of a binary image, so the main problem is to identify the vertical bars in the score. This is done by scanning the columns of the image and counting vertical run lengths of pixels in a column. A straight, thin vertical bar should generate a large run length of black pixels in a column, with white pixels surrounding it on both sides (Figure 15.1b). In practice, however, even this simple problem becomes complicated when a photocopy of the music sheet is scanned and examined. In the photocopy, the vertical bars may not be completely vertical, due to misalignment in the copier, or may be fuzzy, if the copy is itself made from a copy, not

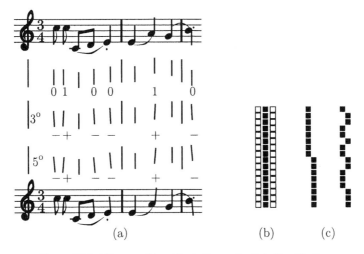

Figure 15.1: Watermarking Music Scores by Rotating Staffs.

from the original (Figure 15.1c).

The developers of the method have experimented with other types of modifications that may be more promising, such as small horizontal shifts of notes, where a group of notes is shifted as one unit. At the time of this writing (mid 2004), this work is still in progress.

15.2 Data Hiding in MPEG-2 Video

The term *MPEG* is an acronym for Moving Pictures Experts Group. MPEG is a general name for a group of methods for video compression, a process that involves the compression of digital images and sound, as well as synchronization of the two.

The MPEG project started in 1988 and employed hundreds of experts under the auspices of the International Standardization Organization (ISO) and the International Electrotechnical Committee (IEC). At present (year 2004), there are several MPEG standards. MPEG-1 is intended for intermediate data rates, on the order of 1.5 Mbit/s. MPEG-2 is intended for high data rates of at least 10 Mbit/s. MPEG-3 was intended for HDTV (high-definition television) compression but was found to be redundant and was merged with MPEG-2. MPEG-4 is intended for very low data rates of less than 64 Kbit/s. A third international body, the International Telecommunications Union (ITU), has been involved in the design of both MPEG-2 and MPEG-4.

To get a feeling for the words *high data rates*, consider a typical example of high-definition video with a resolution of 1080×1920 pixels per frame, a pixel depth of 24 bits, and a refresh rate of 30 frames per second. The image part of this video requires $1080 \times 1920 \times 24 \times 30 = 1,492,992,000$ bits/s. The audio part normally employs two sound tracks (for stereo sound), each sampled at 44 kHz with 16-bit samples. The audio data rate is $2 \times 44{,}000 \times 16 = 1{,}408{,}000$ bits/s. The total is about 1,500 Mbit/s, and this is supposed to be compressed by MPEG-2 to a high data rate of at least 10 Mbit/s, a compression factor of about 150! Another aspect is the decoding speed. An MPEG-compressed movie may end up being stored on a CD-ROM or DVD and has to be decoded and played in real-time. Thus, the decoding algorithm has to be fast.

This section describes the work of [Busch, Funk, and Wolthusen 99] on robust hiding of small quantities of data as a watermark in MPEG-2 video files. This work, in turn, is based on the method of [Zhao and Koch 95] for embedding data in a JPEG still image file. The reader is encouraged to study that method (Section 14.7) before embarking on the present algorithm.

A detailed description of MPEG-2 can be found in [Rao and Hwang 96]. For the purpose of this section, it is enough to note that the various MPEG methods are based on the discrete cosine transform (DCT), introduced in Section 14.6.

A video file consists of *frames*, where each frame is a single image. Those familiar with digital images know that neighboring pixels in an image tend to be similar. If we select a pixel at random in an image, there is a good chance that its immediate neighbors will be similar to it, and even its near (not immediate) neighbors will mostly be similar. We say that the pixels of an image are *spatially correlated* (page 135). Similarly, in a video stream there is temporal correlation, because successive frames are often very similar.

The algorithm described here can embed up to four different watermarks (three secret and one public) in a single video file.

The luminance component of each video frame (Section 5.9.1) is partitioned into blocks of 8×8 pixels each, and one bit of data from each watermark is hidden in each block. Thus, up to four bits can be hidden in a block, but they belong to different watermarks. In principle, the number of data bits from one watermark hidden in each video frame can equal the number of blocks in the frame. In practice, many of the hidden bits may become corrupted by the lossy MPEG compression that follows the watermark embedding, so each bit should be hidden in the frame several times for maximum redundancy. The algorithm therefore hides just 64 data bits from each watermark in each frame. Once these 64 bits have been embedded in the first 64 blocks, they are embedded again in the next group of 64 blocks, and so on, for all the blocks in the video frame.

Given a video frame with 1080×1920 pixels, it is partitioned into 135×240 = 32,400 blocks, so the string of 64 data bits from each of the four watermarks is hidden 506 times in the frame. The next paragraph is a tentative description of the embedding process.

A stego-key is used as the seed of a pseudorandom number generator to select the blocks of a frame in a certain sequence. The DCT is temporarily applied to each block, and two of the DCT coefficients are quantized with the quantization coefficients proposed by the JPEG standard. The single bit for each of the four watermarks is hidden in one of the four bands numbered in Figure 15.2a. Bands 1–3 are used for hiding up to three secret watermarks. Band 4 is for hiding a public watermark. For each watermark, a band is chosen and is used to hide the bits of that watermark in all the video frames. Each band consists of three DCT coefficients, and the bit is hidden by modifying two of the three coefficients. The two coefficients are selected by a pseudorandom number generator and are therefore different for each block. Once two DCT quantized coefficients t_k and t_l have been chosen, a 1-bit is embedded in the block by modifying the coefficients, if needed, such that $t_k \geq t_l + d$ and a 0-bit is embedded by making sure that $t_k + d \leq t_l$, where d is a noise-level parameter. The two (possibly modified) coefficients are then dequantized and the inverse DCT applied to the block in order to recreate a block of (modified) luminance values.

The description in the paragraph above is very similar to that of the Zhao and Koch algorithm for still images (Section 14.7). When the process in the above paragraph was first applied to video files, it resulted in considerable artifacts when the watermarked video was MPEG-compressed and then decompressed and previewed. The algorithm exploits pixel correlations in each frame to hide up to four data bits in the frame, but these modifications change blocks located in the same position in consecutive frames in different ways. It therefore violates the temporal correlation of the frames, resulting in noticeable flickering when the video is played.

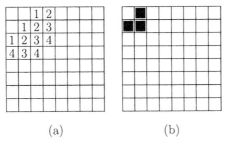

(a)   (b)

Figure 15.2: (a) Four Bands of Three DCT Coefficients Each. (b) DCT Coefficients Used for Edge Detection.

The developers of this algorithm have discovered experimentally that uniform areas in a video frame are especially sensitive to these artifacts, as also are regions with sharp edges. Thus, they added to the process above a step in which each block is checked. If the block turns out to be uniform, the two DCT coefficients are modified by less than the normal amount. A block with edges is considered invalid and is skipped.

There are many algorithms to identify uniform blocks and areas with sharply defined edges, but these are generally complex and slow. An algorithm such as the one described here, where the watermark has to be retrieved and verified in real-time, while the video is playing, has to be fast. Another point is that our algorithm has the DCT coefficients available and can use them to check the block. Experiments indicate that when a block containing an edge is transformed by means of the DCT, the low-frequency DCT coefficients (the ones near the top-left corner) are large. The algorithm therefore uses the three DCT coefficients shown in Figure 15.2b as a test for an edge. The test is: If even one of these three coefficients exceeds the value of a predefined static threshold parameter, the block is considered to have an edge and is declared invalid. The value of the threshold parameter was set by experiments to 40. The test for a uniform block is: If one of the two coefficients t_k and t_l selected for modification is zero, the block is considered uniform.

As a result of these tests, the process described above has been revised and is written here in detail.

Step 1. The DCT is applied to the block (the algorithm uses a revised version of the DCT that operates on 16-bit integers, rather than floating-point numbers).

Step 2. The edge detection test is applied. If the block fails, it is ignored and the next block in the sequence is selected.

Step 3. A pair of DCT coefficients t_k and t_l are chosen from the three coefficients of the band for the watermark being hidden. The two coefficients are quantized.

Step 4. The uniformity test is applied to t_k and t_l. If the block turns out to be uniform, small values are chosen for the future modification of the two coefficients.

Step 5. The two coefficients t_k and t_l are modified, if necessary, depending on the data bit to be hidden in this band in the block.

Step 6. The modified coefficients are dequantized and the inverse DCT (modified to use 16-bit integers) is applied to the entire block.

The decoder retrieves the bits embedded in a frame by using the voting principle. An array with 64 columns and n rows is prepared, where n is the embedding redundancy (506 in the example above). The decoder then selects the blocks in each frame in the same sequence as the encoder. An invalid block is skipped. A bit is retrieved from each valid block (from the band reserved for the current watermark) and stored in the array. The array index is incremented rowwise, such that the first 64 bits are stored in the top row, the next 64 bits in the row below it, and so on. When all the blocks have been scanned in this way, the 64 bits are determined by scanning each of the 64 columns of the array. If column i has mostly bits of 1, then bit b_i is determined by the decoder to be 1.

15.3 Digital Audio

Data can be hidden in an audio file, and such files are becoming more and more common in multimedia applications. This section is a short introduction to audio files and their main features.

A scanner is a device that takes an image drawn or painted on paper and converts it to a digital image. The scanner breaks the original, continuous image up into pixels and writes each pixel, as a number, on the image file. Similarly, it is possible to digitize sound. When sound is played into a microphone, it is converted to a voltage that varies continuously with time according to the amplitude and frequency of the sound. This voltage is the analog representation of the sound (Figure 15.3; see also Exercise 1.9), and it can be digitized by a device called an *analog-to-digital converter (ADC)*. The ADC measures the voltage at many points in time and writes each measurement, as a number called an *audio sample*, on a file. This process is termed *sampling*, and the set of audio samples constitutes an audio file.

The difference between a sound wave and its samples can be compared to the difference between an analog clock, where the hands seem to move continuously, and a digital clock, where the display changes abruptly every second.

Digitized sound has several advantages over analog sound. It can easily be stored on a disk, edited, compressed, and played back. It can also be used to hide secret data. Playback is done by converting the audio samples into voltages that are continuously fed into a speaker. This is done by a digital-to-analog converter (DAC). Intuitively, it is clear that a high sampling rate results in better sound reproduction but also in many (perhaps too many) samples and therefore bigger files. Thus, the main problem in sound sampling is how often to sample a given sound.

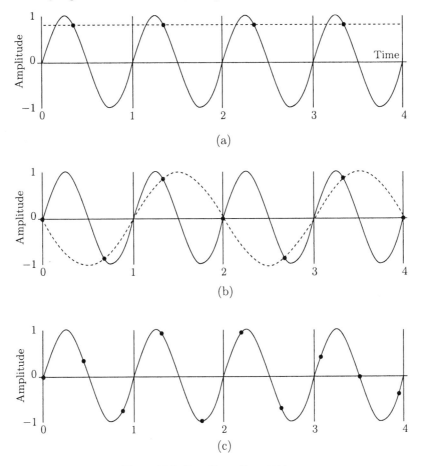

Figure 15.3: Sampling a Sound Wave.

Figure 15.3a shows what may happen if the sampling rate is too low. The sound wave in the figure is sampled four times, and all four samples happen to be identical.

When these samples are used to play back the sound, the result is a uniform sound, resembling a buzz. Figure 15.3b shows seven samples, and they seem to "follow" the original wave fairly closely. Unfortunately, when they are used to reproduce the sound, they produce the curve shown in dashes. There simply are not enough samples to reconstruct the original sound wave.

The solution to the sampling problem is to sample sound at a little over twice the maximum frequency of the sound. Such a sampling rate is called the *Nyquist rate*. The Nyquist theorem guarantees true reproduction of the sound if the sampling is done at this rate. Nyquist rate sampling is illustrated in Figure 15.3c, which shows 10 equally spaced samples taken over four periods. Notice that the samples do not have to be taken from the maxima or minima of the wave; they can come from any point.

The range of audible frequencies is from 16–20 Hz to 20,000–22,000 Hz, depending on the person and on age. When sound is digitized at high fidelity, it should therefore be sampled at a little over the Nyquist rate of $2 \times 22,000 = 44,000$ Hz. This is why high-quality digital sound is based on a 44,100 Hz (or 44.1 kHz) sampling rate. Anything lower than this rate results in distortions, while higher sampling rates do not improve the reconstruction (playback) of the sound.

Many low-fidelity applications sample sound at 11,000 Hz, and the telephone system, originally designed for conversations, not for digital communications, samples sound at only 8 kHz. Thus, any frequency higher than 4000 Hz gets distorted when sent over the phone, which is why it is hard to distinguish, on the phone, between the sounds of "f" and "s." This is also why, when someone gives you an address over the phone you should ask, "Is it H Street, as in EFGH?" Often, the answer is, "No, this is Eighth Street, as in sixth, seventh, eighth."

> The meeting was in Mr. Rogers' law office, at 1415 *H* Street. My slip of paper said 1415 *8th* Street. (The address had been given over the telephone).
>
> —Richard P. Feynman, *What Do YOU Care What Other People Think?*

The second problem in sound sampling is the sample size. Each sample becomes a number, but how large should this number be? In practice, samples are normally either 8 or 16 bits, although some high-quality sound cards may optionally use 32-bit samples. Assuming that the highest voltage in a sound wave is 1 volt, an 8-bit sample can distinguish voltages as low as $1/256 \approx 0.004$ volt, or 4 millivolts (mv). A quiet sound, generating a wave lower than 2 mv, would be sampled as zero and played back as silence. In contrast, a 16-bit sample can distinguish sounds as low as $1/65,536 \approx 15$ microvolt (μv). We can think of the sample size as a quantization of the original audio data. Eight-bit samples are more coarsely quantized than 16-bit ones. Therefore, they result in smaller audio files but also in poorer reconstruction (the reconstructed sound has only 256 levels).

⬦ **Exercise 15.1:** Suppose that the sample size is one bit. Each sample has a value of either 0 or 1. What would we hear when these samples are played back?

Audio sampling is also called *pulse code modulation* (PCM). We have all heard of AM and FM radio. These terms stand for *amplitude modulation* and *frequency modulation*, respectively. They indicate methods to modulate (i.e., to include binary information in) continuous waves. The term *pulse modulation* refers to techniques for converting a continuous wave to a stream of binary numbers. Possible pulse modulation techniques include pulse amplitude modulation (PAM), pulse position modulation (PPM), pulse width modulation (PWM), and pulse number modulation (PNM). (See [Pohlmann 85] for a good source of information on these methods.) In practice, however, PCM has proved to be the most effective form of transforming analog sound to numbers. When stereo sound is digitized, the PCM encoder multiplexes the left and right sound samples. Thus, stereo sound sampled at 22,000 Hz with 16-bit samples generates 44,000 16-bit samples per second, for a total of 704,000 bits/s, or 88,000 bytes/s.

15.4 The Human Auditory System

The frequency range of the human ear is from about 20 Hz to about 20,000 Hz, but the ear's sensitivity to sound is not uniform. It depends on the frequency, and experiments indicate that in a quiet environment the ear's sensitivity is maximal for frequencies in the range 2 kHz to 4 kHz. Figure 15.4a shows the *hearing threshold* for a quiet environment.

⋄ **Exercise 15.2:** Suggest a way to conduct such an experiment.

It should also be noted that the range of the human voice is much more limited. It is only from about 500 Hz to about 2 kHz.

The existence of the hearing threshold suggests an approach to hiding data in audio files: hide bits in any audio samples that are below the threshold. Since the threshold depends on the frequency, the encoder needs to know the frequency spectrum of the sound being compressed at any time, but the encoder's only input is the audio samples. The encoder therefore has to save several of the previously input audio samples at any time ($n-1$ samples, where n is either a constant or a user-controlled parameter). When the current sample is input, the first step is to transform the n samples to the frequency domain. The result is a number m of values (called *signals*) that indicate the strength of the sound at m different frequencies. If a signal for frequency f is smaller than the hearing threshold at f, it (the signal) can be modified to hide data. (This, of course, is just a general approach. Any specific algorithm has to indicate how the hidden data can be retrieved.)

In addition to this, two more properties of the human auditory system can be used in audio steganography. They are *frequency masking* and *temporal masking*.

Frequency masking (also known as *auditory masking*) occurs when a sound that we can normally hear (because it is loud enough) is masked by another sound with a nearby frequency. The thick arrow in Figure 15.4b represents a strong sound source at 800 kHz. This source raises the normal threshold in its vicinity (the dashed curve), with the result that the nearby sound represented by the arrow at "x," a sound that would normally be audible because it is above the threshold, is now masked and is inaudible.

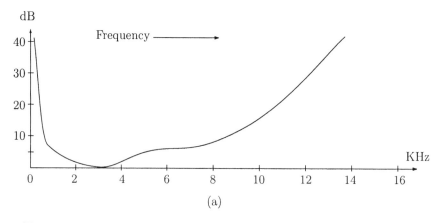

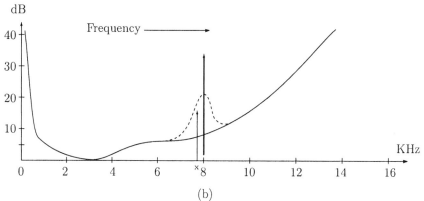

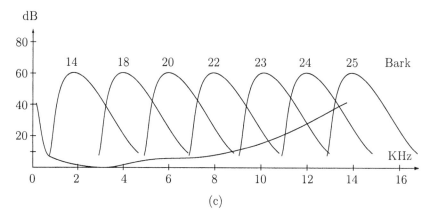

Figure 15.4: Threshold and Masking of Sound.

A sophisticated audio steganography method should identify this case and hide data in the audio samples that correspond to sound "x," since it cannot be heard anyway.

The frequency masking (the width of the dashed curve of Figure 15.4b) depends on the frequency. It varies from about 100 Hz for the lowest audible frequencies to more than 4 kHz for the highest. The range of audible frequencies can therefore be partitioned into a number of *critical bands* that indicate the declining sensitivity of the ear (rather, its declining resolving power) for higher frequencies. We can think of the critical bands as a measure similar to frequency. However, in contrast to frequency, which is absolute and has nothing to do with human hearing, the critical bands are determined according to the sound perception of the ear. Thus, they constitute a perceptually uniform measure of frequency. Table 15.5 lists 27 approximate critical bands.

Another way to describe critical bands is to say that because of the ear's limited perception of frequencies, the threshold at a frequency f is raised by a nearby sound only if the sound is within the critical band of f. This also points the way to designing a practical audio steganography algorithm. The audio signal should first be transformed into its frequency domain, and the resulting values (the frequency spectrum) should be divided into subbands that resemble the critical bands as much as possible. Once this is done, the least significant bits of the signals in each subband can be used to hide secret data. The maximum number of bits that can be used for this purpose is determined as follows. Clear the modified bits to zero and call the result a quantized audio sample. As long as the difference between the original audio sample and the quantized one is still inaudible, more bits can be used for hiding data.

band	range	band	range	band	range
0	0–50	9	800–940	18	3280–3840
1	50–95	10	940–1125	19	3840–4690
2	95–140	11	1125–1265	20	4690–5440
3	140–235	12	1265–1500	21	5440–6375
4	235–330	13	1500–1735	22	6375–7690
5	330–420	14	1735–1970	23	7690–9375
6	420–560	15	1970–2340	24	9375–11625
7	560–660	16	2340–2720	25	11625–15375
8	660–800	17	2720–3280	26	15375–20250

Table 15.5: Twenty-Seven Approximate Critical Bands.

Yet another way to look at the concept of critical band is to consider the human auditory system a filter that lets through only frequencies in the range (bandpass) of 20 Hz to 20,000 Hz. We visualize the ear–brain system as a set of filters, each with a different bandpass. The bandpasses are called critical bands. They overlap and they have different widths. They are narrow (about 100 Hz) at low frequencies and become wider (to about 4–5 kHz) at high frequencies.

The width of a critical band is called its *size*. The widths of the critical bands introduce a new unit, the *Bark* (after H. G. Barkhausen), such that one Bark is the width (in Hz) of one critical band. The Bark is defined as

$$1 \text{ Bark} = \begin{cases} \frac{f}{100}, & \text{for frequencies } f < 500 \text{ Hz}, \\ 9 + 4 \log\left(\frac{f}{1000}\right), & \text{for frequencies } f \geq 500 \text{ Hz}. \end{cases}$$

Figure 15.4c shows some critical bands, with Barks between 14 and 25, positioned above the threshold.

Heinrich Georg Barkhausen

Heinrich Barkhausen was born on December 2, 1881, in Bremen, Germany. He spent his entire career as a professor of electrical engineering at the Technische Hochschule in Dresden, where he concentrated on developing electron tubes. He also discovered the so-called *Barkhausen effect*, where acoustical waves are generated in a solid by the movement of domain walls when the material is magnetized. He also coined the term *phon* as a unit of sound loudness. The institute in Dresden was destroyed, as was most of the city, in the famous fire bombing in February 1945. After the war, Barkhausen helped rebuild the institute. He died on February 20, 1956.

Temporal masking may occur when a strong sound A of frequency f is preceded or followed in time by a weaker sound B at a nearby (or the same) frequency. If the time interval between the sounds is short, sound B may not be audible. Figure 15.6 illustrates an example of temporal masking. The threshold of temporal masking due to a loud sound at time 0 goes down, first sharply, then slowly. A weaker sound of 30 dB will not be audible if it occurs 10 ms before or after the loud sound but will be audible if the time interval between the sounds is 20 ms.

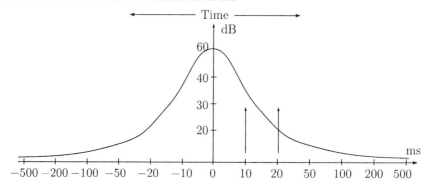

Figure 15.6: Threshold and Masking of Sound.

15.5 Audio Watermarking in the Time Domain

The simplest way to embed secret data in an audio file is to set the least significant bit of each audio sample to the next bit of the data. This is simple: it results in large embedding capacity but has several drawbacks. It is easy to detect, it may be perceptually audible when the cover sound is quiet (since the human auditory system is sensitive to small amplitude variations), and it is not robust. When used to embed data in an image, this method can be based on a key so that consecutive bits of data are hidden in pixels determined pseudorandomly by the key. This is possible because the entire image resides in memory. An audio file, in contrast, may be too big to store in memory in its entirety. The embedding capacity is one bit per audio sample, so in general it is 1 kilobit per second for each 1 kHz of sample rate. With a low, 8 kHz sampling rate, 8 kilobits can be hidden for every second of sound. For a high, 44 kHz sample rate, 44 kilobits can be hidden each second.

In spite of the obvious drawbacks of this basic method, it is still possible to hide bits in audio samples and end up with a sound that is indistinguishable from the original. This can be achieved by hiding bits in those samples that are inaudible, or very nearly so, because of the properties of the human auditory system. Such samples can be identified by a psychoacoustic model. When such a sample is identified, it is possible to modify several of its least significant bits without any audible effect on the final sound. Such a method is not hard to implement because the MPEG audio compression standard shows how to identify such audio samples. However, such a method would not be robust, because MPEG compression works by identifying such samples and quantizing them (removing their least significant bits).

> The most important psychoacoustics fact is the masking effect of spectral sound elements, such as tones and noise, in an audio signal. For every tone in the audio signal, a masking threshold can be calculated. If another tone lies below this masking threshold, it will be masked by the louder tone and will remain inaudible, too.

The method described here works in a similar way, but does not use a complete psychoacoustic model. Instead, it uses only the amplitude of an audio sample to decide how many bits to embed in it. The method is due to [Bassia and Pitas 98], and it embeds a watermark, not arbitrary secret data, in the audio file. It is possible to identify the presence of the watermark with a high degree of certainty (and without the use of the original watermark), but it is impossible to actually retrieve the individual watermark bits. The method also allows embedding multiple watermarks in the same audio file and is robust to lossy compression, filtering, resampling, and requantizing (chopping each 16-bit audio sample to 8 bits and expanding back to 16 bits). Sadly, the original documentation lacks some of the most important details.

The method starts with a watermark key that is used to generate a sequence of *watermark signals* w_i. The mapping from the key to the w_i's has to create signals w_i in the range $[-\alpha, +\alpha]$ (where α is a constant), and these have to be uniformly distributed in this range. This requirement means that a sum of products of the form $\sum x_i w_i$ is zero or close to zero.

We denote the audio samples by x_i, where $i = 1, \ldots, N$. The method is based on a function $f(x_i, w_i)$ that determines, for each sample x_i and each watermark signal w_i, the amount by which x_i can be modified without affecting the perceptual audibility of the audio file. The details of this function are not documented. The watermark is embedded by modifying each sample x_i to $y_i = x_i + f(x_i, w_i)$.

The first step in verifying the watermark is to consider the function

$$S = \sum_{i=1}^{N} y_i w_i = \sum_{i=1}^{N} x_i w_i + \sum_{i=1}^{N} f(x_i, w_i) w_i.$$

Ideally, the first part of the sum should be zero, but in practice it is normally nonzero because the distribution of the w_i's is not ideally uniform. Thus, it is possible to write

$$S = \sum_{i=1}^{N} x_i w_i + \sum_{i=1}^{N} f(x_i, w_i) w_i$$

$$= \sum_{1} x_i w_i + \sum_{2} x_i w_i + \sum_{i=1}^{N} f(x_i, w_i) w_i$$

$$= 0 + \frac{\Delta w}{N} \sum_{i=1}^{N} x_i w_i + \sum_{i=1}^{N} f(x_i, w_i) w_i,$$

where the first sum includes the products $x_i w_i$ that add to zero and the second sum includes the other products. The second sum can therefore be written as a fraction $\Delta w / N$ of the entire sum.

The next step is to approximate S by substituting y_i for x_i. This results in

$$S \approx \frac{\Delta w}{N} \sum_{i=1}^{N} y_i w_i + \sum_{i=1}^{N} f(y_i, w_i) w_i = \frac{\Delta w}{N} |S| + \sum_{i=1}^{N} f(y_i, w_i) w_i.$$

We can now write

$$r \stackrel{\text{def}}{=} \frac{S - \frac{\Delta w}{N} |S|}{\sum_{i=1}^{N} f(y_i, w_i) w_i} \approx 1.$$

The last step is to realize that if no watermark has been embedded in the audio file (i.e., if all $f(x_i, w_i)$ are zero), then

$$S = \sum_{i=1}^{N} y_i w_i = \sum_{i=1}^{N} x_i w_i \approx \frac{\Delta w}{N} |S|,$$

implying that in this case

$$S - \frac{\Delta w}{N} |S| \approx 0.$$

The test for the existence of a watermark is therefore to generate the sequence of w_i's with the watermark's key and use the w_i's to compute r. If r is close to 1, the watermark is present in the audio file. If $r \approx 0$, then this particular watermark is absent from the file.

Several watermarks can be embedded in the same audio file in this way. Naturally, each must have a unique key. The number of watermarks that can be embedded in the same file depends on the values of the w_i's. Smaller values allow the embedding of many watermarks before any audio distortions can be perceived. On the other hand, large values increase the confidence threshold for identifying a watermark.

15.6 Echo Hiding

Audio recording techniques and equipment have come a long way since the days of Thomas Edison. Sound recorded on a CD is perfect in the sense that the recording and playback do not introduce any noise. Nevertheless, there is a difference in what we hear when we listen to the same CD through earphones or through a speaker. In the latter case, echoes from the walls, furniture, and other objects in the room are added to the sound we hear (recording studios also sometimes add a short echo to a singer's voice to add depth). We normally don't mind these echoes, since they seem to add a rich resonance to the sound, and this acceptance can serve as the basis of a steganographic method for hiding data in an audio file. The basic idea is to add two types of echoes to the sound, and hide one bit in each type. The sound is divided into short segments, and one bit is hidden in each segment by constructing an echo of the segment. The echo is a copy of the sound wave in the segment. The copy has a smaller amplitude (because an echo is fainter than the original) and it lags behind the original sound. The amount of lag ($\Delta 1$ or $\Delta 2$) determines the bit (1 or 0, respectively) hidden in the echo.

> "Meet here," Echo answered, and she came out of the woods where she had been hiding. She went up to Narcissus and wanted to throw her arms around his neck.
>
> —Ovid, *Metamorphoses III*

This section follows the ideas described in [Gruhl et al. 96], but the discussion here is nontechnical. The main problem facing a practical implementation of this method is making sure that a person listening to the stego sound perceives the modified sound as innocuous and does not become annoyed or suspicious. If the delay between a sound and its echo is long, the listener hears a distinct echo, which sounds unnatural and may rouse suspicion. If the delay is short enough, the ear interprets the echo as resonance added to the sound. The ideal delay depends on the type of sound, on the quality of the original recording, and on the individual listening to the sound. The delays corresponding to 0 and 1 bits should therefore be parameters, and experiments suggest values in the range 0.5 to 2 ms. The amplitudes of the two types of echoes should also be parameters. Low amplitudes may sound more like an echo, but higher amplitudes are easier to distinguish, so they increase the reliability of retrieving the hidden data. It should be noted that this reliability is never 100%, so an error-correcting code should be added to the data before it is hidden. Typical echo amplitudes are ≈ 0.8 of the original.

The sound is divided into equal-size segments (where the segment size depends on the sampling rate) and one bit is hidden in each segment by creating an echo (a reduced, shifted copy of the segment) and combining it with the segment. For sound sampled at 8 K samples per second, each second is divided into two segments, so two bits can be hidden in each second of sound. For stereo sound sampled at 44 K samples per second, each second can be divided into 32 segments, so 64 bits can be hidden in each second of sound (32 bits in each stereo channel).

Figure 15.7 shows how this is done in principle, assuming that the audio signal is represented as a continuous wave. Part (a) of the figure shows part of a sound wave divided into seven segments. One bit is to be hidden in each segment. Part (b) shows how a low-amplitude copy of the entire wave is made and is shifted by an amount $\Delta 1$ relative to the original signal. This copy represents data bits of 1 to be hidden in all the segments. Part (c) shows how another copy, of a different amplitude, is prepared and is shifted by an amount $\Delta 2$. This represents bits of 0 to be hidden. The original sound wave is then duplicated and each duplicate is combined, by means of a convolution, with one of the low-amplitude, shifted copies. This results in two sound waves, one with hidden 1-bits (part d) and the other with hidden 0-bits (part e). Each wave is then multiplied by a mixer wave that deletes the segments with wrong bits embedded (shown in dashes), and the results are arithmetically added in part (f) to form the final wave, with correct echoes for all the hidden bits.

In practice, the data exists in digital form, as audio samples, not as a wave. Combining a wave and its echo is done by means of the *convolution* operation. In general, the convolution of an infinite discrete signal $x(i)$ (for $i = \ldots, -2, -1, 0, 1, 2, \ldots$) and a finite bank of filter coefficients $h(i)$ (where $i = 1, 2, \ldots, n$) creates a signal $y(j)$ defined by $y(j) = \sum_i x(i)h(j - i)$, where the sum is taken over all possible terms. In our case, there are just two filter coefficients $h(0) = 1$ and $h(1) = \alpha$ (where α is a scale factor that determines the amplitude of the echo). The convolution generates the new signal $y(j)$ (for $j = \ldots, -2, -1, 0, 1, 2, \ldots$) according to $y(j) = x(j)h(0) + x(j - 1)h(1)$. A direct calculation produces the following examples of $y(j)$.

$$y(-2) = x(-2)h(0) + x(-3)h(1) = x(-2) + \alpha x(-3)$$
$$y(-1) = x(-1)h(0) + x(-2)h(1) = x(-1) + \alpha x(-2)$$
$$y(0) = x(0)h(0) + x(-1)h(1) = x(0) + \alpha x(-1)$$
$$y(1) = x(1)h(0) + x(0)h(1) = x(1) + \alpha x(0)$$
$$y(2) = x(2)h(0) + x(1)h(1) = x(2) + \alpha x(1).$$

It's easy to see how this combines $x(i)$ with an echo of itself, an echo with amplitude α lagging one time unit behind $x(i)$.

It's easy to use convolution to create an echo with amplitude β that lags two time units behind the main signal. The filter coefficients are $h(0) = 1$ and $h(2) = \beta$. The combined signal is produced by $y(j) = x(j)h(0) + x(j - 2)h(2)$.

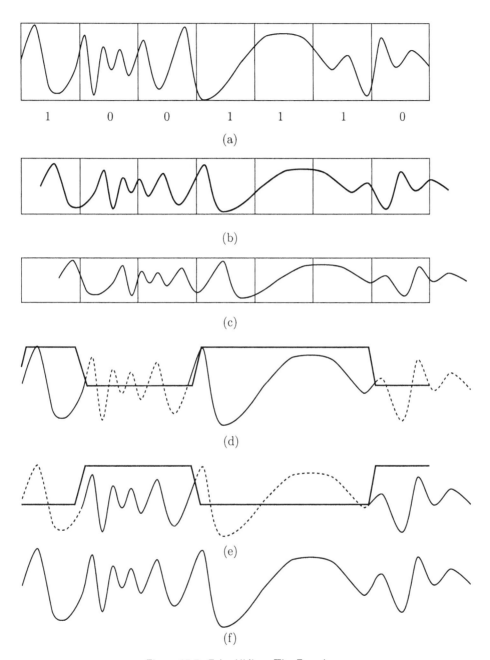

Figure 15.7: Echo Hiding: The Encoder.

⋄ **Exercise 15.3:** (Easy.) Show how convolution is used to create an echo with amplitude β that lags two time units behind the main signal.

In practice, signal $x(i)$ is finite and it starts with $x(0)$. In this case, the convolution starts with $y(1)$, whose value is $x(1) + \alpha x(0)$. The two banks of filter coefficients, for the echoes of 0 and 1, can be expressed graphically as in Figure 15.8.

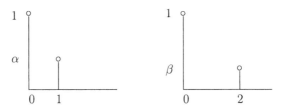

Figure 15.8: Two Banks of Echo Filter Coefficients $h(j - i)$.

Decoding is done by means of the cepstrum transform, whose principles are beyond the scope of this book (see, for example, [Bogert et al. 63]). Results obtained by the developers of the method indicate that with the right choice of parameters, a recovery rate of 85% or better can be obtained. The stego audio, while sounding different from the original, does not sound objectionable but seems to have a richer tone.

15.7 The Steganographic File System

A steganographic algorithm hides data in a larger volume of data. The steganographic file system proposed by [Anderson et al. 98] hides a number of files in a larger collection of files such that a user who knows the password of a file can retrieve it, but someone who does not have the password cannot extract the file or even find out whether the file is present. The hidden files will remain hidden even if an attacker has access to the entire file system and can examine every bit of every file. Such a file system may be useful in cases where the owner denies that certain files exist and would like potential opponents and attackers to believe the denial. This is termed *plausible deniability*. Examples of cases of plausible deniability are the following.

1. Company officials conduct labor negotiations with a trade union. Various informal offers are made but the negotiations fail, the case goes to court, and the trade union obtains court orders for access to company computer files. It helps if the company can plausibly deny the existence of sensitive files.

2. An individual is arrested on suspicion of a crime and is ordered to surrender encryption keys to all encrypted files. This may be a bona fide case, but it may also be a business competitor who had bribed corrupt police in an attempt to obtain private business files. The use of a steganographic file system may help the owner deny that such files exist.

3. An individual is tortured by robbers for the encryption keys to files with private, personal, or financial information. Plausible deniability may help in such a case, since

the robbers would not be able to actually find the files. (An anonymous reviewer's comment: The claimed torture-resistance isn't such a good thing, since it encourages the bad guys to keep torturing until the victim expires. Since there's no way for the victim to prove that they've handed over everything, the bad guys are given an incentive to keep applying the torture indefinitely. This is not a feature.)

It is obvious that plausible deniability can be helpful in practical situations. An owner under duress may provide the passwords of several files and deny that other files exist. An opponent would have no way (short of trying every possible password) to find out whether other files exist. Even if the opponent understands the hardware and software completely and checks the file system at the operating system level, no information about other files would be found. Two approaches for implementing plausible deniability are proposed in the next two sections.

15.7.1 Employing Exclusive OR

This approach exploits the properties of the Exclusive OR (XOR) logic operation, denoted by the symbol $\oplus$ and defined by: The XOR of two identical bits is 0 and that of two different bits is 1. The XOR is associative, so $a \oplus b \oplus c = (a \oplus b) \oplus c = a \oplus (b \oplus c)$. Another important property of the XOR is that if $a = b \oplus c$, then $b = a \oplus c$ and also $c = a \oplus b$. These simple properties yield a technique that some might consider "magical" for hiding data files in a set of cover files.

We assume that a file F to be hidden is n bits long and is protected by a k-bit password P. In practice, the user may pick a strong passphrase of any length, and this phrase, together with the file name, is compressed into k bits and used as the password when F is hidden and again when it is later retrieved. We start with k cover files C_0 through C_{k-1}, each an n-bit random file. The password P is scanned, and for each bit $P_j = 1$ in P, cover file C_j is selected. All the selected C_j files are XORed, the result is XORed with file F, and that result, in turn, is XORed with any of the selected C_js, say, C_a. The process is summarized by

$$C_a \leftarrow \left(\bigoplus_{P_j=1} C_j \right) \oplus F \oplus C_a.$$

Only one of the cover files, C_a, is modified in the process, and there is no need to memorize which one it is. Once F is hidden in this way, it can be deleted and can be retrieved at any time by

$$F = \bigoplus_{P_j=1} C_j.$$

As an example, we choose $n = 4$, $k = 5$, the password $P = 01110$, and the five cover files $C_0 = 1010$, $C_1 = 0011$, $C_2 = 1110$, $C_3 = 0111$, and $C_4 = 0100$. File $F = 1001$ is hidden by using the password to select cover files C_1, C_2, and C_3, XORing them to obtain 1010, which is XORed with F to yield 0011, which is XORed with one of the selected C_j's, say, C_2, to produce a new $C_2 \leftarrow 1101$. Once this is done, file F can be recovered (if P is known) by using P to select C_1, C_2, and C_3 and computing

$$F = C_1 \oplus C_2 \oplus C_3 = 0011 \oplus 1101 \oplus 0111 = 1001.$$

The method is elegant but wasteful. The value of k must be large; otherwise, a knowledgeable attacker could simply try all k-bit passwords. Maintaining a large number of cover files to hide just one file results in a very low embedding capacity. The method must therefore be extended and be made more efficient, and we show how it can be generalized to hide m files F_j, where $m < k$. We initially assume that each F_j is n bits long. The k cover files C_j are arranged as the rows of a $k \times n$ matrix $\mathbf{C}$. Another $k \times k$ matrix $\mathbf{K}$ is constructed to serve as the extraction key. Both $\mathbf{C}$ and $\mathbf{K}$ are binary and are assumed to be over the Galois field GF(2), which means that operations on their elements should be carried out modulo 2 (see Appendix B for a discussion of finite fields). In addition, $\mathbf{K}$ should be orthonormal, meaning that the dot product of a row with itself is 1 (modulo 2), that of two different rows is 0 (also modulo 2), and the same is true for the columns.

Examples of $\mathbf{C}$ and $\mathbf{K}$ for $n = 4$ and $k = 5$ are

$$
\mathbf{C} = \begin{bmatrix} 1010 \\ 0011 \\ 1110 \\ 0111 \\ 0100 \end{bmatrix} \qquad \mathbf{K} = \begin{bmatrix} 11100 \\ 11010 \\ 01110 \\ 10110 \\ 00001 \end{bmatrix}.
$$

Notice that each row and each column of $\mathbf{K}$ must have an odd number of 1s. This way, the dot product of a row (or a column) K_j with itself yields an odd integer, which when computed modulo 2, equals 1. Also, the dot product of two different rows (or two different columns) K_i and K_j must yield an even integer, which when computed modulo 2 equals 0.

We now define hidden file F_j as the product $K_j \times \mathbf{C}$ (mod 2). This is the product of a row vector and a matrix. Each column of $\mathbf{C}$ is multiplied by row K_j to yield a single number which (modulo 2) becomes a 0 or a 1 (a single bit), and the final result is a k-bit row vector. However, since all the operations are carried out modulo 2, the result is simply the XOR of those rows of $\mathbf{C}$ that correspond to 1s in K_j. As an example, the first two data files are

$$
F_0 = K_0 \times \mathbf{C} \ (\text{mod } 2) = C_0 \oplus C_1 \oplus C_2 = 0111,
$$
$$
F_1 = K_1 \times \mathbf{C} \ (\text{mod } 2) = C_0 \oplus C_1 \oplus C_3 = 1110.
$$

These, of course, may not be the files we want to hide. We therefore have to modify $\mathbf{C}$ so it hides the F files we want. For each file F_i we prepare a difference vector D such that $F_i \oplus D$ is the desired file F_i. (If F is already what we want, D should be all zeros. Also, any of the F files can be modified at any time, not just at the beginning.) Matrix $\mathbf{C}$ is modified by XORing it with the special matrix $K_i^t \times D$. The superscript t denotes transpose, so $K_i^t \times D$ is the *outer product* obtained by multiplying the *column* K_i^t by the *row* D. Our calculations are done modulo 2, so the result of the outer product is a matrix where each row that corresponds to a 1-bit in K_i^t is a copy of D and other rows are zeros.

As an example, assume that we want file F_0 to be 1100 instead of the current 0111. We prepare the difference vector $D = 1100 \oplus 0111 = 1011$, compute the outer product

$$K_0^t \times D = \begin{bmatrix} 1 \\ 1 \\ 1 \\ 0 \\ 0 \end{bmatrix} [1,0,1,1] = \begin{bmatrix} 1011 \\ 1011 \\ 1011 \\ 0000 \\ 0000 \end{bmatrix},$$

and XOR it with $\mathbf{C}$ to obtain

$$\mathbf{C} \oplus (K_0^t \times D) = \begin{bmatrix} 1010 \\ 0011 \\ 1110 \\ 0111 \\ 0100 \end{bmatrix} \oplus \begin{bmatrix} 1011 \\ 1011 \\ 1011 \\ 0000 \\ 0000 \end{bmatrix} = \begin{bmatrix} 0001 \\ 1000 \\ 0101 \\ 0111 \\ 0100 \end{bmatrix}.$$

The expression $F_0 = K_0 \times \mathbf{C} \pmod{2} = C_0 \oplus C_1 \oplus C_2$ produces the desired value $F_0 = 1100$, but the modification of $\mathbf{C}$ did not change the original value of F_1, which is still $F_1 = K_1 \times \mathbf{C} \pmod{2} = C_0 \oplus C_1 \oplus C_3 = 1110$. Even though the two rows C_0 and C_1 have been modified, their XOR has been preserved.

$\diamond$ **Exercise 15.4:** Add a third data file $F_2 = 1101$ to $\mathbf{C}$ and verify that this did not change the values of F_0 and F_1.

A straightforward way of using this method is for an administrator to construct the $k \times k$ matrix $\mathbf{K}$ of passwords and allocate individual passwords to users. It is also possible to generate the passwords in $\mathbf{K}$ automatically in such a way that a user given a password K_i (row i of $\mathbf{K}$) will be able to generate all the passwords K_j for $j > i$ (these are termed *low-level* passwords) but not the K_j for $j < i$ (the *high-level* passwords). Such a scheme creates a linear access hierarchy. It is implemented by starting with a random password K_0 and using a one-way function h (Section 12.1) to generate the other passwords via $K_{j+1} = h(K_j)$. Since $\mathbf{K}$ should be orthonormal, two more steps are needed. First, an appropriate mapping is used to convert each row of $\mathbf{K}$ to a pseudorandom binary vector with an odd number of 1s. Second, the Gram–Schmidt orthonormalization process [MathWorld 03] is applied to orthonormalize the rows.

The requirement that the passwords (the final rows of $\mathbf{K}$) be orthonormal restricts the choice of values for the passwords. For example, if $K_1, K_2, \ldots, K_k$ are known, then there is only one choice for K_0. If only $K_2, \ldots, K_k$ are known, then there are only a few choices for K_0 and K_1. A user given a password K_i with a small value of i could conceivably find out the values of K_j for $j < i$ by searching a relatively small number of cases. A possible solution is to limit the number m of files that can be hidden to approximately $k/2$. Now only m rows in $\mathbf{K}$ have to be orthonormalized, making it much more difficult to find a higher-level password.

Another weakness of this method is that it can be broken if an attacker knows more than k bits of plaintexts from one of the hidden files. A practical solution may be to encrypt each file (before it is hidden) with a key derived from the password.

In practice, we want to hide files of different sizes. This can be achieved if the method proposed here is applied to directories instead of to files. Each file F_j being hidden is exactly n bits long, but it is actually a directory containing a number of smaller files (and padded, if necessary, with random bits to make it exactly n bits long).

15.7.2 An Alternative Approach

Imagine a computer with two hard disks. One has the operating system, applications, and those data files that don't have to be hidden. The other disk is used to hide sensitive files. Data are written on a hard disk in blocks of equal size, so the other disk is first filled up with random bits; then any file to be hidden is partitioned into segments, each the size of a disk block; and each segment is encrypted and written in one block on the disk. Since a segment is encrypted, it looks random, so an attacker cannot distinguish between an available disk block and a block containing a segment. The segments of a file must be distributed all over the hard disk, and we want to employ the password of the file, together with the file name, to identify all the segments of a given file. Each segment can be further identified by its serial number. The password of the file, together with the file name, is mapped into a number used as an encryption key, and the key is used to encrypt the serial number of each segment into a block address.

To retrieve the file, the reverse process is applied. The file name and password are used to generate the key, and the key is then used to encrypt each serial number into a block address from which the next segment is read and decrypted.

The obvious problem is collisions. Two segments, either from the same file or from different files, may end up being written to the same disk block, with the result that the second segment overwrites the first one. A little thinking may suggest the following solution: write each segment onto the disk twice, in two different blocks. This doubles the time it takes to read and write but reduces the chance of a collision. After reading a segment from a disk block and decrypting it, the software has to verify that this is indeed the right segment (the next segment from the current file being read). This can be done by writing the file name and the segment's serial number inside the segment before it is encrypted.

A direct extension of this idea is to write each segment to disk several times, instead of just twice. This reduces the chance of a collision even further but also reduces the effective capacity of the disk. Writing each segment m times is equivalent to reducing the capacity of the disk by a factor of m.

Experiments suggest that $m = 4$ is the optimal value, where 7% of the disk can be written before a collision occurs (i.e., before all m copies of a segment are written over). This figure can be increased to perhaps 20% if a sophisticated error-correcting code is included in each file. With such a code, even the loss of 10% of the segments may be fully recoverable. Naturally, an error-correcting code increases the size of the file, so the 20% disk capacity may represent an effective increase of only 15%.

Considering the price/size ratio of current hard disks, a 15% disk utilization may not be a high price to pay for having a secure file system. The use of a Larson table [Larson 84] has been proposed to increase the disk capacity even more, but this option will not be discussed here. This version of the steganographic file system has been implemented for the Linux operating system by [McDonald and Kuhn 99].

15.8 Ultimate Steganography?

We know that the use of a one-time pad cipher provides absolute security in cryptography. Is there an equivalent system in steganography? The answer is still unknown, but it is intriguing to speculate on how a one-time pad can be used to hide data such that it becomes absolutely invisible.

Imagine a video file where one bit is hidden in each video frame by changing the least significant bit of one pixel in the frame, if needed, to equal the hidden bit. The next two numbers in the one-time pad are used to select the pixel's coordinates in the frame. Even without a one-time pad (i.e., just modifying one pixel per frame, always at the same position) this method is very secure.

Sometimes even a small change in one pixel can be noticeable, especially if the pixel is part of a uniform area or is located on a sharply defined boundary. It may be preferable to use the one-time pad to select a region in the video frame (by selecting, for example, the top-left and bottom-right coordinates of a rectangle) and to hide a bit in the region by reversing the parity of the region, if necessary, to equal the bit. Reversing the parity can be done by complementing one bit in one pixel, so this version enables the encoder to examine the region and choose that pixel whose flipping would be the least visible.

The decoder uses the same one-time pad to select the same region chosen by the encoder in each frame. The decoder does not have to know which pixel had been modified. It simply computes the parity of all the bits of all the pixels of the region to come up with the single bit embedded in the region.

Yet another improvement is to choose several nonoverlapping regions in each frame and to embed the same bit in each region. This redundancy increases the reliability of the method, since it enables the decoder to retrieve the original bit even after the frame has been corrupted.

Complementing one bit to reverse the parity of a region has another advantage: namely, it disrupts the image statistics by an amount that can be made arbitrarily small. To understand this claim, consider a binary cover image where 70% of the bits are 1s. If we choose two adjacent pixels (i.e., two consecutive bits) as our region, then out of the four possible cases 00, 01, 10, and 11, the two regions 01 and 10 have a parity of 1. The probabilities of having 00, 01, 10, and 11 in a region are $(1-0.7)(1-0.7) = 0.3^2 = 0.09$, $(1 - 0.7)0.7 = 0.21$, $0.7(1 - 0.7) = 0.21$, and $0.7 \times 0.7 = 0.49$, respectively. The probability that a 2-bit region will be 01 or 10 is $2 \cdot 0.21 = 0.42$. If we now increase the region to three consecutive bits, then of the eight possible 3-bit combinations, only 001, 010, 100, and 111 have parities of 1. The probability of having one of these triplets is $3 \times 0.7 \cdot 0.3^2 + 0.7^3 = 0.532$. Similarly, the probability that a 4-bit region will have a parity of 1 is $4 \times 0.7 \cdot 0.3^3 + 4 \times 0.7^3 \cdot 0.3 = 0.4872$. As the region's size grows, these probabilities converge quickly to 0.5, which implies that with a large enough region, half of all the possible values of the region will have parities of 1 both before and after the modifications, regardless of the bit distribution in the video frame.

⋄ **Exercise 15.5:** The three probabilities above are 0.42, 0.532, and 0.4872. They approach 0.5, but they alternate about this value. Explain this behavior.

Such a method may embed secret data in a video file without changing the image statistics of the individual frames. It therefore has the potential of being absolutely secure, similar to the one-time pad.

15.9 Public-Key Steganography

In the preceding sections, we implicitly assumed that the sender and receiver share the stego-key. In cases where this assumption is not valid, it is still possible, using public-key cryptography, to send hidden messages that can be decoded only by the intended recipient. The main steps are as follows: (1) encrypt the stego-key with the public key of the receiver; (2) suppose that the encrypted data elements are n bits long; encrypt the value of n and embed it in the first b video frames of a video file, where b is a constant; (3) embed the n bits in the following n video frames by modifying (when necessary) the parity of one region in each frame; (4) embed the secret message in the remaining frames using the stego-key. This way, sender and receiver can communicate secretly if they have the same software (using the same constant b) and don't have to share the value of n.

This approach can be extended to the case where an attacker tries to modify randomly selected bits in the stego cover. Clearly, if an attacker is free to stop the message from reaching the receiver, or to modify arbitrarily many bits, the embedded secret data would be lost. However, if the attacker is allowed only bit modifications that leave the stegocover visibly unchanged, then only a limited number of bits can be modified in the attack. This destroys part of the embedded data but not all of it, which suggests the use of redundancy. Embedding the data as before (one bit hidden in each video frame by modifying the parity of a region) but with a sophisticated error-correcting code can result in a robust algorithm where the secret data can be retrieved even after an attacker has randomly modified one bit per frame. The tradeoff, naturally, is the loss of embedding capacity.

15.10 Current Software

Any algorithm published in the professional literature has to be tested by its developer, which requires a software implementation. This author likes to assume that all the methods described in this chapter (and the many others not included here) have been implemented and tested well. However, most of these implementations are of the quick and dirty type, meant to test the algorithm rather than produce fast and efficient results. They may not be user-friendly, may have all sorts of restrictions, perhaps even bugs, and may be available for one platform only (or not available at all from their developers). There are, however, some widely available steganography programs, and a few of them are described here. The programs included are not necessarily the best ones and have been selected simply because their details are easy to come by.

15.10.1 Stego

Stego is perhaps the first steganographic software widely available [Stego 04]. It was conceived and implemented (on the Macintosh) by Romana Machado and is available as shareware. (There are several other programs, for other platforms, also called Stego.) Stego hides data in the least significant bits of a PICT file (PICT is an old image format sometimes still used on the Macintosh). After a PICT image has been selected by the user, the program computes and displays the amount of data that can be hidden in the image. It then embeds the data and displays the image before and after the data is embedded, so the user can evaluate the results. The LSB method and its limitations are described in Section 14.1.

> Featured in the press for being a Very Extropian Person, I consider myself a transhumanist, individualist, and libertarian.
>
> —Romana Machado

15.10.2 Hide and Seek

Hide and seek, by Colin Maroney is another free program (for the PC, source code is also available) that hides data in the least significant bits of an image. The current version (5.0) is a complete rewrite of the program. The image must be in GIF format, must have 256 colors or grayscales, and must have a size of $320 \times 480 = 153,600$ pixels. This size (equivalent to 19,200 bytes of hidden data) is therefore the maximum hiding capacity of the program. Generally, the more data that is embedded in the cover image, the more likely the resulting stegoimage will be degraded.

Hide and seek spreads the data throughout the image in a somewhat random fashion. It uses a stego-key as the seed of a pseudorandom number generator and tries to disperse the hidden bits in the cover image. The program also includes an 8-byte file header encrypted by the IDEA cipher [Salomon 03]. The first two bytes store the size of the file. The following two bytes contain the stego-key. This key is either chosen by the user or is selected at random before the data is embedded. The next pair of bytes is the version number, and the last pair is unused. This last pair is needed to complete the size of the header to 8 bytes, because the IDEA cipher works on blocks of 64 bits.

There is a version (written especially for Windows 95) that uses image files in the BMP format instead of GIF.

15.10.3 S-Tools

The author of this steganography shareware for the PC is Andy Brown (located at a.brown@nexor.co.uk). S-Tools hides data in the least significant bits of WAV audio files or GIF or BMP images. S-Tools can optionally encrypt the data with a key before hiding it, thereby providing an "envelope" that will not rouse suspicion. (The MD5 hash function is used to transform the key to 128 evenly distributed bits.)

S-Tools can hide multiple files of secret data in one cover file. The files can optionally be compressed and encrypted before they are hidden.

The data bits are hidden in the least significant bits of audio samples or pixel values, and the key is used to spread the bits pseudorandomly.

S-Tools employs two techniques for hiding data in a cover image with 24 bits (or three bytes) per pixel. One technique is used when the image can have the maximum number of colors (2^{24} or approximately 16.7 million). The program simply embeds three bits of data in each pixel, one bit in each of the three bytes of the pixel. The other technique is used when the number of colors is limited to 256 (even though each pixel is still three bytes). S-Tools applies a palette optimization algorithm [Heckbert 82] to reduce the number of colors to 32. It follows this by embedding the data (again, each bit becomes the least significant bit of a byte). Each of the 32 colors is defined by three bytes, so changing the least significant bits of those bytes can change the color in at most $2^3 = 8$ different ways. Thus, the total number of new colors can be at most $32 \times 8 = 256$.

S-Tools has an FDD module that can hide data in the free space of floppy disks. To understand how this works, we start with a short discussion of how the old DOS operating system manages files on a disk. When the disk is formatted, it is divided into concentric circles called *tracks* and each track is further divided into several arc segments called *sectors*. Data is written on the disk (and also read from the disk) in sectors, so each piece of data has a two-part address: its track and sector numbers. The sector is the smallest addressable unit on the disk. A 3.25 inch floppy disk, for example, has 2880 sectors, each 512 bytes long, for a total capacity of $512 \times 2880 = 1{,}474{,}560 = 1.44$ Mbytes (a megabyte equals 1024 Kbyte, and 1 Kbyte equals 1024 bytes). Before writing a file on the disk, DOS computes the number of sectors needed for the file and writes this information, together with the start address of the file, in a special table, called the file allocation table (FAT) in a special area at the start of the disk.

The FDD module checks the FAT to determine which sectors are still unused and hides the data by writing it in those sectors. It selects unused sectors pseudorandomly and starts by writing the size of the hidden data and the seed of the pseudorandom number generator. When all the data has been hidden, the module stores random bits in any remaining unused sectors to confuse attackers. Notice that the sectors used to hide the data are still declared unused in the FAT. If a new file is accidentally written on the disk, DOS may write it on the same sectors used to hide the data, thereby erasing the hidden data.

15.10.4 MandelSteg

The Mandelbrot set, first explored by Benoit Mandelbrot [Mandelbrot 82] is perhaps the most famous mathematical object. This is a set of points for which the iteration $z_{i+1} = z_i + c$ converges. In more detail, start with the complex number $z_1 = 0$ and any complex number c. Perform the iteration $z_{i+1} = z_i + c$ several times. If the result converges (i.e., if the difference between z_i and z_{i+1} gets arbitrarily small), then c is added to the Mandelbrot set as a point (recall that any complex number c may be viewed as a two-dimensional point). When the set is drawn by computer, the program should be given the range of values for c and the maximum number of iterations for each c. The set is a self-similar fractal. Many parts of itself (in fact, infinitely many) are identical to the entire set. The number of iterations needed for any c can be used to assign an artificial color to each point in this set, thereby turning it into a colorful, complex-looking image.

MandelSteg hides data in the Mandelbrot set (although it can hide data in any fractal) by modifying the least significant bits of points in the set. The cover image has to be in GIF format. A separate program extracts the data by collecting the least significant bits of all the image pixels.

> Hope is nature's veil for hiding truth's nakedness.
> —Alfred Nobel

Part IV:
Essential Resources

Appendix A introduces the powerful mathematical concept of groups, and especially symmetry groups. This material is used in the Verhoeff method of Section 2.11. Group theory is an excellent example of an abstract mathematical theory, developed by curious people for its beauty with no thought for its practical applications, that eventually found an elegant application in the modern world.

Appendix B is a short introduction to the important topic of finite (Galois) fields. These mathematical abstractions have found many applications in error-control codes and cryptography and are discussed here in some detail for the benefit of advanced readers. As promised in the Preface, however, virtually the entire book can be read and understood without this material.

Appendix C is a brief introduction to the useful concept of CRC. This is an extension of the single parity bit.

Appendix D describes some research and programming projects that should be tried by anyone who wants more than the basic "book knowledge" provided by this book.

> Idleness is an appendix to nobility.
> —Robert Burton

Appendix A
Symmetry Groups

A mathematical group G is a set of objects (the group's elements) with a binary operation denoted by "+" or by "$*$" defined on the elements that satisfies the following requirements.

1. Closure: for any $a, b \in G$, the sum $(a + b)$ is an element of G.
2. Associativity: any $a, b, c \in G$ satisfies $(a + b) + c = a + (b + c)$.
3. Identity: there exists $e \in G$ such that for all $a \in G$ $(a + e) = (e + a) = a$.
4. Inverses: for each $a \in G$, there exists a unique element $a^{-1} \in G$ such that $a + a^{-1} = a^{-1} + a = e$.
5. If the group operation is commutative, i.e., if $a + b = b + a$ for any $a, b \in G$, the group is called Abelian.

> Question: What's purple and commutes?
>
> Answer: An Abelian grape.

Examples of groups:

1. The set of all the integers with integer addition. The identity element is the integer 0. This is an infinite group.
2. The (finite) set of the integers 0, 1, 2,...,$m - 1$ with modulo-m addition.
3. The integers 1, 2,...,$q - 1$ for a prime q with modulo-q multiplication.
4. The set of all rotations in two dimensions under the operation: The sum of the two rotations by α and β degrees is a rotation by $\alpha + \beta$ degrees.

   The set $(0, 1, 2, 3)$ with modulo-4 addition is a group denoted by $G(4)$. It obeys the addition table

+	0	1	2	3
0	0	1	2	3
1	1	2	3	0
2	2	3	0	1
3	3	0	1	2

The *order* of a group (its cardinality) is the number of elements. It is denoted by ord(G). The order of $G(4)$ is 4.

A *subgroup* is a subset of the elements of a group that is closed under the group's operation. A theorem by Lagrange states that if S is a subgroup of G, then ord(S) divides ord(G). For example, if S is the subgroup $(0, 1)$ of $G(4)$, then ord(S) = 2 divides ord($G(4)$) = 4 and $G(4)$ can be partitioned into the *cosets* S and $S + 2$.

This appendix deals with symmetry groups. The elements of such a group are symmetry operations (or transformations) on an object; they are not numbers. Figure A.1a shows four symmetric objects: a rhombus, a rectangle, a square, and a pentagon. The term *symmetric* means an object that retains its shape and location under certain transformations. A square, for example, is highly symmetric, because it preserves its shape and position when rotated by a multiple of 90° or when reflected about the four axes shown by dashed lines in Figure A.1b. A rectangle is less symmetric because a rotation of 90° changes its shape from horizontal to vertical or vice versa.

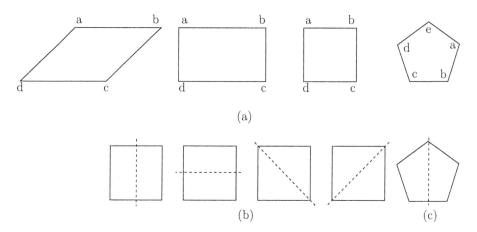

(a)

(b)   (c)

Figure A.1: Symmetries of Rhombus, Square, and Pentagon.

For simple geometric objects, it is possible to express rotations and reflections by listing the new position of each vertex of the object. When the square is rotated 90° clockwise, for example, vertex a moves to b, b moves to c, and so on, which can be expressed as the permutation

$$\begin{pmatrix} a\ b\ c\ d \\ b\ c\ d\ a \end{pmatrix}.$$

Reflections of the square about a vertical axis and about the main diagonal are expressed by

$$\begin{pmatrix} a\ b\ c\ d \\ b\ a\ d\ c \end{pmatrix}, \quad \begin{pmatrix} a\ b\ c\ d \\ a\ d\ c\ b \end{pmatrix}.$$

The connection between symmetry transformations and groups becomes clear when we consider combinations of transformations.

The rectangle is transformed to itself after (1) a 0° rotation, (2) a reflection about a central horizontal axis, (3) a reflection about a central vertical axis, and (4) a 180° rotation. Examining the diagram, the following properties become clear:

1. Transformation 1 followed by transformation i (or i followed by 1) is equivalent to just transformation i for any i.
2. Any of the four transformations followed by itself returns the rectangle to its original shape, so it is identical to transformation 1.
3. Transformation 3 followed by 2 is equivalent to 4.

An analysis of all the combinations of two transformations of the rectangle yields Table A.2a. The table can be considered the definition of a symmetry group of four elements, because it specifies the group operation for the elements. A direct check verifies that element 1 (the null transformation) is the group's identity, that the operation is closed, and that it is noncommutative. This symmetry group is denoted by D_4 (D for *dihedral*, meaning *bending* the arms up; anhedral means the opposite).

(A dihedral group is a group whose elements correspond to a closed set of rotations and reflections in the plane. The dihedral group with $2n$ elements is denoted by either D_n or D_{2n}. The group consists of n reflections, $n-1$ rotations, and the identity transformation.)

$*$	0	1	2	3	4	5	6	7	8	9
0	0	1	2	3	4	5	6	7	8	9
1	1	2	3	4	0	6	7	8	9	5
2	2	3	4	0	1	7	8	9	5	6
3	3	4	0	1	2	8	9	5	6	7
4	4	0	1	2	3	9	5	6	7	8
5	5	9	8	7	6	0	4	3	2	1
6	6	5	9	8	7	1	0	4	3	2
7	7	6	5	9	8	2	1	0	4	3
8	8	7	6	5	9	3	2	1	0	4
9	9	8	7	6	5	4	3	2	1	0

$*$	0	1	2	3	4	5	6	7
0	0	1	2	3	4	5	6	7
1	1	2	3	0	6	7	5	4
2	2	3	0	1	5	4	7	6
3	3	0	1	2	7	6	4	5
4	4	7	5	6	0	2	3	1
5	5	6	4	7	2	0	1	3
6	6	4	7	5	1	3	0	2
7	7	5	6	4	3	1	2	0

$*$	1	2	3	4
1	1	2	3	4
2	2	1	4	3
3	3	4	1	2
4	4	3	2	1

(a)   (b)   (c)

Table A.2: The D_4, D_8, and D_{10} Symmetry Groups.

Similarly, the rhombus has limited symmetry. Its four symmetry transformations are (1) the null transformation, (2) a reflection about the line bd, (3) a reflection about line ac, and (4) a 180° rotation. An analysis of all the combinations of two of these transformations, however, results in the same symmetry group. Thus, even though the rhombus and rectangle are different objects and their symmetry transformations are different, we can say that they have the same symmetries and we call them *isometric*.

Intuitively, a square is more symmetric than a rectangle or a rhombus. There are more transformations that leave it unchanged. It is easy to see that these are the four rotations by multiples of 90° and the four reflections about the vertical, horizontal, and two diagonal axes. These eight transformations can be written as the permutations

$$0 = \begin{pmatrix} a\ b\ c\ d \\ a\ b\ c\ d \end{pmatrix}, \quad 1 = \begin{pmatrix} a\ b\ c\ d \\ b\ c\ d\ a \end{pmatrix}, \quad 2 = \begin{pmatrix} a\ b\ c\ d \\ c\ d\ a\ b \end{pmatrix}, \quad 3 = \begin{pmatrix} a\ b\ c\ d \\ d\ a\ b\ c \end{pmatrix},$$

$$4 = \begin{pmatrix} a\ b\ c\ d \\ b\ a\ d\ c \end{pmatrix}, \quad 5 = \begin{pmatrix} a\ b\ c\ d \\ d\ c\ b\ a \end{pmatrix}, \quad 6 = \begin{pmatrix} a\ b\ c\ d \\ a\ d\ c\ b \end{pmatrix}, \quad 7 = \begin{pmatrix} a\ b\ c\ d \\ c\ b\ a\ d \end{pmatrix},$$

which can immediately be used to construct the symmetry dihedral group D_8 listed in Table A.2b.

Finally, the pentagon is used to create the larger symmetry group D_{10}, because it has 10 symmetry transformations. Figure A.1a shows that the pentagon is transformed to itself by any rotation through a multiple of 60°, while Figure A.1c shows that it can be symmetrically reflected about five different axes. These ten transformations give rise to the D_{10} symmetry group of Table A.2c (identical to Table 2.14a), and it is this group that is used by the Verhoeff check digit method of Section 2.11.

> The mathematical sciences particularly exhibit order, symmetry, and
> limitation; and these are the greatest forms of the beautiful.
>
> —Aristotle, *Metaphysica*

Appendix B
Galois Fields

This appendix is an introduction to finite fields for those who need to brush up on this topic. Finite fields are used in cryptography in the Rijndael (AES) algorithm and in stream ciphers. In the field of error-control codes, they are used extensively. The Reed–Solomon codes of Section 1.14 operate on the elements of such a field.

B.1 Field Definitions and Operations

The mathematical concept of a *field* is based on that of a group, which has been introduced at the start of Appendix A. A *field* F is a set with two operations—addition "+" and multiplication "×"—that satisfies the following conditions.

1. F is an Abelian group under the + operation.
2. F is closed under the × operation.
3. The nonzero elements of F form an Abelian group under ×.
4. The elements obey the distributive law $(a + b) \times c = a \times c + b \times c$.

   Examples of fields are

1. The real numbers under the normal addition and multiplication;
2. The complex numbers; and
3. The rational numbers.

   Notice that the integers do not form a field under addition and multiplication because the multiplicative inverse (reciprocal) of an integer a is $1/a$, which is generally a noninteger. Also, a finite set of real numbers is not a field under normal addition and multiplication because these operations can create a result outside the set. In order for a finite set of numbers to be a field, its two operations have to be defined carefully so that they satisfy the closure requirement. Finite fields are intriguing because the finite number of elements implies that the two operations could be performed by computers exactly (with full precision). This is why much research has been devoted to the use of finite fields in practical applications.

A Galois field, abbreviated GF, is a finite field. These fields were "discovered," studied, and precisely defined by the young French mathematician Evariste Galois, and today they have many applications in fields as diverse as error-control codes, cryptography, random-number generation, VLSI testing, and digital signal processing. Galois has proved that the size of a finite field must be a power m of a prime number q and that there is exactly one finite field with any given size q^m. This justifies talking about *the* finite field with q^m elements, and this field is denoted by $GF(q^m)$.

If $m = 1$, the size of the field $GF(q)$ is a prime number q, its elements are the integers $0, 1, \ldots, q - 1$, and the two operations are integer addition and multiplication modulo q. The simplest examples are $GF(2)$ and $GF(3)$.

The simple field $GF(2)$ consists of the two elements 0 and 1 and is the smallest finite field. Its operations are integer addition and multiplication modulo 2, which are summarized by

+	0 1		×	0 1
0	0 1		0	0 0
1	1 0		1	0 1

Notice that the addition is actually an XOR and the multiplication is a logical AND.

The next field is $GF(3)$, whose elements are 0, 1, and 2. Its operations are integer addition and multiplication modulo 3, summarized by the truth tables

+	0 1 2		×	0 1 2
0	0 1 2		0	0 0 0
1	1 2 0		1	0 1 2
2	2 0 1		2	0 2 1

The additive inverse of 1 is 2 because $1 + 2 = 2 + 1 = 0$. Similarly, the multiplicative inverse of 2 is itself because $2 \times 2 = 1$.

◇ **Exercise B.1:** Write the addition and multiplication tables of $GF(5)$.

> He is the only candidate who gave poor answers. He knows absolutely nothing. I was told that this student has an extraordinary capacity for mathematics. This astonishes me greatly, for, after his examination, I believed him to have but little intelligence or that his intelligence is so well hidden that I was unable to uncover it. If he really is what he appears to be, I doubt very much that he will make a good teacher.
>
> —French physicist Jean Claude Eugène Péclet, one of Galois's examiners in 1829.

◇ **Exercise B.2:** Compute the addition and multiplication tables of $GF(4)$ as if 4 were a prime and show why these tables don't make sense.

If $m > 1$, the elements of $\text{GF}(q^m)$ are polynomials of degree less than m over $\text{GF}(q)$ [i.e., polynomials whose coefficients are elements of $\text{GF}(q)$], and the operations are special versions of polynomial addition and polynomial multiplication. Hence, if the polynomial $a_{m-1}x^{m-1} + \cdots + a_1x + a_0$ is an element of $\text{GF}(q^m)$, then $a_0, a_1, \ldots, a_{m-1}$ are elements of Galois field $\text{GF}(q)$. The degree of the polynomial is the largest i for which $a_i \neq 0$.

Adding elements of $\text{GF}(q^m)$ is easy. If the polynomials $a(x)$ and $b(x)$ are elements of $\text{GF}(q^m)$, then the sum $c(x) = a(x) + b(x)$ is a polynomial with coefficients $c_i = (a_i + b_i) \bmod q$. The sum is a polynomial whose degree is the greater of the degrees of $a(x)$ and $b(x)$, so it is an element of $\text{GF}(q^m)$. Also, the rule for addition implies that this operation is associative and that there is an identity (the polynomial whose coefficients are all zeros).

⋄ **Exercise B.3:** In order for $\text{GF}(q^m)$ to be a field, each element must have an additive inverse. What is it?

Multiplying elements of $\text{GF}(q^m)$ is a bit trickier, because the normal multiplication of two polynomials of degrees m and n results in a polynomial of degree $m+n$. Multiplication of polynomials in $\text{GF}(q^m)$ must therefore be defined (similar to addition) modulo something. In analogy to addition, which is done modulo a prime integer, multiplication is performed modulo a prime polynomial. Such a polynomial is called *irreducible*. Much as a prime number is not a product of smaller integers, an irreducible polynomial is not a product of lower-degree polynomials. The irreducible polynomials we are interested in are irreducible in $\text{GF}(q)$, which means that such a polynomial cannot be factored into a product of lower-degree polynomials in $\text{GF}(q)$. (Note. A polynomial irreducible over $\text{GF}(q)$ has no roots in $\text{GF}(q)$. The opposite, however, isn't true. A polynomial with no roots in $\text{GF}(q)$ may be reducible over $\text{GF}(q)$.) Section B.2 shows how to multiply two polynomials modulo a third polynomial.

The polynomial $x^2 - 1$ over the reals can be factored into $(x - 1)(x + 1)$, so it is reducible. Its relative, the polynomial $x^2 + 1$, is irreducible over the real numbers. This same polynomial, however, is reducible over $\text{GF}(2)$ because the polynomial product $(x+1)(x+1)$, which equals $x \times x + 1 \times x + x \times 1 + 1 \times 1$, can also be written $x^2 + (1+1)x + 1 \times 1$, and in $\text{GF}(2)$ this equals $x^2 + 1$. Another example is the polynomial $(x^2 + x + 1)^2$. It is easy to verify that neither zero nor 1 are roots of this polynomial. It therefore does not have any roots in $\text{GF}(2)$, but it is not irreducible in $\text{GF}(2)$ because it is obviously a product of two lower-degree polynomials.

⋄ **Exercise B.4:** Show that the polynomial $x^8 + 1$ with coefficients in $\text{GF}(2)$ is reducible.

No doubt this style and this efficiency were due to his peasant heredity. Perhaps also to the fact that manual work (whatever the demagogues may say) does not demand a veritable genius, since it is more difficult to extract a square root than a gorse root.

—Marcel Pagnol, *Jean de Florette*

The simplest example of a Galois field of the form $GF(q^m)$ for $m > 1$ is $GF(2^2) = GF(4)$. Its elements are polynomials $a_1x + a_0$ over $GF(2)$ (meaning that it has coefficients that are 0 or 1). If we denote such an element by the two bits a_1a_0, then the four field elements are $0 = 00_2 = 0 \times x + 0$, $1 = 01_2 = 0 \times x + 1$, $2 = 10_2 = x + 0$, and $3 = 11_2 = x + 1$. If we now select the polynomial $x^2 + x + 1$, which is irreducible over $GF(4)$, and multiply modulo this polynomial, then the two field operations become

+	0	1	2	3		×	0	1	2	3
0	0	1	2	3		0	0	0	0	0
1	1	0	3	2		1	0	1	2	3
2	2	3	0	1		2	0	2	3	1
3	3	2	1	0		3	0	3	1	2

The multiplication table shows that $2 \times 2 = 3$. In polynomial notation, element 2 is the polynomial x and element 3 is $x + 1$. This is why the product $x \times x$, which over the reals is x^2, equals $x + 1$ in $GF(4)$.

Notice that the multiplication table implies that $2^3 = (2 \times 2) \times 2 = 3 \times 2 = 1$, so we can consider element 2 the cube root of unity. Over the real numbers, this cube root is $(i\sqrt{3} - 1)/2$, which shows that the names 0, 1, 2, and 3 are arbitrary.

Choosing a different irreducible polynomial of degree m produces a different multiplication table, but all the tables that can be generated in this way are isomorphic; they have the same essential structure in terms of the two operations and differ by the names of the field's elements. However, as we already know, the names are arbitrary.

◇ **Exercise B.5:** Explain why $GF(6)$ does not exist.

Another simple example is $GF(2^3) = GF(8)$. Its elements are polynomials $a_2x^2 + a_1x + a_0$ with coefficients a_i in $GF(2)$ (i.e., bits). We denote such an element by the three bits $a_2a_1a_0$, so element $6 = 110_2$ is the polynomial $x^2 + x$. Addition is simple: the sum of $x^2 + 1$ and $x + 1$ is $x^2 + x + 1 + 1 = x^2 + x$. For multiplication, we select the irreducible polynomial $x^3 + x + 1$. The results are summarized in Table B.1.

+	0	1	2	3	4	5	6	7		×	0	1	2	3	4	5	6	7
0	0	1	2	3	4	5	6	7		0	0	0	0	0	0	0	0	0
1	1	0	3	2	5	4	7	6		1	0	1	2	3	4	5	6	7
2	2	3	0	1	6	7	4	5		2	0	2	4	6	3	1	7	5
3	3	2	1	0	7	6	5	4		3	0	3	6	5	7	4	1	2
4	4	5	6	7	0	1	2	3		4	0	4	3	7	6	2	5	1
5	5	4	7	6	1	0	3	2		5	0	5	1	4	2	7	3	6
6	6	7	4	5	2	3	0	1		6	0	6	7	1	5	3	2	4
7	7	6	5	4	3	2	1	0		7	0	7	5	2	1	6	4	3

Table B.1: Addition and Multiplication in GF(8).

As an example, the $GF(8)$ multiplication table indicates that $5 \times 3 = 4$, or in binary $101 \times 011 = 100$, or in polynomial notation $(x^2 + 1)(x + 1) = (x^3 + x^2 + x + 1) =$

$x^2 \bmod (x^3 + x + 1)$. The modulo operation results in the remainder of the polynomial division $(x^3 + x^2 + x + 1)/(x^3 + x + 1)$.

⋄ **Exercise B.6:** Choose some of the elements of the GF(4) and GF(8) multiplication tables and show how they are computed.

⋄ **Exercise B.7:** List the additive and multiplicative inverses of the eight elements of GF(8).

The existence of the additive and multiplicative inverses makes it possible to subtract and divide field elements. To subtract $a - b$, just add a to the additive inverse of b (since the additive inverse of b is b itself, subtraction in GF(8) is identical to addition). To divide a/b, multiply a by the multiplicative inverse of b.

The particular definition of multiplication in $GF(q^m)$ satisfies the requirements for a field. The product of two field elements is a polynomial of degree $m - 1$ or less, so it is an element of the field. The multiplication is associative and there is an identity element, namely, the polynomial **1**. In order to figure out the inverse of element $p(x)$, we denote by $m(x)$ the particular irreducible polynomial that we use for the multiplication and apply the extended Euclidean algorithm. This algorithm (next paragraph) finds two polynomials $a(x)$ and $b(x)$ such that $p(x)a(x) + m(x)b(x) = 1$. This implies that $a(x)p(x) \bmod m(x) = 1$ or $p^{-1}(x) = a(x) \bmod m(x)$.

The extended Euclidean algorithm solves the following problem. Given two integers r_0 and r_1, find two other integers s and t such that $sr_0 + tr_1 = \gcd(r_0, r_1)$. This employs Euclid's algorithm, where in each iteration the current remainder r_i is expressed in the form $r_i = s_i r_0 + t_i r_1$. The signal for the last iteration is $r_m = \gcd(r_0, r_1) = s_m r_0 + t_m r_1 = s \cdot r_0 + t \cdot r_1$. This algorithm can be expressed recursively as

$$s_0 = 1, \quad t_0 = 0,$$
$$s_1 = 0, \quad t_1 = 1,$$
$$\text{repeat}$$
$$s_i = s_{i-2} - q_{i-1} s_{i-1}, \quad t_i = t_{i-2} - q_{i-1} t_{i-1},$$
$$\text{for } i = 2, 3, \ldots.$$

As an example, we compute the extended Euclidean algorithm for $r_0 = 126$ and $r_1 = 23$:

$$126 = 5 \cdot 23 + 11, \quad t_0 = 0,$$
$$23 = 2 \cdot 11 + 1, \quad t_1 = 1,$$
$$11 = 11 \cdot 1 + 0, \quad t_2 = 0 - 5 \cdot 1 = -5,$$
$$t_3 = 1 - 2 \cdot (-5) = 11.$$

The Exponential Representation of Galois Fields. We start with the simple field GF(q) and define the *order* of a field element. Let β be an element in GF(q). The order of β is denoted by ord(β) and is defined as the smallest positive integer m such that $\beta^m = 1$.

It can be shown that if t is the order of β for some β in GF(q), then t divides $(q - 1)$.

In those days, my head was full of the romantic prose of E.T. Bell's *Men of Mathematics*, a collection of biographies of the great mathematicians. This is a splendid book for a young boy to read (unfortunately, there is not much in it to inspire a girl, with Sonya Kovalevsky allotted only half a chapter), and it has awakened many people of my generation to the beauties of mathematics. The most memorable chapter is called "Genius and Stupidity" and describes the life and death of the French mathematician Galois, who was killed in a duel at the age of twenty. ... "All night long he had spent the fleeting hours feverishly dashing off his scientific last will and testament, writing against time to glean a few of the great things in his teeming mind before the death he saw could overtake him. Time after time he broke off to scribble in the margin 'I have not time; I have not time,' and passed on to the next frantically scrawled outline. What he wrote in those last desperate hours before the dawn will keep generations of mathematicians busy for hundreds of years. He had found, once and for all, the true solution of a riddle which had tormented mathematicians for centuries: under what conditions can an equation be solved?"

—Freeman Dyson, *Disturbing the Universe* (1979)

An element with order $(q - 1)$ in GF(q) is called a *primitive element* in GF(q).

Every field $GF(q)$ contains at least one primitive element α. The elements of $GF(q)$ can be represented as zero followed by the $(q - 1)$ consecutive powers of any primitive element α:

$$0, \alpha, \alpha^2, \alpha^3, \ldots, \alpha^{q-2}, \alpha^{q-1}, \alpha^q = \alpha, \ldots.$$

This is the exponential representation of $GF(q)$. Notice that we don't have to know the value of any particular root α. All we need is this particular sequence of powers of α.

A simple example is element 2 of GF(3). The multiplication table of GF(3) shows that the smallest n for which $2^n = 1$ is $n = 2 = 3 - 1$. Thus, element 2 is primitive and GF(3) can be represented as the set $(0, 2, 2^2 = 1)$. Another example is GF(5). Exercise B.1 shows that element 2 of GF(5) is primitive because the smallest n for which $2^n = 1$ is $n = 4 = 5 - 1$. Hence, the exponential representation of GF(5) with respect to 2 is $(0, 2, 2^2 = 4, 2^3 = 3, 2^4 = 1)$.

◊ **Exercise B.8:** Show that 3 is also a primitive element of GF(5).

The exponential representation of Galois fields can be extended to fields GF(q^m) where $m > 1$.

An irreducible polynomial $p(x)$ of degree m in GF(q) is said to be *primitive* if the smallest positive integer n for which $p(x)$ divides $x^n - 1$ is $n = q^m - 1$.

It can be shown that the roots α_j of an mth-degree primitive polynomial $p(x)$ in GF(q) have order $q^m - 1$. This implies that the roots α_j of $p(x)$ are primitive elements in GF(q^m). The exponential representation of GF(q^m) can therefore be constructed from any of these roots.

As an example, we show the construction of the exponential representation of GF(2^3). The polynomial $p(x) = x^3 + x + 1$ is primitive in GF(2). Let α be any root of $p(x) = x^3 + x + 1$. From $\alpha^3 + \alpha + 1 = 0$ we get $\alpha^3 = \alpha + 1$ (this is done by adding $\alpha + 1$ to both sides, since in GF(2) $1 + 1 = 0$) and from this, the exponential representation of GF(8) can be constructed (Table B.2). The second column of the table is the power of α. These are the field elements in the exponential representation (notice how element zero is termed 7 in this representation). The rightmost columns list the field elements in the polynomial representation.

The exponential representation listed in Table B.2 also makes it clear that the nonzero elements of any Galois field form a *cyclic* group.

exp rep		polynomial representation		
0	7	0	000	0
α^0	0	1	001	1
α^1	1	α	010	2
α^2	2	α^2	100	4
α^3	3	$\alpha + 1$	011	3
α^4	4	$\alpha^2 + \alpha$	110	6
α^5	5	$\alpha^3 + \alpha^2 = \alpha^2 + \alpha + 1$	111	7
α^6	6	$\alpha^2 + 1$	101	5
α^7		1	001	1

Table B.2: Exponential and Polynomial Representations of GF(8).

Which representation is better? The exponential representation (the second column of Table B.2) is useful for multiplication. Adding two elements in this column (modulo 7) produces their product. Thus, $\alpha^4 \times \alpha^5 = \alpha^{9 \bmod (2^3 - 1)} = \alpha^2$. The polynomial representation (the rightmost three columns of Table B.2) is useful for addition. Thus, adding $4 + 7 \bmod 8$ produces 3.

Notice that the sum (i.e., the XOR) of all the field elements is zero. This is a general result.

Notice also how all the powers of α are expressed in terms of $\alpha^0 = 1$, $\alpha^1 = \alpha$, and α^2. These three powers of α are the *basis* for the polynomial representation of GF(8).

A direct check using Table B.1 shows that elements 2, 4, and 6 of GF(8) are primitive. Each can be the α of Table B.2.

⋄ **Exercise B.9:** Show that elements 2 and 3 of GF(4) are primitive elements of this field.

⋄ **Exercise B.10:** Given that the polynomial $x^4 + x^3 + 1$ is primitive in GF(2), construct the exponential representation of GF(2^4) = GF(16).

Any root α is therefore a *generator* of a finite field. A generator is defined as an element whose successive powers take on every element of the field except the zero. It is possible to check every field element for this property, but this process is time consuming. For example, we can test elements of GF(7) by computing successive powers modulo 7 of each nonzero element. It is clear that element 1 cannot be a generator. Successive powers of 2 modulo 7 produce 2, $2^2 = 4$, $2^3 = 1$, but $2^4 = 2$, implying that 2^5 will be

4, the same as 2^2. Next, we try element 3. Its successive powers taken modulo 7 are 3, $3^2 = 2$, $3^3 = 6$, $3^4 = 4$, $3^5 = 5$, and $3^6 = 1$, which establishes 3 as a generator of this field.

The following discussion attempts to shed light on the nature of the elements of $GF(q^m)$ and on the mysterious α. Perhaps the best way to understand finite fields and their elements is to consider algebraic equations of various degrees (Galois himself developed the concepts of groups and fields when trying to answer the question, "Under what conditions does an equation have a solution?"). Consider the linear (degree-1) equation $2x - 1 = 0$. Its coefficients are integers, but its solution is not: it is the rational number $1/2$. Similarly, the quadratic equation $x^2 - 2 = 0$ has the irrational solution $x = \sqrt{2}$. Continuing along the same line, we examine the quadratic equation $x^2 + 1 = 0$. Its coefficients are 0 and 1 (the coefficient of x is zero). If we consider the coefficients real numbers, then the solutions are $x^2 = -1$ or $x = \pm\sqrt{-1}$. There is no real number whose square is -1, so we extend the concept of number and construct the field of *complex numbers*. We can say that when the equation $x^2 + 1 = 0$ is over the reals, its solutions are over the field of complex numbers. Alternatively, we can say that the *base field* of our equation is the reals and the *extension field* is the complex numbers. This shows that the solutions of an equation may sometimes lie in a field different from that of the coefficients. Thus, in order to solve an equation, we sometimes have to extend the concept of numbers and develop new types of mathematical entities.

Next, we consider the equation $x^2 + x + 1 = 0$. When we assume its coefficients to be over the reals, the solutions are the complex numbers $(-1 \pm \sqrt{-3})/2$. They are obtained by the well-known general solution of the quadratic equation. However, when we consider the coefficients elements of $GF(2)$, we have to use $GF(2)$ arithmetic to solve it. It is easy to see that no element of $GF(2)$ is a solution. Trying $x = 0$ produces $0 \times 0 + 0 + 1 = 0$ and trying $x = 1$ yields $1 \times 1 + 1 + 1 = 0$, both contradictions. Thus, we realize that the solutions are not in $GF(2)$ and we have to extend our concept of a field. We therefore denote one of the two (unknown) solutions by α and observe that α satisfies $\alpha^2 + \alpha + 1 = 0$ or $\alpha^2 = \alpha + 1$. We still don't know what mathematical entity α is, but we know that (1) α is neither 0 nor 1, since neither of those elements of $GF(2)$ is a solution to our equation and (2) that the two solutions are α and α^2 [the latter is a solution because $\alpha^2 + \alpha + 1 = (\alpha + 1) + \alpha + 1 = (1 + 1)\alpha + 1 + 1 = 0$]. We don't know how to express α in terms of real or complex numbers. We don't even know if this is possible. However, we also don't "know" what $\sqrt{-1}$ is; it also cannot be expressed in terms of elements of "simpler" fields. We simply accept the "existence" of $\sqrt{-1}$ and use it to perform calculations. In much the same way, we can accept the existence of α and use it to denote elements of finite fields.

The entire finite field $GF(2^2)$ can now be constructed as the 4-tuple $(0, 1, \alpha, \alpha^2)$. Clearly, elements 0 and 1 are needed; they are the identities for the two operations. Elements α and α^2 complete the field because higher powers of α reduce to 1, α, or α^2.

B.2 Polynomial Arithmetic

This section describes the four arithmetic operations on polynomials, especially division, which is needed to compute one polynomial modulo another.

Polynomial Addition/Subtraction. Adding two polynomials is done by adding corresponding coefficients. Thus, adding $P(x) = \sum_0^{m-1} a_i x_i$ and $Q(x) = \sum_0^{n-1} b_i x_i$ is done by adding $(a_i + b_i)$. Subtraction is done similarly by subtracting the coefficients (subtraction is defined over the reals, but in general, a field has only addition and multiplication defined). A simple example is the sum $(5x^2 + 3x - 2) + (-x^3 + x^2 + 7)$ which over the reals equals $-x^3 + 6x^2 + 3x + 5$. It is clear that the degree of the polynomial sum is $\max(m, n)$.

Polynomial Multiplication. Multiplying two polynomials P and Q is done by multiplying every coefficient a_i in P by every coefficient b_j in Q. A simple example serves to make this clear

$$(x^3 - 3x + 4)(-x^2 + 2x + 1)$$
$$= x^3(-x^2 + 2x + 1) - 3x(-x^2 + 2x + 1) + 4(-x^2 + 2x + 1)$$
$$= (-x^5 + 2x^4 + x^3) + (3x^3 - 6x^2 - 3x) + (-4x^2 + 8x + 4)$$
$$= -x^5 + 2x^4 + 4x^3 - 10x^2 + 5x + 4.$$

The degree of the product polynomial is the sum of the degrees of the multiplied polynomials. [Notice that this example is done over the reals. When done over a different field, the rules may be different. When polynomials are multiplied over GF(2), for example, the arithmetic rule $1 + 1 = 0$ applies.]

Polynomial Division. Dividing two integers produces a quotient and a remainder. If m and n are integers, then $m \bmod n$ is the remainder of the integer division $m \div n$ and is therefore in the range $[0, n - 1]$. Similarly, if P and Q are polynomials, then the polynomial division $P \div Q$ produces a quotient polynomial and a remainder polynomial. The latter is denoted by $P \bmod Q$, and its degree is less than that of Q. We illustrate polynomial division with an example. We use the compact notation $(8, 5, 4, 1, 0)$ for the polynomial $x^8 + x^5 + x^4 + x + 1$ and show the steps of dividing $P = (13, 11, 9, 8, 6, 5, 4, 3, 0)$ by $Q = (8, 4, 3, 1, 0)$.

Step 1: Divide x^{13}/x^8 to obtain x^5. This is the highest term of the quotient polynomial.

Step 2: Multiply $(5) \times (8, 4, 3, 1, 0)$ to obtain $(13, 9, 8, 6, 5)$.

Step 3: Add modulo 2 (i.e., XOR) $(13, 11, 9, 8, 6, 5, 4, 3, 0)$ and $(13, 9, 8, 6, 5)$ to obtain $(11, 4, 3, 0)$. Repeat the three steps for this polynomial.

Step 4: Divide x^{11}/x^8 to obtain x^3. This is the second term of the quotient polynomial.

Step 5: Multiply $(3) \times (8, 4, 3, 1, 0)$ to obtain $(11, 7, 6, 4, 3)$.

Step 6: XOR $(11, 4, 3, 0)$ and $(11, 7, 6, 4, 3)$ to obtain $(7, 6, 0)$. This is the final result $P \bmod Q$, since the next step would have to divide x^7 by x^8.

> In Galois Fields, full of flowers
> primitive elements dance for hours
> climbing sequentially through the trees
> and shouting occasional parities.
> The syndromes like ghosts in the misty damp
> feed the smoldering fires of the Berlekamp
> and high flying exponents sometimes are downed
> on the jagged peaks of the Gilbert bound.
>
> —S. B. Weinstein, *IEEE Transactions on Information Theory* (1971)

⋄ **Exercise B.11:** Compute the three polynomial divisions (quotients and remainders) $(x^5 + x^2 + x + 1)/(x^2 + 1)$, $(x^5 + x^2 + 1)/(x^2 + 1)$, and $(x^4 + x^3 + x)/(x^4 + 1)$. Consider the coefficients elements of GF(2) and add them modulo 2.

In expanding the field of knowledge we
but increase the horizon of ignorance.
—Henry Miller

Appendix C
Cyclic Redundancy Codes

The idea of a parity bit is simple, old, and familiar to most computer practitioners. A parity bit is the simplest type of error-detecting code. It adds reliability to a group of bits by making it possible for hardware or software to detect certain errors that occur when the group is stored in memory, is written on a disk, or is transmitted over communication lines between computers. A single parity bit does not make the group absolutely reliable. There are certain errors that cannot be detected with a parity bit, but experience shows that even a single parity bit can make data transmission reliable in most practical cases.

The parity bit is computed from a group of $n-1$ bits and then added to the group, making it n bits long. A common example is a 7-bit ASCII code that becomes 8 bits long after a parity bit is added. The parity bit p is computed by counting the number of ones in the original group, and setting p to complete that number to either odd or even. The former is called *odd parity* and the latter is *even parity*. Instead of counting the number of ones, odd parity can be computed as the exclusive OR (XOR) of the $n-1$ data bits.

Examples: Given the group of seven bits 1010111, the number of ones is 5, which is odd. Assuming odd parity, the value of p should be 0, leaving the total number of 1s odd. Similarly, the group 1010101 has four 1s, so its odd parity bit should also be a 1, bringing the total number of 1s to five.

Imagine a block of data where the most significant bit (MSB) of each byte is an odd parity bit, and the bytes are written vertically (Table C.1a).

When this block is read from a disk or is received by a modem, it may contain transmission errors, errors that have been caused by imperfect hardware or by electrical interference during transmission. We can think of the parity bits as *horizontal reliability*. When the block is read, the hardware can check every byte, verifying the parity. This is done by simply counting the number of ones in the byte. If this number is odd, the

(a)	(b)	(c)	(d)
1 01101001	1 01101001	1 01101001	1 01101001
0 00001011	0 00001011	0 00001011	0 00001011
0 11110010	0 11010010	0 11010110	0 11010110
0 01101110	0 01101110	0 01101110	0 01101110
1 11101101	1 11101101	1 11101101	1 11101101
1 01001110	1 01001110	1 01001110	1 01001110
0 11101001	0 11101001	0 11101001	0 11101001
1 11010111	1 11010111	1 11010111	1 11010111
			0 00011100

Table C.1: Horizontal and Vertical Parities.

hardware assumes that the byte is good. This assumption is not always correct, since two bits may get corrupted during transmission (Table C.1c). A single parity bit is thus useful (Table C.1b) but does not provide full error-detection capability.

A simple way to increase the reliability of a block of data is to compute vertical parities. The block is considered to be eight vertical columns, and an odd parity bit is computed for each column (Table C.1d). If two bits in one byte get corrupted, the horizontal parity will not detect the error, but two of the vertical parity bits will. Even the vertical bits do not provide complete error-detection capability, but they are a simple way to significantly improve data reliability.

Vertical parity is the simplest example of a CRC. CRC stands for Cyclical Redundancy Check (or Cyclical Redundancy Code). It is a rule that specifies how to compute the vertical check bits (they are now called *check bits*, not just simple parity bits) from all the bits of the data. Here is how CRC-32 is computed (CRC-32 is one of the many standards developed by the CCITT). The block of data is written as one long binary number. In our example, this will be the 64-bit number

101101001|000001011|011110010|001101110|111101101|101001110|011101001|111010111.

The individual bits are considered the coefficients of a *polynomial*. In our example, this will be the degree-63 polynomial

$$P(x) = 1 \times x^{63} + 0 \times x^{62} + 1 \times x^{61} + 1 \times x^{60} + \cdots + 1 \times x^2 + 1 \times x^1 + 1 \times x^0$$
$$= x^{63} + x^{61} + x^{60} + \cdots + x^2 + x + 1.$$

This polynomial is then divided by the standard CRC-32 *generating polynomial*

$$\mathrm{CRC}_{32}(x) = x^{32} + x^{26} + x^{23} + x^{22} + x^{16} + x^{12} + x^{11} + x^{10} + x^8 + x^7 + x^5 + x^4 + x^2 + x^1 + 1.$$

When an integer M is divided by an integer N, the result is a quotient Q (which is irrelevant for CRC) and a remainder R, which is in the interval $[0, N-1]$. Similarly, when a high-degree polynomial $P(x)$ is divided by a degree-32 polynomial, the result is two polynomials: a quotient and a remainder. The remainder is a polynomial whose degree is in the range $[0, 31]$, implying that it has 32 coefficients, each a single bit. (If the degree of the remainder polynomial is less than 31, some of its leftmost coefficients are zeros.) Those 32 bits are the CRC-32 code, which is appended to the block of data as four bytes. As an example, the CRC-32 of a recent version of the file with the text of this Appendix is $586DE4FE_{16}$.

The CRC is sometimes called the *fingerprint* of the file. Of course, since it is a 32-bit number, there are only 2^{32} different CRCs. This number equals approximately 4.3 billion, so in principle there are different files with the same CRC, but in practice this is rare. The CRC is useful as an error-detecting code because it has the following properties.

1. Every bit in the data block is used to compute the CRC. This means that changing even one bit may produce a different CRC.
2. Even small changes in the data normally result in very different CRCs. Experience with CRC-32 shows that it is very rare that introducing errors in the data does not change the CRC.
3. Any histogram of CRC-32 values for different data blocks is flat (or very close to flat). For a given, nonmaliciously chosen data block, the probability of any of the 2^{32} possible CRCs being produced is practically the same.

Other common generating polynomials are $CRC_{12}(x) = x^{12} + x^3 + x + 1$ and $CRC_{16}(x) = x^{16} + x^{15} + x^2 + 1$. They generate the common CRC-12 and CRC-16 codes, which are 12 and 16 bits long, respectively.

> All motion is cyclic. It circulates to the limits of its possibilities and then returns to its starting point.
>
> —Robert Collier

Appendix D
Projects

The projects proposed here can serve either as extra work, voluntarily done by conscientious readers, or as class projects, assigned and graded by the instructor.

Chapter 1: Error-Control Codes

1. Construct a 1-bit error-correcting Hamming code for 16-bit codes ($m = 16$).

2. Investigate the reliability of voting codes when the data is copied five times. Repeat the analysis of Section 1.3 for five copies, identify the most probable case where the decoder makes the wrong decision, and compute the probability of that case.

3. Search the Internet and the professional literature for the error-control code used to protect data on DVDs.

Chapter 2: Check Digits For Error Detection

1. Find some ISBNs of books and compute the check digit of each.

2. Obtain software that prints barcodes, use it to print several barcodes, and then read these manually.

3. According to Hamming ([Hamming 86], p. 27) the two most common errors humans make, when keying numbers, dialing them, or reading and saying them, are transposing adjacent digits and changing a triplet of the form aab to abb. Select one of the check digit methods described in this chapter and try to estimate its reliability for the latter type of error.

4. In addition to American Express, other financial and travel organizations such as Barclays, Visa, Citibank, and Thomas Cook also issue travelers checks. Select one of them and find out how it computes its check digit.

5. Try to use mathematical induction to prove that there are $n!$ permutations of n objects.

Chapter 3: Statistical Methods

1. Figure 3.7 shows a Huffman code for the 26 letters. Use the figure to calculate the average size, entropy, and variance of this code.

2. Repeat Exercise 3.10 for another short string of your choice.

3. Search the Internet for a free source code of an arithmetic codec (a good place to start is [faqs 04]) and adapt it to run on your computer.

4. Facsimile compression (Section 3.7) is vulnerable to transmission errors because it uses no error-control codes. Redesign this standard to use a simple error-correcting code, such as the SEC-DED code (Section 1.9). Implement your design and demonstrate its error-correcting capabilities by sending data between computers and artificially corrupting some bits.

Chapter 4: Dictionary Methods

1. Implement one of the dictionary compression methods of this chapter and explore its behavior for random data and data that's close to random. Specifically, find out whether random data is expanded when compressed by the algorithm.

2. The performance of the LZ77 method (Section 4.1) depends on the sizes of the search and look-ahead buffers. Implement this method and experiment with different sizes of these buffers. The point is to find the best sizes for your implementation.

3. This chapter describes only a few of the many dictionary-based compression methods currently known. Use a reference, such as [Salomon 04], to study more such methods.

Chapter 5: Image Compression

1. Use a text on statistics to familiarize yourself with the statistical concepts of variance, covariance, and correlation.

2. Use a Web search engine for images to locate continuous-tone and discrete-tone images on the Internet. In the latter type, identify those parts of the image (such as straight lines and flat planes) that are the hallmarks of a discrete-tone image.

3. Study the main color models, such as RGB, HLS, and CMYK, and how to convert a given color between them.

4. Write a program that takes a color image, separates its bitplanes and replaces the standard binary codes of the pixels in each bitplane with Gray codes (Section 14.2.1).

5. In a programming language of your choice, write a program, similar to the one of Figure 5.8, that rotates the pixels of an image and computes their distributions before and after the rotation.

Chapter 6: Basic Concepts of Cryptography

1. Search the cryptographic literature for encryption methods whose supposed security turned out to be an illusion.

2. Search the Web for private and government organizations involved with secure codes.

Chapter 7: Monoalphabetic Substitution Ciphers

1. In a programming language of your choice, write a program to input several text files and compute tables of digram and trigram frequencies.

2. Implement homophonic substitution codes based on the ideas of Exercise 7.6.

3. Search the Internet and the professional literature for monoalphabetic substitution ciphers not described in this chapter.

4. Implement one of the methods described in this chapter, use it to encrypt a large text file and then try to manually break the code with letter frequencies and by applying your knowledge of the language.

Chapter 8: Transposition Ciphers

1. Implement the substitution–transposition combined cipher proposed at the start of Section 8.6.

2. Design a 12×12 turning template with 36 holes and use it to encrypt long messages.

3. Implement the book method proposed on page 237 without the use of computers. Have some friends agree on a book and a formula and have each compute a new key every day for a week. Finally, compare the keys to see how robust this method is.

Chapter 9: Polyalphabetic Substitution Ciphers

1. Use a reference such as [Salomon 03] to study the traditional methods for breaking the Vigenère cipher.

2. Complete Table 9.1 to include every digram.

3. Use wood or cardboard to construct the encryption device of Figure 9.2b.

4. Implement the variation on the Vigenère cipher described in Section 9.6.

Chapter 10: Stream Ciphers

1. Implement one of the nonlinear stream ciphers described in Section 10.4.

2. Implement the SEAL stream cipher of Section 10.8. This algorithm makes extensive use of the 32-bit hexadecimal constant `000007fc`, so part of your task is to test it with various other constants to find out whether the output is sensitive to this constant (different constants will produce different outputs, but the point is that some constants may produce nonrandom output).

3. (For those with interest in and access to hardware construction.) Construct the generators proposed in Exercises 10.7 and 10.8.

4. Section 10.7 discusses the Latin square combiner. Consult [Ritter 04] for the details of this method and implement it.

Chapter 11: Block Ciphers

1. Implement DES or obtain it from the Internet and experiment with weak keys. Encrypt a block of data with a weak key and then try to break that code.

2. Use the many cryptographic resources available on the Internet, as well as new books on cryptography, to study block ciphers not included in this chapter, such as AES (Rijndael) and IDEA.

Chapter 12: Public-Key Cryptography

1.   Virtually all public-key encryption software uses the RSA algorithm, but other algorithms exist that employ the concept of asymmetric key. Locate resources for the Rabin and El Gamal methods and study them.

2. Study and implement a digital signature algorithm that uses the Diffie–Hellman–Merkle key exchange method. See, for example, the excellent site [Savard 03] for a description.

3. Implement one of the threshold schemes of Section 12.5 for sharing secrets and use it in practice, sharing secrets with friends.

Chapter 13: Data Hiding

1. Examine several of the methods described in this chapter and the next one. For each method, evaluate its embedding capacity, invisibility, undetectability, and robustness.

2. Use the resources available in [WatermarkingWorld 03] (such as FAQs, books, and links) to study methods for watermarking and how they can be defeated.

3. Use the source code in [Wayner 02] to implement a simple version of mimic functions following the basics of this method, described in Section 13.8.

Chapter 14: Data Hiding in Images

1.   Implement the eight variants of LSB Encoding (Section 14.1) and evaluate the embedding capacity, invisibility, undetectability, and robustness of each.

2. Study the technique of Section 14.1.1 for hiding data in a color lookup table and apply it to the BMP graphics file format. For two current references for this useful format, see [Miano 99] and [Swan 93].

3. Search the Internet for new techniques for the lossless hiding of secret data in images.

4. The Patchwork method of Section 14.5 is based on slightly changing the brightness values of many pixels. Write a program that converts an image from RGB to a luminance–chrominance color space such as YCbCr and then changes the brightness of certain regions by a certain amount, specified by the user. Experiment with this program on a group of friends to find out the maximum amount of brightness change that's still undetected by most persons.

5. The Zhao–Koch Method (Section 14.14) is based on partitioning the image into blocks of 8×8 pixels each and hiding one bit in each block by modifying the pixels of the block, if necessary. Implement this method and make the block size a user-controlled parameter. Experiment with different block sizes to find the strengths and weaknesses of small blocks and large blocks.

6. Project 4 of Chapter 3 is about implementing the fax compression standard with parity bits for added reliability. The present project asks you to implement the same method with the features discussed in Section 14.18 for data hiding.

Chapter 15: Data Hiding: Other Methods

1. Search the professional literature for new algorithms to hide data in other than text or image files.

2. Implement the steganographic file system as described in Section 15.7. Use this implementation to actually hide files on your computer, and demonstrate the usefulness of such a system to friends.

> But my grandmother had been obliged to abandon this project, at the instance of my father who knew, whenever she organised any expedition with a view to extracting from it the utmost intellectual benefit that it was capable of yielding, what a tale there would be to tell of missed trains, lost luggage, sore throats and broken rules.
>
> —Marcel Proust, *Within a Budding Grove* (1921)

Answers to Exercises

> If there's some magic in this world, it must be
> in the attempt of understanding someone else,
> sharing something. Even if it's almost impossible
> to succeed, but who cares, the answer must be in
> the attempt.
>
> —Julie Delpy as Celine in *Before Sunrise* (1995)

1.1: Bribe, gibe, glib, jibe, kibe, vibe, brie, babe, bab, bleb, lobe, blob, lube, blue, blub, lice, bide, life, like, bike, bile, lime, line, bine, blin, blip, lire, bise, bite, live, belie, bible, libre, libel, bribee, bribed, briber, bribes, and bolide.

1.2: The case where p is large, say 0.9, $n = 2$, and $j = 1$. In this case, $p^j = 0.9$ and $(1 - p)^{n-j} = 0.1$. Including the term $(1 - p)^{n-j}$ in this case is important, since it reduces the probability to one-tenth the size of p^j.

1.3: The receiver for the $(7, 1)$ voting code makes the wrong decision when a set of seven bits that should be identical features 4, 5, 6, or 7 bad bits. The probability of this happening is

$$p_e = P_4 + P_5 + P_6 + P_7 = {}^7C_4 p^4 (1 - p)^3 + {}^7C_5 p^5 (1 - p)^2 + {}^7C_6 p^6 (1 - p) + {}^7C_7 p^7.$$

Substituting $p = 0.01$ yields $p_e = 3.4 \times 10^{-7}$, implying that, on average, one error in every $1/(3.4 \times 10^{-7}) \approx 2.94 \times 10^6$ bits sent will not be detected and corrected. This should be compared to one undetected bad bit in every 100 without the voting code.

1.4: Adding check bits makes the codewords longer, so they require more storage space and take longer to transmit. The key to data reliability is a tradeoff between the size of a codeword and its efficiency (the number of errors it can detect and/or correct).

1.5:   This code has a Hamming distance of 4, and one way of generating it is to duplicate $code_3$.

1.6:   It is identical to the Hamming code for a set of 256 symbols, except that information bit b_{12} is not needed.

1.7:   Only codes that require information bit b_{17} and higher. The smallest such code has the 12 information bits b_3, b_5, b_6, b_7, b_9, b_{10}, b_{11}, b_{12}, b_{13}, b_{14}, b_{15}, and b_{17}. It can therefore code a set of $2^{12} = 4{,}096$ symbols.

1.8:   Append five artificial segments with data bits of zero and parity bits that will be determined by the data bits of segment n.

1.9:   Figure Ans.1 (compare with Figure 15.3) shows a simple, uniform wave sampled at precisely twice its frequency. It's easy to see that all the samples are identical, so playing them back generates a fixed signal, very different from the original wave.

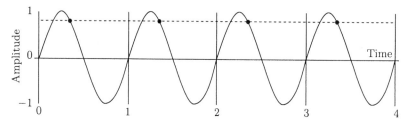

Figure Ans.1: A Wrong Sampling Rate.

1.10:   A general parabola can be expressed by its standard equation $c_1 x^2 + c_2 x + c_3 y + c_4 = 0$ or by its alternate equation $c_1 y^2 + c_2 x + c_3 y + c_4 = 0$. Given the three points (x_1, y_1), (x_2, y_2), and (x_3, y_3), the two equations of the unique parabola passing through them are computed by solving the determinant equations

$$\begin{vmatrix} x^2 & x & y & 1 \\ x_1^2 & x_1 & y_1 & 1 \\ x_2^2 & x_2 & y_2 & 1 \\ x_3^2 & x_3 & y_3 & 1 \end{vmatrix} = 0, \qquad \begin{vmatrix} y^2 & x & y & 1 \\ y_1^2 & x_1 & y_1 & 1 \\ y_2^2 & x_2 & y_2 & 1 \\ y_3^2 & x_3 & y_3 & 1 \end{vmatrix} = 0.$$

1.11:   This is straightforward and Table Ans.2 lists the 14 codes.

0000000	1111111
1000110	0111001
1110000	0001111
0011100	1100011
0100101	1011010
1001001	0110110
0010011	1101100
0101010	1010101

Table Ans.2: Fourteen Codes With Hamming Distance 3.

2.1: Given the 2-digit decimal integer $A = d_1 d_2$, a possible choice for n is 9. Given $A = 49$, it is easy to compute $T = (4 + 9) \bmod 9 = 4$ and $C = 9 - 4 = 5$. However, the number 40 also satisfies $T = (4 + 0) \bmod 9 = 4$, so it has the same check digit 5. Thus, an error that corrupts 49 to 40 will not be detected. This check digit is therefore not very reliable for reasons that have to do with 9 not being a prime number (this is explained in the text).

2.2: A Web search yields few results. Among them is
Joseph Muscat, *Maltese Ports (1400–1800)*, Pubblikazzjonijiet Indipendenza, Malta 2002, ISBN 99932-41-29-6. Price LM3 (3 Maltese lira).

2.3: A bit is a base-2 digit and there are two such digits, 0 and 1. Similarly, a trit is a base-3 digit, so there are three such digits, 0, 1, and 2. Imagine a 3-digit number $d_3 d_2 d_1$, where the digits are trits and the check digit is computed by $T = 3d_3 + 2d_2 + d_1 \bmod 4$ and $I = 4 - T$. Since the base 4 is a multiple of the weight 2, it is easy to come up with $3 \cdot 2 + 2 \cdot 0 + 2 \bmod 4 = 0$ and also $3 \cdot 2 + 2 \cdot 2 + 2 \bmod 4 = 0$. Thus, the two numbers 202 and 222 have the same check digit.

2.4: The answer is trivial, so let's check the effect of 7 as a weight. Using 7 in addition to 1 and 3 doesn't improve the UPC check digit much. If two adjacent digits d_i and d_{i+1} are assigned weights of 3 and 7, then swapping them alters T by $4(d_i - d_{i+1})$, which equals 20 whenever the difference $|d_i - d_{i+1}|$ is 5. Similarly, if two adjacent digits d_i and d_{i+1} are assigned weights of 1 and 7, then swapping them alters T by $6(d_i - d_{i+1})$, which equals 30 whenever the difference $|d_i - d_{i+1}|$ is 5.

2.5: This is 9781579550080 (*A New Kind of Science*, by Stephen Wolfram).

2.6: Either use three bar sizes (but this may lead to more errors in reading the bars) or use six bars in a group. With two long and four short bars, there can be $\binom{6}{2} = \binom{6}{4} = 15$ groups.

2.7: Perhaps the simplest proof of this is by induction.

2.8: The explicit representation of σ is

$$\begin{pmatrix} 0\ 1\ 2\ 3\ 4\ 5\ 6\ 7\ 8\ 9 \\ 1\ 2\ 4\ 6\ 8\ 1\ 3\ 5\ 7\ 9 \end{pmatrix}.$$

2.9: This product can be written as $p = d \times 10^i = d \times 2^i \times 5^i$ where d is a digit and 2 and 5 are primes. The prime 97 is therefore not any of the prime factors of p, so p is not a multiple of 97.

3.1: The unary code satisfies the prefix property, so it can be used as a variable-size code. Moreover, the length of the unary code of the integer n is n bits, so it makes sense to use it in cases where the input data consists of integers n with probabilities $P(n) \approx 2^{-n}$. If the data lends itself to the use of the unary code, there is no need to execute the Huffman algorithm, and the codes of all the symbols can easily and quickly be constructed as unary codes before compression or decompression starts.

3.2: Figure Ans.3a,b,c shows the three trees. The code sizes (in bits per symbol) for the trees are

$$(5 + 5 + 5 + 5 \cdot 2 + 3 \cdot 3 + 3 \cdot 5 + 3 \cdot 5 + 12)/30 = 76/30,$$
$$(5 + 5 + 4 + 4 \cdot 2 + 4 \cdot 3 + 3 \cdot 5 + 3 \cdot 5 + 12)/30 = 76/30,$$
$$(6 + 6 + 5 + 4 \cdot 2 + 3 \cdot 3 + 3 \cdot 5 + 3 \cdot 5 + 12)/30 = 76/30.$$

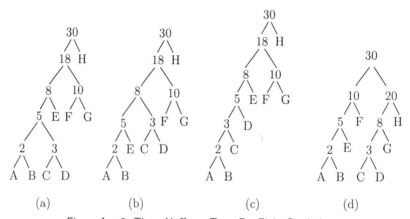

Figure Ans.3: Three Huffman Trees For Eight Symbols.

3.3: After adding symbols A, B, C, D, E, F, and G to the tree, we were left with the three symbols ABEF (with probability 10/30), CDG (with probability 8/30), and H (with probability 12/30). The two symbols with lowest probabilities were ABEF and CDG, so they had to be merged. Instead, symbols CDG and H were merged, creating a non-Huffman tree.

3.4: The second row of Table 3.6 corresponds to a symbol whose Huffman code is three bits long, but for which $\lceil -\log_2 0.3 \rceil = \lceil 1.737 \rceil = 2$.

3.5: The size of the Huffman code of a symbol a_i depends just on the symbol's probability P_i. This probability, however, depends indirectly on the size of the alphabet. In a large alphabet, symbol probabilities tend to be small numbers, so Huffman codes are long. In a small alphabet, the situation is the opposite. This can also be understood intuitively. A small alphabet requires just a few codes, so they can all be short; a large alphabet requires many codes, so some must be long.

3.6: Figure Ans.4 shows Huffman codes for 5, 6, 7, and 8 symbols with equal probabilities. In the case where n is a power of 2, the codes are simply the fixed-size ones. In other cases the codes are very close to fixed-size. This shows that symbols with equal probabilities do not benefit from variable-size codes. (This is another way of saying that random text cannot be compressed.) Table Ans.5 shows the codes and their average sizes and variances.

3.7: The number of groups increases exponentially from 2^s to $2^{s+n} = 2^s \times 2^n$.

3.8: The binary value of 127 is 01111111 and that of 128 is 10000000. Half the pixels in each bitplane will therefore be 0 and the other half 1. In the worst case, each bitplane will be a checkerboard, i.e., will have many runs of size one. In such a case, each run requires a 1-bit code, leading to one codebit per pixel per bitplane, or eight codebits per pixel for the entire image, resulting in no compression at all. In comparison, a Huffman code for such an image requires just two codes (since there are just two pixel values) and they can be 1 bit each. This leads to one codebit per pixel, or a compression factor of eight.

3.9: A symbol with high frequency of occurrence should be assigned a shorter code and should therefore appear high in the tree. The requirement that at each level the frequencies be sorted from left to right is arbitrary. In principle it is not necessary, but it simplifies the process of updating the tree.

3.10: Figure Ans.6 shows the initial tree and how it is updated in the 11 steps (a) through (k). Notice how the *esc* symbol gets assigned different codes all the time, and how the different symbols move about in the tree and change their codes. Code 10, e.g., is the code of symbol "i" in steps (f) and (i) but is the code of "s" in steps (e) and (j). The code of a blank space is 011 in step (h) but 00 in step (k).

The final output is s0i00r100⎵1010000d011101000, a total of $5 \times 8 + 22 = 62$ bits. The compression ratio is thus $62/88 \approx 0.7$.

3.11: A typical fax machine scans lines that are about 8.2 inches wide (≈ 208 mm). A blank scan line produces 1,664 consecutive white pels, making this run length very common.

3.12: These codes are needed for cases such as example 4, where the run length is 64, 128, or any length for which a makeup code has been assigned.

3.13: Currently, there is no need for codes for longer runs. However, there may be fax machines (now or in the future) built for wider paper, so the Group 3 code was designed to accommodate them.

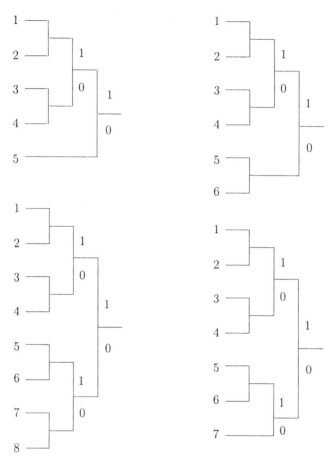

Figure Ans.4: Huffman Codes for Equal Probabilities.

n	p	a_1	a_2	a_3	a_4	a_5	a_6	a_7	a_8	Avg. size	Var.
5	0.200	111	110	101	100	0				2.6	0.64
6	0.167	111	110	101	100	01	00			2.672	0.2227
7	0.143	111	110	101	100	011	010	00		2.86	0.1226
8	0.125	111	110	101	100	011	010	001	000	3	0

Table Ans.5: Huffman Codes for 5–8 Symbols.

Initial tree

(a) Input: s. Output: 's'.
$esc\, s_1$

(b) Input: i. Output: 0'i'.
$esc\, i_1\, 1\, s_1$

(c) Input: r. Output: 00'r'.
$esc\, r_1\, 1\, i_1\, 2\, s_1 \rightarrow$
$esc\, r_1\, 1\, i_1\, s_1\, 2$

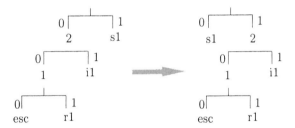

(d) Input: ␣. Output: 100'␣'.
$esc_{␣1}\, 1\, r_1\, 2\, i_1\, s_1\, 3 \rightarrow$
$esc_{␣1}\, 1\, r_1\, s_1\, i_1\, 2\, 2$

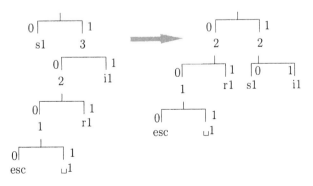

Figure Ans.6: Exercise 3.10. Adaptive Huffman Example: Part I.

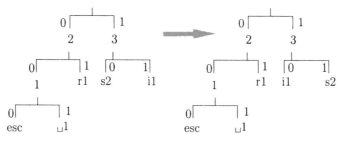

(e) Input: s. Output: 10.
$esc_{\sqcup 1}\, 1\, r_1\, s_2\, i_1\, 2\, 3 \rightarrow$
$esc_{\sqcup 1}\, 1\, r_1\, i_1\, s_2\, 2\, 3$

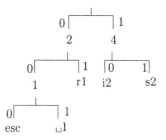

(f) Input: i. Output: 10.
$esc_{\sqcup 1}\, 1\, r_1\, i_2\, s_2\, 2\, 4$

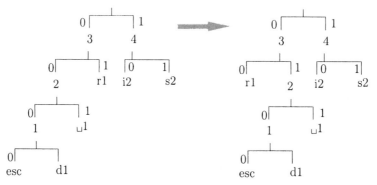

(g) Input: d. Output: 000'd'.
$esc\, d_1\, 1_{\sqcup 1}\, 2\, r_1\, i_2\, s_2\, 3\, 4 \rightarrow$
$esc\, d_1\, 1_{\sqcup 1}\, r_1\, 2\, i_2\, s_2\, 3\, 4$

Figure Ans.6: Exercise 3.10. Adaptive Huffman Example: Part II.

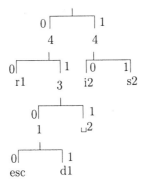
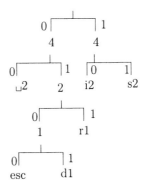

(h) Input: ␣. Output: 011.

$esc\, d_1\, 1\, ␣_2\, r_1\, 3\, i_2\, s_2\, 4\, 4 \rightarrow$
$esc\, d_1\, 1\, r_1\, ␣_2\, 2\, i_2\, s_2\, 4\, 4$

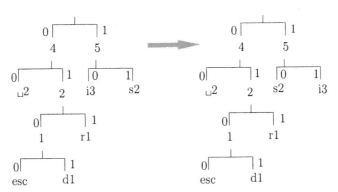

(i) Input: i. Output: 10.

$esc\, d_1\, 1\, r_1\, ␣_2\, 2\, i_3\, s_2\, 4\, 5 \rightarrow$
$esc\, d_1\, 1\, r_1\, ␣_2\, 2\, s_2\, i_3\, 4\, 5$

Figure Ans.6: Exercise 3.10. Adaptive Huffman Example: Part III.

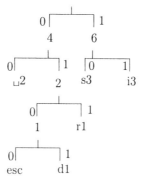

(j) Input: s. Output: 10.
$esc\, d_1\, 1\, r_1\, {\sqcup}2\, 2\, s_3\, i_3\, 4\, 6$

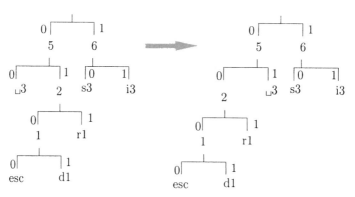

(k) Input: $\sqcup$. Output: 00.
$esc\, d_1\, 1\, r_1\, {\sqcup}3\, 2\, s_3\, i_3\, 5\, 6 \rightarrow$
$esc\, d_1\, 1\, r_1\, 2\, {\sqcup}3\, s_3\, i_3\, 5\, 6$

Figure Ans.6: Exercise 3.10. Adaptive Huffman Example: Part IV.

3.14: The codes of Table 3.18 have to satisfy the prefix property in each column but not between the columns. This is because each scan line starts with a white pel, so when the decoder inputs the next code, it knows whether it is for a run of white or black pels.

3.15: The code of a run length of one white pel is 000111 and that of one black pel is 010. Two consecutive pels of different colors are therefore coded into nine bits. Since the uncoded data requires just two bits (01 or 10), the compression ratio is $9/2 = 4.5$ (the compressed stream is 4.5 times longer than the uncompressed one—a significant expansion).

3.16: Figure Ans.7 shows the modes and the actual code generated from the two lines.

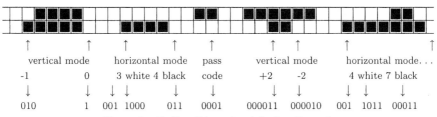

↑	↑	↑	↑	↑		↑	↑	↑	↑
vertical mode		horizontal mode		pass		vertical mode		horizontal mode...	
-1	0	3 white 4 black		code		+2	-2	4 white 7 black	
↓	↓	↓ ↓		↓		↓	↓	↓ ↓	↓
010	1	001 1000	011	0001		000011	000010	001 1011	00011

Figure Ans.7: Two-Dimensional Coding Example

3.17: Table Ans.8 shows the steps of encoding the string $a_2a_2a_2a_2$. Because of the high probability of a_2, the low and high variables start at very different values and approach each other slowly.

a_2 $\quad\quad\quad\quad 0.0 + (1.0 - 0.0) \times 0.023162 = 0.023162$
$\quad\quad\quad\quad\quad\quad 0.0 + (1.0 - 0.0) \times 0.998162 = 0.998162$
a_2 $\quad\quad\quad\quad 0.023162 + .975 \times 0.023162 = 0.04574495$
$\quad\quad\quad\quad\quad\quad 0.023162 + .975 \times 0.998162 = 0.99636995$
a_2 $\quad\quad 0.04574495 + 0.950625 \times 0.023162 = 0.06776322625$
$\quad\quad\quad\quad 0.04574495 + 0.950625 \times 0.998162 = 0.99462270125$
a_2 $\quad 0.06776322625 + 0.926859375 \times 0.023162 = 0.08923124309375$
$\quad\quad 0.06776322625 + 0.926859375 \times 0.998162 = 0.99291913371875$

Table Ans.8: Encoding the String $a_2a_2a_2a_2$.

3.18: It can be written either as 0.1000... or 0.0111... .

3.19: In principle, the eof symbol has to be included in the original table of frequencies and probabilities. This symbol is the last to be encoded, and decoding it serves as a signal for the decoder to stop.

3.20:   The encoding steps are simple (see first example on page 96). We start with the interval $[0, 1)$. The first symbol a_2 reduces the interval to $[0.4, 0.9)$, the second one to $[0.6, 0.85)$, the third one to $[0.7, 0.825)$, and the eof symbol to $[0.8125, 0.8250)$. The approximate binary values of the last interval are 0.1101000000 and 0.1101001100, so we select the 7-bit number 1101000 as our code.

The probability of the string "$a_2a_2a_2$eof" is $.(0.5)^3 \times 0.1 = 0.0125$, but since $-\log_2 0.125 \approx 6.322$, it follows that the theoretical minimum code size is 7 bits.

4.1:   The size of the output file is $N[48 - 28P] = N[48 - 25.2] = 22.8N$. The size of the input file is, as before, $40N$. The compression factor in such a case is $40/22.8 \approx 1.75$.

4.2:   The decoder doesn't know whether the encoder has selected the first match or the last match, but the point is that the decoder does not need to have this information! The decoder simply reads tokens and uses each offset to locate a string of text in the search buffer without having to know whether the string was a first or a last match.

4.3:   The next step matches the space and encodes the string ␣e,

sir␣sid	␣eastman␣easily␣	$\Rightarrow$ (4,1,e)
sir␣sid␣e	astman␣easily␣te	$\Rightarrow$ (0,0,a)

and the next one matches nothing and encodes the **a**.

4.4:   This is straightforward. The resulting steps are listed in Table Ans.9.

Dictionary		Token	Dictionary		Token
15	␣t	(4, t)	21	␣si	(19,i)
16	e	(0, e)	22	c	(0, c)
17	as	(8, s)	23	k	(0, k)
18	es	(16,s)	24	␣se	(19,e)
19	␣s	(4, s)	25	al	(8, 1)
20	ea	(4, a)	26	s(eof)	(1, (eof))

Table Ans.9: Next 12 Encoding Steps in LZ78.

4.5:   Table Ans.10 summarizes the steps. The output emitted by the encoder is

97 (a), 108 (l), 102 (f), 32 (␣), 101 (e), 97 (a), 116 (t), 115 (s), 32 (␣), 256 (al), 102 (f), 265 (alf), 97 (a),

and the following new entries are added to the dictionary:

(256: al), (257: lf), (258: f), (259: ␣e), (260: ea), (261: at), (262: ts), (263: s), (264: ␣a), (265: alf), (266: fa), (267: alfa).

I	in dict?	new entry	output	I	in dict?	new entry	output
a	Y			s	N	263-s	115 (s)
al	N	256-al	97 (a)	␣	Y		
l	Y			␣a	N	264-␣a	32 (␣)
lf	N	257-lf	108 (l)	a	Y		
f	Y			al	Y		
f	N	258-f	102 (f)	alf	N	265-alf	256 (al)
␣	Y			f	Y		
␣e	N	259-␣e	32 (w)	fa	N	266-fa	102 (f)
e	Y			a	Y		
ea	N	260-ea	101 (e)	al	Y		
a	Y			alf	Y		
at	N	261-at	97 (a)	alfa	N	267-alfa	265 (alf)
t	Y			a	Y		
ts	N	262-ts	116 (t)	a,eof	N		97 (a)
s	Y						

Table Ans.10: LZW Encoding of alf␣eats␣alfalfa.

4.6: The encoder inputs the first a into I, searches, and finds a in the dictionary. It inputs the next a but finds that Ix, which is now aa, is not in the dictionary. The encoder therefore adds string aa to the dictionary as entry 256 and outputs the token 97 (a). Variable I is initialized to the second a. The third a is input, so Ix is the string aa, which is now in the dictionary. I becomes this string, and the fourth a is input. Ix is now aaa, which is not in the dictionary. The encoder therefore adds string aaa to the dictionary as entry 257 and outputs 256 (aa). I is initialized to the fourth a. Continuing this process is straightforward.

The result is that strings aa, aaa, aaaa,... are added to the dictionary as entries 256, 257, 258,..., and the output is

$$97 \text{ (a)}, 256 \text{ (aa)}, 257 \text{ (aaa)}, 258 \text{ (aaaa)},\dots.$$

The output consists of pointers pointing to longer and longer strings of a's. Thus, the first k pointers point at strings whose total length is $1 + 2 + \cdots + k = (k + k^2)/2$.

Assuming an input file that consists of 1 million a's, we can find the size of the compressed output file by solving the quadratic equation $(k + k^2)/2 = 1000000$ for the unknown k. The solution is $k \approx 1414$. The original 8-million-bit input is thus compressed into 1414 pointers, each at least 9 bits (and in practice, probably 16 bits) long. The compression factor is thus either $8M/(1414 \times 9) \approx 628.6$ or $8M/(1414 \times 16) \approx 353.6$.

This is an impressive result, but such input files are rare (notice that this particular input can best be compressed by generating an output file containing just "1000000 a" and without using LZW).

4.7: We simply follow the decoding steps described in the text. The results are as follows:

1. Input 97. This is in the dictionary so set I=a and output a. String ax needs to be saved in the dictionary but x is still unknown..

2. Input 108. This is in the dictionary, so set J=l and output l. Save al in entry 256. Set I=l.

3. Input 102. This is in the dictionary, so set J=f and output f. Save lf in entry 257. Set I=f.

4. Input 32. This is in the dictionary, so set J=␣ and output ␣. Save f␣ in entry 258. Set I=␣.

5. Input 101. This is in the dictionary, so set J=e and output e. Save ␣e in entry 259. Set I=e.

6. Input 97. This is in the dictionary, so set J=a and output a. Save ea in entry 260. Set I=a.

7. Input 116. This is in the dictionary, so set J=t and output t. Save at in entry 261. Set I=t.

8. Input 115. This is in the dictionary, so set J=s and output s. Save ts in entry 262. Set I=t.

9. Input 32. This is in the dictionary, so set J=␣ and output ␣. Save s␣ in entry 263. Set I=␣.

10. Input 256. This is in the dictionary, so set J=al and output al. Save ␣a in entry 264. Set I=al.

11. Input 102. This is in the dictionary, so set J=f and output f. Save alf in entry 265. Set I=f.

12. Input 265. This has just been saved in the dictionary, so set J=alf and output alf. Save fa in dictionary entry 266. Set I=alf.

13. Input 97. This is in the dictionary, so set J=a and output a. Save alfa in entry 267 (even though it will never be used). Set I=a.

14. Read eof. Stop.

4.8: We assume that the dictionary is initialized to just the two entries (1: a) and (2: b). The encoder outputs

  1 (a), 2 (b), 3 (ab), 5(aba), 4(ba), 7 (bab), 6 (abab), 9 (ababa), 8 (baba),...

and adds the new entries (3: ab), (4: ba), (5: aba), (6: abab), (7: bab), (8: baba), (9: ababa), (10: ababab), (11: babab),...to the dictionary. This behavior is regular, so it can easily be analyzed and the kth output pointer and dictionary entry predicted, but the results are not worth the effort required.

4.9: The answer to Exercise 4.6 illustrates the relation between the size of the compressed file and the size of the largest dictionary string for the "worst case" situation (input that creates the longest strings). For a 1 Mbyte input stream, there will be 1,414 strings in the dictionary, the largest of which is 1,414 symbols long.

5.1: No. An image with no redundancy is not necessarily random. Page 60 discusses two types of image redundancy, the more important of which is pixel correlation. In rare cases, an image may have little or no correlation between its pixels and yet be nonrandom and even interesting.

5.2:   Figure Ans.11 shows two 32×32 matrices. The first one, a, has random (and therefore decorrelated) values and the second one, b, is its inverse (and therefore with correlated values). Their covariance matrices are also shown, and it is obvious that matrix $\mathrm{cov}(a)$ is close to diagonal (the off-diagonal elements are zero or close to zero), whereas matrix $\mathrm{cov}(b)$ is far from diagonal. The Matlab code for this figure is also included.

5.3:   No. If pixel values are in the range $[0, 255]$, a difference $(P_i - Q_i)$ can be at most 255. The worst case is where all the differences are 255. It is easy to see that such a case yields an RMSE of 255.

5.4:   The code of Figure 5.9 yields the coordinates of the rotated points

$$(7.071, 0),\ (9.19, 0.7071),\ (17.9, 0.78),\ (33.9, 1.41),\ (43.13, -2.12)$$

(notice how all the y coordinates are small numbers) and shows that the cross-correlation drops from 1729.72 before the rotation to -23.0846 after it. A significant reduction!

5.5:   The *Mathematica* code of Figure Ans.12 produces the 8 DCT coefficients 140, -71, 0, -7, 0, -2, 0, and 0. They are quantized to 140, -71, 0, 0, 0, 0, 0, and 0, to which the IDCT is applied. The result is 15, 20, 30, 43, 56, 69, 79, and 84. These are close to the original values, with a maximum difference of 4. Figure Ans.12 lists *Mathematica* code for this example.

```
Clear[Pixl, G, Gq, RecP];
Cr[i_]:=If[i==0, Sqrt[2]/2, 1];
DCT[i_]:={(1/2)Cr[i]Sum[Pixl[[x+1]]Cos[(2x+1)i Pi/16], {x,0,7,1}]};
IDCT[x_]:={(1/2)Sum[Cr[i]Gq[[i+1]]Cos[(2x+1)i Pi/16], {i,0,7,1}]};
Pixl={11,22,33,44,55,66,77,88};
G=Table[SetAccuracy[N[DCT[m]],0], {m,0,7}]
Gq={140.,-71,.0,0,0,0,0,0};
RecP=Table[SetAccuracy[N[IDCT[m]],0], {m,0,7}]
```

Figure Ans.12: Mathematica Code for One-Dimensional DCT Example.

5.6:   Looking at Figure 5.16, it is obvious that the block can be represented as a linear combination of the 8×8 patterns in the leftmost column of the figure. These eight transform coefficients will therefore be the only nonzero ones among the 64 coefficients. The actual calculation yields the eight weights 4, 0.72, 0, 0.85, 0, 1.27, 0, and 3.62 for the patterns of this column.

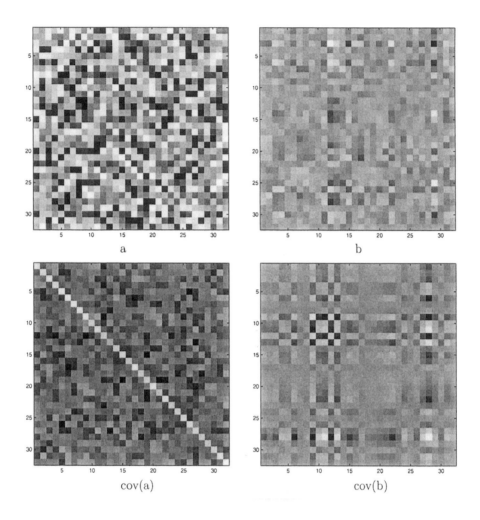

```
a=rand(32); b=inv(a);
figure(1), imagesc(a), colormap(gray); axis square
figure(2), imagesc(b), colormap(gray); axis square
figure(3), imagesc(cov(a)), colormap(gray); axis square
figure(4), imagesc(cov(b)), colormap(gray); axis square
```

Figure Ans.11: Covariance Matrices of Correlated and Decorrelated Values.

5.7: Figure Ans.13a is a uniform 8×8 image with one diagonal line above the main diagonal. Figure Ans.13b,c shows the first two steps in its pyramid decomposition. It is obvious that the transform coefficients in the bottom right subband (HH) indicate a diagonal artifact located above the main diagonal. It is also easy to see that subband LL is a low-resolution version of the original image.

12 16 12 12 12 12 12 12	14 12 12 12	4 0 0 0	13 13 12 12	2 2 0 0
12 12 16 12 12 12 12 12	12 14 12 12	0 4 0 0	12 13 13 12	0 2 2 0
12 12 12 16 12 12 12 12	12 14 12 12	0 4 0 0	12 12 13 13	0 0 2 2
12 12 12 12 16 12 12 12	12 12 14 12	0 0 4 0	12 12 12 13	0 0 0 2
12 12 12 12 12 16 12 12	12 12 14 12	0 0 4 0	2 2 0 0	4 4 0 0
12 12 12 12 12 12 16 12	12 12 12 14	0 0 0 4	0 2 2 0	0 4 4 0
12 12 12 12 12 12 12 16	12 12 12 14	0 0 0 4	0 0 2 2	0 0 4 4
12 12 12 12 12 12 12 12	12 12 12 12	0 0 0 0	0 0 0 2	0 0 0 4
(a)	(b)		(c)	

Figure Ans.13: The Subband Decomposition of a Diagonal Line.

5.8: This is shown by multiplying the largest n-bit number, $\underbrace{11\ldots1}_{n}$, by 4, which is easily done by shifting it two positions to the left. The result is the $n+2$-bit number $\underbrace{11\ldots1}_{n}00$.

5.9: The zigzag sequence of these coefficients is $1118, 2, 0, -2, \underbrace{0,\ldots,0}_{13}, -1, \underbrace{0,\ldots,0}_{46}$.

5.10: Perhaps the simplest approach is to manually figure out the zigzag path and to record it in an array **zz** of structures, where each structure contains a pair of coordinates for the path as shown, for example, in Figure Ans.14.

(0,0)	(0,1)	(1,0)	(2,0)	(1,1)	(0,2)	(0,3)	(1,2)
(2,1)	(3,0)	(4,0)	(3,1)	(2,2)	(1,3)	(0,4)	(0,5)
(1,4)	(2,3)	(3,2)	(4,1)	(5,0)	(6,0)	(5,1)	(4,2)
(3,3)	(2,4)	(1,5)	(0,6)	(0,7)	(1,6)	(2,5)	(3,4)
(4,3)	(5,2)	(6,1)	(7,0)	(7,1)	(6,2)	(5,3)	(4,4)
(3,5)	(2,6)	(1,7)	(2,7)	(3,6)	(4,5)	(5,4)	(6,3)
(7,2)	(7,3)	(6,4)	(5,5)	(4,6)	(3,7)	(4,7)	(5,6)
(6,5)	(7,4)	(7,5)	(6,6)	(5,7)	(6,7)	(7,6)	(7,7)

Figure Ans.14: Coordinates for the Zigzag Path.

If the two components of a structure are `zz.r` and `zz.c`, then the zigzag traversal can be done by a loop of the form

```
for (i=0; i<64; i++){
row:=zz[i].r; col:=zz[i].c
...data_unit[row][col]...}
```

5.11: The third DC difference, 5, is located in row 3, column 5, so it is encoded as 1110|101.

5.12: Thirteen consecutive zeros precede this coefficient, so $Z = 13$. The coefficient itself is found in Table 5.32 in row 1 column 0, so $R = 1$ and $C = 0$. Assuming that the Huffman code in position $(R, Z) = (1, 13)$ of Table 5.33 is 1110101, the final code emitted for 1 is 1110101|0.

6.1: We know that m can be one of the 12 numbers 1, 3, 5, 7, 9, 11, 15, 17, 19, 21, 23, and 25. These numbers are of the form $2n + 1$ for certain nonnegative integers n, but $m = 2n + 1$ implies $(m - 1)/2 = n$, so $(m - 1)/2$ is a nonnegative integer. From this we conclude that

$$13m \bmod 26 = (13 + 13(m - 1)) \bmod 26 = \left(13 + 26\frac{m-1}{2}\right) \bmod 26$$
$$= (13 + 26n) \bmod 26 = 13.$$

We therefore conclude that any multiplicative cipher transforms "n" into "N."

6.2: For $m = 1$, there are 25 such keys, because $a = 0$ is the only value that results in a fixed point. For the 11 values $m > 1$, odd values of a result in no fixed points. There are 13 such values, so the total number of no-fixed-point affine ciphers is $25 + 11 \times 13 = 168$.

To see why odd values of a have this property, we observe that a fixed point, i.e., the case $x = x \cdot m + a \bmod 26$, is equivalent to $x(m - 1) = -a \bmod 26$. Since m is relatively prime to 26, it is odd, implying that $m - 1$, and therefore also the left-hand side, $x(m - 1)$, is even. In order for a solution to exist, the right-hand side must also be even. If the right-hand side (i.e., a) is odd, there are no solutions to the fixed-point equation $x = x \cdot m + a \bmod 26$, so there are no fixed-point ciphers for those keys.

6.3: The inverse of $y = x \cdot 23 + 7 \bmod 126$ is

$$x = 23^{-1}(y - 7) \bmod 126$$
$$= 23^{-1} \bmod 126(y - 7) \bmod 126$$
$$= 11(y - 7) \bmod 126$$
$$= 11y - 77 \bmod 126$$
$$= 11y + 49 \bmod 126.$$

6.4:   The number of 64-bit keys is $2^{64} = 18,446,744,073,709,551,620$ or approximately 1.8×10^{19}. The following examples illustrate the magnitude of this key space.

1. 2^{64} seconds equal $584,942,417,355$ years.

2. The unit of electrical current is the Ampere. One Ampere is defined as 6.24×10^{18} electrons per second. Even this huge number is smaller than 2^{64}.

3. Even light, traveling (in vacuum) at $299,792,458$ m/s, takes $61,531,714,963$ seconds (about $1,951$ years) to cover 2^{64} meters. This distance is therefore about 1951 light years.

4. In a fast, 5 GHz computer, the clock ticks five billion times per second. In one year, the clock ticks $5 \cdot 10^9 \cdot (3 \cdot 10^7) = 1.5 \cdot 10^{17}$ times.

5. The mass of the sun is roughly $2 \cdot 10^{31}$ kg and the mass of a single proton is approximately $1.67 \cdot 10^{-27}$ kg. There are therefore approximately 10^{58} protons in the sun. This number is about 2^{193}, so searching a keyspace of 193 bits is equivalent to trying to find a single proton in the sun (ignoring the fact that all protons are identical and that the sun is hot). The proverbial "needle in a haystack" problem pales in comparison.

6. The term *femto*, derived from the Danish *femten*, meaning *fifteen*, stands for 10^{-15}. Thus, a femtometer is 10^{-15} m, and a cubic femtometer is 10^{-45} cubic meters, an incredibly small unit of volume. A light year is 10^{16} meters, so assuming that the universe is a sphere of radius 15 billion light years, its volume is $(4/3)\pi(15 \times 10^9 \times 10^{16})^3 = 1.41372 \times 10^{79}$ cubic meters or about 10^{124} cubic femtometers. This is roughly 2^{411}, so searching a keyspace of 411 bits is like trying to locate a particular cubic femtometer in the entire universe.

These examples illustrate the power of large numbers and should convince any rational person that breaking a code by searching the entire key space is an illusion. As for the claim that "there is a chance that the first key tried will be the right one," for a 64-bit keyspace this chance is 2^{-64}. To get a feeling for how small this number is, consider that light travels 1.6×10^{-11} meters (about the size of 10 atoms laid side by side) in 2^{-64} seconds.

7.1:   Regardless of the particular monoalphabetic cipher used, once the ciphertext is ready, a computer counts the number of times each symbol appears and appends random symbols to the ciphertext such that each symbol appears the same number of times. Thus, if the most common symbol occurs 768 times in the ciphertext and symbol A appears 269 times, the random text will include $768 - 269 = 499$ occurrences of A. The process of deciphering results in the plaintext, followed by random gibberish that can easily be identified and discarded.

7.2:   For tables of digrams and trigrams in English and other languages, see [Gaines 56].

7.3:   Figure Ans.15 illustrates such an alternative. The 26 letters are placed in a 5×5 grid (where I and J share the same place), where each grid location can be described by horizontal and vertical segments and an optional dot.

7.4:   Follow each letter in the key `polybiuscher` with its first successor that is still not included in the key. Thus, p should be followed by q and o should be followed by p,

A	B	C	D	E
F	G	Ḣ	IJ	K
L	·M	N	O·	P
Q.	R	Ṣ	T.	U
V	W	X	Y	Z

Figure Ans.15: A Variant Of The Pigpen Cipher.

but because p is already included in the key (as are q, r, and s), the o is followed by t. This process produces first the 22-letter string `pqotlmyzbcikuvswhnefrx` which is then extended in the same way to become the 25-letter string `paqdogtlmyzbcikuvswhnefrx`.

7.5: FO → MF, LX → PU, LO → SM, WM → HL, EX → NE, EA → AT, YX → ZY. The ciphertext is FOLLOWMEEARLY → MFPUSMHLNEATZY.

7.6: The simplest choice is to use 3-digit numbers, where the leftmost digit is 0 or 1. Thus the numbers are 000 through 199. A more sophisticated approach selects 200 binary prefix codes (Section 3.3) and assigns the short codes to the common letters.

7.7: An integer N in the range $[a, b]$ can be converted to an integer in the range $[c, d]$ by the transformation

$$\text{round}\left((N - a)\frac{d - c}{b - a} + c\right).$$

A simpler method is to use a generator that generates random real numbers R in the range $[0, 1]$. For each R, the value $\lfloor 12 \times R \rfloor$ is examined. If it is in the right range (in the interval $[1, 3]$ for a D), then it is used; otherwise, another random R is generated and examined.

8.1: A space-filling curve completely fills up a square (or, in general, part of a multi-dimensional space) by passing through every point in it. It does this by changing direction repeatedly. Figure Ans.16a–c shows examples of the well-known Hilbert, Sierpiński, and Peano curves. It is obvious that any square can be completely scanned by such a curve. Each space-filling curve is defined recursively and can be refined to fill a square grid of any size.

8.2: Collection can be done by diagonals, zigzags, or a spiral, as suggested by Figure 8.3. Collecting the plaintext of Figure 8.5 by diagonals from top right to bottom left results in the ciphertext BEJAIDHOCGNRFKQMPL. (See also Exercise 8.1.) There are, of course, many other ways to scan a square, such as going down the first column, up the second column, and alternating in this way.

8.3: After removing the spaces, the string is cut in two equal parts WAITFORMEA and TMIDNIGHT, that are interlaced to form the ciphertext WtAmIiTdFnOiRgMhEtA (where the lowercase letters make it easy to recognize symbols from the second half).

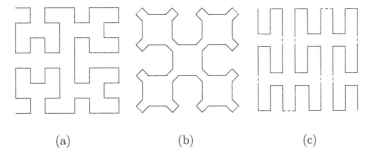

Figure Ans.16: The Hilbert, Sierpiński, and Peano Curves.

8.4: A transposition method encrypts by a permutation, and the result of two consecutive permutations is another permutation. Thus, just combining several transposition methods does not, by itself, increase security. A combination of transposition ciphers may be more secure than any of its individual methods if the methods being combined use keys. A combination of several methods requires several keys, and the security provided by such a combination may be equivalent to that provided by a long key. Also, combining a transposition method and a substitution method (as in Section 8.6) may result in improved encryption.

8.5: This is trivial. The Caesar shift of one position results in the simple permutation

abcdefghijklmnopqrstuvwxyz

BCDEFGHIJKLMNOPQRSTUVWXYZA

which obviously has one cycle.

8.6: The three groups are BFIKMRV03, DLNQU2579, and GJOSXZ148.

8.7: In an 8×8 template there should be $8 \cdot 8/4 = 16$ holes. The template is written as four 4×4 small templates, and each of the 16 holes can be selected in four ways. The total number of hole configurations is therefore $4^{16} = 4{,}294{,}967{,}296$.

8.8: The letter D is the fourth one in the alphabet, implying that the template size should be 4×4. Of its 16 squares, only $16/4 = 4$ should be holes. The first four letters of the key are DOGO, so they produce the numeric string 1324. The resulting template is shown in Figure Ans.17.

Figure Ans.17: A 4×4 Turning Template.

8.9: For 12 November 2001, the weighted sum is

$$50 \cdot 1 + 51 \cdot 2 + 52 \cdot 1 + 53 \cdot 1 + 54 \cdot 0 + 55 \cdot 1 = 312$$

and 312 mod 190 = 122. Thus, the page number is 123.

8.10: The second key is six letters long, so the initial rectangle has six columns. The length of the ciphertext is 32 letters. The quotient of $32 \div 6$ is 5, so the rectangle has $5 + 1 = 6$ rows. The remainder is 2, so the first two columns are full (six rows each) and the remaining four columns have five rows each. The second key is TRIPLE, which corresponds to the numeric sequence 652431. The ciphertext starts with the 5-letter string thbnc that's written into the last column (whose number is 1). This column has just five rows. The ciphertext continues with the 5-letter string rtttn that is placed in the third column (the one labeled 2), and so on. After six steps, the rectangle looks like the one in Figure 8.10b, and a similar process ends up with the rectangle of Figure 8.10a. Reading this rectangle in rows yields the plaintext.

8.11: Two simple variations on AMSCO are shown in Figure Ans.18. They are easy to figure out. AMSCO has been named after its developer, A. M. Scott, so if your name is Claude Isaac Fairchild, you would name your cipher CIFAIR.

Q	U	A	L	I	T	Y		Q	U	A	L	I	T	Y
4	6	1	3	2	5	7		4	6	1	3	2	5	7
C	H	I	D	E	L	L		CO	M	EH	O	ME	I	MM
OM	OM	MM	IA	LY	LI	OS		D	IA	T	EL	Y	AL	L
E	E	E	T	A	S	T		IS	L	OS	T			

Figure Ans.18: Two Variations on AMSCO.

9.1: Assume that the key is an integer with digits $d_1 d_2 \ldots d_k$. To encode plain symbol i, examine digit d_i. If it is in the interval $[0, 4]$, encode symbol i with cipher alphabet 1; otherwise, encode it with cipher alphabet 2. When plain symbol $k + 1$ is reached, go back to key digit d_1.

9.2: The first key letter, l, selects row 6, where c is replaced by U. The second key letter, o, selects row 8, where cipherletter H replaces plainletter o and vice versa.

9.3: We ignore the rightmost column for now. Without this column, the table consists of 27 rows, each a shifted copy of its predecessor. The bottom row is identical to the top row. This creates a table that is symmetric about the diagonal that starts at the bottom-left corner and goes toward the top-right corner. It is this symmetry that makes it easy to use the table. Because of this symmetry, we can either start on the left, slide to the right, stop, and slide up or we can start at the top, slide down, stop, and slide to the left, and end up at the same letter. The rightmost column is identical to the leftmost column and is added as the last step in the construction of the table.

9.4: A string of 26 letters specifies a permutation of the 26 letters because we can envision it written under the string `ab...z`. The idea is to find a permutation σ that doesn't equal any of the 25 powers $\sigma^2, \sigma^3, \ldots, \sigma^{26}$. The table whose rows are the powers from σ to σ^{26} will have 26 different rows and will be fully specified by σ, which is a string of 26 letters.

9.5: `BUT␣WILL␣SHE␣DECRYPT␣MORE␣AFGHAN` is another good key. It is short and easy to memorize, and it produces the 20-letter string `BUTWILSHEDCRYPMOAFGN`. Appending the six remaining letters `JKQVXZ` to this string results in the permutation

```
abcdefghijklmnopqrstuvwxyz
BUTSHEWILDCRYPMOAFGNJKQVXZ
```

9.6: The four integers relatively prime to 8 are 1, 3, 5, and 7. They generate the following permutations:

$$\begin{pmatrix} a\ b\ c\ d\ e\ f\ g\ h \\ a\ b\ c\ d\ e\ f\ g\ h \end{pmatrix} \quad \begin{pmatrix} a\ b\ c\ d\ e\ f\ g\ h \\ a\ d\ g\ b\ e\ h\ c\ f \end{pmatrix} \quad \begin{pmatrix} a\ b\ c\ d\ e\ f\ g\ h \\ a\ f\ c\ h\ e\ b\ g\ d \end{pmatrix} \quad \begin{pmatrix} a\ b\ c\ d\ e\ f\ g\ h \\ a\ h\ g\ f\ e\ d\ c\ b \end{pmatrix}.$$

9.7: Equation (9.5) implies

$$(1\times3-2\times0)^{-1} \begin{bmatrix} 3 & 0 \\ -2 & 1 \end{bmatrix} \bmod 26 = 9 \begin{bmatrix} 3 & 0 \\ -2 & 1 \end{bmatrix} \bmod 26 = \begin{bmatrix} 27 & 0 \\ -18 & 9 \end{bmatrix} \bmod 26 = \begin{bmatrix} 1 & 0 \\ 8 & 9 \end{bmatrix}.$$

9.8: Imagine a plaintext that's 38 letters long. The first 36 letters can easily be encrypted and decrypted. Encrypting the remaining two letters is also easy, but decrypting them must be done by examining 25 strings of ciphertext and selecting the one whose first two letters are the last two plainletters. This may be ambiguous. Interestingly enough, a purely numeric sequence may sometimes make sense as, for example, in 1984 1949, which may refer to the book *1984*, written in 1949.

9.9: The following table illustrates the idea of balanced codes.

```
ETAOINSHRDLUMWYFCGBPKVXQJZ
01234567890122109876543210
```

The digit 0 is assigned to the most common and also the least common letters, The 1 is assigned to the second most common and the second least common letters, and so on.

9.10: Yes, as is easy to see by examining the following examples (notice the two occurrences of 22 in the ciphertext and how they produce different plaintexts):

Plaintext	+	66	05	66	11	61
Key		66	66	22	11	66
Ciphertext		**22**	**61**	**88**	**22**	**27**

Ciphertext	−	**22**	**61**	**88**	**22**	**27**
Key		66	66	22	11	66
Plaintext		66	05	66	11	61

9.11: Each p_i in the sum $\sum_1^{26} p_i^2$ is a probability, so it lies in the interval $[0,1]$, implying that p_i^2 cannot be bigger than p_i. The sum $\sum_1^{26} p_i$ equals 1, so the sum $\sum_1^{26} p_i^2$ cannot exceed 1. On the other hand, this sum cannot be less than 0.038, as shown below, so this sum lies in the right interval and is therefore a probability.

In order to place the lower limit of 0.038 on our sum, we observe that

$$\sum_1^{26} \left(p_i - \frac{1}{26} \right)^2 = \sum_1^{26} p_i^2 - 2\sum_1^{26} \frac{p_i}{26} + \sum_1^{26} \frac{1}{26^2} = \sum_1^{26} p_i^2 - \frac{2}{26}\sum_1^{26} p_i + \frac{26}{26^2} = \sum_1^{26} p_i^2 - \frac{1}{26},$$

which implies that

$$\sum_1^{26} p_i^2 = \frac{1}{26} + \sum_1^{26} \left(p_i - \frac{1}{26} \right)^2 \geq \frac{1}{26} \approx 0.038.$$

10.1: The logical operation XNOR (the inverse of XOR, denoted by $\bar{\oplus}$) also has the property: If $B = A\oplus K$, then $A = B\bar{\oplus}K$.

10.2: We denote the ith bits of the plaintext, the keystream, and the ciphertext by d_i, k_i, and $c_i = d_i \oplus k_i$, respectively. We assume that the keystream is random, i.e., $P(k_i = 0) = 0.5$ and $P(k_i = 1) = 0.5$. The plaintext isn't random, so we assume that $P(d_i = 0) = p$, which implies $P(d_i = 1) = 1 - p$. Table Ans.19 summarizes the four possible cases of d_i and k_i and their probabilities. The values of c_i and their probabilities for those cases are also listed. It is easy to see from the table that the probability of c_i being 0 is $P(c_i = 0) = p/2 + (1 - p)/2 = 1/2$, and similarly $P(c_i = 1) = 1/2$. The ciphertext produced by the Vernam cipher is therefore random, which makes this simple method unbreakable.

d_i	$P(d_i)$	k_i	$P(k_i)$	c_i	$P(c_i)$
0	p	0	$1/2$	0	$p/2$
0	p	1	$1/2$	1	$p/2$
1	$1-p$	0	$1/2$	1	$(1-p)/2$
1	$1-p$	1	$1/2$	0	$(1-p)/2$

Table Ans.19: Truth Table of a Vernam Cipher.

10.3: The average word size in English is 4–5 letters. We therefore start by examining 4-letter words. There are 26 letters, so the number of combinations of 4 letters is $26^4 = 456,976$. A good English-language dictionary contains about 100,000 words. Assuming that half these words have 4 letters, the percentage of valid 4-letter words is $50000/26^4 \approx 0.11$. The percentage of 5-letter words is obtained similarly as $50000/26^5 \approx 0.004$. Random text may therefore have some short (2–4 letters) words, and very few 5–6 letter words, but longer words would be very rare.

10.4: Any 4-stage shift register where the rightmost stage is not a tap will serve. In such a shift register, the state 0001 is followed by 0000 regardless of which of the three left stages are taps.

10.5: The rightmost and leftmost stages of this shift register are taps. Therefore, a direct check produces the following 15-state sequence:

1000 1100 1110 1111 0111 1011 0101 1010 1101 0110 0011 1001 0100 0010 0001.

10.6: The truth table of a basic Boolean function with 2 inputs has 4 elements (Table 10.1), so there can be $2^4 = 16$ Boolean functions of 2 inputs. Similarly, the truth table of a Boolean function with n inputs has 2^n elements, so there can be 2^{2^n} such tables. For $n = 8$, for example, the (huge) number of Boolean functions is $2^{2^8} = 2^{256} \approx 1.16 \times 10^{77}$.

10.7: The output sequence of R_1 is the 7-bit repeating string 1001011. The output string of R_2 is the string 110101111000100 with a 15-bit period. The output of R_3 is the 31-bit periodic string 1001010110000111001101111101000. The final output is 10111010101000010111101100011110.

10.8: The output sequence of R_1 is the 7-bit periodic sequence 0011101. The output sequence of R_2 is the 31-bit sequence 1010000100101100111110001101110. The final output is 10000101111101110.

10.9: If location a of the table contains byte value a, then no special information is needed to construct the inverse table. It should be identical to the forward table.

11.1: The key is implicit in the particular table used. In the case of 3-bit blocks, for example, the table has 8 entries, so there can be 8! tables, and all the parties using this cipher have to agree upon which table to use.

11.2: Yes, if the cipher has enough rounds. In principle, it is possible to design a block cipher where each bit in the cipherblock is a function of all the bits of the plainblock.

11.3: The fact that an XOR is its own inverse is exploited. The XOR of $(A \oplus B)$ with B produces A.

11.4: The hexadecimal values of the four keys are

0101 0101 0101 0101, 1F1F 1F1F 0E0E 0E0E, E0E0 E0E0 F1F1 F1F1, FEFE FEFE FEFE FEFE.

12.1: When an encrypted message is sent by Alice to Bob, it can be intercepted by Eve and copied. When the key is later sent, Eve may intercept it and use it to decrypt the message.

12.2:   Mixing salt and pepper is a one-way operation in practice (in principle, they can be separated). Heat flow from high to low temperature in a closed system is a one-way process in principle. Giving birth is one-way in principle, while squeezing glue out of a tube is one-way in practice.

12.3:   This is a direct result of the properties of the modulo function. In step 3, Alice computes

$$\beta^a \bmod 13 = (5^b \bmod 13)^a \bmod 13 = 5^{b\cdot a} \bmod 13,$$

and Bob computes the identical expression

$$\alpha^b \bmod 13 = (5^a \bmod 13)^b \bmod 13 = 5^{a\cdot b} \bmod 13.$$

12.4:   The final key is computed, in step 3, as $L^{a\cdot b} \bmod P$ (or, identically, as $L^{b\cdot a} \bmod P$), so it is an integer in the range $[0, P-1]$. Thus, there are only P possible values for the key, which is why P should be large. If we allow values L greater than P, then a user may accidentally select an L that is a multiple of P, which results in a key of 0, thereby providing an eavesdropper with useful information. If P is a prime and if $L < P$, then P is not a prime factor of L^x, so $L^x \bmod P$ cannot be zero.

12.5:   We arbitrarily select $q = 10$ and the two slopes $a_1 = 1$ and $a_2 = 2$. The two lines passing through point $(5, 10)$ are computed by $10 = 1 \times 5 + b_1 \rightarrow b_1 = 5$ and $10 = 2 \times 5 + b_2 \rightarrow b_2 = 0$. Each of the two individuals involved receives one of the two pairs $(1, 5)$ and $(2, 0)$.

12.6:   Denoting the secret by a, we select a number b at random and consider (a, b) a line pair (i.e., a slope and a y-intercept). We then select n different random values x_i and compute a y_i for each by means of $y_i = ax_i + b$. The n pairs (x_i, y_i) are points on the line $y = ax + b$, and they are distributed to the n participants in the secret. Any two of them can use their two points to compute (a, b).

One restriction is that the slope a should not be zero. The line $y = 0x + b$ is a horizontal line where all the points have the same y-coordinate b. This does not mean that any participant will be able to obtain the secret a single-handedly (after all, they do not know that the line is horizontal), but it is cryptographically weak. Another restriction is that no point should have an x-coordinate of zero. If we know that point $(0, y_i)$ is on a line, then b can be obtained from the basic equation $y_i = a\cdot 0 + b$. This does not disclose the secret a, but it amounts to providing the opponent with a clue.

12.7:   We randomly select the two values $q = 1$ and $r = 2$ and compute three planes that pass through the point $(5, 1, 2)$. For the first plane, we select $A = 1$, $B = 2$, and $C = 3$, to obtain $D = -13$. For the second plane we randomly select $A = 0$, $B = 2$, and $C = -1$, and obtain $D = 0$. Similarly, we select for the third plane $A = 1$, $B = 0$, and $C = 2$, to obtain $D = -9$. The three quartets $(1, 2, 3, -13)$, $(0, 2, -1, 0)$ and $(1, 0, 2, -9)$ are handed to the three individuals. Point $(5, 1, 2)$ is obtained when the three simultaneous equations $x + 2y + 3z - 13D = 0$, $2y - z = 0$, and $x + 2z - 9 = 0$ are solved.

13.1:   Data can be compressed because its original representation has redundancies. Secret data can be embedded in a cover in "holes" that exist in the cover because of redundancies. Thus, redundancy plays a central role in both fields (as well as in error-correcting codes).

13.2:   Any phrase with the word *love* may indicate the letter N. Any phrase with a mention of speed may indicate the letter E, and any phrase including the name John may indicate a D. Thus, the text "Make haste. With love. John" indicates the word END.

13.3:   The check digit is zero because

$$0 \times 10 + 3 \times 9 + 8 \times 8 + 7 \times 7 + 9 \times 6 + 8 \times 5 + 6 \times 4 + 8 \times 3 + 2 \times 2 = 286 = 26 \times 11.$$

13.4:   The text "hidden letters will defy simple codebreaking" looks innocent. These six words have 2, 2, 1, 2, 2, and 3 syllables, respectively, thus hiding the two triplets 221 and 223.

13.5:   The data is "meet me at nine," hidden in the second letter of every word.

13.6:   A direct check reveals the bits 00d0dd0d0d0ddd01d0101dd, where d stands for *undefined*.

13.7:   An alternative solution is to have dictionary types with 2, 4, 8, 16, etc. words. If one bit remains to be hidden, a 2-word dictionary type is used to hide it regardless of the dictionary type that is specified by the current syntax rule for the next step.

13.8:   This is straightforward. The sentences are "Alice is sending clean data," "Alice is sending clean clothes," "Alice is sending dirty data," "Alice is sending dirty clothes," then the same four sentences with "Alice is receiving..." instead of "sending," and then eight more sentences with "Bob" instead of "Alice," for a total of 16 sentences.

14.1:   Use the same cover image only once. If two modified versions of the same image fall into the wrong hands, they may provide precious clues for the hiding algorithm.

14.2:   Select two images. Use any of the approaches to produce pixel indexes, and hide the odd-numbered data bits in the pixels of one image and the even-numbered data bits in the pixels of the other image. This idea can be extended to three or more images. In its extreme version, it employs many images (perhaps stored as a personal image gallery in the sender's Web site) and hides one bit in each image.

14.3:   The simplest method is to embed the data at the top of the image, then embed it again lower in the image, and so on, until the bottom of the image is reached. The decoder retrieves all the copies and compares them. The voting principle (Section 1.3) can be applied to correct errors. A slightly different approach is to use multiple images and hide one copy of the data in each image.

14.4:   The bitmap size for this case is $3 \times 2^{10} \times 2^{10} = 3 \times 2^{20} = 3$ Mbytes.

14.5:   The results are shown in Table Ans.20 together with the Matlab code used to calculate them.

43210	Gray	43210	Gray	43210	Gray	43210	Gray
00000	00000	01000	01100	10000	11000	11000	10100
00001	00001	01001	01101	10001	11001	11001	10101
00010	00011	01010	01111	10010	11011	11010	10111
00011	00010	01011	01110	10011	11010	11011	10110
00100	00110	01100	01010	10100	11110	11100	10010
00101	00111	01101	01011	10101	11111	11101	10011
00110	00101	01110	01001	10110	11101	11110	10001
00111	00100	01111	01000	10111	11100	11111	10000

Table Ans.20: First 32 Binary and Gray Codes.

```
a=linspace(0,31,32); b=bitshift(a,-1);
b=bitxor(a,b); dec2bin(b)
```

Code For Table Ans.20.

14.6:   The permutation $0 \leftrightarrow 2$, $1 \leftrightarrow 3$, up to $253 \leftrightarrow 255$.

14.7:   There are $\binom{m \cdot n}{2^r - 1}$ ways to choose $2^r - 1$ objects from a set of $m \cdot n$ objects. We can assign the integers from 1 to $2^r - 1$ to the first $2^r - 1$ elements of W, and this can be done in $(2^r - 1)!$ ways. We can then choose each of the remaining $m \cdot n - (2^r - 1)$ elements at random from the set of $(2^r - 1)$ valid integers, and this can be done in $(2^r - 1)^{m \cdot n - (2^r - 1)}$ ways. The total number of ways to choose matrix W is therefore

$$\binom{m \cdot n}{2^r - 1}(2^r - 1)!(2^r - 1)^{mn - (2^r - 1)}.$$

For $m = n = 8$ and $r = 5$, this number is

$$\binom{64}{31} \times 31! \times 31^{33} \approx 2.397 \cdot 10^{101},$$

too big to allow for a brute force approach where every possible W is checked.

15.1:   Each 0 would result in silence and each sample of 1 would result in the same tone. The result would be a nonuniform buzz. The amplitude is constant but the frequency varies. It is low when the sound contains long runs of zeros and ones.

15.2: The experiment should be repeated with several persons, preferably of different ages. The person should be placed in a sound-insulated chamber and a pure tone of frequency f should be played. The amplitude of the tone should be gradually increased from zero until the person can just barely hear it. If this happens at a decibel value d, point (d, f) should be plotted. This should be repeated for many frequencies until a graph similar to that in Figure 15.4a is obtained.

15.3: This is trivial. The filter coefficients are $h(0) = 1$ and $h(2) = \beta$. The combined signal is produced by $y(j) = x(j)h(0) + x(j-2)h(2)$.

15.4: By definition, F_2 has the value $K_2 \times \mathbf{C} = [0, 1, 1, 1, 0]\mathbf{C} = C_1 \oplus C_2 \oplus C_3 = 1010$. To change it to 1101, we need the difference vector $D = 1010 \oplus 1101 = 0111$. The computation described in the text yields

$$
\mathbf{C} = \mathbf{C} \oplus (K_2^t \times D) = \mathbf{C} \begin{bmatrix} 0 \\ 1 \\ 1 \\ 1 \\ 0 \end{bmatrix} [0, 1, 1, 1] = \begin{bmatrix} 0001 \\ 1000 \\ 0101 \\ 0111 \\ 0100 \end{bmatrix} \oplus \begin{bmatrix} 0000 \\ 0111 \\ 0111 \\ 0111 \\ 0000 \end{bmatrix} = \begin{bmatrix} 0001 \\ 1111 \\ 0010 \\ 0000 \\ 0100 \end{bmatrix} .
$$

A direct check verifies that the new value of F_2 is $K_2 \times \mathbf{C} = 1101$ and that the two older files $F_0 = K_0 \times \mathbf{C} = 1100$ and $F_1 = K_1 \times \mathbf{C} = 1110$ haven't changed. This result has been achieved because rows C_1, C_2, and C_3 of $\mathbf{C}$ were modified such that the XORs of any two of them have been preserved.

15.5: We assume that the probability of a 1-bit is greater than 0.5. Therefore, regardless of the size of the region, the bit configuration with the highest probability is that of all 1s. When the size of the region is odd, this configuration has an odd number of 1s, so it has a parity of 1 and thus contributes to the probability of interest, raising it above 0.5. For an even-sized region, this bit configuration has an even number of bits and so is not included in the probability we compute, resulting in low probability (below 0.5).

B.1: Since 5 is a prime, both addition and multiplication in GF(5) are done modulo 5. The tables are

+	0	1	2	3	4		×	0	1	2	3	4
0	0	1	2	3	4		0	0	0	0	0	0
1	1	2	3	4	0		1	0	1	2	3	4
2	2	3	4	0	1		2	0	2	4	1	3
3	3	4	0	1	2		3	0	3	1	4	2
4	4	0	1	2	3		4	0	4	3	2	1

B.2:   It is easy to add and multiply numbers modulo 4 and produce the tables

+	0 1 2 3		×	0 1 2 3
0	0 1 2 3		0	0 0 0 0
1	1 2 3 0		1	0 1 2 3
2	2 3 0 1		2	0 2 0 2
3	3 0 1 2		3	0 3 2 1

The multiplication table doesn't make sense, since 2×1 = 2×3 and 2×0 = 2×2. Elements 1 and 3 cannot be obtained by multiplying 2 by another element. Also, element 2 doesn't have a multiplicative inverse. This happens because 4 is not a prime and field element 2 is a factor of 4. Trying to define multiplication in GF(6) leads to similar results, because 2 and 3 are factors of 6.

B.3:   The additive inverse of a polynomial $a(x)$ is itself because the coefficients of the sum $a(x) + a(x)$ are either $0 + 0$ or $1 + 1 = 0$.

B.4:   It is easy to show that $x^8 + 1 = (x^4 + 1)^2$

$$(x^4 + 1)(x^4 + 1) = x^4 \times x^4 + x^4 \times 1 + 1 \times x^4 + 1 \times 1 = x^8 + x^4 \times (1 + 1) + 1 = x^8 + 1.$$

B.5:   GF(6) does not exist because 6 is not a prime and cannot be expressed as an integer power of a prime.

B.6:   We start with the product 2×2 in GF(4). In binary this is 10×10 and in polynomial notation it is $(x + 0)(x + 0)$. This equals x^2, and $x^2 \bmod (x^2 + x + 1)$ is the polynomial $x + 1$, which in our notation is 11_2 or 3. (See Section B.2 and especially Exercise B.11 for polynomial modulo computations.) Another example in GF(4) is the product 2×3, which is $x(x + 1) = x^2 + x$. When computed modulo $x^2 + x + 1$, the result is 1. The last example is the product 5×6 in GF(8). This is the polynomial product $(x^2 + 1)(x^2 + x)$. It equals $x^4 + x^3 + x^2 + x$, which when computed modulo $x^3 + x + 1$ yields a remainder of $x + 1$ or $011_2 = 3$.

B.7:   A look at Table B.1 shows that the additive inverse (in some sense it is the "negative") of each element is itself. The multiplicative inverses (reciprocals) of the seven nonzero elements are 1, 5, 6, 7, 2, 3, and 4. Notice that 0 does not have a reciprocal and may sometimes be considered its own inverse.

B.8:   The multiplication table of GF(5) (Exercise B.1) shows that the smallest n for which $3^n = 1$ is $n = 4 = 5 - 1$. Hence, the exponential representation of GF(5) with respect to 3 is $(0, 3, 3^2 = 4, 3^3 = 2, 3^4 = 1)$.

B.9:   This is easy. The multiplication table of GF(4) shows that the smallest n such that $2^n = 1$ is $3 = 4 - 1$, and the same is true for element 3.

B.10: Let α be any root of $x^4 + x^3 + 1$. From $\alpha^4 + \alpha^3 + 1 = 0$ we get $\alpha^4 = \alpha^3 + 1$ and the entire exponential representation of GF(16) can be constructed from this relation (Table Ans.21). Notice how the first four powers of α (elements 1, 2, 4, and 8) form a basis for the polynomial representation of GF(16).

expo. repr.		polynomial representation			expo. repr.		polynomial representation		
0	15	0	0000	0					
α^0	0	1	0001	1	α^8	8	$\alpha^2 + \alpha + 1$	0111	7
α^1	1	α	0010	2	α^9	9	$\alpha^2 + 1$	0101	5
α^2	2	α^2	0100	4	α^{10}	10	$\alpha^3 + \alpha$	1010	10
α^3	3	α^3	1000	8	α^{11}	11	$\alpha^3 + \alpha^2 + 1$	1101	13
α^4	4	$\alpha^3 + 1$	1001	9	α^{12}	12	$\alpha + 1$	0011	3
α^5	5	$\alpha^3 + \alpha + 1$	1011	11	α^{13}	13	$\alpha^2 + \alpha$	0110	6
α^6	6	$\alpha^3 + \alpha^2 + \alpha + 1$	1111	15	α^{14}	14	$\alpha^3 + \alpha^2$	1100	12
α^7	7	$\alpha^3 + \alpha^2 + \alpha$	1110	14	α^{15}	15	1	0001	1

Table Ans.21: Exponential and Polynomial Representations of GF(16).

The only exercise some people get is jumping to conclusions, running down their friends, side-stepping responsibility, and pushing their luck!

—Anonymous

B.11: A polynomial division can be summarized in a form similar to the long division of integers, so Figure Ans.22 employs this form to summarize the results of the three divisions. Figure Ans.22a shows a quotient of $(x^3 + x + 1)$ and a remainder (modulo) of 0. Figure Ans.22b has the same quotient and the modulo x. The quotient of Figure Ans.22c is 1 and the modulo is $(x^3 + x + 1)$.

$$
\begin{array}{r}
x^3 + x\ +1 \\
x^2+1\ \overline{\smash)x^5+x^2+x\ +1} \\
x^5+x^3 \\
\hline
x^3+x^2+x+1 \\
x^3+x \\
\hline
x^2+1 \\
x^2+1 \\
\hline
0
\end{array}
$$

(a)

$$
\begin{array}{r}
x^3 + x\ +1 \\
x^2+1\ \overline{\smash)x^5+x^2+1} \\
x^5+x^3 \\
\hline
x^3+x^2+1 \\
x^3+x \\
\hline
x^2+x+1 \\
x^2+1 \\
\hline
x
\end{array}
$$

(b)

$$
\begin{array}{r}
1 \\
x^4+1\ \overline{\smash)x^4+x^3+x} \\
x^4+1 \\
\hline
x^3+x+1
\end{array}
$$

(c)

Figure Ans.22: Three Polynomial Divisions.

Polynomial Division

If $f(x)$ and $d(x) \neq 0$ are polynomials, and the degree of $d(x)$ is less than or equal to the degree of $f(x)$, then there exist unique polynomials $q(x)$ and $r(x)$, such that

$$\frac{f(x)}{d(x)} = q(x) + \frac{r(x)}{d(x)}$$

and such that the degree of $r(x)$ is less than the degree of $d(x)$. In the special case where $r(x) = 0$, we say that $d(x)$ divides evenly into $f(x)$.

Those who think they have not time for bodily exercise
will sooner or later have to find time for illness.

—Edward Stanley,

Glossary

Adaptive compression.   A compression method that modifies its operations and/or its parameters according to new data read from the input stream. Examples are the adaptive Huffman method of Section 3.6 and the dictionary-based methods of Chapter 4. (See also Semiadaptive compression.)

Adversary.   The eavesdropper, the opponent, the enemy, or any other mischievous person who tries to compromise our security.

AES. Advanced Encryption Standard, adopted by NIST as a replacement for the DES.

Affine cipher.   The term *affine* refers to a linear function, a function of the form $f(x) = ax + b$, where b is nonzero. The affine cipher (in the Introduction) is an extension of the basic Caesar cipher, where a plainletter is multiplied by a key before the Caesar key is added to it. (See also Affine transformations, Caesar cipher.)

Affine transformations.   Two-dimensional or three-dimensional geometric transformations, such as scaling, reflection, rotation, and translation, that preserve parallel lines. (See also Affine cipher.)

Algorithm.   A mathematical procedure where a task is executed in a finite sequence of steps.

Alice.   A term for the first user of cryptography in discussions and examples. Bob's associate.

Alphabet. The set of all possible symbols in the input stream. In text compression the alphabet is normally the set of 128 ASCII codes. In image compression it is the set of values a pixel can take (2, 16, 256, or anything else). (See also Symbol.)

Anagram.   A word, phrase, or sentence formed from another by rearranging its letters: "erects" is an anagram of "secret."

In Bruce Schneier's definitive introductory text *Applied Cryptography* he introduces a table of dramatis personae headed by Alice and Bob. Others include Carol (a participant in three- and four-party protocols), Dave (a participant in four-party protocols), Eve (an eavesdropper), Mallory (a malicious active attacker), Trent (a trusted arbitrator), Walter (a warden), Peggy (a prover) and Victor (a verifier). These names for roles are either already standard or, given the wide popularity of the book, may be expected to quickly become so.

—The New Hacker's Dictionary, ver. 4.2.2

Arithmetic coding. A statistical compression method (Section 3.8) that assigns one (normally long) code to the entire input stream, instead of assigning codes to the individual symbols. The method reads the input stream symbol by symbol and appends more bits to the code each time a symbol is input and processed. Arithmetic coding is slow, but it compresses at or close to the entropy, even when the symbol probabilities are skewed. (See also Model of compression, Statistical methods.)

ASCII code. The standard character code on all modern computers (although Unicode is becoming a competitor). ASCII stands for American Standard Code for Information Interchange. It is a $(1 + 7)$-bit code, meaning 1 parity bit and 7 data bits per symbol. As a result, 128 symbols can be coded (see appendix in the book's Web page). They include the upper- and lowercase letters, the ten digits, some punctuation marks, and control characters. (See also Unicode.)

Asymmetric algorithm. A cryptographic algorithm where different keys are used for encryption and decryption. Most often a public-key algorithm.

Asymmetric key. A cryptographic technique where encryption and decryption use different keys.

Attack. An approach used by a codebreaker to decrypt encrypted data or to reveal hidden data. An attack may use brute force, where every key is tried, or a sophisticated approach such as differential cryptanalysis. An attacker may use only known ciphertext or known ciphertext and plaintext.

Authentication. The process of verifying that a particular name really belongs to a particular entity.

Authenticity. The ability to ensure that the given information was in fact produced by the entity whose name or identification it carries and that it was not forged or modified.

Back door. A feature in the design of an algorithm that permits those familiar with the feature to bypass the security of the algorithm. The term *trapdoor* refers to a similar feature.

Barcodes. A decimal code expressed as a combination of black and white bars of various widths. It employs a check digit for added reliability (see UPC and Section 2.2).

Bark. Unit of critical band rate. Named after Heinrich Georg Barkhausen and used in audio applications. The Bark scale is a nonlinear mapping of the frequency scale over the audio range, a mapping that matches the frequency selectivity of the human ear.

Bi-level image. An image whose pixels have two different colors. The colors are normally referred to as black and white, "foreground" and "background," or 1 and 0. (See also Bitplane.)

Bitplane. Each pixel in a digital image is represented by several bits. The set of all the kth bits of all the pixels in the image is the kth bitplane of the image. A bi-level image, for example, consists of two bitplanes. (See also Bi-level image.)

Bitrate. In general, the term *bitrate* refers to both bpb and bpc. In MPEG audio, however, this term is used to indicate the rate at which the compressed stream is read by the decoder. This rate depends on where the stream comes from (such as disk, communications channel, memory). If the bitrate of an MPEG audio file is, e.g., 128Kbps. then the encoder will convert each second of audio into 128K bits of compressed data, and the decoder will convert each group of 128K bits of compressed data into one second of sound. Lower bitrates mean smaller file sizes. However, as the bitrate decreases, the encoder must compress more audio data into fewer bits, eventually resulting in a noticeable loss of audio quality. For CD-quality audio, experience indicates that the best bitrates are in the range of 112Kbps to 160Kbps. (See also Bits/char.)

Bits/char. Bits per character (bpc). A measure of the performance in text compression. Also a measure of entropy. (See also Bitrate, Entropy.)

Bits/symbol. Bits per symbol. A general measure of compression performance.

Block cipher. A symmetric cipher that encrypts a message by breaking it down into blocks and encrypting each block. DES, IDEA, and AES are block ciphers.

Block coding. A general term for image compression methods that work by breaking the image into small blocks of pixels and encoding each block separately. JPEG (Section 5.9) is a good example, since it processes blocks of 8×8 pixels.

Block decomposition. A method for lossless compression of discrete-tone images. The method works by searching for, and locating, identical blocks of pixels. A copy B of a block A is compressed by preparing the height, width, and location (image coordinates) of A, and compressing those four numbers by means of Huffman codes. (See also Discrete-tone image.)

Block matching. A lossless image compression method based on the LZ77 sliding window method originally developed for text compression. (See also LZ methods.)

BMP. BMP is the native format for image files in the Microsoft Windows operating system. It has been modified several times since its inception but has remained stable from version 3 of Windows. BMP is a palette-based graphics file format for images with 1, 2, 4, 8, 16, 24, or 32 bitplanes. It uses a simple form of RLE to compress images with 4 or 8 bitplanes.

Bob. A term used for the second user in cryptographic discussions and examples. Alice's associate.

BPCS steganography. A sophisticated algorithm for hiding data bits in individual bitplanes of an image. (See Section 14.2.)

Caesar cipher. A cipher where each letter is replaced by the letter located cyclically n positions in front of it in the alphabet. (See also Affine cipher.)

Camouflage. A term in steganography. Any steganography method that hides a data file D in a cover file A by scrambling D and then appending it to A.

Check bits. Bits that are added to data to increase its redundancy and thus make it more reliable. Most check bits are parity bits, but in principle a check bit may be selected at random. (See also Parity bits.)

Check digit. An extra digit appended to an important number (such as a credit card number) that provides redundancy and can detect many common errors that may occur when the number is keyed, dialed, read, or pronounced. See Chapter 2.

Checksum. A numeric value used to verify the integrity of a block of data. (See CRC.)

Chrominance. Components of color. They represent color in terms of the presence or absence of blue (Cb) and red (Cr) for a given luminance intensity. (See also Luminance.)

Cipher. A key-based algorithm that transforms a message between plaintext and ciphertext. A cryptographic algorithm.

Ciphertext. Data after being encrypted with a cipher, as opposed to plaintext.

Circular queue. A basic data structure (Section 4.1.1) that moves data along an array in circular fashion, updating two pointers to point to the start and end of the data in the array.

Code (in cryptography). A cryptographic technique that uses a codebook to replace words and letters in the plaintext with symbols from the codebook.

Codec. A term used to refer to both encoder and decoder.

Codes. A code is a symbol that stands for another symbol. In computer and telecommunications applications, codes are virtually always binary numbers. The ASCII code is the de facto standard, although the new Unicode is used on several new computers and the older EBCDIC is still used on some old IBM computers. (See also ASCII, Code, Unicode.)

Combiner. A mechanism that mixes two data items into a single result. The XOR operation is a common combiner because it is reversible. Other examples are the Geffe generator and the summation generator. (See Latin square combiner, Geffe generator, and Section 10.4.)

Compact disc error control. A special version of the Reed–Solomon code design for use in a CD. (See Section 1.11 and Reed–Solomon codes.)

Compression factor. The inverse of compression ratio. It is defined as

$$\text{compression factor} = \frac{\text{size of the input stream}}{\text{size of the output stream}}.$$

Values greater than 1 mean compression, and values less than 1 imply expansion. (See also Compression ratio.)

Compression gain. This measure is defined as

$$100 \log_e \frac{\text{reference size}}{\text{compressed size}},$$

where the reference size is either the size of the input stream or the size of the compressed stream produced by some standard lossless compression method.

Compression ratio. One of several measures that are commonly used to express the efficiency of a compression method. It is the ratio

$$\text{compression ratio} = \frac{\text{size of the output stream}}{\text{size of the input stream}}.$$

A value of 0.6 means that the data occupies 60% of its original size after compression. Values greater than 1 mean an output stream bigger than the input stream (negative compression).

Sometimes the quantity $100 \times (1 - \text{compression ratio})$ is used to express the quality of compression. A value of 60 means that the output stream occupies 40% of its original size (or that the compression has resulted in a savings of 60%). (See also Compression factor.)

Confidentiality.   Ensuring that information is not disclosed to people who aren't authorized to receive it.

Confusion. The part of an encryption algorithm that modifies the correspondence between plain symbols and cipher symbols. (See also Diffusion.)

Context. The N symbols preceding the next symbol.   A context-based model uses context to assign probabilities to symbols.

Context-free grammar (CFG). A set of rewriting (or production) rules used to generate strings of various patterns. CFGs are used by the steganographic method *Mimic Functions* to generate innocuous text files that hide data. (See Mimic functions.)

Continuous-tone image. A digital image with a large number of colors such that adjacent image areas with colors that differ by just one unit appear to the eye as having continuously varying colors. An example is an image with 256 grayscale values. When adjacent pixels in such an image have consecutive gray levels, they appear to the eye as a continuous variation of the gray level. (See also Bi-level image, Discrete-tone image, Grayscale image.)

Correlation. A statistical measure of the linear relation between two paired variables. The values of R range from -1 (perfect negative relation) to 0 (no relation), to $+1$ (perfect positive relation).

Cover (in steganography). A piece of data in which another datum is hidden. Also known as a host, or a carrier.

CRC. An error-detecting code (Appendix C) based on polynomial operations. It is appended to a block of data to increase its error-detection and correction capabilities. (See Checksum.)

The CRC result is an excellent (but linear) hash value corresponding to the data. Compared with other hash alternatives, CRCs are simple and straightforward. They are well understood. They have a strong and complete basis in mathematics, so there can be no surprises. CRC error-detection is mathematically tractable and provable without recourse to unproven assumptions. Such is not the case for most cryptographic hash constructions.

Cryptanalysis. The science and art of breaking encryption (recovering plaintext from ciphertext when the key is unknown).

Cryptanalyst. One who tries to break encrypted codes.

Cryptographer. One who develops encryption methods.

Cryptography. The art and science of using mathematics to obscure the meaning of data by applying transformations to the data that are impractical or impossible to reverse without the knowledge of some key. The term comes from the Greek for "hidden writing."

Cryptology. The branch of mathematics concerned with secret writing in all its forms. It includes cryptography, cryptanalysis, and steganography.

Indiman drew from a locked drawer in the big centre-table the long strip of bluish paper covered with its incomprehensible dashes. "One of the oldest of devices for secret writing," he remarked. "This slip of paper was originally wrapped about a cylinder of a certain diameter and the message traced upon it, and it can only be deciphered by rerolling it upon another cylinder of the same diameter. Easy enough to find the right one by the empiric method—I mean experiment. Once you recognize the fundamental character of the cryptogram the rest follows with ridiculous certainty. Behold!"

—Van Tassel Sutphen, *The Gates of Chance*

Cryptoperiod. The amount of time a particular key is used. Sometimes refers to the amount of data encrypted with it.

Cryptosystem. An encryption and decryption algorithm (cipher), together with all its possible plaintexts, ciphertexts, and keys.

Data encryption standard (DES). A block cipher based on the work of Horst Feistel in the 1970s that is widely used in commercial systems. DES is a 64-bit block cipher with a 56-bit key organized in 16 rounds of operations.

Data hiding. See Steganography.

Data key. A cryptographic key that encrypts data, as opposed to a key that encrypts other keys. Also called a session key.

Decibel. A logarithmic measure that can be used to measure any quantity that takes values over a very wide range. A common example is sound intensity. The intensity (amplitude) of sound can vary over a range of 11–12 orders of magnitude. Instead of using a linear measure, where numbers as small as 1 and as large as 10^{11} would be needed, a logarithmic scale is used, where the range of values is $[0, 11]$.

Decipher. To transform an encrypted message (ciphertext) back to the original message (plaintext).

Decode. To decipher.

Decoder. A decompression program (or algorithm).

Decryption. To extract encrypted data and make it readable. To decipher. (See also Decipher, Decode, Encryption.)

DES. See Data Encryption Standard.

Dictionary-based compression. Compression methods (Chapter 4) that save pieces of the data in a "dictionary" data structure (normally a tree). If a string of new data is identical to a piece already saved in the dictionary, a pointer to that piece is output to the compressed stream. (See also LZ methods.)

Differential cryptanalysis. A technique for attacking a cipher by feeding it carefully selected plaintext and watching for patterns in the ciphertext.

Diffie–Hellman (DH). A public-key cryptography algorithm that generates a shared secret key between two entities after they publicly share some randomly generated data.

Diffusion. An important principle of encryption. Changing one plain-symbol will change adjacent or nearby cipher-symbols. In a block cipher, diffusion propagates bit changes from one part of a block to other parts of the same block. Diffusion is achieved by mixing, and the step-by-step process of increasing diffusion is described as avalanche. (See also Confusion.)

Digital signature. Data value generated by a public-key algorithm based on the content of a block of data and on a private key. It generates an individualized checksum.

Digram. A pair of consecutive symbols.

Discrete cosine transform (DCT). A variant of the discrete Fourier transform (DFT) that produces just real numbers. The DCT (Sections 5.6.2 and 5.9.2) transforms a set of numbers by combining n numbers to become an n-dimensional point and rotating it in n-dimensions such that the first coordinate becomes dominant. The DCT and its inverse, the IDCT, are used in JPEG (Section 5.9) to compress an image with acceptable loss, by isolating the high-frequency components of an image so that these can later be quantized. (See also Transform.)

Discrete-tone image. A discrete-tone image may be bi-level, grayscale, or color. Such images are (with few exceptions) artificial, having been obtained by scanning a document or grabbing a computer screen. The pixel colors of such an image do not vary continuously or smoothly but have a small set of values such that adjacent pixels may differ much in intensity or color. (See also Block decomposition, Continuous-tone image.)

Discrete wavelet transform. The discrete version of the continuous wavelet transform. A wavelet is represented by means of several filter coefficients, and the transform is carried out by matrix multiplication (or a simpler version thereof) instead of by calculating an integral. (See also Decomposition.)

EAN-13. A 13-digit barcode that may replace UPC as the standard for labeling products. The rightmost digit is a check digit that adds redundancy and thereby increases reliability when the barcode is scanned. (See also Barcodes, UPC, and Section 2.2.2.)

Embedding capacity. A concept in steganography. A measure of the amount of data that can be hidden in a cover.

Encipher. To transform an original message (plaintext) to an encrypted message (ciphertext).

Encode. To encipher.

Encoder. A compression program (or algorithm).

Encryption. The transformation of plaintext into ciphertext through a mathematical process.

Entropy. The entropy of a single symbol a_i is defined (in Section 1.1) as $-P_i \log_2 P_i$, where P_i is the probability of occurrence of a_i in the data. The entropy of a_i is the smallest number of bits needed, on average, to represent symbol a_i. Claude Shannon, the creator of information theory, coined the term *entropy* in 1948, since this term is used in thermodynamics to indicate the amount of disorder in a physical system. (See also Entropy encoding, information theory.)

Entropy encoding. A lossless compression method where data can be compressed such that the average number of bits/symbol approaches the entropy of the input symbols. (See also Entropy.)

Error-control codes. A general term for error-detecting and error-correcting codes.

Error-correcting code. Codes that increase data reliability for errors by adding redundancy. Such codes can automatically correct certain errors and can also detect (but not correct) more serious errors.

Error-detecting code. Codes that increase data reliability for errors by adding redundancy to the data. Such codes can automatically detect (but not correct) certain errors.

Eve. A term used in cryptography discussions and examples for the ubiquitous eavesdropper.

Exclusive-OR (XOR). A logical (Boolean) operation that is also its own inverse, which makes it useful in cryptography. It is identical to adding two bits modulo 2.

Facsimile compression. Transferring a typical page between two fax machines can take up to 10–11 minutes without compression. This is why the ITU has developed several standards for compression of facsimile data. The current standards (Section 3.7) are T4 and T6, also called Group 3 and Group 4, respectively. (See also ITU.)

Factor. Given an integer N, a factor is any integer that divides it without a remainder.

Factoring. The process of finding the prime factors of an integer.

Feistel cipher. A special class of iterated block ciphers where the ciphertext is calculated from the plaintext by repeated application of the same transformation (called a *round function*).

Field. A set of mathematical entities satisfying certain rules. Finite fields, also called *Galois fields* (Appendix B), are used in cryptography in the Rijndael (AES) algorithm and in stream ciphers. They are also used to design sets of channel codes with a given Hamming distance. (See also Group.)

Function. A mathematical relationship between two values called the *input* and the *output* such that for each input there is precisely one output.

Galois field. See Field.

Geffe generator. A method used by nonlinear stream ciphers to combine two streams of pseudorandom bits. (See Combiner and Section 10.4.)

Generating polynomials. Special polynomials used to generate sets of channel codes with a given Hamming distance.

GIF. An acronym that stands for Graphics Interchange Format. This format was developed by Compuserve Information Services in 1987 as an efficient, compressed graphics file format that allows for images to be sent between computers. The original version of GIF is known as GIF 87a. The current standard is GIF 89a. (See also Patents.)

Giga. The quantity giga is defined as $2^{30} = 1{,}073{,}741{,}824$. In contrast, a billion is defined (in the United States) as 10^9. (See Mega.)

Golomb code. The Golomb codes consist of an infinite set of *parametrized prefix codes*. They are the best ones for the compression of data items that are distributed geometrically. (See also Unary Code.)

Gray codes. These are binary codes for the integers, where the codes of consecutive integers differ by one bit only. Such codes are used when a grayscale image is separated into bitplanes, each a bi-level image. (See also Grayscale image,)

Grayscale image. A continuous-tone image with shades of a single color. (See also Continuous-tone image.)

Group. A set of mathematical entities obeying certain rules. (See Field.)

Hamming check digits. An error-correcting method that corrects single-digit errors in a decimal number by appending check digits to it. See Section 2.10.

Hamming codes. A type of error-correcting code for 1-bit error correction, where it is easy to generate the required parity bits. (See also SEC-DED codes.)

Hamming distance. The Hamming distance of two binary codes is the number of positions where the two codes differ. The Hamming distance of a set of codes is the maximum distance of all the pairs of codes in the set. It is easy to show that a code with a Hamming distance of $d+1$ can detect all d-bit errors and a code with a Hamming distance of $2d + 1$ can also correct all d-bit errors.

Hashing. An operation that scrambles the bits of a data item to obtain a value that can be used as a pointer to a data structure called a *hash table*.

Hide and seek. Steganography software to hide data in the least significant bits of an image. (See also LSB and Section 15.10.2.)

Hill cipher. A polyalphabetic cipher that employs the modulus function and techniques of linear algebra. (See Section 9.10.)

Homophonic substitution cipher. A cryptographic technique where each plainletter has several potential cipherletters that can replace it. The word comes from the Greek for *the same sound*. (See Section 7.10.)

> Therefore, though the whole point of his "Current Shorthand" is that it can express every sound in the language perfectly, vowels as well as consonants, and that your hand has to make no stroke except the easy and current ones with which you write m, n, and u, l, p, and q, scribbling them at whatever angle comes easiest to you, his unfortunate determination to make this remarkable and quite legible script serve also as a Shorthand reduced it in his own practice to the most inscrutable of cryptograms.
>
> —George Bernard Shaw, *Pygmalion* (1916)

Huffman coding. A popular method for data compression (Section 3.5). It assigns a set of "best" variable-size codes to a set of symbols based on their probabilities. It serves as the basis for several popular programs used on personal computers. Some of them use just the Huffman method, while others use it as one step in a multistep compression process. The Huffman method is somewhat similar to the Shannon–Fano method. It generally produces better codes, and like the Shannon–Fano method, it produces best code when the probabilities of the symbols are negative powers of 2. The main difference between the two methods is that Shannon–Fano constructs its codes from top to bottom (from the leftmost to the rightmost bits), while Huffman constructs a code tree from the bottom up (building the codes from right to left). (See also Statistical methods.)

IBM check digit. A sophisticated error-detection scheme that employs a single check digit to detect certain errors in an arbitrary number of data digits. (See also Barcodes and Section 2.8.)

IDEA. A patented block cipher developed by James Massey and Xuejia Lai in 1992. It uses a 128-bit key and 64-bit blocks. IDEA uses no internal tables and is known mostly because it is used in PGP. (See also Pretty good privacy (PGP).)

Information theory. A mathematical theory that quantifies information. It shows how to measure information so that one can answer the question "How much information is included in this piece of data?" with a precise number! Information theory is the creation, in 1948, of Claude Shannon, of Bell Labs. (See also Entropy.)

Inline encryptor. A hardware product that automatically encrypts all data passing along a data link.

International Data Encryption Algorithm (IDEA). (See IDEA.)

Invisibility. A measure of the quality of a steganographic method.

Involution. Any mapping that is its own inverse.

ISBN. The international standard book number (ISBN) is an identifying number that is assigned to virtually every book published. It employs a check digit for added reliability (see Section 2.1).

ISO. The International Standards Organization. This is one of the organizations responsible for developing standards. Among other things, it is responsible (together with the ITU) for the JPEG and MPEG compression standards. (See also ITU.)

ITU. The International Telecommunications Union, the new name of the CCITT, is a United Nations organization responsible for developing and recommending standards for data communications (not just compression).

JFIF. The full name of this method (Section 5.9.8) is JPEG File Interchange Format. It is a graphics file format that makes it possible to exchange JPEG-compressed images between different computers. The main features of JFIF are the use of the YCbCr triple-component color space for color images (only one component for grayscale images) and the use of a *marker* to specify features missing from JPEG, such as image resolution, aspect ratio, and features that are application specific.

JPEG. A sophisticated lossy compression method (Section 5.9) for color or grayscale still images (not movies). It also works best on continuous-tone images, where adjacent pixels have similar colors. One advantage of JPEG is the use of many parameters, allowing the user to adjust the amount of data loss (and thus also the compression ratio) over a very wide range. There are two main modes: lossy (also called baseline) and lossless (which typically gives a 2:1 compression ratio). Most implementations support just the lossy mode. This mode includes progressive and hierarchical coding.

The main idea behind JPEG is that an image exists for people to look at, so when the image is compressed, it is acceptable to lose image features to which the human eye is not sensitive.

The name JPEG is an acronym that stands for Joint Photographic Experts Group. This was a joint effort by the CCITT and the ISO that started in June 1987. The JPEG standard has proved successful and has become widely used for image presentation, especially in Web pages.

Kerckhoffs' principle. An important principle in cryptography. It states that the security of an encrypted message must depend on keeping the key secret and should not depend on keeping the encryption algorithm secret.

Key. Information (normally secret) used to encrypt or decrypt a message in a distinctive manner. A key may belong to an individual or to a group of users.

Key distribution. The process (or rather the problem) of safely distributing a cryptographic key to a (possibly large) group of authorized parties.

Key escrow. A scheme for storing copies of cryptographic keys so that a third, authorized party can recover them if necessary to decrypt messages.

Key space. The number of possible key values. For example, there are 2^{64} key values for a 64-bit key. (See Exercise 6.4.)

Kraft–MacMillan inequality. A relation that says something about unambiguous variable-size codes. Its first part states: Given an unambiguous variable-size code, with n codes of sizes L_i, then

$$\sum_{i=1}^{n} 2^{-L_i} \leq 1.$$

The second part states the opposite: Given a set of n positive integers $(L_1, L_2, \ldots, L_n)$ that satisfy the above inequality, there exists an unambiguous variable-size code such that L_i are the sizes of its individual codes. Together, both parts say that a code is unambiguous if and only if it satisfies the above inequality.

Laplace distribution. A probability distribution similar to the normal (Gaussian) distribution, but narrower and sharply peaked. The general Laplace distribution with variance V and mean m is given by

$$L(V, x) = \frac{1}{\sqrt{2V}} \exp\left(-\sqrt{\frac{2}{V}}|x - m|\right).$$

Experience seems to suggest that the values of pixels in many images are Laplace distributed, which is why this distribution is used in some image compression methods.

Latin square combiner. A cryptographic combining algorithm. In a simple Latin square combiner algorithm, two consecutive plaintext symbols A and B are used to select a third symbol C from the square and the resulting ciphertext consists of either A and C or B and C. (See also Combiner and Section 10.7.)

LFSR. A simple, efficient technique to produce a large number of pseudorandom bits. (See Stream cipher, Shift register, and Section 10.3.)

Lossless compression. A compression method where the output of the decoder is identical to the original data compressed by the encoder. (See also Lossy compression.)

Lossy compression. A compression method where the output of the decoder is different from the original data compressed by the encoder but is nevertheless acceptable to a user. Such methods are common in image and audio compression, but not in text compression, where the loss of even one character may result in ambiguous or incomprehensible text. (See also Lossless compression, Subsampling.)

LSB. The least significant (rightmost) bit of a data item. (See also LSB encoding, MSB.)

LSB encoding. Steganographic methods that hide data in the least significant bits of an image. (See also Hide and seek, BPCS, LSB, Steganography, S-tools, Stego, and Section 14.1.)

Luminance. A component of color. Roughly speaking, luminance corresponds to brightness as perceived by the human eye. (See also Chrominance.)

LZ methods. All dictionary-based compression methods are based on the work of J. Ziv and A. Lempel published in 1977 and 1978. Today, these are called the LZ77 and LZ78 methods, respectively. The ideas of Ziv and Lempel have been a source of inspiration to many researchers, who generalized, improved, and combined them with RLE and statistical methods to form many commonly used adaptive compression methods for text, images, and audio. (See also Block matching, Dictionary-based compression, Sliding–window compression.)

LZW. This is a popular variant (Section 4.4) of LZ78, developed by Terry Welch in 1984. Its main feature is eliminating the second field of a token. An LZW token consists of just a pointer to the dictionary. As a result, such a token always encodes a string of more than one symbol. (See also Patents.)

Mega. Mega is defined as $2^{20} = 1{,}048{,}576$. In contrast, a million is defined as 10^6. (See Giga.)

Mimic functions. A steganographic method that uses context-free grammars to generate innocuous text files that hide data. (See Context-free grammar (CFG) and Section 13.8.)

Monoalphabetic substitution cipher. A cryptographic algorithm with a fixed substitution rule. (See Chapter 7.)

MSB. The most significant (leftmost) bit of a data item. (See also LSB.)

Multiple encryption. The process of encrypting an already encrypted ciphertext. Such secondary encryption should be done with a different key, not the key used for the first encryption. Multiple encryption may involve more than two encryption steps. The main advantage of multiple encryption is that the input to the second encryption step is the output of the first step, so it is ciphertext that looks random. An attack on the second encryption step should therefore produce something that looks random, making it extremely hard for the codebreaker to decide whether the attack was successful. Multiple encryption also helps to protect the cipher from a known plaintext attack.

National Computer Security Center (NCSC). A United States government organization that evaluates computing equipment for high-security applications.

National Institute of Standards and Technology (NIST). An agency of the United States government that establishes national standards.

National Security Agency (NSA). A branch of the United States Department of Defense responsible for intercepting foreign communications and for ensuring the security of United States government communications.

Network encryption. Cryptographic services applied to data above the data link level but below the application software level in a network. This allows cryptographic protections to use existing networking services and existing application software in a way that's transparent to the user.

Nomenclator. A cipher that consists of a list where each entry associates a letter, syllable, word, or name with a number. Encryption is done by finding a plain word in the list and replacing it by the corresponding number. If a word is not found in the list, its syllables or letters are individually replaced by numbers.

Nonrepudiation. Accountability. An important but unachievable goal of cryptography. The idea that the reception of a message cannot later be denied by the receiver. Today, after more than a decade of trying to achieve nonrepudiation by technical means, most workers in this area have given up and admit that this goal can be achieved only by legal means.

Nyquist rate. The minimum rate at which an analog signal (a wave) has to be sampled (i.e., digitized) in order not to lose information when the samples are played back.

One-time pad. A random sequence of bits that is as long as the message itself and is used as a key. Alternative definition: A Vernam cipher in which one bit of new, purely random key is used for every bit of data being encrypted. (See Vernam cipher.)

Parity bits. Bits that are added to data for increased reliability. Given a group of bits, the number of 1s in the group is counted and the parity bit is chosen to make this number odd (for odd parity) or even (for even parity). (See also Check bits and Section 1.5.)

Patents. A mathematical algorithm can be patented if it is intimately associated with software or firmware implementing it. Several compression methods, most notably LZW, have been patented, creating difficulties for software developers who work with GIF, UNIX `compress`, or any other system that uses LZW. (An anonymous reviewer's comment: GIF was actually patented twice, once by Welch and again by Miller and Wegman. In addition, the LZW patent has now expired.) (See also GIF, LZW.)

Pel. The smallest unit of a facsimile image; a dot. (See also Pixel.)

Periodic codes. Channel codes designed to correct bursts of errors.

Permutation. Any arrangement or rearrangement of symbols or data items.

Pixel. The smallest unit of a digital image; a dot. (See also Pel.)

Plaintext. An as-yet unencrypted message.

Polyalphabetic substitution. A cryptographic technique where the rule of substitution changes all the time.

Polynomial. A function of the form $P_n(x) = a_0 + a_1 x + a_2 x^2 + \cdots + a_n x^n$. Polynomials are simple functions that have many practical applications.

PPM. A compression method that assigns probabilities to symbols based on the context (long or short) in which they appear. (See also Prediction.)

Prediction. Assigning probabilities to symbols. (See also PPM.)

Pretty good privacy (PGP). Encryption software developed by Philip Zimmermann. PGP (version 2) encrypts a message with the IDEA algorithm and uses public-key cryptography to encrypt the IDEA key. Today (late 2004) GnuPG and OpenPGP are commonly used. (See IDEA and Section 12.4.)

Prime. Any positive integer that's evenly divisible only by itself and by 1. The number 1 is considered neither prime nor nonprime. The integer 2 is the only even prime. Prime numbers have important applications in public-key cryptography.

Private key. The key used to decrypt messages in any implementation of public-key cryptography.

PRNG. A pseudorandom number generator. This is a hardware device or a software procedure that uses deterministic rules to generate a sequence of numbers that passes tests of randomness. (See Pseudorandom numbers, Random numbers.)

Pseudorandom numbers. A sequence of numbers that appears to be random but is constructed according to deterministic rules. (See PRNG, Random numbers.)

Public key. The key used to encrypt messages in any implementation of public-key cryptography.

Public-key algorithm. A cipher that uses a pair of keys, a public key and a private key, for encryption and decryption. Also called an asymmetric algorithm.

Public-key cryptography. Cryptography based on methods involving a public key and a private key.

Public-key cryptography standards (PKCS). Standards published by RSA Data Security that describe how to use public-key cryptography in a reliable, secure, and interoperable fashion.

Public-key steganography. Steganography based on methods involving a public key and a private key. (See Section 15.9.)

Quantum cryptography. An approach to cryptography using the Heisenberg uncertainty principle to generate any number of true random bits and thereby achieve absolute security.

Random numbers. A sequence of numbers that passes certain statistical randomness tests. Only a sequence can be random. A single number is neither random nor nonrandom. (See also PRNG, Pseudorandom numbers.)

Redundancy. This term is normally defined as a needless repetition of an act or as the attribute of being superfluous and unneeded. Source codes are based on decreasing the redundancy of data representation, while channel codes add reliability to data by increasing its redundancy.

Reed–Solomon Codes. Channel codes based on the strength of geometric figures such as a straight line or a parabola. (See also Section 1.14 and Compact Disc Error Control.)

RLE. A general name for methods that compress data by replacing a run length of identical symbols with one code, or token, containing the symbol and the length of the run. RLE sometimes serves as one step in a multistep statistical or dictionary-based method.

Robustness. A measure of the ability of a steganographic algorithm to retain the data embedded in the cover even after the cover has been subjected to various modifications as a result of lossy compression and decompression or of certain types of processing such as conversion to analog and back to digital.

RSA Data Security, Inc. (RSADSI). The company [RSA 04] primarily engaged in selling and licensing public-key cryptography for commercial purposes.

S-box. A substitution box used by many block ciphers as part of the substitution-permutation network of the cipher. Such a box is a table that has internal connections between its inputs and outputs. For any bit pattern sent as input to the box, a certain bit pattern emerges as output.

S-tools. Software for hiding data in the least significant bits of an image or an audio file. (See also LSB and Section 15.10.3.)

SEC-DED codes. A Hamming code with an extra parity bit. It can correct all 1-bit and detect all 2-bit errors. (See also Hamming codes and Section 1.9.)

Secret-key algorithm. Cryptographic algorithm that uses the same key to encrypt data and to decrypt data. Also called a symmetric algorithm.

Secure socket layer (SSL). A protocol enabling the secure transfer of sensitive information on the Internet. The sensitive data is encrypted by a block cipher, and the SSL protocol is used to select a random key for each transfer and communicate it securely through unsecure channels.

Security. The process of protecting vital information from prying eyes. This is done either by encryption or hiding.

Semantic methods. Steganographic methods that hide data in a cover text by slightly modifying semantic elements of the text, such as word usage. (See Syntactic methods.)

Semiadaptive compression. A compression method that uses a two-pass algorithm, where the first pass reads the input stream to collect statistics on the data to be compressed, and the second pass performs the actual compression. The statistics (model) are included in the compressed stream. (See also Adaptive compression.)

Shift register. An array of simple storage elements (normally flip-flops or latches) where the value of each element is moved into the next (or the previous) element. Such registers (implemented in either software or hardware) are used by many stream ciphers. (See LFSR, Stream cipher.)

Signal-to-noise ratio (SNR). A measure of invisibility (or its opposite, detectability) of hidden data.

Sliding window compression. The LZ77 method (Section 4.1) uses part of the previously seen input stream as the dictionary. The encoder maintains a window to the input stream and shifts the input in that window from right to left as strings of symbols are being encoded. The method is thus based on a *sliding window*. (See also LZ methods.)

Spread-spectrum steganography. A steganographic method that hides data bits in an image by adding noise to image pixels and hiding one bit in each noise component without changing the statistical properties of the noise.

Statistical methods. These methods (Chapter 3) work by assigning variable-size codes to symbols in the data, with the shorter codes assigned to symbols or groups of symbols that appear more often in the data (i.e., that have a higher probability of occurrence). (See also Variable-size codes, Huffman coding, and Arithmetic coding.)

Steganographic file system. A method to hide a data file among several other data files. The hidden file can be retrieved with a password, but someone who does not know the password cannot see the hidden file, cannot extract it, and cannot even find out whether the file exists. (See Section 15.7.)

Steganography. The art and science of hiding information, as opposed to cryptography, which hides the meaning of the information.

Stego. Software for hiding data in the least significant bits of an image. (See also LSB and Section 15.10.1.)

Stream cipher. A cipher that encrypts one bit at a time. (See LFSR, Shift register.)

Subsampling. Subsampling is, possibly, the simplest way to compress an image. One approach to subsampling is simply to ignore some of the pixels. The encoder may, for example, ignore every other row and every other column of the image, and write the remaining pixels (which constitute 25% of the image) on the compressed stream. The decoder inputs the compressed data and uses each pixel to generate four identical pixels of the reconstructed image. This, of course, involves the loss of much image detail and is rarely acceptable. (See also Lossy Compression.)

Substitution cipher. A cipher that replaces letters of the plaintext with another set of letters or symbols, without changing the order of the letters.

Symbol. The smallest unit of the data to be compressed. A symbol is normally a byte but may also be a bit, a trit $\{0, 1, 2\}$, or anything else. (See also Alphabet.)

Symmetric cryptography. A cryptographic technique where the same key is used for encryption and decryption.

Syntactic methods. Steganographic methods that hide data in a cover text by slightly modifying syntactic elements of the text, such as punctuation. (See Semantic methods.)

Transform. An image can be compressed by transforming its pixels (which are corre-lated) to a representation where they are *decorrelated*. Compression is achieved if the new values are smaller, on average, than the original ones. Lossy compression can be achieved by quantizing the transformed values. The decoder inputs the transformed values from the compressed stream and reconstructs the (precise or approximate) orig-inal data by applying the opposite transform. Image transforms are also important in steganography. (See also Discrete cosine transform, Discrete wavelet transform.)

Transposition cipher. A cipher where the plaintext letters are rearranged in a different permutation.

Trapdoor. See Back door.

Trit. A ternary (base 3) digit. It can be 0, 1, or 2.

Turing machine. A theoretical model of a computing device, proposed by Alan Turing.

Unary code. A way to generate variable-size codes in one step. The unary code of the nonnegative integer n is defined (Section 3.3.1) as $n - 1$ ones followed by one zero (Table 3.3). There is also a general unary code. (See also Golomb code.)

Undetectability. A measure of the quality of a steganographic method.

Unicode. A new international standard code, the Unicode, has been proposed, and is being developed by the international Unicode organization (`www.unicode.org`). Uni-code uses 16-bit codes for its characters, so it provides for $2^{16} = 64K = 65{,}536$ codes. (Notice that doubling the size of a code much more than doubles the number of possible codes. In fact, it *squares* the number of codes.) Unicode includes all the ASCII codes in addition to codes for characters in foreign languages (including complete sets of Korean, Japanese, and Chinese characters) and many mathematical and other symbols. Currently, about 39,000 out of the 65,536 possible codes have been assigned, so there is room for adding more symbols in the future.

The Microsoft Windows NT operating system has adopted Unicode, as have also AT&T Plan 9 and Lucent Inferno. (See also ASCII code, Codes.)

UPC. A 12-digit barcode that's used to label products in the United States. The rightmost digit is a check digit which adds redundancy and thereby increases reliability when the barcode is scanned. (See also Barcodes, EAN-13, and Section 2.2.1.)

Variable-size codes. These are used by statistical methods. Such codes should satisfy the prefix property (Section 3.3) and should be assigned to symbols based on their probabilities. (See also Statistical methods.)

Vector quantization. This is a generalization of the scalar quantization method. It is used for both image and sound compression. In practice, vector quantization is commonly used to compress data that has been digitized from an analog source, such as sampled sound and scanned images (drawings or photographs). Such data is called *digitally sampled analog data* (DSAD).

Verhoeff check digit. A sophisticated error-detection method that uses a check digit to detect all single-digit and adjacent-digits transpositions in integers of arbitrary lengths. (See Section 2.11.)

Vernam cipher. Cipher developed for encrypting teletype traffic by computing the exclusive OR of the data bits and the key bits. This is a common approach to constructing stream ciphers. (See One-time pad.)

Vigenère cipher. A historically important polyalphabetic cipher where a letter-square and a key are used to determine the rule of substitution for each plainletter.

Voting codes. Channel codes that work by transmitting an odd number of copies of the data. The receiver compares the copies and corrects errors if it finds that more than half the copies are identical.

Watermarking. A steganographic term. A small amount of data that indicates ownership, authorship, or another kind of relationship between the cover and a person or an organization.

Weak key. A key value that results in easy breaking of a cipher. The various weak keys of DES are well known. (See Section 11.3.1.)

XOR. See Exclusive OR.

$\mathcal{Z}_N$. The set of integers modulo N, i.e., $\{0, 1, \ldots, N-1\}$. The notation $\mathcal{Z}_N^*$ denotes the set of integers $\{a \in \mathcal{Z}_n | \gcd(a, N) = 1\}$.

Zip barcode. An 11-digit barcode printed on many letters to help the post office sort the letters. The rightmost digit is a check digit that adds redundancy and thereby increases reliability when the barcode is scanned. (See also Barcodes and Section 2.3.)

> As for my mother, perhaps the Ambassador had not the type of mind towards which she felt herself most attracted. I should add that his conversation furnished so exhaustive a glossary of the superannuated forms of speech peculiar to a certain profession, class and period; a period which, for that profession and that class, might be said not to have altogether passed away; that I sometimes regret that I have not kept any literal record simply of the things that I have heard him say.
>
> —Marcel Proust, *Within a Budding Grove* (1921)

Bibliography

Abramson, N. (1963) *Information Theory and Coding*, New York, McGraw-Hill.

ACA (2003) is URL `http://www.und.nodak.edu/org/crypto/crypto/`.

Aegean Park Press (2001) is URL `http://www.aegeanparkpress.com/`.

AFAC (2003) is URL `http://www-vips.icn.gov.ru/`.

Ahmed, N., T. Natarajan, and R. K. Rao (1974) "Discrete Cosine Transform," *IEEE Transactions on Computers* C-23:90–93.

AMS (2004) is URL `http://www.ams.org/new-in-math/cover/errors4.html`

Anderson, K. L., et al., (1987) "Binary-Image-Manipulation Algorithm in the Image View Facility," *IBM Journal of Research and Development* **31**(1):16–31, January.

Anderson, Ross, Roger Needham, and Adi Shamir (1998) "The Steganographic File System," in David Aucsmith (ed.) *Proceedings of the Second Information Hiding Workshop, IWIH*, pp. 73–82, April. Also available from URL `http://citeseer.nj.nec.com/anderson98steganographic.html`.

Arnold, Michael, Martin Schmucker, and Stephen D. Wolthusen (2003) *Techniques and Applications of Digital Watermarking and Content Protection*, Boston, Artech House.

Aura, Tuomas (1996) "Practical Invisibility in Digital Communication," in *Proceedings of the Workshop on Information Hiding*, Cambridge, England, May 1996, pp. 265–278, *Lecture Notes in Computer Science* **1174**, New York, Springer Verlag. Also available from URL `http://www.tcs.hut.fi/Personnel/tuomas.html`.

Barker, Wayne G. (1984) *Cryptanalysis of Shift-Register Generated Stream Cipher Systems*, Laguna Hills, Calif., Aegean Park Press, vol. **C-39**.

Barker, Wayne G. (1989) *Introduction to the Analysis Of The Data Encryption Standard (DES)*, Laguna Hills, Calif., Aegean Park Press, vol. **C-55**.

Barker, Wayne G. (1992) *Cryptanalysis of the Single Columnar Transposition Cipher*, Laguna Hills, Calif., Aegean Park Press, vol. **C-59**.

Bassia, P. and I. Pitas (1998) "Robust Audio Watermarking in the Time Domain," in *IX European Signal Processing Conference (EUSIPCO'98)*, Rhodes, Greece, vol. I, pp. 25–28, 8–11 September.

Bauer, Friedrich Ludwig (2002) *Decrypted Secrets: Methods and Maxims of Cryptology* 3rd edition, Berlin, Springer Verlag.

BBB (2003) is URL `www.bbbonline.com`.

Bender, W., D. Gruhl, N. Morimoto, and A. Lu (1996) "Techniques for Data Hiding," *IBM Systems Journal*, **35**(3,4)313–336.

Berlekamp, Elwyn R. (1968) *Algebraic Coding Theory*, New York, McGraw-Hill.

Blakley, G. R. (1979) "Safeguarding Cryptographic Keys," in *AFIPS Conference Proceedings*, **48**:313–317.

Bogert, B. P., M. J. R. Healy, and J. W. Tukey (1963) "The Quefrency Alanysis of Time Series for Echoes: Cepstrum, Pseudo-Autocovariance, Cross-Cepstrum, and Saphe Cracking," in *Proceedings of the Symposium on Time Series Analysis*, Rosenthal, M. (ed.), New York, John Wiley, pp. 209–243.

BPCS (2003) is URL `http://www.know.comp.kyutech.ac.jp/BPCSe/` file `BPCSe-principle.html`.

Busch, C., W. Funk, and S. Wolthusen (1999) "Digital Watermarking: From Concepts to Real-Time Video Applications," *IEEE Computer Graphics and Applications, Image Security*, January/February, pp. 25–35.

Cain, Thomas R., and Alan T. Sherman (1997) "How to Break Gifford's Cipher," *Cryptologia*, **21**(3)237–286, July.

Campbell, K. W., and M. J. Wiener (1993) "DES Is Not a Group," *Advances in Cryptology, CRYPTO '92*, New York, Springer Verlag, pp. 512–520.

Chen Yu-Yuan, Hsiang-Kuang Pan, and Yu-Chee Tseng (2000) "A Secure Data Hiding Scheme for Two-Color Images," in *IEEE Symposium on Computers and Communications, ISCC 2000*, pp. 750–755. Also available (in PDF format) from URL `http://citeseer.nj.nec.com/chen00secure.html`

Childs, J. Rives (2000) *General Solution of the ADFGVX Cipher System*, Laguna Hills, Calif., Aegean Park Press, vol. **C-88**.

Chomsky, Noam, and George A. Miller (1958) "Finite State Languages," *Information and Control*, **1**(2)91–112, May.

Cleary, J. G., and I. H. Witten (1984) "Data Compression Using Adaptive Coding and Partial String Matching," *IEEE Transactions on Communications* COM-32(4):396–402, April.

Conceptlabs (2004) is URL `http://www.conceptlabs.co.uk/alicebob.html`.

Coppersmith, Donald, and Philip Rogaway (1994) "A Software-Optimized Encryption Algorithm," *Fast Software Encryption, Cambridge Security Workshop Proceedings*, New York, Springer-Verlag, pp. 56–63.

Coppersmith, Donald, and Philip Rogaway (1995) "Software-Efficient Pseudorandom Function and the Use Thereof for Encryption," United States Patent 5,454,039, 26 September.

Cox, Ingemar J., Joe Kilian, Tom Leighton, and Talal Shamoon (1996) "A Secure, Robust Watermark for Multimedia," *Workshop on Information Hiding*, Newton Institute, Cambridge University, May. Also available in PDF format from URL `ftp://ftp.nj.nec.com/pub/ingemar/papers/cam96.zip`.

Cox, Ingemar J. (2002) *Digital Watermarking*, San Francisco, Morgan Kaufmann.

Crap (2003) is URL `http://www.mat.dtu.dk/people/Lars.R.Knudsen/crap.html`.

Cryptologia (2003) is URL `http://www.dean.usma.edu/math/pubs/cryptologia/`.

Cryptology (2003) is URL `http://link.springer.de/link/service/journals/00145/`.

cypherpunks (2004) is `ftp://ftp.csua.berkeley.edu/pub/cypherpunks/steganography/`.

CSE (2001) is URL `http://www.cse.dnd.ca/`.

CSE (2003) is URL `http://www.cse.dnd.ca/`.

DES (1999) is `http://csrc.nist.gov/publications/fips/fips46-3/fips46-3.pdf`.

Despan (2004) is URL `http://www.oneoffcd.com/info/historycd.cfm`.

DSD (2003) is URL `http://www.dsd.gov.au/`.

Dunham W. (1990) *Journey Through Genius: The Great Theorems of Mathematics*, New York, John Wiley.

Ekstrand, Nicklas (1996) "Lossless Compression of Gray Images via Context Tree Weighting," in Storer, James A. (ed.), *DCC '96: Data Compression Conference*, Los Alamitos, CA, IEEE Computer Society Press, pp. 132–139, April.

FAQS (2004) is URL `http://www.faqs.org/faqs/compression-faq/part1/`.

Feig, Ephraim N., and Elliot Linzer (1990) "Discrete Cosine Transform Algorithms for Image Data Compression," in *Proceedings Electronic Imaging '90 East*, pages 84–87, Boston, MA.

Feige, Uriel, Amos Fiat, and Adi Shamir (1988) "Zero Knowledge Proofs of Identity," *Journal of Cryptology*, **1**(2)77–94.

Feistel, Horst (1973) "Cryptography and Computer Privacy," *Scientific American*, **228**(5) 15–23, May.

Flannery, Sarah, and David Flannery (2001) *In Code: A Mathematical Journey*, Workman Publishing Company.

Fraunhofer (2001) is URL `http://syscop.igd.fhg.de/`.

FreeBSD Words (2003) is URL `ftp://www.freebsd.org/usr/share/dict/words`.

Fridrich, Jiri (1998) "Image Watermarking for Tamper Detection," in *Proceedings of the International Conference on Image Processing, ICIP '98*, Chicago, October.

Fridrich, Jiri (1999) "Methods for Tamper Detection in Digital Images," in *Proceedings of the ACM Workshop on Multimedia and Security*, pp. 19–23, Orlando, Fla., October.

Funet (2003) is URL `ftp://nic.funet.fi/pub/graphics/misc/test-images/`.

Gaines, Helen Fouché (1956) *Cryptanalysis: A Study of Ciphers and Their Solutions*, New York, Dover.

Gallian,, J. A. (1989) "Check Digit Methods," *International Journal of Applied Engineering Education*, **5**(4):503–505.

Gallian,, J. A. (1991) "The Mathematics of Identification Numbers," *College Mathematics Journal*, **22**(3):194–202.

Gardner, Martin (1972) "Mathematical Games," *Scientific American*, **227**(2):106, August.

Garfinkel, Simson (1995) *PGP: Pretty Good Privacy*, Sebastopol, Calif., O'Reilly.

GCHQ (2003) is URL `http://www.gchq.gov.uk/`.

Gifford, David K., et al. (1985) "The Application of Digital Broadcast Communications to Large-Scale Information Systems," *IEEE Journal on Selected Areas in Communications*, **SAC-3**(3)457–467, May.

GnuPG (2004) is `http://www.gnupg.org/`.

Goettingen (2004) is URL `http://www.num.math.uni-goettingen.de/Lehre/Lehrmaterial/Vorlesungen/Informatik/1998/skript/texte/abthesis.html`.

Golay, Marcel (1949) "Notes on Digital Coding," *Proceedings of the IRE*, **37**:657.

Golay, Marcel (1954) "Binary Coding," *Transactions of the IRE (IEEE)*, **PGIT-4**:23–28.

Golomb, S. W. (1966) "Run-Length Encodings," *IEEE Transactions on Information Theory* IT-12(3):399–401.

Golomb, Solomon W. (1982) *Shift Register Sequences*, 2nd edition, Laguna Hills, Calif., Aegean Park Press.

Gonzalez, Rafael C., and Richard E. Woods (1992) *Digital Image Processing*, Reading, Mass., Addison-Wesley.

Grafica (1996) is URL `http://www.sgi.com/grafica/huffman/`.

Gray, Frank (1953) "Pulse Code Communication," United States Patent 2,632,058, March 17.

Gruhl, Daniel, Walter Bender, and Anthony Lu (1996) "Echo Hiding," in *Information Hiding: First International Workshop, Lecture Notes in Computer Science*, volume 1174, R. J. Anderson, ed., pp. 295–315, Springer-Verlag, Berlin.

Guillou, Louis, and Jean-Jacques Quisquater (1988) "A Practical Zero-Knowledge Protocol Fitted to Security Microprocessors Minimizing Both Transmission and Memory," in *Advances in Cryptology, Eurocrypt '88 Proceedings*, pp. 123–128, Berlin, Springer-Verlag.

Gutenberg (2004) is URL `http://www.gutenberg.net/`.

Hamming, Richard (1986) *Coding and Information Theory*, 2nd edition, Englewood Cliffs, NJ, Prentice-Hall.

Heath, F. G. (1972) "Origins of the Binary Code," *Scientific American*, **227**(2):76, August.

Hill, Raymond (1986) *A First Course In Coding Theory*, New York. Oxford University Press.

Hinsley, F. H., and Alan Stripp (eds.) (1992) *The Codebreakers: The Inside Story of Bletchley Park*, Oxford, Oxford University Press.

Huffman, David (1952) "A Method for the Construction of Minimum Redundancy Codes," *Proceedings of the IRE*, **40**(9):1098–1101.

Hunter, R., and A. H. Robinson (1980) "International Digital Facsimile Coding Standards," *Proceedings of the IEEE*, **68**(7):854–867, July.

ISBN (2004) is URL `http://www.isbn-international.org/en/identifiers/`, file `allidentifiers.html`

Johnson, Neil F., et al. (2001) *Information Hiding: Steganography and Watermarking—Attacks and Countermeasures, Advances in Information Security*, volume 1, Boston, Kluwer Academic.

Kahn, David (1996) *The Codebreakers: The Comprehensive History of Secret Communications from Ancient Times to the Internet*, revised edition, New York, Scribner.

Katzenbeisser, Stefan, and Fabien A. P. Petitcolas (eds.) (2000) *Information Hiding Techniques for Steganography and Digital Watermarking*, Norwood, Mass., Artech House.

Kerckhoffs, Auguste (1883) "La Cryptographie Militaire," *Journal des Sciences Militaires*, **9**:5–38, 161–191, January–February. Also available in html format from URL `http://www.petitcolas.net/fabien/kerckhoffs/la_cryptographie_militaire_i.htm`.

Kirtland, Joseph (2000) *Identification Numbers and Check Digit Schemes*, The Mathematical Association of America.

Konheim, Alan G. (1981) *Cryptography: A Primer*, New York, John Wiley and Sons.

Knuth, Donald E. (1984) *The TEXBook*, Reading, Mass., Addison-Wesley.

Knuth, D. E. (1985) "Dynamic Huffman Coding," *Journal of Algorithms* **6**:163–180.

Kundur, Deepa, and Dimitrios Hatzinakos (1997) "A Robust Digital Image Watermarking Scheme Using Wavelet-Based Fusion," in *Proceedings of the IEEE International Conference On Image Processing*, Santa Barbara, Calif., **1**, pp. 544–547, October.

Kundur, Deepa, and Dimitrios Hatzinakos (1998) "Digital Watermarking Using Multiresolution Wavelet Decomposition," *Proceedings of the IEEE International Conference On Acoustics, Speech and Signal Processing*, Seattle, Wash., **5**, pp. 2969–2972, May.

Larson, P. Å., and A. Kajla (1984) "Implementation of a Method Guaranteeing Retrieval in One Access," *Communications of the ACM*, **27**(7)670–677, July.

Lelewer, D. A., and D. S. Hirschberg (1987) "Data Compression," *Computing Surveys* **19**(3):261–297. Reprinted in Japanese BIT Special issue in Computer Science (1989), 16–195. Available at http://www.ics.uci.edu/~dan/pubs/DataCompression.html.

Levy, Steven (2001) *Crypto*, New York, Viking.

Lin, Shu, and Daniel J. Costello (1982) *Error Correcting Coding: Fundamentals and Applications*, Englewood Cliffs, N.J., Prentice-Hall.

Linde, Y., A. Buzo, and R. M. Gray (1980) "An Algorithm for Vector Quantization Design," *IEEE Transactions on Communications*, COM-28:84–95, January.

Loeffler, C., A. Ligtenberg, and G. Moschytz (1989) "Practical Fast 1-D DCT Algorithms with 11 Multiplications," *Proceedings of the International Conference on Acoustics, Speech, and Signal Processing (ICASSP '89)*, pp. 988–991.

McDonald, Andrew D., and Markus G. Kuhn (1999) "StegFS: A Steganographic File System for Linux," in *Proceedings of Information Hiding*, New York, Springer-Verlag, LNCS **1768**, pp. 463–477. Also available from http://www.mcdonald.org.uk/StegFS/.

Mandelbrot, Benoit (1982) *The Fractal Geometry of Nature*, San Francisco, W. H. Freeman.

Marking, Michael P. (1990) "Decoding Group 3 Images," *The C Users Journal*, pp. 45–54, June.

MathWorld (2003) is html file Gram-SchmidtOrthonormalization.html in URL http://mathworld.wolfram.com/.

McConnell, Kenneth R. (1992) *FAX: Digital Facsimile Technology and Applications*, Norwood, Mass., Artech House.

Merkle, R. C., and M. Hellman (1981) "On the Security of Multiple Encryption," *Communications of the ACM*, **24**(7)465–467.

Miano, John (1999) *Compressed Image File Formats*, New York, ACM Press and Addison-Wesley.

Moffat, Alistair (1990) "Implementing the PPM Data Compression Scheme," *IEEE Transactions on Communications* COM-38(11):1917–1921, November.

Moffat, Alistair, Radford Neal, and Ian H. Witten (1998) "Arithmetic Coding Revisited," *ACM Transactions on Information Systems*, **16**(3):256–294, July.

NCM (2003) is URL `http://www.nsa.gov/museum/`.

Newton, David E. (1997) *Encyclopedia of Cryptology*, Santa Barbara, Calif., ABC-Clio.

Nicetext (2004) is URL `http://www.nicetext.com/`.

NSA (2003) is URL `http://www.nsa.gov/`.

NSA (2004) is `http://www.nsa.gov/venona/`.

Nyquist, Harry (1928) "Certain Topics in Telegraph Transmission Theory," *Transactions of the AIEE*, **47**(3):617–644, April.

OpenPGP (2004) is `http://www.openpgp.org/`.

Palmer, Roger C. (1995) *The Bar Code Book*, 3rd edition, Peterborough, N.H., Helmers Publishing.

Pasco, R. (1976) "Source Coding Algorithms for Fast Data Compression," Ph.D. dissertation, Dept. of Electrical Engineering, Stanford University, Stanford, Calif.

Pennebaker, William B. and Joan L. Mitchell (1992) *JPEG Still Image Data Compression Standard*, New York, Van Nostrand Reinhold.

Petitcolas (2003) is URL `http://www.petitcolas.net/fabien/steganography/bibliography/`.

Pfitzmann, B. (1996) "Information Hiding Terminology," in *Information Hiding*, New York, Springer *Lecture Notes in Computer Science*, **1174**:347–350.

Phillips, Dwayne (1992) "LZW Data Compression," *The Computer Application Journal*, Circuit Cellar Inc., **27**:36–48, June/July.

PKCS (2004) is `http://www.rsasecurity.com/rsalabs/node.asp?id=2124`.

Podilchuk, C. I., and W. Zeng (1997) "Digital Image Watermarking Using Visual Models," in *Proceedings of the IS&T/SPIE Conference on Human Vision and Electronic Imaging II*, **3016**, pp. 100–111, February.

Pohlmann, Ken (1985) *Principles of Digital Audio*, Indianapolis, Ind., Howard Sams.

Pohlmann, Ken C. (1992) *The Compact Disc Handbook*, 2nd edition, A-R Editions, Inc.

Polster, Burkard (1998) *A Geometrical Picture Book*, New York, Springer Verlag.

Press, W. H., B. P. Flannery, et al. (1988) *Numerical Recipes in C: The Art of Scientific Computing*, Cambridge, Cambridge University Press. (Also available on-line by anonymous ftp from `http://www.nr.com/`.)

Rao, K., and J. J. Hwang (1996) *Techniques and Standards for Image, Video, and Audio Coding*, Upper Saddle River, N.J., Prentice-Hall, pp. 273–322.

Reed, Irving S., and Gustave Solomon (1960) "Polynomial Codes over Certain Finite Fields," *SIAM Journal of Applied Mathematics*, **8**(10):300–304.

Rescorla, Eric (2000) *SSL and TLS: Designing and Building Secure Systems*, Reading, Mass., Addison Wesley.

RFC804 (2003) is URL `http://www.faqs.org/rfcs/rfc804.html`.

rfc1321 (2003) is URL `http://www.ietf.org/rfc/rfc1321.txt`.

Rissanen, Jorma (1976) "Generalized Kraft Inequality and Arithmetic Coding' *IBM Journal of Research and Development*, **20**:198–203, May.

Ritter (2004) is URL `http://www.ciphersbyritter.com/ARTS/PRACTLAT.HTM`.

Rivest, R. (1991) "The MD4 Message Digest Algorithm," in Menezes, A. J., and S. A. Vanstone, (eds.), *Advances in Cryptology: CRYPTO '90 Proceedings*, pp. 303–311, New York, Springer-Verlag.

Rivest, R. (1992) "The MD4 Message Digest Algorithm," RFC 1320, MIT and RSA Data Security, Inc., April.

Rosen, Kenneth et al. (2000) *Handbook of Discrete and Combinatorial Mathematics*. Boca Raton, Fla., CRC Press.

RSA (2001) is URL `http://www.rsasecurity.com/rsalabs/challenges/factoring/` file `faq.html`.

RSA (2004) is URL `http://www.rsasecurity.com/`.

Rubin, F. (1979) "Arithmetic Stream Coding Using Fixed Precision Registers," *IEEE Transactions on Information Theory* **25**(6):672–675, November.

Salomon, David (1999) *Computer Graphics and Geometric Modeling*, New York, Springer-Verlag.

Salomon, David (2003) *Data Privacy and Security*, New York, Springer-Verlag.

Salomon, David (2004) *Data Compression: The Complete Reference*, 3rd edition, New York, Springer-Verlag.

Savard (2003) is URL `http://home.ecn.ab.ca/~jsavard/crypto/jscrypt.htm`.

Schneier, Bruce (1993) "Fast Software Encryption," in *Cambridge Security Workshop Proceedings*, pp. 191–204. New York, Springer-Verlag. Also available from `http://www.counterpane.com/bfsverlag.html`.

Schneier, Bruce (1995) *Applied Cryptography: Protocols, Algorithms, and Source Code in C*, 2nd edition, New York, John Wiley.

Schneier, Bruce (2003) is URL `http://www.counterpane.com/crypto-gram.html`.

Schotti, Gaspari (1665) *Schola Steganographica*, Jobus Hertz, printer. Some page photos from this old book are available at URL `http://www.cl.cam.ac.uk/~fapp2/steganography/steganographica/index.html`.

Shamir, Adi (1979) "How to Share a Secret," *Communications of the ACM*, **22**(11):612–613, November.

Shannon, Claude E. (1949) "Communication Theory of Secrecy Systems," *Bell System Technical Journal*, **28**:656–715, October.

Shannon, Claude E. (1951) "Prediction and Entropy of Printed English," *Bell System Technical Journal*, **30**:50–64, January.

Simovits, Mikael J. (1996) *The DES, an Extensive Documentation and Evaluation*, Laguna Hills, Calif., Aegean Park Press, vol. **C-68**.

Singh, Simon (1999) *The Code Book*, New York, Doubleday.

Sinkov, A. (1980) *Elementary Cryptanalysis: A Mathematical Approach* (New Mathematical Library, No. 22), Washington, D.C., Mathematical Assn. of America.

Sorkin, Arthur (1984) "Lucifer, A Cryptographic Algorithm," *Cryptologia*, **8**(1):22–41, January. An addendum is in **8**(3)260–261.

Stallings, William (1998) *Cryptography and Network Security: Principles and Practice*, Englewood Cliffs, N.J., Prentice-Hall.

Steganosaurus (2004) is URL `http://www.fourmilab.to/stego/`.

Stego (2004) is URL `http://www.stego.com/`.

Stollnitz, E. J., T. D. DeRose, and D. H. Salesin (1996) *Wavelets for Computer Graphics*, San Francisco, Morgan Kaufmann.

Storer, J. A., and T. G. Szymanski (1982) "Data Compression via Textual Substitution," *Journal of the ACM* **29**:928–951.

Swan, Tom (1993) *Inside Windows File Formats*, Indianapolis, IN, Sams Publications.

Thomas, Steven A. (2000) *SSL and TLS Essentials: Securing the Web*, New York, John Wiley.

Trithemius, Johannes (1606) *Steganographia*. Available (for private use only) from URL `http://www.esotericarchives.com/tritheim/stegano.htm`.

Tseng, Yu-Chee, and Hsiang-Kuang Pan (2001) "Secure and Invisible Data Hiding in 2-Color Images," *IEEE Infocom 2001*. Also available from URL `http://www.ieee-infocom.org/2001/paper/20.pdf`.

UCC (2004) is URL `http://www.uc-council.org/`.

Unicode Standard (1996) *The Unicode Standard*, Version 2.0, Reading, Mass., Addison-Wesley.

Unicode (2003) is URL `http://www.unicode.org`.

Verhoeff, Jacobus (1969) "Error Detecting Decimal Codes," Mathematical Center Tract 29, Amsterdam.

Vinzant, Carol (1999) "What Hidden Meanings Are Embedded in Your Social Security Number?," *Fortune*, **139**, p. 32, January 11.

Vitter, Jeffrey S. (1987) "Design and Analysis of Dynamic Huffman Codes," *Journal of the ACM*, **34**(4):825–845, October.

WatermarkingWorld (2003) is located at URL http://www.watermarkingworld.org/.

Weinberger, M. J., G. Seroussi, and G. Sapiro (1996) "LOCO-I: A Low Complexity, Context-Based, Lossless Image Compression Algorithm," in Storer J., (ed.), *Proceedings of Data Compression Conference*, Los Alamitos, Calif., IEEE Computer Society Press, pp. 140–149.

Welch, T. A. (1984) "A Technique for High-Performance Data Compression," *IEEE Computer*, **17**(6):8–19, June.

Winters, S. J. (1990) "Error Detecting Schemes Using Dihedral Groups," *UMAP Journal*, **11**(4):299–308.

Witten, Ian H., Radford M. Neal, and John G. Cleary (1987) "Arithmetic Coding for Data Compression," *Communications of the ACM*, **30**(6):520–540.

Wayner, Peter (1992) "Mimic Functions," *Cryptologia*, **XVI**(3):193–214, July.

Wayner, Peter (2002) *Disappearing Cryptography*, 2nd edition, London, Academic Press.

Wu, M. Y., and J. H. Lee (1998) "A Novel Data Embedding Method for Two-Color Images," in *Proceedings of the International Symposium on Multimedia Information Processing*, December.

Xia, Xiang-Gen, Charles G. Boncelet, and Gonzalo R. Arce (1998) "Wavelet-Transform Based Watermark for Digital Images," *Optics Express* **3**(12):497–511, December 7.

Zhao, J., and E. Koch (1995) "Embedding Robust Labels into Images for Copyright Protection," in *Proceedings of the International Conference on Intellectual Property Rights for Specialized Information Knowledge and New Technologies*, August 21–25, Vienna, Austria, Oldenbourg Verlag, pp. 242–251. Also available in PDF format from URL http://citeseer.nj.nec.com/zhao95embedding.html.

Zimmermann, Philip (1995) *PGP Source Code and Internals*, Cambridge, Mass., MIT Press.

Zimmermann, Philip (2001) is http://www.philzimmermann.com/.

Ziv, J., and A. Lempel (1977) "A Universal Algorithm for Sequential Data Compression," *IEEE Transactions on Information Theory*, IT-23(3):337–343.

Ziv, J., and A. Lempel (1978) "Compression of Individual Sequences via Variable-Rate Coding," *IEEE Transactions on Information Theory* IT-24(5):530–536.

> Outside of a dog, a book is man's best friend. Inside of a dog it's too dark to read.
>
> —Groucho Marx

Index

Whenever possible, the index indicates the part of the book (channel codes, source codes, or secure codes) to which an index item belongs. Thus, the words "check digit" qualify index item "airline tickets," while "anagram" is identified as a transposition cipher. A special effort was made to include full names (first and middle names instead of initials) and dates of persons mentioned in the book.

A good book has no ending.

—R.D. Cumming